The Salmon P. Chase Papers

Salmon P. Chase (1808–73)

Daguerreotype by L. H. Whitehurst, ca. 1850–55.
Courtesy of the Chicago Historical Society (ICHi-09783).

The Salmon P. Chase Papers

VOLUME 4

Correspondence, April 1863–1864

John Niven, Editor

James P. McClure, Senior Associate Editor

Leigh Johnsen, Associate Editor

Kathleen Norman, Editorial Assistant

The Kent State University Press

KENT, OHIO, AND LONDON, ENGLAND

Library of Congress Catalog Card Number 93-16217
ISBN 0-87338-567-5
Manufactured in the United States of America

06 05 04 03 02 01 00 99 98 97 5 4 3 2 1

Publication of this book has been supported in part by a grant from the National Historical Publications and Records Commission.

Library of Congress has cataloged volume 1 of this series as follows:

Library of Congress Cataloging-in-Publication Data
Chase, Salmon P. (Salmon Portland), 1808–1873.
The Salmon P. Chase papers / John Niven, editor ; James P. McClure, senior associate editor ; Leigh Johnsen, associate editor ; William M. Ferraro, Steve Leikin, assistant editor[s].
p. cm.
Includes bibliographical references and index.
Contents: v. 1 Journals, 1829–1872
ISBN 0-87338-472-5 (cloth : alk. paper) ∞
1. Chase, Salmon P. (Salmon Portland), 1808–1873—Archives. 2. United States—Politics and government—1849–1877—Sources. 3. Legislators—United States—Archives. 4. Judges—United States—Archives. 5. United States. Congress. Senate—Archives. 6. Governors—Ohio—Archives. I. Niven, John. II. Title.
E415.6.C48 1993
977.1'03'092—dc20 93-16217

British Library Cataloging-in-Publication data are available.

Contents

Acknowledgments

CREATION OF this volume would not have been possible without the sponsorship of the Claremont Graduate School and grants from two federal agencies, the National Historical Publications and Records Commission (NHPRC), a branch of the National Archives, and the National Endowment for the Humanities (NEH), an independent federal agency.

As has been the case with all volumes of the *Chase Papers,* detailed labor essential to the completion of this book was provided by graduate student assistants whose efforts and skill deserve recognition. Michael Vanderlan, Peg Lamphier, Heather Wilson, Dorcas Hawker, John Walker, and Nora Farabaugh performed a myriad of assignments, including library research, proofreading, database entry, and citation checking. Dorran Boyle and Laura Pierce assisted in the later stages of work on the volume. Most of the transcription was done in 1992 by Maria Baglien, Scott Birrell, Krista Caufman, Bonnie Khaw, Erika Kreger, and Laura Morrow. Mia Park and Kenneth Osterkamp also transcribed documents.

We owe thanks, for their cheerful endurance, to the staff of the interlibrary loan office at Honnold Library of the Claremont Colleges, as well as to the reference and government documents librarians of the Colleges' libraries. Our research has also benefited from access to the genealogical research library at the Church of Jesus Christ of Latter-day Saints in Upland, California, and the Huntington Library in San Marino. Timothy Connelly and Michael Meier of the NHPRC applied their considerable expertise to our research queries involving records in the National Archives. We are particularly grateful also for the aid given by the office of the curator of the Department of the Treasury, especially Paula Mohr and Mary Edwards, as we sought illustrations for the volume. Some years ago Patrick Delana, as assistant editor of the microfilm edition of Chase's papers, first collated and researched the different versions of Chase's letters to John T. Trowbridge. Charles Young, professor of philosophy at the Claremont Graduate School, helped us identify an oblique classical reference. Linda Thrift, keeper of the Catalog of American Portraits at the National Portrait Gallery, furnished important information about portraits of Chase. With Beverly Wilson Palmer and Holly Byers Ochoa of the Thaddeus Stevens edition, based down the street at Pomona College, we have shared warm camaraderie as well as cordial, if ad hoc, arrangements that gave both projects access to necessary books and materials. Holly helped proofread this volume of the *Chase Papers,* as well. Thanks also to the many institutions that responded to this project's initial search for documents during the 1980s, and to Edwin C. Hoyt, grandson of Chase's daughter Janet, for his abiding consideration.

We would like to thank those people at the funding agencies and our sponsoring institution who were most involved in helping us complete this volume: Nancy Sahli and Kathy Jacob of the NHPRC, Douglas Arnold and Daniel Jones of the NEH, and, at the Claremont Graduate School, Carol Gamble. So too must we express our gratitude to John Hubbell, Julia Morton, Linda Cuckovich, and Will Underwood of The Kent State University Press. In its commitment to the *Chase Papers,* the Press has acted in its own right as one of the project's vital sponsors.

Chronology

1863 Chase visits Philadelphia, New York, and Boston to solicit loan subscriptions (late April–early May)

Federal loss at battle of Chancellorsville; Chase offers to tender resignation over Puget Sound collectorship; Chase visits Gen. Hooker's headquarters in Virginia (May)

Confederate troops cross Potomac River and move into Maryland and Pennsylvania (June)

Battle of Gettysburg; Treasury circular revises trade regulations; Vicksburg, Miss., and Port Hudson, La., fall to U.S. forces; New York City draft riots; Chase escorts daughters to Rhode Island (July)

Chase returns to Washington, attending to Treasury business in New York en route (August)

Treasury issues revised trade regulations; battle of Chickamauga causes Federal disarray in Tennessee (September)

Chase makes campaign speaking tour to Ohio and Indiana and addresses Unconditional Union meeting in Baltimore (October)

Kate Chase and William Sprague marry; battle of Chattanooga (November)

Lincoln touches on Reconstruction in annual message and issues Proclamation of Amnesty and Reconstruction; Chase sends annual report to Congress; Wendell Phillips publicly criticizes Chase for his role in the Margaret Garner fugitive case of 1856 (December)

1864 Subscriptions for 5–20 bonds close (January)

"Pomeroy Circular," promoting Chase as a presidential candidate, becomes public; Union party members of Ohio legislature endorse Lincoln for reelection; Francis Preston Blair, Jr., in speech given in U.S. House, criticizes Chase and Treasury (February)

Ulysses S. Grant commissioned lieutenant general and given command of all U.S. armies; Federal forces under Gen. Nathaniel P. Banks commence Red River campaign; Treasury opens subscriptions for 10–40 bonds (March)

Treasury attempts to curb speculation in gold, and Chase travels to New York and Philadelphia; Francis P. Blair, Jr., delivers another speech condemning Chase and Treasury agents (April)

Radicals select John C. Frémont as presidential candidate (May)

National currency act revises national banking system; Chase consults with bankers in New York; Union party national convention in Baltimore nominates Lincoln-Johnson ticket; Chase and Lincoln contend over replacement for John J. Cisco; Chase offers, and Lincoln accepts, resignation from the Treasury; Congress passes internal revenue act and ways and means act (June)

Chase travels in New England (July–September)

Attempt to nominate Chase for Congress from Ohio fails; Democratic national convention nominates George B. McClellan as candidate for president (August)

Chase stumps through Middle West for Lincoln's reelection (September–November)

Chief Justice Roger B. Taney dies (October)

Lincoln reelected president (November)

Lincoln nominates Chase to be chief justice of U.S. Supreme Court; Senate confirms appointment and Chase joins Court (December)

Introduction by John Niven

THIS VOLUME reflects the lowest point in Chase's career as a public man: Lincoln's acceptance of his resignation from the cabinet. It also depicts his failed campaign to secure the Republican-Union nomination for the presidency in 1864 but closes with his appointment as chief justice of the Supreme Court.

In October 1863, under the pretext of "going home to vote," Chase made what appeared to him a most successful electioneering trip in Ohio and Indiana. In speeches he delivered in both states, he gave his version of the cause of the war (free labor versus slave labor) and reviewed his accomplishments in establishing a successful financial and fiscal policy that was underwriting the Union war effort.[1]

Reluctantly, he had supported the issue of paper or fiat currency that was not backed by specie but only by the government's credit. Denominated greenbacks, these issues, including fractional currency, now amounted to over $400 million. Together with other borrowed funds, in bonds and Treasury notes, Chase managed to finance the war, though not without significant, but sustainable, inflation. His correspondence with John J. Cisco, the department's assistant treasurer in New York, and Jay Cooke, the Philadelphia banker, demonstrates not only a firm grasp of financial policies but also his capacity as a forceful administrator who dealt decisively with the Union's financial community.

Chase's cherished national bank system, however, faced concerted opposition from state-chartered banks and was slow to gain adherents from the financial interests. Nor was the marketing of the new issue of 10–40 bonds, which Chase counted on to meet the increasing costs of military operations, as successful as the sale of the previous 5–20 bonds.

Under congressional pressure during the winter of 1863–64, Chase had to dispense with Jay Cooke's exclusive agency. Without Cooke's energy and merchandizing techniques, the public and the banks were slow to purchase these securities. Apparent military stalemate also hindered the sale of government equities. And the rise of inflation—as gold, in terms of greenbacks, soared in the money market—reflected uncertainty with respect to the Union war effort. Although Congress rejected Chase's requests for higher taxation that would have curtailed speculation in gold, key members insisted that the Treasury sell gold to enhance greenback value. Hesitant to enter such an open-market operation, Chase in mid-April 1864 finally bowed to the pressure and personally directed the sale of $11 million of the government's gold reserves over a five-day period. This action brought a temporary panic in the New York stock market and a temporary rise in the value of greenbacks as measured in gold. But within a month gold had resumed its steady rise and greenbacks continued to fall in specie value. The experiment, for which Chase was blamed and had to accept responsibility, was a failure.

Chase's influence on military policy declined considerably during 1863 and 1864, but he continued to maintain his links with army commanders. And of course his network of Treasury agents, especially those in the Mississippi River Valley, kept him informed about military and political affairs in their respective districts.

Of particular importance to Chase and to Lincoln was the situation in Louisiana, specifically the port of New Orleans and its hinterland. At first Chase sought to carry out his ideas of Reconstruction through his appointees in the New Orleans Custom House and backed the radical Unionist faction in the city. One of his primary objectives was the elimination of the exceptions in the Emancipation Proclamation that sustained the institution of slavery in those areas the Union army controlled (especially New Orleans). During 1863 and the first half of 1864, he pressed Lincoln to rescind these exceptions, but to little avail. At the same time, as his correspondence with his custom house appointees at New Orleans and elsewhere indicates, he played a waiting game, supporting the radical candidates for election to Congress under Lincoln's "ten percent plan" for Reconstruction but ultimately acquiescing in the more moderate regime of General Nathaniel Banks, whom Lincoln had selected late in 1862 to replace the more radical General Benjamin Butler. Chase gave way also to the president's replacement of Chase's cousin George Denison as acting collector with Cuthbert Bullitt, a New Orleans native and conservative Unionist.

The Port Royal experiment, too, was experiencing difficulties. Generally successful, in a modest way, it had fallen prey in some respects to speculators. And agricultural production, especially in sowing cotton seed and in harvesting the crop, was hindered by the military's manpower demands of black males for army duty. When the former plantation came up for sale for taxes that the absentee owners had not paid, Mansfield French, a reformist minister at Port Royal, for one, feared that the former slaves would be deprived of ownership of the plots they were working. In distant Washington, Chase was unable to form a clear view of the problem and finally capitulated to current notions of the free-market economy. Many, if not most, of the resident blacks were unable to meet the cash requirement under the tax sales and were deprived of ownership.

Midsummer of 1863 brought the terrible battle of Gettysburg and the draft riots in northern cities. In a letter to William Sprague, who would soon become his son-in-law, Chase describes how despondent Lincoln felt at the failure of General George Meade, commanding the Army of the Potomac, to finish off Lee's army after repulsing it at Gettysburg.[2] In mid-July, within two weeks of the battle, Chase received messages from Hiram Barney, customs collector in New York, and John J. Cisco announcing the draft riots that were sweeping the city. On July 23, Cisco mailed a full account of the riots and his preparations to defend the subtreasury building. The editors have included this letter as representative of the telegrams and letters from Barney, Cisco, and others in New York detailing the seriousness of the situation.[3] Those interested in the riots and their aftermath will find additional correspondence in the microfilm edition.

In the fall of 1863, Chase converted the wedding of his daughter Kate to the Rhode Island textile magnate William Sprague into a quasi-political event. At the lavish ceremonial in his Washington, D.C., home, Chase made sure that important members of the capital's political society—and that included his cabinet colleagues and the president—were guests to witness the event as he put his beautiful daughter on display. Yet all was not an exhibition of personal politics. Chase wrote sensitive and feeling letters to both the bride and the groom about the responsibility of marriage, revealing a warm and caring side to the austere nature he displayed to the public.

Meanwhile, as the war dragged on, public morale in support of the Union war effort continued to decline. Despite the victory at Gettysburg and the surrender of the last Confederate strongholds on the Mississippi, Vicksburg and Port Hudson, Lee's Army of Northern Virginia and Bragg's Army of Tennessee remained a very potent force in being. In fact Chase was brought into the *ad hoc* council that convened to consider what steps should be taken to relieve Rosecrans's Army of the Cumberland after its defeat at Chickamauga in late September 1863.[4]

During the early fall of 1863, Chase was beginning to position himself for the Republican-Union nomination for the presidency. After his successful electioneering visit to Ohio and Indiana, a small group of politicians and railroad speculators formed a secret campaign committee to boost Chase for the nomination. Chase was aware of their objective and though he personally did not play an active role in their strategy he did nothing to dissuade them. In fact, as his correspondence shows, he wrote carefully constructed letters to such important molders of public opinion as Horace Greeley of the *New York Tribune,* Theodore Tilton of the New York *Independent,* the influential religious daily, and Joseph Medill of the *Chicago Tribune.*[5]

The *New York Tribune,* the *Evening Post,* and a popular weekly, *Wilkes' Spirit of the Times,* began a tentative display of support for Chase's candidacy that featured his ideas on Reconstruction and praise for his financial and fiscal policies. Chase also began providing John T. Trowbridge, a popular writer of juvenile books, with detailed autobiographical information. In all, he was to write twenty-four long letters to Trowbridge that contain valuable material on his life and career. These letters were meant to form the basis of a campaign biography, and did result in a slim volume entitled *The Ferry-Boy and the Financier.* Because of their length, only six of Chase's autobiographical letters to Trowbridge are included in this volume.[6] All of these letters, however, are included in the microfilm edition.

Since the prime movers for Chase's campaign—Senators Samuel Pomeroy of Kansas, John Sherman of Ohio, and B. Gratz Brown of Missouri—were available for strategy sessions in Washington, there is no correspondence that touches on their activities to replace Lincoln with Chase at the forthcoming Republican-Union convention. When the ill-fated Pomeroy Circular, which praised Chase and criticized Lincoln, became public knowledge in February 1864, Chase's letter of explanation to the president and Lincoln's replies formed an interesting dialogue that highlights their relationship in an ongoing political contest.[7] Public reaction to the Pomeroy Circular was negative. When several state legislatures, including Ohio's, backed Lincoln for renomination, Chase publicly withdrew his candidacy.

Coincidentally with the Pomeroy Circular and the collapse of Chase's campaign, Frank Blair, a conservative Union-Republican congressman from Missouri, excoriated Chase in two speeches he made on the floor of the House.[8] Blair's political constituency in Missouri had been under attack from Chase's Treasury agents and radical friends in Missouri. A vibrant politician, Blair was also a distinguished corps commander in General William T. Sherman's army and probably the best nonprofessional major general in the Union ranks.

Chase reacted strenuously to Blair's speeches on the floor of the House. Much of what Blair said when he accused Chase of encouraging corruption among his Treasury agents for political purposes was either spurious or based on grossly inflated hearsay. But there was no doubt that many of Chase's agents, especially those in the Mississippi Valley, were actually using their positions to enrich themselves and incidentally to further Chase's political fortunes.

Chase soon learned that Lincoln had met with Frank Blair and had held Blair's military commission while he was attacking Chase in Congress, then restored his commission so that he could rejoin his command. Jumping to the conclusion that the president, through Blair, was conspiring to ruin him politically, Chase was ready to resign. But when Chase's intermediaries met with Lincoln, the president satisfied them that he had had no hand in the Blair assault and, in fact, was embarrassed by it.[9] When they communicated this information to Chase, he decided to remain in the cabinet.

Relations between Chase and Lincoln remained correct but were decidedly cool. Chase's position toward Frank Blair and his brother Montgomery, a cabinet colleague, became bitterly hostile—an attitude the Blairs reciprocated in full measure. There is little correspondence that bears on this political fallout in the aftermath of the Pomeroy Circular, but the episode is fully documented in other sources.[10]

For the next four months, Chase's patronage position within the party came under steady attack, primarily from conservative Union-Republican politicians such as Thurlow Weed and the Blairs. The battle was joined when John J. Cisco proffered his resignation as assistant treasurer in New York and Chase sought to place his own man in that politically important post. When Lincoln rejected his candidate, Chase offered his resignation. To his surprise and consternation, the president accepted it on June 30, 1864.

A chastened Chase took no active part in the move to back Frémont in place of Lincoln on the Republican-Union ticket. When the radical-inspired Frémont candidacy terminated, Chase took the stump in support of Lincoln's reelection. His motive is at least partially explained by his desire to become chief justice of the United States Supreme Court upon the death of aged and ailing Roger B. Taney. This volume closes with Chase's note to Lincoln that thanks the president for the nomination to the Court.

1. For Chase's assessment of the trip see his letter to Edward D. Mansfield, October 18, 1863 (below). The addresses appeared in pamphlet form as *"Going Home to Vote." Authentic Speeches of S. P. Chase, Secretary of the Treasury, during his Visit to Ohio*... (Washington, D.C., 1863).

2. Chase to Sprague, July 15, 1863 (below).

3. Cisco to Chase, July 23, 1863 (below). For the initial information from Cisco and Barney concerning the situation in New York, see Barney to Chase, July 15, 1863 (below), and Cisco to Chase, July 13, 1863 (Letters Received from Asst. Treasurers, Gen. Recs. Treasury Dept., Nat. Arch.).

4. *Chase Papers,* 1:450–54.

5. Chase to Greeley, Oct. 9, 1863; to Tilton, Oct. 31, 1863; and to Medill, Jan. 30, 1864 (all below).

6. Trowbridge's *Ferry-Boy* was published in Boston in 1864. The autobiographical letters to Trowbridge included in this volume are dated January 25, February 10, and March 13, 20, 21, and 22, 1864.

7. Chase to Lincoln, Feb. 22, 1864 (below); Roy P. Basler, ed., *The Collected Works of Abraham Lincoln,* 9 vols. (New Brunswick, N.J., 1953–55), 7:200, 212–13.

8. For Blair's speeches of February 27 and April 23, 1864, see the notes accompanying Chase's letters of February 22, 1864, to Lincoln and May 5, 1864, to Jay Cooke (both below).

9. See Chase to Jay Cooke, May 5, 1864 (below).

10. Howard K. Beale, ed., *The Diary of Gideon Welles,* 3 vols. (New York, [1960]), 2:17–21; David Herbert Donald, *Lincoln* (New York, 1995), 496–97.

Editorial Procedures

THIS BOOK, like Volumes 2 and 3 of the edition, is a selective representation of Salmon P. Chase's correspondence. That is to say, Volume 4 includes only a small fraction of Chase's letters from April 1863 through December 1864. In specific terms, 269 letters appear here, while the microfilm edition of Chase's papers reproduces over 3,700 documents from that twenty-one-month period of Chase's life. The microfilm edition is itself selective, and does not contain all incoming letters, duplicate versions of letters by Chase, or—an immense body of material—numerous routine Treasury documents and correspondence that provide little illumination of major policy issues or politics.[1]

It has been, needless to say, a difficult task to choose the relatively few letters that space and other resources will admit into this volume. Through a serial process of screening, the chief editor selected those documents that in his judgment were interesting to read and also presented the most important contents. Effort was made to include letters touching on a variety of significant policy matters, to represent Chase's continuing political correspondence, and to illustrate aspects of his personal life. Not every issue that arose during Chase's tenure as secretary of the Treasury appears in these pages, and for many topics only a segment of Chase's relevant correspondence could be reproduced here. Annotation places the letters in general context, but some researchers will want to turn to the microfilm edition and to examine source materials mentioned in this volume's notes.

With the exception of the last letters in the volume, those from July to December 1864, Chase's correspondence in this book all dates from his tenure as secretary of the U.S. Treasury. In this respect Volume 4 is the partner of Volume 3 (*Correspondence, 1858–March 1863*), for together they span Chase's time as head of the Treasury Department. Some of the special characteristics of Chase's correspondence as secretary, including the department's procedures for managing the flow of letters in and out, are discussed in Volume 3 (pp. xxiii–xxvii).

LETTERPRESS AND LETTERBOOK COPIES

As was the case with Volume 3, letterpress copies served as the source texts for transcription of a number of the documents included in this volume. Letterpress copies were facsimile impressions of outgoing letters, retained as file copies. In this process the ink of a handwritten letter left an impression on the retained copy, but the letterhead of printed stationery did not. This characteristic accounts for the appearance of some letterpress copies, which seem to have strangely incomplete dates and to lack any indication of where they were written. For example, in Chase's day U.S. Treasury stationery displayed the department's name at the top of the page, along with a line for the date with the first three digits of the year—"186"—already imprinted. Chase or his clerk would write in the month and day, along with the final digit of the year. The letterpress copy of such a letter preserved no trace of the "Treasury Department" imprint at the head of the sheet and picked up only the ink of the handwritten portion of the date. February 17, 1864, for example, would come through on the letterpress copy as "February 17th,   4." In such cases the editors have not supplied the "missing" information.

On occasion Chase or a clerk wrote on a letterpress file copy to supply information that did not come through in the facsimile process. An example would be a notation of "Washn" to stand in for the printed departmental letterhead that did not leave an impression on the letterpress copy. Such additions are part of the letterpress file copy, if not of the original letter, and we have included them in our transcriptions. However, we have silently omitted filing notations added by Chase's clerks, such as "copied" (to show that a letterbook copy had been made), notes of letterbook page numbers, or a "u" found in the corner of some letters, probably to indicate a filing location.

Sometimes more than one version of a letter was available to the editors. In choosing from multiple versions of a manuscript, we have attempted to reproduce here the text that is closest to the actual signed letter that passed from writer to receiver. Under such a general rule, in the absence of the original letter the editors have given preference to a letterpress copy over a fair-hand letterbook copy. In a few cases, as identified in annotation, we turned to alternate versions of a document to assist in reading difficult text.

Sometimes the only manuscript versions of a letter we have are two fair copies, one an official letterbook copy by a Treasury clerk and another made for Chase's private files. In those instances we give preference to the "official" copy since, according to Treasury Department procedures, it was most likely made from the original or a letterpress copy soon after the letter was written. We do not know when letterbook or fair copies in Chase's private files were made, or what the copyist in such a case used as a source text.

TEXTUAL PROCEDURES

A source note at the top of each letter describes the form of the original—"autograph letter," for example—and gives the repository and collection in which it is located. "Autograph" as used in the source notes means that the letter is in its author's handwriting. Most source notes also contain a designation of *micro* followed by numbers to indicate the location of the document in the microfilm edition (thus *micro* 26:0033 means reel 26, frame 33). If the version of a letter included in this volume did not appear in the microfilm edition the source note will have no *micro* notation, although a footnote may indicate another version that does appear on the microfilm.

In transcribing the letters we have tried to reproduce spelling, capitalization, punctuation, abbreviations, and repetition of words as they appear in the originals. We do not show canceled (marked out) text unless it is significant enough in content to warrant mention in a note. We have silently incorporated interlineations and other insertions. Our intention as expressed by these policies is to report the text of a letter as its author intended it to be read. Readers interested in the nuances of alterations to particular documents will want to consult the originals or, at the least, microfilm facsimiles. If a word's spelling is ambiguous in the original, as can be the case with handwritten manuscripts, we have favored the spelling given preference in *Webster's Ninth New Collegiate Dictionary.*

Uncertain readings, whether of phrases, words, or parts of words, are enclosed in plain square brackets: [ ]. Occasional explanation by the editors within the text of a document is enclosed in the same kind of bracket, but appears in italic type, as in [*illeg.*] or [*torn*] to explain words missing from the text. Thus standard roman type within square brackets means an uncertain reading of the text of the original, while italic type within such brackets signals commentary by the volume's editors. To avoid confusion, any square brackets found in an original document are depicted here as ⁅ and ⁆.

When not enclosed by the editor's brackets, italic type signifies text that was underlined in the original letter. Underlining by two or more strokes is represented by small capitals. Signatures to letters appear as a combination of large and small capitals. Printing convention usually employs small capitals for A.M. and P.M. to indicate time of day. To avoid confusion with other uses of small capitals in this volume, we do not follow that convention in our transcriptions but instead use full capitals for A.M. and P.M. If our source text is a printed document, we follow the original in use of italics and small capitals, except that signatures are always rendered in the volume's standard form. We do not attempt to replicate all details of printed letterheads.

The editors have not supplied any punctuation that may be missing from the original. Readers may encounter, therefore, "closing" quotation marks without their "opening" partners, or vice versa. We have tried to place punctuation marks either inside or outside quotation marks just as they appear in the original. If placement in the original seems ambiguous we follow the appropriate modern rule for that mark of punctuation as given in the *Chicago Manual of Style.* We have brought superscripted characters down to the line and used a period to represent any mark appearing under a superscripted character in the original.

Following the convention of the edition's other volumes, we have introduced one symbol. Sometimes writers of handwritten letters let the right edge of the page serve in place of punctation at the end of a sentence or phrase, and we have indicated those spots with a standard slash: / . In such cases the slash is preceded and followed by space, which—along with the symbol's location—helps distinguish our introduced symbol from slashes that appear as part of original text.

ANNOTATION

Annotation is intended to make references in the letters intelligible to readers, and for practical reasons most of the notes emphasize identification more than full explication of topics. Notes to a letter appear at the foot of the document before the next letter in sequence. In citations, the names of manuscript collections and repositories have been shortened by abbreviation: "L.C." for Library of Congress, for example, "Hist. Soc. of Pa." for the Historical Society of Pennsylvania, "Collec." for Collection, "Lib." for Library, "Univ." for University, and so on. References to the Bible cite the King James version.

Many people mentioned in these letters were identified in earlier volumes of the edition. In most such cases the person's general biographical identification will not be repeated here, and a boldfaced reference in the index directs the reader to data in preceding volumes. Individuals making their first appearance are identified by basic biographical information, with primary emphasis placed on the context of the person's role in these papers.

In searching for publication data on books and periodicals the editors have utilized, without citation in the notes, computerized on-line bibliographic services, including the Online Computer Library Center

(OCLC) and the Research Libraries Information Network (RLIN), as well as the following printed sources: *The National Union Catalog: Pre-1956 Imprints,* 754 vols. (London, 1968–81); *British Museum General Catalogue of Printed Books: Photolithographic Edition to 1955,* 263 vols. (London, 1965–66); Winifred Gregory, ed., *American Newspapers, 1821–1936: A Union List of Files Available in the United States and Canada* (New York, 1936); and Edna Brown Titus, ed., *Union List of Serials in Libraries of the United States and Canada,* 3d ed., 5 vols. (New York, 1965).

For convenience, the bibliography contains works that appear more than once in citations. As a matter of course the bibliography contains more reference works than interpretive studies, and it is not intended to serve as an overview of historical writing on subjects touched in this volume.

1. John Niven, ed., James P. McClure, assoc. ed., and Patrick Delana, asst. ed., *The Salmon P. Chase Papers,* 43 reels (Frederick, Md., 1987). For the search for manuscripts and the selection criteria employed for the microfilm edition, see pp. 7–11 of the printed guide.

The Salmon P. Chase Papers

The Correspondence of Salmon P. Chase, April 1863–1864

FROM EDWARD L. PIERCE

Autograph letter. Chase Papers, Historical Society of Pennsylvania (*micro* 26:0033).

Personal

Beaufort SC 2 April 1863.

My Dear Friend,

I arrived here a week ago Tuesday, and since that time have been busily engaged in visiting plantations and schools.[1] It is now nine months since I left—and a little more than a year since we put our enterprise in operation. In general, I am entirely satisfied with the development of character which has been made among the negroes and more than ever fortified in the opinion that the negroes will work for a living. Indeed I have no doubt whatever on this point. They took hold well this spring— They designated themselves the amount of land they wanted for corn and cotton and were entirely free agents in determining the amount. The testimony of the superintendents is that with the exception of one district which is much disorganized by proximity to soldiers & sailors, they have taken all the land for working that was desired.[2] I see them at work every day as I ride through the fields listing for cotton, corn and potatoes, and with no one to force them. One proslavery dogma is utterly confuted by the experiment here.

The work and the people have been greatly disturbed by the draft and by the generally *capricious* management of affairs in this department. Had Higginson had charge of the enlistments from the beginning, the negroes could have been procured as volunteers.[3] But now things are different. The superintendents were required by Gen Hunter to hand in a list of persons of proper age for military service. They have industriously tried to persuade them to enlist—but have only procured a small number. Detachments of soldiers are going through the islands to enforce the draft. The laborers are hiding in the woods where they pass the night, and even old men who are not fit for service are doing this. The consequence is that the labor is greatly deranged and the greater part of it is being performed by women—and they even are very much affected by the prevailing fear. Besides Gen Saxton had promised the people in church that they should not be forced to enlist—and he has been unable to keep his word. Being Governor of the district—and by his commission put expressly in charge of all persons not in military service here, it was a matter exclusively in his charge.[4] He was and is opposed to the draft, but he did not care to have a contest with Gen Hunter which would have resulted in his being ordered from the Department—and so submitted. The recruits should have been procured from refugees coming in, and not from these worn out islanders who have around them their wives, children, pigs, chickens and local associations—and indeed the best and main part of Higginson's regiment was procured in this way. The soldiers enforcing a draft say they have orders to fire on all negroes running from them—and they have done so. I confess that the way the conscription is being carried on by parties who know nothing of negroes and who do not hold a position where they feel permanently responsible for the developement and welfare of the people, seems to me very unwise and in some respects revolting. There ought to be a distinct order of the government putting the raising of negro soldiers here entirely in the hands of Gen Saxton and entirely out of the hands of Gen Hunter. Until that is done there will be no peace—no confidence reposed by the negroes in the assurances of Gen S. and the superintendents. There should be one mind in the government of the negroes—and that should be the humane, sensible and consistent mind of Gen Saxton—and besides this is his proper function as Governor.

The children are learning well in the schools, tho there are not so many of these as there should have been in the winter. This part has been somewhat overlooked—or rather has not been properly organized. There are 5 regular schools on St Helena—3 on Ladies—three or four on Beaufort—mainly conducted by ladies—and ranging in number from 130 down to 25 of average attendance in each. The advanced classes are reading in Hillards 2d Reader & Nellsons 2d Progressive Reader[5]—and I found that they caught the idea of the little fables or stories.

Generally, there has been a good developement in the consciousness of rights and of their position as self supporting citizens who have their own cause in their own hands. They have a great desire for the comforts of life, and are buying them with the money they receive for their labor.

Yesterday with Gen Saxton I visited Admiral Dupont and Capt Rogers—Fleet Captain and had a free talk.[6]

The iron clads did not answer expectations at the recent attempt on Fort McAllister.[7] They made no impression on the sand defences. They could not however get nearer than 1000 yds because of obstructions. Sumpter can not be protected by sand—but the attempt has been made to protect it by stone.[8] The iron clads are weak on the deck—on the turrets and on the bottom. A 10 in shell injured the deck and a 13 in would have gone through. The most formidable difficulties were expected from obstructions as ropes, torpedoes—and also from insufficient water. The paddles would be disabled if caught on ropes. There is danger of grounding—as the English man of war did a few days ago on coming out, notwithstanding she was guarded by a Charleston pilot. The army could render no assistance—whatever—not even to distract the enemy— Last summer an adequate force at the Stono could have captured the city—but that opportunity had been lost. On the whole the admiral felt that the chances were against us— Still he felt that very often difficulties grow less as you approach nearer to them—and his temperament was such that in doing his duty he was not affected by them. No day had been lost and everything had been done in his power to secure against defeat He felt that the public and the government had counted too much on the invincibility of iron clads. The iron clads had gone as far as Edisto except the Montauk and Passaic which leave today.[9] I should think that it would take not far from a week to get them all before Charleston and everything ready for the final assault—but it is quite sure to occur some day next week. It is fortunate that so able and good a man as Admiral Dupont has charge. I have hardly ever in my life seen a man who impresses me so favorably

I must close my long letter—expecting to leave here by the close of next week.

Yours truly,
P

1. Pierce, a major participant in the "Port Royal Experiment," represented Chase on South Carolina's occupied Sea Islands in dealings with former slaves and confiscated plantations. *Appletons'*, 5:12.

2. The superintendents were Northern volunteers who, under Pierce's direction, supervised former slaves. *Chase Papers*, 3:159–66.

3. On March 6, 1863, David Hunter, commander of the Department of the South for the previous year, had issued orders to draft "able-bodied male negroes between the ages of eighteen and fifty" despite earlier warnings from Chase. Thomas Wentworth Higginson commanded the 1st South Carolina Volunteers, the first black Union regiment, from 1862 to 1864. *OR*, ser. 1, v. 14:1020–21; Chase to Hunter, Feb. 14, 1863, in *Chase Papers*, 3:381–82; *DAB*, 9:17, 400.

4. Rufus Saxton served as military governor of the Department of the South, 1862–65. *Appletons'*, 5:410.

5. George Stillman Hillard, *A Second Class Reader: Consisting of Extracts, in Prose and Verse . . .* (Boston, 1856), published in various editions, and likely *The Progressive Second Reader . . .* (Boston, 1856) of Salem, Mass., co-authored by Nelson M. Holbrook.

6. In the spring of 1863, Samuel Francis DuPont bore responsibility for operations of the South Atlantic blockading squadron of the U.S. Navy. John Rodgers, DuPont's former aide, commanded the monitor USS *Weehawken*. *DAB*, 5:531–32, 16:78.

7. Federal vessels had attempted to take Fort McAllister, south of Atlanta, on March 3. E. B. Long, *The Civil War Day by Day: An Almanac, 1861–1865* (Garden City, N.Y., 1971), 325.

8. On April 7, led by the *Weehawken,* a flotilla of ironclads under DuPont unsuccessfully attacked Fort Sumter in Charleston harbor. Ibid., 335–36.

9. Noted inventor John Ericsson had delivered the 750-ton USS *Montauk* and USS *Passaic* to U.S. Navy officials the previous fall. *ORN,* ser. 2, v. 1:149–50, 170.

TO WILLIAM CURTIS NOYES

Letterpress copy of autograph letter. Chase Papers, Historical Society of Pennsylvania (*micro* 26:0136).

Washington, Apl. 7, 1863,

My dear Sir,

I am often meditating things not exactly in my line, and more inclined to think what can & should be done than what might have been done.

It is among the clearest of my convictions that this rebellion cannot be suppressed, unless we have on the national side the sympathy and active cooperation of a considerable body of people in the insurrectionary districts.

Every thing looks well now except the military side of our cause: and this looks not well only because there have been so few in high places connected with military operations, who have felt the importance of conciliating the Southern people as distinguished from the master-class.

My chief hope of success now is derived from slow development of this conviction which begins to appear among those who control the conduct of the war.

You will remember that some eighteen months ago[1] I expressed my own fixed opinion on this matter by the remark at a dinner where you uttered some wholesome truths, "The blackest loyalist in Carolina is whiter, in my esteem, than [the] whitest rebel." Such is my judgment now.

The Southern people whom we must conciliate are the black Americans, who till the soil, or load the boats, & cars, or pursue the handicrafts. They are the whites, also who are willing to pay or see received by all, days wages for days works. All others are naturally in sympathy with the rebellion.

Now the point to which I wish to draw your attention is this. It seems to me that in no way can a greater good be accomplished just now than by the organization of a National Emancipation Commission which shall charge itself with the promotion of the well being of the emancipees in the states to which the proclamation applies; in states which may emancipate by voluntary legislation; and in all the states where persons are found entitled to freedom under any of the acts of Congress.[2]

Take for example the present condition of things on the Mississippi river. Had our Generals on that river, ten months ago, enlisted all the able bodied blacks willing to serve in military organization, we should today have held the entire river & the entire right bank, if, indeed, the whole rebellion had not been subdued. Had such a commission as

I now suggest existed charging itself with the care of the families of the black soldiers; with the provision of lands for homes & cultivation to those families & to others who could not enlist, & with,—to some extent—the organization of the labor not employed by Government, who can tell what results might not have followed?

So deeply did I feel this at the time that I made myself under many disadvantages & with the smallest possible time for the work a sort of Commission for Port Royal;[3] and [the] results were not contemptible; though I had to endure much remark that was not pleasant, with small sympathy where I should have found much.

It is not too late to organize a Commission which shall do for the whole country what I wished done for Port Royal.

The beginning should be, I think, a meeting of half a dozen gentlemen in New York—not more—prudent, active, resolute, patient men—who should organize themselves as a National Emancipation Commission. The number might be increased by addition from other cities & places, none being admitted at first except unanimously in order to secure harmony & efficiency. Afterwards admissions might be made under less strict regulations, securing, however, always a united & energetic administration.

Now you are the man to begin. Select your five coworkers from the best men in New York. Get together & organize. Then lay your plan of action before the War Department; and I am confident you will have the Secretarys cordial cooperation. You shall have mine & that of my agents.

I verily believe here is a way in which immense good can be done.

Your Friend
S P Chase

Wm Curtis Noyes Esq

1. Chase traveled to New York City four times between August and December 1861 to arrange loans from banks to the Treasury. Bray Hammond, *Sovereignty and an Empty Purse: Banks and Politics in the Civil War* (Princeton, 1970), 109, 111, 113; Jacob W. Schuckers, *The Life and Public Services of Salmon Portland Chase* (New York, 1874), 225, 230; *Chase Papers*, 1:317.

2. Noyes responded to Chase's suggestions on April 20 (below).

3. Formation of the National Freedman's Relief Association in February 1862 had preempted Chase's plans. John W. Edmonds to Chase, Mar. 4, 1862 (Chase Papers, Hist. Soc. of Pa.); Mansfield French to Chase, Feb. 24, 1862 (Chase Papers, L.C.).

TO GEORGE OPDYKE ET AL.

Copy in clerk's hand on letterhead stationery. Chase Papers, Historical Society of Pennsylvania (*micro* 26:0154).

Treasury Department.
April 8th, 1863.

Gentlemen,[1]

Imperative demands on my time compel me to deny myself the gratification of attending the meeting to which you kindly invite.[2]

You will meet to send words of cheer to our brave Generals and soldiers in the field; to rebuke treason in our midst, giving, in the garb of peace, aid and comfort to treason in the panoply of war; to maintain inviolate the integrity of the National Territory and the Supremacy of the National Constitution and Laws; to strengthen the hands and nerve the heart of the President for the great work to which God and the People have called him. For what worthier purposes can American citizens now assemble?

It is my fixed faith, gentlemen, that God does not mean that this American Republic shall perish. We are tried as by fire; but our country will live. Notwithstanding all the violence and all the machinations of traitors and their sympathizers on this or the other side of the Atlantic, our country will live.

And while our country lives, Slavery, the chief source and cause and agent of our ills, will die. The friends of the Union in the South, before rebellion, predicted the destruction of slavery as a consequence of secession, if that madness should prevail. Nothing, in my judgment, is more certain than the fulfillment of these predictions. Safe in the States, before rebellion, from all federal interference, Slavery has come out from its shelter under the State Constitutions and Laws to assail the National Life. It will surely die, pierced by its own fangs and stings.

What matter now how it dies? Whether as a consequence or object of the war, what matter? Is this a time to split hairs of logic? To me it seems that Providence indicates clearly enough how the end of slavery must come. It comes in Rebel Slave States by military order, decree or proclamation, not to be disregarded or set aside in any event as a nullity, but maintained and executed with perfect good faith to all the enfranchised; and it will come in loyal Slave States, by the unconstrained action of the people and their legislatures, aided freely and generously by their brethren of the Free States. I may be mistaken in this; but if I am, another better way may be revealed.

Meantime it seems to me very necessary to say distinctly what many shrink from saying. The American blacks must be called into this conflict, not as cattle, not now even as contrabands, but as men. In the free States, and in the rebel States by the Proclamation, they are free men. The Attorney General, in an opinion which defies refutation, has pronounced these freemen citizens of the United States.[3] Let, then, the example of Andrew Jackson, who did not hesitate to oppose colored regiments to British invasion, be now fearlessly followed.[4] Let these blacks, acclimated, familiar with the country, capable of great endurance, receive suitable military organization and do their part. We need their good will and must make them our friends, by showing ourselves their friends. We must have them for guides, for scouts, for all military service in camps or field, for which they are qualified. Thus employed, from a burden they will become a support; and the hazards, privations, and labors of the white soldiers will be proportionally diminished.

Some will object, of course. There are always objectors to everything practical. Let experience dispel honest fears and refute captious or disloyal cavil.

Above all, gentlemen, let no doubt rest on our resolution to sustain with all our hearts and with all our means the soldiers now in arms for the Republic. Let their ranks be filled up; let their supplies be sufficient and regular; let their pay be sure. Let nothing be wanting to them which can ensure activity and efficiency. Let each brave officer and man realize that his country's love attends him; and inspired by this thought, let him dare and do all that is possible to be dared and done.

So, gentlemen, with the blessing of God, will we make a glorious future sure. I see it rising before me, how beautiful and how grand! There is no time to speak of it now; but from all quarters of the land comes the voice of the Sovereign People rebuking faction, denouncing treason, and proclaiming the indivisible unity of the Republic, and in this heaven-inspired union of the People for the sake of the Union is the sure promise of that splendid hereafter.

With Great Respect, Yours Truly,
S. P. CHASE

Hon. Geo: Opdyke, Geo: Griswold, Esq.[5]
And Others.

1. This letter, but with a date of April 9, was later published by the Loyal Publication League. Chase to Robert Dale Owen, Sept. 6, 1863 (below); Loyal Publication Society, *The Conditions of Reconstruction* . . . (New York, 1863), 22–24.

2. Opdyke, New York's Republican mayor, had apparently invited Chase to a "mass meeting" arranged by the Loyal National League and held in New York on April 10. "The object of the meeting," according to one report, "was to reiterate in the ears of Southern traitors, and before the eyes of Northern sympathizers, the loyalty of New-York to the Union, its confidence in the Administration, its desire for an aggressive war-policy, its extreme abhorrence of all Confederates and absolute detestation of all Copperheads." *New York Times,* Apr. 11, 1863.

3. Edward Bates wrote the opinion in November 1862 after Chase pushed him to rule on the status of blacks who commanded vessels detained along the coast. *Chase Papers,* 1:387–88.

4. Earlier, also—as in a letter to Gen. Benjamin Butler in July 1862—Chase had invoked the example of Andrew Jackson's use of African-American soldiers at the battle of New Orleans. *Chase Papers,* 3:237.

5. Griswold (1819–84) was a director of New York insurance companies and a founder of the city's Union League Club. *New York Times,* Apr. 27, 1884.

FROM HANSON A. RISLEY

Autograph letter. Chase Papers, Library of Congress (*micro* 26:0220).

Albany April 10. 1863[1]

Hon S. P. Chase
Sect. of Treasury
Sir,

The Bank Bill was not reached in Senate yesterday, but will have its third reading and go to the House this morning. I had a conference with Bank Coms. of Senate & House last even'g and *failed* to convince them of the necessity of further legislation, than as provided in Monroes Bill.[2] They urge that *any* and *all* the Banks in our state can wind up at pleasure under existing laws & without legal proceeding. Mr Van Dyck takes the same view.[3] I spent an hour yesterday at the Department with him examining the law and practice in the matter. Banks *are* voluntarily winding up every day. The Clinton Bank at Buffalo is just now proceeding to wind up. They send down to the Superintendant an Official certificate that a majority of the Directors have voted to wind up, they return their circulation $10,000 or $20,000 at a time, as they get it in; and as fast as they send it he returns an equal amount of their secureties, and when they return all their circulation they get back all their secureties. *Practically,* they can not call in *all* their circulation. There will always be $10.000 more or less out. For this amount they deposit with Superintent., an equal amount of money & he surrenders their secureties and assumes the redemption of the remaining circulation. He advertises to that effect & after six years all circulation not presented for redemption is presumed to be lost or destroyed & he gives the Bank or its assigns any of the deposit remaining in his hands. The Bank has in the mean time closed up, divided its assets & gone out of existance.—

In the articles of association of evry Bank there is a Stipulation how it may be dissolved; sometimes by majority, sometimes by 2/3 Vote of Directors; again requiring assent of ½ or 2/3 of stock holders.—

The Bank of Commerce N.Y. have restricted themselves greatly by articles of association. The powers of Directors are defined explicitly. They cannot go beyond the letter of their authority, or incur liabilities not enumerated, without the assent of stock holders. Hence, they never have applied for circulation. They could not have it without imposing on stock holders *personal* liability for its redemption.

The position of the Superintendant & of the Bank Coms. of Senate & House, is this—

1. Evry thing is provided for under Monroes Bill, that is in the power of legislation to accomplish, to harmonize the two systems.

2. All Banks in the State can now wind up at pleasure, without legal proceeding or delay. and the individual stock holders or any number of them, can organize, if they choose, under Act of Congress.—

Hence, they say, no such provision as I urge is necessary.—

In answer to my suggestion, that it will do no harm *to make entirely clear* the right of Banks to wind up at pleasure &c. they say, I had better not press it—it will get up discussion, perhaps opposition & may delay & defeat the Bill.— That there are a good many Bankers in the legislature, loyal men and true, who have not yet contemplated the idea that one State, pet system, is to be merged & lost in the comprehensive, grand & better National scheme; and any thing that suggests to them radical change, is distasteful. That all are united on the Senate Bill & if no unexpected opposition springs up, they will pass it and that it will answer all purposes, at least, until experience shows further legislation necessary.—

So the matter stands up to this time.

Very Respectfully

Your Obt. Servt.
H A Risley

1. Later in the year Risley became a supervising special agent for the U.S. Treasury. *Letter of the Secretary of the Treasury, Transmitting . . . A List of the Special Agents of the Treasury Department and their Assistants,* 38th Cong., 1st sess., 1864, S. Ex. Doc. 31, 2.

2. The New York legislature was considering action to enable formation of state banking associations in accordance with the national currency act of February 1863. Allen Munroe (b. 1819), a Republican from Syracuse, had served in the state's senate since 1859. William Allen Butler to Chase, Apr. 2, 10, 1863, Ira Harris to Chase, Apr. 8, 1863 (Chase Papers, L.C.); William D. Murphy, *Biographical Sketches of the State Officers and Members of the Legislature of the State of New York. In 1862 and '63* (Albany, 1863), 89–92.

3. Henry Herbert Van Dyke (1809–88), New York printer, Republican politician, and superintendent of the state's banking department, 1861–65. *Appletons',* 6:245; *New York Tribune,* Jan. 13, 1864.

TO CUTHBERT BULLITT

Letterpress copy of autograph letter. Chase Papers, Historical Society of Pennsylvania (*micro* 26:0259).

Unofficial

Wash April 1[4]. 1863

My dear Sir,[1]

Accept my thanks for your letters concerning the condition of matters in New Orleans and for your personal expressions of esteem, which I reciprocate very cordially.[2]

It is difficult to judge accurately at this distance of the adaptation of measures to intended results: but it cannot be denied that a general impression prevails that the substitution of what may perhaps be well enough called the Banks policy for the Butler policy has not been useful.[3] I am the friend of each of these generals: and only prefer one to the other where a choice is to be made on public grounds.

I thought the idea of sending Gen. Banks to Texas with Gen. Hamilton as Military Governor & with a force sufficient, aided by the cooperation of loyal Texans, to ensure the possession of Galveston & the occupation of the Rio Grande, a wise one.[4] But had I been consulted as to his being sent to supercede Gen Butler I should have remonstrated against it as unwise & dangerous. It put both those gentlemen in false positions, and imposed on Gen. Banks a task to which it was not quite just to assign him.

All I learn from New Orleans convinces me that this view is correct. The Country has seen the policy of conciliating rebels tried without results until it is heartily weary of it. It prefers now the policy of justice. It is equally weary of the vain endeavor to maintain slavery which crushing the rebellion—to preserve the cause and kill the consequence. It sees no practical results of this policy at New Orleans, except increasing disloyalty or, perhaps more properly, increasing manifestation of disloyalty, and diminishing military strength through the abandonment of that system of recruiting from the colored population inaugurated by Gen. Butler.

I say this with the greatest regret—regret because of my wishes for Gen Banks personal success; deeper regret because of my apprehensions of the evil effects on the welfare of the country.

Let me hope that you will do what you can towards inspiring right sentiments & stimulating right action. At the same time let me frankly say to you that I fear that the generosity and openness of your nature may incline you too far towards lenity—very good in itself and very wise rightly timed; but capable of the worst effects when ill timed. This fear has just had a little quickening from a letter received this morning, about a clergyman lately returned to New Orleans. By the way I may as well send you the letter—it will save my time in writing about it—and you can return it after reading.

From Mr. Dennison I am glad to have good accounts of your success in administration.[5] It is my hope that you two will continue cordially to cooperate.

I enclose the New Regulations and the recent law with an official letter.[6]

Yours sincerely
S P Chase

Cuthbert Bullitt Esq
New Orleans.

1. Chase had appointed Bullitt acting collector of customs at New Orleans earlier in the year. Chase to George S. Denison, Jan. 19, 1863 (Denison Papers, L.C.); *Register of Officers (1863)*, 95; *Chase Papers*, 3:324.

2. Bullitt had sent at least three such communications since arriving in New Orleans early in March. Bullitt to Chase, Mar. 7, 14, 20, 1863 (Chase Papers, L.C.).

3. Control and confrontation had marked Benjamin F. Butler's rule of occupied New Orleans, which started in May 1862. With the arrival of Nathaniel P. Banks as military commander in December 1862, Federal policy became more conciliatory. Later, in November 1863, Butler assumed command of the districts of Virginia and North Carolina. *DAB*, 3:358; Fred Harvey Harrington, *Fighting Politician: Major General N. P. Banks* (Philadelphia, 1948), 140–42; Long, *Civil War Day by Day*, 432.

4. Banks's expedition against Texas did not start until the middle of August. President Lincoln had previously appointed Brig. Gen. Andrew Jackson Hamilton provisional governor of the state. *DAB*, 8:183; Harrington, *Fighting Politician*, 130–34; James Marten, *Texas Divided: Loyalty and Dissent in the Lone Star State, 1856–1874* (Lexington, Ky., 1990), 67.

5. Chase may have referred to George S. Denison's restrained evaluation of Bullitt in March: "Mr. Bullitt does very well," wrote Denison. "I had no high opinion of his business ability & have less now. He is a pleasant gentleman, & what is called generally a first rate fellow. Fortunately he appreciates his inexperience, & is docile & tractable. His presence lightens my labor but little——I have nearly as much to do as heretofore." Denison to Chase, Mar. 21, 1863 (Chase Papers, L.C.).

6. Treasury regulations issued on March 31, 1863, as a result of "An Act to Provide for the Collection of Abandoned Property and for the Prevention of Frauds in Insurrectionary Districts," signed into law on March 12. *Commercial Intercourse with and in States Declared in Insurrection, and the Collection of Abandoned and Captured Property* (Washington, D.C., 1863), 31–38; *Statutes at Large*, 12:820–21.

FROM WILLIAM CURTIS NOYES

Autograph letter. Chase Papers, Library of Congress (*micro* 26:0356).

New York, April 20 1863.

My dear Sir,

The omission to answer your letter has not been owing to any want of an adequate appreciation of its importance,[1] but to my being engaged in a long cause which has been under argumt some weeks & is still continuing; and also, to my desire to consult some experienced & valued friends in regard to the benevolent purpose which it embraces. I am rejoiced to find that the Govt. has finally concluded to avail itself of the services of two classes of men, more in earnest than any other, and whose aid as well as sympathy it for a long time repelled,—the sincere and original friends of the Slaves and the Slaves themselves. It was a grave mistake, to commit the conduct of the war to those who did not seem to appreciate the fierce bararity of those who commenced it, or their great determination to overthrow our free government; and who were not only insensible to the causes which produced it, but were willing to continue them & to guarantee their permanency. Now that this policy is given up—I fear in part only—the practical result seems to be that the able bodied Slaves who come under our control, will be formed into an armed force, & that all other classes of their people, including women & children, will be thrown upon the care of the Govt.; making it necessary that some means of a comprehensive character, should be adopted to put such of them as can work to some profitable labour and thereby, and by other means, to provide for their support, and the means of becoming ultimately a settled free population within the insurrectioning states; to some, if not to a great extent, taking the place of the present inhabitants who are in in rebellion. In short, the Port Royal experiment, which I understand has been a success, is to be tried over again on a large scale, for the great purpose of giving us a loyal population in the seceded states and this must necessarily demand the agency of a large number of persons and considerable pecuniary means in the outset of the scheme at least. After the large drafts upon our city, already made & those now daily required for purposes of benevolence, connected with the War, it is not reasonable to expect that any aid of great moment can, at present, be procured here—certainly it could not be without interfering with other operations, well organized & conducted, of an indispensable character—such as the Sanitary & Christian Commissions &c.[2] [Moreover], my own conclusions agree with those of the judicious friends I have consulted, that any one undertaking to consider your suggestions and disposed to act upon them, should be informed to what extent & under what circumstances the protection and aid of the U.S. will be afforded, where & at what time the trial shall be attempted; & in short, a fuller development of the excellent idea underlying your communication. I think I can secure the active cooperation of some of our best men and perhaps some of the wealthiest, and I have to request that you will give me such further light on the subject as your position may enable you to afford, in order that I may, with them, act understandingly.

I suggest, that the way to secure the colored people & give them a real interest in our institutions and in their preservation, is to confer upon them titles to small parcels of land, thus making them freeholders. There will be enough of these if the confiscation acts shall be enforced,[3] as they should be, and I agree with you that their loyalty is more estimable than all the White rebels in the land. The slaves who have fled to us from their Masters, have hitherto had small reason to count upon our care for them & I regret to say that even here, there is little love for the colored people. A class among us would not only drive them from all employments, but many would take their lives & until this atrocious public sentiment is changed and justice done them, we may count upon a continuation of that Divine vengeance which is now being visited upon us for our countless wrongs against them. If we wish to win the aid of their strong arms and iron muscles, we must first secure their hearts.

I am writing, and listening to an argument & [hope] you will excuse the haste of my letter— Should it be needful to *talk* about this matter, I would go to Washington for a day or so.

Very truly Yours,
WM. CURTIS NOYES.

Hon. S. P. Chase.

1. Chase had written to Noyes on April 7 (above).
2. The U.S. Christian Commission, a religious voluntary organization founded by the Young Men's Christian Association, and the U.S. Sanitary Commission promoted the welfare of Union soldiers. Charles Capen McLaughlin et al., eds., *The Papers of Frederick Law Olmsted,* 6 vols. to date (Baltimore, 1977–), 4:52.
3. The first and second confiscation acts, August 6, 1861, and July 17, 1862. *Statutes at Large,* 12:319, 589–92.

TO ABRAHAM LINCOLN

Autograph letter. Abraham Lincoln Papers, Library of Congress (*micro* 26:0381).

Philadelphia, Apl. 22. 1863.

My dear Sir,

My purpose in visiting Philadelphia & New York at this time is to ascertain, if a loan, say of fifty millions, to pay off all arrears cannot now be obtained. The only difficulty I find in the way springs from the painful uncertainty generally prevalent as to the future of the War. Notwithstanding this, however, I hope to succeed; and I am greatly cheered by the resolved determination which appears to animate all our friends. This is a sentiment which can be easily converted into triumphant gladness by the acheivement of some important successes and above all by the development of some settled and promising plan for the successful termination of the contest.

I have, since I came here, heard a good deal of the facility of communication with the rebels by their friends in loyal states. A lady stated to me the other day—Sunday—that she wrote about the last of March to some friends in South Carolina announcing the death of a relative and that she had just received a reply. The time for going and returning was only a little more than three weeks. A regular mail goes to Nassau under our postal arrangement with Great Britain and letters to the interior of Rebeldom are thence forwarded by the Blockade Runners. A large proportion of these letter mails from Nassau get safely through. In fact it is not difficult to imagine an arrangement by which they might nearly all be safely landed at unfrequented spots. I do not know that there is any remedy for this; but if possible one should be found.

I have just received a letter from my friend Gen Garfield, who is Chief of Rosecrans Staff.[1] It gives me the best idea of that army, its relations and purposes that I have yet obtained from any quarter, and inspires me with great hopes / Unless something decisive is to be done on the Mississippi & done promptly, is it not now clear that Grants Army should be made to cooperate otherwise with Rosecrans? How I wish that Sherman was at the head of that Army instead of Grant. He is certainly an abler & better & more reliable Commander.[2]

Next Saturday I hope to be in Washington again. Meantime I thought you would not be displeased to hear some account of me.

Yours most Sincerely
S: P: CHASE

The President

1. James A. Garfield, Ohio Republican and, at this time, brigadier general of volunteers, had been elected to the U.S. House of Representatives on March 4. He served in Congress from December 1863 to December 1880. Maj. Gen. William S. Rosecrans commanded the Army of the Cumberland, 1862–64. *Bio. Dir. U.S. Cong.*, 1043–44; *DAB*, 7:145–46, 16:163–64.

2. Maj. Gen. Ulysses S. Grant, presiding over the Department of the Tennessee and commanding the Army of the Tennessee, was preparing the Thirteenth Army Corps for a successful assault on Vicksburg, Miss., July 4, 1863. William Tecumseh Sherman, at the time a major general of volunteers, commanded one of two corps in the Army of the Mississippi. *DAB*, 7:496, 17:94–95; Long, *Civil War Day by Day*, 281, 378–79.

FROM WILLIAM H. ASPINWALL AND JOHN MURRAY FORBES

Letter in Aspinwall's hand, also signed by Forbes. Chase Papers, Historical Society of Pennsylvania (*micro* 26:0435).

No. 3.

London 25th April 1863

Hone. S. P. Chase
Secty of the Treasury
Washington
Dear Sir

Since our last respects under date of 18th inst. we have had the bonds conveyed to this City—& have handed over to Messr Baring Bro & Co, as collateral to the loan of £500,000—the bonds from No. 20,001 to 23,999 inclusive, as set forth in the enclosed copy of our letter to them, dated 24th. inst. The remaining 6000 bonds—or rather six millions worth of bonds remain in their vault for safe keeping subject to our order.[1]

We have now to acknowledge rect. of your letter of 30. March handed to us by the Hone. Robt J Walker, & to say that this gentleman has also repeated us the verbal explanations which you made to him before his departure.[2] We have carefully considered both: & we find that the main object of his visit to Europe is to acquaint European capitalists with the actual circumstances & resources of our country.

We think he will render great service in helping to stem the current of ignorance & misapprehension so generally prevalent in Europe; & in compliance with your suggestions we shall confer freely with him on all occasions when we think he can, by his advice or his knowledge of facts, or by his political position, aid us in carrying out the objects of our mission; but we do not consider ourselves called on, either by your letters or by our own judgement of what is expedient, to show him our instructions, altho he has exhibited to us his own; nor do we feel justified, under our understanding with Messr. Baring Brothers & Co, to mention to him or to any one else here the particulars of our temporary loan;[3] we have told him generally that the difficulty did not lie so much in the question of money for the iron clads, as in the difficulty of getting hold of those partially paid for by the rebels, & that if the opportunity offered we felt no fear of obtaining a reasonable Sum to secure them.

We all agree that the policy just now, is to bring the Government, & the public to understand the injustice & impolicy of allowing them to be fitted out—& we feel greatly encouraged by the progress made in this respect. The recent debates in Parliament, especially that of last evening, show that this Government is fully committed to see that the existing law is vigilantly carried out & that their interpretation of it will forbid the sailing of these engines of destruction, if proof of identification can be established.[4] We shall relax no effort in this important matter—& also in the less imperative, but still important, matter of getting control of dangerous smaller vessels fitting out in England & Scotland; full details of these efforts go to the [He.] the Secretary of the Navy by this mail[5]—

We can get no trace of any formidable ram building by Mr. Winans—he is building another Segar-steamer the particulars of which we are promised in a day or two.[6]

We have not been negligent on the last suggestion of your letter; & are prepared to resort to it whenever other means fail; but the institution of criminal prosecutions against Laird & other builders, by us or any American official or individual party, would be liable to raise up such an excitement as would frustrate the object in view.[7] The English Government must be moved to take these proceedings—or failing to do this effectually, we can count on a local English association for action—& either of these must command a support we could not rely on, & both must be exhausted before we take the last chance.

We defer a reply to the alteration in your instructions for the long loan, untill the rect. of promised suggestions from France & Holland & Germany.[8] In the present excited state of the public mind, nothing can be done; but we are not without hope that by the time we receive your decision on the suggestions we hope to send you by the next Cunard mail, a change may have come over the Stock Exchange with reference to the value of a loan from the Federal Government.[9]

We are very truly

Your obt Servts.
WM. H. ASPINWALL
J. M FORBES

1. In March, U.S. entrepreneurs Aspinwall and Forbes had embarked on a mission to encourage British confiscation of Confederate ironclads constructed in British shipyards, to secure a loan from Baring Brothers banking firm, and to sound prospects for a $50 million loan by way of bond sales in Europe. They had taken with them $10 million in 5–20 bonds for use as collateral for the loan from Baring Brothers. In their letter of April 18, Forbes and Aspinwall reported that the bank had agreed to a smaller loan than Chase had hoped, secured by $4 million of the bonds, and with a term of six months rather than the anticipated one year. *Chase Papers,* 3:408–12; Aspinwall and Forbes to Chase, Apr. 18, 1863 (Chase Papers, Hist. Soc. of Pa.).

2. Chase's letter of March 30 contained detailed instructions for Aspinwall and Forbes. Chase had secretly commissioned former Treasury secretary Robert J. Walker to assist the pair and to spread favorable word in Europe of U.S. economic health. *Chase Papers,* 3:408–14.

3. Chase discussed the mission of Aspinwall and Forbes in several letters after recruiting them. On March 21, he had told them to "make the best terms possible" for a temporary loan, "and not go above six percent unless in your judgment a real exigency shall require it." Chase to Aspinwall and Forbes, Mar. 16 (four letters) and 21 (two letters) (Chase Papers, Hist. Soc. of Pa.); same to same, Mar. 30, 1863, *Chase Papers,* 3:408–12.

4. On April 24, the opposition in Parliament had assailed the British government for recently seizing the *Alexandria,* a schooner under construction for the Confederacy in Liverpool. The Foreign Enlistment Act of 1819 forbade British subjects from selling ships for use against governments at peace with England. *London Times,* Apr. 25, 1863; Long, *Civil War Day by Day,* 335; Frank Merli, *Great Britain and the Confederate Navy, 1861–1865* (Bloomington, 1965), 183, 205.

5. Forbes and Aspinwall sent regular intelligence and advice to Secretary of the Navy Gideon Welles, including letters of April 22 and 29 from Forbes to Welles (Welles Papers, L.C.).

6. Inventor and Confederate sympathizer Ross Winans was experimenting with a vessel shaped similar to a cigar. *DAB,* 20:372.

7. In his letter of March 30, Chase had mentioned the possibility of "criminal prosecutions . . . against Laird, in the trial of which all the facts relating to the equipment, in Great Britain of ships of war for the rebels might be fully brought out." British shipbuilders besides John Laird known to have dealt with the Confederacy included Fawcett, Preston and Company, Jones and Company, William C. Miller, Alexander Stephen and Sons, and J. and G. Thomson. Chase to Aspinwall and Forbes, Mar. 30, 1863, in *Chase Papers,* 3:411; Merli, *Britain and the Confederate Navy,* 63, 121, 128, 138–39.

8. Chase's instructions indicated "that I do not regard it as a matter of very great importance that you use the authority given you to negotiate a Loan of Fifty Millions of Dollars in Europe." *Chase Papers,* 3:409.

9. On April 29, Aspinwall informed Chase that the Baring Brothers wanted to be paid in British sterling. Chase approved of this arrangement in a response written on May 14, and told Aspinwall and Forbes at that time that the larger anticipated European loan would not be needed due to improved domestic demand for the bonds. The British and North American Royal Mail Steam Packet Company, operated for the British government by the Cunard Line, had a reputation for fast, reliable, inexpensive delivery. Aspinwall to Chase, Apr. 29, 1863, Chase to Aspinwall and Forbes, May 14, 1863 (Chase Papers, Hist. Soc. of Pa.); Francis E. Hyde, *Cunard and the North Atlantic: A History of Shipping and Financial Management* (London, 1975), 27–35.

FROM BENJAMIN F. FLANDERS

Autograph letter. Chase Papers, Historical Society of Pennsylvania (*micro* 26:0511).

Private

New Orleans April 30th 1863[1]

Dear Sir,

Our friends, with whom we consult, object to Mr. Waples for Judge.[2] He is considered eccentrick, sometimes flighty, and hence an unsafe man for that appointment. We have not yet found one possessing all the essential requisites for the office, who can or will accept it; and we will not recommend any person who has them not. The members of the Bar and the public generally are extremely desirous that the Court should be opened as soon as possible.

To obviate supposed objections and obstacles a number of prominent lawyers, petitioned the President to establish the Court and appoint Judge Peabody to preside over it, but they do not want him appointed if the Court can be opened by any other suitable person.[3] The Provisional Court and its officers are in very bad repute among our union people, and the suppression of the whole establishment would gratify the public.

I hope that before the departure of the next steamer a suitable person will be agreed upon and induced to allow his name to be presented to the President. Most of our lawyers who are competent and fit for the position gain by their practice twice the amount of the salary attached to the Judgeship and, they do not think the honor and permanency of the office an equivalent for the pecuniary sacrifice they would make by accepting it. Some of our best men are ineligible having voluntary held office under Confederate rule.

The union Sentiment here has been much depressed but it is now higher than ever. The recent brilliant success of General Banks, has greatly elated Union men:[4] and the vigorous policy foreshadowed in his late orders gives them great satisfaction.

I now think General Banks will do well, and succeed here; but it is essential to his success, or to that of any Commander placed here, that he should not be hampered by instructions or interfered with by orders from Washington; at this distance from the Government a large discretion should be allowed the Commander both as to his military movements and his civil administration

General Banks is not the equal of General Butler but it will be found, upon investigation, that he has not deserved the complaints made against him. The weak feeling which depressed Union men and made the disloyal insolent and defiant, was not his. That policy was a great mistake, whoever dictated it, but not a greater mistake than the placing of three independent authorities here; A Military Commander, a Military Governor, and a Provisional Judge, who were not in accord[5]

Much evil has resulted from this trinity of powers.

The Military Governor and his people were Butler Men and *he* could direct them. Genl Banks could neither influence or direct them without a *fuss.* The Provisional Court is regarded as Copperhead. I think their notions will improve with time, but you have seen the injury they have done the cause.

I am informed that General Ulman brings orders to take for soldiers the negroes who are working the plantations under Genl. Bank's arrangement with the planters.[6] If that is done it will prove mischievous; a great mistake. I would not have advised such an arrangement, but being in operation, and working pretty well, I would not disturb it at present. This part of the State is now quiet and "making a living" Many plantations are being managed upon Genl. Bank's contract plan, others by free labor, black and white.

The Opelousas country, recently conquered,[7] will supply Genl. Ulman with as many negroes as he wants to make up the force he is authorized to raise, and they are all free.

Genl. Banks has scarcely force enough to occupy and hold that country till Ullman's force is organized, and it would be very unwise to create trouble by disturbing arrangements made in good faith in this part of the State, and which the force of events now in progress will soon render inoperative.

Mr. Bullitt is less fit for the place he holds than I suspected. He is weak and not far from wicked. He *might* get along with the usual Custom House business—but the internal trade is entirely beyond his capacity. An agent for that business should be *immediately* sent or appointed here. Knowing how important you thought the business when you were drawing up the regulations for that trade I have expected an agent to manage it, by every steamer. I think Mr. Plumly would be an excellent appointment.[8] In the brief acquaintance I have had with him I have conceived a high opinion of his character and capacity— If you do not think best to select him for that special agency, and if you can repose sufficient confidence in me I would ask for the appointment.

The internal revenue business is well conducted in both departments / A large revenue will be collected, here.

I have the honor to be,

Very Respectfully,

Your Obt Servant

BENJ. F. FLANDERS

Hon Salmon P Chase

Secretary of the Treas'y.

1. Flanders's single term as a Unionist congressman had ended in March. During the remainder of the year he served as a captain in the Louisiana Volunteer Infantry, received an appointment as special agent of the Treasury Department in May and, in November or December, became president of the First National Bank of New Orleans. In 1864, he ran unsuccessfully against Michael Hahn as a candidate for governor of Louisiana. *Bio. Dir. U.S. Cong.*, 1004; Chase to Flanders, May 16, 1863 (Letters Sent Relating to Restricted Commercial Intercourse and Captured and Abandoned Property, Gen. Recs. Treasury Dept., Nat. Arch.); Thomas J. Durant to Chase, Dec. 4, 1863 (below).

2. In January Abraham Lincoln had appointed Rufus Waples U.S. attorney for the eastern district of Louisiana. U.S. Senate, *Journal of the Executive Proceedings of the Senate of the United States . . .* (Washington, D.C., 1828–; reprint, New York, 1969), 13:368.

3. Charles Augustus Peabody (1814–1901), a prominent Republican and former New York Supreme Court justice, had served on Louisiana's provisional court since its organization on October 20, 1862. Lincoln appointed him chief justice of the state's supreme court later in the year. *Appletons'*, 6:695–96; Roy P. Basler, ed., *The Collected Works of Abraham Lincoln*, 9 vols. (New Brunswick, N.J., 1953–55), 5:467–68; *New York Times*, July 4, 1901.

4. Earlier in the month, Federal forces under Nathaniel Prentiss Banks had conducted a series of successful military movements in Louisiana, culminating in May with the siege of Port Hudson. For the evident new direction of Banks's policy in Louisiana, see Chase's letter to Banks of May 19, 1863 (below). Long, *Civil War Day by Day*, 338, 340, 346, 353.

5. That is, Nathaniel P. Banks; George F. Shepley, military governor of New Orleans, June 1862 to May 1864; and Charles A. Peabody. *DAB*, 17:79.

6. Orders from the War Department authorized Brig. Gen. Daniel Ullmann, a former American party politician, to raise six companies of "Louisiana volunteer infantry," recruited "from the plantations and from whatever source." The "arrangement" assured wages for black laborers, but offered assistance to maintain order on plantations and to prevent former slaves from leaving. *Appletons'*, 6:206; Louis S. Gerteis, *From Contraband to Freedman: Federal Policy Toward Southern Blacks, 1861–1865* (Westport, Conn., 1973), 85–98; *OR*, ser. 3, v. 3:99, 101–2.

7. Union troops had occupied the region since April 20. Long, *Civil War Day by Day*, 340.

8. Benjamin Rush Plumly apparently served under Banks as "general appraiser" at this time. He later helped supervise abandoned plantations. In May, Chase appointed Flanders to the position in question. *Appletons'*, 5:43; Chase to Plumly, Feb. 26, 1864 (Chase Papers, Hist. Soc. of Pa.); Chase to Flanders, May 16, 1863 (Letters Sent Relating to Restricted Commercial Intercourse and Captured and Abandoned Property, Gen. Recs. Treasury Dept., Nat. Arch.); Chase to Plumly, May 23, 1863 (below); Plumly to Chase, Aug. 1, 28, 1863 (Chase Papers, L.C.).

FROM JAMES A. GARFIELD

Autograph letter on letterhead stationery. Chase Papers, Library of Congress (*micro* 26:0599).

HEAD-QUARTERS, DEPARTMENT OF THE CUMBERLAND,
Murfreesboro. May 5 1863.

Hon. S. P. Chase.

My Dear Friend,

Yours from New York of April 25th. came duly to hand, and yesterday your package of letters to the Union League was received.

I am exceedingly gratified with your letter— It is an opportune moment to advance those views. The time is ripe in the army—and there will be heard only a feeble voice of dissent. We are gradually getting educated up to the point of willingness to use the means which God has placed in our hands for ending the war. Gen. Rosecrans read the letter and was greatly pleased with it— He sends his best regards—and tells to say that he fully concurs in the views expressed in your letter.

The situation here is now very interesting. The rebels have been reinforced from Mobile, and have advanced their lines to this side of Duck River.

The two armies now confronting each other here—will, I think have a collision soon.[1] Gen. Hartsuff was sent here by Gen. Burnside, and night before last—a council was held to determine upon a plan of operation by which Gen B's force should or part of it, at least, move in conjunction with ours.[2]

I am been anxious to impress upon the General the truth that our true objective point of operations is the rebel army and not any partical position or territory.

In Europe, if an army becomes master of London, Paris, Vienna or Berlin, it has conquered England, France, Austria or Prussia. Not so with the Confederacy. We may take Richmond, but they can put their government, with all its archives on wheels and trundle it away into the interior in 48 hours— Nothing but hard blows that will break their armies, and pulverize them can destroy the Confederacy— I am therefore for striking, striking, & striking again till we do break them. The two armies here are in fine condition— Indeed they are veteran armies—and there will be a fearfully bloody struggle when the grapple again—& I think the day of conflict is now very near. The movement at which I hinted in my last, is now so far in progress that I may speak of it safely. We have sent a force of near 2000 men—that went down the Cumberland, up the Tennesse, and on the 26th April, under cover of a force from Corinth which we had engaged to act in concert with our own—it left Tuscumbia Alabama for the mountains, and I hope & believe it has by this time reached the Georgia R.R. system and broken it, between Rome & Atlanta. I have set my heart on this expedition more than on any one thing since I have been here. In order to secure it—after I had fully canvassed the ground I offered to lead it myself—Gen. R. could not spare—me—but we chose—one of my old officers that served with me last year, Col Streight of Ind[3]—who will make thorough work—and if at last surrounded he will sell his command as dearly as possible. When the blow has fully fallen upon the rebels—I think we can successfully meet them in front— Should this rear movement be successful—its results can hardly be estimated. The loss of the whole force would be trifling in comparison with the advantages to us—

I hardly know what I ought to do in reference to the Congressional question.[4] But there are so many contingencies hanging on the events of this "Battle Summer" that the question may have adjusted itself long before, the time for decision arrives— When the time comes I shall be glad to hear from you[5]— Of course I shall stay in the army for the present—

Remember me kindly to Miss Kate and when you can—please favor me with a letter. With kindest regards

I am Very Truly Your Friend
J. A. Garfield

1. For the Union, the Army of the Cumberland, under William S. Rosecrans, faced Confederate Braxton Bragg's Army of Tennessee. A series of minor clashes between the armies ceased on June 23, when Rosecrans outflanked Bragg at Tullahoma, Tenn., and thus triggered the Tullahoma, or Middle Tennessee, campaign. Long, *Civil War Day by Day,* 370; James M. McPherson, *Ordeal by Fire: The Civil War and Reconstruction* (New York, 1982), 334.

2. Maj. Gen. George Lucas Hartsuff commanded the Twenty-third Army Corps at this time. In March, Lincoln had assigned Ambrose E. Burnside, also a major general, to head the Department of the Ohio. Burnside gained notoriety there for efforts to find and prosecute opponents of the Union war effort. *DAB,* 3:311–12, 8:369–70.

3. Abel D. Streight (1829–92) of the 51st Indiana Infantry. Rossiter Johnson, ed., *The Twentieth Century Biographical Dictionary of Notable Americans . . . ,* 10 vols. (Boston, 1904; reprint, Detroit, 1968), v. 10.

4. Whether Garfield should give up his army commission to take his seat in Congress. *Chase Papers,* 3:383–84, 389–90.

5. See Chase to Garfield, May 31, 1863 (below).

FROM GEORGE S. DENISON

Autograph letter on letterhead stationery. Chase Papers, Library of Congress (*micro* 26:0659).

Private

United States Internal Revenue,
COLLECTOR'S OFFICE,
DISTRICT OF THE STATE OF LOUISIANA,
New Orleans, May 9th 1863.

Dear Sir—

We are getting along very well in the Office of Internal Revenue. My official Bond will be transmitted next week. The selection of Mr. Higgins as Assessor is a good one, & he is quite popular here, besides being unexceptionable as to politics.[1] His selections of assistant assessors are excellent.

In a recent letter, I suggested to you the propriety of taking from Mr. Bullitt, the internal trade business, & putting it in the hands of a competent person.[2] I now repeat the suggestion emphatically. The fact is I have tried to like Mr. Bullitt, because you sent him here, & to assist him so that the Custom House might be managed creditably. In both those desires I have utterly failed. I know he is a fool & am almost equally sure he is a bad man. He is false in all things & venal in all things, & I cannot help regarding a man whose word cannot be trusted, as past all hope. Probably he or any other man has a right to make money, (if that is his ambition) honorably honestly & without using or compromising his official position, but Bullitt proclaims his object to be money making—in his office or on the street—without shame or sense of propriety.

But he can do no harm, the internal business (Regulations of March 31st) being placed in other hands. If you are not ready to send some one from Washington, appoint temporarily, some one already here, & the sooner it is done, the better.

I hope too, you will have some one here to carry out the law concerning "abandoned and captured property".[3] The Quartermaster[4] is shipping cotton seized by Gov't, to New York for sale, & I cannot collect the Excise tax. They refuse to pay & of course, I cannot help myself. On inquiry at the Quarter Master's Office, I was informed that Gen. Banks had temporarily appointed Col. Chandler to act under that law, until the Special Ag't appointed by you, should arrive.[5] I hope you will see that Gen. Banks shall not make appointments for you. This proceeding throws everything into confusion & will give rise, I fear, to legal questions to be raised by the claimants of the property. I should say that this business & the internal trade might be done by one person, if a good business man.

I hope you will keep Mr. Plumly here, & give Mr. Flanders the best office at your command. Gen. Banks has seized eight or ten thousand bales cotton, and about same number hogsheads Sugar, on which I shall be unable to collect the tax (which should be paid here, of course) unless some one authorized by you, is here to receive it from the Quartermaster.

Very Respectfully

Your Ob't Servant
George S. Denison

Hon S. P. Chase
Secretary of the Treasury

1. As special agent of the Treasury Department and acting surveyor of customs Denison had to post a bond of five thousand dollars. The new assessor of internal revenue was William H. Higgins. Denison to Chase, Feb. 21, 1863 (Chase Papers, L.C.); *New Orleans Times*, June 17, 1865; *Register of Officers (1863)*, 41.

2. "Bullitt is not a smart man," Denison had written on April 25. "I believe this business . . . should be in the hands of a shrewd man who will be your friend through thick & thin," he added, suggesting as a replacement either Benjamin F. Flanders or Benjamin R. Plumly. Denison to Chase, Apr. 25, 1863 (Chase Papers, L.C.).

3. Denison referred to "An Act to Provide for the Collection of Abandoned Property," the enabling legislation for the Treasury regulations of March 31. Later in May, Chase appointed Benjamin F. Flanders to the position. Chase to Flanders, May 16, 1863 (Letters Sent Relating to Restricted Commercial Intercourse and Captured and Abandoned Property, Gen. Recs. Treasury Dept., Nat. Arch.); *Statutes at Large*, 12:820–21.

4. Capt. Samuel Beckley Holabird (b. 1826). *Nat. Cyc.*, 10:122.

5. Banks had appointed professional soldier John Gorham Chandler (1830–1915). Ibid., 17:59.

FROM GEORGE S. DENISON

Autograph letter on letterhead stationery. Chase Papers, Library of Congress (*micro* 26:0656).

Private

United States Internal Revenue,
COLLECTOR'S OFFICE,
DISTRICT OF THE STATE OF LOUISIANA,
New Orleans, May 9th 1863.

Dear Sir

I failed to inform you in my other letter of today,[1] of the course pursued by Gen. Banks in regard to produce in the country recently occupied by him.

By an order (unpublished) of the General, the Quarter Master seizes all cotton & all sugar found as the army advances.[2] This cotton & sugar is brought to the city, & the sugar (as I am informed) is to be sold here, while the cotton will be shipped to New York for sale. Col. Chandler supervises the business. It is said that the loyal owners will be paid what their produce was worth before Banks occupied their country, but one of the principal Quartermasters informs me that Chandler is appointed by Banks to carry out the law concerning "abandoned & captured property," until the regular agent is appointed by you.[3] One gov't steamship leaves tomorrow loaded with Quartermaster's cotton which has not paid Excise tax, but, of course, its seizure by me is a physical impossibility. This cotton is consigned to the Quarter Master at N.Y. to be sold for the Gov't.[4]

Mr. Gray tells me he shall offer you his resignation.[5] Do not accept it. He has been faithful in the service of the Gov't for 25 years, and is the most efficient Deputy Collector I have ever seen.

Dr. Kennedy, Editor of the New Orleans "True Delta" is going on to Washington, but I do not know with what object, unless it be to assist the planters.[6] Dr. Kennedy is a brother-in-law of Bullett's, and is a smart man. His "True Delta", was an anti-Jeff-Davis paper always, but never since the occupation of the city by the Gov't troops, has it contained a single outspoken word in favor of the Union. I believe the planters intend to purchase a controlling interest in it, so that in future it may be the *pro-slavery-Union* organ.

Very Respectfully

Your Ob't Serv't
GEORGE S. DENISON

To
Hon S. P. Chase
Secretary of the Treasury

1. Denison actually wrote two other letters on May 9: one published above and another that discussed military operations in Louisiana and Mississippi. "The prospect of opening the River never seemed brighter than today," he reported, "& when that is done the Rebellion is virtually finished." In the same letter Denison alerted Chase to a delegation of Louisiana planters headed toward Washington, D.C., in pursuit of special consideration. Denison to Chase, May 9, 1863 (Chase Papers, L.C.).

2. "Many protests have been presented by persons claiming to be French or English subjects against this seizure," wrote Banks of the order; "but it will be found, upon full consideration, to be not only the right, but the duty, of the Government to appropriate this property in this manner." Banks to Edwin M. Stanton, May 4, 1863, in *OR,* ser. 3, v. 3:189.

3. See Denison's other letter of May 9 (above).

4. David H. Vinton, a deputy quartermaster general, was chief quartermaster at New York, 1861–66. *Appletons',* 6:301.

5. Formerly of New York, William C. Gray, deputy collector at New Orleans, had apparently received his appointment through Hiram Barney's influence. In June, Gray faced allegations of irregularities related to customs on cigars, and Cuthbert Bullitt suspended him. Later in the summer Gray received successive appointments as acting chief clerk in New Orleans and acting special agent. Chase to Benjamin F. Flanders, Aug. 19, 1863 (Third Special Agency, Incoming Letters, Recs. of Civil War Special Agencies, Nat. Arch.); *Chase Papers,* 3:224; Gray to John Hutchins, June 26, 1863 (Chase Papers, L.C.).

6. Irish-born former druggist Hugh Kennedy (1810–88) was a leading Democratic politician in New Orleans, the brother-in-law of Cuthbert Bullitt, and, until January 1864, editor of the proslavery *True Delta.* In 1865, Kennedy started a turbulent one-year term as appointed mayor of the city. Melvin G. Holli and Peter D'A. Jones, eds., *Biographical Dictionary of American Mayors, 1820–1980: Big City Mayors* (Westport, Conn., 1981), 192; Peyton McCrary, *Abraham Lincoln and Reconstruction: The Louisiana Experiment* (Princeton, 1978), 208.

TO ABRAHAM LINCOLN

Autograph letter. Abraham Lincoln Papers, Library of Congress (*micro* 26:0676).

Treasury Department,
May 11, 1863.

Dear Sir,

Some weeks ago you verbally directed me to investigate the papers connected with the case of the Collector for the Puget Sound District and to report the result to you.[1]

Almost immediately afterwards important business of my Department called me to the Eastern Cities.[2] On leaving I directed the Assistant Secretary[3] to examine all the papers; arrange them in proper order; and make a brief of their contents so that, on my return, I could at once make the investigation you required.

I came back on Friday night (8th) & was informed by the Asst. Secretary that you had already directed him to make out and send to you a Commission for a new Collector.[4]

This information surprised and greatly pained me; for I had not thought it possible that you would remove an officer of my Department, without awaiting the result, although somewhat delayed, of an investigation directed by yourself; and appoint a successor, for whose action I must be largely responsible, without even consulting me on the subject.

Today I have received your note stating that the person for whom, in my absence, a commission was prepared, is deceased; and directing one to be made out for another person of whom I know absolutely nothing.[5]

It has been and is my ardent desire to serve you by faithful service to the country in the responsible post to which you have called me; but I cannot hope to succeed in doing so, if the selection of persons, to fill important subordinate places in the Department, is to be made, not only without my concurrence; but without my knowledge.

I can ask, of course, nothing more than conference. The right of appointment belongs to you; and if, after fair consideration of my views in any case, your judgment in relation to a proper selection, differs from mine, it is my duty to acquiesce, cheerfully, in your determination; unless, indeed, the case be one of such a character, as to justify my withdrawl from my post. I have, however, a right to be consulted. That right was virtually conceded to me when you invited me to assume the charge of the Department and make myself responsible for its administration.

The blank Commission which you direct me to send to you is enclosed; for, to obey your directions, so long as I hold office under you, is my duty. It is enclosed, however, with my most respectful protest against the precedent; and with the assurance that if you find anything in my views to which your own sense of duty will not permit you to assent, I will, unhesitatingly, relieve you from all embarrassment so far as I am concerned by tendering you my resignation.[6]

With very great respect,

Yours truly,
S P Chase

The President.

1. Lincoln was concerned about Joseph Vial ("Victor") Smith, collector of customs for the district and one of Chase's acquaintances from Cincinnati. Smith had antagonized residents of Washington Territory, a Democratic stronghold, and incurred the hostility of Gov. William Pickering and Surveyor General Anson G. Henry, two close friends of Lincoln, through a series of controversial decisions. In July 1862, a local grand jury levied formal charges of corruption against Smith which, however, were dismissed early the following year under pressure from Chase. Lincoln might have made his request for an investigation around March 1863, when he asked Chase to discuss Smith's case directly with Henry. Lincoln to Chase, Mar. 21, 1863, in Basler, *Collected Works,* 6:144; Marian Parks, "A Man for his Season: Victor Smith, 1826–1865" (master's thesis, Claremont Graduate School, 1981), 36–84; Smith to Chase, Aug. 22, 1859 (Chase Papers, L.C.).

2. During the latter part of April and early in May, Chase visited New York, Philadelphia, and Boston in search of subscribers for a loan. Chase to Lincoln, Apr. 22, 1863 (above); Chase to George Harrington, Apr. 30, May 1, 1863, Chase to National Academy, Apr. 24, 1863 (Letters Recd. from Exec. Officers, Secretary's Office, Gen. Recs. Treasury Dept., Nat. Arch.); Chase to Hiram Barney, May 4, 1863 (Chase Papers, L.C.).

3. George Harrington.

4. Lincoln had determined to appoint Henry Clay Wilson of Washington Territory. "I do not decide that the charges against him are true," wrote Lincoln of Smith. "I only

decide that the degree of dissatisfaction with him there is too great for him to be retained." Lincoln to Chase, May 8, 1863 (two letters), in Basler, *Collected Works,* 6:202.

5. Lincoln's letter of May 11 requested a commission for Frederick A. Wilson. Two days later, however, the president agreed to appoint Lewis C. Gunn, in accordance with wishes expressed by Chase. Ibid., 209, 213.

6. According to his endorsement, Lincoln considered this letter Chase's "First offer of resignation."

TO BENJAMIN C. LUDLOW

Letterpress copy of letter in clerk's hand, signed by Chase. Chase Papers, Historical Society of Pennsylvania (*micro* 26:0686).

Washington May 12, 1863

My dear Major,

Yours of the 8th was only received to-day.[1] It was very welcome. While I regret that the movement of the army was not crowned by a decisive victory, I have not been able to see wherein the commanding General, regarding the actual situation under the lights he had, could with prudence have acted otherwise than he did[.] Gen. Hooker had the reputation of a brave general. He now adds to that the reputation of discretion

On one point only am I at a loss. Why was not Lee's rear attacked when he was engaging Sedgwick?[2]

I am looking forward with confident expectation for best results from fresh movements. With God's blessing on a good cause we cannot fail to succeed; though, to my unmilitary judgment, the whole plan of campaign seems not well conceived. I look at the war both under political and military aspects; and it seems to me that occupation must be immediately followed by political reconstitution in order to secure permanent advantages. Hence, I should select, as the theatre of operations, those portions of the country where reconstitution should be easiest and most stable. Those portions are on the Gulf.

I would take Florida, Alabama, Louisiana and Texas, and make free States as rapidly as possible. I would arm the loyal native population, white or black, so as to put them into a condition of self-defense. Then I would push Northward up the Mississippi River, and Southward into East Tennessee and the Mountain Regions.

In some such way as this, I think the rebellion can be most speedily and economically crushed. *I* lay much stress on the "economically"; for the time must come, and is probably not very remote, when financial expedients, hitherto so successful, will be exhausted and great embarrassment must ensue.

I did not mean to go into this speculation when I commenced this letter. I am very thankful that you are yet safe, and pray God that He will protect you in the faithful discharge of your duty.

Give my best regards to Gen. Hooker and Gen. Butterfield,[3] and believe me

Cordially yours,
S P Chase

Maj. B. C. Ludlow

My press of engagements obliges me to dictate my letters to a confidential phonographer.[4]

1. Ludlow, Chase's brother-in-law and since 1862 a major in the Union army, served as aide-de-camp to Maj. Gen. Joseph Hooker. The letter was a participant's account of the battle of Chancellorsville, Va., May 1–4, a disaster for Federal forces, and of the subsequent retreat ordered by Hooker, who at the time commanded the Army of the Potomac. *DAB,* 9:197; Francis Bernard Heitman, *Historical Register and Dictionary of the United States Army* . . . 2 vols. (Washington, D.C., 1903), 646; Long, *Civil War Day by Day,* 344–49; Ludlow to Chase, May 8, 1863 (Chase Papers, L.C.).

2. Robert E. Lee commanded the Confederate Army of Northern Virginia. The attack on troops under Maj. Gen. John Sedgwick (1813–64), who presided over the Fifth and Sixth Corps in the Federal Army of the Potomac, had occurred on May 4. *DAB,* 9:197, 11:125–26, 16:548.

3. Maj. Gen. Daniel Butterfield served as Joseph Hooker's chief of staff in the Army of the Potomac. Ibid., 3:373.

4. Chase added this note in his own hand. The body of the letter is in the handwriting of Homer G. Plantz.

TO RICHARD C. PARSONS

Autograph letter. Chase Papers, Historical Society of Pennsylvania (*micro* 26:0693).

Washington May 13, 1863.

My dear Parsons,[1]

There seems to be some misunderstanding in your mind, about the Permits to buy Cotton. Of course if I could grant special favors to any body while administering a public trust, you would be a little more apt to be the recipient of them than any other person. But it would be wrong to do so, and I am resolved to keep myself absolutely clear of all imputations, not wholly groundless, while I retain the great trust now in my hands. Congress has, of necessity, conferred on me very extensive powers, and I *must* so use them as to give no occasion for accusations of abuse.

Hence I established General Regulations on the subject of intercourse with those portions of the insurgent States occupied by our armies, and confided the execution of them to Selected agents of integrity & capacity.[2] I saw very early that no Special Licences could be granted by the Department without exposing it to great reproach & determined to grant none. And except a few, early granted & long since revoked, none have been granted.

On the other hand in order to facilitate proper & legitimate transactions as far as possible the Collectors & Surveyors of the different ports were authorized to grant permits on conditions specified in the regulations; and it was entirely practicable for you and your associates if you desired to purchase cotton, to obtain permits to do so any where within our lines of occupation; and your resources & character would doubtless have enabled you to succeed if any body could. Naval & Military Commanders would naturally show preference for men of your known positions in Society and in this respect you would have naturally enjoyed some important advantages.

So you see that if no licence could be granted from this Department your way was by no means hedged up.

I have written so much on this subject that I cannot touch the other topics of your letter, except to say that I am delighted that your wife[3] escaped injury by that Railroad accident.

Senter is here.[4] I had a glimpse of him at the War Dept. but he has not called. Is he miffed?

Yours cordially
S P Chase

Col. R. C. Parsons

1. At the time, Parsons was collector of internal revenue at Cleveland, Ohio.
2. The rules were issued on March 4, 1862, in accordance with legislation signed into law on July 13, 1861. "Rules and Regulations Concerning Internal Commercial Intercourse," Mar. 4, 1862 (Letters Sent Relating to Restricted Commercial Intercourse and Captured and Abandoned Property, Gen. Recs. Treasury Dept., Nat. Arch.); *Statutes at Large,* 12:255–58.
3. Sarah Starkweather Parsons.
4. George B. Senter was commandant of Camp Cleveland from July 1862 to April 1864. David D. Van Tassel and John J. Grabowski, eds., *The Encyclopedia of Cleveland History* (Bloomington, 1987), 879–80.

TO WILLIAM H. ASPINWALL AND JOHN MURRAY FORBES

Letterpress copy of letter in clerk's hand, signed by Chase. Chase Papers, Historical Society of Pennsylvania (*micro* 26:0704).

May 14, 63.

Gentlemen.

Your letters have been received and read with much satisfaction.[1]

Your arrangement with Messrs Baring, Brothers & Co. is fully approved. The rate of interest is somewhat higher than would be required on a similar Loan in the United States; but, under the circumstances, was very properly allowed. Under the name interest I include, of course, the commissions arranged for.

I do not regret that you find European capitalists indisposed to make offers for a large loan. Such a loan, though it would not be declined if offered at New-York par for 5–20 Sixes,[2] is not now really desirable.

There is not at this date in the Treasury Department a single unsatisfied requisition for the Naval, Military, or Civil Service. The Army has been paid in full to the 1st. of March; and over ten millions of dollars have been already transferred to various Paymasters for payment of part of the troops to the 1st. of May, now current. The rest of the troops will be provided for during the remainder of this month; so that on the first of June, unless we meet some military reverses of a very serious character, our Army and Navy will have been fully paid off, and every just claim presented will have been fully satisfied.

Meanwhile, the issue of United States Notes for circulation (except some $150,000, daily, for yet a few days, to supply demands for small currency) has wholly ceased.[3] The investments of the people in the Five-twenty Sixes, together with the regular income from Customs and Internal Duties, more than meet our whole expenditure.

My financial measures have thus been crowned with more than expected success. The Banking System is received with great favor, and the National Currency bids fair to become, more rapidly than was anticipated, the only recognized currency of the country.[4] I have been very fortunate in securing the services of Mr. McCullough, the President of the State Bank of Indiana, as Comptroller of the Currency.[5] He leaves a position of larger pecuniary income to take charge of the National Currency Bureau, and will devote to the success of the Banking System all the powers of a vigorous, well-trained and very active mind.

You will not, therefore, think me sanguine, I hope, if I express a pretty strong confidence in our ability to meet all financial exigencies from domestic resources, should success crown the operations of the war

I must not omit to mention, as one ground of my confidence, the fact that, under an improved system of purchases and disbursements for the Army, our expenditures have been considerably reduced; so that our Debt, which I estimated at about $1120.000.000 on the 1st. of July, will not probably exceed $1050.000.000. With the resources created by the more vigorous application to production of all our industries, reinforced by large immigration, and by improved machinery, I think we may safely expect to carry on the war two years longer, if necessary, before we encounter a debt half as large as the present National Debt of Great Britain, or much more than half as burdensome on the people.[6]

You will readily see in these statements my reasons for not being solicitous for a Foreign Loan. A Domestic Loan is at all times to be preferred; and, under existing circumstances, it is cheapest as well as best.

I do not entertain, therefore, the idea of making either principal or interest payable otherwise than in American Gold or elsewhere than at the Treasury of the United States.

It is not my province to speculate on the War. The defeat of Gen. Hooker was a disaster attributable, in my judgment, to two causes[7]—first, and mainly, to the disreputable retreat of the 11th. Corps, attributed, and it may be rightly, to the substitution of Gen. Howard for Gen. Sigel in the command of it;[8] and, secondly, to the temporary, but for a time serious, injury sustained by Hooker from prostration by a ball which struck and shattered a pillar (wooden) on which he was leaning. This injury, perhaps, rendered him less prompt to seize the advantage offered by the situation when Lee was attacking Sedgwick than he should have been. I see no reason, however, for thinking that his army is not now an overmatch for any which the Confederates can probably assemble in Virginia. But on nothing connected with the War, do I wish to express any positive opinion. My Department is the Treasury, and my information as to the action of other Departments is quite limited.

The organizing of the Negro Regiments seems to be working very well. It is said that 50,000 Negro troops will probably be under arms before the end of June. If this be so, it is difficult to estimate the importance of the movement. Slavery cannot co-exist with such an organization; nor can peace be restored on any other basis than entire enfranchisement.

One of the Senators from Virginia (the Old State)[9] expressed to me yesterday his regret that the President had excepted the Norfolk District from the operation of his Proclamation, and said he would support cordially a revocation of the exception. I hope it will be revoked; and also the Louisiana exceptions.[10] I should be glad, indeed, to see Tennessee included in the Proclamation of Freedom

I hope all the documents, intended to go by Mr. Walker but [sent] after him, reached you soon after the date of your letter. Other documents specially asked for by Mr. Walker will be sent as soon as they can be collected. With this letter, you will receive some copies of the Compendium of the Census and of the last number of the Bankers Magazine, which contains an interesting account of the Gold Product of the World.[11]

Wishing and hoping best results from your patriotic labors, I remain

Most truly yours,
S: P: Chase

Wm. H. Aspinwall, Esq.,
& John M. Forbes, Esq.,
London

1. Chase received two letters since corresponding with Aspinwall and Forbes on April 25 (above). The first, written on May 2, enclosed a letter from the Baring Brothers firm that expressed qualified support for a loan of $25 million sold at a rate greater than six percent, but urged the domestic sale of bonds first to bolster the confidence of international investors. In the second, on May 8, Aspinwall and Forbes reported on discussions with French bankers. Aspinwall and Forbes to Chase, May 2 (enclosing Baring Brothers' of May 1), May 8, 1863 (Chase Papers, Hist. Soc. of Pa.).

2. That is, U.S. bonds callable in five years, maturing in twenty, and yielding six percent interest. Hammond, *Sovereignty,* 289; *Statutes at Large,* 12:345–48, 532–33.

3. Congress had authorized several forms of interest- and non-interest-bearing U.S. Treasury notes over the past two years. Hammond, *Sovereignty,* 46–47, 93–94.

4. On February 25, Lincoln had signed the national currency act, which provided the framework for a national banking system. Banking associations authorized under the act participated in the circulation of U.S. notes that would, Chase hoped, supplant the notes of state-chartered banks. *Statutes at Large,* 12:665–82; *Chase Papers,* 3:274, 368.

5. Hugh McCulloch had assumed the position in March 1863 and filled it until March 1865. *DAB,* 12:6–7.

6. Great Britain's national debt stood at $3,871,042,352.76 in U.S. currency on March 31, 1863. *Appletons' Annual Cyclopædia and Register of Important Events . . . ,* 42 vols. (New York, 1862–1903), 3:459.

7. At Chancellorsville early in May. See Benjamin C. Ludlow to Chase, May 12, 1863 (above).

8. West Point graduate Oliver Otis Howard (1830–1909), at the time a major general of volunteers, commanded the Eleventh Corps in the Army of the Potomac, a contingent dominated by German-American soldiers who disliked Howard for taking the place of their former leader, Maj. Gen. Franz Sigel. *DAB,* 9:279, 17:153.

9. Either John S. Carlile or Waitman T. Willey.

10. The Emancipation Proclamation specifically excepted the Louisiana parishes of Ascension, Assumption, Jefferson, Lafourche, Orleans, Plaquemines, St. Bernard, St. Charles, St. James, St. Johns, St. Martin, St. Mary, and Terrebonne, and the southeastern Virginia counties of Elizabeth City, Norfolk, Princess Anne, and York. Despite continuing pressure from Chase, Lincoln declined to revoke the exceptions. The president reminded Chase that the declared legal basis for the proclamation was solely "as a military measure," a justification that did not apply to the exempted districts. To revoke the exemptions, Lincoln explained, "must I not do so, . . . without any argument, except the one that I think the measure politically expendient, and morally right? Would I not thus give up all footing upon constitution or law? . . . Could this pass unnoticed, or unresisted? . . . Would it not lose us the elections, and with them, the very cause we seek to advance?" Basler, *Collected Works,* 6:29, 428–29; Ira Berlin et al., eds., *Freedom: A Documentary History of Emancipation, 1861–1867* (Cambridge, Eng., 1982–), ser. 1, v. 1:59–70; *Chase Papers,* 1:429, 447.

11. The article, which appeared in the May 1863 issue of *Bankers' Magazine,* summarized nine other publications. "Compendium" might refer to Joseph C. G. Kennedy, *Preliminary Report on the Eighth Census, 1860* (Washington, D.C., 1862). Robert J. Walker was preparing to write a collection of pamphlets later published as *American Slavery and Finances* (London, 1864), an explanation and defense of the Union cause. From London he had written on May 8 asking for copies of reports from the secretary of the interior and the commissioner of the General Land Office for 1861 and 1862, as well as "receipts from the tariff for the first three quarts. of the present fiscal year," and "receipts from internal taxation, by months or quarters, up to the latest dates." In addition, he requested a search for evidence that in 1849 Jefferson Davis had supported repudiation of controversial bonds previously sold by Mississippi's Union Bank. *Report of the Secretary of the Interior* and *Report of the Commissioner of the General Land Office,* 37th Cong., 3d sess., 1861, H. Ex. Doc. 1; Walker to Chase, May 8, 1863 (Chase Papers, Hist. Soc. of Pa.); Robert J. Walker, *Jefferson Davis and Repudiation . . .* (London, 1863).

TO NATHANIEL P. BANKS

Letterpress copy of autograph letter. Chase Papers, Historical Society of Pennsylvania (*micro* 26:0797).

Wash
May 19, 1863

Dear General,

Having received a pacquet from Gen Butterfield this evening with a request to read & forward it to you, I comply with pleasure.

I received longsince a letter from you concerning trade in your Department together with copies of some orders relating to social organization. There appeared, at the time, to be no occasion for suggestions on the former topic, and your ideas on the latter seemed so widely different from mine that comment from me seemed quite unlikely to be useful. I did not, therefore, trouble you with a reply.

Of late I rejoice to see that you have used proper severity with rebels and their Sympathizers and that you no longer hesitate to recruit existing or organize new colored regiments.[1] Had I felt at liberty to offer you counsel, I should have advised from the beginning judicious severity towards enemies and most liberal sympathy & support for friends of whatever complexion. We cannot hope, in my judgment, to crush this rebellion with the population of the rebel states practically united against us; and I do not believe that there is now any considerable portion of that population upon whose sympathy we can certainly count except the blacks. I could not help regretting, therefore, in your recent order something like an apology for the Corps d'Afrique, founded on the right of using any thing belonging to rebels, for the suppression of rebellion.[2]

I write very frankly, because I do not wish to leave my views at all in doubt and because I feel a great interest in your success in a trying position, where so much depends on your action. But be assured I do not wish to dogmatize; but greatly prefer to sustain you when differing from me [tho'] finding fault, with measures which I am sure were honestly & patriotically intended & have [*illeg.*] a presumption of soundness in their favor from the fact that your sound judgment exercised on the spot approves them.

Most heartily do I unite in the congratulations of the whole country upon the success of your recent military movements. The possession of Opelousas & Alexandria practically deprives rebellion of Texas.[3] Is it too much to hope that Louisiana & Texas may soon be reorganized with free labor institutions embarrassed by no exceptions.

A few days since I had the pleasure of accompanying Mrs Banks from New York to Boston.[4] It was very pleasant to have that opportunity of becoming better acquainted with her & with Col. & Mrs Howe who were with her.[5]

I enclose with this letter copies of the Acts of Congress & the Orders of the Secretaries of War & Navy and my own Regulation touching commercial intercourse & abandoned property.[6] I have appointed the Hon Mr. Flanders Supervising Special Agent for your Department & hope you will give him such aid as may be in your power.

Yours very truly
S: P: CHASE

Maj. Gen. N. P. Banks.

1. Recent examples of such "severity" included the forced dispersion of ten thousand Louisianans demonstrating in support of Confederate officers during February, and, in March, orders forbidding the use of any currency other than U.S. greenbacks. Banks had recently increased efforts to recruit black troops in response to competition from Daniel Ullman. Harrington, *Fighting Politician,* 94–95, 112; Benjamin F. Flanders to Chase, Apr. 30, 1863 (above).

2. "The Government makes use of mules, horses, uneducated and educated white men, in defense of its institutions," claimed General Orders No. 40 on May 1. "Why should not the negro contribute whatever is in his power for the cause in which he is as deeply interested as other men? We may properly demand from him whatever service he can render." *OR,* ser. 1, v. 15:717.

3. For Banks's successes, see Benjamin F. Flanders to Chase, April 30, 1863 (above). Federal forces had occupied Opelasas and Alexandria, La., on April 20 and May 6, respectively. Long, *Civil War Day by Day,* 340, 350.

4. Mary Theodosia Palmer Banks. For Chase's trip to the Northeast see his letter to Lincoln, May 11, 1863 (above).

5. At the time Frank E. Howe directed the New England Soldiers' Relief Association in New York City. Howe to Chase, May 20, 1863 (Chase Papers, L.C.); *New York Times,* May 24, 1883.

6. Chase apparently referred to acts of Congress regarding "commercial intercourse" and "abandoned and captured property," July 13, 1861, and May 20, 1862; to related orders by the secretaries of navy and war, March 31, 1863; and to Treasury regulations, March 31, July 3, and September 11, 1863—all of which were later printed in the compilation entitled *Commercial Intercourse.*

TO JOSEPH HOOKER

Copy in clerk's hand. Chase Papers, Library of Congress (*micro* 26:0934).

Copy

Washington[1]
May 2[3] 1863

My dear General

I shall try to write this letter in so plain a hand that you will not miss Butterfield in endeavoring to read it

This morning I called on Secretary Stanton with Chandler & Wade and expressed to him my opinion of your late movement & battle giving you the great credit which I honestly think due to you for the courage, ability and prudence you displayed.[2] The subject of increasin your present force was then discussed. In the course of the conversation on this matter the Secretary expressed his perfect readiness & indeed his earnest wish to give you all the support possible; but doubted whether adding the movable column now in front of Washington to your immediate command would help you so much as the retaining of it in its present position & work. He said most distinctly however, that every thing in Virginia east of the Shenandoah Valley was practically tho' not immediately under your orders and that you would be joined by whatever portion of the force before Washington on (on the) the Peninsula or in the vicinity of Norfolk you should think necessary to your most effective action; consulting of course as you certainly would, the general safety and success as well as the safety and success of the movement under your immediate personal direction.

After leaving Mr Stanton I saw the President. He read to me the letter you read to me yesterday at camp.[3] I made, of course, no allusion to the fact that I had heard it before but listened attentively. Having read it he said "you see exactly how the matter is left. At the same time while he seemed to feel the necessity of doing whatever you might desire to strengthen you, he expressed some apprehension lest in trying to do so, other important points might be too much weakened. He evidently regarded every (thing) as left pretty much to your discretion.

While I was with the President Maj Genl Couch was announced, and the President remarked that you were sending up the different commanders of Divisions that he might satisfy himself as to their sentiments in relation to which he had intimated some apprehension in his letter to you.[4]

The result of both interviews satisfied me that three courses are open to you; first inaction where you are until reinforced from the draft, if ever; secondly to fight with the troops you have & at once; thirdly to call earnestly & positively for the additional twenty or thirty thousand men for the movement you discribed as possible.

The first is not to be thought of if it can be possibly avoided; the second should not be risked except as as an alternative to the first; the third seems to me the true course. Ask the President for a correct statement of the troops at Norfolk & Suffolk at Fortress Monroe and on the Peninsula; ascertain as nearly as possible what may be spared without risking too seriously Norfolk or the approaches to the Fortress; make the same enquiries as to the troops before Washington and their work. Then collect all you need to hold your present position and move on the enemy with your main body according to your best judgement with the utmost possible celerity and decision. It really seems to me that all that is possible in months may be accomplished by vigorous work in some days, without seriously endangering the vast stores accumulated here or the important positions which must be held elsewhere.

There must indeed be no disaffection. Better far make new generals of the best captains or lieutenants. I fear it is a mistake to have chiefs of Corps come up here to tell their different stories, though it may be for the best. We all like to be heroes and every body knows so well what he himself has done and how much better every thing else would have been done if his counsel or his ideas had been followed!

Pardon this letter dear General; let it have not a bit of consideration except as hints to be improved or rejected by your better judgement.

Cordially Yours
S P: CHASE

Maj Genl Hooker.

1. The copyist used Treasury stationery, but crossed out the printed *Treasury Department* heading and wrote in *Washington.*

2. U.S. Senators Zachariah Chandler of Michigan and Benjamin F. Wade of Ohio accompanied Chase. Chase was among those in a divided cabinet who continued to support Hooker as commander of the Army of the Potomac after his defeat at the battle of Chancellorsville, May 1–4. Walter H. Hebert, *Fighting Joe Hooker* (Indianapolis, 1944), 227; Long, *Civil War Day by Day,* 344–49.

3. Chase had visited Hooker's camp near Falmouth, Va., May 21–22. In correspondence written on May 14, Lincoln altered previous orders for Hooker to cross the Rappahannock. "I . . . shall not complain if you do no more, for a time, than to keep the enemy at bay, . . . and to put your own army in good condition again. Still, if in your own clear judgment you can renew the attack successfully, I do not mean to restrain you. . . ." Lincoln continued: "I must tell you that I have some painful intimations that some of your corps and Division Commanders are not giving you their entire confidence. This would be serious, if true; and you should therefore, first of all, ascertain the real facts beyond all possibility of doubt." Lincoln to Hooker, May 14, 1863, Chase to Lincoln, May 21, 1863 (Lincoln Papers, L.C.); Chase to Laura Wiggins, May 23, 1863 (Chase Papers, Hist. Soc. of Pa.); *OR,* ser. 1, v. 24:479.

4. West Point graduate and major general of volunteers Darius Nash Couch (1822–97) commanded the Second Corps in the Army of the Potomac. *DAB,* 4:463–64.

TO BENJAMIN RUSH PLUMLY

Letterpress copy of autograph letter. Chase Papers, Historical Society of Pennsylvania (*micro* 26:0889).

Hon B. R. Plumley
New Orleans

Washington May 23, 1863

My dear Sir,

Your letters have not received the prompt replies which would have been given to them had not my engagements, of multiform character, been so exacting.[1]

What the country may think proper to do with me is of far less consequence then what it is my duty to do for my country. It does not so much matter that my services be recognized as that they be performed. Of course, I have little inclination for political arrangements having reference to my personal future; but prefer to leave that to the disposition of events and the will of the People: being myself quite as ready to resume the part of private citizen as to continue in my present or to be transferred to any other public position.

So I shall leave any body whether friendly or hostile to do just as they please concerning me, cherishing meanwhile gratitude and love for friends, but indulging no bitterness toward opposers.

You will see in these brief statements my reason for making no comments on a portion of your letter; for which however you must accept my sincere thanks; for all such information as that you give me is valuable & important many ways.

I had determined to make you Supervising Special Agent of Commercial Intercourse with the portions of the Insurgent States occupied by our troops and of the Collection of Abandoned Property, when I received a letter from Mr. Flanders saying that he would accept the appointment if tendered to him.[2] As you already hold the position of Appraiser General and there is a manifest impolicy not to say impropriety in appointing the same persons to two such positions, if no public exigency really requires it; I did not hesitate to make Mr. F—— the Supervising Special Agent: and his appointment and instructions have been already sent him. In this action I count on your approval & support: and I hope Mr. Flanders will be able, by industry & energy, to reduce everything in his District to as good system as is now established in Mr. Mellens.[3] There is every reason to hope now that intercourse by the River between the two Districts will be soon restored and permanently maintained.

I have contributed with great pleasure to the reestablishment of regular Federal Judicial Authority in New Orleans by securing the appointment of the gentlemen recommended by Messrs Flanders & Hahn as District Judge, District Attorney & Marshal.[4] This will do away with the necessity for the Anomalous Court held by Judge Peabody except so far as it may be needed as a temporary substitute for a State Court.

This will not I hope be long. Hardly anything can be more important to us now than the reorganization of the State of Louisiana and its practical restoration to the Union. But this reorganization & restoration must depend for value on the principles underlying them. The reconstitution of Louisiana as a Slave State would be a calamity. It would perpetuate discord instead of establishing Union. They will show themselves the wisest statesmen and noblest benefactors who go to work most promptly & most earnestly for a Free State Convention to bring Louisiana back into the Union as a Free State with Universal Suffrage or if restricted at all, restricted by a light-property qualification but not by color.

If this movement is entered on boldly & carried out successfully it will defeat the machinations of those who are calculating on the restoration to power of the proslavery factions and on the political overthrow of such men as Flanders, Hahn, Durell, & their friends who have dared to be faithful to the Union & to advocate liberal ideas. It cannot be too strongly impressed on the minds of those who sustained the National Government that halfway measures now are worse than no measures; and that thorough work now is safe work & permanent work.

Suppose for example Louisiana reorganized as a state and restored to the Union on the Universal Suffrage basis. Is it not clear that the restoration of Slavery would be impossible?, that the political ascendancy of proslavery men would be equally impossible?, & that, in case other southern States should adopt a more illiberal policy, Louisiana would gain by rapid accessions of the most useful and intelligent portions of the colored population, and speedily become in fact what she is by position the Empire State of the South?

But I have only space enough for one more consideration. Why does not somebody move for the establishment of the "First National Bank of Louisiana?" I cannot enlarge on this hint; but it has [wide] ramifications.

I have written *very* hastily and illegibly; but I hope that your patience will not be too [*illeg.*]ly tried in your endeavoring to make out what I mean and that what I have written may not be entirely without useful consequences.

Yours truly
S P Chase

1. On March 25, Plumly had reported on his arrival in New Orleans. "I feel, as if I had stepped into a Maelstrom," he wrote, "and had not yet, determined the currents." Plumly to Chase, Mar. 25, 1863 (Chase Papers, L.C.).

2. See Flanders to Chase, April 30, 1863 (above).

3. In April, Chase had appointed William P. Mellen supervising special agent for the middle and upper portions of the Mississippi Valley. Chase to Mellen, Apr. 4, 1863 (Gen. Agent, Letters Recd.: Sec. of Treas., Recs. of Civil War Special Agencies, Nat. Arch.); *Letter of the Secretary . . . Special Agents,* 2.

4. On May 9, Benjamin F. Flanders and Michael Hahn recommended Edward Henry Durell, Rufus Waples, and James Graham to positions as U.S. district judge, U.S. attorney, and U.S. marshal, respectively, for Louisiana's eastern district. All three received the positions later in the year. Like Flanders, Hahn (full name Georg Michael Decker Hahn) had presented his credentials to the U.S. House of Representatives in December 1862 and taken his seat in February 1863 for the Congress that ended on March 3. Hahn then involved himself in journalism in New Orleans and was appointed prize commissioner. In February 1864 he won election as governor of Louisiana on a Free-State ticket. Basler, *Collected Works,* 6:223–24; U.S. Senate, *Journal of Executive Proceedings,* 13:325, 384, 405; *Bio. Dir. U.S. Cong.,* 172, 1109; *DAB,* 5:545, 8:88.

TO BENJAMIN F. FLANDERS

Autograph letter. Special Collections, Dartmouth College Library (*micro* 26:0910).

Unofficial

Treasury Department.
May 24 1863

My Dear Sir,

I have written you so fully lately that I shall confine myself today to two points only.[1]

The first is the necessity of Calling a Convention to reestablish a State Government for Louisiana.[2] In your present relations you can greatly promote this work, and, with the aid of other loyal men in and out of public position, can undoubtedly succeed in it. And the work once done can never be undone.

The best plan of action will be easiest determined by yourselves. The precedent of regarding the loyal people of a large portion of a state, not subjugated by the insurgents, as competant to act for the whole state has been already established in the case of Virginia.[3] All that is required then to inaugurate the movement is a preliminary meeting or Convention of those favorable to the General Object & a call by that body of a State Convention to reestablish the State Government under a State Constitution adapted to the new exigencies. This state Constitution would probably be the old Constitution amended to suit existing conditions and future contingencies. The Amended Constitution should contain articles denying the heresy of secession; establishing freedom for the entire population without exception or delay; and providing for universal suffrage; or, (should a limitation in any form be insisted on,) for suffrage restricted only by a light property qualification. Such a reorganization would be most salutory every way; as an example to other states; as a guaranty of the continued ascendancy of the liberal union sentiment and of its friends; as an extinguisher upon the hopes of those who wish for the revivial of the Slave Power; as a public benefit to Louisiana in ensuring stability to her institutions & prosperity to her Agriculture, Mechanic Arts, & Commerce. All that is needed, as it seems to me, to ensure the absolute success of this movement & great honor to its authors & supporters is common sense courage, energy & promptitude; which four qualities, by the way, win all the battles of the world.

The second matter to which I wish to draw your attention is the establishment of National Banks in Louisiana. The time has come, I think, when no currency other than the national currency should be permitted in that State / Certainly the time has come when no other currency should be received or paid out by persons holding positions under the National Government. It may be difficult, [just now], to supply all the currency that may be needed, in the form of legal tender notes; though the difficulty cannot be by any means insuperable. A provision for a good permanent currency is, however, made by the National Banking Law; and few things could be better calculated to promote loyalty and to ensure a sufficient supply of safe circulation than the establishment of National Banks under that law. Cannot a beginning be made by the establishment of at least one with a capital not less of course than $50.000, but not less, if possible, than $100.000 or $1000000? Such a Bank on giving proper securities, would have, of course, all the Government deposits, except those from customs.

We are rejoicing greatly over the news from Vicksburgh, that Grant, after a series of brilliant marches & successes, has the rebels shut up in the town with every prospect of being able soon to compel them to surrender.[4] If this hope is realized the Mississippi will soon be opened and the rebellion on its west bank virtually suppressed.

Yours most truly
S P Chase

Hon B. F. Flanders.

Be sure to keep me fully advised both officially and unofficially

1. Chase had written on May 16 to appoint Flanders the Treasury's supervising special agent for the lower Mississippi Valley and to enumerate the duties of that office. Another letter, on May 20, discussed other Louisiana appointments in the Treasury Department and in the judiciary. Chase to Flanders, May 16, 1863 (Letters Sent Relating to Restricted Commercial Intercourse and Captured and Abandoned Property, Gen. Recs. Treasury Dept., Nat. Arch.); Chase to Flanders, May 20, 1863 (Spec. Collec., Dartmouth College Lib.).

2. Louisiana's constitutional convention met intermittently throughout the summer of 1864 and finally adopted a constitution on July 22. *New Orleans Daily Picayune,* July 23, 1864.

3. For this Virginia precedent see *Chase Papers,* 3:345–50.

4. Besieged since May 18, the Confederate stronghold of Vicksburg, Miss., finally fell to Union forces under Ulysses S. Grant on July 4, 1863. Long, *Civil War Day by Day,* 354, 378–79.

TO SAMUEL HALLETT AND COMPANY

Letterbook copy in clerk's hand. Letters Sent, Loan Division, Records of the Bureau of the Public Debt (Record Group 53), National Archives (*micro* 26:0932).

Treasury Department.
May 25th. 1863.

Gentlemen.[1]

Yours of the 23d. is just received. You are quite at liberty to say that no proposition for a permanent loan, payable otherwise than in American Gold, or any where else than at the Treasury of the United States, has ever been entertained, or is likely to be entertained, by me as head of the Treasury Department; and that no authority has been given to any one to negotiate a Loan abroad on any other terms than would have been accepted for the same loan from American capitalists.

I had an idea, some time since, of receiving proposals, at home and abroad, for a Loan payable after ten years; but that thought was abandoned, or at least postponed, in consequence of the success of the Five-twenty subscription, and all authority to receive proposals abroad for such a Loan was withdrawn as soon as it was determined not to ask for it at home; for I have never admitted the idea that, under any circumstances, foreign capitalists or business men should be preferred to American. I now think it undesirable to receive a large foreign loan, even for Five-twenties at par in New York. There is not now in the Department a single unsatisfied requisition for disbursement in any branch of the public service. The Army has been paid in full to the first of March, and the payment to the first of May, already largely advanced will soon be completed. Unless very serious military reverses should be experienced—and Grant's successes augur nothing of the kind[2]—there is every reason to believe that, on the first of June, every liquidated demand on the Treasury will have been satisfied, and that our financial condition (putting out of view the great public debt necessarily contracted) will be more satisfactory than at any period since the outbreak of the rebellion. A foreign Loan is, therefore, now less desirable than ever.

You are mistaken in the impression that the Department has any Agents abroad for the negotiation of loans. The authority to which I have referred was given to gentlemen who went to Europe on other business, and as incidental simply. Mr Walker, however, did not go to Europe at my request, not as an Agent to borrow mony, but to lay before business men and the general public those facts with which his former official positions made him best acquainted, and which properly understood, would correct serious misapprehensions in regard to our resources and strength. I thought this sufficiently important to us in a financial point of view to warrant my request to him, especially as he was meditating the journey in reference to private business; and I am quite satisfied thus far, with the results of his action.

This letter, of course, is not designed for publication, but you can make such use of the facts stated, in your circular, as you may think beneficial to the country.[3]

Yours very respectfully.
S. P. CHASE

Messrs Sam'l Hallett & Co.
New York.

1. Hallett (d. 1864), a New York banker, promoted construction of the transcontinental railroad. *New York Dir. (1863)*, 362; *New York Times*, July 30, 1864.

2. On May 14, Grant's army had taken Jackson, Miss., and, on May 16, won the battle of Champion's Hill, or Baker's Creek. Chase had just recently learned of Grant's besiegement of Vicksburg and evidently did not yet know about failed Union assaults there on May 19 and 22. Long, *Civil War Day by Day*, 353–54, 355–56; Chase to Benjamin F. Flanders, May 24, 1863 (above).

3. *The American Circular*, of New York, was a financial periodical published by Hallett that tended to support Chase. *New York Herald*, July 2, 1863.

FROM HENRY B. CARRINGTON

Autograph letter. Chase Papers, Library of Congress (*micro* 26:0961).

Confidential, and of some importance.[1]

Indianapolis Inda. 26th May, 1863,

Dear Sir

Can you spare time, *at home*, to read this statement. Gov *Morton* may have given you the facts.[2] In answer to telegram, Gen Burnside proposed to visit this city 22nd. ult. to consult as to Indiana matters. *Gov.* telegraphed "he should be away that day" & it was deferred two days. At noon, the *22d.* I was relieved from command, &, as ordered went to Cincinnati. I reported to Gen. *Burnside*, what had been *my policy*, which had the *hearty daily support* of *Gov. Morton:* viz.

1st. To treat all *loyal* citizens, of *all parties*, on the same footing.

2d. *Quietly*, but *thoroughly*, to ferret out & expose all disloyal organizations.

3d. To use *civil* tribunals *only*, for trial of citizen offenders, *except* in extreme cases, none of which I anticipated.

4th. To use the military to make arrests, when civil process would fail, but, to at once turn over offenders to Grand Jury of US. Court, which Judge Smith especially ordered,[3] and which indicted a large number, several of whom were convicted by petit Jury & sentenced: the first cases I believe during the war.

5th. I divided the state by school districts, securing the names of good union men everywhere, so that no deserter could be harbored and no disloyal secret society meet, without my knowledge.

6th. Upon taking command, (at Gov. *M*'s suggestion) I invited the Supreme Judges, Senator Hendricks & leading Democrats,[4] to meet leading Republicans, to unite in policy as to the *K.G.C's*[5]—*return* of *deserters*—*resistance* of *Conscript act* &c. My address met unanimous approval before it was issued, and did good. The *Dem. State Com.* formally endorsed it, and upon my advice, it was understood that Vallandigham should not even be invited to speak, at the Convention. Subsequent events must have changed their plans.[6]

The result was, that I had full knowledge of the State, the confidence of good men, and divided the union from the disloyal Democrats, to the promised extinction of the K.G.C's: then very numerous.

Upon reaching Cinti. I regretted to find that Genl. *B.* disapproved my policy saying—*"that the radical defect was my use of the Grand Jury and civil Courts, and that the Military Commission should have been used only."*

When Genl *B. first* reached Cinti. I sent him copy of my statement as to Indiana affairs, which I prepared at Gov *M*.s request for the President & Secretary of War:[7] and up to my removal, received no instructions, or disapproval of my views.

On the 24th. ult Gen *B.* visited Indianapolis. Gov. *M*—Senator *Lane;*[8] *R. M. Thompson;*[9] Judge *Smith,* and about 60 prominent men, waited upon Genl. *B.* to urge my immediate restoration. Gov. *Wright,* and others at Cinti. urged it with emphasis.[10] Without my approval, or sanction, petitions, with names from a majority of the counties, (many thousands of the leading men of the state) have been sent to Mr. Colfax to give the President.[11]

Prominent Union Democrats concur in what *each* of the *above named,* have *declared,* that my fair—firm, and thorough course, *saved this state from disorder* and *held* it, until the evil could smother itself.

It was very painful to me, with my whole soul in the work, to be under a cloud, when so heartily supported by the Governor, and our best friends. I know I had no selfish ends, but to promote the good cause, & I know, *as well,* that more arbitrary treatment would have annihilated the administration party, just at that crisis, or precipitated civil war.

I have worked for nine months night and day; when legal judgment was worth as much as military knowledge. In conflict with the Supreme Court upon the Habeas Corpus cases, I sustained the government, and the *court yielded.*[12] In the use of Military force, (always with the approval of Gov M. and our wisest men) I have quietly and noiselessly done the work, until there was no county where offenders did not expect me, and yet, where the knowledge that I was in *earnest* did not prevent the frequent use of force. I was very much impressed, with your views expressed in August, and they have guided me in my policy.

Permit me, whatever your views may be, and with the highest respect for the judgement of my superior officers, to say: that the people of this state are exceedingly jealous as to trials of Citizens by Military Courts. I could arrest *Vorhes*[13] or *Hendricks,* without a murmur of dissent, if a civil Court were to try their case; and I am candid to say, that I believe the conviction of several citizens by the US. Court, did more good here, than the arrest of Vallandigham. I feel that the civil power should be exhausted at the north, and still *fearlessly appealed to,* before *officers* should try *citizens.* If awe is inspired by the summary proceedings of the latter; does not the reaction tell against us. If we push the war with vigor, will not the people weigh the bad men and reject them, in the end:—and *sooner,* than if there are fictitious issues, that bear upon popular liberty, mingled with their case. Will not northern traitors *die,* as our *arms* prosper, and *die* beyond resurrection? Is not this in accordance with human nature, and sound philosophy? The *great thing* is to be in *earnest,* and *this,* through their accustomed tribunals, will do good, when there is no enemy in arms to require martial law. I feel that while we are pushing war measures, we should turn all the civil power *with us, and we gain* by it. If we retain, proximately, the habitudes of peace at home, are we not the gainers in the end? Do not misunderstand me, or think I would parley with treason or shrink from the largest responsibilities in the proper case. I reason from some knowledge of human nature, and the people of this state, & write you freely; and could I command the three states of Indiana, Illinois and Michigan through the draft, I believe the application of these principles, would secure the draft, invigorate republicanism and strengthen the government.

It has seemed to me that East Tennessee & Kentucky should be together; That West Virginia should be with Ohio, as they afford centres of active operations; but, that the military command in the other states should be so, that, the Governors should practically govern, and the US. officer should hold the check upon disorder, while co-operating with the Civil authorities.

For myself, personally, I ask only that I may not be deprived of influence and position, *provided* my *policy* is *approved.* I ought to be away from here—*north.* My health has suffered and my physicians say I cannot take the field for a long time. I must have work; and administrative labor I believe I can meet. I wish there was some duty for the government that would give me a sea-voyage, northward, or to the lakes; but I know of none. If re-instated, at the West, I shall feel that the work which Indiana has so generously approved is approved by the administration.

I send you my address of 22nd. Feby on the war,[14] and thank you for your interest in my promotion. I felt that it was *just,* but no less deeply do I feel your friendship. Mr. Lane told me of your continued friendship; and Colfax, whom I never saw, wrote me, thanking me for my work in Indiana.

I feel that we have great work to do. In twelve months will come Presidential nominations; and, unless prudent and wise policy is pursued in these western states, a dangerous opposition will be developed against us.

I speak what I know, and I keep my own counsel, while I feel at times as if I would give much to talk an hour with you upon public affairs.

With sincere regard & affection

I am ever your friend
HENRY B. CARRINGTON

Hon. Salmon P. Chase
Washington D.C.

1. The former adjutant general of Ohio, Carrington held the rank of brigadier general while organizing Federal troops in Indiana, where he gained notoriety for prosecuting suspected disloyalty. *DAB,* 3:521.

2. Oliver Hazard Perry Throck Morton, governor of Indiana.

3. Former secretary of the interior Caleb Blood Smith, appointed, in December 1862, judge of the U.S. court for the district of Indiana. U.S. Senate, *Journal of Executive Proceedings,* 13:10, 21.

4. At the time, the Indiana Supreme Court had four justices, all Democrats: Andrew Davison (1800–1871), James M. Hanna (1816–72), Samuel Elliott Perkins (1811–79), and James Lorenzo Worden (1819–84). Thomas Andrews Hendricks (1819–85), U.S. senator from Indiana, 1863–69, was a prominent Democratic critic of the Lincoln administration. *DAB,* 8:534–35, 14:476–77; *Nat. Cyc.,* 18:290–91; Leander J. Monks, ed., *Courts and Lawyers of Indiana,* 3 vols. (Indianapolis, 1916), 1:247–48, 253–54; Emma Lou Thornbrough, "Judge Perkins, the Indiana Supreme Court, and the Civil War," *Indiana Magazine of History* 60 (Mar. 1964): 80.

5. The Knights of the Golden Circle, a secret society in the North suspected of subversion. Frank L. Klement, *Dark Lanterns: Secret Political Societies and Treason Trials in the Civil War* (Baton Rouge, 1984), 7–33.

6. Clement Laird Vallandigham of Ohio led the Peace Democrats in Congress. On May 19, Lincoln had banished him to the Confederacy for allegedly treasonous speech in violation of orders issued by Ambrose Burnside. According to one unsympathetic newspaper, "circumstances over which he had not control" prevented Vallandigham from attending the Indiana State Democratic Convention that assembled in Indianapolis on May 20. *DAB,* 19:144; "Indianapolis Daily Journal," May 21, 1863.

7. Carrington's report, written March 19, 1863, focused on suspected danger from the Knights of the Golden Circle. "The Government must be felt as the protector of the people," he urged. "Now is the time. Come what will, firmness is our safety and the result is certain." *OR,* ser. 2, v. 5:363–67.

8. U.S. Senator Henry Smith Lane, Republican of Indiana, 1861–67. *Bio. Dir. U.S. Cong.*, 1339.

9. Carrington may have referred to Richard Wigginton Thompson (1809–1900) of Indiana, a former Republican state legislator who, during the Civil War, served as provost marshal for the area around Terre Haute. *DAB*, 18:468–69.

10. Former Indiana governor Joseph Albert Wright served as a Unionist in the Senate from February 1862 to January 1863. *Bio. Dir. U.S. Cong.*, 2091.

11. Schuyler Colfax had presided as speaker of the U.S. House since March. Ibid., 809.

12. Proclamations by Lincoln unilaterally authorized suspension of habeas corpus at various times throughout the war. The most notable criticism was *Ex parte Merryman*, a decision issued in chambers by Chief Justice Roger Taney in support of a Maryland resident detained for destroying railroads in April 1861. Congress did not formally suspend the writ of habeas corpus until March 1863. Long, *Civil War Day by Day*, 66, 79, 90, 270–71, 325, 409; Carl B. Swisher, *The Taney Period, 1836–64*, vol. 5 of Paul A. Freund, gen. ed., *The Oliver Wendell Holmes Devise History of the Supreme Court of the United States* (New York, 1974), 841–54; Mark E. Neely, Jr., *The Fate of Liberty: Abraham Lincoln and Civil Liberties* (New York, 1991), 30–31.

13. Peace Democrat Daniel Wolsey Voorhees (1827–97), Indiana congressman, 1861–66. *DAB*, 19:291.

14. "The War, its Nature and Prospects, its Moral and Social Evils, and its Ultimate Success," delivered to U.S. troops in Indianapolis on February 21. *Indianapolis Daily Journal*, Feb. 21, 1863.

TO JAMES A. GARFIELD

Autograph letter on letterhead stationery. James A. Garfield Papers, Library of Congress (*micro* 27:0029).

Treasury Department.
May 31 1863

My dear General,

I am much obliged to you for your letter.[1] You must not write to me however at the expence of any of your duties. My trust in you is as complete as that of the good deacon in his Minister—I can sleep if it is you who preaches. Still the letters give me a sort of inside view which I am exceedingly glad to have and which sometimes it may be useful for me to have.

There is very little here to communicate. Every eye is turned towards Vicksburgh. Our most recent advices are to the 20th; unless credit is to be attached to reports from rebel sources. These reports credited warrant the belief that Vicksburgh is ours; and the latest intelligence which describes the seige operations as well advanced, make some credit of these reasonable

But you will know all long before this reaches you And how idle it seems to speculate on contigencies so rapidly becoming facts.

My disappointment at the failure of Straights expedition was great. It ought to have been as successful as Griersons and more successful than Stonemans.[2] What was the real cause of failure? One can never gather any certainty from newspapers—and except letters newspapers are the chief source of information to me; though, I think, if I were President I would have a system of information which should at least keep my Secretary of the Treasury advised of every thing of importance.

Rumors are rife of a movement in Lee's Army. Since the defeat of May 4'. our Army has been quiet[3]—gradually, indeed, losing strength from the expiration of the nine month terms. If Lee is actually moving he will find no [divided] armies before him as formerly under Pope & McClellan[4] and will have no child's play to encounter. It seems to me indeed the very thing to be desired for us and I am confident that Hooker will make him repent of it. If he does not move, I expect that Hooker will soon take the initiative. The rumor of movement has certainly some support in actual conditions. Just after the late battles an autograph letter from Jeff Davis to a Mississippi Officer under Lee came into our possession in which he spoke of the difficulty of sending reinforcements to Lee, though he was very anxious to do so. The truth is I apprehend that the rebels *cannot* much *increase* their [present] force and that the difficulties of *movement* are constantly becoming greater. Of course as our armies are every where more or less weakening by the expiration of terms, the rebels are now relatively stronger than they will ever be again. If they will take the offensive under any circumstances therefore they will, probably, now.

The enlistment of colored troops is now going on well. The Florida project which we discussed so much seems now likely to be realized; and it is not unlikely that Colored troops will be mainly relied on for its accomplishment. The first regiment from Massachusetts has already gone to Port Royal. The second will probably follow in less than a fortnight. A Regiment is being raised here.[5] Very soon there will be two full and strong brigades at Port Royal and the number will be rapidly augmented. They *can* do much & *will*.

The President is now thoroughly in earnest in this business & sees it much as I saw it nearly two years ago. The Secretary of War has always since he came in been willing to do all that the President would allow to be done. Now the whole business of colored troops is very thoroughly organized. There is a good board for the examination of officers.[6] And it seems likely that these troops from more care in selection both of men & officers will be as effective as any in the service. I wish Gen. Rosecrans had not contented himself with pick & shovel brigades; and hope he will no longer do so.[7]

One item of private intelligence shall conclude this unreasonably long epistle. I am going to lose a daughter & gain a son. Katie is to be married to Gov. Sprague: but the *event* will not probably take place before fall.[8] What changes may take place between now and then: It makes me almost shudder to think of it. But let us hope the best and as one of the best things that you dear General may be with us on the "auspicious occasion"

With best regards to Gen. R——[9] and all other friends believe me

Faithfully yours
S P Chase

Brig. Gen Garfield

1. On May 9, Garfield informed Chase of efforts to destroy Confederate communications in Alabama and Georgia and inquired about the military situation on the Rappahannock River. Garfield to Chase, May 9, 1863 (Chase Papers, L.C.).

2. Abel Streight and 1,300 mounted troops had surrendered on May 3 to Nathan Bedford Forrest at Cedar Bluff, Ala., while on a mission to destroy Confederate railroads. Col. Benjamin Henry Grierson (1826–1911), of the 1st Cavalry Brigade under Ulysses S. Grant, had completed a similar raid that ended successfully in Baton Rouge, La., on May 2. Maj. Gen. George Stoneman, head of cavalry in the Army of the Potomac, had harassed enemy communications between Fredericksburg and Richmond from April 13 to May 2, without significant results. Garfield to Chase, May 5, 1863 (above); *DAB,* 7:613–14, 18:92; Long, *Civil War Day by Day,* 348; Johnson, *Twentieth Century Biographical Dictionary,* v. 10.

3. That is, since the battle of Chancellorsville.

4. Chase referred to the military positions of former general-in-chief George B. McClellan and Maj. Gen. John Pope shortly after the close of McClellan's Peninsula campaign, July 1862, and prior to Pope's defeat the following month at the second battle of Bull Run. Long, *Civil War Day by Day,* 236, 247, 251–57.

5. Two such units were recruited in Washington, D.C.: the 1st and 2d Regiments of U.S. Colored Troops. *OR,* ser. 3, v. 3:1112.

6. General Orders No. 143, issued May 22, 1863, established "a bureau . . . in the Adjutant-General's Office for the record of all matters relating to the organization of colored troops" and authorized boards to be "convened at such posts as may be decided upon by the War Department to examine applicants for commissions to command colored troops." *OR,* ser. 3, v. 3:215.

7. Under general orders issued by William Rosecrans early in 1863, African Americans within the Department of the Cumberland were employed as laborers, teamsters, cooks, hospital workers, officers' servants, and construction workers building fortifications, but were not recruited as soldiers. *OR,* ser. 1, v. 23, pt. 2:17–18, 290–91.

8. Kate Chase and William Sprague married on November 12, 1863. *DAB,* 17:475; Chase to Catherine Ludlow Whiteman, Nov. 12, 1863 (below).

9. Rosecrans.

TO JAMES S. WADSWORTH

Letterpress copy of autograph letter. Chase Papers, Historical Society of Pennsylvania (*micro* 27:0033).

Washington May 31, 1863.

Dear General,[1]

Mr. Stickney has enclosed to me a letter for you which I have read & now forward.[2]

Ever since McClellan's defeat before Richmond[3] I have thought that our military & politico-military operations should be conducted with reference to these objects:

1. Occupation of Florida, & Louisiana and *then* of other Gulf States: Florida & Louisiana to be occupied & held by Colored troops & orga-

nized as Free States & so made the secure base of operations for White, & other troops northward.

2d. The possession of the Mississippi & the defence of its shores by Colored troops; thus securing supplies to Louisiana; [an] outlet for Western products; & the means of reducing to constitutional order the States on its west bank as well as powerful contributory [areas] towards restablishing the National Authority in the States on the East [Bank] & beyond.

3. The occupation of East Tennessee & the connected Mountain region, forming a great central & impregnable fortress giving to the Union all the [interior] lines.

4. Defensive operations simply unless opportunities of [successful] offensive movements should offer, along the northern lines of [*illeg.*]

With these views I naturally take a profound interest in Mr. Stickneys project for the occupation of & [creation] of a free state in Florida;[4] and cordially commend them to your attention. If the President will give *me* the Military power I will undertake the work myself.

Yours faithfully
S P CHASE

Brig. Gen. Wadsworth.

1. Wadsworth, at the time a brigadier general of volunteers, commanded the 1st Division in the First Corps of the Army of the Potomac. *DAB,* 19:309.

2. Lyman D. Stickney served as a U.S. direct tax commissioner in Florida. Stickney to Chase, Apr. 16, 17, 1863 (Chase Papers, L.C.).

3. Signified during the first week of July 1862 by McClellan's withdrawal to Harrison's Landing. Long, *Civil War Day by Day,* 236.

4. Stickney had suggested using military and naval power to drive Confederates out of Florida. "A loyal population is left behind," he continued, "who would welcome the civil Authority of the Government, and speedily elect a Legislature & State officers in harmony with it." Stickney to Chase, May 9, 1863 (Letters Recd. from Exec. Officers, Internal Revenue, Gen. Recs. Treasury Dept., Nat. Arch.)

FROM WILLIAM SPRAGUE

Autograph letter. Chase Papers, Library of Congress (*micro* 27:0036).

Washington May 31. 1863.

My Dear Sir.

For Katy's sake I think a respite necessary, and have concluded to go home tomorrow; unless the excursion is made to Mt Vernon, of which I have written her.

My desire is (and with which Katy concurs) for my elder sister Mrs Nichols and myself to join Katy and her friends at Niagra after your journey west,[1] & go direct to Newport, where a house may be secured, and plesant arrangements made for an agreeable sojourn for August.

In November we would be married, occupying that month in journeying; then settle in Washington. Katy expresses a desire for a temporary relief from the cares of housekeeping; she has formed plans in her own mind as to this, which she will tell you

If more agreeable for us to be of your family; let it be so; we having separate arrangements so far as possible, such for instance as having our own carriage, Horses, servants and the priviledge of as much of the pecuniary burden as possible, causing less interferance with yourself; and so we could have our connection our own as far as possible.

If you should leave Washington, which I hope is not possible, our course would be clear; as it is let us just arrange matters in a way as little objectionable to yourself as can be & secondly let our own well fare be consulted.

I have shadowed these views and will consult you as to them before leaving. Let me here my dear sir, thank you from the bottom of my heart for the treasure you have reared and given to me. God bear me witness that it will be *the* object of my life to see that she receives no detriment in my hands. If a life of devotion to her, and to yourself can make me worthy of it all I shall deem it well spent.

Gratefully yours
WM SPRAGUE

Gov Chase.

1. Chase planned to travel to Ohio in late June and early July, with Niagara as a potential stop in the itinerary, but did not make the trip. Sprague's sister was Mary Ann Sprague Nichols. Chase to Stephen S. L'Hommedieu, June 12, 1863, Chase to George M. Parsons, same date, Chase to Kate Chase, July 7, 1863 (Chase Papers, Hist. Soc. of Pa.).

TO JAY COOKE

Letter in clerk's hand on letterhead stationery, signed by Chase. Jay Cooke Papers, Historical Society of Pennsylvania (*micro* 27:0046).

Unofficial

Treasury Department.
June 1st., 1863.

Dear Sir.

I sent you this morning the following Telegram:—

"From this date, June 1st., inclusive, your compensation as agent, including compensation of sub-agents, will be one-eighth of one per cents, and actual expenses of advertising and transportation":[1]—and soon after received your reply. Thinking that you acted hastily, I sent for Mr. H. D. Cooke (with whom I conferred before sending the original telegram) and showed him your answer.[2] I suggested to him the expediency of advising you not to act precipitately, but to continue your agencies, only restricting their compensation to such a sum as would leave you a fair remuneration for your services. This, I thought, might be obtained for for you and them from one-eighth of one per cent, as was the case with the Agencies for subscriptions to the National Loan[3]—especially, as I had stated in my telegram that all expenses of advertising and transportation would be paid in addition.

Since my first interview with Mr. H. D. Cooke, I have seen him again—indeed he is now with me—and I have read your telegram to him. I notice what you say respecting the propriety of having given more notice to your Sub-agents. There is force in your observations: and I should have given you this notice before, had I known of your being in Philadelphia. I give it now only because it is desirable that the new rate of compensation should commence with the first of the month.

You will remember that my original proposition (which was accepted) fixing the compensation at one-half of one per cent—distributed, one-eighth to local agents, one-half for advertising, etc., and one-eighth to yourself—was limited to the first ten millions, after which the compensation was to be at the rate of one-fourth of one per cent. When the subscriptions had nearly reached ten millions, you advised a continuance of the compensation at the rate fixed for that amount; and I so far yielded to your views, as, in conversation to Mr. H. D. Cooke, to agree to the rate of three-eighths for subscriptions beyond the ten millions. It was my intention, at that time, to continue the new arrangement only up to the amount of about fifty millions; but no definite understanding has since been had.

I prize very highly indeed your services to the Department, and have no disposition to reduce the compensation either of yourself or your agents below what is just and liberal. On the other hand, I have a duty to the country to perform, which forbids me to pay rates which will not be approved by all right-minded men; and I cannot think that now, when your past services must have been fully compensated, and when the necessity for extensive advertising must be greatly reduced and the amount of subscriptions so largely increased that a very low rate will afford you a larger remuneration than a very high rate formerly, the original compensation should be continued.

I shall be very glad, however, to confer with you and with Mr. Cisco,[4] and fix upon some basis for the continuance of your services, which would be honorable to yourself and proper for the Government. If you can come to Washington, please notify me, and I will telegraph Mr. Cisco to meet you. In the meantime I suggest the expediency of allowing your sub-agents to continue as now, rendering bills for reasonable advertising and expenses, and receiving such proportion of the general compensation allowed—which may be considered as 1–5 of one per cent instead of 1–8 until a full understanding can be arrived at—as may be just.

My limitations in this letter will not, of course, take effect on any of your present arrangements with sub-agents, until they can be properly notified and the new arrangement adjusted.

Yours truly
S P CHASE

Jay Cooke, Esq

1. Chase to Cooke, June 1, 1863 (Telegrams Sent, Gen. Recs. Treasury Dept., Nat. Arch.).

2. Henry David Cooke oversaw the Washington office of his brother's banking company.

3. The national loan act of July 17, 1861, had authorized the Treasury secretary to borrow up to $250 million. Cooke had acted as a subscription agent for the loan. In the autumn of 1862, Chase asked him to use his network of subordinate agents to market 5–20 bonds authorized by the legal tender acts. *Statutes at Large,* 12:259; *Chase Papers,* 3:183, 299–301.

4. John J. Cisco, U.S. assistant treasurer in New York. In 1864, he resigned and started his own banking firm on Wall Street. *New York Times,* Mar. 24, 1884.

TO JAY COOKE

Autograph letter. Jay Cooke Papers, Historical Society of Pennsylvania (*micro* 27:0064).

Washington, June 2, 1863.

My dear Sir,

You informed me two or three weeks ago that you had purchased 300 shares of Phila. & Erie R.R. Stock for me. At that time I was expecting means of payment from the sale of a farm in Ohio and would have been glad to hold the stock for income. The sale, however, has not yet been effected and I have, therefore, not been able to make payment.[1]

This morning I have yours of yesterday notifying me that you have sold the stock at an advance which gives a profit of $4200—on the transaction and you enclose me a check for that amount.[2]

As I had not paid for the stock and did not contemplate purchase with any view to resale I cannot regard the profit as mine & therefore return the check for $4200—. It is herewith enclosed.

I am much obliged to you for your willingness to regard the money paid for the Stock as a temporary loan from you to me; but I cannot accept the favor.

When Congress, at the last session, saw fit to clothe me with very large powers over currency and financial movements,[3] I at once determined to avoid every act which could give occasion to suspicion that I would use the powers conferred on me to affect markets unnecessarily or at all with reference to the private advantage of any body. To carry out this determination faithfully I must decline to receive any advantages from purchases or sales made with views to profits expected from the rise or fall of market prices.

For these reasons I must decline to receive the check. In order to be able to render most efficient service to our country it is essential for me to *be* right as well as *seem* right & to *seem* right as well as *be* right.

Yours very truly
S P Chase

Jay Cooke, Esq

1. Chase was trying to sell property that he owned in Butler County, Ohio. Flamen Ball to Chase, June 6, Aug. 14, 28, 1863 (Chase Papers, L.C.); Chase to Ball, May 16, 1863 (Chase Papers, Hist. Soc. of Pa.).

2. The sale involved shares of the Philadelphia and Erie Railroad Company. Cooke to Chase, June 1, 1863 (Chase Papers, Hist. Soc. of Pa.).

3. Among other provisions, the March 1863 "Act to Provide Ways and Means" authorized new loans, provided for issues of 10–40 bonds and interest-bearing Treasury notes, and removed some previous impediments to marketing of U.S. bonds. *Chase Papers,* 3:366–72, 374–75, 397–402; *Statutes at Large,* 12:709–13.

TO JOHN A. BINGHAM

Letterpress copy of autograph letter. Chase Papers, Historical Society of Pennsylvania (*micro* 27:0096).

Washington, June 4, 1863

My dear Bingham,[1]

You may think that out of sight is out of mind: but it is n't so with me, so far as you are concerned, whatever you may think.

The Nevada vacancy has not occurred and is not likely to occur I think. Since it has not seemed likely that the appt. will fall in a certain quarter, those who pressed the removal of one of the Judges seem to have dropped the matter.[2]

You were mistaken if you thought I said you could be appointed District Attorney in California. The office is filled and I know of no ground for the removal of the incumbent.[3] What I did say was that I thought California now offered the finest chance in the Union for a gentleman of your abilities & eloquence, and that I thought it would be in my power to put business in your way there that would be worth four or five thousand dollars the first year. I still think so and so does Mr. Brown who has been there and will return as a Special agent of the Department.[4] Of course however I could not make any contract in advance, though I could give you an appointment as Special Agent on temporary service which would do you some good & be useful to the Govt.

Within the last few days another opening has presented itself. A kind Providence has lately prompted Judge Marvin, the U.S. District Judge at Key West with Circuit Court powers, to resign.[5] It is a most important office and its admiralty jurisdiction is called into constant exercise: and it is of first consequence that a man of superior abilities high legal attainments, and unshrinking patriotism should fill the place. Whoever fills it will exercise a potential influence in the regeneration of Florida, which I hope to see in the Union again as a Free State before the next Congress meets.

So I thought here is a good chance for me to serve Bingham and the Country too, & so I went to the President & proposed to him to appoint you. "To be sure I will" said honest Abe with a promptitude that did equal credit to his head & heart—to use an original phrase. And then he at once wrote a note to the Atty. General directing the appointment to be made.[6]

Now will you take it? The salary is $3000 a year. There is a good chance to be Senator if you like. There is a capital good place for life if you don't want to be Senator. There is a great opportunity of usefulness. There is a pleasant residence.

Of course I prefer as I have told you that you [sh]ould be Governor of Ohio. I want you numbered among *my* Successors. But if you *prefer* another place I must yield my preference.

Your friend
S P Chase

Hon John A Bingham

1. Voters in his home state of Ohio had recently turned down Bingham's bid for a fourth consecutive term in Congress. The following January Lincoln appointed him judge advocate of the army. *DAB,* 2:277.

2. In a letter written on April 29, Bingham had reminded Chase of an apparent promise for an appointment as chief justice of Nevada or as U.S. district attorney for California. In 1863, Nevada's chief justice was George Turner. Bingham to Chase, Apr. 29, 1863 (Chase Papers, L.C.); U.S. Senate, *Journal of Executive Proceedings,* 11:340–41.

3. William H. Sharp and Billington C. Whiting served as the U.S. district attorneys for the northern and southern districts of California. Whiting had been a Democratic candidate for state attorney general in the election of 1855. U.S. Senate, *Journal of Executive Proceedings,* 11:435, 12:92, 382; Peyton Hurt, "The Rise and Fall of the 'Know Nothings' in California," *Quarterly of the California Historical Society* 9 (Mar. 1930): 44, 45.

4. In 1862 and early 1863, Thomas Brown, another Ohioan, had investigated alleged fraud in the San Francisco Custom House. He also examined other Treasury-related matters and reported political intelligence to Chase. He returned to California in August 1863. Chase to Brown, Aug. 25, Dec. 24, 1862 (Letters Sent to Special Agents, Recs. of Bureau of Customs, Nat. Arch.); Brown to Chase, Oct. 28, Nov. 11, 1862, Jan. 6, Aug. 1, Aug. 28, 1863 (Chase Papers, L.C.).

5. Ill health had recently caused the retirement of William Marvin, a federal judge in Florida since 1839. *Nat. Cyc.,* 11:379.

6. On June 3, Lincoln had asked Edward Bates to forward the commission. Bingham eventually declined the offer. Lincoln to Bates, June 3, and Bingham to Lincoln, Aug. 5, 1863, in Basler, *Collected Works,* 6:245, 363.

TO EDWIN M. STANTON

Letterbook copy in clerk's hand. Letters Sent Relating to Restricted Commercial Intercourse and Captured and Abandoned Property (BE Series), General Records, Department of the Treasury (Record Group 56), National Archives (*micro* 27:0115).

June 5. 1863.

Hon. E. M. Stanton,
(Secretary of War—)
Sir:

I am advised by the 5th Auditor of this Department[1] that in a number of instances, under Permits granted by the War Department, very considerable quantities of goods have been taken into Virginia from this city. Among others, a purchase made by Mr. Tayloe, at Perry Brothers, is specified.[2]

If this practice exists, it cannot have attracted your observation, or the permits must have been given without sufficient consideration. The law expressly prohibits intercourse between the States declared in insurrection and the loyal States, except under special License—and under Regulations prescribed by the Secretary of the Treasury. These Regulations have been established and an order to secure its due execution, so far as officers of the army are concerned, was issued by you on the 31st. of March.[3]

A copy of the Regulations is herewith transmitted.

Yours Very respectfully
S. P. Chase
Secretary of the Treasury.

1. Charles Manning Walker occupied the position from 1862 to 1869. *Appletons'*, 6:325.
2. Benjamin Ogle Tayloe resided in Washington, D.C. Augustus E. Perry and Thomas J. S. Perry ran a dry goods store on Pennsylvania Avenue. *Wash. Dir. (1863)*, 162.
3. Chase referred to the act, approved March 12, 1863, "for the Collection of Abandoned Property and for the Prevention of Frauds in Insurrectionary Districts"; to his regulations issued under that law; and to Stanton's War Department General Orders No. 88 of March 31. *Commercial Intercourse*, 31–38, 48–53.

TO WILLIAM SPRAGUE

Letterpress copy of autograph letter. Chase Papers, Historical Society of Pennsylvania (*micro* 27:0136).

Washington, June 6, 1863.

My dear Governor,

Katie showed me yesterday your letters to her and I cannot refrain from telling you how much they delighted me. The manly affection breathed in them satisfied me that I had not given my daughter to one did not fully appreciate her, or to whom she could not give the full wealth of her affections. It is said that there are fathers who wish to retain the love & duty of daughters even in larger measure that they are given to their husbands. If there are I am sure I am not one of them. I want to have Katie honor & love you with an honor & love far exceeding any due to me; and I shall feel happiest when she makes your happiness most complete.

Still I say to her as I say to you that neither must expect perfection from the other. There must be trials, light certainly, perhaps great. The great will be easiest to bear. The soul prepares itself against great trials. Small ones come like surprises, taking the heart off its guard. The only security against them is constant love enabled by constant mutual respect.

But I did not mean to preach a sermon; but simply to express my great gratification. May God bless you both. That's the benediction & of course the sermon is over.

In respect to all matters of domestic arrangement we will take time to think. So too about the summer journey. If Katie had been content I should have preferred to have the marriage take place about the first of September, and have you take your journey in the pleasant months of the fall; but, except the matter of the journey November will do quite as well. And who knows but we may have Florida and Louisiana so securely by that time, that a trip to one or both states will not be the pleasantest of excursions?

I do not believe I shall feel easy with any household arrangement where you will not be the head. If I remain Secretary I shall have obligations which will make it necessary for me to receive people & give dinners which would hardly be compatible with your headship. So probably it will be best for you to take the house just as it is and let me find a place suited to my purpose nearer the Presidents. I merely throw out these ideas. As we cannot tell what events may bring forth, we will let them go subject to the modification of events.

Katie knows nothing of what I have written; but I shall read it to her; for, I think, the fewer reserves between us three the better.

Affectionately & faithfully
Yours
S P Chase

Hon. Wm Sprague

TO HENRY WINTER DAVIS

Letterpress copy of autograph document. Chase Papers, Historical Society of Pennsylvania (*micro* 27:0144).

Wash Monday Morning
June 8, 1863.

My dear Sir,

Accept my congratulations on your nomination, and my thanks for the manly and, in my judgment, wise speech addressed to your rejoicing friends.[1]

In what I did pending the contest for the nomination I trust I had your approbation. You doubtless knew every thing from Mr. Hoffman;[2] from whom I had no secrets. Absolute non-interference was a duty prescribed to me in every consideration of rectitude & honor. Every such consideration now requires that every man, truly loyal to the Union, to Freedom & to the Government, give you an earnest & faithful support.

I cannot but think you have a great career before you.

Sincerely your friend
S P Chase

Hon. H. Winter Davis.

1. On June 5, Davis, a radical Republican from Maryland, received the endorsement of Unconditional Unionists for the state's much-disputed third congressional district. On the same day he gave a speech in support of the Lincoln administration. Davis won the election and sat in the House until 1865. *DAB,* 5:120; *Daily National Intelligencer,* June 6, 1863.

2. Henry W. Hoffman, collector of customs at Baltimore.

TO ROBERT J. WALKER

Letterpress copy of letter in clerk's hand, signed by Chase. Chase Papers, Historical Society of Pennsylvania (*micro* 27:0150).

Unofficial

Washington, June 8, 1863.

My dear Sir,

We are still without decisive intelligence from Port Hudson and from Vicksburg—the first invested by Banks and the other by Grant.

Mr. Denison, Collector of Internal Revenue, just arrived from New-Orleans, brings the last dispatch which was sent from the telegraph station, three miles from Port Hudson, at 2 P.M. on the 9th. It is the last intelligence from that quarter, and I enclose it.

A dispatch from Grant, dated the 3d. inst., expressed the hope and expectation that his guns will be in position for a successful attack on the enemy's works at Vicksburg, to-day.[1] It is not unlikely that they are, at this moment, being carried.

The most remarkable feature of the attack on Port-Hudson was the wonderful bravery displayed by the Negro Regiment.[2] The enemy had sent a Message to Gen. Augur, that, if he brought his negro troops into battle, they would raise the black flag.[3] Gen. Augur replied that he should bring into battle all the troops he thought proper, without regard to complexion. The enemy did not raise the Black Flag; but, expecting the heaviest attack on their extreme right (our left) massed the greatest portion of the garrison in that quarter. The carnage among our soldiers, and particularly in the Negro Regiment, was dreadful. The 2d. Louisiana, composed exclusively of freedmen,—that is, slaves emancipated by the Proclamation and Acts of Congress[4]—marched upon the works, never flinching for a moment and never firing a gun after the first volley, but using the bayonet only, until they stood within the entrenchments and the battery was ours. The Regiment, however, had been so fearfully reduced in number, (having lost between six and seven hundred, out of nine hundred) that it was unable to hold its hard-won position. But this fierce combat on our left so engaged the enemy's attention, that a comparatively weak resistance was made to the attack of Weitzel on the right—I say comparatively, for the resistance there was vigorous and not easily overcome. It was, however, overcome; and Weitzel took the battery by whose fire the "Mississippi" was destroyed some weeks ago, and turned its guns upon the enemy's works below.[5]

This freedmen's charge has settled forever the question whether negroes will fight. There will no longer be any objections to the policy of arming them which will be worthy the least consideration.

Mr. Denison informs me that Gen. Ullman had already recruited about Four Thousand colored men when he left, and that they were coming in as fast as they could be registered, inspected, received, assigned and armed, say, at the rate of One Thousand a day. Gen. Ullman expects to complete his whole number of Eighteen Thousand within two weeks.

These statements are enough to show the utter hopelessness of the rebel cause. They may struggle a while longer—perhaps a year longer—and may achieve some transient success; but, with the whole body of the blacks bound to the Union by their hopes of freedom and their resolve to achieve it, while a large body of the whites prefer Union with Freedom to Disunion with Slavery, the result can be deemed no longer doubtful.

I look with great interest to the occupation of Florida, which will soon be accomplished. The Tax Commissioners there are men of ability and sound judgment.[6] Two of them have resided long in Florida, and are earnest in their resolves to make it a free State as soon as possible.

I have no time to write further by the next steamer, but you may expect another letter very soon. Please show this to Messrs Aspinwall and Forbes.

Yours very truly,
S: P: CHASE

Hon. Robt. J. Walker.

1. Grant to Henry W. Halleck, June 3, 1863, in John Y. Simon et al., eds., *The Papers of Ulysses S. Grant* (Carbondale, Ill., 1979), 8:304.

2. The first Federal attack on Port Hudson, La., May 27, 1863, was a failure. According to the *New York Tribune,* the 1st and 2d Louisiana Regiments nevertheless "fought like tigers." Long, *Civil War Day by Day,* 359; *New York Tribune,* June 9, 1863.

3. Maj. Gen. Christopher Columbus Augur was second in command to Nathaniel P. Banks. *DAB,* 1:427–28.

4. The Emancipation Proclamation and the first and second confiscation acts, August 6, 1861, and July 17, 1862. *Statutes at Large,* 12:319, 589–92.

5. The USS *Mississippi* had succumbed to Confederate guns at Port Hudson in March. Brigadier general of volunteers Godfrey Weitzel served with Union forces in Louisiana from the spring of 1862 to December 1863. *ORN,* ser. 2, v. 1:146; *DAB,* 19:616.

6. The Federal presence at Fernandina did not expand into full occupation of Florida and the complete surrender of Confederate troops there until May 1865. The U.S. direct tax commissioners were Harrison Reed (1813–99), a Massachusetts native and governor of Florida, 1868–73, John S. Sammis, and Lyman D. Stickney. John E. Johns, *Florida during the Civil War* (Gainesville, Fla., 1963), 208–9; *Letter of the Secretary . . . Special Agents,* 2; Robert Sobel and John Raimo, eds., *Biographical Directory of the Governors of the United States, 1789–1978,* 4 vols. (Westport, Conn., 1978), 1:256.

FROM WILLIAM SPRAGUE

Autograph letter. Chase Papers, Library of Congress (*micro* 27:0155).

Providence June 8th. 63.

My dear Sir.

I hasten to acknowledge the recipt of your very kind note of the 6th.[1] It will tend to foster the obligation I am under to you; and it gives me renewed assurance of your willingness to intrust that which is nearest and dearest to you, to my charge. God helping I shall accept the charge with renewed determination to see that your good opinion and anticipations are abundantly realized.

Your council is timely. I do not however expect that all will, at all times, run smoothly, but I do expect, that so far as human happiness can be arrived at, it can be attained by mutual interests, mutual forbearance, mutual love. It will I think be my fault if such is not the future of your daughter and myself. I shall very gladly concur in whatever views your greater experience in such matters may decide for our domestic arrangements. I would that the marriage was in September and the excursion you suggest could be arranged for the contemplated journey.

Affectionately & faithfully

Yours
WM SPRAGUE.

Gov Chase

1. Chase to Sprague, June 6, 1863 (above).

TO WILLIAM B. THOMAS

Letterpress copy of autograph letter. Chase Papers, Historical Society of Pennsylvania (*micro* 27:0163).

Unofficial & private

Washington
June 9, 1863

My dear Sir,

No one has asked for your removal, so far as I know; and certainly I should not entertain such an application very complacently; for all acknowledge your ability, fidelity, and patriotism, and I have always felt honored by your personal friendship.[1]

At the same time I cannot agree with you upon the expediency of forcing all the employees in your Office into a military organization on pain of removal; and could not conscientiously approve removals made *on no other ground* than declining to join such an organization.

I do not object to the military organization. I am far from entertaining the idea that clerks in public offices should be exempt from any military duties required of clerks in private offices. They have no right to any exemption from draft more than other men similarly employed for individuals. I am willing to go farther and say that I should think it a good ground of favor to a clerk that he was zealous and earnest in a military organization intended for the safeguard of public property. But I doubt the right to *exact* of clerks that they enroll themselves in such an organization; and still more do I question the propriety of *requiring* them to become members of an organization pledged to enter the military service of the United States as volunteers on the call of the President or into that of the State on the call of the Governor.[2] Of course I cannot see the right or propriety of enforcing such an exaction or requirement by the penalty of removal in case of noncompliance.

I jot down these ideas hastily and unofficially. Please send me the printed & written papers necessary to enable me to form a correct idea of the military organization you have set on foot and of mode in which connexion with it is formed and enforced. I shall then be able to respond formally to your communication of the 7th.

Yours sincerely
S P CHASE

Wm. B. Thomas, Esq

1. Thomas, at this time collector of customs at Philadelphia, was forming the 192d Pennsylvania Infantry. Frank Hamilton Taylor, *Philadelphia in the Civil War, 1861–1865* (Philadelphia, 1913), 247; *Register of Officers (1863)*, 83.
2. Pennsylvania governor Andrew Gregg Curtin.

TO SUSAN WALKER

Letterpress copy of autograph letter. Chase Papers, Historical Society of Pennsylvania (*micro* 27:0166).

Washn. June 9, 1863.

My dear friend,[1]

For a lady, who does not wish to be charged with the *care* of investments but desires a safe income with the least possible risk, I think the investment in U. States 5–20s the best now offered. There are many ways, doubtless, in which a few thousand dollars could be employed so as to produce larger returns: but I do not know what they are. Any friend, in active business could advise better than I on this point.

With larger returns however would come larger risks; and for a sister situated precisely as you are I should prefer the 5–20s.

It is impossible for me to foresee what loans I may be obliged to offer while I remain at the Head of the Treasury / I shall offer any loan after 10 years if I can help. Whether I *can* help it, I do not foresee.

Nor can I foresee what I shall do in respect to 5–20s after the first of July. The *privilege* of taking them at par for U. S. Notes will then expire. If public necessities require they may again be offered at par. If not, not.

If you conclude to take the 5–20s I advise you to take registered instead of coupon stock.[2] There is less liability to loss from loss of bonds, though a little more inconvenience in collection. The difference however is not great & the coupons command usually the best price in market, because more easily transferred.

Whether you take Coupons or registered deposit with Mr. Cisco & send the original certificate.

There, you have the best advice I can give, and all the information I have myself. I wish I could make it more satisfactory & definite.

Sincerely your friend
S P Chase

Miss S. Walker

1. Susan Walker, the sister of one of Chase's early law partners, served in various philanthropic causes during the Civil War, including efforts to educate former slaves at Port Royal. *New York Tribune,* Dec. 18, 1887.

2. Coupon bonds had coupons printed at the bottom, to be detached and redeemed for interest payments. The February 1862 legal tender law that authorized the 5–20s provided for both forms of bond. *Statutes at Large,* 12:345–46.

FROM DANIEL BUTTERFIELD

Unsigned letter in clerk's hand on letterhead stationery. Chase Papers, Historical Society of Pennsylvania (*micro* 27:0196).

Head-Quarters, Army of the Potomac,
June 11th. 1863.

Hon S. P. Chase.
Washington D.C.
Dear Sir.

Your confidential letter by Major Ludlow received. Any reply to it on my part must from its nature and our relative position be considered as as entirely confidential and unofficial.

Gen. Hookers instructions as they stand now from the President and General in chief do not permit him to cross the Rappahannock if Lees Army should move toward the Shenandoah Valley or toward

Washington and the instructions require him to cover Harpers Ferry and Washington with his army[1]

The views you express in regard to having one head have been anticipated by General Hooker. I enclose you confidentially an extract from a despatch of his to the President dated June 5th.[2] In regard to the numbers of this army for duty you state in your letter that the President gives the return of the 30th. of May of 104.000 effective officers and enlisted men for duty.

This is true so far as it goes but in this 104.000 are counted the Signal Corps Guards and Orderlys the Engineer Brigade, General and Staff Officers the batteries at Acquia Creek[3] and the Artillery reserve. In making up an estimate of our fighting forces we generally take the infantry Corps which include the Artillery with them and the Cavelry. This return for May 31st. shows as follows.

1st. Corps enlisted men for duty	12.651
2d. " " " " "	11.715
3d. " " " " "	12.588
5th.	9.844
6th.	16.274
11th.	10.459
12th.	8.261
Cavelry	9.626
Total	91.418

From this between the time this return was made up to the 15th. of the present month 20 regiments to leave the Army, they are leaving every day / From this you can get an idea of the effective fighting force we have in the field.

I coincide with you entirely in your view that these forces should be under one head and one direction. General Hooker does not desire or ask this, does not seek it; but I feel almost certain that if the enemy has not greatly increased their numbers by reinforcements from North Carolina and elsewhere that such a disposition of the forces operating to effect the movements of Lee's Army under a comprehensive mind would accomplish much for the purposes and objects mentioned in your letter.

I have written you hastily with the aid of a stenographer and wind up by saying in my private opinion that the objects specified in your letter will not be accomplished in the present condition of affairs. Of course you will consider this letter entirely confidential.

I am very truly Yours etc

Maj Gen & Chief of Staff

1. Henry W. Halleck, general-in-chief of Federal forces from July 1862 to March 1864, had issued the orders on June 5. *OR*, ser. 1, v. 27, pt. 1:31–32; *DAB*, 8:151–52.

2. Given his instructions to cover Washington, Hooker asked Lincoln whether he could, if the Confederates started moving toward the Potomac, strike the enemy's rear near Fredericksburg. Hooker also noted that "I cannot too forcibly impress upon the mind of His Excellency the President the necessity of having one commander for all of the troops whose operations can have an influence on those of Lee's army. Under the present system, all independent commanders are in ignorance of the movements of the others; at least such is my situation." *OR,* ser. 1, v. 27, pt. 1:30.

3. That is, Aquia Creek, the landing on the Potomac River that formed part of the supply and communications link to Hooker's army in the vicinity of Falmouth, Va. *Official Atlas of the Civil War* (New York, 1958), pl. 8.

TO EDWIN M. STANTON

Letterpress copy of letter in clerk's hand, signed by Chase. Chase Papers, Historical Society of Pennsylvania (*micro* 27:0223).

Unofficial[1]

Treasury Department
June 12, 1863.

Sir—

I return the letter, dated May 28, 1863, of Brig.-General Shepley, Military Governor of Louisiana, and the paper transmitted by him relating to the reörganization of the State Government of Louisiana under a Constitution to be adopted by the loyal people of that State, which you have submitted to my perusal; and, beg your attention to a few observations & suggestions.[2]

The precedent established in the case of Virginia fully warrants the proposed proceeding for the reëstablishment of a State Government under a State Constitution. The loyal people of a State must by the National authorities, be regarded as the State, unless completely [overborne] and subjugated by a foreign or insurgent force. When so overborne and subjugated, their rights are in abeyance, awaiting the expulsion of the dominating force; and are then subject in their exercise to such control by the National Government as will most certainly ensure the State and the Country against renewed invasion or insurrection.

These general principles being kept in view, it seems highly desirable that the State Government of Louisiana be reconstituted; and the plan of reconstitution proposed by the Committee appears to be, in the main, judicious.

It proposes, indeed, little else than the obvious measures of registring the loyal voters of the State; authorizing them to vote for members of a Constitutional Convention; and providing for the holding of that Convention, and for the framing by it of a State Constitution

The main, and, in my opinion, the vital question is, Who shall be regarded as legal voters?

The plan submitted to Gen Shepley, and by him to the Secretary of War, sufficiently secures the point of loyalty; but restricts suffrage to loyal white citizens and aliens who have declared their intention to become citizens.

Is this restriction politic or just? I think it neither.

The treaty under which Louisiana was acquired stipulated that "the inhabitants should be admitted, as soon as possible according to the principles of the federal Constitution, to the enjoyment of all the rights, advantages and immunities of citizens of the United States"[3] / It excepted no class of inhabitants; and I have always regarded it as an error pregnant with mischief that this stipulation, so far as the colored inhabitants were concerned, was wholly disregarded. They were all disfranchised and many of them enslaved.

Recently, the Proclamation of the President has emancipated the descendants of the people thus enslaved, as well as all other persons enslaved in Louisiana, except those held in certain parishes; and many of the persons there held are also free under various Acts of Congress.[4] Being free, they are, according to the opinion of the Attorney General lately given, citizens of the United States.[5]

Is it not a clear obligation of honor and duty to protect these citizens against the possibility of future enslavement? Can any sure guaranty of such protection be given them, except by recognizing their right to participate in the reconstitution of the State, by voting for the members of the proposed Constitutional Convention?

But, apart from every consideration of the original injustice, and the obligation towards these colored citizens assumed by the Proclamation and the legislation of Congress, there are other weighty reasons for watchful protection of their rights by the National Government. (1st.) They constitute a vast majority of the loyal people of the State. (2d.) Very many of that portion of them who have been long free are intelligent, hold property, maintain schools and churches, and are in all respects as well qualified to exercise the right of suffrage as their white fellow-citizens. (3d.) Those who have been long free and those recently emancipated have alike proved their loyalty by volunteering for the defence of the Union and the National Supremacy. One regiment, at least, of the former shared in the recent bloody conflict at Port-Hudson, while a regiment of the latter signalized its patriotic courage by a persistant attack on the enemy's works which cost more than half its number their [lives].[6] Besides these regiments, it is said that eight more are already mustered in from the colored citizens; whereas not one-tenth of the number of colored soldiers have probably volunteered from the class to which it is proposed to restrict suffrage. These reasons cannot be disregarded with credit, or even with safety.

I take the liberty of suggesting, therefore, that, in any plan of reconstruction which Gen. Shepley may be authorized to sanction, universal suffrage of citizens of the United States be expressly provided for. The possible consequences of omitting this provision may be inferred from the fact that, in the Schedule of Apportionment transmitted with the plan, the population of *all* the parishes, both excepted and not excepted, is divided into White, Free colored and *Slave,* without respect either to the Proclamation or the Acts of Congress. This may have been from inadvertence; but such inadvertences are suggestive.

Yours truly
S P Chase

Hon. Edwin M. Stanton

1. Chase's holograph draft of this letter, unidentified as to receiver or date, is in his papers at the Library of Congress and appears at *micro* 24:0424.

2. George F. Shepley had written to Stanton on May 28, enclosing proposals from Thomas J. Durant and James Graham, in behalf of "various Union associations of New Orleans and Jefferson," to reorganize Louisiana. *OR,* ser. 3, v. 3:231–35.

3. Article 3 of the Louisiana purchase treaty, April 30, 1803. *Statutes at Large,* 8:202.

4. That is, the first and second confiscation acts, August 6, 1861, and July 17, 1862. *Statutes at Large,* 12:319, 589–92.

5. Chase mentioned Edward Bates's opinion in correspondence with George Opdyke et al., April 8, 1863 (above).

6. For Chase's thoughts on fighting by the 1st and 2d Louisiana Regiments at the first battle of Port Hudson, May 27, see his letter to Robert J. Walker, June 8, 1863 (above).

TO WILLIAM P. MELLEN

Letter in clerk's hand on letterhead stationery, signed by Chase. General Agent, Letters Received from Secretary of the Treasury, Records of Civil War Special Agencies of the Treasury Department (Record Group 366), National Archives (*micro* 27:0279).

Treasury Department.
June 15,—1863.

Sir:

It becomes necessary from information which has reached this Department, to again impress upon the minds of its officers the importance of keeping an accurate and detailed record in relation to all captured or abandoned property received or collected by them.

You are instructed, therefore, when any such property comes into your possession, to immediately make and keep a full and correct record of all the facts or information in regard to it known or accessible to you—including, in each case, as nearly as possible, the following: where captured or abandoned; under what circumstances; by whom owned, or alleged to be owned; by whom captured or abandoned; by whom received or collected; from whom received; all names, marks, signs or devices, (whether distinct—indistinct or partially erased,) upon such property; together with all other information which may in any way serve to identify or make known the history of any particular lot, or to trace the same or the proceeds thereof, from the earliest period possible to its final disposition.

Also, to charge against each lot, and keep a true account of all expenses incurred in its receipt or collection, transportation, care and sale, or, where two or more lots are treated together, a fair and just proportion against each; as well as all fees due in any way to the Government therefrom.

You will also promptly transmit to this Department, and to the agent or officer to whom it may be turned over or consigned for sale, a copy of all such record in each case.

You will communicate the substance of these instructions to all persons acting under or with you, and see that they are in every instance faithfully complied with.

S P Chase
Secretary of the Treasury.

Wm. P. Mellen, Esq.,
Sup'g Sp. Ag. Tr. Dep't,
Cincinnati, O.

TO RICHARD C. PARSONS

Autograph letter on letterhead stationery. Chase Papers, Historical Society of Pennsylvania (*micro* 27:0282).

Treasury Department.
June 15—1863

My dear Parsons,

If Vallandigham violated any law he should have been arrested, tried & convicted. To arrest, try & attempt to convict him now seems very much like a confession that the Burnside Court had no jurisdiction;—if the charge be based on the acts which were proved before that Court.[1]

I have never myself been much afraid of words: and when men (Vallandigham among them) have sought to cripple the financial administration by misrepresentation and vilification I have preferred to reply by augmented efforts in the service of the country rather than by arrest & imprisonment.

You will infer, perhaps not unreasonably, that I am no great admirer of Order No 38.

Not that I am at all averse to arrests for sufficient cause [&] in proper time and place. It would have been very well to arrest Lee, & Johnston & others, instead of allowing them to resign and take rebel service.[2] It was very well to arrest the incipient traitors in Maryland who were plotting the consummation of treason by open rebellion.[3] But I think the exercise of such a power ought to be reserved for grave and clear occasions.

But what is the use of writing this. All that I can say will change nothing.

I will suggest to the President what you suggest to me. It may be after all that it will be well enough to have an indictment, if the facts warrant one; & let him plead, in defence, the trial by & sentence of the Burnside Court. There may, too, be other matters warranting an indictment not drawn before the Military Commission.

Before you receive this the Convention will be over. I should have attended it in accordance with the Committees invitation had it been practicable. Tod will doubtless be nominated; and though there are some things about him which are not altogether to my liking, still he has done as much to sustain the War as any other Governor & I should not like to see him refused the nomination if he or his friends desire it.[4] We must be liberal to all who are rowing our boat whether we like them—or are liked by them—or not.

I hope to come to Ohio early in July; but things look now as though I shall not get a chance to do so.[5] Love to Madame.

Yours Ever
S P Chase

Col. R. C. Parsons

Secretary Stanton bluffed me very decidedly as to Dangler.[6]

1. On May 22, a military commission under Gen. Ambrose Burnside had convicted Clement L. Vallandigham of "declaring sympathies for the enemy," in violation of General Orders No. 38, issued on April 13, 1863. *DAB,* 19:144; *OR,* ser. 2, v. 5:480, 633.

2. Upon Virginia's secession from the Union, Joseph Eggleston Johnston, like Robert E. Lee, had resigned from the U.S. Army to serve with the Confederacy. *DAB,* 10:144, 11:122.

3. In September 1861, Federal authorities had arrested a number of Maryland legislators suspected of disloyalty. Long, *Civil War Day by Day,* 118.

4. At a state convention in Columbus on June 18, the Union party of Ohio passed over the incumbent Republican governor, David Tod, and nominated John Brough instead. *DAB,* 18:568; *Daily Ohio State Journal,* June 18, 1863.

5. Chase apparently remained in Washington, D.C., most of July, then late in the month traveled to the Northeast (see Chase to Jay Cooke, July 29, 1863 [below]).

6. In earlier letters to Parsons, Chase also referred to the case of David A. Dangler, an assistant quartermaster of volunteers who had resigned at the end of May, after less than seven months' service, amid allegations of unspecified "misconduct." *Chase Papers,* 3:311, 312, 384; Heitman, *Historical Register,* 1:353.

TO KATE CHASE

Letterpress copy of autograph letter. Chase Papers, Historical Society of Pennsylvania (*micro* 27:0401).

Washington June 22, 1863.

My darling,

You were very good and thoughtful to write me immediately on reaching your [room]. I think you would have done better by going to Col. Howes; where your neuralgia would have been better cared for and I should have felt easier about you. Then you could have looked up Mrs McDowell quite as well the next day &, meantime, your *trunks* might have occupied your room at the 5th Avenue.[1] I hardly expected however, knowing your *setness* of will, that you would go; and, if no harm comes to you, I shall be quite content.

Your letter only came this morning: and I write immediately. I have seen nobody to learn any thing since Saturday night. Then everything looked well. This morning I find all sorts of trashy rumors in the papers; and actually heard a newsboy crying, "Capture of Baltimore." So far as I have heard anything authentic, I find no reason to believe that there are 2000 rebels this side of the Potomac from Cumberland down, including those who made the grand scare in Pennsylvania.[2] One of the most intelligent and candid correspondents I have seen who has just visited all the threatened points, coming here, yesterday, told me that he thought Lee's Army was moving down the Kanawha. This is possible and it is also possible that he may be going to Bragg through East Tennessee:[3] but I don't think either movement probable. The point of destination is too distant to allow of his reaching it with more than a third or at most, a half of the Army he had at Fredericksburgh and he would leave any Atlantic rebel city uncovered. In my judgment he is in the Shenandoah Valley or not far from it, and means to fight any part of Hookers force he can find exposed and avail himself of any opportunities that may be offered to strike blows. My conviction is that he will not accomplish any great *things;* but, on the contrary, will find that he has made a false & disastrous move. Nous verrons.[4] Why may I not *guess* as well as any body else. Mind I dont *prophecy.*

Miss Claire is very well; but misses you dreadfully. She is as good as she can be; but you know I can give her next to no time.[5]

I shall send this under cover to Col. Howe thinking it may reach you a little sooner than if sent to Mr. Barney. If I knew Mrs. McDowell's exact address, the penny post would probably make the earliest delivery.

If Gov. S—— is in New York make to him my most cordial greetings, and assure Mrs McDowell of my kindest souvenirs.

Your affe. father
S P CHASE

Miss Kate Chase

1. Helen Burden McDowell was Gen. Irvin McDowell's wife. The Fifth Avenue Hotel was on Broadway at the corner of West 23d in New York. *New York Dir. (1863),* 284.

2. Lee's Army of Northern Virginia had moved around Hooker's position on the Rappahannock, and, on June 15, the Confederates' leading forces began crossing the Potomac. Their movement into Maryland brought consternation to Harrisburg, Pa., and other locales in their projected path. The Confederate incursion into Maryland and Pennsylvania resulted in the battle of Gettysburg, July 1–3. Long, *Civil War Day by Day,* 364–67, 374–78.

3. Gen. Braxton Bragg commanded the Confederate Army of Tennessee. *DAB,* 2:586–87.

4. "We shall see." For a much earlier use of this phrase by Chase, see *Chase Papers,* 1:110.

5. Swiss-born Claire Albrecht was a family friend who, at least by September 1863, worked in the Treasury counting U.S. notes and postal currency. Evidence suggests that

she later married Charles Manning Walker. *Register of Officers (1863),* 19; *Chase Papers,* 1:499, 501; Chase to Jay Cooke, Sept. 8, 1864 (Chase Papers, Hist. Soc. of Pa.); Walker to Chase, Aug. 30, 186[8], Nov. 28, 1870, Chase to Walker, Dec. 8, 1870 (Chase Papers, L.C.); Chase to Kate Chase Sprague, Nov. 18, 1863, and to Janet Chase, Feb. 2[6], Mar. 15, 1864 (below).

TO KATE CHASE

Letterpress copy of autograph letter. Chase Papers, Historical Society of Pennsylvania (*micro* 27:0478).

Washington June 25, 1863.

My dear Katie,

Matters are becoming more serious, though not at all alarming in this region. The situation as now understood indicates that Lee is about to try an invasion of Maryland & possibly of Pennsylvania. There is an opinion, not held, though, by many, that he may attempt to reach the Ohio at Pittsburgh or Wheeling. The days of six miles a day marches are over, however, and he will get no great distance, in any direction, without feeling Hooker strike him. The severe slaps in the face he has already received at Brandy Station and at Aldie are samples in little of what he is to expect.[1] If God smiles on active and earnest work on the right side Lee will never take his army back to Richmond. Gen. Halleck was in Baltimore yesterday looking after matters there and when he returned found Hooker here who had ridden in to confer with him. Hooker had been already told that a better officer was needed at Harpers Ferry, which you know is out of his command, and had been asked if he could spare one. Halleck repeated the question when they met & said we must have a new commander there tomorrow. "He shall be there tonight" said Hooker: and doubtless some time last night that important fort was put into safe hands. Perhaps it was in safe hands, already, but it is not thought best to risk it again as it was risked before.[2] Where Hooker is this morning it wd. be hard to tell. He is, certainly, with his army and I suppose in motion. Where he will be tonight I cannot guess; but he will be where he thinks he can render most service & he will make no noise about it.

We were all delighted by Capt. Rodgers exploit. It was really "splendid", as Nettie would say. The rebels came out to take and staid out—taken.[3] I told General Halleck last night—Seward[4] Stanton & I rode out to see him—that it was a victory which I specially like, for only five shots were fired, all taking effect save one—& the affair was therefore *so* economical. They all laughed; but seemed to think that behind the joke there was a real care for the peoples cash.

The news from Vicksburgh is to the eighteenth & all was going on well: so also from Port Hudson. I hope we *now* have both those places. Indeed everything looks well now on all sides.

Col Birney has just been in. His first colored regt. has now seven companies & he expects it filled this week. On Sunday he intends marching his soldiers to church down Penna. Avenue. Won't parson Turner be glad & happy to see his church filled with his colored brethren—so lately slaves—now freedmen & more volunteer soldiers of the Union?[5]

Mr. & Mrs Cooke are returned from Phila.[6] Mr C—— has just left me. He did not know of your engagement & modestly asked me & I told him—they would have been among the first to be informed had they been in the city.

It looks very much as though I shall not be able to go to Ohio next week. You can remain in New York as long as you think best, you & Nettie & then go direct to Ohio if you choose or return here. I dont give up the journey but may be obliged to postpone it.

Yours affectionately
S P CHASE

Miss Kate Chase

1. On June 9, Union cavalry under Alfred Pleasonton had surprised and nearly overwhelmed Confederate counterparts under James Ewell Brown ("Jeb") Stuart at Brandy Station, Va. Pleasonton also commanded Union troops in skirmishes at Aldie, Va., on June 17 and 18. Long, *Civil War Day by Day,* 363–64, 368; *OR,* ser. 1, v. 27, pt. 1:903–10.

2. Despite urgent warnings from superiors, Union forces under Maj. Gen. Robert Huston Milroy, commander of the second division of the Eighth Army Corps, had moved slowly on June 14 and 15 to meet Confederates who threatened Federal control of Harpers Ferry. *DAB,* 13:20; Long, *Civil War Day by Day,* 365–67.

3. The *Atlanta,* a Confederate ironclad steamer, had surrendered to John Rodgers, commander of the USS *Weehawken,* after a brief battle in Wassaw Sound, Ga., on June 17. "Nettie" was Chase's younger daughter, Janet Ralston Chase. Long, *Civil War Day by Day,* 368.

4. Secretary of State William H. Seward.

5. William Birney helped supervise the enlistment of black Union soldiers. On May 22, he had received an appointment as brigadier general of volunteers. Henry McNeal Turner, an African Methodist Episcopal bishop, was pastor of Israel Church in Washington, D.C. *DAB,* 2:294, 19:65–66.

6. Evidently, given Chase's comment that they had "returned from Phila.," Henry David Cooke and his wife, Laura S. Humphreys Cooke.

TO JOHN J. CISCO

Letterpress copy of autograph letter. Chase Papers, Historical Society of Pennsylvania (*micro* 27:0493).

Washington June 26, 1863.

My dear Sir,

I enclose the check of Jay Cooke & Co for $350 and beg you to excuse my delay. The *next time* I will improve.

Possibly I may come to New York on Monday.[1] My object would be to consult in respect to the expediency of extending the time for receiving subscriptions at par for 5–20s; and in respect to the issue of Treasury Notes. I have thought also of adding to the 81 Loan[2] say 50 millions at a premium say of 6% or 7%.

My judgment inclines to all three measures. 1st. It seems to me that as the 5–20 subscription has worked so well & the people are becoming habituated to this way of investing their funds that it would be judicious to announce that the receipt of subscriptions will be continued for sixty days. The only doubtful question to my mind is whether the subscriptions should be continued on the present plan through a general agency as well as through the Assistant Treasurers or confined to the Assistant Treasurers[3] / My impression is in favor of letting well enough alone; but of course I want to avoid every avoidable expence.

(2d The issue of interest bearing notes would I think benefit the Treasury without deteriorating the circulation. I incline to the opinion that to avoid the great inconveniences and considerable risks which would attend the payment of interest at short periods on notes of small denominations that it [would] be best to issue these notes for one year with interest at 5% payable with the note at maturity. The first issued—say the first 50,000,000 should be made legal tender for their face. Afterwards if the probable demand should warrant it another series could be issued convertible into legal tenders for their face amount. Few inconveniences & more advantages seem to me to attend this plan than any other.[4]

(3[d)] The present high price of 81s indicates a demand for them which would warrant a loan in that form, of say $50,000,000. The amount thus obtained could be held as a reserve by the subscribed banks or capitalists, only ten or fifteen cent. being paid it; until the demands of the government *un*satisfied from other sources should require it. This would make the Department very strong, and increase probably the value of all securities.

If these suggestions strike you favorably please confer with a few leading friends confidentially and if you think it useful for me to come telegraph me.

Yours truly
S: P: CHASE

J. J. Cisco Esq.

Military affairs look well to me, though I do not profess to see far or know much. It seems as if Lee had "put his foot in it" and I trust Hooker will profit by the mistake.[5]

1. "Circumstances" forced Chase to cancel the trip several days later. Chase to Kate Chase, June 29, 1863 (below).

2. Legislation approved on July 17, 1861, had authorized a national loan of up to $250 million, "irredeemable for twenty years." *Statutes at Large,* 12:259–61.

3. In addition to Cisco in New York, the assistant treasurers were Theophilus P. Chandler in Boston, Archibald McIntyre in Philadelphia, and Benjamin Farrar in St. Louis. *Register of Officers (1863),* 31–33.

4. The ways and means act of March 3, 1863, authorized Chase to issue up to $400 million in interest-bearing notes. To be printed in denominations of ten dollars or

greater, the notes "may be made a legal tender . . . for their face value excluding interest." The new notes were to have a term of no more than three years and "may be disposed of on the best terms that can be obtained." The act authorized an annual interest rate of up to six percent. For details regarding issue of such notes, see Chase to Cisco, August 31, 1863 (below). *Statutes at Large,* 12:710.

5. In recent military correspondence, Joseph Hooker had discussed plans to seal the escape route of Robert E. Lee, whose Confederate troops had crossed the Potomac River in mid-June to threaten Maryland, Pennsylvania, and Washington, D.C. Long, *Civil War Day by Day,* 367, 370–71.

TO KATE CHASE

Letterpress copy of autograph letter. Chase Papers, Historical Society of Pennsylvania (*micro* 27:0573).

Washington, June 29, 1863.

My dear Child,

You must have been greatly astonished by the relieving of General Hooker; but your astonishment cannot have exceeded mine.[1] He was relieved at his own request and the request must have been very suddenly resolved on; for his telegram asking to be relieved was dated at eight on Saturday night; and I received one from Butterfield dated at Six or half past suggesting some military movements in Virginia in which there was not the slightest allusion to Hookers purpose.[2] What prompted his request I do not know. I did not hear of it nor of the appointment of Gen. Meade in his place till Sunday, when at a Meeting of the Heads called for a different purpose, having no connection with Hooker's affairs, the President mentioned it to us.

I understand that Gen. Meade is preferred by the majority of the officers to any one except Hooker & perhaps now to him. He was at once notified of his appointment; and though taken entirely by surprise, accepted it in a modest telegram and at once entered on his duties.[3] By this time I presume he has the army pretty well in hand.

Gen Butler is here. I wish the President would make him General in Chief. I like General Halleck personally, and he seems to me to have capacity; but he does not *work, work,* WORK, as if he were in earnest. Butler would take hold I think with a will. You must not think he came with any idea of superseding Gen H—— His purpose was simply to take one of his daughters who has just finished her course & has a vacation at Georgetown back to Massachusetts.[4]

There has been a good deal of alarm here yesterday and today because of the enemy's cavalry coming very close to the city with supposed designs on the Washington & Baltimore & Baltimore & Ohio Railroads.[5] I should not be surprised by the cutting of either or both of them; but I attach no great consequence to these raids. While the rebels are doing these things near Washington we are doing the same things near Richmond; where as you have doubtless seen a detachment from Gen. Dix's command on Friday or Saturday burnt the bridge across the South Anne & captured Gen. W. F. Lee, other officers & privates & many mules & wagons.[6] Still these things are pleasanter to do than to suffer.

There is of course a great deal of concern about the military operations of the two great armies; a concern naturally increased by the action of Gen Hooker. In respect to these I hope the best, and trust in God. If our cause is just & right will He not bless it? Will He suffer the cause to fail because of the unworthiness of those who sustain it?

Under existing circumstances I cannot come to New York. Will it not be well for you to arrange your visit to Ohio independently of me, taking some trusty servant to look after your baggage. I can send you Schureman, if you desire, who would be delighted to go: or if you prefer one of the gentlemen from the Department—say Mr. French.[7]

Yours Affectionately
S P Chase

Miss Kate Chase

1. Hooker and General-in-Chief Henry W. Halleck had disagreed on how to counter the Confederate invasion. On June 27, Lincoln replaced Hooker with Maj. Gen. George G. Meade as commander of the Army of the Potomac. Long, *Civil War Day by Day*, 367, 371–72; *DAB*, 12:475–76.

2. Daniel Butterfield's telegram, sent at 6:30 P.M. on June 27, suggested an attack on Richmond, Va. Butterfield to Chase, June 27, 1863 (Chase Papers, L.C.).

3. "The order placing me in command of this army is received," replied Meade. "As a soldier I obey it, and to the utmost of my ability will execute it." George Meade, *The Life and Letters of George Gordon Meade*, ed. by George Gordon Meade, 2 vols. (New York, 1913), 2:4–5.

4. Apparently Blanche Butler, a young woman about sixteen years old. Hans Trefousse, *Ben Butler: The South Called Him Beast!* (New York, 1957), 28.

5. Chase referred to raids in the vicinity by troops under Jeb Stuart. Long, *Civil War Day by Day*, 372–73.

6. Maj. Gen. John A. Dix commanded the Department of Maryland. In July he was reassigned to the Department of New York, where he stayed for the rest of the war. From 1863 to 1868 he also presided over the Union Pacific Railroad as its first president. Troops under Dix had burned one of the Central Railroad's bridges near Hanover Junction, Va., on Friday, June 26. William Henry Fitzhugh Lee (1837–91), a son of Robert E. Lee and brigadier general in the 9th Virginia Cavalry, was captured while recuperating from wounds received on June 9. *Appletons'*, 2:184; *DAB*, 5:326, 11:134; *OR*, ser. 1, v. 27, pt. 2:796–97.

7. Possibly E. F. French, a clerk in the Treasury Department. Schureman may have been James H. A. Schureman, listed in the city directory as a messenger. *Register of Officers (1863)*, 20; *Wash. Dir. (1864)*, 244; Chase to Janet Chase, Feb. 2[6], 1864 (below).

TO DAVID DUDLEY FIELD

Letterpress copy of autograph letter. Chase Papers, Historical Society of Pennsylvania (*micro* 27:0596).

Washington June 30, 1863

My dear Sir,

I am much gratified by your assurance that the decision of your Court of Appeals will probably be unanimous in support of the law making U.S. Notes a legal tender. To have your anticipation converted into certainty this week would be still more gratifying. You did quite right in employing Judge Foote.[1]

If I could explain the movements in Pennsylvania and Maryland I should be glad: but no thicker darkness envelopes any one than myself.[2]

After Lee had begun his movement from between Hooker & Richmond, nothing seemed clearer to me than that he had recklessly given us an opportunity to close the War by the destruction of his army and the capture of Richmond; and the movements of Hooker, except so far as they were controlled, otherwise, from Washington, appeared to be calculated for the accomplishment of those objects. But differences arose; Hooker committed some imprudences in counsel and action; confidence was shaken on both sides; and finally he asked to be relieved and his request was promptly granted.[3] Where the fault was I know not. The request was a surprise to me. It was received and granted & Meade appointed Saturday night, & I heard nothing of it until Sunday about noon.

Meade seems to have a large share of the confidence of the officers. It was to him more than any other person that they seemed to look immediately after the battle of Chancellorsville.[4] He has acquitted himself well, also, hitherto; and will do better, I hope, in the future. Time must determine that.

It seems to me now as it has seemed from the first that there need be nothing alarming in this invasion; that on the contrary it offers a capital opportunity to strike the most fatal blows the rebellion has yet received. A raid of rebel cavalry near Washington is not agreeable; but it has not much practical significance, unless followed up by an attack, which Lee will hardly undertake. The same thing may be said of the raid of Spear from Dix's army to Hanover Junction last week—useless unless a prelude to attack on Richmond.[5] But how idle it seems for me to speculate on Military affairs! The President consults only Stanton & Halleck in the management of the War. I look on from the outside and, as well as I can, furnish the means. In my own department I live by works—in the others by faith only. But I *exercise* faith, not forgetting hope & charity.[6]

Cordially your friend
S P Chase

David Dudley Field Esq

I enclose for your perusal a letter of Robert J Walker which I am sure will interest you. Please return it.

1. Chase had hired Field, a prominent New York Republican lawyer, to argue in support of the legal tender acts in the cases of *Metropolitan Bank v. Van Dyck* and *Meyer v.*

Roosevelt, heard by the New York State Court of Appeals on June 26 and 27. Field's associate was Samuel A. Foote (1790–1878), a former state legislator and appellate judge. "I have no doubt, that the decision will be unanimous, in support of the law," wrote Field on June 29. Actually, the court sustained the legislation by a margin of six to two. *DAB,* 6:360; Charles Fairman, *Reconstruction and Reunion, 1864–88, Part One,* vol. 6 of Paul A. Freund, gen. ed., *The Oliver Wendell Holmes Devise History of the Supreme Court of the United States* (New York, 1971), 693–94; Field to Chase, June 29, 1863 (Chase Papers, Hist. Soc. of Pa.); *New York Times,* May 12, 1878.

2. In his letter of June 29, Field enquired about the meaning of movements by Confederate and Union armies that soon culminated in the battle of Gettysburg, July 1–3. "There must be some stronger & better-directed impetus given to the Army, or the people will become disheartened," he wrote. Field to Chase, June 29, 1863 (Chase Papers, Hist. Soc. of Pa.)

3. Chase discussed Hooker's replacement in a letter of June 29 to his daughter Kate (above).

4. May 1–4, 1863.

5. Col. Samuel Perkins Spear (d. 1875), of the 11th Pennsylvania Cavalry under John A. Dix, had destroyed a Confederate railroad bridge near Hanover Junction, Va. Chase to Kate Chase, June 29, 1863 (above); Heitman, *Historical Register,* 1:909; *OR,* ser. 1, v. 27, pt. 2:795–97.

6. Apparent paraphrases of Rom. 3:27 and 1 Cor. 13:13.

TO ULYSSES S. GRANT

Letterbook copy in clerk's hand. Letters Sent Relating to Restricted Commercial Intercourse and Captured and Abandoned Property (BE Series), General Records, Department of the Treasury (Record Group 56), National Archives (*micro* 27:0658).

Treasury Department
July 4, 1863.

Maj. Genl. U. S. Grant
&c &c &c
General,

I find that the establishment of a rigorous line, within districts occupied by our military forces, from beyond which no Cotton or other products can be brought, and within which no trade can be carried on, gives rise to serious, and to some extent, apparently, well-founded complaints.

I have therefore instructed Mr. Mellen, the Supervising Special Agent of this Department for the Mississippi Valley, to confer with you as to the propriety of substituting Bonds, to be given by all parties receiving permits, for the rigorous line now established; or at least, of substituting them partially.[1]

I enclose you a copy of my letter to Mr. Mellen, and beg you to give it, and any suggestions on the subject he may offer, such consideration as the other great demands upon your time and attention will allow.

Yours Very truly,
S. P. Chase.
Secy of the Treasy.

1. Chase's letter of July 3 to William P. Mellen issued instructions about how to deal with each of four major categories of property under his jurisdiction: abandoned,

captured, commercial, and confiscable. The orders permitted substitution in cases that did not entail "the furnishing of supplies." Chase to Mellen, July 3, 1863 (Gen. Agent, Letters Recd.: Sec. of Treas., Recs. of Civil War Special Agencies, Nat. Arch.).

TO WILLIAM P. MELLEN

Autograph letter on letterhead stationery. Clara H. Mellen Papers, Bowdoin College (*micro* 27:0662).

Treasury Department.
July 4, 1863

Dear Sir,

I hope you are not losing sight of the very important matter about which I requested you to confer with Generals Grant & Rosecrans:—I mean of course the Allowance of parties having cotton or other property *any where* within our lines of military occupation to bring it out by their own means and at their own risk, receiving only from the military & naval services such incidental aid as would be rendered any citizens in legitimate pursuits. Such parties should, as I have already stated to you, be required to give bond conditioned that no military or naval officer of the United States & no civil officer serving in any capacity connecting him directly or indirectly with the charge of abandoned or captured property or of commercial intercourse in or with the insurrectionary districts is interested with them in the transaction for which a permit is desired or to their knowledge in any like transactions in which said parties may be interested; that they have disclosed fully the names of all parties in interest in their application for a permit; & that neither they nor any persons interested with them will by means of the permit or otherwise give any information, aid, comfort or support to persons within the lines of rebel military occupation or to rebels or insurgents elsewhere. The penal sum should be stipulated damages.

It does seem to me that such a bond would more effectually protect our military operations than any lines however carefully drawn; though probably some general lines between districts militarily occupied but not surely & completely & districts within which the Authority of the Union is more fully reestablished will still be useful.

It might be well to confine the introduction of supplies into the uncertain districts (except in the smallest quantities for absolute necessaries,) to parties who shall have given such bonds. You can think of this.

I observe the attacks made on you and on me.[1] These must be expected & must not at all affect our action. Our object must be to do our duty & be content with the consciousness of doing it, whether praised or reviled.

Yours sincerely,
S P Chase

Wm P. Mellen Esq

1. On July 2, for example, the *New York Herald* had written with disapproval of Chase's "plans to outwit President Lincoln, his schemes to get ahead of poor Seward, his efforts to organise loyal leagues, and his immense, secret, underground machinery to upset all the other republican candidates and secure his nomination for the next Presidency." *New York Herald,* July 2, 1863.

TO CUTHBERT BULLITT

Letterpress copy of autograph letter. Chase Papers, Historical Society of Pennsylvania (*micro* 27:0723).

Unofficial

Washington, July 9, 1863

My dear Mr. Bullitt,

The very favorable impressions of your character and qualifications made upon me by our personal intercourse during your brief visits to Washington, as well as the cordial testimony borne in your behalf by mutual & valued friends, induced me to appoint you Special Agent and acting Collector at New Orleans at the expence of displacing a gentleman, very dear to me on many accounts, &, according to the testimony of all having business with him, an excellent and most faithful officer.

Under these circumstances I expected that you would confer freely with that gentleman—Mr. Denison—and rely much on his counsel in the administration of your office. You assured me, indeed, that you should do so.

I was greatly pained, therefore, to learn that differences had arisen between you: that after obtaining from him a classification of the Clerks according to his judgment of their efficiency & capacity, you made it known to some if not all of them, when it should have been treated as a communication made to you in confidence; & that, in other matters in connexion with the administration of the office, you acted against his judgment, without any sufficient public reason.

My pain from these things was heightened by the variances between yourself and Mr. Gray, whose life of unimpeached integrity in New York makes it difficult to believe that he was altogether in fault. I shall hope, however, that, in this matter, the report of the Special Agent whom I have instructed to examine into the charges you make against him, will relieve me from the fear that you have acted without sufficient reason in his suspension.[1]

Besides my disappointments in these respects is another, which, though it does not connect itself [directly] with the admn. of the Custom House, has a very serious importance in my mind. Before your appointment I explained to you most candidly my views of the necessity and wisdom of the Presidents proclamation of Emancipation, and understood you, if not as altogether concurring with me, yet as ready to accept the policy of the proclamation as fixed and to give it your hearty support. I also understood that your brother in law Dr. Kennedy, the Editor of the True Delta, concurred with you in general views and purposes.

That I was mistaken as to Dr. Kennedy's position the columns of the True Delta show clearly enough. And I regret it exceedingly; for believing myself most thoroughly that secession has killed slavery, I should have most gladly welcomed the cooperation of so able & accomplished a gentleman in the work of reestablishing the Union & prosperity of the country on the basis of emancipation—the only sure if not the only possible basis.

I regret still more to learn that you do not harmonize in action with the friends of the proclamation and its policy; and that neither your official or personal influence is given to that cause.

You will readily understand that the official relations which exist between us cannot be maintained with any tolerable degree of satisfaction, if, in the important place you occupy, dissensions with gentlemen holding equal positions cannot be avoided; unless, indeed, the fault is with those gentlemen, in which case the same remark applies to them: nor can those official relations continue mutually agreeable if the policy of the President, whether in respect to Emancipation or the War, cannot find in you a cordial supporter, at a place where unanimity about the officers of the government is so essential.

I trust you will appreciate the frankness with which I write and receive what is written in the same spirit of kindness, with which I subscribe myself

Very sincerely your friend
S P Chase

Cuthbert Bullitt Esq

1. The special agent was John Hutchins, a former Ohio congressman appointed to investigate charges that William C. Gray had accepted a bribe. Gray's continued employment in U.S. government service until at least September 1864 suggests that the allegation was never proven. Denison to Chase, May 9, 1863 (above); Hutchins to Chase, June 26, Gray to Hutchins, June 26, 1863, Denison to Chase, Sept. 6, 1864 (Chase Papers, L.C.); *Bio. Dir. U.S. Cong.*, 1239.

TO JAY COOKE

Letter in clerk's hand on letterhead stationery, signed by Chase. Jay Cooke Papers, Historical Society of Pennsylvania (*micro* 27:0797).

Treasury Department.
July 13, 1863

Sir,

I have this moment received, from the Assistant Treasurer at New-York, a letter in reply to one from me enjoining him not to sell with the one-eighth deduction, except to purchasers buying for resale and not for investment.[1]

In that letter of the Assistant Treasurer the following passage occurs: "In no instance have I allowed commissions to parties other than those claiming to purchase for resale, or as agents on behalf of other parties; and in every instance, so far as I am informed, where I have declined to allow it to investers, they have immediately gone to Sub-agents here, *who allow it in all cases.*"

You will at once see the importance of a strict prohibition to the sub-agents from making this allowance.[2] Indeed, I do not see how they can make it except out of their own pockets; for the arrangement of the Department with you since July 1st. allows only 1/8 of one per cent to local agents, and to you, for advertising and transportation, the actual expenses not exceeding 1/8, and also to you, as compensation for your general agency and for sales made by houses of which you are a member a sum not exceeding one-eighth of one per cent

I am fully satisfied that the success of the 5–20 Loan is due, in very large measure, to your zealous and wise agency. I cannot, however, consistently with my ideas of public duty, restrict sales by the sub-Treasurers and designated Depositories with whom subscriptions for loans have always been authorized; nor could I refuse to purchasers who buy for purposes, not of investment, but of resale, the deduction of 1–8 of one per cent, leaving them to pay their own expenses of advertisement and transportation

It is not surprising, perhaps, that under these circumstances some misunderstandings should arise in the minds of of your sub-agents in respect to the Assistant Treasurers, and in the minds of the Assistant Treasurers in respect to your sub-Agents. Such misunderstandings, however, should be avoided as far as possible. I will endeavor to reduce it to the minimum on the part of the Assistant-Treasurers, and trust you to do the same thing in respect to the sub Agents.

Yours very truly,
S P Chase

Jay Cooke, Esq.

1. Agreements with the U.S. Treasury permitted Cooke to deduct one-eighth of one percent from proceeds on the sale of 5–20 bonds to cover commissions and expenses. Henrietta M. Larson, *Jay Cooke: Private Banker,* (Cambridge, Mass., 1936), 148.

2. Subagents were representatives that Cooke engaged on commission to sell bonds directly to the public. Ibid., 125–26.

TO WILLIAM SPRAGUE

Letterpress copy of autograph letter. Chase Papers, Historical Society of Pennsylvania (*micro* 27:0822).

Washington, July 14, 1863.

My dear Governor,

Katie and I have talked over matters and have come to about these conclusions: 1st That you shall have the large rooms on the east side of the house to work your will in, doing with them precisely what you please (2d) That I will keep the rooms I now have for sleeping room & library, in like manner (3d) that the rest of the house shall be for the friends of either or both as may happen, and in common; (4th) that I will pay the rent and servants wages and you the table expences, dividing the stable expences between us.

If this arrangement suits you exactly let it stand. If not modify it till it does suit. What I want is the happiness of both of you and your honor & credit, which must henceforth be ever dearer to me than my own.

Katie says you propose to have a separate carriage & coachman. There is not the slightest necessity for this, and I am sure you will find it an inconvenience. We have two carriages & their horses all very respectable, and nobody makes much use of them but Katie. You and I will hardly ever require either, and it would be useless to double for her. Better give the money it would cost to the Hospitals.

I have given up my idea of taking a house or apartment near the Presidents in deference to Katies wishes, and as she assures me to yours. To do so would be in some respects better all round as I think, and the arrangement would enable me to be of more service with the President should I remain in the Department. But life is short and uncertain and I am not willing to do anything which will grieve my children. So I yield the point and trust all will be best suited in the end.

Our military prospects now look really bright. Meade is pressing Lee closely. Sometimes I think a force on the right bank of the Potomac to harrass them if found too strong to be attacked opposite Williamsport or to attack them in front when crossing should that be found practicable would be an improvement on what is being done: but I don't like to criticize men who seem to be doing all they think it best to do and think it best to do all that can be done.

Bragg is retreating before Rosecrans, who will not I hope stop as some say he will on the left bank of the Tennessee but push steadily on to Chattanooga and fight if need be his way into East Tennessee & permanently occupy the Mountain region, which should have been occupied two years ago.

Jo Johnston is retreating before Sherman eastward through Mississippi. Sherman is pressing him closely with force enough to overwhelm him.

Port Hudson is probably ours: if not it soon will be. There are not rebels enough West of the Mississippi & outside of Jo. Johnstons Army to hurt Banks: though guerillas or raiders may pick up careless officers or men as in some instances

Capt. McGowan of the Revenue Steamer Cuyahoga[1] who left Port Royal on the 8th tells me that the Weehawken, Montauk, & Nahant, ironclads, left at the same time going to Charleston Bay, with intent to take part in an attack on Morris Island, or perhaps should circumstances favor on Sumter on the 9th. The attack probably took place and we may hope good tidings.[2]

Such is the situation. Every thing confirms the impression made, by Jeff Davis intercepted letter to Lee that rebeldom is a shell which only requires vigorous pressure to yield at all points.[3]

Shall we have the vigorous pressure? I hope so—almost believe so.

Meantime what a scandal is the mob in New York? It makes me wish I could have the power for a week.[4]

Where is Col. Miner?[5]

Yours Affectionately
SP CHASE

Hon Wm. Sprague

1. John McGowan (1805–91) had been an officer in the revenue service, 1831–53, and returned with the rank of captain in August 1861. His ship, a 308-ton propeller steamer, had been purchased as the *Santa Anna* earlier in 1863, repaired, and renamed *Cuyahoga* for service as a revenue steamer. Johnson, *Twentieth Century Biographical Dictionary*, v. 7; *Register of Officers (1863)*, 46; U.S. Department of Transportation, *Record of Movements: Vessels of the United States Coast Guard, 1790–Dec. 31, 1933* (Washington, D.C., 1989), 390; William M. Lytle, comp., *Merchant Steam Vessels of the United States, 1807–1868* (Mystic, Conn., 1952), 44.

2. Union forces took Morris Island in Charleston Harbor as a result of military action from August 12 to September 9, but failed to seize Fort Sumter or Charleston itself. Long, *Civil War Day by Day*, 396–407.

3. On July 2, Federal scouts near Gettysburg had captured Confederate correspondence that included a letter written on June 28 from President Jefferson Davis to Robert E. Lee. "Do not understand me as balancing accounts in the matter of brigades" wrote Davis from Richmond; "I only repeat that I have not many to send you, and enough to form an army to threaten, if not capture, Washington as soon as it is uncovered by Hooker's army. My purpose," he continued, "was to show you that the force here and in North Carolina is very small, and I may add that the brigades are claimed as properly of their command." *New York Times*, July 6, 1863; *OR*, ser. 1, v. 26, pt. 1:77.

4. On July 13, violence had erupted in New York and other northern cities in opposition to the Federal draft. Estimated losses in New York after three days of rioting totaled one thousand dead and $1.5 million in property damage. Chase received firsthand accounts of the unrest from Hiram Barney, July 15; Hamilton Fish, July 18; and John J. Cisco, July 23 (all below). Long, *Civil War Day by Day*, 384–86.

5. William Miner of Warren County, Ohio, an old political associate of Chase who in 1862 had received an appointment as assessor of internal revenue for Ohio's third district. Miner to Chase, Sept. 8, Nov. 21, 1862, Sprague to Chase, July 18, 1863 (Chase Papers, L.C.); Chase to Miner, Nov. 24, 1862 (Chase Papers, Hist. Soc. of Pa.); *Register of Officers (1863)*, 39; *Chase Papers*, 1:180.

TO WILLIAM SPRAGUE

Letterpress copy of autograph letter. Chase Papers, Historical Society of Pennsylvania (*micro* 27:0841).

Washington, July 15, 1863.

My dear Governor,

I intend to write you pretty often and pretty freely: so you must keep me advised of your whereabouts.

We were all terribly disappointed yesterday by the news that Lee had escaped with the whole remainder of his Army and all his Artillery and baggage.[1] The President came in to my room and told me of it about two yesterday afternoon. He was more grieved and indignant than I have ever seen him. Ever since the battle of Gettysburgh he had been urging on Halleck the importance of promptitude and vigilance and of activity. His sole fear has been lest Lees Army should get away. He was annoyed by the tone of Meades Address to his troops, which indicated that the main object, conceived by him, was the repulse of the enemy's invasion. He saw the same idea in Meades despatches, and did all he could (except take the responsibility) to make him understand that it was the rout of Lees army not its mere expulsion from Pennsylvania which was desired.[2] And now his worst fears were realized. Lee's Army gone & no blow struck. I reminded him that the last time he came to my room it was very much in the same frame of mind—when he had just received despatches from Hulburt that Grant had been defeated and his army captured at Jackson:[3] and that I then told him that daylight always came after darkness and that all we had to do was to gather new forces & persevere. He thought the cases not exactly similar & I agreed but insisted that the difference was on our side, for had Grant been in fact defeated the case would have been much worse with us than now.

Since this interview with the President I have learned that Meade called a council of his corps commanders on Saturday or Sunday Evening—that Slocum, Sedgwick, French and one or two more opposed a battle while Howard, Wadsworth & Pleasanton decidedly favored it[4]—that the debate was warm & earnest—that Meade's judgment was with the minority but his desire with the majority—that the Army consequently lay idle all day Monday when Lee was crossing the river some six or eight miles off, Meade knowing nothing of it; & that Tuesday Morng they found all gone & clear across.

Meade's laurels are badly stained: for my part I yet put most faith in Hooker.

The News of last night made some amends.[5] It all came through rebel sources & therefore is certainly not *more* favorable to us than the truth.

It seems that the attack on Morris Island was not made on the 9th as I expected but on the 10th & was successful as was anticipated. Gilmore did not expected to reduce the batteries at the northern extremity immediately; but did expect to reduce them in a little while—at most a few days. Forts Wagner & Gregg as I understand it occupy that northern extremity and had not been reduced on the 10th Friday.[6]

Then came from the rebels too the news of the unconditional surrender of Port Hudson to Banks. This is the grand complement of Grants great victory, and opens the Mississippi;—henceforth to remain open though we may be annoyed by guerillas for some time.[7]

Such is the tableau which yesterdays news presented.

Today we have substantial assurances that European Intervention is again postponed—now probably indefinitely—unless we think it best to intervene in Europe.[8]

So the sky clears.

Coleman called on me today with a note from you asking for his transfer from the Interior to the Treasury.[9] He cannot have Baileys place for that is filled:[10] but he can have another & perhaps as good as that he now holds. One thing, however, I ought to forewarn you of. He may not be of as much use to you after appointment here as he is now. Every clerk is required to give the whole of his office hours to the Govt.—that is from 9 till 4—and to serve extra hours when required; and no leaves of absence are given except in the aggregate about four weeks a year & each days absence is set down to that account. We are obliged to be strict in these rules and make no exceptions.

Katie & Nettie are well.

Faithfully & affectionately yours
S P Chase

Hon Wm. Sprague

1. Unchallenged by Union forces, Lee's Army of Northern Virginia had crossed the Potomac from Maryland to Virginia on the night of July 13. Long, *Civil War Day by Day,* 384–85.

2. "Our task is not yet accomplished," claimed Meade on July 4, a day after the battle of Gettysburg ended, "and the Commanding General looks to the army for greater efforts to drive from our soil every vestige of the presence of the invader." In Lincoln's own words, he "left the telegraph office a good deal dissatisfied" after reading the address. *New York Times,* July 7, 1863; Lincoln to H. W. Halleck, July 6, 1863, in *OR,* ser. 1, v. 27, pt. 3:567.

3. Troops under Grant took Jackson, Miss., on May 14, 1863. "The main Federal army at Jackson has surrendered," Maj. Gen. Stephen Augustus Hurlbut (1815–82), commander of the Sixteenth Army Corps, reported on May 19, "except cavalry, which escaped across Pearl River. Said to be two divisions surrendered." *DAB,* 9:425–26; Long, *Civil War Day by Day,* 353; *OR,* ser. 1, v. 24, pt. 3:329.

4. Maj Gen. Henry Warner Slocum (1827–94), commanding the Twelfth Corps; Maj. Gen. John Sedgwick of the Fifth and Sixth Corps; Maj. Gen. William Henry French (1815–81) of the Third Corps; Oliver Otis Howard of the Eleventh Corps; James S. Wadsworth, leading the first division of the First Corps; and Maj. Gen. Alfred Pleasonton (1824–97), who had charge of all Union cavalry under Meade. *DAB,* 7:25–26, 15:8–9, 16:548–49, 19:309, 27:216–17.

5. On July 14, Union forces had seized Fort Powhatan, Va., on the James River. Long, *Civil War Day by Day,* 386.

6. Federal troops did not occupy Forts (or Batteries) Gregg and Wagner until September 7. Brig. Gen. Quincy Adams Gillmore commanded the Department of the South and the Tenth Army Corps. Ibid., 406; *DAB,* 7:295.

7. Vicksburg and Port Hudson had fallen to troops under Ulysses S. Grant and Nathaniel P. Banks on July 4 and 8, respectively. Long, *Civil War Day by Day,* 378–79, 381.

8. An apparent reference to a recent report that discounted as "entirely without foundation" rumors "that the Emperor Napoleon has proposed to the English Government to make some fresh suggestions to the belligerents in America." *New York Times,* July 13, 1863.

9. Rhode Island native Walter H. Coleman, a clerk in the Pension Office, later held a position as an additional clerk in the internal revenue branch of the office of the secretary of the Treasury. *Register of Officers (1865),* 19; *Wash. Dir. (1863),* 66.

10. Very likely John F. Bailey, who had been a clerk in Chase's office and was assigned as a special agent to investigate the New York Custom House, 1863–64. Bailey to Chase, Jan. 13, 1864, Chase to Hiram Barney, Feb. 13, 1864, Horace Greeley to Chase, Feb. 10, 1864, and William Orton to Chase, Jan. 6, 1864 (all below); Lincoln to Chase, Feb. 12, 1864, in Basler, *Collected Works,* 7:181; *Register of Officers (1861),* 15.

FROM HIRAM BARNEY

Autograph letter. Chase Papers, Historical Society of Pennsylvania (*micro* 27:0845).

N.Y. July 15, 1863

My dear Sir,

For the last two days and nights I have been so busy that I have found no time to write a line.

The mob has moved about in large & small bodies since early on Monday morning busy and successful in the work of destruction. At first it was stimulated by opposition to the conscription and to those officers who had in charge the execution of that law; Since then its vengeance has been demonstrated against other officers of the government & its friends—by personal attacks and by the destruction of property—by fire & force— The mob permits neither public nor private carriages of any kind to travel the streets so far as they can prevent it— No regular line of Stages or cars is running and the gas is stopped off.

The City and State Authorities were wholly unprepared for the emergency— On Monday morning I applied by letter to Genl Wool and to Admiral Paulding for a force & arms to protect the Treasury & Customs buildings[1]— Mr Cisco joined in it— The answers from Genl Wool & the Admiral were to the effect that all their forces were employed to protect the City and they could not help me—, Admiral Paulding however sent me last night 25 men & two howitzers— In this emergency I provided arms for the clerks & inspectors and made the best organization in my power for defence / It is difficult to continue long to transact business and be prepared by night & day to resist an attack which may occur at any time— I have therefore authorized the employment of 100 well trained returned soldiers who will be sworn in as temporary Aids to the revenue & assigned as a guard to the buildings and shall assume the responsibility of increasing the force if necessary for the protection of the public Stores.

We have on storage in the Public Stores near 100 thousand enfield & other rifles / I have been very anxious about them lest the mob should get possession of them—but have been obliged to trust to the Police & Military for their protection giving them the proper information

I feel some embarrassment in consequence of the U.S. not owning or having a cession of the jurisdiction of this building—but concluded to stand upon the Common law right of protecting my "Castle"—giving orders to make no offensive movement until the building is actually attacked & then to give the mob cause to regret having done so.

The Mayor has just proclaimed that the Mob is controllable by the authorities—but the facts of the case seem to conflict with this official announcement. The Governor has just sent a carriage requesting me to go to him at the St. Nicholas[2]—

I am truly Yours
HIRAM BARNEY

Hon. S. P. Chase

1. Maj. Gen. John Ellis Wool commanded the Department of the East. Although officially retired from duty, Hiram Paulding (1797–1878) presided over the New York Navy Yard, 1861–65, and also carried out other shore assignments. *DAB,* 14:320–21, 20:514.

2. The St. Nicholas Hotel, on Broadway. George Opdyke, a Republican, and Horatio Seymour, a Democrat, had filled the posts of mayor and governor, respectively, since 1862. Chase went to the War Department with letters and telegrams from John J. Cisco, David Dudley Field, and others. As Chase reported to Field, "I was informed that the Seventh Regiment was on its way; that two or three other New York Regiments had been ordered to New York; that two regular regiments one of infantry, and one of artillery—perhaps only a battery of artillery had also been ordered thither; and that this was thought ample, when added to the force already there." Chase to Field, July 16, 1863 (Chase Papers, Hist. Soc. of Pa.); *DAB,* 17:8; Holli and Jones, *Biographical Dictionary of American Mayors,* 274–75; *Nat. Cyc.,* 11:464–65; *New York Dir. (1864),* 752.

FROM GEORGE S. DENISON

Autograph letter on letterhead stationery. Chase Papers, Library of Congress (*micro* 27:0857).

Private

United States Internal Revenue,
COLLECTOR'S OFFICE,
DISTRICT OF THE STATE OF LOUISIANA,
New Orleans, July 15, 1863.

Dear Sir—

Mr. Hutchins will not leave by the "Creole", as was expected, but will probably go on the "Morning Star" in about ten days.[1]

The Rebel force in the Lafourche and on the Teche is still there. Movements are in progress to cut them off and capture them—or drive them back into Texas, & the matter will be decided in four or five days.

Gen. Banks is expected in the city tomorrow. Mr. Flanders has done but little, as he has been waiting to see the General & have him issue the necessary orders, & it has not been proper or necessary to intrude such matters on his attention while engaged in his great work at Port Hudson.

For the same reason, Mr. Plumly has not seen Gen. Banks since my return, but he will see him and ascertain whatever it may be desirable to know.

Mr. Plumly is devoted to your interest—is a man of perfect honor and cannot betray. Of this I am fully satisfied. And yet he holds this relation to you, at the same time laboring under a conviction that he has been misrepresented to you, and that your confidence in him is impaired. I have ascertained this little by little, & of course, not by direct questioning. For the interests of the colored people he labors unceasingly & unselfishly. He has great & increasing influence. He is enthusiastic & some would say, sometimes visionary, but supplies qualities possessed neither by Mr. Flanders nor myself—qualities more useful in the excitable South than in the North. The feeling that he deserves, but fails to possess your full confidence, seems to him a misfortune if not an injustice, but does not seem to cause his personal loyalty to waver.

The foregoing statement is the result of close & continual observation of which he was not aware. Should my opinion change in the least (which I do not anticipate) you will be informed at once.

I suggest the propriety & expediency of your writing him a private letter such as will remove (in part at least) the impression under which he labors. At any rate it will be a kind action & I believe, worth while.[2]

No State government will be organized for a long time, & I am glad of it, for the time has not yet come for surely succeeding in the plan of *universal* suffrage essential to our permanent success. The chances will improve day by day, & delay is an advantage—but of final success I have little doubt. Men who fight will have to vote, & Gen. Banks will immediately organize all the negroes he can get. Gen. Andrews will command the "Corps d'Afrique"[3]—a more proper man than Ullmann who will command a Brigade.

A strong party is already forming here, whose leading idea is the restoration of Louisiana to slavery *and* to the Union, of which party Kennedy, of the "True Delta", is an active & enterprising leader and advocate. The fact that Gen. Emory, (commanding here in Banks' absence) is a bitter pro-slavery man, gives to this party a great but temporarary advantage.[4] With these, Mr. Bullitt, who is entirely under Kennedy's control, seems to be in perfect sympathy. Emory Kennedy & Bullitt are much together—generally at Bullitt's house.

We already have too many pro-slavery Generals here, & the papers say Gen. Franklin is coming, who is supposed to be of the same stripe.[5]

I have talked with many officers of the old regiments here, & there seems to be much dissatisfaction in the army. No matter what the papers say, Gen. Banks is unpopular in his army. There may be an improved state of feeling since Port Hudson fell, but that cannot make a very great difference. The reason for this dissatisfation, is this. The whole army, from Colonels down, is thoroughly abolitionized. They have seen the negroes drill & fight, & they want to give them a chance & put down slavery. I have not seen a soldier who has not this feeling., But Grover,[6] Emory, Sherman (somewhat) & others, have been ostentatiously pro-slavery all along. (I do not include Weitzel, the best and most popular General here). The army think these men control Banks & his policy, which up to a certain point, was conciliatory.

Besides this they (the army) have acquired a very poor opinion of Banks' ability as a military officer, but this may have changed somewhat since the fall of Port Hudson.

You remember that Gen. Banks changed his mild policy all of a sudden, & issued several severe orders in one day.[7] It may be a *significant* fact that just previous to that time, Mr. Seward's son (who was or is an Ass't Secretary, I think)[8] made a flying visit here, went to the front to see Banks, & after staying here four or five days went back to New York.

Gen. Banks can recover (in part at least) the army's confidence, and remove dissatisfaction, by adopting a decided & severe policy, which I hope & think he will do.

Anti slavery feeling continues to develop & grow steadily.

Mr. Flanders is the very best man you could get for the position occupied by him. I want Mr. Hutchins to come back here in official position, & will gladly give up to him my place as Coll. of Internal Revenue, if that will induce him, for I believe he would be of great use here politically.

Everything I have to write about Custom House matters, will be sent by the hands of Mr. Hutchins.

There is great rejoicing here over the fall of Vicksburg, Port Hudson / over Rosecrans' success,[9] & the defeat of the Rebels at Gettysburg. I am sorry to say that no official answer is yet received to the questions regarding Int. Revenue Tax, which I laid before you in Washington. We can do nothing but wait, until the date from which the tax is to be assessed is determined.

Gen. Banks private Secretary informs me that Port Hudson would have been evacuated, if the investment had been delayed a few hours. The Rebel Commander had the order to evacuate from Johnston, in his pocket, & had commenced its execution when Banks appeared. This fact was not known until after the surrender. Johnston wanted the Port Hudson Garrison to join him back of Vicksburg.[10]

Very Respectfully

Your Obt Serv't
GEORGE S. DENISON

To
Hon S. P. Chase
Secretary of the Treasury

1. Two *Creoles* were in service, one a 316-ton commercial sidewheeler and the other a 1,056-ton screw steamer. The *Morning Star,* a new sidewheel steamer, displaced 2,022 tons. Lytle, *Merchant Vessels,* 42, 132.

2. "It gives me great pleasure that all the friends whom I fully trust have been so well pleased with your action and opinions," Chase wrote Benjamin Rush Plumly on July 25. "Everyone who writes me (and especially Flanders and Hutchins) expresses himself warmly in your praise." Chase to Plumly, July 25, 1863 (Chase Papers, Hist. Soc. of Pa.).

3. In addition to recruiting black troops, Col. George Leonard Andrews (1828–99), a West Point graduate who had been chief of staff of Banks's operation against Port Hudson, was given command of U.S. troops around Baton Rouge. *DAB,* 1:291–92.

4. Maryland native and professional soldier William Hemsley Emory (1811–87), a brigadier general of volunteers. Ibid., 6:153.

5. Briefly dismissed for his part in the Federal defeat at the battle of Fredericksburg, Maj. Gen. William Buell Franklin had recently been reassigned to the Nineteenth Corps in Louisiana. Ibid., 6:602.

6. Col. Cuvier Grover (1828–85) served in the Nineteenth Corps. Ibid., 8:28.

7. Denison may have referred to five orders issued by Nathaniel P. Banks in April that, in Denison's words, gave "great and general satisfaction to all loyal persons." Among these were instructions for "registered enemies of the United States" to leave the Department of the Gulf and for the sale of supplies to Confederates to cease upon "penalty of death." Denison to Chase, Apr. 30, 1863 (Chase Papers, L.C.); *OR,* ser. 1, v. 15:710; *DAB,* 16:613.

8. Frederick William Seward, assistant secretary of state.

9. According to the *New York Times,* Braxton Bragg's Confederates had withdrawn from Chattanooga, leaving Federal troops under William S. Rosecrans in control of the field. "Our army are in high spirits and in splendid condition," the report concluded. *New York Times,* July 15, 1863.

10. Maj. Gen. Franklin Gardner (1823–73) had commanded Port Hudson since December. "Evacuate Port Hudson forthwith," wrote Joseph E. Johnston on May 19, "and move with your troops toward Jackson, to join other troops which I am uniting." Jon L. Wakelyn, ed., *Biographical Dictionary of the Confederacy* (Westport, Conn., 1977), 196; *OR,* ser. 1, v. 26, pt. 1:180, pt. 2:9.

FROM HAMILTON FISH

Autograph letter. Chase Papers, Library of Congress (*micro* 27:0919).

In the Highlands.
opposite West-Point—
(Garrison— P.O.). N.Y[1]—
July 18, 1863—

My dear Governor—

Pardon me for saying a few words upon a matter that appears to me of momentous importance—

Now, that the supremacy of disorder & violence in New York City, is subsiding, we should try to seek its causes, & its incidents[2]— Although order is regaining its ascendancy, the feeling neither of confidence & of safety on the one side, nor of contentment & of submission on the other, is at all apparent—

During the late disturbances I have divided my time between the City, & this place, where my family is— Here, there has been no actual violence—but there is very apparent a very uncomfortable & restless feeling— The population around me, for some miles, is mainly agricultural—but amid this laboring class there is much uneasiness— They are excited & apprehensive— The idea has been industriously impressed upon them (with what object you will imagine) that it is a part of the Emancipation policy of the Administration to bring the emancipated negroes from the South into the Northern States—while many, who do not incline to assign such a rank *as part of the design & policy* of the Government, express the apprehension that it must inevitably be a *consequence* of the Emancipation Measures— "Employment & profits of labor," say they, "will thus be interfered with & the dignity of labor be degraded."— I *know* this opinion to obtain largely—aye, quite generally, among a very large class of very useful, laborious, & quiet citizens— They apprehend that the Negro is to be their competitor & rival—they do not entertain any particular hostility to those now resident here—& would not molest them but for the fear that their numbers are to be largely increased

From a very careful observation during two days of the riot in New York, I am convinced that that apprehension had much to do,—in fact lay at the very bottom of the inception of the bloody, savage outrages to which the poor blacks were subjected— It exists around me here, in the Country, to such extent, that I will not allow my colored servants to go off my own place— A discreet friend in a position that enables him to *know* what he says, called upon me to say that it would be highly dangerous to allow these colored servants to be seen, *just now* at the neighboring village; where a large laboring population is employed—

Now, my dear Sir, cannot & should not, the Government in some way, remove this apprehension, & disabuse the well intentioned but misguided & excited portion of our laboring population?

Scores, of poor negroes, have already fallen victims to this apprehension. And although order seems to be resuming its ascendancy I am *not* mistaken in my conviction, that the feeling which excited the late outrages against the blacks, exists today as strongly as it did three days since;—& will again, on some unexpected occasion, break out in violent action, unless assured and quieted with regard to the policy of the Government—

Humanity, & order, as well as policy seem to me to call for some authoritative assurance, that the policy & measures of the Government will not interfere with the labor & employment of the people of the Free States—

Can there not be some elucidation & announcement of the policy of the Government of this point? some *assurance* that it is no part of their policy to bring the Emancipated negroes, into the Free States?

This fear of a large increase it is that excites & maddens many whose daily labor, is their only & precarious support even without the competition they have been brought to fear—

Excuse me, my dear Sir, for thus pressing these views upon you— I do so, under a firm conviction that something, in the direction suggested is essential to the firm re-establishment & preservation of order—& that without it, the colored population among us will not be secure of peace or of the means of livelihood—

With great regard

Yours faithfully
HAMILTON FISH

The Honorable
S.P. Chase—
&c &c &c
Washington D.C—

1. During the Civil War, Fish was a member of the defense committee for New York state and a commissioner for the relief of prisoners. *DAB,* 6:397.

2. Chase received other reports of the New York draft riots, July 13–15, from Hiram Barney, July 15 (above), and John J. Cisco, July 23 (below).

FROM WILLIAM BIRNEY

Autograph letter. Chase Papers, Historical Society of Pennsylvania (*micro* 27:0968).

Baltimore, July 21, 1863.

Hon. S. P. Chase.
Dear Sir,

There were great obstacles here, arising chiefly from the timidity of all the residents. General Schenck and his Chief of Staff, Col. Piatt, have rendered me invaluable aid.[1] They are admirably fitted for military government. Every thing now promises success. A sure revolution is going on in popular feeling. I feel sure not only of raising a regiment but of striking a heavy blow at the "institution" in this state.

The wretched pay, seven dollars a month, for privates and sergeants alike, stands fearfully in our way every where. If the pay were the same as for whites, I could have raised a division before this time.[2]

A decided influence has been brought to bear to exclude the colored men from the chaplaincies and sutlerships. I fear that the good Major-General Casey has been swept away by this.[3] To me it was clear that those posts should be left to colored men, being the only ones the rapacity of the whites would respect. The chaplain must be united in interest and sympathy with his charge, must be one who knows their families, who can visit them familiarly, counsel them as a friend, teach them, write letters for them, nurse them in sickness. No white man will do this; and yet office seeking white parsons are seeking to get the posts of chaplains to these colored regiments. I am indignant at this; and still more so that any man connected, as officer, with a colored regiment should favor these mousing politicians. On a recent visit of a few hours to Washington, I found a white preacher officiating in the first regiment! For my part, I have steadily excluded white preachers and invited the best black ones. Could not Mr. Stanton be led to declare officially his views on this subject.[4]

A white candidate for a chaplaincy informed me, not long since, that he had a friend for whom he desired to have the sutlership! These two were hunting in couples. The sutlership is the only post of profit in the regiment. Why not let the blacks have it? The customers are colored; and so should be the trader.

I know that your influence will be thrown in favor of equity and fair dealing in this matter. If you can benefit us, do so—in your own way.

My duties as a Mustering officer will take me to Washington, Thursday night. I will endeavor to see you.

Yours very truly,
William Birney.,
Colonel 2d U.S. Colored Troops.

When I first came, I heard frequent reports of threats to assassinate, mob &c / They reminded me of old times in Ohio.

I hear nothing of them now.

1. Maj. Gen. Robert Cumming Schenck had commanded Federal troops in Baltimore since December 1862. His chief of staff was Lt. Col. Donn Piatt. *DAB,* 14:556, 16:428.

2. Federal law finally equalized pay for black and white soldiers on June 15, 1864. *Statutes at Large,* 13:129–30.

3. Maj. Gen. Silas Casey (1807–82) served as president of the board for the examination of candidates for commission as officers of colored troops. *DAB,* 3:560.

4. See Chase to Edwin M. Stanton, July 23, 1863 (below).

TO JAY COOKE

Letter in clerk's hand on letterhead stationery, signed by Chase. Jay Cooke Papers, Historical Society of Pennsylvania. (*micro* 27:0994).

Treasury Department.
July 22, 1863.

Sir,

I have noticed that some of the vouchers connected with your account do not correspond with the Agency contract as understood by me.

I was aware that instead of keeping a regular account of disbursements for advertising by each Sub-Agent, you allowed to some, if not all of them, one-fourth of one per cent., with the understanding that half (that is, one-eighth) was to cover their expenses for making the loan known to the people by adertising and otherwise. But it was my understanding that each Sub-Agent would keep a strict account of the actual expenses incurred for advertising and newspaper notices, and transmit the vouchers to you on settlement, and account for any unexpended balance of the Eighth appropriated to that purpose.

Nor did I understand that the Eighth allowed for advertising and publication of the loan by agents and newspapers was to be appropriated to the expenses of transportation, telegraphing, and like disbursements. I supposed that these would be paid from the one-eighth commission charged as a part of the expenses of business. Are not such expenses ordinarily covered by the commission charged individuals who employ brokers as Agents in the purchase and sale of bonds.

I by no means fail to appreciate the value of your agency or its utility to the Government. I do not doubt that the loan negotiated through you has furnished means for meeting public disbursements more economically than could have been obtained in any other way, and that the certainty and regularity with which demands upon the Treasury have been met from the proceeds of this loan, have materially lessened the cost of supplies, and in this way, saved several times the cost of the Agency. But I wish to have all contracts made by the Department definitely understood at the outset, and then exactly fulfilled, without any departure not mutually and definitely agreed upon before-hand.

Very Respectfully,
S: P: CHASE
Secretary of the Treasury.

Jay Cooke, Esq., Subscription Agent,
Philadelphia, Penna.

TO EDWIN M. STANTON

Letterpress copy of autograph letter. Chase Papers, Historical Society of Pennsylvania (*micro* 27:1017).

Washington July 23, 1863.

Dear Sir,

I hear that officers appointed to Colored Regiments are trying to get White Chaplains, and White Sutlers.[1] However convenient this may be for Officers who have friends or partners whom they wish to provide for and at the same time get the rewards due to the patriotism which induces them to take commissions to command blacks, it can hardly be beneficial to the service or promotive of the grand objects you have in view.

If you have already heard of this, the proper action has doubtless been taken. If not, you will doubtless make the proper enquiries & do what seems to you right.

Yours
S P CHASE

Hon E M Stanton.

1. See the letter from William Birney, July 21, 1863 (above).

FROM JOHN J. CISCO

Letter in clerk's hand on letterhead stationery, signed by Cisco. Letters Received from Assistant Treasurers, General Records, Department of the Treasury (Record Group 56), National Archives (*micro* 27:1028).

United States Treasury,
New York, July 23d. 1863

My dear Sir:—

During the continuance of the recent riots in this city, I kept you advised, day by day, by the wires, as fully as I could, of the progress of affairs. In your telegram of the 15th. you authorized me to "take every responsibility necessary to the safety of the public buildings and property."[1]

I now propose giving you a short and succinct account of the arrangements which I made for the defense of this building and the Government property contained in it—arrangements the efficacy of which there was fortunately no occasion to test.

The first outbreak took place in the upper part of the city early on monday morning the 13th. inst. Immediately after being informed of what had occurred and was occurring I sent a communication to Admiral Paulding at the Navy Yard,[2] asking for a guard of Marines. He replied that he intended to place every marine that he could spare at the disposal of General Wool. I then made a similar application to the General, who replied in substance that he could do nothing for me, and that I must take care of myself. I may here state that permanent authority has been lodged at this office, since the bread riots some years ago, to call upon the armed forces of the Government both at the Navy Yard and at Governor's Island for protection, at any time, in case of need; and such requisitions of mine have been ordered to be obeyed.

Such being the state of the case, I determined at once to put this building in a position to withstand the assault of any mob. My first act was to arm all the employees of every grade, including those of the Assay Office. I then procured carboys of *sulphuric acid* from the Assay Department, and placed them, with pitchers to throw the acid from, at the various windows of the second story of this building, which are not protected, as are those below, by iron shutters. (My *sulphuric acid battery* has become famous.) About this time Col. Adams, of the regular army, called upon me and suggested that I should procure a supply of 6 or 8 inch shells to be thrown by hand.[3] I sent a messenger to Admiral Paulding with a letter asking for them and for two men to handle them. He replied that if I would make a regular requisition in writing, and send for the shells, I could have them with one man. I made the requisition, sent an express-waggon for the shells, and procured them, with the man, as promised.

On tuesday I asked the Admiral for one or more howitzers with crews to man them, and for cutlasses. He promised them to me, but subsequently notified me that he was afraid to send them, lest they should be captured by the mob, on being landed at the foot of Wall street. In my opinion, his fears were absolutely groundless. Tuesday morning some 25 men of the 10th. Regt. (Col. Bendix's)[4] were sent to me, and quartered in the building. The Captn. told me that his instructions were to remain here until I should have no further occasion for his services, but on wednesday morning he abruptly was ordered to report elsewhere. They were replaced shortly afterwards by about the same number of men, who were again abruptly taken from me early in the evening when I most required their services. My own people were, of course, becoming very weary, watching all night, and working all day. At a later hour, however, some 80 men of the N.Y. 65th. were sent to me—also a battery of the 8th. militia, consisting of two small howitzers. That morning Captn. Sluyter, commanding the Gun boat "Tulip",[5] who had been placed at the foot of Wall street by Admiral Paulding, with his guns bearing upon the street, volunteered to go to the Navy Yard, and procure the guns for me for which I had asked the day before, provided I would make a peremptory demand for them. This I did, and in the afternoon he brought me two 24 pound howitzers, with a supply of cutlasses, but only 6 men. I was compelled to send a force of labouring men from the melting and Refining Department to drag the guns from the landing to the Treasury. These men were subsequently trained to handle the guns. I had previously procured and placed in the hall commanding the Pine street entrance a rifled battery, which appeared a very effective weapon.

At the beginning of the difficulties several persons volunteered to take the military command of the garrison. I finally accepted the services of Lieut. Col. Manchester, of the Naval Artillery.[6] Night and day I was well provided with scouts, both on foot and mounted, and had arranged signals to communicate with the gun boat and the Custom House, in case I should be attacked. After your telegram authorizing me to make use of the Cutters, I found that they had all been appropriated by Mr. Barney for the defense of the Custom House. That it was the intention of the mob at one time to attack me I have no doubt, as I received several distinct warnings— Of course all proper barricades for doors and windows had been provided.

On wednesday morning at 3 o'clk two of my scouts reported that a mob of 5.000 persons was moving from Greenwich street in this direction. It was very satisfying to see how rapidly and determinedly the whole garrison got themselves in readiness for action. I have no doubt that any attempt upon my fortress would have failed and met with a terrible retribution. My business went on as usual during business hours. My employees were so trained that in case of an attack during those hours the whole building (including the vaults) could have been closed in a minute. We had one false alarm, and this was actually done.

I was greatly indebted to Col. Manchester and his subordinates for the energy and intelligence which they displayed from first to last. They were untiring. Mr. Dunning, Superintendent of the Assay Office,[7] and his clerks and workmen were most efficient. My own subordinates deserve my commendation. My Deputy, Mr. Field,[8] displayed very commendable energy and fidelity, not having left the building from monday morning until friday night.

Of course a very moderate expense had to be incurred in these arrangements, such as rations for the military and my own people, the hiring of arms, compensation of a few persons, scouts &c. I will let you know the amount as soon as possible.

I think that a battery of two howitzers should immediately be procured for the permanent defense of this building—also an addition to my stock of small arms. My own people and those of the Assay Office, being thoroughly trained to use them, we should have the means, in case of a sudden attack, to protect ourselves, without waiting for extraneous aid. How shall these things be got? Shall they be purchased expressly, or procured by requisition upon the Army or Navy Department? Please reply upon this point.

Here ends the first *military* report which I have had occasion to make to you.

Ever Faithfully Yours
JOHN J. CISCO

The Honle. S. P. Chase,
&c &c &c

1. Cisco telegraphed at least once each day during the crisis. Chase replied by wire on the fifteenth: "Have conferred with President and Secretary of War and am assured that adequate force is on its way to New York, and that all has been done that can be." Chase suggested that revenue vessels in New York harbor and their crews might be able to assist Cisco and Collector of Customs Hiram Barney. Chase's telegram closed with the sentence quoted by Cisco in this letter. Cisco to Chase, July 14, Chase to Cisco, July 15, 1863 (Telegrams Sent, Gen. Recs. Treasury Dept., Nat. Arch.); Cisco to Chase, July 13, 15 (twice), 1863 (Letters Received from Asst. Treasurers, Gen. Recs. Treasury Dept., Nat. Arch.); Cisco to Chase, July 15, 1863 (Chase Papers, Hist. Soc. of Pa.)

2. The New York Navy Yard was in Brooklyn, on the east side of the East River. *New York Dir. (1863).*

3. During the riots, Julius Walker Adams (d. 1865), who held the regular army rank of captain but had been colonel of the 1st Long Island Volunteers, helped organize former U.S. military officers in the city for service. Heitman, *Historical Register,* 1:153; *New York Times,* July 14, 1863.

4. Col. John E. Bendix (d. 1877) of the 10th New York Infantry. Heitman, *Historical Register,* 1:209.

5. Only the previous month the Navy had purchased the merchant steamer *Chih Kiang* and converted it for government service as USS *Tulip.* New York native Stephen G. Sluyter, the vessel's commander, had been appointed to the rank of acting ensign on May 19, 1863. *Register of the Commissioned, Warrant, and Volunteer Officers of the Navy of the*

United States . . . to January 1, 1864 (Washington, D.C., 1864), 137, 241; *ORN*, ser. 2, v. 1:226; Lytle, *Merchant Vessels*, 31.

6. Lt. Col. Horace A. Manchester of the 1st New York Marine Artillery. *OR*, ser. 1, v. 18:105.

7. George Freeman Dunning had supervised the U.S. Mint's New York assay office since 1862. *Register of Officers (1863)*, 45; *Who Was Who*, 1:348.

8. Maunsell B. Field, deputy assistant treasurer at New York. In October 1863 he began service in Washington as an assistant secretary of the Treasury. *Chase Papers*, 1:440, 449, 457.

TO JAMES MORRISON MCKAYE

Letterpress copy of autograph letter. Chase Papers, Historical Society of Pennsylvania (*micro* 28:0024).

Washington, July 25, 1863.

Dear Sir,

The points stated by me were suggested by Mr. Owen's interesting account of the heads of your report.[1] From that report I expect great good & thought that the ideas which I roughly shadowed could have the advantage of its endorsement they would be received into the public mind, and add somewhat to its fruits.

I do not know that I recall them now exactly but they were somewhat as follows.

1st. The persons enfranchised by the Presidents proclamation cannot now be properly called contrabands.

"Contraband" was the embodiment of Gen. Butlers idea that negroes belonging to rebels & used for aid to rebellion might be used for trenching, teaming &c by National Commanders without infringement of rights of property because those rights of property had been forfeited by such use just as right to other property adapted to military uses & destined to such uses would be forfeited. It does not describe at all the condition established by the proclamation; which regards the negroes as men and, as such while subjected to slavery, important auxiliaries to rebellion; and, therefore, with a view to military consequences permanent in character & in the expectation that these men, enfranchised, will be auxiliaries to the national cause declares them permanently freemen. Thenceforward they might be called properly enough freedmen, Afric-Americans, blacks, negroes, colored citizens—this last designation by the way that employed by Andrew Jackson[2]—but never contrabands.

2. The condition of freedom established by the Proclamation is a permanent condition, so declared in express terms. The National honor and especially the honor of the President is engaged to make this condition permanent. It should therefore be distinctly declared in every public document treating with any considerable fullness the condition of the colored population of the insurgent states that no state,

which has carried rebellion into a formal act of secession & included in the proclamation, can be readmitted into the full enjoyment of the rights of a member of the Union, until it has by a fundamental provision or act incorporated in its constitution recognized & sanctioned the condition established by the Proclamation.

These if I recollect rightly were the ideas on which I laid some stress. They appear to me to possess great importance.

Very truly yours
S P CHASE

Col. J. McKaye.

1. As members of the American Freedmen's Inquiry Commission, Col. James Morrison McKaye of New York and reformers Robert Dale Owen and Samuel Gridley Howe had the responsibility "to investigate the condition of the colored population emancipated by acts of Congress and the President's proclamation of January 1, 1863." McKaye, Owen, and Chase had recently discussed the commission's preliminary report, issued on June 30. McKaye to Chase, July 23, 1863 (Chase Papers, L.C.); *OR*, ser. 3, v. 3:73–74, 430–54; McLaughlin, *Papers of Olmsted*, 4:612.

2. See, for example, Jackson to W. C. C. Clairborne, Sept. 21, 1814 (Jackson Papers, L.C.).

TO JAY COOKE

Letter in clerk's hand, signed by Chase. Jay Cooke Papers, Historical Society of Pennsylvania (*micro* 28:0071).

New York.[1] July 29th. 1863.

Dear Sir.

Yours of the 28th. was received this morning; and I have considered carefully what you say, and consulted fully with Mr. Cisco.

I have determined to continue the sales of Five Twenties under present arrangements, until after ten days notice, given hereafter by me.

Mr. Cisco seems to have the impression that you do not regard yourself as liable for monies received by or through your sub-agents if illegally diverted or employed by them. I am confident that this impression is incorrect: your bond would avail little, if it secured only your own acts, without creating any liability for the acts of those whom you employ.

I have not time at present to go into particulars as to the terms of your existing agency. Please refer to my last letter to you;[2] which expresses clearly my understanding, and by which, I desire that you will consider yourself as instructed as to it.

I can now only mention, that I observe, that for sales made by your houses, the second eighth is charged precisely like sales made by houses, in which you have no interest. Mr. Henry D. Cooke, and I, have several times conversed on this subject, and it has always been clearly understood, and is indeed expressed in writing, that these sales are to be considered as compensated by the general one eighth allowed to you.

I will write you hereafter more fully.

Yours Very truly
S P Chase
Secy of the Treasy

1. During the last week of July, Chase departed Washington for a trip that took him to Philadelphia, New York City, and Rhode Island, where he left his daughters for a visit at the Sprague family's summer residence. Chase negotiated with bankers in New York over subscriptions for interest-bearing Treasury notes, then returned to Washington on August 7. Chase to Kate Chase, Aug. 19, 1863 (below); Chase to George Harrington, July 28, 30, Aug. 6, 1863 (Harrington Papers, Mo. Hist. Soc.); Chase to John J. Cisco, July 29, 1863 (Letters Sent, Loan Division, Recs. of Bureau of Public Debt, Nat. Arch.); Cisco to Chase, telegram, Aug. 7, 1863 (Letters Recd. from Asst. Treasurers, Gen. Recs. Treasury Dept., Nat. Arch.).

2. Chase to Cooke, July 22, 1863 (above).

TO EDWARD B. JUDSON

Letterbook copy in clerk's hand. Letters Sent, Loan Division, Records of the Bureau of the Public Debt (Record Group 53), National Archives (*micro* 28:0157).

Treasury Department.
August 11th. 1863.

Sir.[1]

Yours of the 4th. of August, having been referred in my absence to Comptroller McCullough,[2] was sent to me yesterday. My unvarying statement to all gentlemen concerned in organizing banking associations under the national law has been that it was my purpose to use them as depositories of the internal revenue, requiring, of course, proper security. The extent and nature of the security to be required have much occupied my thoughts, and my final conclusion is to ask from the national banks desiring to receive such deposits, to place in the Treasury of the United States, six per cent bonds to an amount equal to ten per cent of their capital stock, and to give the bond of the directors and others to an amount equal to their capital stock, as security for the punctual payment of all lawful checks for deposits, and on receiving this security, to direct the collector of internal revenue to make deposits with the bank or banks giving it.[3]

Inasmuch, however, as a number of banks have been organized and as yet are without circulation, I propose to direct deposits to be made with such, on receiving from them the consent of their respective boards of directors that the bonds already deposited as security for circulation may be held also as security for deposits, leaving the additional bonds, as well as the bond of the directors and others to be given afterward at any time before the furnishing of circulation.

Enclosed you will find a form of assent, on returning which to this Department, after execution of it by the directors under seal of the association, direction will be immediately given to the collector of internal revenue to make his deposits with your institution.

Very truly yours.
S. P. CHASE.
Secretary of the Treasury.

E. B Judson. Esq. President.
First National Bank.
Syracuse, N.Y.

1. Judson (b. 1814), a New York politician and banker, was organizing the First National Bank of Syracuse and became its president. *Nat. Cyc.*, 7:198–99.

2. Hugh McCulloch, comptroller of the currency.

3. Chase sketched his plans for national banking associations in accordance with the national currency act (or "bank bill") of February 25, 1863. The collector of internal revenue for Syracuse at this time was Alfred Wilkinson. *Register of Officers (1863)*, 38; *Statutes at Large*, 12:665–82.

FROM GEORGE S. DENISON

Autograph letter. Chase Papers, Library of Congress (*micro* 28:0188).

Private

New Orleans August 12th 1863.

Dear Sir—

I returned two days ago from Memphis. My journey was partially unsuccessful, because Mr. Mellen was absent, but I had interviews with Gen. Grant, and other Generals commanding Posts, & acquired considerable information from Mr. Yeatman.[1]

The people all along the River, and throughout Western Mississippi, are abjectly submissive. I never supposed a people who had boasted so much, could be so thoroughly subjugated. The organization of negro troops is progressing tolerably well both here & in Gen. Grant's Department, but in Grant's army I perceive a prejudice against negro troops which does not exist here. I don't mean to say it is general, but it is noticeable, although every one spoke highly of the fighting qualities of the negro troops as displayed at Milliken's Bend & other places.[2] The great trouble in organizing negro troops anywhere along or near the River, is that the "prime hands" have all been removed to Texas, or Eastwardly into Alabama. We shall get at them before long however.

Mr. Plumly has gone to Natchez & will return in two or three days. I think I told you that one of his sons is colonel of a negro regiment here. His other son commanded a battery in Ellett's Marine Brigade, but Mr. Plumly has caused him to be transferred to this Department, and he is now raising a colored battery. Both these young men are fine officers.[3]

A great expedition against Mobile is in preparation. I do not know how many men will be used, nor in what manner nor at what time the attack will be made, but a portion at least of Grant's Army will go, & I think the expedition will start very soon—say in three or four weeks. After the capture of Mobile, I understand the long-deferred Texas expedition will start, & will advance from here probably by way of Red River.[4]

Mr. Plumly has had a full conversation with Gen. Banks concerning political matters. I have seen him but once since the conversation & then for a few minutes only & therefore I cannot now give you a full report of the conversation. I only can say that Gen. Banks states positively that he has no alliance with Mr. Seward & never has had any. That he was approached with a proposition to make such an alliance, which he did not accept. That Seward's friends, for their own purposes, have frequently created the impression that such an alliance existed, when it never has existed, & that he is under no obligation to them. That he regards you as the *power* at present in the Government, & would be willing to come to an understanding with you.

I believe what Gen. Banks says, & think I have correctly reported the substance of his statements. Mr. Plumly will return in three or four days, when I write you *fully* concerning this matter. He left two days before my return from Memphis, & probably expected to meet me somewhere on the River.

I now know that the letter I wrote you from Memphis was unnecessary. The Collector at St. Louis, advertised the collection of 5 per cent on shipments to New Orleans, as I told you, but rec'd proper instructions from you before the tax was exacted.[5] Shipments of of Produce & live Stock, are coming here from St. Louis, & have already much diminished the cost of living here.

I am satisfied I did right in recommending the appointment of Mr. Hutchins in my place, as Collector of Internal Revenue. I have more than I can do, although I leave the business of the Internal Revenue almost entirely to Mr. Whitaker, the Deputy.[6]

A great pressure is brought to bear on Mr. Flanders & myself by holders of cotton & speculators, who are urgent to bring their crops to the city by the River. Gen. Banks agreed to furnish Mr. F.—— with a plan whereby all interests would be protected. He submitted to Mr. F. today, a general order on the subject, of which I quote two sections, which are the main features of the order.

"The owners of cotton & other staple products of the country are hereby authorized to transport the same to the Mississippi River at New Orleans, Donaldsonville, Plaquemine, Port Hudson, or other points occupied by troops of the United States, & deliver the same to the authorized Agents of the Treasury Department to be disposed of for the benefit of the Gov't according to law. Such owners or their Agents shall be entitled to receive upon such delivery, in the Treasury notes of the United States, at the rate of——— cents per pound for cotton, & a proportionate sum for other staple products."

"Loyal persons will be permitted, in addition to this payment, to present claims to the Government for such additional payment hereafter as may be deemed equitable & just. But no person shall be held or considered to have an absolute claim against the Gov't except for the sum specified which is to be paid upon delivery of the property."

I do not approve, & shall advise Mr. Flanders, not to accept the foregoing, for various reasons—viz—because I suppose the Gov't does not wish to speculate in cotton—because I do not think it will bring in large amounts—because I have understood that the Gov't have once considered the purchase of southern products by itself, & decided not to do it—because the labor will be immense much dissatisfaction will necessarily be created, & because the whole thing being managed by Treasury Officers, the responsibility, blame if there be any, will fall upon the Treasury Department. I should not want to consent to such a new & decided project, without your previous sanction.

I should rather Gen. Banks would increase the tax to $50 per bale, or say, ten cents per pound, which should be the aggregate of all taxes imposed, & then permits would be issued to purchase anywhere on the Mississippi. In this case, the Gov't would be saved great labor & would receive large returns—& would not act as speculator. Besides I think this would bring forward much more cotton, after it was generally known. Gen Banks and Mr. F. will, I suppose, settle on some plan in three or four days.

The city is very healthy and there are no signs of yellow fever. There are a few cases at Quarantine, as there always are, but probably we shall have none in the city this season.

I failed to mention, that Gen. Banks does not define our military lines within which trade can be permitted & probably cannot, as they frequently change. The Lafourche is the only section strictly & wholly within our lines, but that is not a cotton country.

Very Respectfully

Your Obedient Serv't
GEORGE S. DENISON

To
Hon. S. P. Chase
Secretary of the Treasury

1. Thomas H. Yeatman of Cincinnati served as U.S. Treasury agent at Memphis and government purchasing agent at Vicksburg. Charles Robson, ed., *The Biographical Encyclopædia of Ohio of the Nineteenth Century* (Cincinnati, 1876), 254.

2. Denison apparently referred to the near defeat of Federal troops at Milliken's Bend, La., on June 7. Long, *Civil War Day by Day,* 363.

3. Benjamin Rush Plumly's sons were evidently Col. Murdon W. Plumly of the 14th Infantry and Maj. John L. Plumly, 4th Regiment of Engineers. Both units were in the Corps d'Afrique. Brig. Gen. Alfred W. Ellett commanded the Mississippi Marine Brigade during the siege of Vicksburg. *Appletons',* 2:327; *OR,* ser. 1, v. 24, pt. 1:473; U.S. Adjutant-General's Office, *Official Army Register of the Volunteer Force of the United States,* 8 vols. (Washington, D.C., 1865–67), 8:266.

4. Neither undertaking started until the following year. Led by Banks, the Red River campaign, March 10 to May 19, 1864, ended in failure. Federal forces took Mobile, Ala., on April 12, 1865. Long, *Civil War Day by Day,* 474, 505, 673.

5. In June, Chase had taken away from acting collector of customs Cuthbert Bullitt, and given to Denison as collector of internal revenue, the authority to issue trade permits for the lower Mississippi Valley under the regulations issued March 31, 1863. The collector of internal revenue at St. Louis was Samuel H. Gardner. In Memphis, Denison had tried to resolve a jurisdictional dispute between Benjamin F. Flanders and William P. Mellen. "Shipments are made *by sea* to New Orleans from New York and other Ports, unrestricted by any such tax," Denison complained. "The exaction of this tax on goods *going down the River* to the same destination, is a distinction of 5 per cent in favor of Eastern & against Western Ports." Denison to Chase, Aug. 6, 1863 (Chase Papers, L.C.); *Register of Officers (1863),* 39; Chase to Denison, June 10, 1863 (Letters Sent Relating to Restricted Commercial Intercourse and Captured and Abandoned Property, Gen. Recs. Treasury Dept., Nat. Arch.); Chase to Flanders, June 10, 1863 (3d Spec. Agency, Incoming Letters of Super. Spec. Agent, Recs. of Civil War Special Agencies, Nat. Arch.).

6. Denison had recommended John Hutchins in July. Denison's deputy was J. S. Whitaker's nephew, William R. Whitaker, later named collector of internal revenue for Louisiana. Denison to Chase, July 15, 1863 (above); B. R. Plumly to Chase, June 20, 1862, Denison to Chase, July 24, 1863 (Chase Papers, L.C.); U.S. Senate, *Journal of Executive Proceedings,* 13:470.

TO JAMES A. GARFIELD

Letterpress copy of autograph letter. Chase Papers, Historical Society of Pennsylvania (*micro* 28:0258).

Aug 17, 3

My dear friend,

Your most interesting letter came while I was absent for a few days partly on financial business and partly to establish my children on the Seashore for the summer.[1] It followed me but I have not hitherto had time for a reply.

You cannot tell how much disappointed I have been that Rosecrans did not move sooner and that he came to a pause so soon after he began to move. His great battle at Murfreesboro made me thankful that I had been instrumental in giving him his first position and I looked with confidence to his following up his success just as rapidly as possible.[2] I felt no wish to urge him for my confidence was strong. But when week followed week and month, month and still no advance, I felt sad enough. I saw that the confidence he had inspired was growing weaker and weaker and that however popular he might be with his army he was not keeping his hold on the country. Of course I was delighted when he moved once more; nor was the result different from what I anticipated.

What I had heard of Braggs force convinced me that he could not make head against Rosecrans advance; nor do I believe he would have made head had Rosecrans pushed on to Chattanooga. My disappointment was great when I found he did not intend to do so. He took away, by his halt, and by his return to Nashville, for administration (military) purposes I suppose, from me the ability to defend him against the censures of the War Department—by which, I mean the Secretary & the Comg. General.[3] The Secretary feels most deeply the importance of activity and aggressive movement: and as his temper is not the most patient in the world, he expresses himself very decidedly against dilatoriness: and I saw with real pain his admiration of Rosecrans change to painful doubt and then to positive disapproval. As things stand now I should not be surprised by some action which would be very disagreeable to him and all his friends. The President, who is always disposed to make great allowances and to admit the possibility of good reasons for action which disappoints & pains him, could not I think oppose what the Secretary & General should agree on as necessary to be done.

I rejoice that you have always been on the side of movement, and I earnestly wish your counsels might now prevail. If you think it will do any good you may read what I have written to the General. I am sure it is written in no unkind spirit to him, but exactly the reverse. I cannot, however, help thinking how much *he could* do with his splendid army and how much the country needs his doing it. This war apart from its cost in generous blood is costing immense treasures. The last forty five days have added Ninety millions to our public debt, and I begin to be really alarmed about the possibilities of getting on. With any tolerable economy I think that I can carry the country along financially, if the best use possible is made of our military means, through the rebellion; but it must be substantially suppressed so that our expences can be paid without loans within the current fiscal year—that is before the 1st of July next—I see no clear path otherwise.

It is little that I know about the war. The System (if system it be) of departmental administration allows nothing like the concert of action which is indispensable to good conduct by concerts of public affairs. But I pick up facts & draw my own conclusions. And I feel quite sure that all the rebels that can be drawn together in arms in all the States south of Kentucky and not belonging to the Atlantic Slope are not a match for Rosecrans army alone. Why not then push them to the Gulf and the ocean? Why not drive them from East Tennessee at least. The rebellion is demoralized & discouraged: but will make vast efforts to recruit & make head again. Why give it time?

I wish you would let me know the particular views of as many officers as you can touching reconstruction & slavery; generals, Colonels & others if you please. These are the first questions of the hour. In my judgment there should not be a thought of admitting back a state without such amendments of its constitution as to recognize the freedom conferred by the proclamation, and limiting suffrage, for a time at least, to those who give ample proof of loyalty. The Union Men of the South & those who have been made free by the proclamation must be protected the former against the political despotism of disloyal [*illeg.*] & the latter against personal enslavement to masters from whom they have been declared free.

Katie & Nettie were very glad to hear from you & of you & would join in heartiest greetings were they here. Katies Wedding will take place (D.V.)[4] in October or November. Why can't you be here?

Rousseau[5] goes back somewhat disappointed; but not without expectation that a portion of the Army will be mobilized in the way he proposes. He is a cordial friend to me, even to thinking the country would be safe under such an administration as I should give it! I wonder whose the next admn. will be? Somebody's, I [trust], who will be positive at least & earnest. I certainly shall lose no sleep through hopes or fears.

Cordially your friend
S P Chase

Brig Gen Garfield

1. Chase visited the Northeast during late July and early August. Chase to Richard C. Parsons, June 15, 1863 (above).

2. Despite early Confederate success, Federal forces under William S. Rosecrans had prevailed at the battle of Murfreesboro, or Stone's River, Tenn., December 31, 1862, to January 3, 1863. After delays, Rosecrans advanced on troops under Braxton Bragg in the Tullahoma campaign during late June and early July and the Chickamauga campaign, which started on August 16 and culminated in battle around Chickamauga Creek, September 19–22. Other officials also "instrumental" in securing Rosecrans a position as brigadier general in 1861 included George B. McClellan and Winfield Scott. Chase to Rosecrans, Oct. 25, 1862, in *Chase Papers,* 3:304–5; William Mathias Lamers, *The Edge of Glory: A Biography of General William S. Rosecrans, U.S.A.* (New York, 1961), 186; Long, *Civil War Day by Day,* 302, 306–8, 370–83, 397–413.

3. Henry W. Halleck.

4. *Deo volente,* "God willing."

5. Lovell H. Rousseau, at the time a brigadier general of volunteers. *DAB,* 16:194.

TO JOHN AUSTIN STEVENS, JR.

Autograph letter. John Austin Stevens Papers, New-York Historical Society (*micro* 28:0274).

Washington, Aug. 17, 1863.

My dear Sir,

I enclose the resolutions; but they will be of little use to you.[1]

The only ideas which it seems to me important to keep fully in view just now are

1. That the rebellion *must* be suppressed & the integrity of the Republic maintained.

2. That states desiring to reestablish their relations as loyal members of the American Union should in all proper ways be encouraged to do so, through the voluntary action of the loyal people of *each* state.

3. That this action should be through [separate] Conventions, composed of the *loyal* people or their representatives, framing state Constitutions which repudiate secession; recognize the freedom of all established by the proclamation; and provide adequate securities against future rebellion.

4 That reconstitution in this mode is the only safe reconstitution practicable; & alone promises a prosperous & commanding future.

It will be well also to make some appropriate declarations in favor of exemption & economical administration & I need hardly say that I should be gratified by some recognition of the financial success which seems to me—may I say so without immodesty—not the least important victory of the war.

Of course these [are only] hints, which you will know best how to dispose of & I shall not be dissatisfied with any disposition.

Your friend
S P CHASE

John Austin Stevens Jr Esq

1. Attached to the letter are five printed resolutions from an unidentified source regarding Unconditional Union politics in Maryland.

TO JANET CHASE

Letterpress copy of autograph letter. Chase Papers, Historical Society of Pennsylvania (*micro* 28:0329).

August 19, 3

My darling Nettie,

Your somewhat ragged looking letter came yesterday. I am afraid you do not take with you a very good supply of paper, pens, and ink. If you used the writing case I gave you you would do better. And don't you think yourself that, knowing as you do how it pains me to have you careless in any thing, that you owe me enough to make it your duty to be more attentive to my wishes—saying nothing of your duty to yourself. Think of these things now, and you will save yourself much pain in thinking about them hereafter. Count nothing trifling which involves the idea of duty.

I wrote your Sister yesterday and very little has happened since.[1] To be sure Nellie comes to see me every evening after dinner and puts her nose up in my face in a sort of sympathetic way—whether offering or asking sympathy it is hard to say. But Nellie is almost the only individual whom I have seen & cared to see.[2]

Mr. Cooke (H. D.) was seized by a violent attack of Cholera Morbus last Sunday night and for a time seemed to be in great danger. He is much better now however, and will I hope soon be well again. I am going to see him this morning as soon as I finish this and a little note to Katie.[3]

The workmen are still busy about the house. What *they* are doing I do not know; for I was not consulted in their employment and have not thought it best *to* enquire. They have painted the blinds white which makes no very agreeable contrast with the oak coloring of all the other woodwork. They have really improved the looks of the bath room however; and I suppose when they get through we shall see a general bettering. Very few however would think it worth while to put so much expence on a house which at most can be occupied under the existing lease only some eighteen months.[4]

But Thomas is waiting and I must write a line to Katie and go. I hope your trip to the White mountains is pleasant and beneficial. Love to Katie, Eliza,[5] the Governor[6] & all

Your Affe. father
S P Chase

1. Chase's letter of August 18 congratulated Kate Chase on her twenty-third birthday, on August 13, and conveyed family news. Chase to Kate Chase, Aug. 18, 1863 (Chase Papers, Hist. Soc. of Pa.).

2. The affectionate Nellie, as confirmed by other letters from Chase to his daughter, was a dog. Chase to Janet Chase, Aug. 17, 1863 (Chase Papers, Hist. Soc. of Pa.); Chase to Janet Chase, May 2, 1866 (Chase Papers, L.C.).

3. See Chase to Kate Chase, August 19, 1863 (below).

4. Chase leased his Washington, D.C., residence, which stood at the northwest corner of 6th and E Streets, N.W., from New York lawyer Joseph Bradley Varnum, Jr. Chase to Varnum, Aug. 27, 1863 (Chase Papers, New Hamp. Hist. Soc.).

5. Apparently Eliza Chase Whipple, Chase's niece. William Sprague to Chase, Aug. 20, 1863 (Chase Papers, L.C.).

6. William Sprague.

TO KATE CHASE

Letterpress copy of autograph letter. Chase Papers, Historical Society of Pennsylvania (*micro* 28:0332).

Aug. 19

My dear Child,

Your note added to Netties informs me that you borrowed $200 of Prentice for the expences of your trip. Had you informed me of your intention to make it, when I was at South Pier and of the sum you wanted it would have been furnished, and the borrowing would have been unnecessary.[1] It would also have been much more agreeable to me to be called on in the first instance, than to have you resort to borrowing—which cannot but seem somewhat strange to lenders. However I prefer that you should *borrow,* rather than omit anything which the proper care of your health may seem to require. To protect *that* is the first object: all I ask is that you avoid *unnecessary* expence, for as I have told you the present scale of our expenditure cannot be met from income; but must be supplied, as to the the excess over income, by loans: or, in other words, from the principal.

The money you borrowed will be sent Prentice today.

Your affe. father
S P CHASE

You were quite right in not allowing the Gov.[2] to pay your bills—including Netties and Eliza's.

1. Josiah Prentice Tucker, assistant deputy surveyor of customs at Boston, was the husband of one of Chase's nieces, Hannah Ralston Whipple Tucker. South Pier was in Rhode Island on Narragansett Bay, where the Sprague family had a summer home. Janet Chase to Chase, Aug. 26, 1865, Tucker to Chase, July 21, Oct. 10, 24, 1863 (Chase Papers, L.C.); Chase to Tucker, Oct. 20, 1863 (Chase Papers, Hist. Soc. of Pa.); Thomas Graham Belden and Marva Robins Belden, *So Fell The Angels* (Boston, 1956), 86.

2. William Sprague.

TO WILLIAM H. ASPINWALL

Letterpress copy of autograph letter. Chase Papers, Historical Society of Pennsylvania (*micro* 28:0347).

Washington, August 20, 1863.

My dear Mr. Aspinwall,

Your kind note with the letters of Mr. Bright and Mr. Baring came yesterday, and I read the letters which I now return to the President.[1] He seemed most interested in that of Mr. Bright. The position in which he is placed before the civilized world & before history is not unappreciated by him. He feels bound to stand by his proclamation and will I am sure do so.

At the same time I can see clearly what pressure may be brought to bear on him; not to set aside the proclamation by his own acts but to allow it to be set aside by others. The symptoms of discontent with the Confederate Govt. (so called) in several of the rebel states have not escaped your notice. North Carolinians appear to be most dissatisfied; and you have doubtless seen in the New York papers a significant article which has recently appeared in the Raleigh Standard & is said, by persons apparently well informed to express the views of the rebel governor or at least of men near him & influential with him.[2] If you have read this paper you will have been struck by the terms of reunion suggested—namely the adoption by the loyal states of Mr. Corwins proposition to guarantee perpetual slavery in the states by an amendment of the Federal Constitution.[3]

This proposition ignores the proclamation altogether—not even alluding to it. By implication it more than nullifies it.

Now suppose the controlling influences in North-Carolina conclude that to insist on this is insisting on too much, and determine simply to cease hostilities, and elect Senators & Representatives to Congress of the United States and, perhaps to repeal the ordinance of secession.[4] And suppose farther that the Senate & House receive the Senators & Representatives so elected. What, under these circumstances, becomes of the proclamation?

It is the possibility that some such case as this may arise that excites the only fears I have that we may be humiliated & disgraced before the world by an abandonment of the proclamation. And nothing is more true than Mr. Brights observation that by such an abandonment we should be humiliated and disgraced. It would be a repudiation of faith plighted to millions of oppressed and loyal people, the stain of which could never be effaced.

You know my habit of mind is to look at circumstances and their relations as matters of fact & without taking much trouble to philosophize about them, to ask simply "What is to be done?"

Following this habit I ask what is to be done to avoid this humiliation and disgrace? And the way seems to me very clear. *First;* The Administration (President, I should say) ought to give it to be distinctly understood that no state affected by the proclamation can be regarded as loyal or as having any right to representation in Congress until it has proved its loyalty by a Constitutional provision recognizing and establishing the conditions created by the Proclamation. In other words the Proclamation is today one of the Constitutional National laws to which each rebel state must conform, before it can be regarded as other than rebel. Such a declaration as this, plainly made & firmly adhered to, would give the needed security. But, secondly, even without such a declaration the Administration—the President in his office & the several Heads of Departments in theirs—can secure the same result by simply recognizing the loyal *people* of the state, willing to accept the proclamation, as the State, and encouraging them to form State Constitutions & Governments on the basis of Freedom & Free Labor. If properly supported and encouraged the loyal people of Florida would form such a state Constitution & Government in two months or at most in three; and this action so far as Florida is concerned would settle the question forever: and not only so but would form a most important precedent & example for other states. This example too would be followed and so the whole difficulty may be got rid of quietly, peacefully & without any shock. All that is wanted is some tact & courage.

I have written you a long letter when I only intended to write you a few lines. It will give me pleasure to know what you think of my ideas.[5]

I will only add that the Messrs B—— were long since notified of my acceptance of their proposition.

Very cordially yours
S P Chase

Wm. H. Aspinwall, Esq

1. Noted English reformer and member of Parliament John Bright championed the Northern cause in Britain during the Civil War. The other correspondent was probably British financier Thomas Baring. "As I understand Mr Seward is absent," wrote Aspinwall, "I send Mr Baring's letter to you & you may shew both to the President if you think proper." Aspinwall asked Chase to return the letters, "as yet they are unanswered." Aspinwall to Chase, Aug. 18, 1863 (Chase Papers, Hist. Soc. of Pa.); *DNB,* 1:1113, 22:273–91.

2. Zebulon Baird Vance (1830–94) had been governor of the state since 1862. The article, which appeared in the *Raleigh Standard* on July 31, criticized the rationale and consequences of secession and appealed for an end to the conflict. "The one great demand of the *people* of this part of the State is *peace,*" wrote "Davidson" from Clemsonville; "*peace* upon any terms that will not enslave and degrade us." *New York Times,* Aug. 19, 1863; *DAB,* 19:158–61.

3. The proposal, offered in the House of Representatives on March 18, 1861, by former U.S. senator and Ohio governor Thomas Corwin, would have prohibited any constitutional amendment to "authorize or give to Congress the power to abolish or interfere, within any State, with the domestic institutions thereof, including that of persons held to labor or service by the laws of said State." *Congressional Globe,* 36th Cong., 2d sess., 1861, 1263.

4. Enacted on May 21, 1861. Edward McPherson, *The Political History of the United States of America, During the Great Rebellion . . .* (Washington, D.C., 1864), 5.

5. For Aspinwall's response, see his letter of August 26 (below).

TO CYRUS W. FIELD

Letterpress copy of letter in clerk's hand, signed by Chase. Chase Papers, Historical Society of Pennsylvania (*micro* 28:0365).

Washington, August 21st., 1863.

My dear Sir,

I thank you for sending me a copy of Mr. Bright's letter. It is marked by the comprehensive sagacity which distinguishes his statesmanship.[1]

Have you read "Callirrhoé"?—a fanciful story of George Sands', which has appeared in the late numbers of the "Revue des deux Mondes".[2] It is founded upon the idea of transmigration; and especially upon the notion that the souls of those who have lived in former times reappear, with their characteristic traits, in the persons of new generations. If I adopted this notion, I might believe that Hampden and Sidney live again in Bright and Cobden.[3]

A letter expressing the same general ideas as are contained in that addressed to you, was lately sent by Mr. Bright to Mr. Aspinwall.[4] This letter Mr. Aspinwall kindly enclosed to me, and I read it to the President. I had repeatedly said the same things to him, and was not sorry to have my representations unconsciously echoed by a liberal English statesman. The President said nothing, but I am sure he is more and more confirmed in the resolution to make the Proclamation efficient, as well after peace as during rebellion.

My own efforts are constantly directed to this result. Almost daily, I confer more or less fully with loyalists of the insurrectionary States, who almost unanimously concur in judgment with me that the only safe basis of permanent peace is reconstruction by recognition, in the fundamental law of each State, through a Convention of its loyal people, of the condition of universal freedom established by the Proclamation. It was only yesterday that I had a full conversation with Gov. Pierpont, of Virginia, and with Judge Bowden, one of the United States Senators from that State, on this subject.[5] Both these gentlemen agree in thinking that the President should revoke the exception of certain counties in South Eastern Virginia from the operation of the Proclamation; and that the Governor should call the Legislature together and recommend the assembling of a Convention for the amendment of the existing Constitution; and in expecting that the Convention will propose an Amendment prohibiting Slavery. I think there is some reason to hope that the President may determine to revoke the exception, and more reason to hope that the Convention will be called and Freedom established in Virginia through its agency.

I do not know that you are perfectly familiar with the present condition of things in Virginia. Soon after the outbreak of the rebellion, the loyal people of Virginia organized under the old Constitution, through a Legislature at Wheeling; and subsequently, through a Convention, consented to a division of the State by organizing the North-West portion as the State of West Virginia. If you look at the map, you will see that the line forming the Southern and Eastern boundaries of this new State commences on the Tug fork of the Big Sandy in the West line of McDowell County, and thence proceeds irregularly, so as to include McDowell and Mercer Counties, along the crest of the Alleghenies to Pendleton County, where it diverges to the Shenandoah Mountains and proceeds North-East to the Potomac River at the North East corner of Berkeley, including Pendleton, Hardy, Hampshire, Morgan and Berkeley counties. Congress consented to the admission of this State; and it is now in the Union, fully organized under a free-labor Constitution. Its organization, of, course, left the Government of old Virginia in the hands of Gov. Pierpont and his associates, by whom the seat of Government has been established at Alexandria. At present, only a comparatively narrow belt of counties from the Atlantic to the East line of Berkeley is practically controlled by the loyal State Government; but the loyal men of these counties [are] recognized by the National Government as the State, and as County after County is recued from rebel control, it will come naturally under this organization, until, probably at no distant day, Gov. Pierpont will be acknowledged as the Governor of Virginia at Richmond.[6] When this takes place, the State will be necessarily a Free State, under a Constitution prohibiting Slavery.

The loyal people of Florida are ready to take the same course which Gov. Pierpont proposes to take in Virginia; and the same is true of the loyal people of Louisiana to a great extent. It will be found, doubtless, as the authority of the Union is reëstablished in other States included by the Proclamation, that the same sentiments will prevail; so that it will be quite easy for the National Government, if the President feels so disposed, to secure the recognition of the Proclamation and the permanent establishment of its policy through the action of the people of the several States affected by it.

In this way the great ends to be accomplished can be most certainly reached. My own efforts are constantly directed to their attainment; and I never admit in conversation or otherwise the possibility that the rebel States can *cease* to be *rebel States* and *become loyal members* of the Union except through the recognition of the condition created by the Proclamation, by the establishment of Free Institutions under Slavery-prohibiting Constitutions. I not only labor for these ends, but hope quite sanguinely that they will be secured. The public sentiment of the country has undergone a great change in reference to Slavery. Strong Emancipation parties exist in every Slave State not affected by the Proclamation, and a general conviction prevails that Slavery cannot long survive the restoration of the Republic. The Proclamation, and such recognition of it as I have mentioned will have finished it in the Proclamation States. In the other States, the people will finish it by their own action.

I do not care to sketch the picture of the great and powerful nation which will then exhibit its strength in America. Your own foresight must have anticipated all I could say.

The war moves too slow and costs too much; but it moves steadily and rebellion falls before it. Our financial condition remains entirely sound. The new National Banks are being organized as rapidly as prudence allows; and no doubt can, I think, be longer entertained that, whatever else may happen, we shall have gained, through the rebellion, an opportunity, not unimproved, of establishing a safe and uniform currency for the whole nation—a benefit in itself compensating in some degree, and in no small degree, for the evils we have endured.

I trust you are succeeding well in your great scheme of the inter-Continental telegraph. It is an enterprise worthy of this day of great things. If I had the wealth of an Astor,[7] you should not lack the means of construction.

Yours very truly,
S P Chase

Cyrus W. Field, Esq.

1. New York merchant and entrepreneur Cyrus Field had gained notoriety for efforts to lay a telegraph cable across the Atlantic. In the summer of 1863, he traveled to Britain to raise capital for the project. According to Field's biographer, Chase referred to a letter from Bright on February 27 that expressed impatience for news from the U.S. "There is great effort without great result and we fear the divisions in the North will weaken the government and stimulate the South," wrote Bright. "Sometimes of late I have seemed to fear anarchy in the North as much as rebellion in the South." *DAB,* 6:357–59; Isabella Field Judson, ed., *Cyrus W. Field: His Life and Work [1819–1892]* (New York, 1896), 155–69.

2. "Callihroé" was actually written by Maurice Sand, the pen name of Jean François Maurice Dudevant (1823–89), son of novelist Amandine Aurore Lucie Dupin, Baronne Dudevant (1804–76), better known as George Sand. The story appeared in the June 1, 15, and July 1 issues of the periodical. *Dictionaire de Biographie Française,* 18 vols. to date (Paris, 1967–), 11:1350–52; J. O. Thorne, ed., *Chambers's Biographical Dictionary,* rev. ed., (New York, 1969), 1129.

3. John Hampden (1594–1643) and Algernon Sidney (or Sydney) (1622–83) were outspoken critics of royal abuses shortly before and during the English Civil War. British reformer Richard Cobden (1804–65) earned his political reputation as a leader of the Anti-Cornlaw League, an association dedicated to free trade in agriculture. *DNB,* 4:604–10, 8:1138–46, 18:202–10.

4. See Chase's letter of August 20 to William H. Aspinwall (above).

5. Francis Harrison Pierpont and Lemuel Jackson Bowden (1815–64), who held the position from March 1863 to January 1864. *Bio. Dir. U.S. Cong.,* 649.

6. Final approval for the admission of West Virginia into the Union occurred on December 31, 1862. Pierpont officially declared Alexandria to be Virginia's seat of government by early the next September and moved it to Richmond on May 23, 1865. Charles H. Ambler, *Francis H. Pierpont: Union War Governor of Virginia and Father of West Virginia* (Chapel Hill, 1937), 213; Long, *Civil War Day by Day,* 689; *New York Times,* Sept. 6, 1863; *Statutes at Large,* 12:633–34.

7. Offspring of American fur magnate John Jacob Astor (1763–1848), in his time the richest man in the U.S. *DAB,* 1:397–99.

TO CHARLOTTE S. EASTMAN

Letterpress copy of autograph letter. Chase Papers, Historical Society of Pennsylvania (*micro* 28:0374).

Washington, August. 22, 1863.

My cherished friend,

What a sweet letter you have sent me! I have read and reread it. What a charming picture you draw of the old house, hallowed by the portrait of your grandmother and so many associations; the near flowing river; the gay passers by; the fisher[mens] boats and their [songs]. It made half feel myself with you & quite wish to be. I took up the map and found that York is on York River which looks like an arm of the sea, and not very far from Portsmouth.[1] And then I thought that on Sunday, just two days before you wrote Katie and Nettie were at Portsmouth, spending the day with a friend Mrs. Bridge,[2] and how glad I should have been if you had known it & could have been there too. I am so sorry that you & Katie—one so dear to me as a friend and the other as a daughter don't exactly *jee.* But I think you would more and more, if you could only be thrown together awhile accidentally. The two children were on their way to the White Mountains, having determined to take a vacation from "Tuckers"[3]

I wish you had told me a little more about the old house. Who lives in it now? What sort of a place is it? Have you a charming little library there too? How I should like to exchange hot Washington for the dear old house library or no library, with or without the moon, that so brightly silvered the ocean at Beverly! But I confess that what I would most like would be to exchange the calls of business people for the "sweet society" of the dear friend whose presence brightens it. I would like to see too if the "beautiful grandmother" from Copley's brush is more lovely than her handsome grandchild?[4] There now, don't scold. But I am sure you wont for you dont know how.

The gossip about my friend Dr. Stone could hardly have come at more unsuitable moment. I had already heard of his dangerous illness, and was anxiously hoping better news—news of his improvement or recovery, when this morning—your letter came yesterday—a telegram announced his death.[5] He was a faithful friend, a sincere lover of his country and his kind, and an excellent public officer. No office was more ably or honestly conducted than his: and neither to me nor to the country can his loss be easily made good: Those who censured him will now let censure sleep.

I wont complain any more of your remarks about my ambition; but take it for true that I *am* ambitious and forget in ambitious hopes and wishes, some duties of friendship & charity. I will only try to direct my ambition to public ends and in honorable ways, and forget friends and claims as little as possible.

This letter has been written at the Department / It would amuse you if I could describe the interruptions. and interrupters. *Now,* I must go to the President.

Goodbye, my dear friend.

Yours Affectionately & faithfully
S P Chase

Mrs. C. S. Eastman,

1. York, Maine, near Portsmouth, N.H.

2. Charlotte Marshall Bridge, the wife of Navy bureau chief Horatio Bridge, a native of Maine who some years earlier had served at the Portsmouth Navy Yard. *Appletons',* 1:372–73.

3. Josiah Prentice Tucker and his wife Hannah Ralston Whipple Tucker.

4. John Singleton Copley (1738–1815), Colonial American and British painter best known for portraits. *DAB,* 4:423–30.

5. A year before, Chase had nominated James W. Stone collector of internal revenue for the third district of Massachusetts. Stone's brother, Anson Stone, had sent the telegram. Chase evidently misdated either his reply to Anson Stone or this letter to Charlotte Eastman; according to their contents they were written on the same day, yet one is dated August 21 and the other August 22. Chase to Anson Stone, Aug. 21, 1863 (Chase Papers, Hist. Soc. of Pa.); Chase to Abraham Lincoln, Aug. 26, 1862 (Lincoln Papers, L.C.).

FROM MANSFIELD FRENCH

Autograph letter. Chase Papers, Library of Congress (*micro* 28:0388).

Beaufort. S.C.
Aug 22. 1863

My dear Mr. Chase,

I am constrained by the present condition of the colored people in this Department,[1] to make a few suggestions concerning them.

Many have laid up, little sums, from their hard & scanty earnings, during the summer, while others are about to realize larger amounts, from their harvest of corn, & particularly, of cotton. They have been told that the lands would be in market, and on such conditions that they could purchase homes.

If the lands were surveyed into tracts of 20, 30, & 40 acres, and sold at, say $1,25, or $1,50 per acre, very many, if not most, of the families would, no doubt, be able to purchase a home. It seems very desirable, if it be possible, that the Government should throw around them every possible safeguard to insure permanency of possession.

If the lands should not be offered to the people in season, their hard earnings will, it is to be feared, quickly melt away, and they will be *obliged* to *float another year.* Demoralization, and that of the *worst kind,* in many instances, would *necessarily follow.*

The future interests, as well as honor of the Government, seem to urge a speedy provision for *permanent homes,* as the only means, of subserving the social, intellectual & spiritual interests of this, yet to be, under God, mighty people.

As the present freedmen, as well as the millions yet to be borne into freedom, with all their sacred & complicated interests, lay with great weight upon your heart, and as you have direction, in a great degree, of the doings of the Tax Commissioners, but *most of all,* because God our Common Father, has given you a heart to feel for, and a holy boldness to defend & protect the rights of, this great people, I have been induced thus to write you.

I pray God to guide you with his counsel into such action as will be for the greatest good of the people & for his glory.

Genl. Gilmore moves *slowly,* but in harmony with what seems to have been the Divine order heretofore, viz. Success *only* at the *most costly* rate, but with national purity in equal ratio, as the reward. *God's will be done.*

Yours with highest regards
M. French.

1. The army's Department of the South.

TO HENRY WILSON

Letterpress copy of autograph letter. Chase Papers, Historical Society of Pennsylvania (*micro* 28:0410).

Washington, Aug. 24, 1863.

Dear Wilson,

Thanks for your 1st August speech. It was a timely & nobly spoken word. I shall try to have the President read it.

The Chronicle (which I believe you see) has an article this morning, communicated, which, I think, comes from somebody not far from the Post Office. At any rate it reflects the sentiments of those who call themselves supporters of the Administration & yet either desire or are willing to consent to reconstitution, with slavery preserved, notwithstanding the proclamation, in the rebel states.

I have looked over the article from the Tribune which you sent me. It is from a Md. correspondent & had escaped my notice.[1]

Part of its statements are correct & part otherwise. Swann is as *much* of an Emancipationist as Davis but not so *zealous*. He was a candidate for the Union Nomination & Davis beat him.[2] Blair was for Davis. I rather preferred Swann, though because of my admiration for the bold & explicit manner in which Davis put forth his views and my concurrence in the views themselves, I refused to *express* any preference for him, to the officers of the Government who sought to know my opinions.

When Davis was declared nominated I urged all our friends to support him. But I soon found great dissatisfaction among the friends of Swann. They complained of military interference by bringing to the City special friends of Davis & leaving out the friends of Swann and of unfair play generally. Swann was urged to come out as an independent candidate, but has not done so and I hope will not.

Then came in a new element of trouble. The State Convention of the Union Party had organized a State Union Committee. Our friends who most sympathize with Mr. Davis thought that this Committee was not to be trusted; and through the Committees of the Union Leagues called a State Convention. The Union State Committee called, also, a Convention. The two Conventions met and disagreed in their state ticket. The Union State Convention men insist that theirs is the regular nomination; claim to be emancipationists & many of them administration men; while the Union League Convention men deny these claims & insist on their own.

My sympathies are with the Union League men; because I believe them to be the most in earnest. But I cannot shut my eyes to the fact the the other side have the advantage, whatever it is of regular organization or be surprised if many of our best men go along with them.

This is a slight sketch of the situation, but I believe correct as far as it goes. You will see that there are *faults* as well as *virtues* on both sides.

If we had any means of reconciling all the true men & bringing them together I should be very glad. But at present the prospect is not bright. We must keep our temper & be ready to make the best of every thing.

Your friend
S P Chase

Hon H Wilson.

1. In "My Maryland," "C" criticized Republican appointees from the state—particularly Montgomery Blair—for allegedly opposing key policies of the Lincoln administration. "It is proper that the country should know that the *whole* Emancipation policy is jeopardized in Maryland by its professed friends in the Cabinet and in office in the State," suggested the article. *New York Tribune,* Aug. 20, 1863.

2. Thomas Swann, Jr., had lost to radical Henry Winter Davis in a recent bid for the Union party's nomination as candidate for Maryland's third congressional district. Ibid.; *Chase Papers,* 1:435–36; Chase to Davis, June 8, 1863 (above); John F. McJilton to Chase, Aug. 28, 1863 (below).

TO GEORGE S. DENISON

Letter in clerk's hand, signed by Chase. George S. Denison Papers, Library of Congress (*micro* 28:0462).

Unofficial

Washington, August 26, 1863.

My dear Sir,

I have your private letter of the 12th.[1] I have for some weeks devoted what time I could spare to the revision of the Regulations,[2] and for the last few days have had the assistance of Supervising Special Agents Mellen and Risley. I observe that a good deal of complaint is made against restrictions on trade—some of it altogether unreasonable, and some of it entitled to great consideration. My purpose has been to make the restrictions as moderate as possible, and as little inconvenient in their practical operation as possible, keeping in view, however, the important object of preventing supplies to rebels either direct or by accumulation at points from which they can be easily furnished. I hope that the new Regulations will be more satisfactory than those of March 31, though I cannot hope that they will be altogether so.

The proclamation of August 16, 1861, excepted from the general prohibition of commercial intercourse in the Act of July 13, 1861, certain named portions of States in insurrection, and also such portions as might "be, from time to time, occupied and controlled by the forces of the United States engaged in the dispersion of the insurgents"[3] The exceptions left those parts of the rebel States occupied by our troops open to trade, very imperfectly restricted by Treasury Regulations and military Orders. Great embarrassments in the prosecution of the war arose, and great complaints of misconduct of the military officers and of traders within the lines of the army and even beyond them.

To remove the ground of these complaints, and to introduce, if possible, a better condition of things, the President, on the 31st. of March, 1863, revoked the exceptions as to districts occupied by our troops, and placed the whole of the States declared in insurrection, except the ports of New-Orleans, Key West, Port Royal and Beaufort in North Carolina, under the prohibition of commercial intercourse contained in the Act of Congress, and, at the same time, to relieve as far as practicable the inconveniences arising from that prohibition, licensed limited commercial intercourse, under the Regulations of the Treasury Department.[4] The effect of this was to transfer the regulation of trade from various and sometimes differing military authorities to the Treasury Department, thereby insuring a tolerable degree of uniformity and, at the same time, such deference to the orders of Generals commanding Departments as would prevent interference with the operations of the war. It has been my aim to accomplish these results. The Regulations of March 31, 1863, which were approved by the President and by the Secretaries of War and Navy, were framed with this view. The Regulations shortly to be issued will be made with the same view. It is impossible to accomplish all that could be desired or redress by any endeavors the mischief of the rebellion. I hope, however, that something has been and that more will be done through the action of the Department towards the accomplishment of the purposes of Congress and of the President and for the benefit of all concerned.

I have lately seen in the "*True Delta*" of the 14th. of August, an article entitled "Louisiana's Appeal to the West".[5] It is inspired by a very unjust and ungenerous spirit. No one knows better than yourself how untrue is the allegation that the Treasury Department has sent forth any swarm of electioneering spies and agents. All the appointments of the Department have been made with a simple desire to secure the honest execution of the Acts of Congress with as little inconvenience and as much benefit as possible to the people, and at the same time to sustain the President in the measures adopted by him for the suppression of the rebellion. No one can say with the slightest approach to truth that anybody has been appointed for electioneering purposes.

I suppose that the allegation that purchasers of family supplies in the city are subjected to the five per cent tax is untrue;[6] and the other allegations in respect to internal commerce, are either absolutely untrue or, at least, highly colored. If the Form of Application for a Permit is correctly given, there is a mistake in the mode of framing it. All such applications go to the Collector of Internal Revenue and not to any Special Agent of the Treasury Department. Would it not be well to have proper explanations of these matters printed for public information in the papers? I want no vindication of the action of the Treasury Department; but I do want that the people shall be made to understand, as far as possible, the practical operations of its Regulations, and wherever these practical operations can be made more beneficial by amendment of them, I want to know it in order that the amendments may be made.

I am glad to see that Gen. Banks does not propose to let his troops remain idle.[7] I hope that not only will Mobile be soon taken but that the whole country West of the Mississippi will be cleared of rebels so that trade may be resumed there without restrictions.

I have had no letter from Mr. Plumly in relation to his interview with Gen. Banks. I appreciate both his talents and his services. No one can be more ready than I am to manifest that appreciation on all proper occasions. I want him to feel that I desire to give him a cordial support in his position, and want from him a cordial support in mine. If we ever differ, the fault shall not be on my side.

In your action as Permit Officer I wish you, as I also wish Mr. Flanders in his action as Special Agent, to confer fully with the Commanding General and to do nothing in any case which will embarrass his military operations. The two sections which you quote from his plan correspond exactly with my own views; and I endeavored, at the last session of Congress, to obtain authority to receive property and pay for it in the mode, and with the further provision for contingent additional payment, which he suggests. Congress, however, refused to confer this authority, and, of course, I do not feel at liberty to exercise it.

Please read the letter which I address to-day to Mr. Flanders.[8] It contains some information in regard to public measures, with which I wish you to be acquainted.

Please continue to write me fully and frequently, and believe me

Very sincerely yours
S P Chase

Geo. S. Denison, Esq.

1. See Denison to Chase, August 12, 1863 (above).
2. Formally issued on September 11, 1863. *Commercial Intercourse,* 13–30.
3. *Statutes at Large,* 12:255–58, 1262.
4. Basler, *Collected Works,* 6:157.
5. The piece warned that "incomprehensible" trade regulations jeopardized "the revival of the old, lucrative, reciprocally advantageous trade" along the Mississippi River and criticized the Treasury Department for "its swarm of electioneering spies and agents."
6. The phrase *is untrue;* is an interlineation in Chase's hand.
7. In the middle of August, Banks had embarked on an invasion of Texas, the most notable accomplishment of which was the capture of Brownsville on November 6. Harrington, *Fighting Politician,* 130–34; Long, *Civil War Day by Day,* 431.
8. Chase to Flanders, Aug. 26, 1863 (below).

TO BENJAMIN F. FLANDERS

Letter in clerk's hand on letterhead stationery, signed by Chase. Special Collections, Dartmouth College Library (*micro* 28:0469).

Treasury Department.
August 26, 1863.

Dear Sir,

Your private letter of the 12th instant was duly received. I am much obliged to you for your frank statement concerning Mr. *T.* I am glad that he has a place which suits him better than an Assistant Agency.[1]

As a general rule I think that the compensation of Assistant Agents ought not to exceed five dollars a day and actual necessary expenses when traveling. There are cases, however, in which exceptions should be made. For example, I have recently addressed you in relation to making Gen. Hamilton an Assistant Special Agent for Texas.[2] His compensation should, I think, be on the same footing with your own. In fact, Texas might well constitute a Supervising Special Agency; but, for the present at least, I think it can be more easily managed as an Assistant Agency, and Gen. Hamilton no doubt will find his duties lighter and will be able to perform them better under you, than if acting independently. I presume that you both will before long be called to important political positions, and I hope you will be looking out for competent and faithful men to take these places when you will retire from them. I have devoted for some time past—what time I could command—to a revision of the General Regulations, and for the last two or three days have had the assistance of Mr. Mellen and Mr. Risley, the last the Supervising Special Agent for this Agency. I hope to complete the revision this week and to be able to send you a copy by the mail of next week. They are an improvement, I think, upon the former Regulations, though no doubt still defective.[3] I observe that the "True Delta" of the 14th instant contains an attack on the Department and its regulations and officers. Such assaults must be expected, but I mean that my conduct shall give as little occasion to them as possible, and I trust that the conduct of the officers of the Department will be regulated by such principles of impartial integrity and strict duty as will challenge investigation.[4]— In the new Regulations the limits of the Supervising Special Agencies will be defined as accurately as possible. So much of Mississippi and Arkansas as may be within the lines of military operations from the South will be in yours; the residue in Mr. Mellen's. You will see also that the granting of permits to trade is to be strictly subordinate to military exigencies, and therefore to the directions of the General commanding the Department.

The subject of the re-organization of the State of Louisiana is one of great interest here now. The President, I am inclined to think, would not be unwilling to revoke the exception of the two districts, including New Orleans, from the operation of his Proclamation if such revocation should be recommended to him by any considerable number of influential and intelligent loyal citizens of Louisiana. Cannot such a recommendation be sent him? and would not a revocation greatly strengthen the truly loyal men and aid, and materially aid, in securing a free-labor re-organization?

Some two weeks since, on my return from New England after a few days absence, the President read to me a letter which he had addressed to General Banks. It expressed a preference for a Constitution recognizing the condition established by the Proclamation: in other words, prohibiting Slavery. The letter was worded with that caution and respect for the opinions and wishes of others which is characteristic of the writer, and did not express, I think, his preference as strongly as he feels it.[5] I am sure that few things could gratify him so much as the reorganization of the State with a free-labor constitution. Such an act, in my judgment, would contribute more powerfully than anything else to the restoration of union upon a solid and permanent basis.

General Shepley called on me to-day to speak about clearances to blockaded ports in military occupation. He will take instructions on this subject from the War Department, and I shall send instructions on the same subject to Mr. Denison. General Shepley will also take instructions on the subject of a Convention to re-organize the State.[6] These instructions have been framed with great care. You will doubtless see them, and I need not state details. The great feature of them is, that they direct the apportionment of delegates according to the number of loyal citizens of the United States, and a registration of these loyal citizens with reference to the selection of delegates. You are aware that the Attorney General has given an opinion that all free persons born in the United States or naturalized of whatever color, are citizens of the United States, and the instructions have been framed with this opinion in view. I send you several copies of this opinion.[7] I do not know whether public sentiment will admit the application of this doctrine in Louisiana, but it seems to me that a class of people from whom volunteers for the defence of the Union are furnished by thousands is quite as well entitled, though colored, to the rights of citizenship as a class, though white, from which volunteers come by hundreds.

The "True Delta," I see, charges the officers of this Department with being electioneering agents. If it means by this that they are zealous for the restoration of the Union and for the principles of the Proclamation, I trust its statement is true. As to their personal preferences, I have never inquired and never shall. Let us save our country, and postpone personal questions till that great object is accomplished.

Let me hear from you as often and as fully as practicable.

Yours very truly,
S P Chase

I have omitted to say anything about a National Bank. I hope the time for the establishment of one at New Orleans is not far distant.

Hon. Benjamin F. Flanders,
New Orleans.

1. On July 8, Chase had enquired about Thomas Bangs Thorpe (1815–78), a Louisiana artist, author, and former staff officer for Benjamin F. Butler who sought an appointment as U.S. marshal. According to Flanders, Thorpe lacked "sense and discretion" and was "an unsafe man to trust with business." Thorpe soon abandoned his quest for the position to pursue "privileges of trade" after learning that government employment paid no more than five dollars a day. Elsewhere in the letter, Flanders told of plans to start a bank "at the first favorable moment," objected to the removal of Mississippi from his jurisdiction, and reported on tension with U.S. military authorities over trade policies. Chase to Flanders, July 8, Flanders to Chase, Aug. 12, 1863 (Chase Papers, Hist. Soc. of Pa.); *DAB,* 18:509.

2. In September Chase appointed Andrew Jackson Hamilton an assistant special agent of the Treasury, but within a few days President Lincoln, expecting a reassertion of Union control in Texas, gave Hamilton a new commission as military governor of the state. Chase to Hamilton, Sept. 15, 1863 (Chase Papers, Hist. Soc. of Pa.); Basler, *Collected Works,* 6:465–66.

3. The new regulations, formally announced on September 11, replaced those of March 31, 1863. *Commercial Intercourse,* 13–38.

4. On the same day Chase also discussed the *True Delta* article in correspondence with George S. Denison (above).

5. "I would be glad for her to make a new Constitution recognizing the emancipation proclamation," wrote Lincoln about Louisiana, "and adopting emancipation in those parts of the state to which the proclamation does not apply." Lincoln to Banks, Aug. 5, 1863, in Basler, *Collected Works,* 6:365.

6. Edwin M. Stanton wrote both sets of Shepley's instructions on August 24. For those to Denison, see Chase to Denison, August 26, 1863 (above). *OR,* ser. 1, v. 26, pt. 1:694–95.

7. Chase had discussed the opinion in correspondence with George Opdyke et al., April 8, 1863 (above).

FROM WILLIAM H. ASPINWALL

Autograph letter on letterhead stationery. Chase Papers, Historical Society of Pennsylvania (*micro* 28:0481).

Rockwood.
Tarrytown N.Y.
Aug 26 /63

My dear Mr. Chase

As I was absent from home your letter returning that of Mr. Bright did not reach me in course of mail[1] / I now thank you for the interesting views which it contains, & for the assurance that the President will prove true to himself & to the Country. You ask me a question which it is hard to answer—& the difficulties which surround it are not such as we have to cope with in our private affairs— There, we can weigh well all the circumstances, & having made a plan can carry it out with a singleness of will & purpose which political questions do not admit of. Under ordinary circumstances I would prefer that a gradual emancipation of the slaves still held in bondage—say covering 5 or 7 years, should leave on their masters the care & expense attending the change / No individual who has been able & willing to avail of the proclamation should under any circumstances be again enslaved—& I only refer to those who could not or would not leave their mast[ers]

But time is an important element—as the direction of public affairs may in 18 months be in different hands & we must do what we can be sure to finish up, during this & the next session of Congress— I would therefore consider all slaves as free and establish such laws for the employment of those still held by their masters, as apprentices for a limited period as will ensure their services— The difficulty in the way is the great desire of many earnest advocates of the war, to see it brought to a close, & the disposition of the Democrats to make a party issue on the rights of the Rebel states to claim the representation they had in Congress before their treason. The best way to meet this is your second alternative—to encourage & protect the *individuals* of the rebel states in forming conventions acknowledging the proclamation, & which shall send representatives to Congress— I have been surprised since my return to find this desire to have the war brot. to a close overruling the judgement & perseverance of men who hitherto have shown an unwavering determination to exterminate all cause for future wars—& especially in the case of the Louisianians who called on the Prest. last month—& who afterwards came to New York, I was amazed to be asked to meet them, by one of the staunchest Republicans among us, who expressed a decided opinion that these men had not been treated liberally in Washington— I believe no meeting was held, or at any rate if held it was stillborn, as most sensible men would refrain interfering with such question after the Cabinet had passed on it.

As to the return of the states we can expect nothing but opposition from those rebels now in power there—& therefore neither with them as states nor with the Confederacy, can we expect to do any thing satisfactory— The work must be begun with the people of the different States, & even if at first feeble, the Govt. ought to give them strength— It seems to me clear that efforts should be centered on that one state most likely to come back—for the example of one will soon be followed by others—& as this subdivision of authority favored Secession, so will it facilitate the restoration of the Union

I was one of those most opposed to the war 'till it was forced on us— but once in it I would rather have it last five years than to leave half done the task imposed on us— I only mourn that we cannot bring unity of purpose & action to the aid of abundant phisical power, to end it speedily & honorably—& forever.

With true regard

Your friend & Servt.
Wm. H. Aspinwall

I have heard as coming from a high official that there is an unpublished opinion of the Supreme Court that all those in rebellion are aliens & have forfeited all existing political rights— Has such an opinion been given?

1. Chase to Aspinwall, August 20, 1863 (above).

TO GEORGE WILKES

Letterpress copy of autograph letter. Chase Papers, Historical Society of Pennsylvania (*micro* 28:0518).

August 27, 3

My dear Sir,

Your article on the designs of Napoleon is replete with instructive suggestions. It had already attracted my attention in the Spirit of the Times; but I thank you none the less for sending it to me.[1]

It is painful for one to be so near the springs of action and yet unable to touch them. It is almost like the nightmare in oppressiveness, and worse because there is no illusion. I can only counsel; and that without any certainty of being understood, or, if understood, of being able to obtain concurrence, or, even after concurrence, action.

The Proclamation as you say was providential; and you are right in saying it saved us. Made complete now by revocation of its exceptions (of which I do not despair) and efficient, permanently, by being insisted on as the basis of loyal reorganization, it will make us strong enough, if we have wisdom & courage to use our strength, to thwart and baffle all aggressive plans.

We ought long since to have anticipated all Europeans all European schemes by taking the advantages offered to our acceptance in Central America & Mexico.

Yours truly,
S P CHASE

Geo Wilkes, Esq

1. Wilkes owned *Wilkes' Spirit of the Times, A Chronicle of the Turf, Field Sports, the Army and the Stage,* published in New York. The article, published on August 8 and sent to Chase on the twenty-fourth, expressed concern over Napoleon III's invasion of Mexico. According to Wilkes, the French emperor, in league with the Confederacy, envisioned "'a vast kingdom of the earth,' stretching from the Potomac to the Isthmus, embracing all the islands of the Gulf, the cotton and tobacco fields of North America, and surmounted by a Bonaparte, whose dockyards and arsenals, upon the Western Ocean, would domineer over the Pacific and the East." To Wilkes, this "plot" suggested the need for an alliance between the North and Great Britain to defend "constitutional liberty and freedom over all the earth." "Texas is the key to the situation for which we must contend with this new combination between the European Lucifer and his confederate allies, . . ." the article continued. "The sooner Grant is turned from the inadequate object of Mobile, and sent into that region, . . . the better will it be for the fate of the mighty conflict that most surely is approaching." *Wilkes' Spirit of the Times,* Aug. 8, 1863; Wilkes to Chase, Aug. 24, 1863 (Chase Papers, L.C.); *DAB,* 20:218.

FROM HORACE GREELEY

Autograph letter on letterhead stationery. Chase Papers, Historical Society of Pennsylvania (*micro* 28:0524).

Office of The Tribune,
New York, Aug. 27, 1863.

My dear Sir:

I have yours of the 25th, and must answer it very hastily.[1]

Of course, I know, as all know, that any peace not based on the virtual destruction of Slavery can be but a truce after a drawn battle. So much is clear enough. But that is by no means the worst possible result of our great struggle.

In all human efforts, two ends must be kept distinctly in view: 1. What is desirable; 2. What is practicable. To confound these or ignore the distinction between them, is the reverse of statesmanship.

We have embarked on the critical experiment of impelling a Pro-Slavery people to sustain a (necessarily) Anti-Slavery War. It is an experiment inevitably dangerous and requiring not to be pressed too far.

The country is fearfully weary of the cost, the sacrifices, the burthens inseparable from a great war. The Draft—a most necessary step—increases the popular impatience. "Peace! Peace!" is the aspiration of almost every heart. Hence our Elections are quite likely to result worse than those of last year, except where (as in Ohio) the soldiers did not vote then but do vote now. I fear that, even with the great lift given us by Seymour and his friends we cannot carry this State.[2]

Now, then, *we must not let the Opposition make this issue on us—that on their platform we might have instant Peace and Reunion, while on ours we must prosecute interminable War.*— On any such issue, we must go at once to the wall, and give place to men who are more thoroughly Pro-Slavery to-day than the Rebels.

To maintain even a footing with the People, we must not seem to let Anti-Slavery stand in the way of Peace. On the contrary, we can only live while we make at least half the people believe that Peace with Union is as obtainable and as near on our platform as on our adversaries'.

I believe this is enough to enable you to comprehend me. It is possible that I may be able to just run to Washington about the 10th–12 of September; but I do not feel sure of it. In any case, believe me,

Yours, truly,
HORACE GREELEY.

Hon. S. P. Chase,
Washington, D.C.

1. Chase had accused Greeley, who edited the *New York Tribune,* of underrating "the importance of the question of reconstruction" and invited him to visit Washington to discuss the issue. Chase to Greeley, Aug. 25, 1863 (Pierpont Morgan Lib.).

2. Legislation enacted in Ohio earlier in the year enabled soldiers to vote by absentee ballot. Greeley had recently assailed Horatio Seymour, a leading Democratic critic of Lincoln, for failing to support the draft act of March 1863 and for demonstrating insufficient vigor in suppressing the New York riots. *New York Tribune,* July 24, Aug. 11, 1863; Eugene H. Roseboom, *The Civil War Era, 1850–1873,* vol. 4 of Carl Wittke, ed., *The History of the State of Ohio* (Columbus, 1944), 394, 403, 405.

FROM JOHN F. MCJILTON

Autograph letter. Chase Papers, Library of Congress (*micro* 28:0559).

Baltimore, August 28th, 1863.

Dear Governor;

After a very agreeable interview with our mutual friend Smith, I suggested the propriety of my addressing you a few lines on the subject of our conversation, which he cordially approved and requested me to say so to you.[1]

I feel no little hesitation, and, indeed, embarrassment, in addressing you in this *friendly* way, as our relations have been, almost exclusively, of an official character; but, being assured by mutual friends, (and having no cause myself to think otherwise,) that you will receive a communication, of this sort, in the same spirit which dictates it, I take the liberty thus to address you.

I shall state a few things as briefly as possible, prefering, if it could be, to have a personal interview with a few of your *true* friends, at some time entirely convenient to yourself.

Maryland politics are, in many respects, different from those of any other State. We have an Eastern and a Western Shore—a tier of Counties bordering on Pennsylvania, and a large and populous City. Each division represents different, and, in some respects, conflicting interests. Their educational, agricultural and political pursuits and tastes are diverse the one from the other. In former years, when the contest was between the Whigs and Locos,[2] Balto. City and the border counties, almost invariably, cast their vote for the Locos; while the counties on the E. & W. Shores gave large Whig majorities. The Locos then, as now, were a unit; the Whigs then, as are the Union men now, were clamorous and contentious—manifesting more anxiety in putting forward certain men representing cliques and combinations than in supporting the cardinal principles of the party. The Whig party was divided into two parts—one known as the "Court House Clique" and the other as the "Conservative". The former worked for the few—the latter for the many. The Clique were the wire-pullers and always succeeded in having their choice nominated for Governor, but never elected him but once, in 1844, when Tho. G. Pratt (now a rebel) was, on Henry Clay's popularity, successful by less than 500 majority. He was the only Whig Govr. Maryland ever elected by a popular vote—altho' Genl. Harrison,

Genl. Taylor & Mr Clay carried the State by thousands.[3] The reasons can be easily explained, and, like means, in the opinion of many discreet, far-seeing gentlemen, will produce like results this fall.

We have now two divisions of the Union men styled the "radical" and "Conservative"—both desiring the same thing but opposed as to the mode of effecting it. The first believes that the emancipation question should be the prominent, and perhaps, the *only* "rallying cry"—the other prefers the *entire* policy—among which looms up, conspicuously, the *financial* feature, of the Administration. In some few sections, it is thought, the former will succeed, but in most of the counties it is firmly believed it will not, while, it is also believed, the success of the latter is certain. For illustration: Balt. City and probably Allegany and Cecil counties, might be carried on the open and naked question of emancipation, but, if the other counties make that the chief "rallying cry" they would be defeated, while the most of them can be carried on the *whole-policy* platform. I merely re-echo the opinions as they have been promulgated by each division.

The question is now agitated whether slavery shall be abolished against law or by constitutional enactments. It is the opinion of many of our very best Union men that the President, in his proclamation, and the Cabinet, as far as their views are known, favor the latter. The contrary, however, is asserted by some. Just here the embarrassment of the *real* friends of the Administration becomes exceedingly painful. It would greatly relieve the perplexity of *your* personal and political friends if they could be informed on this point. I think much depends on this. I mean as to the success or defeat of the *vital* question. If the Administration advise its friends to adopt the revolutionary side, the Conservative portion do not hesitate to express the opinion that the State will be lost to the Union cause. The opposite portion, however, think differently.

Many would prefer, and so declare themselves, that the Administration take no part in the controversy now, as they took none previous to the Congressional nominations. Its friends now belong to both divisions and they will remain "stedfast and unmovable", but this may not be if *either* side is accepted at Washington to the rejection of the other.

I have, so far, taken no active part, on either side, in this unhappy struggle. I have done all I could to prevent a fatal collision. Nothing would cause me more regret than to see the good cause we have espoused, and, for the consummation of which, we have so long contended, "wounded in the house of its friends,"[4] and, that Maryland shall be cursed with slavery a decade of years longer, merely to gratify the personal ambition of a few local, selfish politicians, to be found in the ranks of both divisions.

The Union men of Maryland I trust may be made willing, for this once at least, to act the patriot instead of the politician—to aid in promoting concord among them—to draw gently the cords of fraternal union—to use kind words and cease from all offensive epithets—to bear and forbear, and by this means soothe and heal instead of chafing and wounding. Who are to do this and how it is to be done, may be, hereafter, profitably discussed. I do not think the disease has reached a point beyond recovery. The proper remedies, judiciously applied, *will* cure. The subject may be so discussed and managed that these divisions and differences may be all healed, and all the Union voters see eye to eye and work shoulder to shoulder—the grand and glorious object achieved and Maryland be forever liberated from the scars of Locofocism and the infernal curse of human slavery.

I have perhaps already written more than I ought, and yet there are many other things I wish to say; but as our friend Smith, whose clear mind and practical suggestions are worthy of note, is so anxious for you to see a few of your true friends, some evening after working hours, I trust you may find it convenient to give them an audience at no distant day, so that the whole subject may be laid before you truthfully and impartially, and, in the tone and emphasis, which it is impossible to do on paper.[5]

I am, Very Truly,

Your friend & Obt Servant,
JNO. F. MCJILTON

1. McJilton edited the Baltimore *Patriot* and was surveyor of customs at Baltimore. The "mutual friend Smith" might have been William Prescott Smith, master of transportation for the Baltimore and Ohio Railroad. *Chase Papers,* 1:454–56; Edward Hungerford, *The Story of the Baltimore & Ohio Railroad, 1827–1929* . . . (New York, 1928), 2:51; J. Thomas Scharf, *History of Baltimore City and County* . . . (Philadelphia, 1881), 497–98.

2. From "locofocos," a term often used during the late 1840s and 1850s in reference to the Democratic party. William Trimble, "Diverging Tendencies in the New York Democracy in the Period of the Locofocos," *American Historical Review* 24 (Apr. 1919): 416.

3. William Henry Harrison, Zachary Taylor, and Henry Clay. During the Civil War, Federal officials briefly imprisoned former governor Thomas George Pratt because of his support for the Confederacy. *DAB,* 15:178.

4. Zech. 13:6.

5. Chase granted the request, and a conference took place on September 3 that discussed Maryland's rival Union party factions and their leaders, Henry Winter Davis and Thomas Swann. Chase to Henry Wilson, Aug. 24, 1863 (above); *Chase Papers,* 1:435–36.

TO JOHN J. CISCO

Letterbook copy in clerk's hand. Letters Sent, Loan Division, Records of the Bureau of the Public Debt (Record Group 53), National Archives (*micro* 28:0584).

Treasury Department.
August 31, 1863.

Sir.

The pay of the army for the current six months will require an addition to the ordinary receipts for bonds, of about twenty-five millions of dollars; and must be provided for immediately.

The best mode of doing this so as to guard against all contingencies, is to obtain subscriptions from the banks and bankers for fifty millions of Treasury Notes; by which name, as you know, Legal-tender Interest bearing Notes are described in the Act of Congress.[1]

The plates for these notes are now being engraved, and the issues of them will be ready during the month of September. They will be in denominations of 10s, 20s, 50s, 100s, 500s, and 1000s, and will be payable one year from date, with interest at five per cent. Being Legal-tender for their face value, excluding interest, they cannot fall below the legal-tender par; bearing interest, they cannot materially affect the circulation with reference to gold.

I will receive subscriptions for these notes, and will authorize the Assistant Treasurers to issue Certificates, on deposit of five per cent. of the amount subscribed to the Assistant Treasurer in New York, Philadelphia or Boston, and placing ninety-five per cent to the credit of the Treasurer of the United States, on the books of the banks or bankers subscribing. Subscribers will be entitled to six per cent interest on the whole amount subscribed from date of certificate of deposit of five per cent of subscription till delivery of the Treasury Notes. The amount placed to the credit of the Treasurer, will be drawn out as wanted, by checks in favor of the Treasurer or an Asst. Treasurer, during the months of September and October, say half in each month.

Please see the best men immediately, and ascertain whether thirty-five millions of this subscription will be made in New York.[2]

Yours very truly
S. P. Chase.

John J. Cisco. Esq.
Copies of the above sent to
T. P. Chandler. Boston.
A. McIntyre. Philadelphia.

1. That is, the ways and means act of March 1863 that provided for the issue of interest-bearing legal tender notes. Chase to Cisco, June 26, 1863 (above).

2. Chase, who considered the banks' subscriptions for the notes as a form of temporary loan, needed $20 million for army pay during September but initially sought $50 million "in order to be strong and avoid all possible disturbance." Rumors incited by his proposal, however, caused some concern in financial quarters. Banks in Boston and Philadelphia agreed to subscribe under the terms he outlined in this letter, but financial institutions in New York asked for notes with a term of two or three years, with interest paid semiannually, and wanted future issues of the notes to be restricted to banks that joined in the initial subscription. Chase would not allow his options to be limited by the latter provision but agreed to the longer term. Chase to Cisco, Sept. 3, 5, 1863 (Letters Sent, Loan Division, Recs. of Bureau of Public Debt, Nat. Arch.); Cisco to Chase, telegrams, Aug. 7, Sept. 3, 4, 7, 1863 (Letters Recd. from Asst. Treasurers, Gen. Recs. Treasury Dept., Nat. Arch.); Chase to Cisco, Sept. 4, 1863 (Telegrams Sent, Gen. Recs. Treasury Dept., Nat. Arch.).

TO JAY COOKE

Autograph letter on letterhead stationery. Jay Cooke Papers, Historical Society of Pennsylvania (*micro* 28:0605).

Treasury Department.
Sept. 1, 1863

My dear Sir,

Let my first letter of this month be a remonstrance against meanness and oppression

Why cannot colored people ride in the Washington & Georgetown Street Railroad Cars?[1] Who volunteers now a'days except colored men? And do they not volunteer under circumstances in which no white man would volunteer? The compensation of the colored man is ten dollars a month: the white mans thirteen; the white regiments are officered by whites: no commission in a colored regiment is given to a colored man; the white private may hope promotion—the colored soldier can hope none, as laws and regulations now stand. Yet the colored men are coming to the standards with a degree of alacrity & earnestness which does them honor. Banks writes he could not have taken Port Hudson without his colored recruits. Grant writes that the colored regiments are indispensable.[2] I repeat why cannot people of this race ride in the W. & G. Street R.R. cars?

Their exclusion is a shame & disgrace. I see, in the Star, a statement that the Company is getting cars for their use.[3] What kind of cars? if poorer than the others I desire as one of the stockholders of the company to protest against it. If the colored people are to be confined to special cars, let them be *better* than the others so as to compensate in some measure for exclusion from the others by superior accommodation.

But have no such cars. Let all cars be free to all. Let all decent people ride in any car convenient when they get in.

What is to be feared if this simple & just rule be adopted. I know not; but of this I am sure that nothing is so much to be justly feared as the doing of injustice and the acting of meanness.

You can stop it on these cars. Stop it then I pray you.

Yours truly
S P CHASE

Jay Cooke Esq

1. The Washington and Georgetown Street Railroad Company had been incorporated in 1862 with Cooke's brother, Henry D. Cooke, as its president. DeB. Randolph Keim, *Keim's Illustrated Hand-Book: Washington and Its Environs* . . . , 4th ed. (Washington, D.C., 1874), ix; *Wash. Dir. (1863)*, 302.

2. In correspondence to Lincoln on August 17, General Banks praised the role of African-American troops in the fall of Port Hudson: "I think it may be said with truth that our victory at Port Hudson could not have been accomplished at the time it was but for

their assistance." Chase might also have referred to a letter that Ulysses Grant wrote to the president on August 23: "By arming the negro we have added a powerful ally." *OR*, ser. 1, v. 26, pt. 1:689; Simon, *Papers of Grant*, 9:196; Long, *Civil War Day by Day*, 381.

3. A notice appearing in the *Washington Evening Star* on September 1 suggested that the company had ordered several cars built specifically for black passengers.

TO THE COMMITTEE OF THE ST. LOUIS UNION MERCHANTS EXCHANGE

Letterbook copy in clerk's handwriting. Letters Sent Relating to Restricted Commercial Intercourse and Captured and Abandoned Property (BE Series), General Records, Department of the Treasury (Record Group 56), National Archives.

Treasury Department
September 3d. 1863

Messrs. S. M. Breckinridge, Barton Able, Charles L. Tucker and J. H. Alexander, Committee.[1]

Gentlemen.

Your letter of the 1st. inst., addressed to me in behalf of the Union Merchant's Exchange of St Louis, has been carefully considred.[2]

You desire that the Mississippi "may be opened to the free use of the loyal people occupying the territory it drains, limited only by such restraints as the good of the whole country and the successful prosecution of the war for its redemption may impose."

Such also is my desire; not in regard to the Mississippi alone, but in regard to every river and every road that passes through States now unhappily in rebellion. I ardently desire, also that by all just and honorable means, the war for the enforcement of the laws and the restoration of the Union may be so effectively prosecuted that all necessity for restraint may speedily disappear, and commerce be resumed in perfect freedom, and with the old benefits under the old flag.

Mean time, while the war yet continues, the only question in reference to commercial intercourse is, what restraints are necessary for the "good of the whole country" and "the successful prosecution of the war"[3]

Acts of Congress authorize the Secretary of the Treasury to prohibit and prevent the transportation of goods intended for the insurgents, or for places where there is imminent danger that they will fall into their possession or control,[4] and these acts prohibit all commercial intercourse with States and parts of States declared in insurrection, except under License of the President and under Regulations prescribed by the Secretary of the Treasury

The President, by his proclamation, has declared that Virginia, North Carolina, Tennessee, South Carolina, Georgia, Florida, Alabama, Mississippi, Arkansas, Louisiana and Texas, except the Ports of Key West, New Orleans, Port Royal and Beaufort in North Carolina, are in insurrection, and has prohibited all commercial intercourse not licensed and conducted as authorized by Congress.[5]

To mitigate the general prohibition, the President has seen fit to license limited commercial intercourse under the Regulations of the 31st. March, 1863, sanctioned by the War Department and Navy Department orders of the same date.[6]

These Regulations were framed, on full consideration of all known circumstances and all suggestions made by parties in interest, with a view to avoid all restrictions on trade not really necessary to ensure obedience to the Acts of Congress and the injunctions of the Proclamation, by preventing supplies to rebels and to residents within rebel lines, and by securing the operations of the Army against hindrances and embarassments much complained of by commanding Generals. The principle of the Regulations is enforcement of the laws—their policy, mitigation of restrictions on trade so far as compatible with the prevention of supplies to rebels.

Keeping this policy strictly in view, the river trade between the river ports of the loyal States of the Centre and the city of New Orleans, was placed at once on the same footing as the ocean trade between New Orleans and the ports of the loyal Atlantic States, as soon as the capture of Port Hudson was ascertained.[7] In the same spirit, the regulations of the 31st. of March have been undergoing careful revision, and some modifications have been introduced, which it is hoped, will prove generally beneficial / In some respects, the wishes you express in behalf of the Union Merchants Exchange will be found to have been partially anticipated; though I have not felt myself warranted to admit the change which you seem to regard as most desirable, namely, the substitution of the points of receipt and distribution in insurrectionary States, instead of the points of shipment, near these States, as the places where supervision is to be exercised. This change would, in my judgment, defeat the objects of the Act of Congress and the Proclamation. It would for example, remove all supervision from shipments at St Louis, and substitute for it such supervision as could be exercised at Helena Vicksburgh and other places in the rebel States on the Mississippi & its tributaries. It needs no argument to show that civil supervision after such a change, would be ineffectual. Nor, in my judgment, would the change secure any substantial benefits to the merchants who desire it. It would almost certainly cause serious embarrassment to military operations and lead to severe military restrictions.

I have already intimated that you are mistaken in supposing that the trade of Atlantic ports with New Orleans enjoys any favor not accorded to the river ports of the Central Valley. If any discrimination exists it is unknown to me; if any be made known it will be promptly corrected. In the administration of public trusts I know no geographical lines except those which include my country; and no distinctions except those which divide rebels and traitors and their friends, from citizens faithful to the Constitution and the Laws, and earnest in their support of the Goverment which is striving to maintain both in just supremacy throughout the Republic.

Let us hope gentlemen that Victory may continue to attend our brave armies, and that the rebellion may be speedily and permanently suppressed throughout the land. As that blessed consummation draws near, restrictions on trade will become less and less important, and therefore less and less stringent, and with its final accomplishment will alltogether disappear.

Meantime may it not be expected that liberal construction and generous support to measures believed by those charged with the grave responsibility of executing the laws to be indispensable to their due enforcement, will be given by all who, to use your own well-chosen words, "are not only willing but eager to endure whatever inconveniences, burdens and privations may be necessary to ensure, or, in any way contribute to the success of the struggle in which the country is engaged."

With pert. respect,[8]

Yours truly
S. P. CHASE

1. Samuel Miller Breckinridge was a jurist and Republican state legislator. St. Louis merchant Barton Able (1823–77) had ties to the conservative branch of the party. Tucker had served as president of the Miller's and Manufacturer's Insurance Company. Steamboat and omnibus entrepreneur Joshua Henry Alexander at one time occupied the office of city comptroller. Johnson, *Twentieth Century Biographical Dictionary,* v. 1; J. Thomas Scharf, *History of Saint Louis City and County* . . . , 2 vols. (Philadelphia, 1883), 1:604; *St. Louis Dir. (1854–55),* 194; Walter B. Stevens, *St. Louis, The Fourth City, 1764–1911,* 2 vols. (St. Louis, 1911), 2:682.

2. Breckinridge et al. to Chase, Sept. 1, 1863, copy enclosed in Breckinridge et al. to Abraham Lincoln, Sept. 3, 1863 (Lincoln Papers, L.C.).

3. Chase quoted from the committee's letter.

4. In legislation of July 13 and 31, 1861, and March 3, 1863. *Statutes at Large,* 12:257, 284, 820–21.

5. Lincoln's proclamation concerning trade was dated April 2, 1863. Basler, *Collected Works,* 6:159–60.

6. Lincoln issued the license with a statement that "partial restoration of such intercourse between the inhabitants of sundry places and sections heretofore declared in insurrection . . . and citizens of the rest of the United States, will favorably affect the public interests." Navy and War Department orders established military policy on the subject. Ibid., 6:157; *Commercial Intercourse,* 51–56.

7. On July 16, eight days after the Confederate capitulation at Port Hudson, Chase unofficially acknowledged that "The Mississippi is open." On July 23, in response to a request from William P. Mellen, Chase telegraphed instructions to surveyors of customs at Ohio River cities and at St. Louis: "Clear boats and cargoes except of prohibited articles to New Orleans if desired, taking bond not to land goods at intermediate points, except under permits authorized by existing Regulations." Chase to Nathaniel P. Banks, July 16, Chase to Henry T. Blow, July 25, 1863 (Chase Papers, Hist. Soc. of Pa.); Mellen to Chase, and Chase to surveyors of customs, July 23, 1863 (Telegrams Sent, Gen. Recs. Treasury Dept., Nat. Arch.).

8. The clerk likely misread the original. A copy of this letter in Abraham Lincoln's papers at the Library of Congress and a version printed in the *New York Times,* September 25, 1863, both give the line as: "With great respect."

TO ROBERT DALE OWEN

Letterpress copy of autograph letter. Chase Papers, Historical Society of Pennsylvania (*micro* 28:0715).

Septr. 6 3

My dear Sir,

Your note to me, with a copy of your letter to Mr. Seward, and an enclosed letter to the President came a day or two ago.[1] The letter to the President was sent to him immediately with a memorandum which, I hope, has secured its perusal. If he has not yet read it, I mean he shall, if my words have any weight with him.

I have read it with attention and *intention;* and I thank God for it. Just such an exposition, so plain, so direct, so convincing and so eloquent was greatly needed just now. That we have it is evidence that we are not to be abandoned to the unutterably loathsome infamy of consent to the reenslavement of men made free by a great National act—or rather by two great National Acts; by the Proclamation & by the Act of Congress.[2] You know how full of anxiety I have been on this subject; and you know a very little of my labors in season and out of season with the President & Secretary of War and though in less measure with other Heads of Departments. Your letter greatly lightens that anxiety; though no labor is yet to be spared nor any counted won till the rebel slave states are back in the Union as loyal free states. To make this consummation sure I hope the Loyal Publication Society will put your letter in the hands of every officer of the Army, every civil officer of the Government, every member of Congress & every member of a State Legislature.[3] I should count it an honor if My letter to the Loyal National League, stating but not arguing the same doctrine, could go along with it.[4]

Some progress has been made, for which we are in great measure indebted to Mr. Stanton to whom how much the country owes will never be known. Sometime ago he sent me Gov. Shepley's plan for the reorganization of Louisiana.[5] It proposed a Convention to frame a State Constitution or amend the old, and apportionment of the delegates to it to districts according their free white population, & was accompanied by a census of the inhabitants distinguishing them as free white, free colored & slave. I returned the plan with some written comments on the absurdity of such a census since the proclamation and suggesting that those who furnished nearly twenty to one of the volunteers could hardly be excluded decently from some representation in a body of such importance to them. Nothing was then done: but lately Gov. Shepley has been here, and has gone back with authority to make districts having regard to the number of *loyal Citizens of the United States* resident in them & to call a convention to be elected by these loyal citizens / And I believe he has taken with him one or more copies of the Attorney General's opinion on Citizenship. For the instructions we are indebted to Mr. Stanton & the President.[6] I cannot tell to whom Gov Shepley is indebted for the copies of the Opinion.

It seems to me that all our efforts should now be directed to the reorganization of the rebel states by the loyal citizens: and that no one should be counted loyal who does not sincerely and cordially accept the proclamation as the law or is not willing to join in framing a constitution & state Government on its basis. You remember that the Ordinance of 1787 declared its articles of Compact (among them the perpetual interdict against slavery, to be the basis of basis of all laws constitutions & governments which forever thereafter should be formed in the Northwest Territory.[7] Why should not the Proclamation be declared the basis of all laws, constitutions & governments in the States affected by it? What a pity that it did not embrace all rebeldom & so stand on a clear principle admitting no exception, just like the Ordinance.

Why can't you write one more letter on "What to do"? as a practical question, taking these points: The Proclamation in all parts of rebeldom included by it is law: The Act of Congress as to all slaves of persons enumerated in it or found in places previously occupied by the rebel troops—such as New Orleans, Newbern Fernandina & almost *every* other town in rebeldom, are free; that upon every theory of reorganization the Government may confide that work to citizens of the state to be reorganized; that loyal citizens alone are entitled to participate in such a work; that no man is a loyal citizen who does not acccept the Proclamation & the acts of Congress as law, and is not willing to make the principle of that, namely freedom of all, the basis of the reorganization.[8]

Mr. Heaton Special Agent from N. Carolina has been with me this morning and assures me that the people of that state within our lines are ready for such a reorganization.[9] Such is the fact also in Virginia, in Florida & in Louisiana. Why not avail ourselves of it; and by wise & prompt action now ensure the future?

Most sincerely your friend
S P Chase

Hon. Robt. Dale Owen

1. Enclosed in Owen's letter to Lincoln was an identical copy to Seward, both written on August 27, that urged slavery's permanent eradication as the foundation for Reconstruction. To Lincoln, Owen recommended this message as "one of the most important . . . now before the American people." "The vast importance of the present juncture of the subject therein treated," Owen further informed Chase, "may explain my anxious desire that it may get to the Presidents hands in such a way that he will be likely to read it." Owen to Chase, Sept. 3, 1863 (Chase Papers, Hist. Soc. of Pa.); Owen to

Lincoln, Aug. 27, Sept. 3, 1863 (Lincoln Papers, L.C.); Owen to Seward, Aug. 27, 1863, in *New York Tribune,* Sept. 3, 1863; Owen to Seward, Sept. 3, 1863, in Loyal Publication Society, *Conditions of Reconstruction,* 3–21.

2. That is, the Emancipation Proclamation and the second confiscation act, July 17, 1862. *Statutes at Large,* 12:589–92.

3. The Loyal Publication Society of New York was a private organization formed on February 14, 1863, to distribute "journals and documents of unquestionable and unconditional loyalty." Frank Friedel, "The Loyal Publication Society: A Pro-Union Propaganda Agency," *Mississippi Valley Historical Review* 26 (Dec. 1939): 360.

4. Chase referred to his letter written to George Opdyke and others on April 8, 1863 (above), which the Loyal Publication Society later published in *Conditions of Reconstruction,* 22–24. Formed earlier in the year under the leadership of John Austin Stevens, Jr., the Loyal National League was one of several major private societies in New York that promoted the Union. Guy James Gibson, "Lincoln's League: The Union League Movement during the Civil War" (Ph.D. diss., Univ. of Illinois, 1957), 204–31.

5. Chase had discussed George F. Shepley's plan in correspondence with Stanton on June 12, 1863 (above).

6. Authorized by Lincoln, Stanton had written Shepley's instructions for reorganization on August 24, 1863. For discussion of the attorney general's decision of November 1862 that declared free blacks U.S. citizens, see Chase's letter to Opdyke et al., April 8, 1863 (above). *OR,* ser. 3, v. 3:711–12.

7. In accordance with articles 5 and 6 of the ordinance. Worthington Chauncey Ford et al., eds., *Journals of the Continental Congress, 1774–1789,* 34 vols. (Washington, D.C., 1904–37), 32:342–43.

8. In correspondence to Lincoln on September 30, Owen suggested that office-holding in reconstructed states be extended only to voters who acknowledged and supported "all the laws passed by the Congress of the United States and all the Proclamations issued by the President of the United States, during the progress of the Rebellion, including the laws providing, under certain conditions, for the enfranchisement of slaves, and including also the Proclamation of January 1, 1863." Owen to Chase, Oct. 3, 1863 (Chase Papers, Hist. Soc. of Pa.); Owen to Lincoln, Sept. 30, 1863 (Lincoln Papers, L.C.).

9. Chase had appointed David Heaton to the position earlier in the year. At breakfast, Heaton reported that hostility to the Emancipation Proclamation among North Carolinians was "confined principally to the former slave owners, who wish to re-enslave the Emancipees." *Chase Papers,* 1:438; *Appletons',* 3:155.

TO HENRY C. WHITMAN

Letterpress copy of autograph letter. Chase Papers, Historical Society of Pennsylvania (*micro* 28:0792).

Washington, Sept. 12, 1863.

My dear Judge,[1]

Enclosed with this you will find a letter, which I hope is a fulfilment of Mr Stanton's promise, in regard to your son.

It rejoices my heart that you follow democratic principles in this crisis, rather than the party which audaciously assumes the name. Why cannot all democrats, who believe that slavery is not to be excepted from the application of fundamental principles, come together in a democracy worthy of success? I hoped for such a union years ago when you voted for me as Senator, though greatly preferred another, who, I am sorry to see now supports Vallandigham.[2] I have never given up the idea; though it has never been in my power to do more for its realization than talk.

Slavery seems now likely to fall, & with it will disappear the evil influence of Oligarchy. The Proclamation if resolutely adhered to & made the basis of new constitutions in the States included by it puts an end at once & forever in those states: in the Nonincluded States the People are themselves taking hold of the evil; and already in all of them except Kentucky Emancipation seems to have secured a majority of suffrages?

The End of slavery will be the beginning of the glory of the Republic.

Yours truly
S P Chase

Best regards to Mr. Kebler;[3] & better to Mrs W.

Hon H. C. Whitman

1. Whitman had served as a common pleas judge in Ohio, 1852–62. Elliot Howard Gilkey, *The Ohio Hundred Year Book: A Hand-Book of the Public Men and Public Institutions of Ohio . . .* (Columbus, 1901), 563.

2. In 1849, Whitman, then a member of the Ohio Senate, had favored William Allen (1803–79) over Chase as U.S. senator. *Chase Papers,* 2:214–15; *DAB,* 1:210.

3. John Kebler, Whitman, and F. F. Manning were legal partners in Cincinnati. *Cinc. Dir. (1863),* 215; Kebler to Chase, Mar. 4, 1862 (Chase Papers, L.C.).

FROM GEORGE S. DENISON

Letter in clerk's hand, signed by Denison. Chase Papers, Library of Congress (*micro* 28:0798).

Unofficial

New Orleans, Sept. 12, 1863.

Dear Sir,

I have the honor, to acknowledge the receipt of your letter (unofficial) of 26th August.[1]

Of late my letters have been, necessarily, hastily written and imperfect. I supposed, however, you were kept fully informed by Mr. Hutchins, and more lately by Mr. Plumly, in person.

The new regulations of which you speak have not yet reached me, but are expected by the next steamer. So far as I have observed, most of the complaints concerning the restrictions and taxes imposed come from people who are anxious to make large gain by trading with the enemy. I understand that a petition has been forwarded to you from here, asking for the removal of the five per cent tax; but I do not think this would ever have been done, had it not been for the active exertions of Mr. Sarjeant, Custom House Appraiser.[2]

Five per cent tax is collected on all shipments of supplies from this port to any point outside the city, whether for trade or family supplies. This is done by order of Mr. Flanders, with whom at first I did not agree as to the propriety of the order, but I now think it just and expedient.

The poorer class generally buy their supplies from traders who have paid their five per cent. The planters and wealthier people generally send orders to their commission merchants in the city, who make the shipments. I do not see any impropriety in regarding these transactions as trade. If, in this community, only what was for trade should be taxed, I think government would receive but little, for many people would not hesitate to ship, as for plantation use, what they really intended for sale, and, owing to the size of plantations, in most cases without detection.

The military authorities have interfered much with trade. Provost Marshal General Bowen allows nothing to go out of the city without the permit has his endorsement.[3] He allows no one to use permit to trade, except the permit be first endorsed by the Pro. Marshal of the place where the goods are to be sold, and afterward endorsed in his office. On all permits to Baton Rouge two per cent is collected by the Pro. Marshal. All cotton arriving here is taxed five dollars per bale for hospital fund. I think these unnecessary military restrictions are more vexatious to the public than all those imposed by the regulations of the Treasury Department, and I have endeavored to have them removed, and, at last, with promise of success. Gen. Bowen today informs me he will cease to interfere, but the promise is not yet fulfilled.

I have issued several permits to purchase cotton at points within our lines and below the mouth of the Red river. Considerable cotton has already arrived here and more will arrive. The guerillas in Mississippi are burning a good deal, and have captured two or three cotton traders in the vicinity of Baton Rouge, and, it is said have hanged one or two of them.

It is important that the extent of Mr. Flanders jurisdiction be defined. You intimate that his authority will have the same geographical boundaries as that of the Commanding General of this Department. General Banks informs me that his command terminates, and Gen. Grant's commences, at or near the mouth of Red river. Now the whole country up to points above Vicksburg has always drawn supplies from, and sent their produce to, this port. Any attempt to force trade out of its fixed and natural channels by turning the produce up the river, would be attended with difficulty, expense and inconvenience; though the inconvenience would not be so much felt in the country between Vicksburg and Memphis. Of the truth of these statements I am reminded every day, by persons applying for supplies for Natchez and points above which have always been supplied from here, and from which the cotton has always come hither. You are aware that the factor generally makes advances on crops, and that the planter generally spends the proceeds of his crop before it goes to market. Most of these factors lived in this city, and, claims being still unsettled, they come to me for permits to bring down their cotton. I suggested to you that Mr. Flanders district should include all South of the Northern boundary (on West side of the river) of Louisiana, said line being extended right across the State of Mississippi.[4] At any rate, it should go as high as Vicksburg or Natchez, at least,—on both sides of the river. You can tell better than myself whether this is objectionable because Mr. F's. district would then extend into two military departments; but I should think this no objection.

Under instructions from the Treasury Department, spiritous liquors have been regarded as contraband of war, and have not been allowed to be brought to this port.[5] On the first of September, the steamer Julia arrived here from Saint Louis, having on board more than one hundred bbls. whiskey, which was cleared (somewhat irregularly) from the Custom House at St. Louis.[6] I detained it in Government Warehouse, not permitting it to go into consumption, until receipt of instructions from you, when it will be delivered to claimants, or turned over to the District Attorney,[7] as you may direct. Kennedy & Co., of this city,[8] agents of the owners, have addressed a letter to you on the subject. Thirty barrels more arrived today, which was seized by Mr. Bullitt. If you have authorized the officers of Customs at Saint Louis to clear whiskey for this Department, I should like to be informed of it.

What you say of the "True Delta" is quite correct, but I am sure you overestimate the influence of that paper.[9] It makes a business of assailing all persons in office without regard to merit or demerit, and with an apparent disregard of truth. Where the character of the paper is well understood, as it is here, its influence is small. I have reason, however, for stating that no more articles will be written in the same strain; and for the reasons above mentioned, I do not think any printed explanation is necessary.

In my former letter,[10] I quoted two clauses of a proposed order of Gen. Banks, for the purchase of cotton on behalf of government; said cotton to be paid for at such a price as might be deemed sufficient. In your letter of the 26th, you say, "that these two sections correspond exactly with my own views; and I endeavored, at the last session of Congress, to obtain authority to receive property, and pay for it in the mode, and with the further provision for contingent additional payment, which he suggests. Congress, however, refused to confer this authority, and, of course, I do not feel at liberty to exercise it."[11]

I wish to be distinctly informed if you are in favor of this project being carried into execution by military order, myself or other officers of the Treasury Department attending to the execution thereof. The quotation above made merely expresses your preference for this mode, to be executed in a certain manner, and I cannot conclude therefrom that you would desire its execution in the manner proposed by Gen. Banks. It is not too late to adopt Gen. Banks's plan here. Texas will soon be occupied, and then no obstacle will be in the way of the execution of the plan.[12] Please inform me if you would approve doing this thing in the manner proposed (military order, the agents of the Treasury Department executing such orders. I deem this matter of importance.

There are three distinct ways of managing the cotton trade, each having its merits and objections. First; that the military authorities should seize all produce and turn it over to the Treasury Department. Second; that they should seize nothing, but that permits should be issued to traders to purchase it. Third; that the Government should purchase at a fair price according to Gen. Banks's proposed order. These distinct plans, or a combination of two or three of them, are, I think, the only methods whereby cotton may be brought out. This is not a subject that can be neglected and allowed to take care of itself, because heavy pecuniary interests are involved.

I have conversed with Gen. Banks upon this subject. If you approve of the adoption of his order, in the manner indicated, please inform me unofficially, and I can have it carried into effect, I have no doubt, without responsibility on your part.

I enclose, for your information, a copy of letter relating to salaries this day transmitted to Commissioner of Internal Revenue.[13]

Very Respectfully,

Your Obt. Svt.
GEORGE S. DENISON

Hon. Salmon P. Chase,
Secretary of the Treasury,
&c., &c., &c.,
Washington.

1. See Chase to Denison, August 26, 1863 (above).

2. Robert Sargeant, originally from New York. B. R. Plumly to Chase, Oct. 3, 1863 (Chase Papers, L.C.); *Register of Officers (1863)*, 95.

3. Brig. Gen. James Bowen (1808–86), provost marshal of the Department of the Gulf, was a former New York legislator. *Appletons'*, 1:336.

4. Denison made the suggestion on August 8 while visiting Memphis to settle a jurisdictional dispute between Benjamin F. Flanders and William P. Mellen. Denison to Chase, Aug. 8, 1863 (Chase Papers, L.C.); same to same, Aug. 12, 1863 (above).

5. In accordance with section 8 of "Regulations concerning internal and coastwise commercial intercourse," dated August 28, 1862 (Letters Sent Relating to Restricted Commercial Intercourse and Captured and Abandoned Property, Gen. Recs. Treasury Dept., Nat. Arch.).

6. The commercial sternwheel steamer *Julia* displaced twenty tons. Lytle, *Merchant Vessels*, 104.

7. Rufus Waples.

8. S. H. Kennedy and Company, New Orleans merchants. *New Orleans Dir. (1855)*, 131.

9. See Chase's letter of August 26 (above).

10. Denison to Chase, Aug. 12, 1863 (above).

11. Chase to Denison, Aug. 26, 1863 (above).

12. Federal troops did not pacify Texas until after the Civil War ended. In fact, not until August 20, 1866, did President Andrew Johnson formally declare the rebellion over in Texas. Long, *Civil War Day by Day*, 696–97.

13. Joseph Jackson Lewis.

TO WILLIAM G. BROWNLOW

Letterpress copy of autograph letter. Chase Papers, Historical Society of Pennsylvania (*micro* 28:0814).

Washington, Septr. 13, 1863.

My dear Sir,[1]

I thank you for your interesting letters. You will see from the Revised Regulations that I have not been unmindful of your wishes in respect to Nashville. I hope soon to have the pleasure of putting Knoxville in the same category.

It does the heart good to read your announcement of the Knoxville Whig. Please send it to me as a subscriber regularly. If your duties to it will prevent you from serving as Asst. Agent let me have somebody in your place equally faithful.

You will soon be reorganizing your State Government. It is of vast importance that it be established on such foundations as to exclude the possibility, of sympathy with rebellion becoming hereafter ascendant. I earnestly hope you will make *free labor* one of these foundations.

Tennessee is not touched by the proclamation; but the slaves of many of her rebel citizens must be free under acts of Congress.[2] The freedom of these must be respected of course. As to the rest, why not boldly inaugurate Emancipation? In all the so called seceded States except Tennessee the Proclamation has freed the slaves, and wherever our armies go or the authority of the Government is acknowledged this freedom becomes actual. In all the loyal border states strong emancipation parties exist. In Delaware & in Missouri they are sure to triumph. In Virginia & West Virginia they have already achieved success. In Maryland the struggle between the Unconditional Unionists & their opponents who also *claim* to be Union men is sharp; but emancipation is sure to prevail. Kentucky is the only state in which, through the fears of the friends of the Administration & Emancipation, the proslavery party has achieved an apparent success. Thus, with the single exception of Kentucky all the border States are committed to Emancipation. Will not Tennessee set a noble example to Kentucky? And will not you who have suffered so much & have done so much for the Union lead in this great act which will make the Union indissoluble & invincible?

Please write me your views on this subject and any other you please and believe me

Sincerely your friend
S P Chase

Rev. Wm G. Brownlow.

1. William Gannaway Brownlow of Tennessee was a Unionist leader and future governor of the state. Since late 1862, he had served as a Treasury agent in Nashville. In November 1863, he revived the "Knoxville Whig and Rebel Ventilator," a newspaper he

had previously edited until suppressed by the Confederates. Brownlow to Chase, Dec. 1, 1862 (Chase Papers, Hist. Soc. of Pa.); Ellis Merton Coulter, *William G. Brownlow: Fighting Parson of the Southern Highlands* (Knoxville, Tenn., 1971), 251; *DAB,* 3:177–78; *OR,* ser. 1, v. 23, pt. 2:524.

2. Particularly the second confiscation act, July 1862. *Statutes at Large,* 12:589–92.

TO JANET CHASE

Letterpress copy of autograph letter. Chase Papers, Historical Society of Pennsylvania (*micro* 28:0888).

Washington Septr. 19, 1863.

My darling Nettie,

You and Sister or one of you try my patience a good deal. Some time ago you wrote me that you were going to return promptly to your school &, try, this year, to make improvement which would fully satisfy my wishes. Instead of that, I learn that on the evening of the very day before your school was to open in New York you all went off from Providence to Boston, and Gov. Sprague, who tells me this, adds "I don't know their further movements."[1] This pains me very much. If your sister wanted to go to Boston & could not possibly manage to go in time to take you to New York before your school was to open, you ought to have insisted on going yourself, and should have asked Gov Sprague to have the goodness to send an escort with you to New York. Had I supposed that you would be prevented from returning by want of somebody to go with you I would have sent some one from Washington, for Mrs Macaulay had written me, particularly desiring that you should be present at the opening of the school.[2]

I am not at all certain that this letter will find you in New York but I hope it will: and I hope also most earnestly that you will now give your mind to the duties of the school & set every thing else aside.

If you and Katie could only realize how much distress it occasions me to have you treat so lightly the plain every day duties—such as that of being present when your school opens—you would, *I hope,* be more careful. I say, "I hope"—I wish I could say, "I am sure."

I have had no letter from your sister for a long time: and your last dated the 13th did not state where you were or what you intended to do

Your affe. father
S P Chase

1. Janet Chase attended a school for girls in New York operated by Mary E. Macaulay, a widow who lived on Madison Avenue. William Sprague had reported on the young women's travels in a letter written on September 15. Chase to Janet Chase, Nov. 23, 28, 1863 (below); *New York Dir. (1863),* 568; Sprague to Chase, Sept. 15, 1863 (Chase Papers, L.C.).

2. According to Macaulay's schedule, school opened on the sixteenth. In her letter to Chase, Macaulay described Nettie as "full of talent—but erratic—and must be *compell'd* to apply herself systematically— . . . It is no easy task," wrote Macaulay, "to enforce

application when a child has wrapp'd herself around one's heart as closely as she has around mine." Macaulay to Chase, Sept. 9, 1863 (Chase Papers, L.C.).

TO MURAT HALSTEAD

Letterpress copy of autograph letter. Chase Papers, Historical Society of Pennsylvania (*micro* 28:0908).

Washington, Septr. 21, 1863.

My dear Sir,

I am not responsible for the management of the war; and have no voice in it; except that I am not forbidden to make suggestions; and do so now and then when I cant help it.

You are wrong in blaming Stanton as you do.[1] You ought to allow for the great difficulties of his position and remember that it much easier to criticize than to act so as to avoid even just criticism. Nor should you forget that a war managed by a President, a commanding General,[2] and a Secretary cannot, especially when the great differences of temperament, wishes, and intellectual characteristics of these three are taken into account, reasonably be expected to be understood in the best possible manner. This condition can only be remedied by the President &, as yet, he fears the remedy most.

Don't be so impatient.

Your friend
S P Chase

M. Halstead Esq

I am anxious about Rosecrans but hope the best.[3] Last night I was looking at the maps & studying the [intervals] I could put together from the papers, in the light of such facts as had casually come to my knowledge here. It seemed to me that he might have 100,000 men together—say [(originally) after] reinforcements to Johnston & desertions &c 30,000; from John[ston] 20,000; from Buckner 10,000;[4] from paroled prisoners 15,000; from Lee and Longstreet 10,000; from all other quarters 10,000, in all 100,000. It seemed to me also that it would be seen that the best way of defending Atlanta wd be to attack Rosecrans; and that Atlanta must be defended all hazards. There appeared also to be indications, especially that of pushing forward through one of the gaps in front of Lafayette[5] that the rebel generals meant to attack. I am not therefore surprised by this mornings telegrams; or rather the telegrams of yesterday which appear this morning. I am afraid that Rosecrans has another Stone River on his hands; but trust that the Providence which protected him there will give or has given him the victory now.[6]

P.S. Since writing the above I have called at the War Dept.— No *good* news—but the bad not *so bad* as might be—failure at Sabine Pass may be soon retrieved &, I think, will be[7]—defeat (for so I fear it must be called) [south] of Chattanooga will also, I hope, be also retrieved. I find the Dept. estimate of rebel force less than 75,000— I trust it is nearer the truth than mine.

1. "The arrangement of the Government on the conscription is awful," wrote Halstead, editor of the *Cincinnati Commercial,* on August 28. "Is Lincoln absolutely and hopelessly a fool, or is Stanton?" Halstead to Chase, Aug. 28, 1863 (Chase Papers, L.C.).

2. Henry W. Halleck.

3. At the battle of Chickamauga, in which the heaviest fighting occurred September 19–20, the Army of the Cumberland, under William S. Rosecrans, faced Confederate Braxton Bragg's Army of Tennessee reinforced by troops from generals Joseph E. Johnston and James Longstreet. Long, *Civil War Day by Day,* 411–13; *New York Times,* Sept. 21, 1863.

4. Maj. Gen. Simon Bolivar Buckner commanded Confederate troops under Bragg. *DAB,* 3:236.

5. La Fayette, Ga., southwest of Chickamauga.

6. Rosecrans reported from Chattanooga on September 20: "We have met with a serious disaster; extent not yet ascertained. Enemy overwhelmed us, drove our right, pierced our center, and scattered troops there." Reporting to Stanton from Tennessee, Assistant Secretary of War Charles A. Dana declared Chickamauga "as fatal a name in our history as Bull Run." At Stone's River (Murfreesboro) on the last day of December 1862, Bragg's troops initially drove the Army of the Cumberland against the river, thus threatening the Federal army's destruction. *Chase Papers,* 1:449; Long, *Civil War Day by Day,* 302–3, 307–8; *OR,* ser. 1, v. 30, pt. 1:142–43, 192.

7. The battle of Sabine Pass, Tex., September 8, 1863, slowed the Federal advance into the Confederate southwest. After the battle of Chickamauga, defeated Federal troops under Gen. George Henry Thomas retreated northeast to Chattanooga and formed a defensive position. Long, *Civil War Day by Day,* 406–7, 412.

TO HENRY T. BLOW

Letterpress copy of autograph letter. Chase Papers, Historical Society of Pennsylvania (*micro* 28:0956).

Washington, Septr. 23, 1863.

My dear Sir,[1]

Accept my sincere thanks for your kindness in sending me the no. of the Democrat containing the article on the Report of the Committee headed by Judge Breckenridge. I think, also, that I am indebted to you for some previous vindication of my official conduct.[2]

You shall never have cause to be ashamed that you have done so. My public acts are dictated by my public duties: and I defy the utmost scrutiny of malice to show that in any instance I have been governed by considerations personal to myself.

In all my course in relation to Missouri I have nothing to regret. When the question was between rebels and loyalists I spared no labor in aid of the lamented Lyon, with whose name I then delighted to associate that of Francis P. Blair Jr.[3] When the rebel schemes were defeated and Jackson driven from the state and Gov. Gamble became the representative of the organized Union sentiment, I was prompt and cordial in my endeavors to sustain him;[4] and neither he nor the Attorney General will question the value of these endeavors. When Gov. Gamble lagged behind the Emancipation spirit in the State and more earnest men took up the cause in its more advanced progress, I should have belied all my antecedents had I not sympathized with the Progressives; though sympathy, I am sorry to say, was pretty much all I had to give them. For this sympathy, however, I am now assailed. So be it. I shall go on quietly performing my duty.

The truth, however, is transparent to anyone willing to see. The act of Congress of July 13, 1861 interdicted *all trade* with insurrectionary states & forfeited all goods going either way with the vehicles carrying them except under Licence of the President & the Regulations of the Secretary of the Treasury. The Licence of the President, under *all the trade that exists* is allowed, was suggested & drawn by me and all the Regulations under which it has been conducted, except the Local Regulations of Agents have been framed by me.[5] I early adopted the maxim, Let Commerce follow the Flag, and both Licence and Regulations have been *in mitigation* of the *Non-Intercourse* decreed by Congress.[6] And as circumstances have permitted the mitigation has been mitigated, and will continue to do so. The clamor of selfishness and political malice will neither hasten or retard that mitigation one jot. When rebellion ends the restrictions made necessary by it—(there is now just so much restriction & no more—) will cease and no one will be more rejoiced than I.

One word only on another point—I have never enquired as to the personal likes or dislikes of any agent I have appointed. Most of them are strangers to me personally. All I ask of them is that they faithfully sustain the measures which the President has adopted for the suppression of the Rebellion & give their cordial support to the loyal men of the sections of country in which they may be called to work.

Perhaps I ought not to have written this letter. But I have yielded to the impulse which prompted it. Let it go.

Very cordially & faithfully

Yours
S P CHASE

Hon H. T. Blow.

1. Blow, a St. Louis merchant, was also a member of Congress beginning in March 1863. *Bio. Dir. U.S. Cong.*, 636.

2. Chase responded to the committee on September 3 (above). In commentary published on September 18, the *Daily Missouri Democrat* had criticized the group's final report for "furnishing the Conservative press of this city a text for gross attacks upon Secretary Chase. The zeal with which they rush to the assault," claimed the article, "proves clearly that they wanted nothing more than a pretext for attacking him, and strongly confirms the suspicion that the entire movement was managed by a few persons with a view to create a prejudice against the Secretary of the Treasury for political purposes." Early in

August, Blow had sent Chase warning of the committee's alleged motives. Blow to Chase, Aug. 4, 5, 1863 (Chase Papers, L.C.).

3. Brig. Gen. Nathaniel Lyon commanded Union forces in St. Louis from May 1861 until his death three months later. A former Republican congressman from Missouri, Blair ultimately held the rank of major general in the Union Army. *DAB,* 2:333, 11:534–35.

4. State officials with secessionist leanings had fled Missouri in June 1861. On July 31 of that year, members of the Missouri state convention replaced incumbent Gov. Claiborne Fox Jackson, a Confederate sympathizer, with Hamilton Rowan Gamble, a Conditional Unionist. *DAB,* 7:120–21, 9:538.

5. See Chase's September 3 letter to the St. Louis committee (above).

6. That is, legislation enacted on July 13, 1861, and amended on May 20, 1862. *Statutes at Large,* 12:255–58, 404–5.

FROM HORACE GREELEY

Autograph letter on letterhead stationery. Chase Papers, Historical Society of Pennsylvania (*micro* 28:1042).

Private.

Office of The Tribune,
New York, Sept. 29, 1863.

Dear Sir:

I have hoped to visit Washington this Autumn, but do not now see any chance of doing so before the 1st of December or thereabout. But my late partner (as stockholder in The Tribune) and always devoted friend, Mr. Benj. F. Camp, recently came home from the South, and presented some views with regard to next President, which impel me to seek a confidential talk with you[1]—or rather *to* you, for I do not desire any response. I only wish you to understand me clearly: nothing more.

I know no man in our country who is in my view better qualified for President than yourself, nor one whom I should more cordially support. Yet I am by nature a devotee of ideas, of principles, of measures, and accustomed to regard men merely as means to ends. It does not seem credible to me that a great man should much care to be or not to be President: hence Webster was all his later life one of my deep enigmas.[2] In '60, I heartily supported Judge Bates,—with a perfect understanding that there could never be any sympathy or cordiality between us—because I thought him the man of all men best calculated to bridge over our National transition from the side of Slavery to that of Liberty without provoking a desperate and bloody Civil War. I knew he was an Old Fogy; but I thought him for that reason just the man to maintain a powerful body at the South throughout our passage through the dreaded state of transition before us. Men insisted that I had quarreled with Seward, and, *therefore* took the course I did to defeat him; when in fact I liked him (not his gang) as well as ever, and would have nominated and elected him if I could have done so without risking a reign of anarchy and bloodshed in the country and of corruption (not *his*) and profligacy at the Capital. That was all there was of my anti-Seward issue. By-and-by, I shall talk this all over with Gov. Seward himself—should we both live.

You know that our National sky looks darker to me than to most others. I see men intent on what we shall do, after 1864 if the War is not finished meantime. In *my* view, if the Rebellion is not put down meantime, the Government goes to the Copperheads at the next Presidential Election, and no earthly power can prevent it. On the other hand, should we *promptly*—that is, within six or eight months—put down the Rebellion and uproot its pestilent cause, I *think* we may retain our hold on power. But be sure the Rebellion will be put down during the present term, or it will never be.

If in 1864 I could *make* a President (not merely a candidate) you would be my first choice. Yet it may be that I shall see, six months hence—what I do not now see—that the National existence and well-being requires a concentration of our strength on some one else. In that case, I shall put the country first and individual preferences no where.

Frankly Yours,
HORACE GREELEY.

Hon. S. P. Chase.

1. Camp, a New York builder, delivered this letter to Chase on October 2. *Chase Papers,* 1:459.
2. Daniel Webster.

FROM NORTON S. TOWNSHEND

Autograph letter. Chase Papers, Historical Society of Pennsylvania (*micro* 28:1046).

Private

Avon Septr 29th 1863

Hon S. P. Chase
My dear friend.

Through your kindness in procuring for me a "Leave of absence" I am able to write you from home[1]— The *Leave* did not reach N.O. until the 2nd. of Septr & then because all the steamboats had been taken for the Texas expedition I could not get passage up the River until the 8th. Our progress on the River was so slow owing to the low stage of water that I could not reach Cleveland before the 18th the last day of the State Fair. When I reached home I was quite sick with jaundice & one of the thinest & yellowest men you ever saw— To reach N.O by the 1st of Octr when my leave expired I should have been compelled to return turn about & journey back from Cleveland without visiting my home at all. I reached home on the 19th quite sick & have scarcely been able to leave the house yet, though two days since I felt obliged to go to Cleveland &

obtain a certificate of my sickness from an army surgeon on which to found an application for an extension of my leave— I have mailed the application today & think it will be granted

In your kind letter of the 18th. ult. you ask me for as much information in detail as I can furnish of the state of affairs in New Orleans[2]— If I were well enough to write at length, I could furnish some facts bearing on two or three important points which I will mention & leave the detail until I see you or am better able to write— The foremost and deepest conviction which I have recieved regards the necessity of mending the President's patchwork proclamation— The exception from its effects of all parts of Louisiana held by Union troops is a great injustice & a great inconvenience & it has this ridiculous look it applies to all localities where we have no means of enforcing it while every place where we could enforce it is excepted from its application & there the worst kind of traitors (viz, those who have taken the oath of allegiance to save their property) enjoy their slaves in spite of our efforts to enlist or conscript them

Another conviction at which I have arrived is that there are not enough loyal white citizens to make a State government without the aid of the loyal blacks—there are doubtless a few good men like Mr Flanders—Judge Hiestand & Mr Durand[3] but I think there are ten times as many open or concealed secesh— I know of no way to keep the State loyal but to open the elective franchise to the blacks all of whom almost are true friends of the Fed Govt & infinitely superior to the white aristocracy in business capacity & general morality. Cant the military governor authorize an election for the choice of delegates to form a new constitution for the State & give to all citizens alike black or white a vote in the choice of those delegates? It is time the blacks of Louisiana were secure in their persons & had the common rights of property, education & legal & political equality.

I trust no attempt at reconstruction will be made in Louisiana or any other slave state without considering the interests & rights of the colored people slave & free— I dont believe that God will show himself on the side of this nation until all our oppressions of the African race have been repented of & reparation to some extent made / The colored people of Louisiana are a very interesting people & the pleasantest work I have found in New Orleans has been in their Sunday Schools Day schools & churches—

Yours truly
N. S. Townshend

1. Earlier in the year, Townshend, a physician and former antislavery politician from Ohio, had received an appointment as a U.S. Army medical inspector at New Orleans. He was also president of the Ohio State Board of Agriculture. During August he asked Chase to obtain a leave of absence from Edwin M. Stanton so that Townshend could

attend the Ohio State Fair in Cleveland, September 16–18. *Appletons',* 6:151; Townshend to Chase, Aug. 26, 1863 (Chase Papers, Hist. Soc. of Pa.); *Cleveland Plain Dealer,* Sept. 16–18, 1863.

2. "I feel exceedingly solicitous to have a Convention called of the loyal men, and Louisiana restored to the Union as a Free State," explained Chase. Chase to Townshend, Aug. 18, 1863 (Chase Papers, Hist. Soc. of Pa.).

3. New Orleans Unionists Ezra Heistand and Thomas Jefferson Durant, attorney general of Louisiana since June and, later in the year, commissioner of registration. *DAB,* 5:543; Durant to Emerson Etheridge, Nov. 6, 1863 (Chase Papers, L.C.); McCrary, *Lincoln and Reconstruction,* 161–62, 168.

TO JANET CHASE

Letterpress copy of autograph letter. Chase Papers, Historical Society of Pennsylvania (*micro* 28:1054).

Washington, Sept 30, 1863

My darling Nettie,

You want just one word: there is only one which comes near expressing my feeling for you & that is *love.* Take it, darling.

I bought a beautiful writing table for you the other day, which is your birthday present from me.[1] How old *we* grow!

Those little girls you write about are not *much* smarter or more political than you were at the same age: but it is so far back that you have forgotten. You were "preco*c*ious" too. Mind, I spell precocious, preco*c*ious—not preco*s*ious. Overhaul your dictionary, and "when found make a note of it."[2]

Your affe. father
S P Chase

1. Janet Chase had turned sixteen years of age on September 19, 1863. "Family Memoranda" (Chase Papers, L.C.).

2. A phrase often used by Captain Cuttle in Charles Dickens's *Dombey and Son* (London, 1846–48), which was available in various editions.

TO JOSHUA LEAVITT

Letterpress copy of autograph letter. Chase Papers, Historical Society of Pennsylvania (*micro* 29:0139).

Strictly Private

Washington, Oct. 7, 1863.

My dear friend,[1]

Receive my warm thanks for your kind, generous, warmhearted, old time letter.[2]

And do not mistake me. If I know my own heart a judicial would be more *agreeable* to my personal feelings than *any* political position. So I have felt for years; but Providence has kept me hitherto, in political positions; and I now think I have done more good than I could have effected on the bench. And so I think, also, concerning the future. Perhaps I am overconfident; but I really feel as if, with God's blessing, I *could* administer the Government of this country, so as to secure and *imperdibilize* (there's a new word for you)[3] our institutions; and create a party, fundamentally & thoroughly democratic, which would guarantee a succession of successful administrations. I may be overconfident, I say; and I shall take it as a sign that I am, if the People do not call for me, and I shall be content.

God does not need any of us;—and I know very well that His world & work will go on, whether I live or die, just as He pleases to order. He is working now; and oh! how sublimely! He has come down to plead the cause of the poor and the needy and is compelling the wrath—*and the weakness*—of man to praise Him. What mad wrath of the traitors! What compromising weakness [in] attempted suppression of treason! What demands to "let my people go"! What hesitation—half decision—retraction! What *plagues!* What faltering consent at last![4] I tremble when I think how little People or Administration yet realize of the dread significance of the grand march of events.

In the midst of such things I dare not *ask* any thing except to work in my place, whatever that place may be. I assert no claim—I only recognize obligation. Neither friends nor country owe me any thing. I owe to them all that I can do for both.

And there I leave the matter. I know that very many of the best and truest men of our land desire that my services may be required in the highest office of administration: and there seems to be a general popular confidence in me which warrents the belief that those desires might be realized without any very extraordinary exertions. But I shall not complain if these exertions are not put forth. I shall have no right to complain—*no* right and, I hope, *less* inclination.

There, you have my ideas, roughly & hastily dashed down. Consider them indulgently & believe me

Your old friend
S P Chase

Rev. Dr. Leavitt

1. A Congregational clergyman, abolitionist, and doctor of divinity, Leavitt had edited the New York *Independent* since 1848. Chase to Leavitt, Jan. 24, 1864 (below); *DAB,* 11:84–85.

2. Leavitt's letter of September 30 expressed support for Chase as chief justice, instead of president. Leavitt to Chase, Sept. 30, 1863 (Chase Papers, L.C.).

3. A variant of the obsolete adjective "imperdible," indicating permanence. J. A. Simpson and E. S. C. Weiner, eds., *The Oxford English Dictionary,* 2d ed., 20 vols. (Oxford, 1989), 7:708.

4. Chase alluded to ancient Israel's flight from Egypt. Exod. 8–12.

TO HORACE GREELEY

Letterpress copy of autograph letter. Chase Papers, Historical Society of Pennsylvania (*micro* 29:0172).

Washington, Oct. 9, 1863.

My dear Sir,[1]

It was my duty to reply promptly to your last letter.[2] My only plea in mitigation of censure is the constant pressure of perplexing duties which, as Mr. Wirt used to say, put me "out of tune for decent correspondence".[3] I am still "out of tune" but I must not longer omit this duty.

Be assured that I appreciate fully the patriotic spirit in which your letter was written. No man has a right to ask a moments consideration, when public interests require that it should be withheld: and I think I can truly say that I have never hesitated to give way to others or even to put others forward where I might have taken myself the place of prominence, when the good of the cause of Freedom & Just Government seemed to require it. I hope that I love our country and the cause of Human Progress, so intimately connected with the fate of our country, too well to allow any personal wishes or aspirations, from which I do not claim to be more free than other men, to interfere with any duty to her or it.

I am proud of your approval and your preference. It is a great reward for the little I have done to have it. No man has so powerfully promoted the increase of just sentiments concerning political and social rights and duties as you have, through speech and press. Postage Reform, the Homestead, Liberality towards Immigrants, Freedom of the Territories, Constitutional Emancipation, and all kindred movements, have found in you an advocate, animated by genuine principle and therefore steadfast amid the changing currents of expediency. The immense audiences which have heard your voice through the Tribune have been constantly inspired by generous & progressive sentiment. Because of this I greatly value your approval; and that confidence which induces you to express a preference for me as the next Union candidate for the Chief Magistracy. Should circumstances justify your final action in accordance with this preference and should it be my fortune (which does not seem probable enough to affect me much) to be called to that responsible position I shall take to it whatever capacity God has given me, and just the same spirit & industry which I have brought to other duties. Should the choice fall on another I shall retire to private life equally content to devote myself to its less conspicuous but not less healthful duties.

Your suggestions in a preceding letter were promptly attended to. Indeed I had before urged repeatedly on Mr. Stanton and the President substantially the same views, and you will have observed a gradual progress towards their complete adoption.[4] Mr. Stanton is thoroughly in earnest; Mr. Lincoln, with sentiments which divide him between the border state and the progressive policy, advances slowly but yet advances. On the whole, when we think of the short time, and immense distance in the matter of Personal Freedom, between the 1st of March 1861 & the 1st of October 1863 the progressives cannot be dissatisfied with results.

I wish the war could be more efficiently & more economically conducted: but see little ground to hope for much improvement, so long as divided counsels prevail in its conduct. I say conduct for, as you are doubtless aware, there is no such thing in Washington as an Administration in the accepted sense of the word. There is a Heptarchy or seven Administrations—State, Treasury, War, Navy, Interior, Post Office, Law. All except the third are left, almost absolutely to their several Heads, each of whom is expected to "run his machine" as well as he can. The War comes under a divided Jurisdiction. The President, Mr. Stanton and Gen Halleck, each take part in the conduct of military operations as well as in the organization & administration of the army. Nobody else has more than an incidental and casual influence. I cannot think this divided Headship is best, but see not how it can be remedied.

I will not bore you with another sheet, but stop just here

Yours most truly
S P Chase

1. The recipient can be inferred from the letter's contents, including allusions to letters from Greeley, and the index of the bound volume of letterpress copies that contains the original.

2. Greeley to Chase, Sept. 29, 1863 (above).

3. Chase referred to his law mentor, William Wirt.

4. On August 30, Greeley had suggested a plan to allow payment of Federal bounty funds to loyal slaveholders who permitted their slaves to enlist and then granted them freedom. The War Department implemented similar policies on October 3. Greeley to Chase, Aug. 30, 1863 (Chase Papers, Hist. Soc. of Pa.); *OR*, ser. 3, v. 3:816, 861.

TO JOHN J. CISCO

Letterbook copy in clerk's hand. Letters Sent, Loan Division, Records of the Bureau of the Public Debt (Record Group 53), National Archives (*micro* 29:0245).

Treasury Department.
Oct. 17th. 1863.

Sir,

The letter of the Treasury Note Loan Committee to you of the 14th. instant was laid before me on my return to day.

In reply will you have the goodness to state to the Committee that the Treasury Notes to be issued to the subscribers to the recent loan are regarded as evidences of public debt, and that all public debt is expected to be paid when due in lawful money of the United States.

I hope that when these notes become due, nothing will be regarded as lawful money except gold and silver and their equivalents issued by the United States.

It is impossible however to foresee the future. It may be that some emergency will exist which will require the payment of the Treasury Notes in U.S. Notes made legal tender by law.

The Notes of the National Banking Associations have not been made legal tender, and the subscribers to the Loan will therefore not be expected to receive them in payment unless they desire so to do.

Yours truly
S. P. CHASE.

John J. Cisco. Esq.

TO JOHN CONNESS

Letterbook copy of letter in clerk's hand, signed by Chase.
Historical Society of Pennsylvania (*micro* 29:0256).

October 18th, 3.

My dear Sir,

Yours from Chicago reached me yesterday on my return from Ohio.[1] I went there to vote and found a reception such as I had not dreamed of; was almost forced to Indianapolis, where the people gave me another welcome such as I cannot forget. I had supposed that while my part of the work was receiving full, if not undue, consideration from the business community, it was too quiet to attract much attention from the masses; but I found it appreciated by everybody to a degree which made me actually ashamed of myself—comparing my work with the value set on it.[2]

You are unjust to Sumner. You ought to have read his entire speech. It is a repository of all the information extant on the subject he discusses, and has great value as such. It will besides do us good abroad. When I first read it, I felt the apprehensions you express; but I am now satisfied they had no sufficient warrant. The London Star—which has alone among the great dailies stood by us—comments on it in a tone which makes me certain that it strengthens our friends abroad and alarms our enemies. Sumner has his faults; but of whom must not this be said? He has also rare virtues—and he has eloquence and learning. Don't allow yourself to be prejudiced against him by those qualities which his associations with the literary aristocracy—unlike our associations with the practical working men of the land and its institutions—have given him; but take his real worth and real attainments and real abilities, and let them have their place in the battle against treason and its accomplices; and let him do his share of the work in his way, while you and I do our share in our way.

My apprehensions of intervention are not serious. The great victories in the recent elections prove that the people are in earnest; and will push on the war and will maintain the integrity of the Republic against home traitors.[3] Vigor and efficiency in the field will secure us against foreign enemies. I long for more of both; and hope you will do your share toward giving us more. I don't like "bold retreats." Give us "bold advances."

I wish you had spoken in Ohio and Pennsylvania during the late-closed contest. You would have found *such welcome and such hearing* as you never had before.

When will you be in Washington? Have you provided yourself with Winter quarters.

Some friends in California write that you are supposed there to be obtaining removals and securing appointments in the interest of Gen. Banks for the succession.[4] If this were true, I should only regret it so far as I think any such special object, just now, must create the divisions you so justly condemn. The General deserves his friends; and among the men from whom the next choice must be made he holds such a place that no one should or could feel that any other had been wronged by a preference for him. Most sincerely do I wish that in so grave a matter as the selection of a candidate for the Chief Magistracy all petty jealousies could be laid aside, and the choice made solely with reference to the qualities needed in the time of trial which is to come on us immediately after the compressions of the War which now holds our political organization together, shall be relaxed and broken off.

Yours most truly
S. P. Chase

Hon. John Conness,
Solon Mills, Illinois.[5]

1. Written on October 12, the letter criticized a speech on U.S. relations with Britain and France that Senator Charles Sumner of Massachusetts had delivered at New York's Cooper Union on September 10. "I cannot help regarding the speech as mischievous, . . ." wrote Conness. "It appears to me that as we are not able to fight all the world at once we should not scold like a very shrew at the world." Conness to Chase, Oct. 12, 1863 (Chase Papers, L.C.); *New York Times,* Sept. 11, 1863.

2. State elections were held on October 13. From October 10 to the sixteenth, Chase visited Ohio and Indiana to vote and to campaign for Republican candidates. Speeches he made on the tour were published, under the auspices of the Union League of America, as a pamphlet entitled *"Going Home to Vote."* Chase to Edward D. Mansfield, Oct. 18, 1863 (below); Salmon P. Chase, *"Going Home to Vote." Authentic Speeches of S. P. Chase, Secretary of the Treasury, during his Visit to Ohio . . .* (Washington, D.C., 1863).

3. In recent balloting, Union candidates had swept state elections throughout the North and secured control of the U.S. Congress. Allan Nevins, *The War for the Union,* 4 vols. (New York, 1959–71), 3:177–79.

4. "There may be no truth in these rumors," wrote special agent Thomas Brown from San Francisco, "but it is *certain* that they have grown out of threats made by Senator Conness." *Appletons',* 1:411; Brown to Chase, Sept. 21, 1863 (Chase Papers, L.C.).

5. Elected earlier in the year to represent California in the U.S. Senate, Conness was spending time in Illinois and elsewhere while en route to Washington, where the first session of the Thirty-eighth Congress would open on December 7. Conness to Chase, Oct. 12, 24, 29, 1863 (Chase Papers, L.C.); *Bio. Dir. U.S. Cong.*, 175, 818.

TO EDWARD D. MANSFIELD

Letterpress copy of autograph letter. Chase Papers, Historical Society of Pennsylania (*micro* 29:0259).

October 18th 3

My dear friend,[1]

I seize a moment to write you a few lines.

Never in my life have I felt such emotions as were excited by my recent visit to Ohio and Indiana.[2]

I went out expecting to vote for the Union Ticket and so discharge a single duty. It had been told us here in Washington that there was possibility of failure at the polls; and so I took pains to see that all in my Department who had a right to vote should go home, & thinking that example was the best precept determined to go myself. I little imagined the reception that awaited me.

The best of it was that it was entirely spontaneous and popular. The masses seemed to move of themselves. And it was wonderful to me that so many people whom I never supposed to know any thing of my work seemed to understand it perfectly and to appreciate it at a higher rate than myself.

Such appreciation & such manifestation of warm personal esteem—moved me deeply. I cannot tell you how grateful I am for them. All the time I ask myself what can I do to deserve them.

Not among the least of my gratifications was the cordial recognition I experienced from the Press. As you have opportunity I hope you will assure Mr. Smith and the other gentlemen of the Gazette that I shall never forget their kindness.[3]

I have just been reading your letter to the Times of Oct. 2. It is very clear & able.[4] But is it quite correct to say that "a system of Finance must relate mainly to the the three elements capital, currency & credit." Can transactions or business be properly comprehended under either or all of these heads? And is it not transactions or business which mainly determines the quantities of currency acquired and so controls the workings of financial systems at all given periods? Suppose that in 1830 the condition of business was so benumbed as to require only 5½ dollars for each individual of the population. then 5½ for 1 was as much as 12 for 1 in 1853, supposing the condition of business then to require only that amount. Now all transactions are for money & hence no redundancy.

You are right as to the gold product and as to the ability of the government to control it. I cannot but regret however to observe the general tendency to believe that as we have got along so well thus far we must continue to get along no matter what my happen. But this is not so. By seizing (so to speak the currency of the country for the use of the Government & thus checking measurably bank expansion I did great good in more ways than one. I imparted solidity to transactions which established confidence & I obtained for the Government a great resource almost without cost. But this resource is now exhausted. The Govt. currency cannot be increased safely. The National Bank Currency can only be introduced by the withdrawal of a part of the Govt. or a part of the state Bank Circulation. But this is aside from my main object. What I mean is simply that the Govt. can no longer borrow without interest to any appreciable extent. And payment of interest necessitates taxes. We now get gold only from import duties. Suppose a revenue from this source of 75,000,000. You once demonstrated I think that it could not exceed a certain ratio to capital & population—say 85,000 000 under the Census of 1860. Suppose 75,000,000. Take 15,000,000 for *expences* which must be met in coin—diplomatic intercourse, navy on foreign stations & the like—and the remainder is 60,000,000. Now suppose an interest bearing debt 6% debt of 1000,000,000; and you suppose the exhaustion of your means to pay the interest. Here is one danger. Capitalists must see it. Hence more danger still in depreciation of currency and securities together.

I have just given you roughly what most disquiets me. I should fear nothing if we had An *Administration* in the first sense of the word guided by a bold, resolute, farseeing, & active mind, guided by an honest, earnest heart. But this we have not. Oh! for energy & economy in the management of the War. But how can we have it with these heads? But I must stop.

Your friend
S P Chase

Hon E. D. Mansfield.

1. Mansfield edited the *Cincinnati Gazette,* 1857–80. *DAB,* 12:255.

2. Chase also discussed his visit to Ohio and Indiana, October 10–16, in correspondence with John Conness on October 18 (above).

3. Richard Smith was affiliated with the *Cincinnati Gazette. Appletons',* 5:584.

4. Mansfield's correspondence, written on October 2, appeared in the *New York Times* on October 17 with his customary signature as "A Veteran Observer." In the letter, Mansfield minimized inflationary dangers from an oversupply of currency and pointed with reassurance to recent infusions of California gold which, according to him, served as a reserve in support of paper money. "It is *credit,*" he declared, "which is expanded and causes inflation." *DAB,* 12:255.

TO JANET CHASE

Letterpress copy of autograph letter. Chase Papers, Historical Society of Pennsylvania (*micro* 29:0325).

Washington Oct. 21, 1863.

Darling Nettie,

I enclose this note with $90 to Mrs Macaulay because I do not want to do anything concerning you while under her care except with the sanction of her judgment.

Katie and you talked over the matter of allowance. Katie thinks $300 enough for clothing & I add $60 for incidentals: making $75 for clothing and $15 for incidentals each quarter. The check now sent is for fall quarter—1 Sep to 1 Decr. You shall the next sometime in December.

If you take charge of your own affairs in this way you must consult Mrs. Macaulay in what you do; & be very careful not to spend beyond your means. You must make no debts & keep within your allowance at all events.

Your affe. father
S P Chase

Miss Nettie Chase

TO ROBERT B. WARDEN

Letterpress copy of letter in clerk's hand, signed by Chase. Chase Papers, Historical Society of Pennsylvania (*micro* 29:0373).

October 23d, 3.

My dear Judge,[1]

Yours of the 20th is just received and touches me deeply. The loss of your noble son moves my profoundest sympathies, and it is fit that just such a monument as your book will make for him should be constructed by your hands.[2] Is it the will of God that the precious blood poured out in this terrible struggle shall nourish the vine which he planted in America to a fresher and nobler growth! I reverently hope so. The effects of the fiery trial to your mind and many other spirits of like reach and culture confirm the hope. It is a real gratification to be assured that any words of mine have contributed to your present convictions.

I was never an Abolitionist of that school which taught that there could never be a human duty superior to that of the instant and unconditional abolition of slavery. He who sees the tower in the quarry and the oak in the acorn requires no impossible task from his creatures. But for more than half my life, I have been an Abolitionist of that other school which believed slave holding wrong, and that all responsible for the wrong should do what was possible for them, in their respective spheres, for its redress. I shall be very glad to see your book.

Hon. R. B. Warden,
Cincinnati, Ohio

Sincerely your friend
S. P. CHASE

1. A former common pleas judge and, briefly, justice of the state supreme court, Warden practiced law in Ohio. *DAB,* 19:444.

2. Sgt. Ernest Warden (1844–63) of the 83rd Ohio Volunteer Infantry died on May 15 during the siege of Vicksburg. Robert Warden had written Chase of his intention to publish a manuscript entitled *Ernest and the Flag he Followed.* "Since Ernest's death," wrote Warden, "my eyes have been opened wonderfully, and at last I am an Abolitionist of the new school developed by the rebellion." Elsewhere in the letter, Warden complimented Chase on his "grand and beautiful expression of a noble doctrine" in a recent Cincinnati speech. Warden also declared a preference for keeping "rebellious states" in the Union with slavery abolished, but he foresaw a possibility of putting them out altogether and creating free states to replace them. *OR,* ser. 1, v. 24, pt. 2:37; Warden to Chase, Oct. 20, 1863 (Chase Papers, L.C.); William A. Warden, *The Ancestors, Kin and Descendants of John Warden and Narcissa (Davis) Warden, His Wife . . .* (Worcester, Mass., 1901), 124.

FROM WILLIAM TECUMSEH SHERMAN

Autograph letter. Letters Received from Executive Officers (AB Series), General Records, Department of the Treasury (Record Group 56), National Archives (*micro* 29:0434).

Head Qrs. Army of the Tennessee.
Iuka Miss. Oct 25. 1863.

Hon S. P. Chase.
Sec. U.S. Treasury. Washington DC.
Dear Sir

By the vicissitude of war, I am again forced into the command of a Department.[1] I almost shrink from a command that involves me with Civil matters which I do not understand. Politics or the means to influence a Civil Poeple are mysteries I do not comprehend, but am forced to act.

Matters involving the navigation of Our Great Rivers must necessarily fall somewhat under my jurisdiction but I assure you I have no inclination to influence the officers of your Department.

I extract parts of a letter I have just written to Admiral Porter at Cairo which express my general opinions on the main points.[2]

"My notions about the Mississippi are these. We must never again allow the enemy to make a lodgement on its Banks with artillery: and therefore Columbus,[3] Memphis, Vicksburg and Mouth of Yazoo must be held with troops. All else may be trusted to your Gun boats and a surplus force kept at Memphis and Vicksburg available to float to any threatened point to prevent a lodgement.

Through traffic on large steamboats manned and properly officered should be encouraged by all means. Each boat might be required to carry a Gun, 25 muskets and men, and a Musket proof Barricade at each Bow & Quarter from which to fire. Also the boilers might be better sheltered.

Regular Packets should be encouraged to keep up daily and rapid communication which increases a feeling of security. It brings private Enterprise to aid the General Purpose, viz uninterrupted navigation of the River.

Trading Boats will of course be regulated by the Treasury Department. I dont see as we have any Right to interfere further than as to "Contraband of War", and to make this more clear you & I ought to say what is "Contraband of War". The Term is very indefinite, but I am clear of opinion that the Laws of War give the Army and Navy a Legal Right to protect themselves against Contraband Traffic and its agents. Merchants as a Class are governed by the Law of Self Interest and the temptation to import and sell Contraband goods is so great that many will engage in it, but this is confined to a Class of men that you & I know well. The Real Merchant, the Man who loves his Country as we do, would not ask to send down the River Arms and Ammunition or anything that would endanger our lives or the lives of Our Command. There are some things such as salt for curing meats, medicines for curing wounds & sickness that I am not so clear about, and care less.

If you will prepare a list of Contraband and send it to Secretary Chase I know he will make it public, and save us a world of trouble

I have announced in orders that any officer of my Command who makes a Cent of profit by selling permits, passes, &c, or by any species of Trade, & speculation is corrupt and criminal.[4] I hear of such things but really find few or no real cases, but I must stop scandal. Also I contend I have a right to impress for Military service any men who have run from the North and come here to make a living and avoid the Draft. I will pick up a few such and this will stop that Class of meddlers and unauthorized hangers on that has given us so much trouble."

I beg to convey to you direct these ideas, with the assurance that I wish to make all my acts conform to the Law & Policy of the Govt. whatever it may be, only like many other poeple having my own notions I find it easier to execute them.

With great respect

Yr obt Servt.
W. T. SHERMAN

Maj Genl. vols.

1. On October 24, Sherman succeeded Grant as commander of the Army of the Tennessee. Long, *Civil War Day by Day,* 425.

2. Rear Adm. David Dixon Porter, U.S.N., commanded the Mississippi Squadron. *DAB,* 15:87.

3. Columbus, Ky.
4. Outlined in General Orders No. 2, issued on October 25, 1863. *OR*, ser. 1, v. 31, pt. 1:731.

TO EDWARD D. MANSFIELD

Letterpress copy of autograph letter. Chase Papers, Historical Society of Pennsylvania (*micro* 29:0463).

Washington, Oct. 27, 1863.

My dear friend,

Yours of 21st is just received. I fear the substitution of Thomas for Rosecrans was well warranted:[1] but I knew nothing of it till after it was made: nor more of its reasons than anybody could find in the papers, till Mr. Stanton mentioned various grounds to me today. Among other things he mentioned the statement of an officer whom we both know & in whom we both have confidence concerning Gen. R——s action or rather non action after his centre was broken, which amazed as much as it pained me. In my judgt. the whole matter should be made a subject of investigation immediately either by order or by the Generals demand for a Court of Enquiry.

Your comments on Charleston express in the main my own views.[2]

Ditto as to Mr. M. Blair.[3] But I cant agree with you that the President should take no sides in what are called local questions. He ought to be known distinctly as on the side of the Unconditional Union men and support them heartily in every practicable way. They are all for Emancipation where slaves remain to be emancipated and all for the exclusion of slavery where the Proclamation has (as I understand its sense & purpose) abolished it. These are the only local questions now-adays. Around these all other local questions turn.

And why do you talk about a Cabinet? Blair is P.M. General but not a member of the Cabinet for there is no Cabinet to be a member of. You have been in Washington and you know that each Head of a Department is expected to "run his own machine," as Mr. Lincoln expresses it. And each runs his machine, without any help of the others, pretty much as he pleases; and no one knows, except as matter of news, what either of the others are doing. The President & General Halleck however, do help carry on the war.

I confess I don't like these separate Administrations: but the glorious people will take us through if they have even a moderate chance. All I fear is that even the chance may not be given: for exhaustion through delay, mismanagement, and waste is not impossible.

Wont you be here at the wedding. Do come and bring your daughter.[4]

Faithfully yours
S P Chase

Hon E D Mansfield.

1. Mansfield's letter criticized the War Department's decision, on October 17, to relieve Rosecrans from command of the Army of the Cumberland and replace him with George Henry Thomas, major general of volunteers, who during October was made a brigadier general in the regular army. Mansfield to Chase, Oct. 21, 1863 (Chase Papers, L.C.); Long, *Civil War Day by Day,* 423; *DAB,* 18:433.

2. Mansfield had expressed alarm over Federal inability to take Charleston, S.C. Mansfield to Chase, Oct. 21, 1863 (Chase Papers, L.C.).

3. In his letter of October 21, Mansfield had complained about a speech delivered by Postmaster General Montgomery Blair in Rockville, Md., October 3, which assailed radical Republicans for making "the manumission of the slaves the means of infusing their blood into our whole system." *New York Times,* Oct. 11, 17, 1863; *Daily National Intelligencer,* Oct. 6, 1863.

4. Chase referred to the impending marriage of his daughter Kate and William Sprague on November 12. Mansfield had three surviving daughters: Elizabeth Phipps Mansfield (b. 1843), Eleanor Strode Mansfield (b. 1845), and Margaret-Edith Mansfield (b. 1853). Horace Mansfield, *The Descendants of Richard and Gillian Mansfield . . .* (New Haven, 1885), 133–34.

FROM EDWARD JORDAN

Autograph letter. Chase Papers, Library of Congress (*micro* 29:0472).

Private

New York October 27th 1863

Sir,

I ascertained, on arriving here, that the purpose for which Mr. Dennison had telegraphed for me was that I might inquire into the grounds of charges which had been made that Mr. H. B. Stanton, Deputy Collector, had been induced by bribery, to permit the cancellation or destruction of bonds for the production of evidence of the consumption outside of the Confederate States, of goods exported to Bermuda, Nassau &c, without the production of any such evidence, and even before the goods could have reached their ostensible destination.[1] I regret to say that the examination I have made has shown that there is too much reason for believing the charge to be well founded. It is beyond question that bonds of the description mentioned have been permitted to be withdrawn from the rooms in the Custom House under the control of Mr. Stanton, and destroyed; as not only one of the obligors upon the bonds, and the broker through whose agency the negotiations in the premises were conducted testify to the fact, but the mutilated bonds themselves, five in number, have been placed in my possession, and I now hold them. It is equally certain that this permission was granted in consideration of money, paid by the parties interested. The only open question is as to the delinquent official, and the only doubt is as to whether that delinquent is Mr. Stanton or his son,[2] or whether both are guilty. I hope to be able, in a day or two, to obtain such further evidence as will make this point clear. It is asserted that there is a general understanding among persons engaged in the trade subject to these bonds that they can be cancelled at any time, in payment of a suitable consideration in money, to Mr. Stanton.

I had, last night, a long conversation with Mr. Barney. I will recapitulate this, in detail, on my return, and will now simply state the result in the form of several propositions.

First. You are Mr. B.s first choice for the presidency

Second. He is willing to labor to secure your nomination, provided he be permitted to labor in his own way.

Third. He is of opinion that you should take no action and that none should be taken on your behalf looking directly to your candidacy, and especially, that no issue should be made with the President or his friends.

Fourth. He holds himself free, and will continue to do so, to judge for himself when the nomination is actually to be made, whether yourself, the President, or some other person should receive it.

Fifth. He thinks it possible that you may be nominated if *his* policy is pursued, but if it is not he considers it certain that you will not be nominated, and doubtful whether either you or the President will be.

Sixth. He denies that he has acted in bad faith towards you, insisting on the contrary that he has pursued the only course consistent with your best interests.

Seventh. He avers that Mr. Palmer entirely understands his views and has acted in perfect accordance with them; and that furthermore Mr. P. is thoroughly cordial in opinion and a warm friend of yourself.[3]

Such, I believe, is the essence of what Mr. Barney said to me. I may state one other proposition which I inferred from the whole tenor of the conversation; viz; That Mr. B. thinks it *probable* that the President will be renominated, but quite *improbable* that you will be.

I have also seen and conversed with several other persons here, but I reserve an account of what I have thus heard and observed, until my return. One thing, however, I will state here. I have been given to understand that should the removal of Mr. Barney be considered desirable, *that object might be attained without your intervention or even that of your friends.*

Reserving all further particulars until I shall be in Washington, which will be so soon as I shall have satisfied my self whether or not the extent of Mr. Stanton's criminality is susceptible of clear demonstratio[n] and within a few days at all events,

I am, with high respect,

Yours truly
EDWARD JORDAN

Hon. S. P. Chase,
Secretary of the Treasury.

1. Jordan, the solicitor of the Treasury, had also investigated earlier instances of fraud by customs officials in New York. George Denison, naval officer in the New York Custom House, led investigations on the scene. The deputy collector was Henry Brewster Stanton. Jordan to Chase, Jan. 25, 29, Feb. 9, 1863 (Letters Recd. from Exec. Officers, Gen. Recs. Treasury Dept., Nat. Arch.); *Chase Papers,* 3:317–18.

2. Bond clerk Daniel Cady Stanton (1842–91). Both Stantons were removed from office on October 28. A House investigating committee later found evidence to support the allegations. William J. Hartman, "Politics and Patronage: The New York Custom House, 1852–1902" (Ph.D. diss., Columbia University, 1952), 102; *New York Custom-House*, 38th Cong., 1st sess., 1864, H. Rep. 111, 5; William Alonzo Stanton, *A Record, Genealogical, Biographical, Statistical, of Thomas Stanton, of Connecticut, and his Descendants, 1635–1891* ([Boston], 1891), 462–3.

3. Albert Marshman Palmer (1838–1905), in later life a noted New York theater manager, received an appointment as Barney's private clerk in May 1861. *New York Custom-House*, 148; *DAB*, 14:172–73.

TO HORACE GREELEY

Autograph letter. Horace Greeley Papers, Library of Congress (*micro* 29:0522).

Washington, Oct. 31. 1863.

My dear Mr. Greeley

Mr. Chittenden, the present Register of the Treasury, was a Member of the Peace Congress and took notes. Lately he has written out from his notes the speech I made in defence of the Republican & against the Anti-Republican proposition; and I have revised it.[1] Some to whom it has been read have thought its publication would do good. I doubt it; but have consented that he should send it to you & let you judge. Do just as you please about it. I shall be sure you are right whichever way you decide.

I attach a great deal of importance to that Baltimore meeting last Wednesday. My speech was intended as a sort of announcement of the existence of a great unconditional Union Party, with *Emancipation as a Cardinal principle.* It was received with an enthusiasm which assures me that the time is ripe. I got Judge Kelley to follow up the announcement with what he said so admirably concerning the universality nationality[2] of the Unconditional Union Party; & its permanence if faithful to its ideas of Freedom and Justice; and its identity with real Democracy.[3]

I will send you tomorrow a corrected copy of my speech and hope you will turn to your files for Judge K——'s. The idea of both, it seems to me ought to receive the imprint of our press & made national currency.

Your friend
S P Chase

Hon H. Greeley

1. Lucius Eugene Chittenden, a former Vermont legislator, represented that state at the Washington, D.C., Peace Conference of February 1861. Chittenden published Chase's speech as *How the South Rejected Compromise in the Peace Conference of 1861: Speech of Mr. Chase of Ohio* (New York, 1863) and the minutes as *A Report of the Debates and Proceedings in the Secret Sessions of the Conference Convention for Proposed Amendments to the Constitution of the United States Held at Washington, D.C., in February, A.D. 1861* (New York, 1864). *Nat. Cyc.*, 13:553.

2. Chase wrote *nationality* as an interlineation above *universality* without striking through the latter word.

3. According to one report, the meeting of Unconditional Union supporters in Monument Square, October 24, "was an assemblage of the loyalty of Baltimore such as has not been witnessed in this city during the great National struggle." Chase's brief speech followed one by Henry Winter Davis. "The Unconditional Union cause is one and the same throughout this land," proclaimed Chase. "It is one here in Maryland; it is one in Ohio; it is one in Missouri. . . ." Others on the podium included Benjamin F. Flanders, James A. Garfield, and William Darrah Kelley (1814–90), congressman for Pennsylvania's fourth district. Chase's address was published in *"Going Home to Vote"* along with his Ohio and Indiana speeches. *Baltimore American,* Oct. 29, 1863; Chase, *"Going Home to Vote,"* 35–36; *DAB,* 10:299.

TO ABRAHAM LINCOLN

Autograph letter. Abraham Lincoln Papers, Library of Congress (*micro* 29:0524).

Treasury Department.
Oct. 31, 1863

My dear Sir,

The enclosed paper was sent to me because of the communication about liquor speculation.[1]

I take the liberty of sending it to you hoping you may find time to read the Editorial on the Missouri Election.

The real issue in Missouri,—somewhat embarrassed by the action of a portion of those who have sustained your administration—is undoubtedly between those who make no conditions about the support to be given to the measures of your administration and those who really sympathize with its opponents and will finally act with them.[2]

It seems to me a plain duty, without going at all into details, to give all the support which can be given [legi]tmately & honorably to the former.

You can now give them a moral support, without impeachment of anybody by sending Gen. Rosecrans to the Department which includes Missouri: and either sending Gen. Schofield honorably to the field, or leaving him to take his proper place under General Rosecrans as his superior in rank.

At the same you can, by this action, relieve the friends of the Administration in Ohio and elsewhere from all unnecessary embarrassment, arising from the recent orders consolidating the Military Departments of the Tennessee the Cumberland & the Ohio and their effect in superceding General Rosecrans as Commander of the Army of the Cumberland.[3]

Pardon me if I seem too earnest in this matter, and believe me

Very truly yours,
S P Chase

The President.

1. According to a filing endorsement on the letter, Chase enclosed issues of two St. Louis newspapers, the *Evening News* and the *Daily Union.*

2. Chase alluded to memorials that a group of radical Republicans from Kansas and Missouri presented to Lincoln on September 30 and October 3. Chase was in contact with

the delegation, which he had entertained at his home the evening of September 30. The petitioners asked Lincoln to remove Brig. Gen. John McAllister Schofield for demonstrating insufficient vigor in efforts to apprehend Confederate guerrilla William Clark Quantrill after the Quantrill band's notorious raid on Lawrence, Kans., August 21–22. Suggesting Benjamin F. Butler as a replacement for Schofield in command of the army's Department of Missouri, the memorialists also wanted the president to put Unionist forces in Missouri under Federal control. Lincoln's response, on October 5, turned down the requests. Chase had learned from a report in June that popular sentiment in Missouri questioned the loyalty of Schofield, who had commanded a state organization, the Army of the Frontier. Basler, *Collected Works,* 6:499–507; *Chase Papers,* 1:457; *DAB,* 16:453; Long, *Civil War Day by Day,* 399–400; William P. Mellen to Chase, June 27, 1864 (Chase Papers, Hist. Soc. of Pa.).

3. General Orders No. 337, issued on October 16, united the three departments into the Military Division of the Mississippi under Ulysses S. Grant. *OR,* ser. 1, v. 30, pt. 4:404.

TO WILLIAM SPRAGUE

Letterpress copy of autograph letter. Chase Papers, Historical Society of Pennsylvania (*micro* 29:0528).

Washington, Oct 31, 1863.

My dear Governor,

Your last letter gave me a great deal of pleasure, with which—I could not help it mingled not a little sadness. Katie is very dear to me, and I cannot the solicitous care of her and for her, which I have used for so many years, even to you, without emotion. As she has gained experience in life she has constantly become more thoughtful, more affectionate, more loving; and, at this hour, is dearer than ever. I begin to realize how changed every thing will be when she is gone. Your letter comes when these feelings are very vivid; and, though it does not dispel them wholly, brightens the prospect with the assurance that in [parting] with her to you, I shall place under a guardianship not less watchful & tender than my own. I am glad that she so honors and loves you as she does, and that your affection for her is so respectful & so true. Mutual honor is hardly a less sure pledge of future happiness than mutual love.

There is another circumstance which is a great comfort to me. Katie has known almost nothing of a mothers care.[1] Now she will find in yours, her own. It is a great satisfaction to me to think of the happiness and benefit she will from her wise & kindly counsels and from the pure example of her life. She already reveres and loves her; and will not, I think, be likely to miss gaining her confidence and affection in return.

So I look to the future, not without uneasiness—for who can raise the veil, which hides it, ever so little without trembling—but with hope and trust. May the blessing of God, without which there is neither honor, nor happiness nor true success in this life, rest upon what we do and fulfil all our desires.

I felt quite concerned about your health when you were here: and am glad to learn from your letter that it is now quite restored. You will need your full vigor for the duties of the winter—

Things move on here very much as usual. There is if possible less of a Government than ever. I do not know now if even any meetings of Heads of Departments takes place at the White House. I don't go to any. When I have any matter to talk to the President about I go and see him; but I have no relish for meetings nominally for administrative business but at which really no business at all is done.

Grant seems to have taken hold of affairs in his enlarged Command with spirit & vigor. The last intelligence shows important successes below Chattanooga, on the left bank of the River.[2] The war, I think, will culminate & end in that region.

At Baltimore the other evening I said a [few] words to an immense concourse.[3] My reception [was] all that any friend could wish. I do not see [*several words illeg.*] [little I said] in any Eastern [*several words illeg.*] you.

[Faithfully &] affectionately yours
S P Chase

I must not omit saying that Gov. Dennison was here a day or two since and expressed the warmest respect & regard for you & desired to be remembered when I next wrote[4]

1. Kate Chase's mother, Eliza Ann Smith Chase, died when Kate was five years old. Chase subsequently wed Sarah Bella Dunlop Ludlow, who died when Kate was eleven. "Family Memoranda" (Chase Papers, L.C.).

2. On October 27, forces under Grant successfully constructed a pontoon bridge on the Tennessee River below Chattanooga, thus creating a supply line that relieved the besieged city from Braxton Bragg's Confederates. For Grant's new command of the Military Division of the Mississippi, see Chase's October 31 letter to Abraham Lincoln (above). Long, *Civil War Day by Day*, 426.

3. The meeting of Unconditional Union supporters held on October 24, discussed in Chase's correspondence with Horace Greeley, October 31 (above).

4. William Dennison, former Republican governor of Ohio. In 1864 he presided over the Republican national convention and became U.S. postmaster general. *DAB*, 5:241.

TO THADDEUS STEVENS

Letterpress copy of autograph letter. Chase Papers, Historical Society of Pennsylvania (*micro* 29:0531).

Washington, Oct. 31, 1863.

My dear Sir,

It will give me great pleasure to designate your friend Dr. Freeland for a clerkship in the Department. He will of course have to begin in the first class.[1]

Your great victory in Pennsylvania did my heart good, because it was won, as I am assured, on no *modified* issue.[2]

Some days ago I had your note about Blair.[3] I did not know what to say and therefore said nothing. He claims to speak for the President. I don't believe he had any authority to do so: but the President does not & I suppose will not, publicly at least, disclaim.

For my part I manage the Treasury Department as well as I know how; and, since it is not the pleasure of the President to have a cabinet in the usual sense of that term, but simply expects each Head of a Department to "run his own machine", with such help as he finds it convenient to give, I just run mine and let the rest run theirs. Nobody interferes with me and I interfere with nobody, except that I cannot help talking a little now and then to Stanton and to the President about the progress & conduct of the war and its relations to the political condition of the states. What good I do by talking I cannot say; perhaps none.

Sincerely your friend
S P Chase

Hon Thaddeus Stevens
Lancaster, Pa.

1. On November 10, Chase appointed J. B. Freeland of Pennsylvania a temporary clerk in the third auditor's office. *List of Clerks and Others Employed in the Treasury Department,* 38th Cong., 1st sess., 1863, H. Ex. Doc. 62, 19.

2. Stevens's recent reelection to Congress was part of the overwhelming victory that Union candidates in Pennsylvania and throughout the North enjoyed earlier in the month. Stevens continued to preside over the House Committee on Ways and Means. *Bio. Dir. U.S. Cong.,* 1872; Nevins, *War for the Union,* 3:177–79; *New York Times,* Oct. 14, 1863.

3. "If such men are to be retained in Mr. Lincoln's cabinet," wrote Stevens in relation to Montgomery Blair's "infamous" Rockville, Md., speech of October 3, "it is time we were consulting about his successor." Stevens to Chase, Oct. 8, 1863 (Chase Papers, Hist. Soc. of Pa.); Edward D. Mansfield to Chase, Oct. 21, 1863 (Chase Papers, L.C.).

TO CHARLES SUMNER

Autograph letter. bMS Am 1, Houghton Library, Harvard University (*micro* 29:0533).

Treasury Department.
Oct. 31, 1863.

My dear Sumner,

The letter you sent me will have prompt attention but I fear the writer is more sensitive than he need be. I know him. He is honest but nervous.

I am glad you are pleased with what I said in Ohio. Was not the Baltimore reception still more remarkable?[1]

The view changes little. Too much delay and irresolution in military affairs & on vital questions; but gradual progress which will take us through if it don't cost too much.

Yours faithfully
S P Chase

Hon C. Sumner.

1. That is, the Unconditional Union gathering on October 24, 1863. Chase to Horace Greeley, Oct. 31, 1863 (above).

TO THEODORE TILTON

Autograph letter. Misc. Mss. Chase, Salmon P., New York Historical Society (*micro* 29:0535).

Washington, Oct. 31, 1863.

My dear Mr. Tilton,[1]

I was rather out with you for saying on your return from Washington that I and the other Heads of Departments were mere Presidents Clerks;[2] when the fact is so notorious that with no Department, except the War and to a limited extent the State, does the President at all interfere. I wish somebody could and would relieve me of responsibility in mine; but I am left alone to devise and execute as I best may.

But let this pass. I know your sincere heart and that nothing out of the way was intended.

My views of Missouri matters differ widely from the conclusions the President has announced. I have frankly stated, and he has respectfully heard my statement of, these differences. I have even sought to induce him to modify his conclusions and his action in regard to the Unconditional Unionists of Missouri, by sending Gen. Rosecrans to the Department, whose rank would of course give him Command.[3] It is not for me to criticise his determinations. The responsibility and duty of decision are with him. It is my part to sustain his action when I can and when I cannot, to differ in respectful silence.

With the sincerest esteem

Yours cordially
S P Chase

Dr. Leavitt[4] has just left me. I have talked with him frankly.

Theodore Tilton Esq

1. Tilton, a radical Republican, edited the *Independent,* an influential Congregationalist periodical published in New York. *DAB,* 18:552.

2. "Each Secretary seems to have performed the local and technical duties of his bureau with industry and fidelity . . . ," claimed the *Independent* on October 30. "The men in power do the best they know how. But they are not adequate to their situation."

3. Chase had corresponded with Lincoln about Missouri and apparently tried to convince him in a cabinet meeting on October 23. Chase to Lincoln, Oct. 31, 1863 (above); Howard K. Beale, ed., *The Diary of Gideon Welles,* 3 vols. (New York, [1960]), 1:474.

4. Joshua Leavitt.

TO JAMES A. GARFIELD

Letterpress copy of autograph letter. Chase Papers, Historical Society of Pennsylvania (*micro* 29:0554).

Washington, Nov. 1, 1863.

My dear General,

I ought to have written you the result of our interview with the President, & so I should have done had the result affected your movements.

But it did not: and I had no heart to write. We accomplished nothing but a long talk. Our devoted friends in Missouri are to be left without support.[1] May God give them the victory! So I pray but with little faith.

The election takes place on Tuesday next—not the week following as I supposed when we talked. Of course, little time remains for useful action; and none here (the little in my power excepted) is to be expected.[2]

Please daguerreotype to me your impressions & observations in Maryland. Do you go to Delaware?

Your friend
S P Chase

Brig. Gen. Garfield

1. By "our interview" and "a long talk," Chase may have alluded to a two-hour meeting that Missouri and Kansas radical Republicans had with Abraham Lincoln on September 30. Chase to Lincoln, Oct. 31, 1863 (above); Earl Schenck Miers, ed., *Lincoln Day by Day: A Chronology, 1809–1865*, 3 vols. (Washington, D.C., 1960), 3:210.

2. The Missouri election centered on candidates for the state's supreme court and presented a choice between factions the *Missouri Democrat* starkly labeled as "Radical" and "Conservative." The legislature would also soon fill two seats in the U.S. Senate to replace senators expelled for disloyalty in January 1862. *Daily Missouri Democrat,* Nov. 9, 1863; *Appletons' Annual Cyclopædia,* 3:657; *Bio. Dir. U.S. Cong.,* 176, 680, 1171, 1272, 1658; Chase to Thomas J. Durant, Nov. 19, 1863 (below).

TO GRANVILLE A. W. WALDEGRAVE

Letterpress copy of autograph letter. Chase Papers, Historical Society of Pennsylvania.

Washington, November 1st, 1863.

My dear Lord,[1]

Your note introducing Capt. Harrison was presented by him today, and I thank you for the pleasure of a few moments conversation with so intelligent a gentleman. I shall be very glad to be of service to him during his visit to Washington—which, I understand, will be very short.

I rejoice that the action of your Government has removed a cause for most disquieting apprehensions of conflict between two nations of the same blood, lineage & traditions. Had the rebel rams been permitted to come out, no human wisdom could fathom the consequences.[2]

Knowing your Lordships interest in whatever concerns humanity, I take the liberty of enclosing to you a newspaper, of great respectability, conducted wholly by colored men and representing as an organ the African Methodist Episcopal Church.[3] This is a large religious body, organized precisely like the Methodist Episcopal Church of the United

States with Bishops and Preachers and Conferences & Book Concerns & Newspapers. The latter church admits colored persons to membership, but, hitherto, hardly if at all to the ministry: the former is composed, both in ministry and membership, exclusively of colored persons.

I think you will be especially interested in the visit of a correspondent to Norfolk & Portsmouth in Virginia; in the accounts, by others, of the colored regiments with which they are connected; and in the appeal in behalf of Wilberforce University by Bishop Payne (whom I know, black as the ink I write with and very capable and intelligent) and his associates[4]

The paper itself speaks well for the improvement of the colored people in this country; and there are several other papers conducted by them, of no less merit. This improvement is destined to go on steadily and with increasing speed, for the repressive influences of Slavery will disappear, with slavery itself, before the great forces which the rebellion has brought into action.

My daughter, Miss Kate, desires me to express to you her pleasant remembrance of your visit and to say (in all which I join) that you will be most welcome should you ever again incline to visit America. You will not, however, find her *Miss Kate;* for she is to be married in a few days to Ex-Governor Sprague of Rhode Island, and now a Senator (and the youngest in the body) from that State.

With the greatest respect and esteem,

Yours very truly,
S P Chase

Lord Radstock

1. Granville Augustus William Waldegrave, Baron Radstock of Castletown (1833–1913), later gained notoriety as a lay evangelist. A clerk's copy of this letter is in Chase's papers at the Historical Society of Pennsylvania and appears at *micro* 29:0559. *The Complete Peerage: Or a History of the House of Lords and All Its Members . . .*, 13 vols. (London, 1910–59), 10:723.

2. Early in September, a decision by the British government to detain two ironclad rams under construction for the Confederacy resolved a standing dispute between the United States and Great Britain and thus averted a major international crisis. William H. Aspinwall and John M. Forbes to Chase, Apr. 25, 1863 (above); Long, *Civil War Day by Day,* 405.

3. Chase had enclosed a copy of the October 24 edition of the *Christian Recorder.*

4. The correspondent was Alexander Walter Wayman (1821–95), a bishop in the African Methodist Episcopal Church. Daniel Alexander Payne held the post of president of Wilberforce University, Xenia, Ohio, 1863–76. In "One Hundred or More Grand Bazaars for Wilberforce University," Payne and his committee appealed for assistance to retire a debt of eight thousand dollars. Other members of Payne's group included James G. Mitchell, a teacher at the University who often helped with fund raising, E. D. Davis, R. Conrad, and H. S. Mount. *Christian Recorder,* Oct. 24, 1863; Frederick A. McGinnis, *A History and Interpretation of Wilberforce University* (Wilberforce, Ohio, 1941), 141; *Nat. Cyc.,* 4:187–88.

FROM JOSEPH HOOKER

Letter in clerk's hand, signed by Hooker. Chase Papers, Library of Congress (*micro* 29:0613).

Look-out Valley, Tenn.
November 3d. 1863.

Governor S. P. Chase,
Secretary of the Treasury.
Dear Governor:

I have a few moments, and I believe they are the first at my command, to tell you that your very kind letter of the 28th. Septr. was duly delivered to me at the Relay House, on my way to the West.[1]

I regretted very much that I could not see you before leaving, but in the absence of that I was constrained to console myself with your few written words on parting.[2] They were precious ones, and only those a generous friend would venture to address me.

The only part of your note that was at all unsatisfactory, was that relating to my habits—indicating that you were still in doubt in this regard. As no endorsement of myself will be likely to remove your apprehensions, I will only relate to you the partial contents of a letter I received a day or two since from my old Professor at West Point, Prof. Mahan— He says that General Seth Williams informs him that I am not a member of the Church—that I sometimes make use of profane language—but, in example, many professors of religion would do well to imitate me.[3]

The character of Seth Williams you probably know. I am no member of the church, and never expect to be, and only claim to be governed by the laws of honor and of duty, and if I have ever departed from those I must go further back than my memory extends. It is impossible for me to personate a character I do not possess, for if there is anything in this wide world that I abhor it is the character of a hypocrite and imposter. I hope that I am honest in word and deed, and I desire to have no relations with those who are not so— I find no fault with those who differ from me in opinion, nor am I in the habit of wasting time in attempting to make them converts to my opinions or actions— Rather let it be as Pope has it—"all natures difference makes all natures peace."[4]

I find everything here, so unlike the service in the East that I do not feel exactly at home. Here there is a total lack of system and administrative ability— It is felt in all branches of service, and to such an extent that I cannot avoid feeling that whatever is accomplished is the result of accident rather than design— There is not a Post Master, a rail road agent, or officer of the Staff Departments of the Army that I have met with who should remain an hour if I could find some one to put in his place. From what I have seen, this Army instead of being a splendid piece of machinery, working smoothly and harmoniously in all of its parts, is as ricketty and disorganized as when the troops of which it is composed were first brought together— The material is as good as that of any Army— It will be in vain to ascribe this to any peculiarity of Western troops, for the Western troops in the Army of the Potomac are as distinguished for discipline and instruction as the Eastern. There, if a Corps Commander, the head of a Staff Department or his subordinates are removed, a dozen stand ready to fill his place, and often-times more than fill it— Here it is far otherwise— To find an officer capable of doing his duty is really a luxury.

Meigs is here, laboring with all of his might to bring order out of chaos, but it is more than one man can do.[5] He requires a dozen assistants.

I had hoped that Grant would appoint Butterfield the Chief of his Staff—this would effect much, but I do not know that he will do it[6]— If he should not, you will allow me to say that the best position to assign Butterfield is to organize and instruct twenty thousand negro troops in Kentucky and Tennessee. No officer of my acquaintance can do it in so short a time or so thoroughly. His knowledge of the right sort of officers in the Army of the Potomac and here afford him a great advantage over those now engaged in this service. This I know will be acceptable to him, and you may be assured that he will make troops faster and at less cost than they can be raised by conscription or voluntary enlistment.

As you know, the Army of the Cumberland was in an extremely critical condition on my arrival with reinforcements, nor are its embarrassments yet removed. It is by no means certain to my mind that it will be able to maintain its position at Chattanooga. The whole of the Army, except that portion necessary to guard the lines of communication, are established on the south side of the Tennessee, with the enemy holding the intermediate ground between the two wings, and commanding the river, the line of rail road, and the land routes on the south side of the river— They hold Look-out Mountain which is the great spinal ridge of this part of the continent. No attempt has yet been made to dispossess them of this, and I do not know that any is in contemplation. In brief our present position is with the Tennessee in our rear—my command connected with the opposite bank by a pontoon bridge, and another connects the force at Chattanooga, but both bridges have been carried away two nights in succession, by trees and rafts the enemy have thrown against them, while they hold the commanding ground between the two wings of our Army. In my judgment the most critical position our Army could be placed in.

All of these difficulties proceed directly from the effort of the Army of the Cumberland to advance beyond Chattanooga before its communications had been established to that point— These required the erection of expensive bridges over the Tennessee and Falling Water, both of which had been burned by Bragg on his retreat.[7]

It is alleged that it was necessary to fight the battle of Chickamauga before possession by all the forces could be taken of Chattanooga—this is a mistake—Rosecrans had force enough to take and hold that position and Look-out Mountain, despite all the forces the enemy could send against him, and it was madness not to have done it— He was compelled to return and do this work before making any considerable advance, whether successful or not—by no other means could he replenish his supplies.

Until my arrival the enemy occupied the whole of the south side of the river from Chattanooga to Bridgeport, and beyond—compelling Rosecrans to wagon his supplies from Stevenson to his position, over horrible roads, and sometimes for a distance of eighty four miles— This, of course, wore out and destroyed his animals, and in the end, had he been compelled to fall back, it would have been at the expense of his Artillery, and the greater part of his transportation, from want of animals— As his forage and rations were exhausted the condition of the Army was extremely perilous.

At this juncture I was ordered to cross the Tennessee, at Bridgeport, with the 11th. Corps and one Division of the 12th. Corps, and open and secure the line to what is called Brown's Ferry.[8] This required me to advance within two miles of the enemy's lines of investment around Chattanooga, with nothing to prevent his detaching two thirds of his Army, and throwing it on me— I regarded it precisely as I did sending my Corps across the Antietam Creek to attack the whole rebel Army. I could not know whether I was advancing against a mouse or an elephant—

The second day out, and near the end of my journey, I encountered small bodies of Infantry, which were easily knocked out of the way, and at night established one Division under Geary at Wauhatchie, and Howard's Corps about three miles from it, and nearer Brown's Ferry, with my small force it being impossible to establish and keep up communication between them.[9] These points were determined by the intersection with the Look-out Valley road the two branches of the road which unite about two miles distant at the Gap through Raccoon Mountain[10] to the Tennessee River— This being the new line over which it was intended to draw our supplies.

About one O'clock two of Longstreet's Divisions sprang on my command like tigers—they first bounced Geary and immediately Schurz' Division[11] was directed to double quick to his relief, but before they had proceeded far they received a sheet of musketry from the left, when one Brigade was detached to attack this force, and the others proceeded as before directed. Meanwhile Howard's second Division came up, when two Regiments of that were ordered to carry a hill in possession of the enemy still further to the rear of the heights Schurz was attacking. It was held by a full Brigade of the enemy who were tolerably well entrenched—notwithstanding which it was wrenched from them in the most glorious style, almost without firing a gun— More resolute, unflinching, masculine courage was never displayed by troops.

During this time the enemy had enveloped Geary on three sides, and in that condition he fought like a lion, and actually repulsed and scattered them before reinforcements could reach him.

My losses will fall between four and five hundred men—among them some of the bravest officers of the command. We took a respectable number of prisoners, and killed and wounded a goodly number of the enemy. Geary alone buried one hundred and fifty who had bitten the dust in his front. Although in the night, the fight was a very animated one, from the splendid conduct of the troops, and would have had splendid results, had not the forests and the night covered the routes of the enemy's escape.

One amusing incident occurred, which I must relate, as I know no parallel to it in history. In the middle of the fight about thirty of Geary's mules became stampeded, and, true to their nature, instead of running from danger, charged on the enemy, spreading consternation wherever they went. One entire Regiment threw away their arms and broke in the wildest confusion. I have found much to admire in mules in the course of my experience—now I will add another feather to their cap. I cannot refrain from smiling when I think of the services of these mules— They certainly deserve preferment.

I am now in Look-out Valley, protecting our communications, and command the district of the south side of the river, with nothing to live on but the excitements of service. It is a wretched country, and the natives only one or two removes from Indians.

I cannot understand the recent operations of the Army of the Potomac. At this distance I conclude that I have lost nothing in not being identified with them.

I hope you are well, and only regret that you cannot be here to renew our rides. I read your speeches in Ohio with great pleasure.[12] I thought they were just the thing, but of that you know better than I; I only know the effect was good on your servant.

My kindest regards to Miss Kate or Mrs S., as the case may be.[13]

Please ponder on what I have written regarding Butterfield, for the business of organizing black regiments should be in the hands of one of his capacity and dispatch. Many of the natives are removing from here to Kentucky and some to the free states. All are heartily sick of the war, and this feeling pervades the rebel Army. I think there never has been the animosity in the Army of the South and West that we find in that of Virginia— The opposite is the case in our Armies— The reason is to be found in the character of the two Governments— The one is a unit in feeling and in action, the other almost neutralizes itself by its diverse views.

Excuse this long letter, and believe me

Truly your friend,
JOSEPH HOOKER
Maj. Genl.

1. Relay House stood between Baltimore and Washington, D.C., on the Baltimore and Ohio Railroad. Long, *Civil War Day by Day,* 70.

2. As ordered by Lincoln, Joseph Hooker and the Eleventh and Twelfth Corps departed the Army of the Potomac on September 25 to relieve beleaguered U.S. forces in Chattanooga under William S. Rosecrans. Ibid., 414; *Chase Papers,* 1:450–54.

3. Hooker, class of 1837, had studied under Dennis Hart Mahan, professor of civil and military engineering at the U.S. Military Academy, 1832–71. At the time Hooker wrote this letter, Williams (1822–66) was adjutant general in the Army of the Potomac. *Appletons',* 6:530; *DAB,* 9:196, 12:209.

4. *An Essay on Man,* epistle 4, line 56, by British poet Alexander Pope (1688–1744). John Butt, ed., *The Poems of Alexander Pope* (New Haven, 1963), 537; *DNB,* 16:109–27.

5. In the aftermath of the Chickamauga disaster, Quartermaster General Montgomery C. Meigs went to Tennessee, where he helped reestablish supply lines for the Army of the Cumberland and supervised the construction and repair of steamboats, bridges, and railroads. *OR,* ser. 3, v. 4:879–82.

6. Daniel Butterfield never held the position under Grant. Beginning in January 1863 Butterfield had served as chief of staff of the Army of the Potomac under Hooker and subsequently under George Meade, and in October he had become Hooker's chief of staff in the Army of the Cumberland. *DAB,* 3:373.

7. Threatened by William S. Rosecrans and the Army of the Cumberland, Braxton Bragg's Confederate Army of Tennessee had abandoned Chattanooga, Tenn., on September 9. Long, *Civil War Day by Day,* 407.

8. Hooker received the orders on October 24. Brown's Ferry spanned the Tennessee River, west of Chattanooga. *OR,* ser. 1, v. 31, pt. 1:43–44; *Official Atlas of the Civil War* (New York, 1958), pl. 50.

9. Brig. Gen. John White Geary served with the Twelfth Corps. Maj. Gen. Oliver O. Howard commanded the Eleventh Corps. *DAB,* 7:203, 9:279–80.

10. South of the Tennessee River, slightly west of Chattanooga and northwest of Lookout Mountain. *Official Atlas,* pl. 50.

11. The Third Division of the Eleventh Corps, under Maj. Gen. Carl Schurz. *OR,* ser. 1, v. 31, pt. 1:110–11; *DAB,* 16:468.

12. Chase, *"Going Home to Vote."* Chase had discussed the speeches he gave in Ohio and Indiana, October 10–16, 1863, in correspondence to John Conness and to Edward D. Mansfield, October 18 (above).

13. Hooker referred to Kate Chase's imminent marriage to William Sprague.

FROM CHARLES F. SCHMIDT

Autograph letter. Chase Papers, Historical Society of Pennsylvania (*micro* 29:0624).

Confidential

Washington, Nov. 3d. 1863.

Hon. S. P. Chase.
Sir,

You kindly instructed me last evening to say in writing what means I wished to obtain and for what object.[1]

To organize New York and Penna. as thoroughly as possible is of the utmost importance, particularly the former State; to commence at once agitation for the *One* term principle and to secure the election of Some representatives in the Coming National Convention,[2] are among the foremost objects to be attained. To carry out these ideas, I asked for letters to some of your friends, that I might lay my plans before them and obtain necessary means to execute them.

At the same time Mr. Bittmann should go West and prepare matters in the same direction.[3] Every day shows more plainly, that great efforts are making in *other* Quarters, to secure the Germans. To prevent this, a stand must be taken at once, for the single term principle; the Spirit among my Countrymen is excellent just now and no time ought to be lost to secure all, that can possibly be obtained.

Mr. Bittman has completed his official labors for the Quarter and can be absent without detriment to the service. In my own case, the Desk to which I am assigned is still occupied by the former incumbent, who is waiting to be transferred to other duties. I am moreover still suffering from incipient Amaurosis and there is some hope, that travelling and abstinence from writing, might possibly be of use to me.

My foremost wish however, is to secure and improve, what has been begun so successfully and for this I ask your kind assistance.

You will not, I trust, think me presumptuous, when I beg of You most earnestly, not to allow any importunity to prevail upon you, to make many Public Speeches, much less to write letters to be published. Your late, most admirable efforts in the West and at Baltimore, may well close your carreer before the people, for the present.[4] To remain in the hands of your friends henceforth, would render success certain.

Hoping that my presumption to advise, has not offended, I remain with highest esteem & gratitude

Sir

Your Sincere humble servt.
CHAS. F. SCHMIDT

1. A native of Germany with connections to Ohio, Schmidt was a clerk in the office of the Treasury's fifth auditor and evidently served at times as a liaison with German-Americans. Chase to Schmidt, Aug. 12, 1864 (William Howard Taft Papers, L.C.); Schmidt to Chase, Aug. 28, 1864 (Chase Papers, L.C.); *Register of Officers (1863)*, 27; *Wash. Dir. (1863)*, 178.

2. In 1864, the National Union party, a coalition of Republicans and War Democrats, met in Baltimore, June 7–9. Long, *Civil War Day by Day*, 516–18.

3. Treasury employee John Bittman had worked as a clerk in the secretary's office responsible for cases involving damaged merchandise and for statistics of exports and imports. *Wash. Dir. (1863)*, 47; list of clerks, [1863] (Letters Recd. from Exec. Officers, Secretary's Office, Gen. Recs. Treasury Dept., Nat. Arch.).

4. Schmidt referred to Chase's speeches in Ohio and Indiana during mid-October and to the address at Baltimore on October 24. Chase to John Conness, Oct. 18, to Edward D. Mansfield, Oct. 18, and to Horace Greeley, Oct. 31 (all above).

FROM WILLIAM SPRAGUE

Autograph letter. Chase Papers, Library of Congress (*micro* 29:0647).

Providence Novr 4th. 1863

My dear Governor,

Your letter has filled me with a great deal of pleasure.[1] When you was writing to me, probably the same hour, I wrote Katie that her fathers care was attributable far more to his anxiety for her future, than to other causes. This could not well be otherwise. I think I realize the delicate link which has so long united father & daughter. I think I realize something of that high & holy relation, and that I know something of the great soul of the one, and its counterpart in the other, hightened & electrified by the extreme delicacies of female character. My dear Sir you will not think less of me, for being in love with both these characters— I shall strive to so conduct myself to be worthy of the connection, and shall never be happier than when contributing to continue the same relation between father & daughter—that has heretofore existed, excepting if possible to share something of it, myself. If resolves are anything, If a single mind & heart absorbed in the happiness of another, can be my guarantee of a bright and happy future for Katie, I think I can faithfully and truly promise it to her.

I have taken little or no care for myself during my past life. It has been my luck to have others interests in my keeping; from my earliest youth, I have neglected both mind & body—I have for some time given more attention to the latter, & think I have worked out a remedy for physical ills so that with good health and a proper exercise of the talent God has been pleased to give me, I hope to to do something usefull for my day and generation

I am not satisfied with having done well

Past honors or acts have no attraction to me,—the very much over estimated ability given me, whatever of real talent I may have of business or family, they all have no charms for me unless they are contributing to something more usefull for the future than has been done in the past. My creed was (tho somewhat blurred by my hurried advent into public life) was to prove a worthy son of my father & mother & of the superior advantages of this day over those of the past.

Infirmities of nature, increased by improper remedies to asuage the disease, has made my life an excited & excentric one.

I feel I have found a remedy against all this, & with good health & disposition I have more hopes for a successfull accomplishment of the work God has for me to do in the future than I ever have had in the past. I need not say here I rely much upon your guardianship, expecting to receive a fathers council & the benefits of a fathers experience, and a faithfull reliance upon Him who always smiles upon the efforts of those who in relying upon Him make every effort to help themselves, and having another and better half I think I have a right to feel I commence my new life in great hopefullness for myself & for those who are dependent upon me. Dont think me weaker my dear Sir for thus uncovering so much of my real nature I believe they are true ones, & I am far happier to be weak if such must be weakness. I have not had a fathers care for 20 years, Katie has missed a mother's, while my mother with her whole heart has gone out to her; I shall, repeating again, try to desire from you a fathers guidance, council & affection. I note your remark as to the Govt, and am gratefull at the Baltimore meeting appreciation / I have been so many times interupted while writing my letter that I hope you will overlook its hurried style, & get Katie to read it if you cannot

Faithfully & affectionatly

Yours
WM SPRAGUE

1. See Chase to Sprague, October 31, 1863 (above).

TO HIRAM BARNEY

Letterpress copy of autograph letter. Chase Papers, Historical Society of Pennsylvania (*micro* 29:0704).

Washington, Nov. 7, 1863.

My dear Mr. Barney,

Your private letter should have received an earlier answer; but my delay I believe is not greater than your own.[1]

Nothing was farther from my purpose than to add the weight of a feather to your anxieties. I prefer to endure rather than give pain.

Indeed I thought I had so worded my note as to avoid any expression that even looked like the withdrawal of personal confidence or that could possibly occasion any annoyance; beyond that which is inseparable from the recognition of the simple fact, which your conversation when here first made me imagine the [existence] of; which further conversation made me discredit as only imagined; but which subsequent statements of gentlemen who had conversed with you compelled me to accept as real:—namely, that you had come to the conclusion that the political support you had always given me should now be withdrawn.[2]

The recognition of such a fact is, of course, painful on both sides: but you will do me the justice to say that no one could accept such a fact with less manifestation of personal unkindness than my letter contained. Far from any such unkindness that letter and all my conversation since with gentlemen about you, uttered & has uttered nothing but perfect confidence in you personally & officially.

I claim no right to any one's political support. Were I to consult my [own] personal interests and true happiness I should [*blotted*] myself very promptly out of the entire circle of political influences. But a very large number of citizens, most of them strangers to me personally,—some of them friends of the cause to which I have devoted my life and entitled to every consideration on my part—manifest a strong disposition to require my services in another & higher sphere of duty than any I have heretofore filled. It seems to me neither modest to assume that the people will concur in these sentiments and make haste to decline an honor which may never be tendered; nor even to repel that manifestation of confidence and interest. So I let them take their course; wishing naturally enough the concurrence with them of my old friends; but asking nothing & claiming nothing.

I say this much to set myself right. Your letter assures me that my conclusion that you proposed to withdraw your political friendship was erroneous. I accept the assurance and dismiss the whole matter: only begging you to "keep a stiff upper lip" & never join the doubters & croakers. If success becomes an impossibility let it come from the efforts of those who from interest or policy prefer others not from fears or misgivings among ourselves.

One word more. Mr. Jordan tells me that you took the recall of Mr. McElrath to New York as evidence of unkind feeling. It was not. Your wishes in that matter had gone out of my recollection when I acted. Had they been present to my mind I should have refrained from action. I shall write Mr. McE—— urging him to adopt & act on your views in his official business.[3]

You must not fail to come to the wedding & bring your daughters. I am sanguine in my hopes of happiness for both Kate & the Governor. I had a delightful letter from him this morning.[4]

Sincerely your friend
S P Chase

H. Barney Esq.
Thank Mr. Palmer for his telegrams.

1. Barney wrote Chase two letters on October 19. One introduced Albert M. Palmer, Barney's personal clerk, who planned to visit Washington, D.C. The other, headed "Private," described Palmer as one who "will perhaps satisfy you about the policy of the N.Y. Custom House & its political integrity & influence." Barney also alluded to strained relations between Chase and himself due to growing doubts over his own support for Chase's presidential bid. "I have felt since I left you that your faith in me has been somewhat shaken, . . ." ventured Barney. "I do not see how it could be otherwise unless you are prepared to doubt the veracity & judgment of very respectable gentlemen." Barney to Chase, two letters, Oct. 19, 1863 (Chase Papers, Hist. Soc. of Pa.).

2. Suggested, for example, in correspondence from Edward Jordan to Chase on October 27, 1863 (above).

3. Thomas McElrath (1807–88) had previously worked as Horace Greeley's partner and publisher of the *New York Tribune.* In 1861, Abraham Lincoln appointed McElrath

general appraiser of New York, a position he still occupied in 1863. *DAB,* 12:36; *Register of Officers (1863),* 73.

4. Evidently Sprague's letter of November 4 (above).

TO JAMES WATSON WEBB

Autograph letter. James Watson Webb Papers, Manuscripts and Archives, Yale University Library (*micro* 29:0724).

Washington, Nov. 7, 1863.

My dear General,

It is very discouraging to write to a friend who cannot get your letter till two months after the date of it; when the folly of his speculations may have become apparent, or his history proved fable, or his prophecies refuted by events. This may not be received by you as a sufficient excuse for not not having written you as I ought; and so I put my manifold duties into the scale and hope you will permit it to descend & carry my negligence to the beam.

Last August I began a letter to you which was intended as quite a decent epistle; and had gone so far as to thank you—(let me repeat those thanks here—) for the very kind manner in which friends report you as having spoken of me & to assure you of the high esteeem in which I hold you and your services & to tell you of what Butterfield Chief (acting) of Meades Staff reported to me concerning your son's conduct at the battle of Gettysburgh, ascribing to his intelligence and bravery & that of another Colonel the repulse of one of the fiercest assaults of the enemy, and thus a large share in saving the day.[1] But I was compelled to break off and then one thing after another prevented me from resuming until the letter would not bear finishing.

You have long since doubtless been made aware by Mr. Seward that affairs had changed so much at the time he received yours accompanied by the very remarkable letter addressed to you by the French Emperor from the condition in which they were when that letter was written, that he did not think it expedient to make any change at Paris:[2] and in all matters relating to diplomatic intercourse his decision is substantially final as is mine in all matters relating to the Treasury.

It is a peculiarity of this Administration that there is very little concert of action among those who are popularly regarded as members of it. The President limits his participation in the conduct of affairs very much to the War Department. His authority is, of course, respectfully recognized in all, & Mr. Seward, I think, generally reads to him the dispaches sent to our Ministers, & he appoints such officers as he thinks fit. But there is almost never any consultation on matters of importance; so that what are called Cabinet Meetings have fallen pretty much into disuse. Each Head of a Department, therefore, the War only excepted administers within his Sphere pretty much as he thinks best—excepting only that of War.

I cannot say that I approve or like this disjointed method of administration and rather than have a share in it have been often tempted to retire: but the President has always treated me with such personal kindness and has always manifested such fairness and integrity of purpose, that I have not found myself free to throw up my trust, especially while so many of our best men seem to think it important that I should retain it. So I still work on.

All my financial measures—thanks to a kind Providence and a generous people—have succeeded wonderfully and I have now no apprehensions except those excited by What I cannot help thinking the needless protraction & waste of the War. We have passed great financial perils, grazing the very rocks of shipwreck, though the passengers in the ship seemed unconscious. We can pass all but one—the accumulation of debt beyond the possibility of paying interest without large & permanent direct taxation for that purpose. We should now be on that rock had I not contrived to make interest low and it is not now so far distant as I could wish.

The War lags. The progress is steady and irresistible. But it is the progress of an enormous pressure, rather than that of vigorous, intelligent & well directed action. We are looking for the downfall of Charleston; for the advance of Grant into Georgia; for the reoccupation of Arkansas and Texas.[3] All these things should have been & might have been accomplished this year—&, I almost venture to think,—last year. They will be accomplished in time, and surely—but when? Qui le sait?[4]

I am very busy just now with my report: when completed I shall take great pleasure in sending you a copy.[5] Meantime I will send you sooner some offhand speeches which I was obliged to make when I went home to vote, which are now being printed.[6]

Please present my best respects to Mrs Webb and your family and remember me affectionately my excellent friend Monroe.[7] He will be glad to learn that our friend Garfield is made a Major General and richly deserved it. He will however resign & take his place in Congress where he will be needed.

Yours cordially
S: P: Chase

His Excellency
James Watson Webb. &c &c &c

1. Lt. Col. Alexander Stewart Webb (1835–1911), a West Point graduate, led a brigade of the Second Corps at the battle of Gettysburg, where his troops held the Bloody Angle against Confederate general George E. Pickett's famous charge. In 1891, Webb received the Congressional Medal of Honor for his performance there. *DAB,* 19:571–72.

2. Napoleon III and Webb first met in 1835. Webb had renewed the acquaintance during a visit to France en route to his position as U.S. minister to Brazil. Napoleon's letter of May 22, in response to one from Webb, explained France's invasion of Mexico. "My desire is, at all events, to withdraw as soon as honor and the exigencies of our present position will permit," wrote the emperor. Webb's correspondence with Seward discussed the background of Napoleon's letter and disavowed any desire by Webb to become U.S. minister to France, in spite of pressure from Napoleon for the appointment. Napoleon III to Webb, May 22, Webb to Seward, June 20, 1863 (Seward Papers, Univ. of Rochester Lib.), in *The Papers of William H. Seward* (Woodbridge, Conn., 1981), microfilm reel 78; *DAB,* 19:575.

3. Little Rock, Ark., had fallen to Federal troops on September 10. Early in May 1864, U.S. forces under William Tecumseh Sherman began to advance toward Atlanta. Charleston, S.C., did not surrender to U.S. forces until February 1865. For Nathaniel P. Banks's operations in Texas, see Chase's August 26, 1863, letter to George S. Denison (above). Long, *Civil War Day by Day,* 407–8, 483, 495, 639–40.

4. French for "Who knows?"

5. *Report of the Secretary of the Treasury, on the State of the Finances, for the Year Ending June 30, 1863,* 38th Cong., 1st sess., 1863, H. Ex. Doc. 3.

6. Chase, *"Going Home to Vote."*

7. Former Ohio educator and legislator James Monroe served as U.S. consul at Rio de Janeiro, 1863–69. Webb's wife was Laura Virginia Cram Webb (c. 1825–90). The couple had five sons: William Seward Webb (1851–1926), a physician and businessman; Henry Walter Webb (1852–1900), a New York attorney; George Creighton Webb (b. 1853), a lawyer and diplomat; Jacob Lewis Webb (b. 1856); and Francis Egerton Webb (b. 1858). James Watson Webb also had children from an earlier marriage, including Alexander Stewart Webb. *Appletons',* 4:358; James L. Crouthamel, *James Watson Webb: A Biography* (Middletown, Conn., 1969), 112, 153; *DAB,* 19:575; *Nat. Cyc.,* 1:532, 12:18; *Who Was Who,* 1:1312; Reynold Webb Wilcox, *Wilcoxson-Wilcox, Webb and Meigs Families* (New York, 1938), 187–88.

TO CATHERINE LUDLOW WHITEMAN

Letterpress copy of autograph letter. Chase Papers, Historical Society of Pennsylvania (*micro* 29:0812).

Washn. Nov. 12, 1863

My dear Kate,

Netties $2 is recd.[1]

I snatch a moment to say that Israel is quite well. Dr. Goldsborough, a fellow prisoner, released on parole to bear some message, concerning the exchange of surgeons, to the War Dept, was at our house on Friday, with word from Israel that he was quite well.[2] He and Israel had it seems become very good friends in the prison & the Doctor manifested great interest in him. He told us that Israel had a narrow escape, the ball striking the angle of his [jaws], glancing off & passing round over the carotid artery and lodging in the back of his neck. The wound is now healed but the ball remains & the Doctor thinks it best for it to remain as it gives no trouble until he is exchanged, when it can be removed without danger & with little inconvenience.

Ben is here at the wedding—so is Jep Garrard. We shall Israel some wedding cake.[3] Ben sent him a box of provisions lately. The Doctor says the rebels let them get what is sent but allow no correspondence

Kate received your beautiful gift & would send many thanks if she knew of my writing. She has been literally overwhelmed with kindness.

Love to all. I am so sorry you are not all here

Yours affectionately
S P Chase

Mrs C. L. Whiteman
Ludlow, O

1. Whiteman was the sister of Janet (Nettie) Chase's deceased mother, Sarah Bella Dunlop Ludlow Chase. Earlier in the year, Whiteman had discussed the possibility of renting a lot that Nettie owned at Ludlow Station, Ohio, for three dollars annually. Whiteman to Chase, Apr. 5, 1863 (Chase Papers, L.C.).

2. Confederates captured Whiteman's brother, Capt. Israel Ludlow of the 5th Regular U.S. Artillery, at the battle of Chickamauga in September 1863. Ludlow regained his freedom in March 1864 after serving time in Libby Prison. Ludlow's "fellow prisoner" there was evidently Charles Goldsborough, an assistant surgeon with Maryland's 5th Regiment. Chase to Whiteman, Mar. 8, 1864 (Chase Papers, Hist. Soc. of Pa.); Long, *Civil War Day by Day,* 411–13; *New York Times,* Nov. 6, 1863; *OR,* ser. 1, v. 6:886–87; Robson, *Biographical Encyclopædia,* 629; U.S. Adjutant-General's Office, *Official Army Register of the Volunteer Force of the United States,* 8 vols. (Washington, D.C., 1865–67), 3:1077.

3. The wedding of Kate Chase and William Sprague took place during the evening of November 12 in the Chase residence at the corner of 6th and E Streets, N.W. Family members in attendance included Kate Whiteman's brother Benjamin C. Ludlow and their cousin, Jeptha D. Garrard. President Lincoln, members of the cabinet, prominent political figures, and foreign diplomats were also among a "large and brilliant concourse of guests" who enjoyed a banquet and danced to music played by the Marine Band. *Daily National Intelligencer,* Nov. 13, 1863; *Washington Evening Star,* Nov. 12, 13, 1863; Anna Russell des Cognets, *Governor Garrard, of Kentucky, His Descendants and Relatives* (Lexington, Ky., 1898), 33–34.

FROM HOMER G. PLANTZ

Autograph letter. Chase Papers, Library of Congress (*micro* 29:0820).

New York, Nov. 13th., 1863.

My dear Governor.

Greatly to my disappointment, I was unable, after every possible effort, to secure accommodations for my people by the Navy transport which sailed yesterday. No other government vessel will sail for some time, and I have, therefore, procured passage by the "Evening Star", the regular New-Orleans packet, which leaves here tomorrow. I feel that I ought to respond to the trust reposed in me by all possible promptness[1]

I received your letter, enclosing one to Mr. Curtis, and thank you for your confidence. I will confer with Mr Curtis as soon as I arrive and report to you the result of my investigations.[2]

I happened to meet to-day Hon. M. M. Benton, of Covington.[3] He mentioned Gov Bramlette as a prominent candidate for the Senatorship. On my expressing some surprise at this after the Inaugural Address, Mr. Benton defended him warmly[4]—said we must take things in Kentucky as they are and not as we wish them to be—and upon the whole left the impression that he was favorable to Gov. Bramlette's candidacy. I thought you might like to know this.

Since I have been here, Winchell has called on me, and we have had quite a talk. He is now General Agent of the Union Pacific R.R. He says that Frémont is "in earnest" as a candidate for the Presidency.[5] With his usual unreliability, however, he has disappointed the pecuniary expectations which he authorized in connection with the Rail Road; and the influence of the Road will be used against him.

Winchell himself has purchased a controlling interest in the Leavenworth Times, the oldest daily paper in Kansas. He will be in Washington on the business of the R.R. during the earlier portion of the coming session; but expects to assume the editorship of the Times early in the Spring. His standing in Kansas; his influence in the R.R., and over Hallett personally, who, though perhaps not a very good, is certainly a very energetic man; and his ability, would make him, I think, a valuable friend. He is an earnest anti-Slavery man, and regards you as the natural representative and leader of the Cause; but is not free, I have been sorry to find, from the notion that it may be expedient to re-elect Mr. Lincoln. He assured me however that the "Times" would not commit itself before the Spring.

I have myself more confidence in Winchell than in most Kansas politicians. He is frank and steadfast. He will not promise support and afterwards withhold it; nor will he abandon one whom he once supports. He is much more likely to do more than less than he engages to do. He says Lane and Pomeroy are both advocates of Mr. Lincoln's reelection.[6]

Excuse so long a letter. I hope you may find enough in it to pay for its perusal, and no answer is needed. I will write you immediately on my arrival at Key West.[7]

I would thank you here, as I do daily, for your great confidence and kindness to me through all the time I have been with you; but I think you know my heart, and I mean to prove my gratitude by faithfully doing my duty.

With great respect and affection
HOMER G PLANTZ

1. Chase had recently helped secure Plantz, the Treasury clerk who acted as his private secretary, a position as U.S. district attorney at Key West, Fla. The *Evening Star* was a side-wheel steamer out of New York. Plantz to Chase, Nov. 23, 1863 (Chase Papers, L.C.); *Chase Papers,* 3:xxv–xxvi; Lytle, *Merchant Vessels,* 60.

2. In October, Cornelius Curtis of Key West sent Chase an enumeration of "treasonable" trade practices that local residents allegedly conducted in the open. Chase, on November 9, promised to investigate and asked Plantz to conduct an "impartial inquiry." Plantz responded in December with a series of reports that supported Curtis's assertions and depicted Federal officeholders in the area as lukewarm Unionists at best. Curtis to Chase, Oct. 23, Plantz to Chase, Dec. 1, 12 (two letters), 1863 (Chase Papers, L.C.); Chase to Curtis, Nov. 9, 1863, Chase to Plantz, same date (Chase Papers, Hist. Soc. of Pa.).

3. Mortimer M. Benton (1807–85), first mayor of Covington, Ky. H. Levin, ed., *Lawyers and Lawmakers of Kentucky,* (Chicago, 1897), 725–26.

4. Running as a Union Democrat, Thomas E. Bramlette had won election on September 2 as governor of Kentucky. His recent inaugural vowed to employ state resources

"to crush the present causeless and wicked rebellion," but also warned of his intention to oppose "all unconstitutional, all wicked, unwise, or hurtful measures of policy, which may be suggested or adopted in the prosecution of our defensive war." *Appletons' Annual Cyclopædia,* 3:569; *DAB,* 2:595–96.

5. Kansas journalist, Republican politician, and railroad manager James Manning Winchell (1823–77) openly urged Chase's election to the presidency in 1864. On May 31, 1864, radical Republicans meeting in Cleveland chose former major general John C. Frémont as their presidential standard-bearer. *DAB,* 7:22; Long, *Civil War Day by Day,* 511–12; *New York Times,* Feb. 7, 1877.

6. James Henry Lane and Samuel Clarke Pomeroy, U.S. senators from Kansas. For the "Pomeroy Circular," Pomeroy's effort in February 1864 to promote Chase's candidacy over Lincoln's, see Chase's correspondence with Lincoln, February 22, 1864 (below).

7. Plantz wrote on November 23, announcing his arrival at Key West two days earlier and promising to send detailed political analyses. "I cannot speak the gratitude I feel to you for giving me my great opportunity here," he concluded. Plantz to Chase, Nov. 23, 1863 (Chase Papers, L.C.).

FROM CHARLES H. RAY

Autograph letter. Chase Papers, Library of Congress (*micro* 29:0833).

Chicago, Nov 14th 1863.

Hon. S. P. Chase,
Secretary &c,
My Dear Sir,

Within the next ten days, I shall be in Washington to talk to you about a matter in the future, in which you are intimately concerned. You may guess what I refer to. I hope, as your time is wholly occupied by public duties, that you will, between the receipt of this and the day of my arrival, designate in your own mind some one to whom I can open my budget—somebody upon whom you can rely. I have not much to say, but the little is important to you and I think to the country.[1]

Yours Very Sincerely,
C. H. Ray

1. Ray was an antislavery journalist, Republican activist, and former business associate of Horace Greeley. Poor health had forced Ray to sell his interest in the *Chicago Tribune* earlier in the year. *Nat. Cyc.,* 29:327.

FROM GIDEON WELLES

Letter in clerk's hand on letterhead stationery, signed by Welles. Letters Received from Executive Officers (AB Series), General Records, Department of the Treasury (Record Group 56), National Archives (*micro* 29:0838).

Navy Department,
Washington, Novr. 14th 1863.

Sir,

I am in receipt of your letter of the 10th. inst, suggesting a revision of the estimates of this Department for the year 1864–5, with a view to their reduction.[1]

These estimates were based upon carefully considered data as to the number of Vessels and men in the service and its prospective increase.

At the breaking out of the rebellion there were in the Navy but 76 Vessels. By construction and purchase the number was increased to 264 in Dec, 1861; to 427 in Dec, 1862, and my report to be submitted to Congress at the commencement of the ensuing session will show a total of 588 Vessels completed and in process of construction.[2]

Vessels now building and hereafter to be built cannot be completed at the prices at which contracts could have been made a year since. Not only is the cost of constructing Vessels largely increased, but the expense of repairing and maintaining those already in commission is greatly in excess of any former period. The rate of wages is already about fifty per cent in advance of 1861, and a movement is now on foot with the large class of mechanics and artisans whose labor enters into the construction and repair of Vessels, having in view a farther increase of 25 per cent. If the movement is successful the estimates under the heads of "Construction and repair," Armor plated Sea Steamers" and "Steam Engineering" embracing nearly two thirds of the entire amount required, should be increased rather than diminished.

A large advance, too, has been made since the estimates were submitted, in the cost of fuel, which forms no inconsiderable item in the expense of keeping a steam navy afloat. At the commencement of operations upon the Mississippi river coal was readily obtained at ten cents per bushel. The price has been gradually increasing, and within a few days the Department has been notified of an advance to fifty cents per bushel, and as the estimates were based upon a lower figure a revision of them could lead to no other result than their increase. The price of Coal on the Atlantic Coast has doubled within a year past, and it would not be surprising were there a still greater advance.

The estimates are upon a War basis and no reduction can safely be made except in view of a cessation of hostilities. A return of peace alone will justify a reduction.

The estimate for personal expenses for the year ending June 30th., 1865, is upon a basis of 50.000, men. There are in the service at the present time about 34.000, and it is easy to foresee that if the war continues an increase of 16.000, will be required within the coming twenty months.

The entire resources of the country are employed in the construction of Vessels and to place them in commission the large number of men for which estimates have been made, will be required.

The extraordinary bounties offered by the National and State Governments for enlistments in the Army, naturally draw into that service many who would otherwise enlist in the Navy and it is not improbable that bounties will be required to enable the Navy to secure the number of men indispensably necessary to keep its Vessels afloat.

Vessels on foreign service have been gradually increasing and more are required. The high rate of exchange render their maintenance abroad very expensive, and has had its influence in swelling the estimates submitted.

In view of these facts and others not necessary to enumerate, I am not prepared to reduce the estimates already made. I trust the efforts of this Department for economy have been such as to assure you that no greater amount will be expended, whatever the appropriation, than is absolutely required. I cannot think it wise, or for the interests of the country, to under estimate expenditures or to cramp the service financially and thus impair its efficiency.

I have the honor to be

Sir, Very respectfully , &c
GIDEON WELLES
Secretary of the Navy.

Hon.
S. P. Chase
Secretary of the Treasury.

1. Welles had suggested an allocation of $142 million for the Navy Department during the next fiscal year, a figure $74 million greater than that for 1863–64. Chase to Welles, Nov. 10, 1863 (Letters Recd. by Sec. of the Navy from the President and Exec. Agencies, Naval Records Collec., Nat. Arch.).

2. *Annual Report of the Secretary of the Navy,* 38th Cong., 1st sess., 1863, H. Ex. Doc. 1, xi.

FROM HENRY C. BOWEN

Autograph letter on letterhead stationery. Chase Papers, Library of Congress (*micro* 29:0849).

private

United States Internal Revenue,
COLLECTOR'S OFFICE,[1]
Brooklyn, November 16th. 1863

Honl S. P. Chase
Secy. Treasury
My dear Sir

The time has come, in my judgement, when, in the most quiet way, your friends—the friends of freedom and lovers of the Union—should take action in reference to the political welfare of the country. There is only one way, now, in which we can be defeated and that is by inaction. Every proper, *judicious,* movement, of late, has brought forth abundant fruit. I have good reason to know that what your friends have done, without much concert of action, has resulted in great good. The copper heads begin to fear and tremble and are preparing for all sorts of unholy alliances. To allow them to go forward without counteraction, to prevent their mischievous work, would be both indiscreet and wrong. For one I am afraid to act for fear I shall not move in accordance with some general plan. To be plain with you, if you are prepared directly or through confidential friends, to communicate your views I should be glad to know them believing that through our paper (The Indt.) & in other ways I can render important service.

If you were here I should like to tell you some things which might help on matters and make them go more smoothly than they now do.

I suppose your duties—those of your office—may call you here before many days. I wish you could be here next sabbath—the 22d inst—as our Mr Beecher will then make his first public appearance in our church.[2] It will be a memorable day and the occasion will bring a vast throng of distinguished people—including M.C's on their way to your city[3]— On many accounts, not necessary to mention, I hope business will open the way for you to come to New York at that time. It will give me great pleasure, in a most informal way, to give you a resting day at my house, if agreeable to you.

I think, when I see you, I can convince you, that you are suffering personally, greatly, and the country is losing largely, for the want of better management in the collection of Internal Revenue. *This however is strictly private*

I know you will pardon this intrusion upon your valuable time and believe that I remain as ever

Your faithful friend
HENRY C BOWEN

1. New York businessman and Congregational leader Henry Chandler Bowen (1813–96) published the *Independent.* In 1862 he had become, with Chase's endorsement, collector of internal revenue for New York's third district, one of two districts that covered Brooklyn. *DAB,* 2:505; *Register of Officers (1863),* 38; Chase to Abraham Lincoln, Aug. 22, 1862 (Lincoln Papers, L.C.).

2. Henry Ward Beecher presided over Brooklyn's Plymouth Church. His appearance in its pulpit on November 22 was his first since returning from a recent trip to Britain. Despite Bowen's wish that he could attend, Chase was busy preparing his annual report and remained in Washington on the twenty-second. *New York Tribune,* Nov. 23, 1863; Chase to ———, Nov. 22, 1863 (Chase Papers, Hist. Soc. of Pa.); Chase to Kate Chase Sprague, Nov. 18, 1863 (below); *DAB,* 2:132.

3. That is, members of Congress.

FROM JAY COOKE

Autograph letter on letterhead stationery. Jay Cooke Papers, Historical Society of Pennsylvania (*micro* 29:0872).

Office of Jay Cooke, Subscription Agent,
114 SOUTH THIRD STREET.
Philadelphia, Novr 17th 1863

Honl S. P. Chase
Secretary of the Treasury
Dear Sir

I have fully appreciated the desire which you have ever manifested to reduce the expenses attending the negotiation of the "Five twenty"

Loan to the lowest possible point and I think you will give me credit for the economy with which I have conducted the expenditures and also that I have frequently for the success of the Loan encroached heavily upon the very small commission of ⅛ per cent assigned to me as general agent & in consideration of which I assumed all the risks & labors attending this agency—

You are doubtless aware that similar negotiations, but without similar risks—on the part of agents of European nations are not undertaken upon such economical terms / A commission of one half to one per cent is the usual allowance, In this case the Government assumed no risk whatever for any of the vast preliminary Expenditures nor indeed for any of the expenditures thereafter, but in case of sales being made the whole expense of these negotiations was limited by you to three eighths per cent & it was your desire that this sum should be divided as follows as near as possible viz an allowance of ⅛ to subagents, ⅛ to be expended in necessary expenses of advertising printing, circulars Editorial aid travelling agents exchanges, sub allowances &c &c—& the balance ⅛ per cent to be my compensation as agent for subscriptions, Your suggestion in July last that this ⅛ to myself should include thereafter the services rendered by the Houses with which I am connected as partner I have *acceded to* altho' I dont think such reduction from the original compensation offered me should have been required. I know your determination to economize in this and all other expenditures & that you would not willingly do me injustice in view of the value of the services I have rendered yet as my Houses in Philada and Washington are doing a vast amount of work which is wholly gratuitous on their part & which properly should be done by the Treasury Department & at its expense—& involving the employment of many additional first class clerks at heavy expense I can see no good reason why a large portion of my commission should be thus applied, Still I desire fully to meet your views & I agree cheerfully to this reduction

Knowing your desire to reduce the allowance for other purposes also—I have carefully and I trust earnestly gone over & over again the whole subject, but arriving always at the conclusion that any reduction would be ruinous to the working of the plan, & in fact the history of the world presents no such example of vast results upon so little expenditure—

I think that by this time the wisdom of your plans in respect to the employment of a direct agency, by which to reach the people & draw from them the supplies of money needed for the successful maintenance of the public credit and suppression of the rebellion—must be fully apparent not only to your own mind but entirely satisfactory to the public whom you represent.[1] I think it is conceded by all that amongst the wonderful results attending your management of the finances the success of the 5–20 Loan has been the most gratifying. There is nothing on record in History to compare with the triumphs of [this] appeal of yours to the people of our land, and I feel a just pride in having been—under your instructions one of the instruments in this great work

The success attending your former efforts to popularize the 7.30 Loan[2] together with motives of economy and a desire that the *people* should participate in the advantages of the Loans to government led you after a full conference with some of the most eminent financial minds in the country to adopt a similar course in disposing of the 5.20. Loan, You became convinced that negotiations with Banks & capitalists at that time for any considerable sums would involve a loss to the Treasury of at least two to three per cent to be followed by still greater sacrifices as the Banks & capitalists found your wants pressing upon them, already heavily tasked as they would be, to carry the immense sums already advanced to the Treasury— You anticipated the benefits that have since been realized by a direct appeal to the people & the distribution of the Loan through the medium of this agency into every nook & corner of the loyal States & *rightly* relied upon the patriotism of the people to sustain the Treasury of the nation. some influential parties urged that the interest of our Bonds should be payable together with the principal in Europe & that agents should be despatched thither to negotiate a Loan— This course you declined to take and we now owe it to your decision in this matter that our nation has the proud consciousness of having upon its own unaided resources supplied the Treasury with ample means wherewith to meet promptly all demands upon it—

If you could have negotiated from time to time the whole of the Loan with Banks & capitalists even at 97. the loss would have amounted to *Fifteen Millions* of dollars / The plan which you decided to adopt does not involve the expenditure of one tenth this sum. & therefore you have saved to the Treasury in this item over thirteen Millions & a half of dollars by availing yourself of the popular mode

But to my mind this is a very low view to take of the matter for who shall estimate the value to the nation from this direct communication [with] the whole people through the daily efforts of over fifteen hundred active and enthusiastic agents, all intent on convincing the people of the superiority of the Loans of the Government as a safe investment of their earnings & means, Who can calculate the extent & value of the information conveyed as to the true state of the nations finances—the prejudices & fears removed & the confidence awakened & restored? This is all beyond the power of any one to reduce to figures & it is not too much to say that your plans—thus after careful & anxious thought matured by your own brain & then confided to this agency to carry out in detail have saved the credit of the nation, given confidence to our people—convinced those in rebellion of the utter hopelessness of their bankrupt cause and advised Foreign nations of our entire ability to take care of ourselves and provide promptly from our own resources all that our Treasury might need, How all this has cheered and delighted our brave officers & soldiers in the field & our Farmers. Merchants Mechanics & capitalists / How it has improved & strengthened the public credit—what *perfect* confidence all now have in the final success of our cause & in your ability to save us from the incalculable evils of a bankrupt Treasury & a deranged & depreciated currency

Why! if needed I could bring abundant proofs before you showing that the competition engendered by prompt pay & restored confidence which the sale of the 5.20 Loan with the circumstances attending its distribution—has produced—has saved during the last twelve months upon the expenditures for supplies—an average of fifteen per cent at least on the full amount of Loan sold say on three hundred & fifty Millions of dollars—a saving of Fifty two Millions five hundred thousand dollars!!! This is no exaggeration but plain, simple truth well known to contractors in every department of the public service!

I trust that your own mind is fully satisfied with the results thus far of the agency system. I have struggled through the year with a weight of care and anxiety upon me that, had I foreseen the extent of them I should have shrunk from with dismay— The securities lodged by me in the Treasury Department & amounting to nearly one and a half Millions of dollars all of which I have had at risk—together with the expenditure of large sums made prior to sales of Bonds, the increase of the clerical force of my offices more than three fold & other large expenditures over & above the allowance for that purpose—must convince all that the work has been transacted by me upon terms most liberal to the Government

It has been calculated that if it had been possible for the Treasury Department to have accomplished the work we have done throughout the vast extent of this agency system—the correspondence alone connected with it would have required the employment of one or two hundred additional clerks in the Department at an expense nearly equal to the commission paid to me and if a division of the agency had been made at the start it would not have saved one dollar to the Treasury—but would doubtless have proved a costly & dangerous experiment, besides being devoid of that unity of action that is necessary to success in all such undertakings

My estimate of the number of individuals subscribing to the Loan to date is 536.000 Five Hundred & thirty six thousand of all classes, high & low, rich & poor white & black & of all nations & tongues, trades occupations & professions!

I wish I had time at present to enter more largely into the statistics & facts connected with this negotiation & coming under my immediate notice / This I will do at the final winding up of the sales— In meantime let me assure you again as I have done before of my entire and cheerful willingness to resign at any time my connection with the Loan if you deem that the public interests will be better served by the appointment of any other agent or number of agents or I will cheerfully give my services without compensation if relieved of all risk & responsibility for the future—only requiring the repayment of actual expenditures, but at same time I assert without reservation that the allowance heretofore received by me is wholly disproportioned to the amount of risk assumed & work performed—

I am indeed deeply grateful for the confidence you have shown towards me & I rejoice that I have been instrumental in carrying out your plans for the public good— I have endeavored to perform faithfully the duties imposed upon me

Most truly your frd
& obt Servant
JAY COOKE
Subn Agt

1. Chase apparently got the idea of a direct agency for the sales of 5–20 bonds in 1862 from successful French precedents during the 1850s. Larson, *Jay Cooke,* 121.

2. On July 17, 1861, Congress had authorized the sale of U.S. Treasury notes "not less than fifty dollars, . . . to be payable three years after date, with interest at the rate of seven and three tenths percentum per annum, payable semi-annually." *Statutes at Large,* 12:259.

TO KATE CHASE SPRAGUE

Autograph letter. Private collection (*micro* 29:0903).

Washington, Nov. 18, 1863.

My darling child,

Your letter—so full of sweet words and good thoughts—came yesterday and I need not tell you how welcome it was.

I rejoice greatly in all your happiness, & fervently pray that it may be continued to you. But I rejoice with trembling. Few lives are so unclouded as yours has been hitherto; and I fear the dark days. But you are beginning right; and there is one infallible security against unhappiness. I thank God that He puts it into your heart to take shelter under this security. "The fear of the Lord is a strong tower; the righteous man runneth into it & is safe."[1] I don't know that I quote the precise words; but I preserve the idea. It is this that trust in God, proved by conformity to His will, is a sure defence against all the ills of life. The same idea was expressed by the great Roman Orator when he said that "no ill can befall a good man."[2] He meant that the man who conforms his life to the principles of rectitude is in harmony with the everlasting laws and therefore cannot miscarry. But who can conform his life to the unvarying rule of rectitude? Who does? Here the Christian faith comes in to save us from despair. For perfect conformity it substitutes repentance and faith—repentance which is unfeigned sorrow for transgression, proved by steadfast endeavors to keep the law & faith, which is trust in God & His appointed Salvation through Christ, proved by constant endeavors towards conformity & tranquil reliance on His merits instead of our own.

Dear Katie, I desire nothing so much for you and your beloved husband as that you may be Christians in heart & life. Then though sickness & misfortune may come, and death must come, you will indeed be safe: and many will be blessed through you. No duty will be neglected belonging to your station nor any work appropriate to it omitted. But duty will be made easy by the spirit of its performance and the work lifted out of its grosser material character, by the nobleness of the motives which prompt the doing of it.

Things are going on very nicely at the house. Marshall & Richard seem to be doing their best and Eliza is beginning to take on housekeeping ways: while Claire is pleasant and ornamental.[3] Wilson has not yet gone; but I shall send him off tomorrow. I hate to do so: but see no alternative.[4]

The President, with all the "Heads" except Mr. Stanton & myself go to Gettysburgh today. I should like to go; but cannot leave my work. The Report is hardly begun, and I must finish, if possible, before Congress comes together.[5]

I shall send with this a short letter to the Governor, and so send no special Messages to him:[6] but warm love for him, & for dear Nettie and Allie.[7]

Please remember that Dudley Walbridge is at the Custom House[8] & get Mr. Barney to have him come to see you. Try also to see John Wallace & the Bakers.[9]

Your very Affectionate father
S P Chase

Mrs Kate Sprague

P.S. I enclose a bill and a check for $50. Please pay all little bills made prior to your marriage; and have the large ones made out & sent to me at once or as early as practicable. The Governor as a good business man will approve of this I am sure.

1. A paraphrase of Prov. 18:10.

2. "For no evil can befall any good man either in life or in death nor will his welfare ever be neglected by the immortal gods." Cicero, who made the comment in his *Tusculan Disputations* (1.42.99), derived it from Socrates as recorded in Plato's *Apology* (41cd). A. E. Douglas, ed. and trans., *Cicero: Tusculan Disputations* (Chicago, 1985), 75; B. Jowett, ed. and trans., *The Dialogues of Plato,* 4th ed., 4 vols. (London, 1953), 366.

3. Chase's niece Eliza Chase Whipple and, evidently, Claire Albrecht. Eliza Whipple had been in Boston at the home of her sister, Hannah Ralston Whipple Tucker. Earlier in November, when Hannah's husband, Josiah Prentice Tucker, left on a Treasury assignment to New Orleans, he escorted Eliza to Washington, where she visited in Chase's household until around the beginning of February 1864. Marshall and Richard were household employees. Chase once described the latter, who worked in the Chase-Sprague household as late as 1867, as "a colored American Citizen." J. Prentice Tucker to Chase, Oct. 24, Nov. 27, 1863, Eliza Whipple to Chase, Feb. 5, 1864, Chase to Janet Chase, Mar. 27, 1867 (Chase Papers, L.C.); Chase to Tucker, Oct. 20, 1863 (Chase Papers, Hist. Soc. of Pa.); *Chase Papers,* 1:503, 535, 557, 603.

4. Chase had decided to dismiss domestic employee Charles Wilson due to "intoxication." Chase to ———, Nov. 22, 1863 (Chase Papers, Hist. Soc. of Pa.); *Chase Papers,* 3:126.

5. On November 19, Lincoln delivered his famous Gettysburg Address. Actually, the only cabinet members to travel with the President were Montgomery Blair, William H. Seward, and Secretary of the Interior John P. Usher. Work on his annual report to Congress prevented Chase from attending. Chase to David Wills, Nov. 16, 1863, in *New York Herald,* Nov. 20, 1863; Miers, *Lincoln Day by Day,* 3:220–22.

6. The letter to William Sprague discussed recent military action near Knoxville, Tenn., that involved Ambrose E. Burnside, and solicited intelligence about preparations for the upcoming Democratic national convention (held in Chicago, August 29–31, 1864). Chase to Sprague, Nov. 18, 1863 (Chase Papers, Hist. Soc. of Pa.); Long, *Civil War Day by Day,* 434, 562–63.

7. Likely Chase's niece Alice Skinner, who with Nettie Chase accompanied Kate's bridal party to Rhode Island. Skinner to Chase, Nov. 22, 1863 (Chase Papers, L.C.); *Washington Evening Star,* Nov. 14, 1863.

8. Dudley H. Walbridge, the son of Chase's sister, Helen Walbridge, clerked in the New York Custom House. *Register of Officers (1863),* 72; Henry B. Walbridge to Chase, July 2, 1862, Dudley Walbridge to Chase, July 9, 1863 (Chase Papers, L.C.).

9. Possibly John William Wallace, reporter for the U.S. Supreme Court, 1863–75. Evidence suggests that Chase was acquainted with a family named Baker through John and Amelia Garniss, the parents of Chase's first wife. John Garniss had dealings with a Jacob S. Baker (d. 1859?) of New York, who was likely the husband of Garniss's sister. John P. Garniss to Chase, June 2, 1847, Sept. 28, 1854, Mar. 3, 1859, Chase to Kate Chase, Oct. 22, 1856 (Chase Papers, Hist. Soc. of Pa.); Jacob S. Baker to Chase, Nov. 6, 1837 (Chase Papers, L.C.); *DAB,* 19:374.

TO THOMAS J. DURANT

Letterpress copy of autograph letter. Chase Papers, Historical Society of Pennsylvania (*micro* 29:0913).

Washington, Nov. 19, 1863.

My dear Sir,

Yours of the 6th has just reached me[,] with copy of the letter to Mr. Etheridge enclosed.[1]

Mr. Colfax, who is a very prominent candidate for Speaker, was present when I read them.[2] He assures me that Etheridge has abandoned all intention (if he ever had any—*I* think he had) of placing the names of the La. pretended members on the roll.[3] There is nothing now to apprehend on that score. My own opinion is that the wise & prompt action of the Free State Committee has been the principal Means of preventing very serious trouble.

I see you are carrying on the registry. Do you register any names of colored citizens? My own impression is that it is safest as well as most just to do so: and I know that the instructions to Gov Shepley were framed in view of the opinion of Attorney General Bates on the citizenship of colored freemen, natives of the U. States.[4] I do not know however, nor have I any reason to believe that the instructions were intended to establish any imperative rule of registration.

It seems to be pretty well settled now that in the regards of the National Government the loyal citizens of a state are to constitute the state. It is, of course, important that the loyalty should be unquestioned and that the numbers of unquestioned loyalty should be as large as possible.

We—that is those who think & feel as I do—are rejoicing exceedingly over the triumphs in Maryland & Missouri—to which will be hope be added today a triumph in Delaware.[5]

"What hath God wrought!"[6]

I shall be always most happy to hear from you. You know not, to how many your name has become dear.

Yours very truly
S P CHASE

Thos J Durant Esq
New Orleans

1. Durant complained to Chase about a recent unauthorized congressional election in Louisiana that favored the proslavery faction. According to Durant, the victors reputedly had assurances from Emerson Etheridge (1819–1902), a conservative Unionist and clerk of the House, that they would be seated in the next Congress. Subsequent events indicated that Etheridge planned to manipulate the credentials of newly elected congressmen throughout the U.S. and thus take control of the House away from radicals. Writing as attorney general and commissioner of registration for Louisiana, Durant warned Etheridge on the same day that the unauthorized election was "contrary to law." Herman Belz, "The Etheridge Conspiracy of 1863: A Projected Conservative Coup," *Journal of Southern History* 36 (Nov. 1970): 549–67; *Bio. Dir. U.S. Cong.*, 972; Durant to Chase, Nov. 6, 1863, Durant to Etheridge, same date (Chase Papers, L.C.).

2. The House of Representatives chose Indiana Representative Schuyler Colfax as speaker on December 7. *Bio. Dir. U.S. Cong.*, 175, 809.

3. Neither New Orleans physician Thomas Cottman nor attorney A. P. Field, the "members" elect, actually served in Congress. Ibid., 176; Jefferson Davis Bragg, *Louisiana in the Confederacy* (Baton Rouge, 1941), 280; McCrary, *Lincoln and Reconstruction*, 178; *New Orleans Dir. (1855)*, 86.

4. The War Department had issued Shepley's instructions on August 24, 1863. The attorney general's opinion dated from November 1862. Chase to Opdyke et al., Apr. 8, 1863 (above); *OR*, ser. 3, v. 3:711–12.

5. In recent congressional elections, Maryland voters had elected four out of five Unconditional Union candidates. Radical (Unconditional Union) candidates had carried the Missouri elections for supreme court justices, and the legislature had recently chosen two radicals, Benjamin Gratz Brown and John Brooks Henderson, as U.S. senators. In Delaware, opponents of Lincoln's administration boycotted polls and thus insured victory for the Unconditional Union nominee in the state's only House race. *Appletons' Annual Cyclopædia*, 3:337, 625, 657; *Daily Missouri Democrat*, Nov. 9, 14, 1863; Chase to James A. Garfield, Nov. 1, 1863 (above).

6. Num. 23:23.

TO GEORGE HARRINGTON

Autograph letter. HM 23407, The Huntington Library, San Marino, California (*micro* 29:0916).

Washington, Nov. 19, 1863.

My dear Mr. Harrington,

I have received two letters from you since you arrived in Europe; but in neither of them did you inform me where a reply would reach you.[1] I now write at a venture; but supposing you will get my letter as soon through our Legation at London as any other way.

It is a great grief to me that you give so little hope of your speedy return in renovated health. I begin to fear that in recommending a journey to Europe your friends were not altogether wise. The cares attendant on travelling with a considerable party are, I am told, quite harrassing even with a good courier & what you needed was good air, plenty of exercise but not too much, & absolute repose. Perhaps you would have found more of all in an overland journey to California or in a sojourn in the region west of the Mississippi. But I will hope better—the best news in your next letter.[2]

Affairs here move on pretty much as when you left. Our arms have made no real progress since Rosecrans fell back to Chattanooga;[3] and a sort of mystery envelopes all military movements. I suppose I could penetrate it if I had time; and I would take time if I had the least reason for supposing that with a perfect understanding of the situation I could impress any conclusions I might reach as practical guides of action, on the President.

In the Treasury Department there has been pretty much the usual work & pretty much the usual results. The 5–20 Loan has been a great success, and has enabled me to meet all the vast demands with promptitude. For some time past there has been a stringency in the money market which has caused an immense reduction in the temporary loan. In less than two weeks I redeemed over forty millions of dollars of the Certificates of 4% & 5% deposit, waving for accommodation of holders the ten days notice. My receipts for the 5–20 Loan enabled me to do this without inconvenience.

The National Banking Scheme is working well. About one hundred & thirty banks have been organized. The organization of one in San Francisco is expected and one in New Orleans is making good progress. It will not be long before they exist in all parts of the Country; and then it will be an easy matter to bring all the present capital of the State Banks into it. The Nationality of the currency will then be complete, and our finances will work much more smoothly than heretofore.

The Fractional Currency has not succeeded as well as was expected: but Mr. Clark is still sanguine: The washable paper was a failure.

Dr. Gwynn has now improved it so that he thinks it will answer perfectly. But it is no longer washable as before: though still impervious to wear because of the middle layer which is of the same substance as the exterior surfaces of the paper first used. If we dont succeed now we shall resort to the ordinary bank note paper. If possible I will send you some specimens of the new fractional notes in the same envelope with this letter.[4]

A week ago my daughter was married to Gov Sprague. The Wedding was not general quoad[5] invitations; though a good many were present: among the rest the Prest. & all the "Heads" except Mr. Blair.

I see that the Times and some other papers are down on my poor speeches in Ohio.[6] They were wholly unpremeditated and not malicious, and when read in full will not seem so harsh. But I meant they should be decided. The people demand decision & firmness. I will send you some copies in a few days.— The Political caldron begins to boil. Many names are mentioned in connexion with the next canvass—the Presidents for reelection, Sewards, Grants, Banks, Seymours[7] Butlers, my own. Nobody can tell who will be taken or who will be left. I mean to be satisfied any how and meanwhile not anxious. With best regards to Mrs H & Mary my sweet friend believe me[8]

Yours Cordially
S P Chase

1. Harrington had departed for Europe in September to seek relief from an unidentified malady. Written from London and Paris, respectively, Harrington's letters of October 4 and 20 reported on his travels, assessed attitudes toward the U.S., and warned about Confederate propaganda successes. From Paris he wrote of being "compelled to be quiet my head having been very troublesome." Harrington to Chase, Oct. 4, 20, 1863 (Chase Papers, Hist. Soc. of Pa.); *Chase Papers,* 1:449.

2. Harrington wrote from Rome in December, describing an "attack" on "the nerves of my back, right shoulder, arm & hand." He had been bedridden "for weeks, a portion of the time unable to move without the assistance of two men." Harrington to Chase, Dec. 12, 1863 (Chase Papers, Hist. Soc. of Pa.).

3. After the Federal defeat at the battle of Chickamauga in September. Long, *Civil War Day by Day,* 411–12.

4. A large funding act passed in March 1863 authorized new fractional currency to replace previous versions of stamps, "postal currency," and fractional notes that had been issued as substitutes for coins of low denomination. Since the fall of 1862, under the supervision of Spencer Morton Clark, who directed the Treasury's printing of bonds and currency, contractor Stuart Gwynn had experimented to develop a new "membrane paper." Those efforts failed, but resulted eventually in what Chase characterized as an "improved product called National paper." Criticism of Gwynn's experiments, which involved expenditures for new printing processes and equipment, generated official investigations of Clark's operation. However, the complaints were fueled at least in part by bank-note engraving and printing companies displeased with the Treasury's assumption of currency and bond printing that previously had been done by private firms. For congressional investigations of Clark, see Chase's letter to John Brough, May 19, 1864 (below). H. A. Risley to Chase, Dec. 8, 1864, with replying endorsement by Chase, Dec. 21 (Corres. and Bids: Distinctive Paper, Engraving Notes and Bonds, Recs. of Bureau of Public Debt, Nat. Arch.); L. C. Baker, *History of the United States Secret Service* (Philadelphia, 1868),

263–89; *Chase Papers,* 1:432; Clark to Chase, Jan. 8, 186[4], Alexander C. Wilson to Chase, Aug. 13, 17, Oct. 6, 1863 (Letters Recd. from Exec. Officers, Comptroller of Currency, Gen. Recs. Treasury Dept., Nat. Arch.); Chase to Wilson, Aug. 15, 27, Oct. 2, 1863 (Misc. Letters Sent, Gen. Recs. Treasury Dept., Nat. Arch.); Chase to Wilson, Oct. 8, 1863, Chase to Fitch Shepard, May 26, 1864 (Chase Papers, Hist. Soc. of Pa.); *Statutes at Large,* 12:711.

5. Latin for "as far as."

6. According to the *London Times,* Chase's campaign speeches of October 10 to 16 "were prompted by the most unrelenting warlike spirit and in accordance with the narrowest views of uncompromising Abolitionism." *London Times,* Oct. 31, 1863; Chase, *"Going Home to Vote."*

7. Horatio Seymour.

8. Mary was evidently Harrington's daughter. Chase to Harrington, June 11, 1865 (Huntington Lib.).

TO JANET CHASE

Letterpress copy of autograph letter. Chase Papers, Historical Society of Pennsylvania (*micro* 29:0976).

Washington, Nov. 23, 1863

My darling Nettie,

I send back your letter with some corrections. I hope you will find time to copy it and return it to me, together with the corrected letter, that I may see whether you understand the corrections I make.

You ought always to have a book about composition, including punctuation, together with a dictionary at your side, until by practice you become perfect in spelling and writing. You may think, I lay too much stress on these matters: but I do not: and some time hereafter you will be convinced of it, by painful mortifications, if you do not now correct your faults.

Your great defect is in heedlessness and it pains me more than I can well tell you. It will cost you an effort and a continued effort to amend. Have you the courage and the conscience to make it? Let your letters show.

I am very glad you have enjoyed yourself so much. It would have suited me better, had you, yourself, showed your sense of the value of your time & insisted on going back to school. Today I think you would have been happier had you done so. But I was not willing even to seem harsh to you: especially when all united in desires that you should go. Of course I did not doubt what was *pleasantest* for *the week to come;* though I preferred for you the more self denying & beneficial course.

It is over now and I rejoice in your rejoicing for all the pleasure you can have, if innocent, is pleasure to me.

It pleases me also to read your resolutions of improvement. May God help you to keep them.

If you determine to come home for the holidays instead of making up lost time by remaining in New York—(if indeed Mrs Macaulay thinks you can thus make up lost time—) I will very gladly invite Minnie Vail to accompany you.[1] It seems to me however that you are so breaking up the first half of your year that it will be of little benefit to you.

Your affectionate father
S P Chase

Miss Nettie Chase

1. Minnie, mentioned again in Chase's letter to Janet on November 28 (below), was evidently one of Nettie's schoolmates.

FROM WILLIAM CULLEN BRYANT

Autograph letter. Chase Papers, Historical Society of Pennsylvania (*micro* 29:0991).

New York Nov. 24. 1863.

My dear Mr Chase

Some years since, Congress took in hand the subject of the emoluments of the Collectors Naval Officer and Surveyor at the several ports of entry, and the members thought they had accomplished a reform.[1] The salaries were fixed, and the public in general supposed that, since that time, their salaries are their only compensation. That Congress supposes this to be so, I have no doubt, and it has occurred to me that you might have the same impression. The proof that the fact is not so, and that each of these officers, at the port of New York, recieved larger emoluments than the President of the United States, is only to be found in certain accounts which, unless there was some obvious reason for looking into them, would not be examined, either by yourself, or any of the members of Congress.

When Mr John Cockle, an old Custom House officer under honest Michael Hoffman, and now a clerk in your department, was in New York the other day, I obtained some information of him on this subject, and if you desire to be informed in regard to the matter, I will take the liberty to refer you to him.[2]

It happened, that when the act of Congress fixing the compensations of the three officers I have mentioned was enacted, certain portions of previous acts, one of them as old as 1799, were left unrepealed, at least as the Custom House officers choose to construe the later statute.[3] By these acts, the "fines penalties and forfeitures" for frauds on the revenue are divided into two equal parts, one of which is recieved by the government, and the other is shared equally between the Collector, the Naval Officer and the Surveyor.

The amount recieved from this source by the Naval Officer of our port in the space of 25 months and four days from his appointment, was $44.640.67, which with his salary of $5.000 yearly for that time would make a total of $56.049.20.[4]

The Collector has recieved some two thousand dollars more than this; the Surveyor some five hundred less—each of them is better paid than the President of the United States—and you will agree with me exorbitantly paid.[5]

I am, Sir,

very truly yours,
W. C. BRYANT.

Hon. S. P. Chase.

1. Bryant, who edited the *New York Evening Post,* evidently referred to legislation signed on February 11, 1846. *Congressional Globe,* 29th Cong., 1st sess., 1846, 310–11; *Statutes at Large,* 9:3–4.

2. A native of New Jersey, John Cockle worked in 1863 as a clerk in the solicitor's office at the Treasury Department in Washington. In 1861, Michael Hoffman was deputy collector in the New York Custom House. *Register of Officers (1861),* 53; *Register of Officers (1863),* 42; *Wash. Dir. (1863),* 128.

3. Congress had established the framework for compensation through legislation on March 2, 1799, and passed numerous related laws since then. *Statutes at Large,* 1:704–9, 3:693.

4. George Denison (not to be confused with George S. Denison in New Orleans) served as naval officer of the New York Custom House for an offical annual salary of $4,950. *Register of Officers (1863),* 81.

5. Hiram Barney's official salary as collector was $6,340 per year, and Rufus F. Andrews, surveyor of customs at New York, received $4,900. Lincoln's annual salary in 1863 was $25,000. *Register of Officers (1863),* 68, 81; *Wash. Dir. (1863),* 279.

TO JOHN A. DIX

Letter in clerk's hand on letterhead stationery, signed by Chase. Chase Papers, New Hampshire Historical Society (*micro* 29:1011).

Treasury Department.
November 25, 1863.

My dear Sir,

Your kind invitation to write something that may be read at the breaking of ground on the Union Pacific Railroad in Nebraska, found me in the midst of engagements so exacting that it has been impossible to write anything worth the reading.[1]

I could not, however, omit writing altogether, for that would imply an indifference to the work which no American feels.

It is among my most pleasing recollections of service, as a Senator from Ohio, that the first practical measure looking to the construction of a Pacific Railroad, which received the sanction of Congress, was moved by me. That measure was an amendment to the Army Appropriation Bill, placing at the disposal of the Secretary of War one hundred and fifty thousand dollars, to be expended in Surveys and Explorations of routes for the road. It was adopted by the Senate in February 1853 and subsequently concurred in by the House.[2] Its results are embodied in the volumes known as the Pacific Railroad Reports, printed by order of Congress.[3]

It is another pleasing recollection that I had the honor in March 1850 of presenting and commending to the Senate the memorial of Dr. Pulte, an intelligent physician of Cincinnati, praying that measures might be taken for the connexion of New York with London by extending the existing lines of telegraph to the Pacific, by way of the coast and Behring's Straits through Northern Asia to St. Petersburgh, and there forming connexions with the lines to the cities of Western Europe.[4]

This great work has since been completed to the Pacific by the indomitable energy of Hiram Sibley, a private citizen of New York, aided by the simple promise of employment and compensation by the Government.[5] On the other side of the Pacific, the Russian telegraph lines from St. Petersburgh constructed by the Imperial Government approaches, if it has not already reached, the Pacific; and American Enterprise is earnestly enlisted in the task,—now certain to be accomplished,[6]—of completing the wonderful work which the Cincinnati physician suggested more than thirteen years ago.[7]

Steam moves more slowly than lightning. The progress of the Railroad has been necessarily slower than that of the telegraph. When the Surveys and Explorations for a Route had been partially reported, the subject of the Railroad was again brought before Congress; and I again had some connection with it,—now, however, of a less pleasant, tho' still significant character. Solicitous for the progress of the work, I submitted a resolution, in January 1854, instructing the Committee on Roads and Canals, to enquire into and report upon the construction of a Railroad from some point on the Western lines of the Western[8] States to some point on the Eastern line of California.

On the motion of Mr. Gwinn the reference to the Committee on Roads and Canals was stricken out and the whole subject referred to a select Committee of nine[9] Senators; from which Committee I was excluded, because I then held about the same relations to the Democratic Party on the subject of slavery as the War Democrats now hold on the question of the Rebellion.[10]

Mr. Gwinn's Committee reported a bill which after much discussion and sundry amendments passed the Senate in 1855; but failing to receive the sanction of the House did not become a law.[11]

Nothing further of importance was done in relation to the Pacific Railroad during the next seven years.[12] The attention of the country was absorbed by other questions; and it remained for the Thirty-Seventh Congress to give a grand proof of the stability of the Republic and the worth of Democratic Republican Institutions by taking up this great measure, in the midst of our terrible Civil War, and framing it into a law.

The Thirty-Seventh Congress will be forever memorable in history as the author of many acts of legislation of transcendent importance and far-reaching consequences. Among these great acts the Pacific Railroad bill will remain as one of the most illustrious monuments of the wisdom and courage of its members.[13]

I shall not attempt any discussion of its importance to our industry, our commerce, or our Union. I have elsewhere said something on these themes; but now the Road is its own most eloquent advocate. I rejoice in the belief that under your charge and that of the eminent citizens associated with you, it will go steadily forward to completion; and vindicate, by perfect success, the most sanguine predictions and hopes of its advocates and promoters.

Very truly Yours,
S P Chase

General John A Dix,
President Union Pacific R.R. Company.

1. Dix issued the invitation on November 23. The ceremony, near Omaha on December 2, featured letters written for the occasion by Chase, John Hay, George Opdyke, William H. Seward, and others. Dix to Chase, Nov. 23, 1863 (Chase Papers, Hist. Soc. of Pa.); *New York Times,* Dec. 4, 1863.

2. *February* is an interlineation in Chase's handwriting.

3. Chase had discussed the Senate action in previous correspondence with Edward S. Hamlin. On March 7, 1853, Jefferson Davis became secretary of war and retained the position until 1857. Altogether, the War Department published twelve volumes of its *Reports of Explorations and Surveys . . .* (Washington, D.C., 1855–61). *Bio. Dir. U.S. Cong.,* 17; Chase to Hamlin, June 6, 1853, in *Chase Papers,* 2:355.

4. Chase presented the memorial of Joseph Hippolyt Pulte on March 15, 1850. *Memorial of J. H. Pulte,* 31st Cong., 1st sess., 1850, S. Ex. Doc. 109.

5. Sibley's name in this sentence is an interlineation by Chase. In 1856, Sibley (1807–88) helped found the Western Union Telegraph Company and served as its first president. He enjoyed a $40,000 annual subsidy from Congress starting in 1860. *DAB,* 17:145–46; *Statutes at Large,* 12:41–42.

6. The phrase originally read: *to be completed.* Chase struck through *completed* and substituted *accomplished.* The word *now* is Chase's interlineation.

7. Successful completion of Cyrus W. Field's transatlantic telegraph during the summer of 1866 destroyed plans for a line across the Pacific. *DAB,* 6:359, 17:146.

8. The clerk left a blank in the line which Chase filled with this word.

9. Chase wrote this word in a blank left by the clerk.

10. Chase actually presented his resolution on December 14, 1853. The successful motion by William McKindree Gwin (1805–85), a California Democrat, passed the Senate on January 4, 1854. Besides Gwin, senators who served on the select committee studying the issue of a rail connection to the Pacific were Democrats Stephen A. Douglas of Illinois, Jesse David Bright of Indiana, Josiah James Evans (1786–1858) of South Carolina, and Thomas Jefferson Rusk (1803–57) of Texas; and Whigs John Bell of Tennessee, Edward Everett of Massachusetts, Henry Sheffie Geyer of Missouri, and William H. Seward of New York. Solomon Foot, a Vermont Whig, and David Settle Reid (1813–91), a Democrat from North Carolina, replaced Bright and Everett during the second session of the Thirty-third Congress. *Congressional Globe,* 33d Cong., 1st sess., 1854, 44, 118–20, 144, 33d Cong., 2d sess., 1855, 52; *Bio. Dir. U.S. Cong.,* 975; *DAB,* 8:64–65, 15:476, 16:236–37.

11. "An act to authorize and facilitate the construction of a northern, a southern, and a central Pacific railroad and magnetic telegraph through the Territories of the

United States" passed the Senate by a margin of 24 to 21 on February 19, 1855. *Congressional Globe,* 33d Cong., 2d sess., 1855, 814.

12. The word *seven* is Chase's insertion in a blank left by the clerk.

13. Lincoln signed the bill on July 1, 1862. *Statutes at Large,* 12:489–98.

TO ABRAHAM LINCOLN

Letter in clerk's hand on letterhead stationery, signed by Chase. Abraham Lincoln Papers, Library of Congress (*micro* 29:1015).

Treasury Department.
November 25, 1863.

My dear Sir,

The conclusions you have come to concerning the reconstruction of the rebel States gives me very great satisfaction, in which I am sure almost all loyal men will share.

There are some points of detail and form, however, which seem to me essential to the completeness of your act; and as I can best make myself understood in that way, I submit them to your consideration in writing.[1]

1. Your act will fitly complete your Proclamation[2] by ensuring the incorporation of the principle of emancipation in the constitution of every reconstituted State.—

Permit me again most respectfully to urge on you the expediency and the duty of making the Proclamation itself complete within the States in which it operates by revoking the exceptions of certain parts of two of them from its operation.

The representations of Gov. Pierpont and of the officers of the Treasury Department connected with the Internal Revenue satisfy me that the whole military necessity which justified the original Proclamation, now justifies and requires the revocation of the exceptions so far as Virginia is concerned: and so far as Louisiana is concerned, the representations of Mr. Flanders and other loyal citizens of that State are to the same effect. They show indeed that in a considerable part of the region covered by the exceptions the rebels were at the time in full possession and are yet in substantial control.

It cannot be doubted that the revocation is warranted. It seems to me necessary to complete for the present generation and for history the great act of the Proclamation.

Sometime since I took the liberty of handing you a sketch of such an order of revocation as I thought least liable to criticism, which you may have retained among your papers. If so, I beg leave to refer you to it as embodying the views I have just offered in practical form.[3]

2. I respectfully advise that in the Proclamation you now propose to put forth,—virtually inviting the people of the rebel States to reorganize their political institutions on the basis of free labor,—no suggestion be made of any apprenticeship of the freedmen or other special legislation for them.

There is great difference of opinion as to this; and it seems to me that it is right to leave the whole subject, without any intimation from Washington, to the judgment of those immediately concerned. My own strong impression is that special legislation for colored citizens will be as unnecessary as for white citizens. The demand for labor will secure them employment, and freedom will enable them to buy and build with the proceeds of their labor; while the voluntary charities, already so widely awakened, will, with proper countenance and support from the Government, secure to them the benefits of education and religion. Whether I am right or wrong in this, it seems to me clear that no, even apparent sanction of legislation which may be easily perverted into virtual re-enslavement should be contained in the document you are about to put forth.—

3. I respectfully suggest the expediency of omitting all reference to the subject of the admission of Senators and Representatives before the reconstitution of the States.

It seems to me quite clear that no such Senators or Representatives shall be admitted. Representatives to the last Congress, who were admitted, were elected under the old apportionment; as were all other members of that Congress.— To the present or a future Congress no member can be elected except under a new apportionment to be made by a loyal legislature, and no Senator can be elected except by such a legislature. There may be, possibly, one or two Senators, elected before the rebellion, who have never taken an active part in it; but they will hardly present themselves, or be admitted to seats if they do, after residing for years within rebel lines in passive acquiescence if not in open participation in rebellion—at least until they shall themselves have taken the benefit of your proposed amnesty, and their States have been reconstituted by those who have also done so.

The introduction therefore of this topic is not likely to do good and may do harm.

There are one or two other points which might warrant a suggestion, but they are comparatively unimportant. I trust you will pardon [my] freedom in those I submit, and attribute it to its true cause, a sincere wish that all you do may be done so as to produce the greatest amount of good, and reflect the greatest honor upon yourself.

Yours very truly
S P Chase

The President.

1. Chase had seen a draft of a Proclamation of Amnesty and Reconstruction that Lincoln issued on December 8. Among other provisions, the proclamation offered to readmit Confederate states into the Union when ten percent of qualified voters took the oath of allegiance. The proposal's key measures became known as the "ten percent plan." Basler, *Collected Works,* 7:53–56.

2. That is, the Emancipation Proclamation.

3. Chase gave the draft to Lincoln on August 29 and the president responded on September 2. Basler, *Collected Works,* 6:428–29; *Chase Papers,* 1:429.

TO WILLIAM SPRAGUE

Letterpress copy of autograph letter. Chase Papers, Historical Society of Pennsylvania (*micro* 30:0004).

Washington, Nov. 26, 1863.

My dear Governor,

This letter is to you, but to Katie almost as much. I have written her a line to Cleveland, which I fear she will hardly get, in which I promise to write fully to Columbus.

My heart is full of love for you both, and I rejoice as I never expected to rejoice in the prospects of happiness opening before both of you. I feared some inequalities of temper—some too great love of the world, either of its possessions or its shows—something I hardly know about. But I find that you each trust the other fully; that each desires to yield whatever is for the real happiness of the other; that you are both taking rational views of life; and above all that you both look to God for his blessing & guidance. It is this last which most assures me. To them that seek Him his blessing will be given & where His blessing is no *real harm* can come though trial may.

I fear that Katie may be a little too anxious about my political future. She must not be so. There is not so uncertain as the political future of any man: and especially as the future which must be determined by popular preferences founded quite as much on sentiment as on reason.

If I were myself controlled merely by personal sentiments I should prefer the reelection of Mr. Lincoln to the election of any other man. But I doubt the expediency of reelecting any body, and I think that a man of different qualities from those the President has will be needed for the next four years. I am not anxious to be regarded as that man; but I am quite willing to refer that question to the decision of those who agree in thinking that some such man should be had.

I can never permit myself to be drawn into any hostile or unfriendly position as to Mr Lincoln. His course towards me has always been so fair & kind; his progress towards entire agreement with me on the great question of slavery has been so constant, though rather slower than I wished for; and his general character is so marked by traits which command respect & affection; that I can never consent to anything, which he himself could or should consider as incompatible with perfect honor & good faith, if I were capable, which I hope I am not, of departure from either even where enemies might be concerned.

It seems to me that prospects look well politically: but my judgment must necessarily be very defective on this subject.

But whatever the political prospects may be I shall not yield my share in the general rejoicing on the news from Grant, concerning the great success of yesterday.[1] It was grand & inspiriting. Oh, that it may be now followed up by a series of crushing blows delivered right on the head of the rebellion.

Katie says nothing about your purchase of this house. Mr. Watson the Asst. Secrty of War, a good man & good judge of property told me the other day that he thought it worth $32,000. He had just sold his own on F. St, diagonal from this across the square & Street & near the Patent Office for 17,000 and he thought it worth not much more than half as much as this house & grounds.[2] Mr. Varnum wrote Col. Graham that he had offered it to you for 30,000, or rather had accepted your offer of that sum for it, with some conditions as to some small matters which he did not explain but to which he thought you would not object. He said he had received no reply from you. I mention all this, lest, in your other concerns, you may have forgotten Mr. Varnum; but without desiring to influence your decision in any way.[3]

Eliza & I have just returned from the Cookes where we took our thanksgiving dinner.[4] We are all well. My report has the framework up & will I hope be ready in time.[5] Wilson has gone finally. All goes well in the house. Love to your darling & mine & may God evermore bless and keep you both

Yours faithfully
S. P. Chase

1. At the battle of Missionary Ridge. Long, *Civil War Day by Day,* 437–38.

2. Peter H. Watson's house stood at 404 F. St., N.W., not far from Chase's residence at 6th and E. *Wash. Dir. (1862),* 178.

3. New York attorney John Lorimer Graham (1797–1876), former postmaster of New York City, claimed his military rank from service in the state militia. In 1863, he was a clerk in the third auditor's office. "It is very annoying," wrote Varnum on November 20 of the pending sale to Sprague of the house at 6th and E, "as I wish a decision one way or the other before I go to Washington." Sprague did complete the purchase. He and Kate Chase Sprague used the house as their Washington residence and shared it with Chase, who lived there until the fall of 1869. *Appletons',* 2:703; *Register of Officers (1863),* 25; Varnum to Graham (extract), Nov. 20, 1863, Chase to J. D. Hoover, Oct. 4, [1869], Chase to Anna P. Hoover, Sept. 27, [1870] (Chase Papers, L.C.); James M. Goode, *Capital Losses: A Cultural History of Washington's Destroyed Buildings* (Washington, 1979), 52.

4. Chase and his niece, Eliza Chase Whipple, dined at the Georgetown residence of Henry D. Cooke. On October 3, a presidential proclamation had set aside the last Thursday of November as a day of Thanksgiving. Basler, *Collected Works,* 6:496; *Wash. Dir. (1863),* 64; Chase to Kate Chase Sprague, Nov. 18, 1863 (above).

5. *Report of the Secretary of the Treasury . . . 1863.*

TO JANET CHASE

Letterpress copy of autograph letter. Chase Papers, Historical Society of Pennsylvania (*micro* 30:0060).

Washington, Nov. 28, 1863.

My darling Nettie,

You wish I would write you one letter of praise. Well, I will try. There are plenty of things to admire and love in you: and it is not because I am insensible to them that my letters have so much criticism in them. There is no one who feels so deep an interest in your welfare as I do and I am naturally prone to think most of those things which most endanger it. This is the reason, why I generally leave the more pleasing office of commendation to others, and take the less agreeable part of pointing out errors & faults to be corrected. What I write however I hope is not *always* in censure, though it is oftener doubtless than you like. Still if you would only make up *your mind to like it,* you would find it most useful.

However I have promised this time to write in praise.

So I will begin by commending your last letter. The sweet grace with which you took my correction of your last letter and the patience with which you wrote it over again is admirable. The letter you sent with your rewritten copy is also marked by a decided improvement. The handwriting is very good and the spelling quite faultless. The style too is very agreeable. Indeed all your letters lately have been so pleasing in this respect that I have only regretted they were so short. We all laughed heartily over your account of James' sentimental speeches.

Your letter has quite convinced me that you should come home at the holidays. I could not think of your staying at New York with almost all the girls and Mrs Macaulay too away and especially after labouring so faithfully to make up lost time. So we shall expect you and Minnie Vail with you, or, if she will not come, any other of your young friends you may select.

It is really very praiseworthy in you to go to work so much in earnest to make up what you have lost. I hope,—indeed I feel quite sure—you will succeed perfectly; and what a satisfaction that will be to Mrs Macaulay, to me, to sister, to all who love you.

Everybody here is rejoicing over the great victory at Chattanooga. I have just been reading a telegram from Gen Meigs—sent to me from the War Department—giving a full account of the three days fighting, and its grand results.[1] I suppose you will see it all in the papers; but I meant to send you the telegram itself; but Aunt Eliza wanted it to send home to Hannah & I could not deny her.[2]

Aunt Eliza received a letter today from Mrs Lander who said she was at Mrs Sprague's reception in Providence and that you filled your new part of Miss Chase, charmingly.[3] And we hear nothing but good of you from every one.

There, darling, have I not kept my promise. May our Heavenly Father bless you and make you understand that there is a grace, which adds charm to all other graces,—that comes down from Heaven & lifts those to whom God gives it—and He gives to all freely & withholds from none who sincerely ask—to Heaven. May that Christian grace be yours.

Your affectionate father
S P Chase

1. Grant's defeat of Confederate forces under Braxton Bragg, November 23–25, broke the siege of Chattanooga and facilitated the Federal invasion of Georgia. Mont-

gomery C. Meigs submitted his report of the battle to Edwin M. Stanton on November 26. Three days later it appeared in the *New York Times.* Long, *Civil War Day by Day,* 436–38; *New York Times,* Nov. 29, 1863; *OR,* ser. 1, v. 31, pt. 2:77–80.

2. Although she was properly the first cousin, not the aunt, of Janet Chase, the "Aunt Eliza" of this letter was Eliza Chase Whipple. She would have sent the telegram "home" to her sister Hannah Ralston Whipple Tucker, with whom Eliza customarily resided. Hannah had remained in New England when her husband, Josiah Prentice Tucker, traveled to New Orleans earlier in November on assignment for the Treasury. In other contexts Chase used the name "Aunt Eliza" to refer to at least two other women: Mary Eliza Chase of Lockport, N.Y., the widow of his deceased brother, Edward Ithamar Chase; and an elderly "Aunt Eliza" Chase who resided in Hopkinton, N.H. J. Prentice Tucker to Chase, Oct. 24, Mary Eliza Chase to Chase, Dec. 29, 1863, Eliza Chase Whipple to Chase, Feb. 5, 1864, Chase to Janet Chase, Aug. 22, 1867 (Chase Papers, L.C.); Chase to Tucker, Oct. 20, 1863, Chase to Mary Eliza Chase, Feb. 12, Chase to Kate Chase Sprague, Aug. 29, 1864 (Chase Papers, Hist. Soc. of Pa.); Chase to Jane Chase Auld, Jan. 2, 1864 (below); *Chase Papers,* 1:612, 613.

3. Jean Margaret Davenport Lander evidently reported on a reception at the Providence, R.I., home of Fanny Morgan Sprague, William Sprague's mother.

FROM THOMAS J. DURANT

Autograph letter. Chase Papers, Library of Congress (*micro* 30:0181).

Neworleans. 4. December. 1863.

Hon. S. P. Chase,
Secretary of the Treasury,
Washington City:
Dear Sir,

I have the honor to acknowledge receipt of your letter of 19 November which reached me on the 30th of the same month.[1] It is very gratifying to me to know that the action of the Free state Committee, of which I have the honor to be President, has been useful to the Government.

Mr. Flanders on his recent arrival here showed me a letter from the President to General Banks on the subject of state organization.[2] This letter had the effect of causing the Free state Committee to wait on the Military Governor, Brig. Gen. Shepley and ask him to name a day for electing members of a Constitutional Convention, and pointing out the 25th of January 1864, as the proper day. Genl. Shepley replied that he would order an election to be held at, about, that time. The opinion of our committee is that we can elect an entire delegation from Neworleans in favor of the abolition of slavery; and this would give us a majority of the whole number of members that could be elected in such portion of the state as an election can be held.

I have had long and intimate business relations with the leading free men of african descent in this city, and believe that I enjoy their confidence to as great an extent as any other in the city. They are a well behaved, and intelligent class; they are eminently loyal and patriotic. They think that the persons of African descent born free before the rebellion and of age to vote should be admitted to the registration. I think the claim well founded in justice, and have advocated it in my public speeches here. These men have petitioned Gov. Shepley to allow them to be registered; to this he promised to reply but has not yet done so.[3]

Mr. Flanders has been elected President of the First National Bank of Neworleans, and it may possible be the case, that there is some incompatibility between that position and the official one he holds in your department. I hope there is not, for it would be exceedingly useful to our cause that he should continue his position in the Internal Revenue branch, until we shall have finished the Constitutional election.

I rejoice as you do in the triumph of the holy cause of human freedom in Delaware, Maryland and Missouri, and hope for equal results in Louisiana.[4] You must give your sympathies to those who for the sake of the country are willing to be called abolitionists in the extreme south; there is some sacrifice in it.

As for myself I hope you will be pleased to think of me and command me as one desirous of devoting all his humble abilities to the cause of the country and of freedom.

I have the honor to be
With the highest respect
Your most obdt. servt.
THOMAS J. DURANT.

1. Chase's letter of November 19 (above).

2. Benjamin F. Flanders consulted with Lincoln in Washington on November 5 and 9. Lincoln's letter to Banks, on November 5, expressed disappointment that preparations to organize a new government for Louisiana had proceeded too slowly. "Time is important," warned Lincoln in apparent reference to plans masterminded by conservative Emerson Etheridge to gain control of the U.S. House. "There is danger, even now that the adverse element seeks insidiously to pre-occupy the ground." Chase to Durant, Nov. 19, 1863 (above); Lincoln to Banks, Nov. 5, 1863, in Basler, *Collected Works,* 7:1–2; Miers, *Lincoln Day by Day,* 3:217–18.

3. The petition emerged from a meeting of New Orleans free blacks on November 5. Shepley never responded or took action on the request, nor did Banks. *Appletons' Annual Cyclopædia,* 3:591–92; McCrary, *Lincoln and Reconstruction,* 181, 182, 186.

4. Durant referred to the success of Union candidates throughout the North in fall elections. He evidently anticipated the selection of delegates for a constitutional convention in Louisiana, which did not take place until March 28, 1864. Nevins, *War for the Union,* 3:177–79; *Appletons' Annual Cyclopædia,* 4:478.

FROM BENJAMIN F. FLANDERS

Letter in clerk's hand on letterhead stationery, signed by Flanders. Chase Papers, Historical Society of Pennsylvania (*micro* 30:0184).

Private

Office Supervising Special Agent Treasury Department.
New Orleans, Dec. 4th. 1863.

Dear Sir,

Without my solicitation, I have been chosen President of the 1st. National Bank of New Orleans. The acceptance of the position may render necessary, my resignation of the office of Supervis: Special Agent. This necessity will not exist, I think, until the Bank is in operation, about a month hence, and perhaps not then.

The office of Supervising Special Agent here, is an exceedingly responsible one, requiring in a high degree, sterling qualities, intelligence, firmness, integrity, prudence, self command and large capacity, for its succesful administration.

Our great cause is prospering well here. It is understood, that Gov. Shepley will soon order an election, to be held about the 25th. of January, next, for a State Convention.[1] We are preparing for the election, and have little doubt, of a favorable result.— All the influence and legitimate power, that we can exert, will be brought to bear in the election. We are at work, full of courage and hope.

The Bank promises to be a power in the land. At the outstart, subscriptions dragged. Mr. A. C. Graham came in and electrified the friends of the institution by a subscription of Seventy five Thousand Dollars.[2] This large subscription at once made the stock popular, and the amount of the Capital was soon subscribed. His experience in Banks, and his zeal and tact contributed largely, in effecting the prompt organization.

Mr. Denison also deserves much credit, for his efficient efforts to promote the Bank. His election and my own, as directors, was apparently so spontaneous, and so nearly unanimous, that the edge of criticism, which might have been raised, upon the point of Treasury influence, had we gotten in by effort and by a small majority, is effectively turned.

I learned yesterday, through Mr. Durant, who had the facts the day before from Gov. Shepley, that Bullitt and Higgins, the Assessor, were active members of the "Masonic Hall Clique", which attempted the copperhead election.[3] I have never seen Mr. Durant so deeply moved, as he was with indignation at this complicity of officers of the Government with the enemies of the Administration and its declared policy.

I kept back Bullitt's Commission for several days, as long as it was proper, enquiring of Mr. Denison and others, if Bullitt had taken part in that movement. They were ignorant of it.[4]

Hahn has behaved well; he is thoroughly with us, in our free state movement, and in other matters he will be right.

Mr. Morse is here, waiting for lumber for the roof to go to work.

Mr. Tucker pleases me much; he is intelligent, true and firm as a rock. I hope he will decide to come here to remain permanently.

Mr. Kauffman is also here, diligently informing himself in regard to the affairs of my Department; he will return by the next steamer.[5]

I am informed, that Mr. Mellen is on his way here. I hope, he will arrive, before Mr. Kauffman leaves, We shall have a harmonious and useful conference.

Very Respectfully, Your Obt. Sert.
BENJ. F. FLANDERS

Hon. Salmon P. Chase.
Secretary of Secretary
Washington. D.C.

1. The election finally occurred on March 28, 1864, after voters selected state officers in accordance with instructions issued by General Banks on January 11. The convention itself convened on April 6. *Appletons' Annual Cyclopædia,* 4:475–79.

2. Graham later became president of the First National Bank of New Orleans. Graham to Chase, Sept. 30, 1864 (Chase Papers, L.C.).

3. Louisiana conservatives who had recently cooperated with Emerson Etheridge's conspiracy to manipulate membership in the U.S. Congress were known to meet in the New Orleans Masonic Hall. Chase to Durant, Nov. 19, 1863 (above); McCrary, *Lincoln and Reconstruction,* 175–78.

4. Chase had appointed Cuthbert Bullitt special agent for the Treasury and collector of customs. Chase to Bullitt, Nov. 6, 1863 (Chase Papers, Hist. Soc. of Pa.).

5. Special Agent John F. Morse was overseeing construction of the New Orleans Custom House. In October, Chase had offered to appoint Josiah Prentice Tucker surveyor of customs at New Orleans. Tucker had recently arrived in the city to consider the position and evidently accepted in 1864. Chase had ordered S. H. Kauffman, a clerk in the Treasury Department, to prepare a report "in relation to the practical operations of the Regulations concerning Commercial Intercourse and Captured and Abandoned Property in the different Agencies of the Treasury Department." *The Biographical Cyclopædia and Portrait Gallery with an Historical Sketch of the State of Ohio,* 6 vols. (Cincinnati, 1883–95), 3:730; Chase to Flanders, Nov. 20, 1863 (Spec. Collec., Dartmouth Coll. Lib.); Chase to Tucker, Oct. 20, 1863 (Chase Papers, Hist. Soc. of Pa.); Kauffman to Flanders, Dec. 8, 1863 (3d Spec. Agency, Incoming Letters of Super. Spec. Agent, Recs. of Civil War Special Agencies, Nat. Arch.); Tucker to Chase, Oct. 24, 1863, Sept. 30, 1864, Eliza C. Whipple to Chase, Feb. 5, 1864 (Chase Papers, L.C.); *Register of Officers (1863),* 18.

FROM JOSEPH C. BUTLER

Autograph letter on letterhead stationery. Chase Papers, Library of Congress (*micro* 30:0218).

Confidential

La Fayette Bank.[1]
Cincinnati, 7 Decr 1863.

Hon. S. P. Chase
Secretary of Treasury
Washington D.C.
Dear Sir,

Much distrust is felt among some of the Bankers here as to the responsibility of Jay Cooke & Co or Jay Cooke Subn. Agent in the delivery of the U.S. 5.20 Bonds. This has been more especially manifest in last few days by the publication of the charges against Capt. Hurtt, in which Mr. Scott their sub agent here seems to have been especially implicated.[2] Mr. Scott valued largely on the Phila. house in his operations and established most of the Agencies here at the outset for sale of the Bonds.

The question often asked is whether the deposit here in U.S. Depository or remittance to Jay Cooke & Co establishes the responsibility of the Government to deliver the Bonds. This Bank has had as high as $600,000— and at present has $380,000— remitted to Jay Cooke & Co by certificate or exchange on New York or Phila. and for which they hold now Jay Cooke & Co acknowledgement. The other Banks and Agents are I suppose as largely interested.

Some authoritative statement from the Department would I think relieve anxiety and increase efforts to dispose of the Bonds. With much respect

Your Obt Srvt
JOSEPH C. BUTLER

1. Joseph Curran Butler (1823–73) was the president of Cincinnati's Lafayette Bank. Charles Theodore Greve, *Centennial History of Cincinnati and Representative Citizens* (Chicago, 1904), 2:57–60.

2. Francis W. Hurtt (d. 1884), an assistant quartermaster of volunteers, faced charges of using "Government money for his private purposes." He was dismissed from the army in June 1864. His alleged accomplice might have been George Scott, local agent for an unidentified firm. *Cincinnati Daily Commercial,* Sept. 18, 1863; *Cinc. Dir. (1863),* 328; Heitman, *Historical Register,* 1:559.

FROM BENJAMIN F. FLANDERS

Autograph letter on letterhead stationery. Chase Papers, Historical Society of Pennsylvania (*micro* 30:0296).

Private

Office Supervising Special Agent Treasury Department.
New Orleans, Decr. 12th 1863

Dear Sir:

There was a full attendance at the Free State Committee meeting last evening; the proceedings were earnest and harmonious. A letter was read from yourself to Mr. Durant, and it elicited warm applause, not so much for what it expressed as because it was from Mr Chase.[1]

A mass meeting was ordered for the 22nd to ratify the action of the committee in calling on Gov. Shepley to order an election for delegates to a State Convention.[2] The Committee are unanimously for radical measures

The letter from the President to General Banks urging him and all under his authority to aid us to establish a State government has had the desired effect.[3] All Departments of the Government now appear on the same side

Mr. Mellen's non arrival before the departure of Mr Kauffman is a disappointment. But Mr. Kauffman's visit has been very useful. He is an intelligent and sterling man; just the man for Supervising Special Agent here. Permit me to suggest, that if he can be spared from Washington, you send him to act as my deputy until after the elections, then to take my place. I know but two of our citizens who have all the essential requisites for this Office, Mr. J. S. Walton and Mr James Graham; the former is city Treasurer the latter U.S. Marshall; both having high salaries could not be expected to accept it.

Maj Plumly has been recommended for the office; You have known him longer than I have and I need not therefore speak of his qualifications for the place

Mr Hutchins is assisting me and I find him competent; A little experience in the affairs of the office will enable him to perform its duties satisfactorily.

Both Mr Kauffman and Mr Tucker, understand the position of affairs here and I respectfully refer you to them for particulars. Mr Tucker pleases me very much and I hope that he will decide to return to New to remain permanently. He is intelligent industrious; and if I am a judge of character, as firm as the hills, in his integrity. He and Mr. Kauffman are the kind of men we want to help to establish the new order of things before us.

Our Convention election will be held about the 25th of January next.

Very respectfully,

Your obt, Servt.
BENJ. F. FLANDERS.

Hon S. P. Chase
Washington D.C.

1. Probably Chase's November 19, 1863, letter to Thomas J. Durant (above).

2. Flanders had discussed the movement for a convention in correspondence with Chase, December 4, 1863 (above).

3. Explained in Durant to Chase, December 4, 1863 (above).

FROM BENJAMIN RUSH PLUMLY

Autograph letter. Chase Papers, Library of Congress (*micro* 30:0320).

New Orleans,
Decr. 12th. 1863

My dear Sir

The letters of our friends, with the reports of Kauffman & Tucker leave little for me to say.

Mr Hutchins sends you the Delta Editorial, Its venom exists, as you will see, in the effort to drive us into the demonstration it suggests, The good of it, is, in the admission of your strength, and of the unity & power of your friends, here[1]

Mr Denison thinks that I did Mr Flanders some injustice, by the intimation that he leans to Lincoln, more than to you. Possibly, I did, Mr Flanders and I have no difference in feeling; none in general policy; none in principles. But, in the specific case, of business, and of the immediate means of success, in political effort *here,* at the time, we do differ materially

I defer to him, altho' I feel, each time, that we lose power by such deference, The truth is he is so good a man, that I almost always, doubt my judgment when I differ, and especially if the difference seems to threaten division:

If the differe[nt] opinion simply affected myself, I should let it go, but when it seems to me, to have political significance, I may grow [*illeg.*].

He is a little hurt I fear, by my sending such strong credentials to you, It is natural, that he should not like to see any new comer, stronger than himself, I say, to him, that the letters were volunteered that I did not send them to you, for *influence; that,* I do not need. I repeat to him that I thank nobody for place, bestowed by you—except yourself. That my appointment, if made, will be because of my supposed fitness for the occasion; or fitness that might diminish under another Commander, or from other circumstances,

Mr Flanders thinks that he should hold on till after the Election, Our friends think not, I agree with them, The Fire Dpt., so much of it, as is worth anything, is in the hands of Mr Denison & myself, by peculiar circumstances after much effort, It never can be in Mr Flander's hand, But, the Bank & money interest may. The political management of the *people* must depend upon Denison's Office, and on his & my management, With the unity of all our force, and the hearty support of the Military; the Provost Marshall;[2] the Chief of Police &c &c, I do not see how we can be beaten, If we win here, we shall surely win in the great national contest,

I think Mr Hutchins rather agrees with Mr Flanders, He is less frank with me, than in his previous visit, which I attribute to a desire not to take sides. He is doing a capital work, both professionally, and in public speaking.

I have just read him this, paragraph, he smiles, at my suspicion of him.

I have such faith in your just judgment that I state it all, and leave it all,

Dr Price goes to Texas, temporarily.[3] He should go to Natches. He is the man for that place. He has good sense and sound judgment,

I hope you may be able to send Kauffman here, for a month, towards April, His advice & aid are invaluable. I am willing to leave all things to his statement,

Very truly
B Rush Plumly

To Hon S P Chase
Secy of the Treas.
Washington DC,

PS. Since writing the above, Mr Hutchins has sent me his letter to you, It is proper to state that my "leaving Mr Flander's Office was in no anger or pique, but simply a prudential measure advised by Mr Denison and, by my own judgment but delayed several days in the hope of its working easier, When Mr Flanders was elected to the Presidency of the Bank, he called me to his room and requested me to act as his Deputy Supg Spl Agt until your decision was heard, I went, but, he never allowed me t[o] anything more than a simple amanuensis—*That* I *could* not be, & would not for a King, It was not my fault that ten people asked for me, to one, for him,

After trying it a week, humiliated not a little, I quietly went back to my place in the other office. So much is needed to avoid any impression of a quarrel or ill feeling, which I will *not* have—

1. On December 11, an editorial in the *Daily True Delta* compared Lincoln and Chase as presidential candidates and suggested that Federal employees in New Orleans "without many exceptions" supported Chase. "If we incorrectly state the fact," challenged the newspaper, "they can very easily get up a demonstration expressive of their confidence" in Lincoln. John Hutchins evidently enclosed the article in a letter to Chase, written on December 12, which reported that Flanders and Plumly "cannot work well together," and cited as evidence Plumly's recent decision not to work in the same office with Flanders. Hutchins to Chase, Dec. 12, 1863 (Chase Papers, L.C.).

2. James Bowen.

3. Edward V. Price was a former auditor in the New York City Hall of Records and, at this time, an assistant special agent for the Treasury. *Letter of the Secretary . . . Special Agents,* 2; *New York Dir. (1863),* 703; Price to Chase, Aug. 26, 1863 (Chase Papers, L.C.).

FROM GEORGE WILKES

Autograph letter on letterhead stationery. Chase Papers, Library of Congress (*micro* 30:0324).

George Wilkes,
Editor

OFFICE
Wilkes' Spirit of the Times,
201 WILLIAM STREET.
New York. 12th Decr 1863.

Hon S. P. Chase
Dear Sir

A movement is on foot, starting I believe with Senator Sumner to have Genl Thomas called to the Army of the Potomac. Should this succeed Hooker would be permanently shelved with a corps, for Foster will be assigned to Burnside's army and Grant will certainly give the Cumberland to Sherman.[1]

Senator Sumner yesterday, not reminding himself of my regard for Hooker, told me he had suggested Thomas to Mr Stanton and that Mr Stanton had very favorably entertained the proposition. I write to you therefore in the hope you may head it off, and I will come to Washington again on Wednesday to rally some senatorial aid. Both Wade and Chandler[2] have promised to work with me in the matter, and Mr Conness will go with me to Mr Stanton.

Fee did accompany me to Mr Stanton's house yesterday but being told by the porter he was quite unwell we did not force our cards up stairs[3]

In the matter of the revenue stamp I would much prefer you would not refer it to the arbitrament of Mr Clarke.[4] I do not know but he is entirely favorable to it, but have reason to think he has a dislike to me, and I fancy I have reasons why I ought not to like him.

The thing has passed through the scrutiny of the examiners in the process of the patent and I think its utility stands proved in the simple observation which any one can exercise while sticking it on paper. It has been experimented on for two months already at the instance of Treasury, and prints equally well on wood and steel. But aside from the specimens now presented the inventor expects to bind himself to furnish them as perfect as you wish

Very Respectfully

Your Obt Svt
GEO. WILKES

P.S. I have just recd a private letter from Genl Hooker, which shows that Grant is endeavoring to overshadow him for Sherman.

G. W.

1. Maj. Gen. John Gray Foster had in fact already succeeded Ambrose E. Burnside as commander of the Army of the Ohio on December 9. *DAB,* 6:549–50; Long, *Civil War Day by Day,* 445.

2. Michigan Republican and U.S. Senator Zachariah Chandler.

3. Possibly John Gregg Fee (1816–1901), expatriate Kentucky abolitionist and founder of Berea College. *DAB,* 6:310–11.

4. Evidently Spencer Morton Clark.

FROM NAPOLEON BONAPARTE BUFORD

Letter in clerk's hand on letterhead stationery, signed by Buford. Letters Received from Executive Officers (AB Series), General Records, Department of the Treasury (Record Group 56), National Archives (*micro* 30:0336).

Head Quarters, District Eastern Arkansas,[1]
Helena, Ark., December 13th. 1863.

Hon: S. P. Chase
Secy: of the Treasy:

I had the honor of communicating to you my views on re-establishing our Government in the South a year ago,[2] The experience derived from my command here confirms those views, It can only be done by conquest, and planting loyal people in place of the disloyal, After two and a half years command in the South I have not seen a man of fortune or standing who was to be relied on as a Union man, Every slaveholder sticks to the institution as his only hope for future respectability and means of living, The poor people are afraid of negro equality and feel as savage a hotility to the *race* as animals that by nature devour each other.

It is said that the State of Arkansas is redy to come back into the Union, It is not true, In this vicinity a few of the slaveholders continue to live on their plantations, and feed and clothe their negroes, though for the last year they have raised no crops, in the hope that slavery will be restored, but the greater number of them have moved their slaves within the Confederate lines, Every family of any note has its representatives in the Confederate Army.

I am firmly of the opinion that we are unnecessarily prolonging the war by permitting trade, with its numerous restrictions to exist on the Mississippi, we should have maintained a strict a blockade at Cairo and New Orleans as at Charleston or Mobile, without our supplies the Rebels would not have been able to have held Vicksburg and Port Hudson, nor at this time to maintain a Guerrilla force which annoys our Commerce and burns our Boats,

I am a witness here to the workings of a permit system, Trade is carried on by the most unscrupulous and disloyal persons, False oaths are taken on both sides, The oath of allegiance is taken whenever interest dictates it, and its violation is held as no crime

I emphatically say to you, if we want the Cotton on this great river, let us have free trade, until it is all removed, Let us make friends by our magnanimity, or if our purpose is to crush the rebellion as early as practicable, let us maintain a strict blockade, The present system makes us no friends, Let us either make friends or conquests.

If it were not for the interests of the rebels to exchange commodities with us, they could blockade the river with Artillery at any place they pleased as they hold the Rail Road which is parallel to the river, and that would require a new army to dislodge them.

To return to my plan, if I was authorized to occupy a certain district, my present one for instance:— Had the power to exclude from it every person who would not obey the laws:— Had two Judges to hold Courts and confiscate the property of persons who are now in arms against us, which could only be bought by loyal people, a new infusion of population would be had; the laws of the State, with the exclusion of Slavery could be re-established:— Officers elected whose interests were with the Union, and peace secured within its border.

I have 16 Companies of Black troops in my command, It would interest you, and all the friends of humanity to see how much their condition has been improved by making them soldiers and giving them the rights of men.[3]

I have also a Contraband School with more than 200 pupils, and should I continue here, hope to exhibit to you the evidence of great amelioration in the condition of these people.

Besides calling your attention especially to the district I command, I also wish to remind you of the sincere affection of

Your friend
N. B. Buford

1. Buford, a brigadier general of volunteers, commanded the District of Eastern Arkansas from September 1863 to March 1865. *DAB*, 3:245.

2. The two had corresponded on the subject in October 1862. *Chase Papers*, 3:294–96.

3. Buford's command included two regiments of African-American soldiers, the 3d Arkansas and the 1st Iowa, and two partial units, the 2d and 4th Arkansas regiments. *OR*, ser. 1, v. 34, pt. 2:201.

TO ELI A. SPENCER

Letterpress copy of letter in clerk's hand, signed by Chase. Chase Papers, Historical Society of Pennsylvania (*micro* 30:0345).

December 14th, 3.

My Dear Sir.[1]

Your letter of the 8th. inst. is just received. I have not yet seen Judge Hood, but shall remember your suggestions when I do.[2]

I have not the slightest wish to press any claims upon the consideration of friends, or the public. There is certainly, however, a purpose to use my name, and I do not feel at all bound to object to it. On the contrary, were the post in which these friends desire to place me, as low as it is high, I should feel bound to render in it all the service possible to our common country.

I sympathize with your feelings about your son. I have a brother-in-law in precisely the same predicament, taken prisoner in the same battle, and now lodged in the same prison.[3] The question for the President and the War Department to determine is, whether, in order to release these young-men, so dear to us, it is best to give up forty thousand rebels for thirteen thousand union prisoners, or to surrender the officers and men of colored regiments to all the barbarities which the rebel government proposes to inflict upon them.

Much as I desire the release of our prisoners, I cannot see that the War Department errs in refusing such unequal terms. Nothing, I believe, is left undone that can be done, without yielding to these terms. Please give me your views.[4]

Yours very cordially
S P Chase

E. A. Spencer Esq.
Madison, Wis.

1. Eli A. Spencer, an attorney from Dane County, Wisconsin, became assistant secretary of state for Wisconsin in January 1864 and later gained notoriety for compiling *A Digest of the Laws of Wisconsin, from the year 1858 to the year 1868 . . .* (Madison, Wis., 1868). J. R. Berryman, *History of the Bench and Bar of Wisconsin,* 2 vols. (Chicago, 1898), 1:298; Spencer to Chase, Dec. 8, 1863 (Chase Papers, L.C.).

2. Spencer's letter explored the possibility of nominating Chase to the presidency in Wisconsin's Republican convention and introduced Thomas Hood, a former circuit court judge and newly elected state senator who was visiting Washington, D.C. "If you propose to permit your name to go before the National Convention," wrote Spencer, "see to it that you conciliate him & if for this purpose it is necessary to give him some aid in any little (decent) enterprise he may have on hand, please extend it." In addition, Spencer complained of a "technical difficulty" that prevented the exchange of his son, evidently Capt. R. H. Spencer of the 10th Wisconsin Infantry, a prisoner of war captured at the battle of Chickamauga in September 1863 and later held in Libby Prison, Richmond. Spencer to Chase, Dec. 8, 1863 (Chase Papers, L.C.); Richard W. Hantke, "Elisha W. Keyes and the Radical Republicans," *Wisconsin Magazine of History* 35 (Spring 1952): 205; Long, *Civil War Day by Day,* 411–13; *New York Times,* Nov. 6, 1863.

3. Chase discussed the capture of his brother-in-law, Israel Ludlow, in correspondence with Catherine Ludlow Whiteman, November 12, 1863 (above).

4. Chase wrote this sentence in his own hand.

FROM WILLIAM ORTON

Autograph letter on letterhead stationery. Chase Papers, Historical Society of Pennsylania (*micro* 30:0365).

No. 1.[1]

unofficial & private.

U.S. Internal Revenue,
6th DISTRICT, STATE OF NEW YORK,
New York, Monday Eve. Dec. 14/ 1863.

My dear Sir:

At an interview with Messrs Mayor Opdyke and Surveyor Andrews this P.M., I promised to write you this eve. concerning a matter of which my only knowledge is derived from them.

It appears that at our primary elections in several of the Wards on Friday night last, (While I was in Washington,) your friends and others opposed to the machine dynasty in this city ran opposition tickets which were defeated in nearly every case.

It is alledged that this result was, in several instances, mainly due to the exertions of Mr. Palmer, who called up the employees of the Custom House and instructed them how to vote—threatening them with removal in the event of their refusal to obey his behests. Further, that Mr. P. now sets himself up for the Presidency of our political organization for the coming year.

Mr. Andrews expresses the opinion that Pal[mer] will undertake to procure the removal of som[e] of our friends, and I therefore respectfully suggest the propriety of withholding your approval of any changes which may be forwarded to you from that office, until carefu[l] inquiry can be instituted concerning the truth of the alledged causes therefor.

Andrews now takes positive ground in favor of your nomination, and while you may properly refuse to make removals for the sole purpose of aiding to procure this result, it will not do to permit your friends to be turned out of offices controlled by you, on account of their zeal in your behalf.

I shall seek an interview with Mr. Barney tomorrow, and believing it impolitic to have Palmer made President of our Central Committee, will advise Mr. B. to interfere to prevent it; and at the same time I will learn the other side.[2]

Messrs Opdyke and Andrews heartily concur in my suggestion to appoint Mr. Stevens Dep. Comr. Intl. Revenue.[3] I feel that this city which has paid about 15% of all the internal duties collected during the past year, was really entitled to the Comr., and that our claim to the Depy., under the circumstances, should be conceded without much debate. I am desirous to see at least one person in that office who, in addition to a faithful performance of official duties, will be competent and willing to cöoperate with your friends whenever such service could be made available. In respect to both these requirements Mr. Stevens is eminently qualified.

With great respect,

Sincerely yours,
WILLM. ORTON,

Hon. S. P. Chase,
Washington. D.C.

1. Orton was a Republican politician and collector of the sixth district, one of a half-dozen U.S. internal revenue districts located in New York City. He labeled this letter "No. 1" because he did not send it to Chase until December 16, with a letter of that date labeled "No. 2," after Orton spoke with Hiram Barney. Orton to Chase, Dec. 16, 1863 (Chase Papers, Hist. Soc. of Pa.); *DAB*, 14:65; *Register of Officers (1863)*, 38.

2. Orton, as promised, met with Barney on the fifteenth. According to Orton, Barney denied that he or Palmer had made any attempt "to coerce their employees" and pledged to disavow any effort to give Palmer "the Presidency of our Committee." Orton confided that "I do not consider Mr. Barney the most sagacious man living, nor is he bursting with executive force; but my impression of his frankness, sincerity, and fidelity to his friends, as originally expressed to you, remains unshaken. I doubt however if it will be possible to restore the old good feeling between him and some others of our friends here." Orton to Chase, Dec. 16, 1863 (Chase Papers, Hist. Soc. of Pa.).

3. On January 20, 1864, Lincoln nominated Edward A. Rollins of New Hampshire to be deputy commissioner of internal revenue, and the Senate confirmed the appointment on February 2. Rollins later served as commissioner of internal revenue, 1865–68, then entered the life insurance business in Philadelphia. Orton's preferred candidate may have been John Austin Stevens, Jr. U.S. Senate, *Journal of Executive Proceedings*, 13:388–89; Charles Lanman, *Biographical Annals of the Civil Government of the United States* . . . (Washington, D.C., 1876), 363.

TO WILLIAM CULLEN BRYANT

Letterpress copy of autograph letter. Chase Papers, Historical Society of Pennsylvania (*micro* 30:0400).

Washington Decr. 1[5], 18[63]

My dear Sir,

Some two or three weeks ago I received a letter from you touching the compensation to Custom House Officers in New York.[1] My answer has been delayed by the extraordinary demands on my time & working [power] during the last [few] weeks.

My impression is that some mistake exists as to the amount of their compensations: though they certainly exceed any legitimate reward for services performed. This, however, is the case in regard to many compensations for services, private and public: when the interest of the giver and receiver are both thought to be promoted—that of the former by stimulus to industry & activity by a fixed proportion of reward to result rather than to labor & that of the latter by the prospect of gain measured by vigilance & diligence

I am in favor of the most moderate compensations compatible with honesty towards workers of whatever work; and there are some men and a good many I hope who are just as diligent and just and vigilant with little as with great pay. I do not know, however, that this is universally the case. Indeed I think the universal practice of contingent or proportioned rewards indicates that the general rule is otherwise.[2]

All I desire is to know in what way the public interest will be best promoted & then to adopt that way. My reflections heretofore have inclined me to the adoption or rather to the continuance of the rule of proportioned compensation as I found it established. Your letter will require me to review the ground & to correct my judgment if erroneous

The steady accumulation of expenditure makes my task a very difficult one. If our State Banks would come into the National System and make a circulation which the Government could use it seems to me that specie payments could be restored without great difficulty;[3] and thus one great cause of rapid augmentation of debt, high prices, be in some degree overcome. But after all with the universal tendency to waste—the increase of pay—the lavish disbursem[*illeg.*] of the Qr. Masters Department—the multitude of useless officers of all military grades pensioned on the country by appointments with which no service is connected or has been for some time—I confess myself uneasy

Very sincerely yours
S P Chase

Wm. Cullen Bryant, Esq

1. See Bryant to Chase, November 24, 1863 (above).

2. Chase's handwriting in this paragraph of the letterpress copy is too faint to read but was overwritten in pencil by a clerk.

3. Payment of specie by the Federal government and many U.S. banks ceased on December 30, 1861. According to legislation of January 14, 1875, the Treasury received authorization to resume payments in two stages: first through redemption of fractional currency in silver coins, effective immediately, and second, through exchange of legal tender notes for coins, to begin on January 1, 1879. Hammond, *Sovereignty,* 150–59; Long, *Civil War Day by Day,* 152; *Statutes at Large,* v. 18, pt. 3:296.

TO WILLIAM P. MELLEN

Letter in clerk's hand on letterhead stationery, signed by Chase. General Agent, Letters Received: Secretary of the Treasury, Records of Civil War Special Agencies of the Treasury Department (Record Group 366), National Archives (*micro* 30:0439).

Treasury Department.
December 17th, 1863.

Sir,

I transmit a letter from General Wadsworth, together with a copy of his Report to the War Department on leased plantations.[1] You have already had some conversation with him and with myself on the subject. The Secretary of War has as yet arrived at no definite conclusion in respect to the permanent policy to be adopted. In the meantime his Order, committing the charge of abandoned plantations to the Supervising Special Agents, stands.[2] I am clearly of opinion that you should immediately proceed to lease these plantations, substantially in accordance with the plan partially executed under the arrangements of General Thomas. You can designate Mr. Field as an Assistant Special Agent under you, and if you think proper others also, and provide them with the necessary clerical aid.[3] I agree fully with the views expressed by General Wadsworth in his Report, and you will see the importance of prompt action. Mr. Field I think deserves great credit for his consideration of the colored people & for leasing, when he could, to them directly. They should all be got out of the Camps and restored to their accustomed employments under the free labor system with as little delay as possible. As the season is advancing, please act promptly.

Yours very truly,
S: P: CHASE
Secretary of the Treasury.

Wm. P. Mellen, Esquire,
Sup. Special Agent, Cincinnati

1. Gen. James S. Wadsworth's report of December 16 recommended that former slaves be allowed to lease abandoned plantations as free agents directly from the U.S. government as soon as possible. "The improvement in the condition of the Black will begin when he is thus assured of his freedom," claimed Wadsworth, "when he sees that his support & comfort depend upon his own industry & that he is respected & confided in as far as his conduct may seem to merit." Berlin, *Freedom,* ser. 1, v. 3:757–62.

2. The War Department issued the order on October 9, 1863. *OR,* ser. 3, v. 3:872.

3. Regulations for commissioners of leased plantations issued by Adjutant General Lorenzo Thomas on October 27 stressed the need "to line the banks of the Mississippi River with a loyal population and to give aid in securing the uninterrupted navigation of the river," and "at the same time to give employment to the freed negroes whereby they may earn wages and become self-supporting." George B. Field was a New York attorney who toured the Mississippi Valley early in 1863 and reported to Edwin M. Stanton. In addition, Thomas had appointed Field a commissioner to oversee plantation leasing. *OR,* ser. 3, v. 3:939–40; Berlin, *Freedom,* ser. 1, v. 2:38, v. 3:496; *DAB,* 18:441–42.

TO THOMAS SWANN

Letterpress copy of autograph letter. Chase Papers, Historical Society of Pennsylvania (*micro* 30:0449).

Washington Decr. 18, 1863

My dear Swann,

I have just finished reading you excellent address and resolutions. The actions of your committee upon them make Maryland a unit on the question of Free Labor; and the thanks of all her citizens are due to your wise and prompt suggestion of it.[1]

Pardon me if I add a word of, it may be importunate counsel. Do not attempt any scheme of apprenticeship. Such schemes have always failed and would have the very consequences you so justly apprehend, under present circumstances, from gradualism.[2] Make all free: give fair & even liberal wages: provide schools: and let Christian philanthropy and aspiration for a better condition do the rest.

Cordially your friend
S P Chase

Hon. Thomas Swann

1. Swann was chair of Maryland's Union State Central Committee, which met in Baltimore on December 16. His speech and resolutions, which the committee approved unanimously, proposed a state convention to draw up a plan for immediate emancipation "with such a system of wages, or apprenticeship, as shall be deemed advisable, to guard against too sudden a revulsion in the inauguration and establishment of the new system of labor." *Baltimore American,* Dec. 18, 1863.

2. Maryland's revised constitution of November 1, 1864, outlawed slavery but permitted former slaves to be held as indentured servants. Later, when he was chief justice, Chase ruled on the issue. In a circuit court case, *In re Turner,* decided on October 16, 1867, Chase struck down the Maryland apprenticeship system as a violation of prohibitions against involuntary servitude in the Thirteenth Amendment and the civil rights act of April 9, 1866. Fairman, *Reconstruction and Reunion,* 1309; Bradley T. Johnson, ed., *Reports of Cases Decided by Chief Justice Chase in the Circuit Court of the United States for the Fourth Circuit . . . ,* intro. Ferne B. Hyman and Harold M. Hyman (New York, 1876; reprint, 1972), 157–61; *New York Times,* Oct. 17, 1867.

TO JOSEPH HOOKER

Letterpress copy of letter in clerk's hand, signed by Chase. Chase Papers, Historical Society of Pennsylvania (*micro* 30:0489).

December 21, 3.

My dear General,

I have been quite unwell of late and my correspondence is a good deal in arrears. Still I must take time to dictate a few lines to you.— I cannot tell you how much I have been gratified by your brilliant achievements in Tennessee and Georgia. How Providential it was that you were sent West at the head of the Eleventh and Twelfth Corps! It seems clear now that but for Mr. Stanton's determination in insisting upon these reinforcements going promptly and going under you, Rosecran's Army would have experienced the gravest disasters.[1] And then it seems equally Providential, that the assault on Lookout Mountain had to be made under your direction. The only thing, I do not clearly see the value of, is your magnificent achievement near Ringgold.[2] It was a splendid battle splendidly won. But what is the use of sacrificing so much to take a town if after all the town is to be abandoned? and the army is to fall back? Whether it was necessary to fall back or not I find myself unable to form any judgment. General Grant ought to know best. I most sincerely hope that he was governed only by the best and most patriotic motives. Grant's whole career has excited my admiration and commanded my respect, and there certainly ought to be no jealousies between two such officers as you and he. Each should rejoice in what adds to the honor of the other

Things here go pretty much at the old rate. There has been a deal of talk about recalling you and placing you in command of the Army of the Potomac, which one of its chaplains in a recently published letter calls, not altogether without reason, "This poor old strategy possessed Army." I wish it might be done. But of course my wishes go for little in such matters. What right indeed has a Secretary of the Treasury, whose business it is to provide money for other people to spend, to have any wishes at all about the results of the expenditures? Is not that exclusively the concern of the President and of Congress?— I suppose I ought to shut my eyes and suppress my feelings, but really it is a little hard when one *thinks* one *sees* how much might be economized of action, power and resources, not to say something of what he thinks and feels.

Gillmore is still firing away at Charleston, and the rebels still keep their flag flying on Sumter. It is said that a storm has removed the obstructions. Possibly the fleet may do something now. It is as cheap, I suppose—(You see my head always runs on the question of cost—) to have a monitor sunk by rebel batteries as by the knocks of Father Neptune, as was the case recently. So [Dalgrehn] may possibly risk it.[3]

Give my best regards to Butterfield. I mean to write to him in a day or two. If matters in which he is interested were under my control, his wishes would not be ungratified, for you cannot say a kind or appreciative word of him which does not find an echo in my heart and judgment.

We all missed you at the wedding. But you were best where you were.— The time is not remote, I hope, when we may once more meet.

May God mercifully keep us all till then.

Faithfully Your Friend,
S P Chase

Major General Hooker.

1. In a cabinet meeting on the night of September 23–24, Edwin M. Stanton had successfully argued in favor of sending two corps from the Army of the Potomac by rail to

relieve the endangered Army of the Cumberland at Chattanooga. Hooker discussed the situation in Tennessee in correspondence to Chase on November 3 (above), shortly after his troops completed the novel maneuver. *Chase Papers,* 1:450–54.

2. The battle of Lookout Mountain, a Federal victory, occurred on November 24. Hooker took Ringgold, Ga., three days later. Long, *Civil War Day by Day,* 437; *OR,* ser. 1, v. 31, pt. 2:35.

3. USS *Weehawken* had sunk near Morris Island in Charleston Harbor on December 6. According to one report, "the disaster was occasioned through neglect of parties on board." Rear Adm. John Adolphus Bernard Dahlgren commanded the South Atlantic blockading squadron and, with Quincy Adams Gillmore, directed the attack on Charleston, S.C. Despite continuing bombardment, the city did not surrender until February 1865. *DAB,* 5:31; Long, *Civil War Day by Day,* 640; *New York Times,* Dec. 19, 1863; *ORN,* ser. 2, v. 1:238.

TO SUSAN WALKER

Letterpress copy of autograph letter. Chase Papers, Historical Society of Pennsylvania (*micro* 30:0547).

Washington Decr. 23, 1863.

My dear friend,[1]

Your last postmarked Woburn is just received. Be assured you *have* my sympathy in all your trials and bereavements.[2] But it is one of the afflictions of absorbing public service that no bereavement seems so great, as when one is at liberty to think & feel as in a quiet home & in a time of peace. I can almost realize the indifference, almost, to life which one is said to come to feel in the Army & in battle. But every now and then there seems to come to me a sort of breath from some unseen region of emotion & sympathies and all the currents, just hardening into ice, seem to melt & flow freely again. So, dear friend, I do feel for you. May God bring you nearer and nearer to Him & make you feel that He is more than father or mother or sister or brother.

This Morning as I lay awake in the early dawn my thoughts turned towards God & his Majesty. What worlds of meaning, I thought are in these words, God is! and in these, God is ruler! And then the idea of God's omnipresence—beyond the limits of remotest space—there in my little chamber came home to me as seldom or never before. And so too the idea of Gods active omnipotence—not an idle power, but every action, forming, ordering, placing, moving all things, came to me. I cannot describe what I felt—indeed, I do not think I felt much—the Majesty was too awful to be felt

Does this great God care for us? Certainly or He could not be this great God! And will He forgive what I have done amiss? I will not doubt it. I will trust and hope and strive to work with his working for purity, penitence & faith.

But I must stop. The hard work of the day calls for me. Good bye—

Your friend
S P Chase

1. A clerk's index to the volume in which this letterpress copy was bound indicates that Susan Walker was the letter's recipient.

2. Walker had apparently sent word of the death of a brother. Chase to Susan Walker, Jan. 2, 1865 (Chase Papers, Hist. Soc. of Pa.).

TO HENRY WARD BEECHER

Autograph letter on letterhead stationery. Beecher Family Papers, Manuscripts and Archives, Yale University Library (*micro* 30:0585).

Treasury Department.
Decr. 26, 1863

My dear Sir,

I have been looking for your half promised return to Washington; but my own experience teaches me too well how difficult it is for a man to whom many daily resort for this and that to change locality even for a few days, to let me feel greatly disappointed. Still I hope you *will* come as soon after Congress gets together again as possible and make my house your home as before. We all cherish the most agreeable recollections of your visit: and have made Gov Sprague & my daughter very desirous to share our gratification

The Presidents Message and proclamation on Slavery corresponded mainly with my expectations.[1] I hoped it would be more positive and less qualified; and urged him to it in conversation & in writing; but he could not make up his mind to it. I really expected that he would have revoked the exceptions—now seen to be so unfortunate—in his 1st Jany proclamation, of portions of Virginia & Louisiana, from its operation; and I expected this the more confidently as Mr. Seward joined me in recommending it and no one seemed to object.[2] But I was disappointed. The effects of the omission are seen in the embarrassments experienced by our friends in Virginia and Louisiana in their endeavors to make free States notwithstanding the exceptions. I was not so much, though a good deal disappointed by his determination to limit his plan for reconstitution so that colored freemen could take no part in it: and to retain the suggestions of qualified involuntary Servitude in the form of apprenticeship of the freed people: & to leave the door open for the admission of Senators & Representatives from States not reconstituted even according to his proclamation[3]

I should have been very Glad to have had a clear, distinct, & positive declaration of fundamental principles & of the practical mode of applying them to the restoration to the Union of States which have been in rebellion against it: but I am thankful that we have at least an affirmation that the loyal white citizens of a State, entitled to vote under the law in force before rebellion constitute the State & if equal in number to one tenth of the voters at the last Presidential election may proceed to reform their State [Conditionally] & come back. I should have greatly preferred the simpler & clearer declaration that the loyal citizens of a State constitute the State and that they only are loyal who bear true faith & allegiance to the Union & the Constitution; accept unreservedly the acts done by the National Government in the suppression of the rebellion; and especially the acts of Congress & the Proclamation of the President touching slavery;[4] and are ready to prove their sincerity by such changes of the State Constitution as are necessary to confirm & perpetuate the condition of freedom established by them.

But I suppose I must use Touchstone's philosophy & be thankful for skim milk when cream is not to be had.

Mr. Wendell Phillips, I see, has been renewing his assault on me.[5] Well, I can bear it. In fact I think it an advantage rather than injury. The injury accrues rather to him who invents & then propagates the falsehood. I have honored the constancy with which Mr. Garrison & his friends have proclaimed anti-slavery truth; while in most of their ideas concerning the Constitution and their whole notion of practical action by disunion I have constantly dissented from them.[6] In the case of Margaret Garner I felt the profoundest sympathy for the unhappy mother & did every thing in my power to save her as the record proves. Nor on looking back through my whole life do I now see a single opportunity of advancing the cause of Human Freedom, offered by God's Providence which was left unimproved. I have not wasted strength in vain attempts; nor have I abused confidence reposed in me by exercising official powers for other purposes than those for which the people conferred them; but whatever was possible I have done promptly and no legitimate use of official power—whatever responsibility might be incurred—has been neglected.[7] And so, God helping, I mean to continue to the end.

Faithfully your friend
S P CHASE

Rev. Henry Ward Beecher.

1. Lincoln's annual message to Congress, December 8, included a brief proposal for Reconstruction, set forth at greater length the same day in his Proclamation of Amnesty and Reconstruction. Basler, *Collected Works,* 7:36–56.

2. In a letter to Lincoln on November 25 (above), Chase discussed the December 8 proclamation, then in draft form, and its relationship to the exemptions in the Emancipation Proclamation (referred to here by its effective date of "1st Jany").

3. That is, Lincoln's Proclamation of Amnesty and Reconstruction.

4. The first and second confiscation acts, August 6, 1861, and July 17, 1862, and the Emancipation Proclamation. *Statutes at Large,* 12:319, 589–92.

5. Phillips, a noted abolitionist, had assailed Chase in a speech at New York's Cooper Union on December 22. According to Phillips, Chase had demonstrated inadequate dedication to the antislavery cause in the case of Margaret Garner, a fugitive slave expatriated from Ohio as Chase started his first term as governor in 1856. Chase discussed the Garner incident at length in letters to William Dennison, December 31, 1863 (below), and to John T. Trowbridge, March 13, 1864 (below). *DAB,* 14:546–47; *New York Times,* Dec. 23, 1863; Julius Yanuck, "The Garner Fugitive Slave Case," *Mississippi Valley Historical Review* 40 (1953): 47–66.

6. Phillips, William Lloyd Garrison, and their followers believed that the North should secede from a union whose constitution tolerated slavery. *DAB,* 7:170, 14:546.

7. Chase repeated similar arguments regarding the Garner case in letters to other correspondents, at least two of whom, John A. Corwin and Edward L. Pierce, wrote defenses of Chase, with his complicity, which later appeared in the *Cincinnati Gazette* and the *National Anti-Slavery Standard.* "The Case of Margaret Garner. A Vindication of Gov. Chase," *National Anti-Slavery Standard,* May 28, 1864; Pierce to Chase, Dec. 28, 1863, Mar. 28, May 18, 1864, Chase to Corwin, Jan. 12, 1864, James M. Gitchell to Chase, Apr. 25, 1864 (Chase Papers, L.C.); Chase to Corwin, Jan. 20, Chase to Gitchell, May 20, Pierce to Chase, May 28, 1864 (Chase Papers, Hist. Soc. of Pa.).

TO WILLIAM P. MELLEN

Letter in clerk's hand on letterhead stationery, signed by Chase. General Agent, Letters Received: Secretary of the Treasury, Records of Civil War Special Agencies of the Treasury Department (Record Group 366), National Archives (*micro* 30:0601).

Treasury Department.
December 27th, 1863[1]

Sir,

Some days since I advised you, in executing the Order of the Secretary of War touching abandoned houses and plantations, to follow, in the main, the System which had been adopted by Gen. Thomas.[2]

Since then I have received important information concerning the practical operation of that System, and the condition of plantations and of the freedmen. Much of it from Mr. Yeatman of St. Louis.[3]

I am informed that two at least of the three Commissioners appointed by Gen. Thomas to lease plantations are themselves lessees.[4] This is wrong. If you appoint Assistant Agents to take charge of this business of leasing, you will take care, I trust, that no one of them shall have the least pecuniary interest, direct or indirect, in plantations, or in supplies furnished for them, or in the results of the labor hired upon them. Clean hands and absolute disinterestedness are primary requisites for Agents connected with the disposition of these plantations. Let them be honest, conscientious, competent men, earnestly desirous for the amelioration and elevation of the freedmen, and ready to make sacrifice of comfort and pecuniary gain for the sake of doing good.

Mr. Yeatman has taken great interest in the welfare of our soldiers as a most active and efficient officer of the Western Sanitary Commission, and has of late given much special attention to the condition of the new made colored citizens, whose recent enfranchisement, in the midst of War, has exposed them to much suffering.

I have read with much interest a good deal of what he has written, and have conversed with him quite freely on the whole subject. No man has more impressed me by the sincerity of his humanity and the general soundness of his views. If I do not subscribe absolutely to all his suggestions, I am quite willing to commend all to your careful consideration; with the assurance that you will adopt such of them as you find expedient and practicable.—

There are some leading ideas which I especially approve.

All leases for the coming year, made under the authority of Gen. Thomas since he was notified of the Order of the Secretary of War, and especially all leases, whenever made, by the Commissioners to one of their own number, should be regarded, I think, as void. Lessees from these Commissioners, however, not of their own number, who have taken leases in good faith, should be considered as entitled to preference in new leases, and as little occasion for complaint as possible should be given.—

In leasing plantations care should be especially taken of the interests of the laborers; and the lessees should be bound to prompt weekly or at least monthly payments of wages, and these wages should be sufficiently liberal to induce laborers to *desire* the employment. To every contract for labor the employee should be a party as well as the employer; and the practice which, as I learn, has obtained to some extent, of assigning the freedmen to labor on this or that plantation or with this or that person, with little or no regard to his consent, should be discontinued and broken up.

When it is found possible to lease plantations to associations or partnerships of the laborers themselves, the opportunity of doing so, should be promptly embraced.

So, too, when leases can be made of a part or parts of a plantation to a single freedman or other person or to two or three freedmen or other persons in partnership, there should not only be no hesitation but great readiness to make them.[5]

Few things will more contribute to the improvement of the condition of the freedmen and to the productiveness of the country than their occupation of the soil as managers under leases made directly to them.

With the same view, proprietors of plantations should be encouraged to sell in small parcels of forty, eighty or a hundred and twenty acres to the freedmen, who can raise sufficient sums to make the necessary payments. I am not at present authorized to speak for the President, but I am very confident he would relieve the plantations of any proprietor remaining or coming to remain within our lines, and desirous to sell it in this manner, from the effects of the confiscation acts. You will, yourself, be warranted, under your present authority, in providing for the necessary surveys. To expedite matters, boundaries might be arranged and marked roughly at first, subject to correction on more regular measurement.

It will be well, I think, to commit the business of leasing and supervising plantations to Assistant Special Agents for Plantations, of whom there should be one for each State, and perhaps, in some cases, more than one. In case you should think it best to appoint more than one in any State, let the jurisdiction of each be limited to specified counties or parishes, and let all be required to report fully every month, and for each month within ten days of its close. These reports are important and should embrace all the suggestions of the practical experience of the Assistant Agents who make them. Until Congress shall place this whole business under definite legislative sanction, these Assistant Special Agents for Plantations may be considered as upon the same footing as to compensation and general responsibility as the Assistant Special Agents provided for in the General Regulations of September 11, 1863.

I have thus given you the leading ideas which should, I think, be kept prominently in view. Details will readily occur to you, or will be suggested by Mr. Yeatman.

I wish Mr. Yeatman could be prevailed on to Act as General Assistant Agent and take the personal oversight of these matters in your Agency. But this is, I suppose, impossible. He desires to keep himself independent of official trammels, thinking he can thus accomplish most good; and perhaps in this he may be right. Possibly you may find Mr. Field a good and useful Assistant Special Agent. But all this belongs properly to you, and with you I am content to leave it.

Very truly Yours,
S: P: CHASE

Wm. P. Mellen, Esquire, Sup. Special Agt.,
Cincinnati, Ohio.

1. Chase's holograph draft of this letter is located in his papers at the Historical Society of Pennsylvania and reproduced at *micro* 30:0607.

2. See Chase to Mellen, December 17, 1863 (above).

3. James Erwin Yeatman (1818–1901), a St. Louis merchant and president of the Western Sanitary Commission, had recently investigated the condition of former slaves along the Mississippi River. "The leasing system as adopted by the Government is an admirable one to put dollars into the pockets of sharpers and sharks who have hovered around and followed up the army," he reported in November 1863. "It does the greatest possible injustice to the poor negro, who I found disheartened, depressed, and discouraged." Yeatman to ———, Nov. 28, 1863 (Chase Papers, L.C.); *DAB,* 20:606–7.

4. Lorenzo Thomas had appointed Louis Dent (1822–74), a St. Louis lawyer and merchant who was Ulysses S. Grant's brother-in-law; George B. Field; and Robert V. Montague, a Louisiana planter. Dent and Montague had already leased plantations. Yeatman to ———, Nov. 28, 1863 (Chase Papers, L.C.); *Appletons',* 2:143; Berlin, *Freedom,* ser. 1, v. 3:496; Gerteis, *From Contraband to Freedman,* 126.

5. In this sentence, the phrases *a part or, or other person;* and *or other persons* are interlineations in Chase's handwriting.

TO THOMAS J. DURANT

Letterpress copy of autograph letter. Chase Papers, Historical Society of Pennsylvania.

December 28 3[1]

My dear Sir,

Your letter recently received afforded me singular gratification.[2] It rejoices my very heart to know that there is a prospect that Louisiana may soon return to the Union under loyal and free state auspices. The country will owe you much for your patriotic labors.

I am particularly gratified by your wise & courageous advocacy of the right of native free born colored citizens to participate in the reorganization of the State Governments. I informed the President of your views in this respect and he said he could see no objection to the registering of such citizens [or to] their exercise of the right of suffrage. You will have observed doubtless that in his message & proclamation he does limit reorganization to the precise forms or modes proposed by him, but is willing to accept any form or mode whereby the great ends of restoration to the Union with permanent free state institutions can be best secured.[3]

Before he sent in his message I urged him very earnestly to leave the general principles perfectly clear of details; but this is not his way and I did not prevail.[4]

Judge Stickney has gone to Florida—went before the Message—after a conference with me, at which I handed him a sketch of resolutions which I thought might be adopted by public meetings in the State & a Convention called through popular action.[5] I send you this paper—a copy—from which you will gather my ideas. They are really only two 1st That the loyal citizens of a State Constitute the State; 2d. That those citizens only can be accounted loyal who bear true faith and Allegiance to the Constitution and the Union; accept candidly the measures of enfranchisement adopted for the suppression of the rebellion, and desire to make these measures efficient & permanent by incorporating a prohibition of Slavery in the reformed Constitution of their State.

These ideas I have been urging on the President more than a year. He has adopted them in the main. I am sorry he could not see his way clear to their adoption without restriction or qualification. I am at the same time duly grateful for what he has done. The lever and the fulcrum are given. Let voluntary work do the rest

I hope your Convention will be wise enough to adopt the principle of universal suffrage of all men, unconvicted of crime, who can read & write and have a fair knowledge of the Constitution of the State & of the United States.[6] What a glory for Louisiana to be the first state to adopt a constitution basing the right to suffrage on virtue & intelligence alone. The object might be easily attained by establishing Commissions to make examinations & give certificates for which a small fee, fifty cents or a dollar might be required. These certificates would naturalize the recipients into the great electoral community. There might be a little hard working of the machinery at first but it would soon wear smooth & find universal approval

Very truly yours
S: P: Chase

Hon Thomas J. Durant

1. A later copy of this letter made by Jacob W. Schuckers, also in Chase's papers at the Historical Society of Pennsylvania, appears at *micro* 30:0635.

2. Durant's letter of December 4 (above).

3. Chase referred to Lincoln's annual message to Congress and the Proclamation of Amnesty and Reconstruction, both presented on December 8. Chase to Lincoln, Nov. 25, Chase to William P. Mellen, Dec. 27, 1863 (above).

4. See the letter Chase wrote to the president on November 25 (above).

5. On December 19, Florida Unionists had called for a constitutional convention to be held in St. Augustine on March 1, 1864, but the meeting did not actually occur until after the war. *New York Tribune,* Dec. 29, 1863; Jerrell H. Shofner, *Nor Is It Over Yet: Florida in the Era of Reconstruction, 1863–1877* (Gainesville, Fla., 1974), 7–8.

6. Louisiana's revised constitution, adopted on September 5, 1864, granted the legislature "power to pass laws extending suffrage to such other persons, citizens of the United States, as by military service, by taxation to support the Government, or by intellectual fitness may be deemed entitled thereto." Soon after, the legislature considered a bill that would have granted suffrage to African Americans, but then overwhelmingly rejected it. *Appletons' Annual Cyclopædia,* 4:479.

FROM HENRY WARD BEECHER

Autograph letter. Chase Papers, Library of Congress (*micro* 30:0645).

Brooklyn Monday 28 Decr. 63

My dear Mr Chase.

Your letter of Dec 26 has just reached me.[1] I mean to be in Washington again. But, I do not yet see the time. It may slip entirely. But it will not alter the fact of my desire & intention.— You speak of Gov. Sprague and his wife, whom I should be greatly pleased to meet, & just now, I am in a very amiable mood, my own son, Harry, a lieutenant in the Artillery, regulars,[2] having brought to my house a charming wife, & they together are ruling both father & mother, & having everything their own way.—

I agree with the views which you express of the Presidents Message & Proclamation.[3]— His mind works in the right *directions,* but seldom works clearly & cleanly

His bread is of unbolted flour, & much straw, too, mixes in the bran & sometimes gravel stones— Yet, on the whole the loaf will sustain life, tho' it makes eating a difficulty—rather than a pleasure— — But, will not *the Legislation* of Congress, be of a kind to make up, in some degree? I have been inclined to hope that we could get from Congress what we lack in the President— —

I do not think that Mr. Phillips *meant* harm—or *did* harm, even with those who are most under his influence[4]— Certainly he cannot shake the conviction of the great mass of intelligent men that you have been soundly, consistently & wisely faithful to the doctrines of liberty, tho' good report & evil, in office & out of it.— But, I confess, that I have a sort of pleasure, in having lived to see a day when the way to diminish a man's influence is to charge him with not having been enough a hater of slavery! During all my life time till now, any suspicion of a love for liberty has been fatal to political aspirations

I do not know that I mentioned to you, when I was in Washington, the very great esteem which I found for you in Gr Brittain.[5] All were not agreed as to the soundness of the financial policy of the Administration, ultimately: but all were united in praising the great skill & administrative ability which had been shewn—

I wish you, and all your family, the best wishes of the Holidays—a Merry Christmas & a Happy New Year

I am very truly yours
H W BEECHER

1. See Chase to Beecher, December 26, 1863 (above).
2. 1st Lt. Henry Barton Beecher. Heitman, *Historical Register,* 1:206.
3. Lincoln's annual message to Congress and the Proclamation of Amnesty and Reconstruction.
4. For Wendell Phillips's criticism of Chase see the December 26 letter to Beecher (above).
5. Beecher had visited Britain between June and November. *New York Times,* May 25, Nov. 5, 18, 1863.

TO QUINCY ADAMS GILLMORE

Letterpress copy of autograph letter. Chase Papers, Historical Society of Pennsylvania.

December 29, 63.[1]

Dear General,

I have for some time had it in mind to write you; but my personal acquaintance seemed to slight to warrant it; and I do not know that I should now overcome my disinclination even to seem intrusive had not Secretary Stanton informed me within the last few days that you have been authorized to employ such part of your force as is not needed for Charleston in whatever military enterprizes may seem best to you; and that you will probably undertake the complete reestablishment of the National Authority in Florida. I may not give the precise ideas of the Secretary but something like them. At any rate he said enough to induce me to think that an enterprize—namely the restoration of Florida—which I have for more than a year been urging on the Executive here is at length to be undertaken, and under your conduct,—so that there need be now no apprehension of failure.[2]

Ever since the retreat of McClellan from the Peninsula[3] it has seemed to me that instead of fighting our way Southward through Virginia, our immediate efforts in the interior should be confined to the repossession of East Tennessee and of the Mississippi River; and that all other operations should be conducted from the coast, supplied by sea transportation, & directed to the reoccupation & reorganization on a free labor & free suffrage basis of state after state from the Gulf upwards as rapidly as possible. With East Tennessee and the Mississippi in our possession, it seemed to me that powerful aid could be contributed to these operations & that they could not fail to be successful.

The late orders to you are not, I suppose, based on this idea; but they allow opportunity to some extent for its realization.

You can, I am sure, drive the enemy in a very few weeks from every part of Florida; and there are loyal men enough in the state to ensure its reorganization on a permanently safe basis.

Judge Stickney lately went from this place after full conference with me, resolved to begin the work of reorganization without delay. I have a letter from him today stating that he has held a large meeting at Saint Augustine, where Resolutions agreed on here were cordially & unanimously adopted: looking to the early reorganization of the State with free institutions.[4] Judge Stickney is one of the Direct Tax Commissioners, and a very clearsighted man. I believe you know him. If not, I trust you will invite him to a Conference & give him your cordial cooperation.

It is of great importance to press this war to the earliest possible termination; and the reestablishment of loyal state governments under free state constitutions will do much to afford rallying points for all the loyalty of the South, of whatever physical complexion; and to discourage exceedingly the hope of restoring the rebel sway. It will mark the two civilizations—or rather the civilization of freedom & the barbarism of Slavery—by distinctly recognizable limits. Where the former has been once fairly established I have no fears of the latter coming back again.

For the sake of the earliest possible and the most economical possible termination of the war, I exceedingly desire this reorganization: and I shall be exceedingly gratified if it can be accomplished for Florida under your Military auspices. You have accomplished much, and have won just titles to respect & honor—every where freely conceded to you. But to secure the reorganization of Florida will be an achievement, which will constitute a yet higher claim on the gratitude of your countrymen.

Besides my anxious desires for the secure & permanent reestablishment of Union in the shortest possible time, I feel a special anxiety for prompt and efficient action, arising from my responsibilities as Head of the Treasury Department. Thus far the administration of the finances has been successful beyond my hopes: but I can see clearly that we can go no further without heavy taxation; and he has read history to little purpose who does not know that heavy taxes will excite discontent; and that the possibility of crippled finances & deranged payments & greater evils is not as remote as one could wish. We *must* put forth all our strength if we want to come out of this struggle, not only with success, but with honor and unsullied credit

I am an Ohio man & so are you. May I not look for your sympathy and trust that the motives which have such power with me will not fail to influence you.

I shall be very glad to hear from you; but will not *claim* a moment of your time from more important duties than that of replying to this letter.

With the greatest respect and esteem,

Yours faithfully
S P Chase

Maj. Gen. Gillmore.

1. Jacob Schuckers later made a copy of this letter, which is also among Chase's papers at the Historical Society of Pennsylvania and appears at *micro* 30:0677.

2. Henry W. Halleck issued the orders on December 22. Despite Chase's confidence, the offensive in Florida failed in wake of a major defeat at the battle of Olustee (Ocean Pond) on February 20, and Federal authority was not reestablished in the state until May 1865. Johns, *Florida during the Civil War*, 208–9; Long, *Civil War Day by Day*, 466; *OR*, ser. 1, v. 28:134.

3. Marked by McClellan's withdrawal from Harrison's Landing, Va., on August 16, 1863. Long, *Civil War Day by Day*, 251.

4. Lyman Stickney referred to the December 19 meeting of Unionists. The *New York Daily Tribune* published the resolutions on December 29. Stickney to Chase, Dec. 21, 1863 (Chase Papers, L.C.).

TO HORACE GREELEY

Autograph letter on letterhead stationery. Horace Greeley Papers, Rare Books and Manuscripts Division, The New York Public Library, Astor, Lenox, and Tilden Foundations (*micro* 30:0681).

Treasury Department.
December 29 1863.

My dear Mr. Greeley,

It rejoiced my heart yesterday to hear from Judge Stickney that he had already held a meeting in Florida & that the meeting had unanimously adopted the resolutions I had drafted for his use, (if approved,) just as they were written.[1] He had promised to do so when we parted in November & I had urged him not to lose a day needlessly. And he has been fully up to his word. He is a man to be sustained.

I had a letter last week from Mr. Durant of New Orleans, to whom I wrote some time ago urging the policy as well as duty of allowing suffrage to colored citizens.[2] I find that almost all who are willing to have colored men fight are willing to have them vote. They agree with me generally that ballots in their hands are as useful as bullets. Mr. Durant in his reply comes almost to this ground: but for the present advocates only the right of the free-born native colored men. The first fruits of this were apparent in the admission of the colored delegates to sit in the recent Convention at New Orleans.[3] Mr. Durant is very honest, very earnest & very able—taken for all in all, I think, about the ablest man on our side in the gulf States.

In this unusual portrait painted in 1864, Ohio-born artist Caroline Ransom depicted Chase at the south entry of the Treasury building. In the background are building stones (probably for construction of the Treasury Extension), military tents, and, in the distance, the unfinished Washington Monument. *Courtesy of the Political History Collection, National Museum of American History, Smithsonian Institution (photo courtesy of the U.S. Treasury Department).*

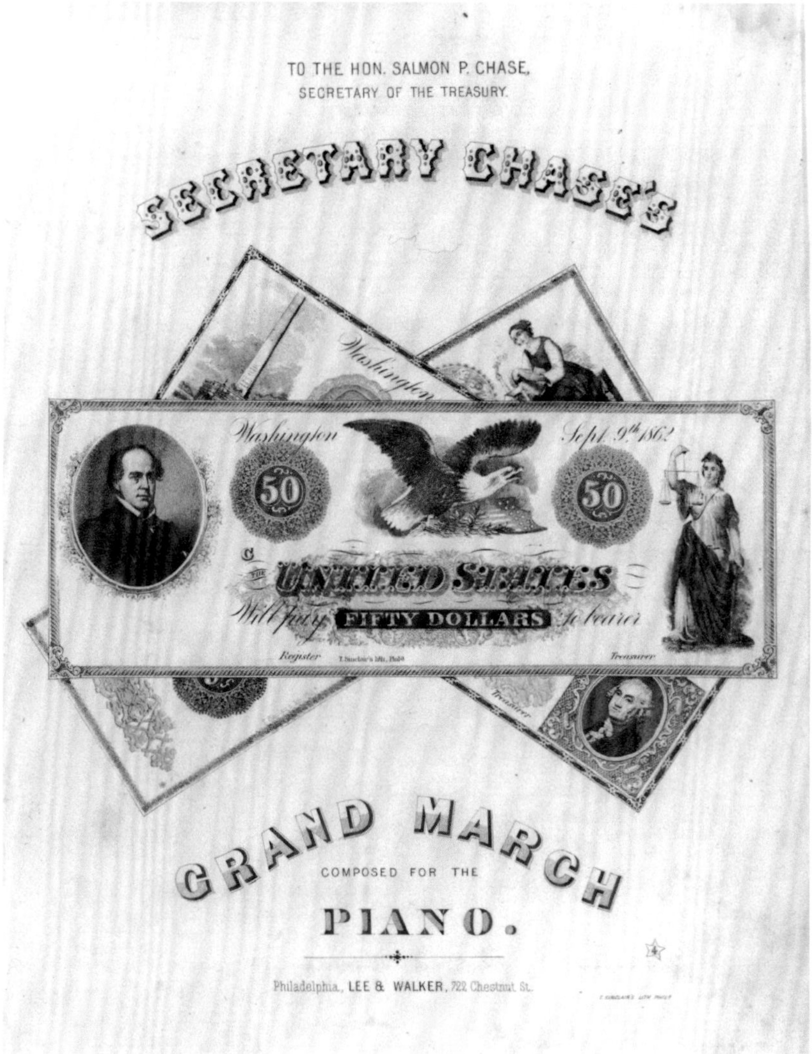

Music composed by Edward Mack in 1863, illustrated with mock currency, demonstrates the popular association of Chase with greenback notes. *Courtesy Collection of the U.S. Treasury Department.*

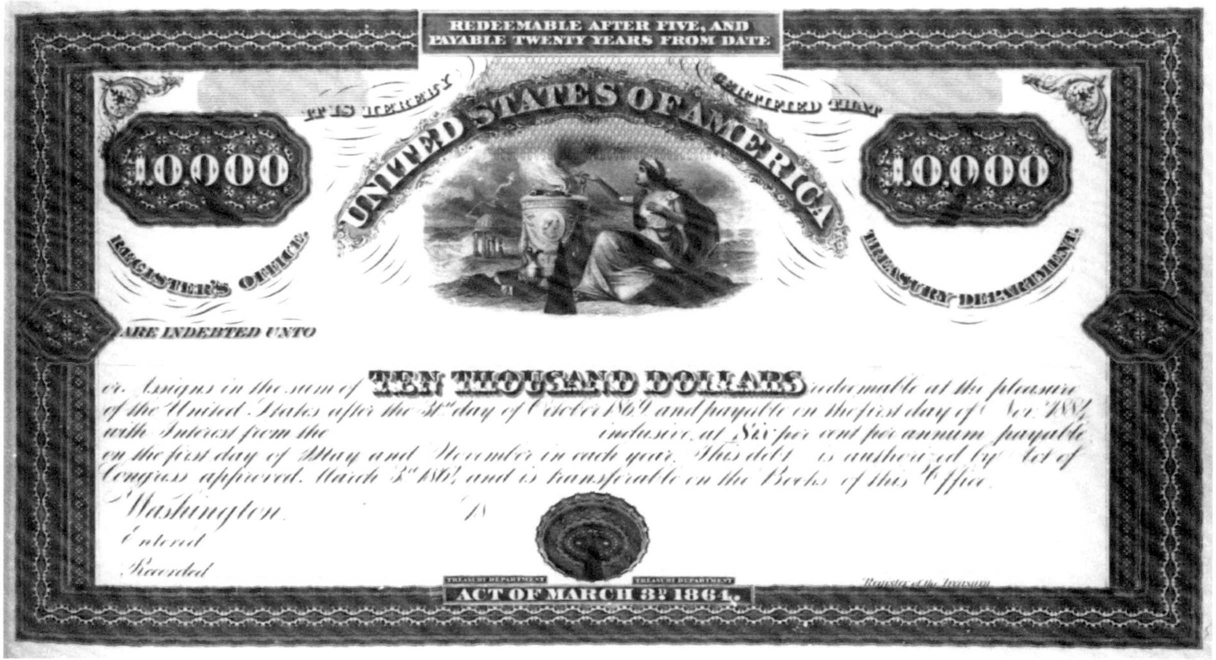

This plate from *The American Bond Detector* (Washington, D.C., 1869) illustrates a 5-20 bond, one of the mainstays of U.S. financial policy during the Civil War. *Courtesy of the National Numismatic Collection, Museum of American History, Smithsonian Institution.*

In a rainy scene from *Harper's Weekly* (February 18, 1865), female workers leave the Treasury building. During the Civil War, women performed such tasks as counting notes and signing interest coupons on bonds. Their pay ($600 a year in 1863) was less than a messenger's salary and only half of what the most junior male clerks received. *Courtesy Collection of the U.S. Treasury Department.*

This 1866 photograph by George Wakely shows the Treasury's south and west facades, wings added to expand the original building. The south wing, in the center and right side of this photo, was completed in 1860, with the secretary's office at its east end (to right in picture). Construction of the large west wing of the Treasury Extension, on the left in the picture, was finished in 1864. *Courtesy Collection of the U.S. Treasury Department.*

Shown here as it appeared long after Chase's death, this stately house on the corner of 6th and E Streets, N.W., in Washington was Chase's home during the Civil War. The house, which no longer stands, was also the Washington residence of Kate Chase and William Sprague after their marriage. *Courtesy of the Library of Congress.*

In November 1863, Kate Chase married Rhode Island textile manufacturer and politician William Sprague. *Courtesy of the National Archives.*

In 1864, author John T. Trowbridge drew on autobiographical letters from Chase to write a book meant—as shown by the scenes depicted on its decorative title page—for young readers.

Mr. Lincoln. "Mike, remove the Salmon and bring me a Tod."
Mike. "The Tod's out; but can't I fitch something else, Sir?"

After Chase's resignation from the Treasury, a cartoon in *Harper's* depicted Abraham Lincoln disappointed in his wish to follow his picked-over "Salmon" with a "Tod" (former Ohio governor David Tod, who declined the Treasury post). *Courtesy of the Library of Congress.*

Gillmore, in his Department, you probably learn more about than I do. All I learn of him inspires me with the highest confidence. Among our wise, energetic, true hearted generals, I think I should put him about at the head. He is thoroughly with such men as Stickney in their efforts at reorganization. I have written him so as to possess him of my views on this head.[4]

How would it do to *advocate* something like this—which I have already proposed to Stickney & Durant:[5] that the new Constitution contain a Suffrage Article, providing for Commissioners for each County or other more convenient subdivision of the State; that all citizens, not in prison for crime or a convicts, who desire to exercise the right of suffrage being twenty one years of age present themselves for examination to these Commissioners & on being found able to read & write & possessed of a competent knowledge of the Constitution of the State & the United States receive certificates, describing each recipient so as to identify him, in virtue of which the citizen receiving it shall be entitled to exercise the right of suffrage. Would it not be very honorable for Louisiana and Florida to lead the way in thus creating an electoral community with no test except virtue & intelligence

I am doing what I can for progress and freedom in such ways as these and devote to the work all the time I can command from my special duties. But oh! how little it seems that I can do compared with what ought to be done! Every thing seems to go so slow whether civil or military and the need of despatch is so urgent.

Your friend
S P CHASE

I must thank you for your word of vindication from the strange attack of Phillips. How little he knows or how perversely he misrepresents.[6]

1. The same day he wrote to Greeley, Chase also discussed the St. Augustine meeting of December 19 and Lyman D. Stickney's letter of December 21 in correspondence to Quincy A. Gillmore (see letter to Gillmore, December 29, 1863 [above]).

2. See the correspondence between Chase and Thomas J. Durant, November 19, December 4, and December 28, 1863 (above).

3. On December 15, a convention of "Free State men" meeting at Lyceum Hall in New Orleans had selected delegates for a "Convention of the Union men of the Slave States, to be held in Louisville, Ky." McCrary, *Lincoln and Reconstruction,* 196–97; *New York Times,* Dec. 27, 1863.

4. Chase to Gillmore, Dec. 29, 1863 (above).

5. See Chase's December 28 letter to Durant (above).

6. Chase had also complained about the incident in a letter to Henry Ward Beecher, December 26, 1863 (above). Greeley had responded on the floor of the Cooper Union directly after Wendell Phillips's reproach of Chase on December 22. "I think it may be demonstrated . . . ," asserted Greeley, "that about the largest brain and the steadiest arm that have given their best efforts to preserve the life of the Nation throughout the gigantic struggle forced upon us by slave-holding treason are those of the statesman who has

been made the object of special assault in the eloquent address to which we have just listened." *New York Tribune,* Dec. 24, 1863.

TO THE DIRECT TAX COMMISSIONERS FOR SOUTH CAROLINA

Letter in clerk's hand on letterhead stationery, signed by Chase; "Additional Instructions" in clerk's hand, signed by Abraham Lincoln. Special Collections, Miller Library, Colby College, Waterville, Maine (*micro* 30:0703).

Treasury Department.
December 30th, 1863.

Gentlemen,

By direction of the President I transmit the following instructions, which you will observe in disposing of lands struck off to the United States.[1] You will consider them as applying to all lands in your district which are now or may be hereafter owned by the United States, except such as are or may be set apart for military, naval, school or revenue purposes, and the plantations on St. Helena Island, known as "Land's End" and the "Ben Chaplin Place,"[2] and the City of Beaufort on Port Royal Island.

All previous instructions or parts thereof which conflict with those now given are hereby rescinded.

Yours Respectfully,
S P Chase
Secretary of the Treasury.

Messrs.
W H Brisbane, A. D. Smith
and Wm. Wording, Direct Tax Commissioners[3]

Additional Instructions to the Direct Tax Commissioners for the District of South Carolina in relation to the disposition of Lands:

1.— You will allow any loyal person of twenty-one years of age or upwards who has at any time since the occupation by the national forces resided for six months or now resides upon, or is engaged in cultivating any lands in your district owned by the United States, to enter the same for pre-emption to the extent of one or, at the option of the preemptor, two tracts of twenty acres each paying therefor One dollar and Twenty-Five cents per acre. You will give preference in all cases to heads of families and to married women whose husbands are engaged in the service of the United States or are necessarily absent.

2.— You will permit each soldier, sailor or marine actually engaged in the service of the United States, or any who may have been or hereafter shall be honorably discharged to pre-empt and purchase in person or by authorized agent at the rate of One dollar and twenty-five cents per acre one tract of twenty acres of land if single, and if married, two tracts of twenty acres each in addition to the amount a head of family or married woman in the absence of her husband is allowed to pre-empt and purchase under the general privilege to loyal persons.

3.— Each pre-emptor on filing his claim and receiving his certificate of pre-emption must pay in United States Notes two-fifths of the price and the residue on receiving a deed for the parcels of land pre-empted, and a failure to make complete payment on receipt of deed will forfeit all rights under the pre-emption as well as all partial payments for the land.

4.— When persons authorized to purchase by pre-emption desire to enter upon and cultivate lands not yet surveyed, they may do so; but they will be required to conform in their selections as nearly as possible to the probable lines of the surveys, and to take and occupy them subject to correction of title and occupation by actual surveys when made.

5.— In making surveys, such reservations for paths and roadways will be made as will allow easy and convenient access to the several subdivisions entered for sale and occupancy by pre-emption or otherwise.

A. LINCOLN.

Approved, Dec. 31, 1863.

1. Legislation of June 1862 and February 1863 authorized the appointment of commissioners in each seceded state to dispose of lands forfeited for nonpayment of a Federal direct tax. *Chase Papers,* 3:352–57; *Statutes at Large,* 12:422–26, 640–41.

2. Lands End stood on the southwest corner of St. Helena Island. The plantation of Chaplin (1776–1851), a local planter, adjoined to the northeast. Theodore Rosengarten, *Tombee: Portrait of a Cotton Planter* (New York, 1986), 324–25, 328–29.

3. Previously, William H. Brisbane had been an antislavery leader in Cincinnati and chief clerk of the Wisconsin state senate. As a judge in Wisconsin, Abram D. Smith had gained notoriety for a decision that denied the constitutionality of the fugitive slave law. William E. Wording was apparently a physician. *Appletons',* 1:378; Willie Lee Rose, *Rehearsal for Reconstruction: The Port Royal Experiment* (Indianapolis, 1964), 202.

TO WILLIAM DENNISON

Letterpress copy of autograph letter. Chase Papers, Historical Society of Pennsylvania (*micro* 30:0713).

Washington, December 31, 1863.

My dear Governor,

A good many friends are writing me from time to time, and especially since Wendell Phillips has made me the subject of his censures, about the Margaret Garner case.[1]

The general history of it so far as I can recall it was something like this

Margaret Garner, with her husband Simon, & several children and two or three other slaves escaped from the Gaines place & vicinity, some fifteen or twenty miles from Cincinnati, [*blotted*] of course in Kentucky, into Storrs Township just below the city.[2]

There with or without a Commissioners warrant they were seized. Some resistance was made & some shots fired, & Margaret, becoming frenzied with horror of being taken, with her children, back to slavery, attempted to kill them & succeeded in killing one.[3] The slaves were seized however and held for examination. In accordance with my uniform rule I determined they should have every advantage which the law would allow them; and my sympathy was especially moved for the unfortunate Mother. She was arrested, therefore,—for such was the unhappy condition of law & opinion both at the time that no other course to save her from dreaded slavery was open—for the homicide of her child & the others as her accomplices. While they were thus held under the State law, & after I believe an indictment against Margaret, Judge Leavitt, about four weeks after the escape issued a habeas corpus, not to enquire into the question of their detention by the sheriff, but to determine the right of the marshal to their custody as against the sheriff.[4] Contrary to expectation, and even to assurances which Judge Hoadly thought he had from Judge Leavitt, he decided that the custody of the sheriff under the criminal law of the State must give way to the custody of the marshal under the fugitive slave act; and under this decision the slaves, Margaret included were immediately turned over by Sheriff Brashears to Marshal Robinson, who hurried them across the river.[5]

They could not properly be regarded as fugitives from the justice of Ohio, for they did not escape from her jurisdiction, but were taken from it against their will, and I hesitated about making a demand for them on the Governor of Kentucky. I hesitated the more because I was unwilling to characterize the homicide as murder. I yielded however to my sympathies for the poor mother & to my wishes in some way to vindicate the outraged laws of the State, & sent an agent to Kentucky with a formal demand for the fugitives.[6] Probably somebody telegraphed the claimants, for though the Governor issued his warrant, Margaret & the rest had been shipped south from Louisville before the agent arrived there with it.

I always regarded Judge Leavitts conduct as entirely unjustifiable & so characterized it in my next message.[7] His unexpected & unwarranted decision & the grab game played under it allowed not the least opportunity for interference by me as Governor: or I should have instructed the sheriff not to regard the order made by him but maintain his custody under the criminal law; or, if I could have done no better, caused a new habeas corpus to be obtained from the State Court.

As it was I did every thing that could be done by any body in my place: and have now no omission to regret.

What I desire of you is to have the files & records of the Governors Office examined & transcripts made of all the papers & correspondence relating to this case, with dates of writing & filing. The whole is between the 28th Jany & the last of April 1856—chiefly in February & the first half of March. Please employ some good copyist and I will pay him whatever you think reasonable.[8]

Cordially your friend
S P Chase

Hon Wm Dennison.

1. "Have you time to prepare for me—or have you already among your papers—a full statement of your action in the Margaret Garner Case?" queried Edward L. Pierce on December 28. "I should like one very much, not perhaps for present use, but I wish to have the facts fully at command." Chase had complained about the attack by Phillips in correspondence to Henry Ward Beecher, December 26, and to Horace Greeley, December 29 (both above), and later discussed the Garner case extensively in a letter to John T. Trowbridge, March 13, 1864 (below). Pierce to Chase, Dec. 28, 1863 (Chase Papers, L.C.).

2. Archibald K. Gaines, who owned the Garner family, had a plantation near Richwood Station, Boone County, Ky. Escaping with the Garners early in 1856 were Simon, Sr., his wife Mary, nine slaves from other plantations, and four children of Simon, Jr., and Margaret: two boys, aged four and six, a nine-month-old girl, and three-year-old Mary. Levi Coffin, *Reminiscences of Levi Coffin: The Reputed President of the Underground Railroad*... (Cincinnati, [1876]), 562–63; Yanuck, "Garner Fugitive Slave Case," 50–52; Chase to John T. Trowbridge, Mar. 13, 1864 (below).

3. Mary Garner, age three. Chase to Trowbridge, Mar. 13, 1864 (below).

4. Humphrey Howe Leavitt, judge of the U.S. district court for Ohio, had a reputation for upholding the fugitive slave law. *DAB,* 11:84.

5. Gazoway Brashears, Hamilton County sheriff, surrendered the fugitives to U.S. Marshal Hiram H. Robinson. Chase's former law student, George Hoadly, Jr., assisted his law partner at the time, Edward Mills, as counsel for Brashears. Mills believed that he had definite assurance from Leavitt "that all rights of mere service or labor being civil claims are inferior to the claims of the State to enforce criminal laws." Hoadly and Mills advised Brashears that a hearing on the writ of habeas corpus would provide judicial validation of the sheriff's custody of the fugitives and protect Brashears against legal action threatened by Archibald Gaines. "This turned out to be a fatal error," Hoadly later stated. "I have never been able . . . to comprehend how Judge Leavitt persuaded himself out of his earlier opinions." Hoadly to Chase, Jan. 6, 1864 (Chase Papers, L.C.); *Cinc. Dir. (1856),* 35, 229; Yanuck, "Garner Fugitive Slave Case," 54–55.

6. Charles Slaughter Morehead (1802–68) had recently won election to the governorship as an American party candidate. Chase's request for extradition, written on March 4, 1856, argued that, in constitutional terms, "the mode in which such persons might come into states where found was entirely unimportant." The agent was Joseph Cooper. Chase to Morehead, Mar. 4, Cooper to Chase, Mar. 11, 1856 (Chase Papers, L.C.); *DAB,* 13:157–58.

7. Although the published version of Chase's next annual message, on January 5, 1857, made no specific mention of the Margaret Garner case, campaign speeches he delivered later in 1856 did include references to the "rescue case." *Message of the Governor of Ohio, to the Fifty-Second General Assembly, at the Adjourned Session, Commencing January 5, 1857* (Columbus, 1857); *New York Times,* Aug. 29, 1857; *Ohio State Journal,* Aug. 25, 1857.

8. Dennison responded with copies of "all the papers on file in the Ex dept., relating to the Margaret Garner Case." Expenses totaled $10. Dennison to Chase, Jan. 30, 1864 (Chase Papers, L.C.).

TO JANE CHASE AULD

Letterpress copy of autograph letter. Chase Papers, Historical Society of Pennsylvania (*micro* 30:0746).

Washn. Jany 2, 1863.[1]

Dear Jane,

I did *not* receive your letter—at least do not remember it. Yours of the 28th has just come and I remember with shame how I thought of writing so that the children should have nice holiday presents & telling you to keep your boy, & how I put it off.[2] Oh! how wrong procrastination is in every thing!

I now enclose $150 & have telegraphed you to relieve your anxiety.[3] Fifty dollars is for the childrens holiday presents. You must not use it for any thing else. One hundred dollars is for your general use: and you shall have more as you need it. May God bless you & restore dear little Jennie. Kiss the children for me.

In haste your affectionate Uncle
S P Chase

Mrs Jane Auld

I received, dear Jane, this morning from your Aunt Eliza a check for a thousand dollars an amount of money lent brother Edward years ago. I have made this a New Year's gift to you & placed it in the hands of Jay Cooke Esq of Philadelphia as a trustee for you to be turned to the best advantage for your benefit. I hope it will prove a good investment for you and your little ones. I will send you his receipt for the money.[4]

1. Chase erred in writing the date, which should have read *1864*. Auld, Chase's niece, had been a widow for over a decade. She worked as a teacher and school principal to support herself and her daughters. Salmon P. Chase to Kate Chase, July 4, 1853 (Chase Papers, Hist. Soc. of Pa.); *Chase Papers,* 2:404.

2. Auld's letter of December 7, written from Loveland, Ohio, reported that her daughter Jane (Jennie) had fallen ill. Auld also explained her decision to hire a "German boy" to help with chores. "Please do not think me idle or extravagant," wrote Auld in a plea for assistance: "I have it is true spent money for Jennie without any good to the poor child, but I meant it for the best." The letter of December 28, written with urgency, told about running out of money, dismissing the boy, and seeing Jennie's condition worsen. Auld had two other children besides Jennie: Alice and Amy. Auld to Chase, Dec. 7, 28, 1863 (Chase Papers, L.C.); "Family Memoranda" (Chase Papers, L.C.).

3. Chase's telegram, marked with a request for immediate delivery, advised Auld to expect his letter and financial aid: "take back the boy—I will pay his wages." Chase to Auld, letterpress copy of draft telegram, [Jan. 2, 1864] (Chase Papers, Hist. Soc. of Pa.).

4. Mary Eliza Chase sent the money to fulfill a debt incurred by her husband, Chase's brother Edward, who had died on October 13, 1862. Calling the gift a "noble act," Jay Cooke acknowledged receiving the money on January 21. Mary Eliza Chase to Chase, Oct. 14, 1862, Dec. 29, 1863 (Chase Papers, L.C.); Chase to Cooke, Jan. 2, Cooke to Chase, Jan. 21, 1864 (Chase Papers, Hist. Soc. of Pa.).

TO BENJAMIN F. BUTLER

Letterbook copy in clerk's hand. Letters Sent Relating to Restricted Commercial Intercourse and Captured and Abandoned Property (BE Series), General Records, Department of the Treasury (Record Group 56), National Archives (*micro* 30:0748).

Treasury Department
January 2d. 1864.

Maj. General Butler
Fort Monroe, Va.
Sir.

I have been reading your General Orders Nos. 38, 39 and 40 in relation to trade.[1] The first order No. 38 was intended, I presume, as a simple recision of permits issued on request and certificate by your predecessor to the end that you may be assured that no abuses were intended under them.[2] And it seemed to me wise and proper,— Order No. 39 forbids all permits to trade unless approved at your Head Quarters for the District of Virginia and of the commanding Officer of the District of North Carolina for that District. Under Regulations 34, 35 and 36, sanctioned by the President, and by the Order of the War Department, No. 88 amended September 11, 1863 which you will find in the pamphlet "Trade Regulations pages 12, 24 51 and 53, licenses and clearances for opened ports are authorized to be given by the proper Collectors and Surveyors, and these clearances and permits are not subject to military control, except where imperative military necessity requires it.[3] No permits at all are granted for shipments to any ports affected by the blockade, except upon the certificate and request of the Commanding General of the Department authorized for that purpose by the Secretary of War, and these certificates and requests are to contain the matters specified in Regulation No. 32.[4] It seems to me that your Order No. 39 has a broader scope than you probably intended, and may lead to difficulties through interference with the proper action of the Agents of this Department under the law, regulations and orders of the War Department. I beg also to call your attention to the tax imposed by order No. 40 upon goods brought into and taken out of your military Department. A charge of 5 per cent is already imposed by the regulations on the goods taken from a loyal State into a State declared in insurrection. Whether it is expedient to impose an additional tax is worthy of consideration—I have requested Mr. Risley, the Supervising Special Agent of the second Agency which includes Virginia, and Mr. Thomas Assistant Special Agent for the Third Agency which includes North Carolina,[5] to call upon you and confer with you fully in regard to matters of trade.— I intended to visit you, and talk over this subject of trade, but find myself prevented by indispensable public duties.

These gentlemen, however, are fully acquainted with my views, and have much practical knowledge of the workings of the regulations.

They as well as all other Agents of the Department, are instructed to execute the duties imposed upon them in harmony with, and if necessary in subordination to, Commanders of Departments within which they act. I recognize and direct them to recognize, the primary necessity of suppressing the rebellion, and of their conformity to the decisions of the Commanding Generals entrusted with that most important work.

I send you a copy of the Regulations.

Very truly yours.
S. P. Chase
Secretary of the Treasury.

1. Order No. 38, published on November 25, 1863, revoked "all permits for the shipment of goods issued prior to the 15th instant." The next order, on the following day, required all trade permits in occupied Virginia and North Carolina to be issued from district headquarters. Also published on November 26 was Order No. 40, which levied taxes of one percent on the invoice value of each shipment, one dollar for every passport, and three dollars per permit for commercial vessels. *OR,* ser. 1, v. 29, pt. 2:489, 494.

2. In November 1863, Butler had replaced Maj. Gen. John Gray Foster as commander of the districts of Virginia and North Carolina. *DAB,* 3:358; Long, *Civil War Day by Day,* 432.

3. Chase referred to Treasury regulations issued on September 11, 1863, and a War Department order originally published on March 31, 1863. All can be found in the compilation *Commercial Intercourse,* on the pages Chase listed.

4. That is, "character, quantity, value, and destination." *Commercial Intercourse,* 24.

5. Uriah Thomas. *Letter of the Secretary . . . Special Agents,* 2.

TO JOHN J. CISCO

Letter in clerk's hand on letterpress stationery, signed by Chase. Chase Papers, Historical Society of Pennsylvania (*micro* 24:0494).

Treasury Department.
January 4th, 1863.[1]

Sir,

Mr. Field has shown me your private letter to him. In my financial arrangements I have seldom consulted the Assistant Secretary of the Department, either before or since Mr. Field took that position temporarily. My confidence in him is entire, but it is inconvenient for me to confer with anybody relating to financial matters beyond what I find necessary to satisfy my own judgment. When you desire explanations, please address your letters to me. The answers will be frank and explicit.—

The recent authority to Mr. Cooke to confer with Bankers and Capitalists as to subscriptions for Treasury Notes to the extent of Thirty-Five millions of dollars was prompted by the emergency created by the bi-monthly payment of the Army, and my desire to make this payment without interfering beyond absolute necessity with the subscriptions for the Five-Twenties required to meet other disbursements. I wished to act quietly, disturbing the ordinary course of business as little as possible. Mr. Cooke thought he could accomplish my wishes. He was to receive no commission whatever for his services, and no advantage could result to him from the operation beyond the comparatively small amount of deposits with the National Banks in which he is interested. Indeed it was and is my desire to receive the money and return it at once, through payments to the army, into the channels of circulation, leaving nothing on deposit a moment longer than necessary for that purpose.

What there is in all this to excite a commotion among the banks and newspapers is more than I can see.[2] One thing is certain, the commotion does not in the least disturb me. I wanted money for important public objects, and took that mode of obtaining it which seemed to me most certain, most convenient and most economical. I am still satisfied with the mode which I adopted. I mean to treat the Banks with scrupulous good faith, and to do nothing which will unnecessarily prejudice any interest they represent. Neither my conscience nor my judgment are in their keeping.

Mr. Haight,[3] in conversation, says you do not feel yourself authorized to receive deposits on account of subscriptions for the Treasury Notes. I supposed you received them precisely as for subscriptions to the 5–20 bonds. There may be some omission in instructions to you, which should have been given. I am confined to the house to-day, but hope to be able to make everything straight tomorrow.

Yours very truly,
S P Chase
Secretary of the Treasury.

John J. Cisco, Esquire, Asst. Treas. U.S.,
New York.

1. Actually January 4, 1864, as confirmed by a Treasury Department letterbook copy and by Chase's reference to Maunsell B. Field, who in October 1863 became acting assistant secretary of the Treasury to fill in for an ailing George Harrington. Chase to Field, Sept. 19, 1863 (Chase Papers, Hist. Soc. of Pa.); Chase to Cisco, Jan. 4, 1864 (Letters Sent Relating to Subtreasury System, Gen. Recs. Treasury Dept., Nat. Arch.); *Chase Papers,* 1:457.

2. In a circular distributed on December 30, 1863, Jay Cooke, as the government's subscription agent, announced a new subscription of up to $35 million in legal tender Treasury notes bearing five percent interest. Larger denominations would pay interest every six months over two years, while smaller notes of the issue were to mature in one year. The notes themselves were not yet available, but Cooke would accept subscriptions for them in exchange for deposits, at par, of non-interest-bearing greenbacks or national banks' notes. "The entire negotiation . . . has not been creditable to the Treasury Department," complained the *New York Tribune.* According to commentary in newspapers, bankers were unhappy over Cooke's role and over the Treasury's inability to manufacture notes quickly enough to fulfill earlier subscriptions of interest-bearing legal tender notes. Concerning this new Treasury note subscription see also Chase's January 13 letter to Hiram Price (below). *New York Tribune,* Dec. 31, 1863; *New York Times,* Dec. 31, 1863, Jan. 1, 1864; Chase to Cisco, June 26, Aug. 31, 1863 (above); *Statutes at Large,* 12:710.

3. Probably Edward Haight, Democratic congressman and president of the Bank of the Commonwealth in New York City. *Bio. Dir. U.S. Cong.*, 1109.

TO RALPH S. HART

Letterpress copy of letter in clerk's hand, signed by Chase. Chase Papers, Historical Society of Pennsylvania (*micro* 30:0783).

Private

January 5th, 64.

My dear Judge,[1]

I have your kind letter of the 21st ultimo.[2]— Fortunately I ha[ve] no aspirations which would tempt me to deviate at all from the path which my own judgment and sincere convictions require me to walk in. You need, therefore, be under no apprehensions that I shall be induced by clamor to abrogate or modify existing Regulations of Trade. I shall keep steadily in view the general principles which I laid down in my Report.[3] First, Absolute freedom of trade where there is no danger where there is no danger that supplies may be taken to rebels; Second, Restricted trade where there is such danger, either in portions of loyal States bordering upon rebels States, or in rebel States occupied by our military forces; Third, No intercourse at all between those within rebel lines and those within national lines. In carrying out the second principle my intention is that the restrictions shall be stringent enough to prevent supplies to rebels beyond our lines, and yet no so stringent as to prevent supplies to the population within our lines.— In carrying out the last, I do not mean to have Agents of the Department so very strict as to presume against the legitimacy of transactions apparently made in good faith. For example, if a quantity of cotton is brought out from within rebel lines by some person bold enough to go there and seize it, or by some Union man escaping from rebel jurisdiction, I would not have this cotton seized as forfeited. Neither the spirit of the Act nor sound public policy require it. If, however, a person within our lines should undertake to trade with people in the rebel lines, and in that way get out their products, such products ought to be seized; for such trade is the very thing prohibited by the Acts of Congress.— I am looking daily for letters from Mr. Mellen, showing precisely the location of the Assistant Special Agents.— Your [letter] [*two words? illeg.*] [supposes] that you may have been stationed at Memphis: if so, you [*several words illeg.*] [will require] all your judgment and all your courage. You are kind enough to warn me against certain influences likely to be brought to bear upon me. As the little negro boy said [to his] [*illeg.*] when saluted by a wish more emphatic than refined, "Same to yourself, massa."

Yours very Sincerely,
S P CHASE

Hon. R. S. Hart,
Memphis, Tennessee.

1. Chase had recently appointed Ralph S. Hart (d. 1864), a personal acquaintance and former Ohio legislator and judge of common pleas, as assistant special agent on the lower Mississippi River. Later in the year, Hart was accused of illegally taking "money for the performance of official duties and otherwise," and, on May 24, Chase formally suspended him. Chase to Hart, Nov. 19, 1863 (Chase Papers, Hist. Soc. of Pa.); Chase to Hart, May 24, 1864 (Letters Sent to Special Agents, Recs. of Bureau of Customs, Nat. Arch.); Chase to Benjamin F. Wade, June 21, 1864 (below); *Letter of the Secretary . . . Special Agents,* 2; Schuckers, *Chase,* 328–29.

2. Writing from Natchez, Hart warned Chase of a conspiracy by speculators to remove valuable stores of Confederate cotton for illegal trade. Hart to Chase, [Dec. 21, 1863] (Chase Papers, L.C.).

3. The Treasury's most recent trade regulations dated from September 11, 1863. Chase mentioned the three "principles" in his recent official report to Congress, issued in December and covering the fiscal year ending June 30, 1863. *Report of the Secretary of the Treasury . . . 1863,* 23.

TO EDWARD D. MANSFIELD

Letterpress copy of letter in clerk's hand, signed by Chase. Chase Papers, Historical Society of Pennsylvania.

January 5th, 64.[1]

My dear Sir,

I am greatly obliged to you for sending me a "Veteran Observer's" Letter to the *Times* of the 2d December.[2] I generally look for these letters, but this one es[caped] me. I am glad you have written this letter. I think it cannot fail to do good. You state the whole case in a nut shell when you say that John [Bell has] no more political rights this day in Tennessee than his slave Pompey.[3] When this [truth sha]ll have gained a lodgement in the thinking brain of the people the problem of [the] status of the rebel states will be solved.

It has long seemed to me that the simple idea that the loyal [people of the] State constitute the State boldly proclaimed and honestly acted on—(perhaps I should say, fearlessly instead of honestly; for honesty without courage in times like these is almost of less value than courage without honesty)—would [save us] from all the troubles that beset our path.

Have you seen the account of the recent meeting at St. Augustine?[4] These Floridians embrace the true idea. I may confess to you per[sonally, that] I had some hand in connection with one of the ablest among them, in [drawing up the Resolutions some time last] November.[5] They solve the question, "[Who] are [the] loyal men?" and it will solved every where the same way if the Presi[dent will only] give the aid and encouragement to the earnest and unconditional Union men which they are entitled to.

If he does not give them aid there is some danger, and a good deal of danger that his late Proclamation of Amnesty will be sadly abused. A gentleman just from Norfolk tells me that the worst sympathizers are taking the oath prescribed by the President, and expect to be numerous enough to frustrate the efforts of the Union Emancipationists to put

Virginia into the list of Free States. I hope he is mistaken; but yet I see clearly enough how such consciences as most of the sympathizers with rebellion have, can be reconciled to taking an oath which contains in itself an admission that in contingencies which the sympathizer expects will certainly come, that the oath will bind him to nothing. I was very sorry to have Mr. Lincoln put the provisoes concerning the possible repeal of the Acts of Congress touching Slavery and a possible judicial decision against the validity of the Proclamation into the oath, but could not prevail on him to omit them.[6]

So much the more reason for you, a "Veteran Observer," and me, "General Greenbacks," to work hard to get the right ideas into the public mind and heart.

Yours very Cordially,
S P Chase

Hon. E. D. Mansfield,
Morrow, Ohio.

1. The editors used a copy of the letter by Jacob Schuckers (Chase Papers, Hist. Soc. of Pa., reproduced at *micro* 30:0788) to help read faint portions of the letterpress copy.

2. The letter, printed in the *New York Times* on December 20, praised an address Chase had made at Mozart Hall in Cincinnati during his trip to Ohio and Indiana in the autumn. Mansfield maintained that, by rebelling, citizens of the Confederacy had forfeited their right to vote. He argued in favor of reconstruction policies based only on loyal citizens and the permanent eradication of slavery. Chase, *"Going Home to Vote,"* 10–19.

3. Former Whig politician John Bell of Tennessee had run for the presidency on the moderate Constitutional Union ticket in the election of 1860 and reluctantly supported the Confederacy during the Civil War. *DAB,* 2:158.

4. The *New York Tribune,* December 29, had published an account of the December 19 meeting and its resolutions.

5. For Chase's role, with Lyman Stickney, in drawing up the Florida resolutions see Chase's correspondence to Thomas J. Durant, December 28, and to Quincy Adams Gillmore, December 29, 1863 (above).

6. The oath in Lincoln's Proclamation of Amnesty and Reconstruction included a promise to "abide by and faithfully support all acts of Congress passed during the existing rebellion with reference to slaves, so long and so far as not repealed, modified or held void by Congress, or by decision of the Supreme Court." Basler, *Collected Works,* 7:54.

FROM WILLIAM ORTON

Autograph letter on letterhead stationery. Chase Papers, Historical Society of Pennsylvania.

U.S. Internal Revenue,
6th District, State of New York,
New York, Jany 6th. 1864.

Dear Sir:

The enclosed letter reached me yesterday, postmarked "Washington Jan. 4." and *appears* to come from the office of Internal Revenue.

I have just learned that one of the Proprietors of the Magazine is in town boreing and begging your friends for contributions, and is representing in every case that your friends in Phila. and Washington are largely interested in the scheme, Mr. Jay Cooke having subscribed $5.000.[1]

Will you permit me to say in that frankness which you have sometimes invited, and prompted by a friendship always watchful of your interests, that in my judgment this movement is ill-advised, and its results so much to be feared, that immediate steps should be taken to check and suppress it.

Assuming that Mr. Jay Cook is your friend, and willing to evidence his regard practically, the very best investment he can make will be to buy up the edition of this before-unheard-of "Magazine," rub out Sartain's mezzotint counterfeit of your person, and commit the whole concern to the flames.[2]

No matter how able or "faithful" the biography may be, the medium through which it is introduced to the public, accompanied by the clap trap of publishers of "yellow-covered-literature," and the venders of Patent Medicines, will stamp it as a flimsy political trick, which will afford our enemies more working capital for injury than they can legitimately procure during a whole campaign well conducted.

I must believe that you are entirely ignorant of the movement, and that it has its origin in the cupidity of some seedy publisher, whose regard for you is based solely upon his presumed ability to make money out of the attachment of your friends to you, without regard to the effect upon your and their best interests.

Respectfully and truly

Your friend
WILLM. ORTON.

Hon. S: P: Chase,
Washn. D.C.

P.S. I have recently met Mr. Bailey, and spent last evening with him and Mr. Barney—at their request. Mr. Barney goes to Washington in day or two, and I hope to see you before the end of the month.[3]

W. O.

1. The publisher of Philadelphia's *American Exchange and Review* intended to issue what was evidently meant to be a campaign biography of Chase. Chase to Lincoln, Jan. 13, 1864 (below).

2. Publishers of biographical works in particular prized illustrations by Philadelphia engraver Samuel Sartain (1830–1906). *DAB,* 16:372–73.

3. Orton evidently visited Washington sometime during the week of January 17–22. Orton to Chase, Jan. 15, 1864 (Chase Papers, Hist. Soc. of Pa.).

FROM BENJAMIN F. FLANDERS

Autograph letter on letterhead stationery. Chase Papers, Historical Society of Pennsylvania (*micro* 24:0438).

Private

Office Supervising Special Agent Treasury Department.
FIFTH AGENCY.
New Orleans, 186[1]

Sir.

Gen. Banks has a letter from the President, giving to him full control of all matters civil and military here; and directing him to take measures to organize a State government for Louisiana![2]

As I was entering the meeting last evening[3] Mr. Durant took me aside, and informed me that General Banks had shown him a letter which he had just received from Mr. Lincoln, in which the President, says, "You are the "master" there and you will organize a State governt;" And that Gen. Banks declared that he would not have a Convention elected until after an election is held for a Legislature and State officers!

How, or upon what basis of representation the Legislature is to be chosen, Gen. Banks could not explain; nor is it easy to see how a loyal State government can be organized under the Constitution of 1852, and the existing State laws.[4] The General also said he should order an election for members of Congress. How this is to be done, the State not being districted, is not explained. Perhaps the General will district the States. To do what he proposes he must do the work which it has been thought by our citizens can only be done by a Convention of the people—

We have, after much trouble got prepared to effict an organization upon a plan adopted by the Union men several months ago, and approved by the President. The mass meeting, last evening, was to be the close of what we regarded as the necessary preliminary work. In twenty days we were to have an eliction for a Convention, twenty days thereafter an election for a Legislature and State offices, and (if the Convention could district the State) for members of Congress. Sixty days was consided by the Union men as the time required to have a full free State Government organized and in operation.

You may imagine; I shall not attempt to describe—the feelings of those who have labored incessantly for months in developing and organizing the union Sintiment, for a free State Govermt, at this turn of affairs.—

This is the Missouri case over again[5]— I fear the result will be less favorable in the second than it was in the first trial.

Very respectfully
BENJ. F. FLANDERS

Hon. S. P. Chase

1. Flanders did not fill in the blanks provided in the printed letterhead for the date and the last digit of the year. He wrote this letter on January 9, since the meeting "last evening" to which he referred took place on the eighth. *New Orleans Daily Picayune*, Jan. 10, 1864; *New York Tribune*, Jan. 21, 1864.

2. Lincoln to Banks, December 24, 1863, in Basler, *Collected Works*, 7:89–90.

3. The meeting of Louisiana Unionists, at the St. Charles Theater on January 8, emphasized the necessity for a new state constitutional convention based on the "principle of liberty and equality." *New York Tribune*, Jan. 21, 1864.

4. Louisiana's 1852 constitution was the frame of government in effect at the time of secession. Perry H. Howard, *Political Tendencies in Louisiana*, rev. ed. (Baton Rouge, 1971), 70–71.

5. The previous autumn, Chase had complained about Abraham Lincoln's apparent lack of support for Missouri radicals. Chase to Lincoln, Oct. 31, 1863 (above).

TO EDWIN M. STANTON

Autograph letter. Edwin M. Stanton Papers, Library of Congress (*micro* 30:0923).

Washn. Jany 11, 1863.[1]

Dear Sir,

I enclose a copy of my letter to the Committee on Finance relating to bounties. You will see that I preferred to send an extract from your letter rather than the letter itself.[2]

My reason was that my recollection of some matters does not correspond with yours; and I do not wish to seem, even, again, to differ from you in any matter which concerns the administration of your Department.

I have no recollection whatever of being present at a consultation where the President, Secretary of State, General in Chief, Adjutant, Quartermaster & Provost Marshal General were present and at which General Order no 191 was agreed on.[3]

What I do remember is this. You sent for me and, the Provost Marshal General being present, explained your purpose of raising a body of veterans, by allowing $302 in addition to the regular bounty of $100, making for premium & bounty $402. I understood that the $300 extra bounty was to come from the Commutation fund, and that your expectation was to obtain speedily in this way a body of at least ten thousand veterans. I was much gratified by the idea of securing the reenlistment of such a body of veterans; but expressed the opinion that the object could be attained by a less bounty & that the commutation fund could then be made to go a great deal farther. You thought a less bounty would not answer the purpose and I acquiesced. This is all I remember about the order. There was some other conversation about the veterans & the bounties at different times, but nothing varying my impression as just stated.

My remark in relation to the estimate of 5,000,000 refers to it as made for 1865. It should have referred to it as for 1864. The statements of the Estimates for 1864 & 1865 are on the same page & in parallel columns of the pamphlet I handed you. It was my error to write "1865."

Of course, your observations, entirely just as referring my remark written, would not have been applied to the remark intended.[4]

Had you been the writer & I the commentator I think I should have noticed the inadvertence, and spared the comment.

I cannot help feeling, and must say it frankly, that you are displeased with my insisting on refraining from appropriations beyond estimates unless accompanied with provisions for taxation which will ensure the means to meet them: and are not unwilling to place me in the attitude of objecting to what I have myself approved and of making a remark upon the estimate for 1865 which could have no reasonable application to it.

If I am not mistaken in this feeling, I can only say that if you were charged with the responsibilities which oppress me, you would be even more unwilling than I am to see new difficulties added to those which already threaten to make provision for the disbursements of the war impossible.

Yours very truly
S P Chase

Hon. E. M. Stanton

1. Actually 1864, as confirmed by the letter's contents.

2. Earlier in the day Chase had addressed a letter to William Pitt Fessenden, chairman of the Senate Committee on Finance, who had requested information about the potential effect of pending legislation to extend the period allowed for enlistment bounties. In response, Chase used extracts of a letter from Stanton, January 8, 1864, that addressed the issue. Chase to Fessenden, Jan. 11, 1864 (Letters Sent to Committees of Congress, Gen. Recs. Treasury Dept., Nat. Arch.); Fessenden to Chase, Jan. 7, Stanton to Chase, Jan. 8, 1864 (Letters Recd. from Exec. Officers, War Dept., Gen. Recs. Treasury Dept., Nat. Arch.).

3. That is, Abraham Lincoln, William H. Seward, Henry W. Halleck, Lorenzo Thomas, Montgomery C. Meigs, and James Barnet Fry. General Orders No. 191, issued on June 25, 1863, established War Department policy for recruiting volunteer veterans. *OR*, ser. 3, v. 3:414–15.

4. Chase had made the mistake in a letter to Stanton requesting information to help Chase frame his reply to Fessenden. Chase to Stanton, Jan. 7, 1864 (E.B. 5, Letters Recd. by Sec. of War from President, Exec. Depts., [etc.], Recs. of Office of Secretary of War, Nat. Arch.).

TO ABRAHAM LINCOLN

Letterpress copy of autograph letter. Chase Papers, Historical Society of Pennsylvania (*micro* 30:0971).

January 13, 3.[1]

My dear Sir,

I am today fifty six years old. I have never, consciously & deliberately, injured one fellow man. It is too late for me to begin by sacrificing to clamor the reputation of a man whom I have known more than twenty years, and whose repute for honesty has been all that time unsullied. I shall not recommend the removal of Mr. Barney unless upon such showing of misconduct or incapacity as makes it my duty to do so.[2] In such a case I shall not shrink from my duty.

I pretend no indifference to the consequences, personal to myself, which you refer to as likely to follow this avowal on my part. But the approval of my own conscience is dearer to me than political position: and I shall cheerfully sacrifice the latter to preserve the former.

You wrote some days since in relation to a biographical sketch to be printed in a Philadelphia periodical.[3] It was a matter in which I had no concern. If any body wants my autograph, & I have time, I give it; if any body wants to take my daguerreotype or photograph, & I have time, I sit for it; if any body wants *to take my life,* in the way of a biographical sketch, *I let him take it,* & if I have time give such information as is wanted that he may take it the more readily. Some friends wanted such a sketch prepared & engaged a gentleman to prepare it. The publisher of the American Exchange & Review, a respectable periodical by the way, I am told, was about to print a series of such sketches and proposed to begin with that of me. How could I object? He asked for subscriptions; & obtained them. How could I control that or supervise that? I was very busy with the affairs of my department, & had no time to look after such matters, even had I been aware of what was being done. If I had been consulted I should certainly have objected to any subscription by Mr. Jay Cooke or his brother; except such a moderate one as any friend might have made. Not that any wrong was intended or done; but because the act was subject to misconstruction; and there are so many ready to misconstrue. Mr. Jay Cooke is a friend, & though he did not subscribe to the sketch, doubtless sanctioned the subscription of his brother Henry who is also a friend, (and the son of a friend,)[4] whose friendship was proved when I was powerless to bestow favors. Neither of the brothers nor the father have ever received at my hands, since I have had some power, any favor which they have not earned by strenuous and untiring labors for the public interest; or any which my worst enemy would not have received as freely had he rendered the same services. What Mr. H. D. Cooke did about the unfortunate biography was done of his own accord without any prompting from me; and his brothers approval was given in same way.

You will pardon me if I write as one somewhat moved. It makes me hate public life when I realize how powerless are the most faithful labors and the most upright conduct to protect any man from carping envy or malignant denunciations; & how little he can expect even from the best and most intelligent when such noises prevail. It is almost equally painful to think how little friends are disposed to bear with the mistakes & inadvertencies of other friends & how ready to make me responsible for these as well as my own.

Very sincerely yours
S P Chase

To the President.

1. Misdated in original; should be 1864.

2. "I am receiving letters and dispatches indicating an expectation that Mr. Barney is to leave the Custom House, at New York," wrote Lincoln on January 11. "Have you anything on the subject?" Chase replied the next day: "Nothing at all, except urgent representations of the necessity of reform, which do not at all impeach Mr. Barney; in whose integrity I have undiminished confidence." Lincoln to Chase, Jan. 11, 1864, in Robert B. Warden, *An Account of the Private Life and Public Services of Salmon Portland Chase* (Cincinnati, 1874), 556; Chase to Lincoln, Jan. 12, [1864] (Lincoln Papers, L.C.).

3. William Orton, writing on January 6 (above), had warned Chase about the biography proposed by a proprietor of the *American Exchange and Review.*

4. Jay and Henry D. Cooke were sons of Martha Cooke and her husband, Eleutheros Cooke (1787–1864), U.S. congressman from Ohio, 1831–33. *Bio. Dir. U.S. Cong.*, 823; *DAB*, 4:383.

TO HIRAM PRICE

Letterbook copy in clerk's hand. Letters Sent to Individual Senators and Representatives (E Series), General Records, Department of the Treasury (Record Group 56), National Archives.

Treasury Department
13. January 1864.

Hon. H. Price.[1]
House Reprs.—
My dear Sir:

Excuse the delay of my reply to your letter. Incessant engagement have alone occasioned it— I now answer fully.—

First.— The Statements of the Circular you have referred to are not correct.— It is only true that the First National Bank of Washington, and Mr. Jay Cooke, the General Subscription Agent for the 5–20 Loan, undertook at my request to distribute Treasury Notes, and if possible to the amount of thirty-five millions of dollars, in order to provide means for the payment of the Army for the last two months.[2] No compensation direct or indirect was to be allowed to them for the service.—

Second. I cannot state precisely, what part of the thirty-five millions has been subscribed for; not more, however, than from three to five millions.— The subscription falls far below my hope, but will I trust improve.—

Third.— I am anxious to pay all creditors in money, except those who expect to receive payment in certificates of indebtedness, and upon Checks in their favor for certificates. I pay as large proportion in money as the condition of the Treasury allows.— I desire, to avoid the payment of Treasury Notes to the creditors of the Government on account of the inconvenience of calculating accrued interest.[3]— I fear, however, that I shall be obliged to make some payments in this form.—

Fourth.— All subscriptions, whether from banks or individuals will be received by the Treasurer[4] or Assistant Treasurers, and all applications for these notes will be received, as made and the applicant will receive the notes in the order of application until $35,000,000, shall have been issued.—

Fifth.— It is desirable, in my opinion, to strengthen the National Banks as much as is legitimately possible.— No preference, however, is given to them in applications for these notes.— The Government wants the money, and will take from anybody who will supply it.— It is due to candor to add, that had the National Banks promptly taken the $35,000,000, the notes would have been furnished to them in preference to other applications, for in that way the money would have been most promptly obtained, and the general interests of the Government, in my opinion, best promoted.—

Sixth.— Applications for these notes may be made to the Treasurer, or to any Assistant Treasurer, or to any Depositary designated to receive them.—

Seventh.— A portion of the thirty five millions is now ready for delivery, and is being delivered to applicants in the order of their application.— Any application now made can probably be satisfied within the next two weeks; perhaps sooner.— If you desire to apply, your application can be considered as made at the date of your letter, as the delay of my answer may have occasioned your delay in making it.—

Eighth.— I am not sure but it will be well to pay Treasury Notes to soldiers in the Army.— We have none, however, of any denomination lower than fifty dollars.— I am endeavoring to arrange a plan in accordance with which soldiers will find it easy and safe to invest such portion of their wages, as they think fit in bonds or notes.—

Very truly &c.
S P. Chase.—

1. Price (1814–1901) represented Iowa in Congress, 1863–69 and 1877–81, and served as president of the state bank of Iowa from 1860 to 1865. Chase's papers at the Historical Society of Pennsylvania contain another letterbook copy of this letter (reproduced at *micro* 30:0975). *DAB,* 15:212–13.

2. Chase also discussed the $35 million subscription for interest-bearing Treasury notes in his letter to John J. Cisco, January 4 (above). Henry D. Cooke was president of the First National Bank of Washington, the largest banking institution in Washington at the time. *Wash. Dir. (1864),* 86.

3. Jay Cooke's announcement of the Treasury note subscription late in December was directed at financiers "who may have considerable sums of Legal-Tender Notes idle on their hands." By accepting deposits of legal tender notes as payment for the new interest-bearing notes, the government would acquire greenbacks to pay creditors. *New York Times,* Dec. 31, 1863.

4. Francis E. Spinner.

FROM JOHN F. BAILEY

Autograph letter. Chase Papers, Library of Congress (*micro* 30:0982).

New York Jan'y 13, 1864.

Hon. S. P. Chase.
Dear Sir:

I should have written you before but work has been pressing.— There has been a very strong feeling developed against Mr. Barney in consequence of successive developments at the C.H.[1] Even Mr. Orton gave him up, and said it was impossible to hold him up longer. I urged, that I had secured an understanding with Mr. Barney that should be every way satisfactory to your friends, and that in the event of change should they be unable to control the succession not only would the plans of administrative reform initiated be embarrassed and postponed, but the result politically would be much less favorable than those promised under Mr Barney. I failed to satisfy him. This was on Monday. Since which time I have not seen him. That evening I went see Mr. Greeley and found him very violent against Mr. B, but he finally said he would allow his columns to be used by me in his defense, if it was thought best. The same evening I had conference with Mr. Opdyke, and convinced him fully that it was best to hold Mr. Barney up, and he engaged to influence his friends in that direction. Sunday last I wrote an article which was made the leader in the *Evening Post* of Monday, copy of which I enclose. Last evening (Tuesday) I was with Mr. Greeley again and satisfied him more fully. I made statements to Mr. Gay on which he prepared an article which was in *Tribune* of this morning.[2] I shall follow up in these papers, & in *Times* unless I receive different instructions with statements in defense & explanation of transactions here.[3] Strongly as I was impressed with the conviction that Mr. Barney should be displaced three or four months ago, I am just as strongly convinced that unless the succession can be absolutely assured, it is essential that he should be held in now. The demands for administrative reform will be fully and generously met by the plans approved by you when I was in Washington.[4] I can help Mr. Barney out in current business and I feel assured not only save your Department from the odium of his inefficiency, but reflect credit upon it. He feels that he is entirely dependent upon those who represent you, here, and is fully inclined to put all matters in their hands, official & others. I can manage matters with the press so as to bring credit from the transactions of the past months, to the Department at Washington, if not very much to Mr. Barney. I have secured sufficient consent to the policy of holding him in, to smooth matters down in three or four weeks with all your friends. I feel I have a right to say this, when I have appeased the most intractable, Mr. Opdyke, and brought him not only to acquiesce, but to co-operate. As for general public sentiment that can be made to acquiesce in his retention. Some dozen good positions will be available during the week, and I think as many more next week.— I will make up & send the reports spoken of in Washington to-morrow, I have had to give so much attention to Mr. Barneys personal matters that I have been obliged to give the go-by to many other matters.— Mr. Weed has now turned openly against Mr. Barney.[5] I feel safe in saying that your friends can all be made satisfied with Mr. B's retention within the next three or four weeks, and that general public sentiment can be satisfied. A change now would sacrifice much careful preparation. I think this could be a favorable opportunity for Mr. Barney to be impressed, from Washington, with the idea that if he is carried through this, officially & politically it is due to the support rec'd from your friends in consequence of the understanding with me. Pardon the abruptness of my statements.

Will you send me list of such merchants as you would be glad to have considered in any changes that may occur.[6]— I have agreed with Mr. Greeley upon some articles for *Tribune* the plan of which, he thinks well of.

Cannot you have sent to me, the bare facts in the connection of Jay Cooke & Co. with the financial measures of the last two years. I can have them worked up so as to be of great service.[7]

Would it not be well to write to the Chamber of Commerce at once inviting the appointment of a Committee to confer with the special agent of the Department on desired changes.[8] The association of the Collector with me would be only an embarrassment, and it seems to me not necessary as the movement originates and will be carried through from the Dept.

With high respect,
J. F. BAILEY.

1. That is, the New York Custom House.

2. Bailey's unsigned article, "Official Frauds," and "The Custom House," written by Sydney Howard Gay, managing editor of the *Tribune*, admitted that instances of corruption had occurred, but blamed them on previous Democratic administrations and assured readers that Chase had already started to implement reforms. *New York Post*, Jan. 11, 1864; *New York Tribune*, Jan. 13, 1864; *DAB*, 7:195.

3. Unsigned defenses of Treasury action related to the New York Custom House scandals appeared in the *New York Tribune*, January 14, 16, and 22, and the *New York Times*, January 16.

4. Bailey evidently visited Washington, D.C., on December 29, 1863. Reforms under consideration included the dismissal and prosecution of corrupt officials, restrictions on private pay for official business, a decrease in the number of clerks, and consultations with a special committee from the New York Chamber of Commerce. *New York Tribune*, Jan. 13, 1864; Bailey to Chase, Dec. 26, 1863 (Chase Papers, L.C.).

5. Thurlow Weed, former editor of the *Albany Evening Journal* and a close associate of William H. Seward, masterminded opposition against radicals within the New York Republican party. *DAB*, 19:599.

6. Bailey wrote Chase later the same day after reading a recent telegram sent to Horace Greeley. According to the message, Hiram Barney's opponents were supposedly "carrying everything" because Chase and the New York radicals had not suggested a replacement. The following day, Chase wrote Greeley suggesting Daniel S. Dickinson for the position, "should the collectorship of the port become vacant." Bailey to Chase, Jan. 13, 1864 (Chase Papers, L.C.); Chase to Greeley, Jan. 14, 1864 (Greeley Papers, L.C.).

7. On January 22, Chase promised to send Bailey a statement prepared for Congress regarding Jay Cooke, along with "such statements of a historical character as will enable you to compare what has been accomplished through him and his sub-agents." Chase sent the statement to Congress on April 2. Chase to Bailey, Jan. 22, 1864 (Chase Papers, Hist. Soc. of Pa.); *Jay Cooke & Co.: Letter from the Secretary of the Treasury . . .*, 38th Cong., 1st sess., 1863–64, H. Ex. Doc. 66, 1–4.

8. Chase seems to have decided eventually against such consultations. Chase to Bailey, Jan. 22, 1864 (Chase Papers, Hist. Soc. of Pa.).

FROM GEORGE OPDYKE

Autograph letter. Chase Papers, Library of Congress (*micro* 30:1045).

Confidential

New York Jany 15th. 1864

My dear sir:

From all I hear in relation to political movements growing out the late Custom House developments here, I anticipate an earnest effort on the part of Weed, Seward and their friends to secure the removal of Mr Barney and the appointment of Mr Wakeman in his place. The movement in this direction was started immediately after Palmer's arrest. Mr. Wakeman himself started at once for Albany, where he secured the cooperation of Benj Field and perhaps others of our professed friends.[1] By their joint efforts, aided by the general dissatisfaction with Mr Barney's management, they have, as I understand, secured for Mr W. the signatures of all the state officers (every one of which are radicals) and nearly all of the Union members of both branches of the Legislature, state Central Committee, &c. Thus backed Weed has gone on to Washington declaring, I understand, that the change above indicated must be made,—that it would break down the Administration to retain Mr Barney under such developments! &c.

You are aware that Mr Wakeman never fails to carry out to the letter the wishes of W. & S. Consequently, if they succeed in their scheme they will have full sway in the Custom House patronage which would probably enable them to control the political action of the State. Our radical friends at Albany, who have joined in this movement, have therefore, in my opinion, made a sad mistake. There they have been badly dealth with by Mr Barney, who has apparently given Mr Weed full sway of late. And yet Weed, at the first moment of his troubles deserts him and their joint pet, Palmer. Under these circumstances it seems to me to be the duty of the radicals to oppose any change for the present unless it shall appear that Mr Barney is implicated in these corrupt and treasonable practices, which I do not believe, nor does any one that I know believe it. At all events he is entitled to demand a full examination of the facts, and a fair hearing. I trust you will view the matter in this light, and firmly resist the proposed change. So far as I know this is the wish of all our friends here. They are not in favor of any change at present, unless such men, as Judge White, David Dudley Field C. H Dana, D. S. Dickinson or Genl W. K. Strong could secure the appointment, and this is supposed to be impracticable.[2] I should be glad to know from you how the matter stands—at least so far as you may feel at liberty to inform me.

I understand that since your letter to me in reference to Jamess Mackin, Assessor in the Dutchess Cy Dist, complaints have been actually made against him, and a vigorous push is now making to oust him.[3] It is all because he is your friend and mine and an honest man. I am confident that he has committed no other offence, and that he makes a first rate officer. If you find any thing in the charges that you deem worthy your notice I hope you will have a copy of them sent to Mackin that he may have an opportunity to rebut them. I saw a letter from Senator Dutcher today, in which he declared that if you refused to remove him they would appeal to the President.[4]

as ever,

faithfully yours
GEORGE OPDYKE

Hon S. P. Chase

1. On January 7, 1864, detectives had arrested Albert M. Palmer for allegedly helping to secure bonds for shipments of restricted goods that were destined, via Nassau, for the South. Abram Wakeman (1824–89) represented New York in Congress as a Whig, 1855–57, was postmaster of New York, 1862–64, and received an appointment as surveyor of customs for the district of New York in March 1865. Benjamin Field (1816–76), a New York politician from Albion, sat on the Republican state committee. *New York Times,* Jan. 8, 1864; *New York Custom-House,* 22, 137–60; *Appletons',* 2:446–47; *Bio. Dir. U.S. Cong.,* 1992; U.S. Senate, *Journal of Executive Proceedings,* 14:220.

2. James W. White (1807–67) served on New York's superior court and, subsequently, on the state supreme court. Later in the year, New York legislator Daniel Stevens Dickinson contended unsuccessfully for the Union party's vice presidential nomination. Brig. Gen. William Kerley Strong (1805–68), a former wool merchant, had commanded troops at Cairo, Ill., under John C. Frémont until October 1863. *Appletons',* 5:723–4; *DAB,* 5:294–5; Lanman, *Biographical Annals,* 460.

3. Chase's letter to Opdyke, written on December 16, 1863, denied hearing any news about efforts to supplant James Mackin, assessor of internal revenue for New York's twelfth congressional district in Dutchess County. "You may be assured that no removal will take except for cause and at present I know of no cause," wrote Chase. "Should any be alleged, your wish that he should a fair opportunity for defense will not be forgotten." Chase to Opdyke, Dec. 16, 1863 (Letters Sent to Collectors and Assessors of Internal Revenue . . . , Gen. Recs. Treasury Dept., Nat. Arch.); *Register of Officers (1863),* 38.

4. Luther S. Dutcher, a Democratic politician from Dutchess County. *New York Times,* Nov. 8, 1862.

FROM THOMAS J. DURANT

Autograph letter. Chase Papers, Library of Congress (*micro* 31:0020).

Neworleans. 16. January. 1864.

Hon. S. P. Chase.
Washington City D.C.
My Dear Sir,

Your valued favor of the 28th ult reached me on the 9th of this month, and was read with great interest.[1] That the call of a convention was the first and only step to be taken by the loyal people of an insurrectionary state in order to enter the Union had always been so firmly fixed in my mind that I was greatly surprised when General Banks informed me he had determined to order an election of state offices before the assembling of such a convention. The General read to me on the 8th January a letter he had just received from the President under date of Dec. 24.[2] The letter worried me because it had evidently been written by the President when inspired by in correct information about affairs in Louisiana; it contains the word *master* as signification of General Banks powers here repeated four times, which grated harshly upon my ears. The President has virtually urged upon Genl Banks to take the matter of the organization of the Civil Government out of the hands of Gov. Shepley and the civilians associated with him in the work on the ground that it was going on too slowly when in point of fact it had been pushed forward as rapidly as the nature of things would permit and was on the eve of its accomplishment, for a general meeting of the people had been called for that very day, 8th Jany, in order to ratify the action of the free state committee's call upon Govr. Shepley to order an election of members of a constitutional convention, and upon the request of which meeting the Governor was to issue his call, thus giving the whole movement a popular rather than a military aspect.

A few days after this Genl Banks issues a proclamation superceding in effect all that the Union men had done under the sanction of the President as conveyed through the secretary of war in August last and ordering an election of state officers prior to the election of the members of the constitutional convention, which amounts to a recognition of the obligatory character of the slave constitution of 1852, in force at the date of secession.[3] This act of the Generals I consider a great mistake, and told him so but was, of course, unable to convince him. He has endeavoured to do away with the evil of such a recognition of the state constitution by declaring in his proclamation that all the parts of the constitution of Louisiana, and of her laws in regard to slavery are null and void, but such a declaration is an assumption of power similar to that which was rebuked in the case of General Hunter,[4] and is more than the President himself has ever attempted to exercise, and after all its force and effect must be tested by the action of the civil tribunales, if as the President says, his proclamations on the same subject must be.[5] It would have been better for the Major General commanding here to have been kept out of the spheres of civil politics which must necessarily have a bad effect upon him.

Your views as to the elective franchise are full of wisdom.[6] I do not know whether I shall be a member of our constitutional convention, but if placed in that position the lesson you have conveyed will not be lost upon me. The difficulties which beset us here in our efforts to vindicate the principles of universal justice, founded on civil and political equality are very great, and constantly demand all our fortitudes, prudence and patience, but I hope that we shall not have struggled in vain.

With sentiments of the highest esteem I have the honor to be

Your most obdt. servt.
THOMAS J. DURANT.

1. See Chase to Durant, December 28, 1863 (above).

2. Benjamin F. Flanders had already informed Chase about the letter and surrounding circumstances. Flanders to Chase, [Jan. 9], 1864 (above).

3. Banks had issued the proclamation on January 11. *OR,* ser. 3, v. 4:22–23.

4. As commander of the Department of the South, David Hunter had, on April 12 and May 9, 1862, attempted to emancipate all slaves in Georgia, Florida, and South Carolina, only to be overruled by Lincoln on May 19. Basler, *Collected Works,* 5:222; *OR,* ser. 1, v. 14:333, 341.

5. In correspondence with Edward D. Mansfield on January 5, 1864 (above), Chase discussed the possibility of a court decision regarding Lincoln's Proclamation of Amnesty and Reconstruction.

6. Durant referred to Chase's letter of December 28 (above).

FROM RUFUS SAXTON

Autograph letter. Letters Received from Executive Officers (AB Series), General Records, Department of the Treasury (Record Group 56), National Archives (*micro* 31:0148).

Beaufort So: Ca:
Jan 22nd. 1864.

My dear Mr Chase—

I can scarcly express the gratification I experienced a few days since on the reception of your new instructions to the U. S. Direct Tax Commissioners of this District[1] / The measures to be adopted in regard to the disposition of the government lands, seemed to me to be so wise, so humane and fraught with good, that I hastened to announce them to the people under my charge, advising them to lose no time in availing themselves of the beneficent provisions of these instructions. To my great surprise as well as regret, two of the Commissioners have declined to carry them out. Judge Smith, to his honor be it said, gives them his cordial and hearty support. I am at a loss to account for the opposition manifested by the other two Commissioners. It seems to me that one of them, Dr Brisbane, in the course pursued by him, has been false to the record of his whole life.

The delay which is occasioned by this unaccontable conduct of the Commissioners I am afraid will prove exceedingly disastrous to the interests of the people who should now be preparing their lands for the coming harvest in order to prevent them from becoming a tax upon the bounty of the government

I most respectfully ask, if, one of these two Commissioners cannot be displaced and another appointed whose head and heart are more in sympathy with your own enlightened policy[2]—

I am with great respect

Sincerely Yours
R. Saxton
Brig: Genl Vol.

1. The instructions accompanied Chase's letter to the commissioners, December 30, 1863 (above).

2. Others besides Saxton later complained to Chase about William H. Brisbane and William E. Wording, but it was Abram Smith who eventually lost his position as direct tax commissioner, to be replaced by John F. Potter on March 18, 1864. U.S. Senate, *Journal of Executive Proceedings,* 13:447–48; Rose, *Rehearsal,* 289–90.

FROM BENJAMIN F. FLANDERS

Autograph letter on letterhead stationery. Chase Papers, Historical Society of Pennsylvania (*micro* 31:0169).

Private

OFFICE OF SUPERVISING
SPECIAL AGENT OF
TREASURY DEPARTMENT.
New Orleans, Jan. 23d 1864

Dear Sir,

Hahn, is Bank's candidate for Governor, and he is to be put in by the soldiers enlisted here, voting in their camps, controlled by non-voting officers most of whom were I believe appointed by Banks himself

Hahn as Governor will appoint two Senators, probably Roselius and Kennedy, certainly men of their stamp[1]

The General has sent out a private order for the soldiers to be registered.

The qualifications of a voter is left in great uncertainty by the Generals Proclamation and he seems unwilling to clear it up. The Free State men believe that he will purposly leave the matter in doubt until it will be too late for them to correct any mistakes or errors they may have committed in preparing their men to vote.[2] The feeling among the old Union men, against Gen Banks for the course he has taken is gitting to be intense, but it has no public expression. Not a word disrespectful to the General has ever dropt from any speaker at our meetings; nor will he be treated otherwise at least before the election

The union men represented by the Free State Committee are in earnest and thus far firmly united. With half a chance left them they will beat the Copperhead Conservative faction led by the Maj General out of sight. But they are not to have such chance even.

Mr Worthington who will hand you this letter will be able to inform you somewhat of the state of affairs here, and I would respectfully refer you to him for information.

Very respectfully

Your obt Servt
BENJ. F. FLANDERS

Hon S. P Chase
Secretary of the Treasury.

1. Prominent New Orleans attorney and politician Christian Roselius had opposed Louisiana's secession. Both of the state's U.S. Senate seats remained vacant throughout the rest of the war. *Bio. Dir. U.S. Cong.*, 176; *DAB,* 16:165.

2. According to Nathaniel Banks's proclamation of January 11, "The registration of voters, effected under the direction of the Military Governor and the several Union associations, not inconsistent with the proclamation, or other orders of the President, are confirmed and approved." Banks issued detailed eligibility requirements for voters on February 13, in General Orders No. 24. *OR,* ser. 3, v. 4:22–23, 96–98.

TO JOSHUA LEAVITT

Letterpress copy of autograph letter. Chase Papers, Historical Society of Pennsylvania (*micro* 31:0187).

Washington Jany 24, 1864

My dear friend,

Some time ago I received a letter from you about the publication of your article on the Monroe Doctrine in pamphlet.[1] My impression is that I did not reply—my intention to do so being frustrated by demands on my time & attention which pushed it out of my thoughts for the time. Recently my thoughts were recalled to the subject by receiving a copy of the pamphlet, and I now wish to say that if in consequence of my remissness you have been put personally to any expence I want the privilege of reimbursing it to you. I am not a rich man & I am glad to be able to say that I have become poorer instead of richer from public employments; but still I can better afford, I fancy, to pay such a contribution to a public object, than most editors of religious newspapers.

In the main I concur in your views—wholly in their principle and spirit. I believe that the statesmen whose views were represented by Mr. Monroes Message[2]—including Mr. Monroe himself—intended to be understood in the plain sense of the language employed—meant that any attempt to force the European System on America would be dangerous to our safety and that any interference with any American Government by European powers for the purpose of oppressing it or forcibly controlling its destiny would be regarded as an unfriendly manifestation. In this sense the declaration was understood and accepted by the American People and became a cardinal principle of American policy. After all, however, it is not so important to enquire into the history as into the soundness of the principle and the propriety of insisting on its application to recent events in San Domingo & Mexico.[3]

It certainly would have suited my temper and taste much better to do so; and yet I cannot blame Mr. Seward for not having done so. He never renounced it: he only forbore to insist on it; when insisting would probably have been counted as a menace & would have precipitated recognition of the Rebel Confederacy and that recognition would have been followed by war.

Had there been here an administration in the true sense of the word—a President conferring with his cabinet and taking their united judgment & with their aid enforcing activity, economy & energy in all Departments of Public Service—we could have spoken boldly & defied the world. But our condition here has always been very different. I preside over the funnel—every body else & especially the Secretaries of War & the Navy, over the spigots, and keep them well opened too—Mr Seward conducts the foreign relations with very little let or help from any body. There is no unity & no system except so far as it is departmental. There is progress—but it is slow and involuntary—just what is coerced by the irresistible pressure of the vast force of the people. How under such circumstances can any body announce a policy, which can only be made respectable by union, wisdom & courage?

But I have written more than I intended. Have you seen Baptist Noel's book on our American Rebellion. He errs sadly in his account of parties as connected with slavery?[4] Can't you write an article like that on the Monroe Doctrine, giving the true view of political action as influenced [*illeg.*]ly by the Liberty Party & the Independent Democracy, or,—as our Whigish friends preferred to call it,—the free soil party.

Who *could* do that as well as you?

Your friend
S P Chase

Rev. J. Leavitt D.D.

1. Leavitt's letter of January 9 enclosed a copy of the article from an unidentified Brooklyn newspaper, also published separately as *The Monroe Doctrine* (New York, 1863), which urged enforcement of the doctrine as a matter of "utmost consequence to the future of the country." Leavitt to Chase, Jan. 9, 1864 (Chase Papers, L.C.).

2. James Monroe (1758–1831), fifth president of the United States, presented the doctrine that bears his name in his annual message to Congress, December 2, 1823. *Annals of Congress,* 18th Cong., 1st sess., 1823, pt. 1, 22–23; *DAB,* 13:87–93.

3. In March 1861, Spain annexed Santo Domingo, and the islanders revolted soon after. By January 1864, French military forces controlled Mexico as a result of Napoleon III's invasion. Jan Bazant, *A Concise History of Mexico from Hidalgo to Cárdenas, 1805–1940* (London, 1977), 85–86; *New York Times,* Mar. 30, July 11, 1861.

4. In *The Rebellion in America* (London, 1863), British author Baptist Wriothesley Noel argued in support of emancipation and reunion and depicted U.S. antebellum politics as a simple contest between the Republican and Democratic parties.

TO JOHN T. TROWBRIDGE

Letterpress copy of autograph letter. Chase Papers, Mss. qC487, ser. 2, letter 85, Cincinnati Historical Society Library, Cincinnati Museum Center for Natural and Cultural History and Science (*micro* 31:0201).

Washington Jany. 25, 1864.[1]

My dear Sir,

These letters are necessarily written in such haste, in the few moments I can spare each morning before breakfast, that they must needs be unfit for any eye but your own. You may find in them some helps to your work.[2]

My uncle, at the time I went to him, was in the maturity of his intellectual & physical powers.[3] He was a great worker, a thoroughly practical man, always thinking of something to be done, and then doing it with all his might. There was not a particle of flam or cant in his make up. Thoroughly religious he always looked to God. His motto was Jehovah Jireh—God will provide.[4] But his faith in God only animated him to most strenuous personal labors. It was not passive but active. If any thing was to be done he felt that he must do it; and that, if he put forth all his energy, he might safely & cheerfully leave the event to Divine Providence. Usually exceedingly kind & a delightful companion to young and old he was often very harsh & severe: not because he liked to be but because he was determined to have every thing just as he thought it ought to be. He was thoroughly imbued with a sense of the importance of his Episcopal office and a thorough believer in the subordination of the other orders to the Episcopate. Certainly he liked to Govern: but he liked to govern for the good of others, not his own. He liked to overcome too—great obstacles stimulated but did not discourage him. Among us boys he was almost and sometimes, indeed, quite tyrannical; but he was not disliked—much less hated—he was revered & feared. He was not loved by them then—but afterwards when they had left him & looked back on the days they had spent under his charge & saw him more as he really was, love mingled with their reverence and became its equal in their hearts.

About this time my cousin Philander, who had been at sea on the Guerrier with Commodore McDonough, in the capacity of teacher or chaplain, & had returned recently, came to Ohio and under the Bishop as President took charge of the school he had established at Worthington.[5] I was a scholar at this school. Some of the boys were from the town and country around it—but many from distant places & from other states. Charles D. Drake, from Cincinnati, son of the celebrated Dr. Drake & now now a distinguished citizen of St. Louis;[6] Allan McArthur from Chillicothe son of Gen. McArthur of the War of 1812;[7] Tom & Nat James, also of Chillicothe sons of a prominent citizen of that place;[8] Alexander & Bazal[ee]l Wells, sons of a wealthy manufacture at Steubenville[9] Mortimer Talbot son of Isham Talbot of Kentucky, were among these last. I was the only boy from New England and the other boys, whose ideas of a Yankee, derived from their parents & their friends, were, I fear, not altogether just, were much inclined for a time to [taunt] me on being one. Every now and then they called me Yankee in tones not altogether respectful / At length I couldn't bear it any longer & said to Tom James when one day he called me "Yankee", "Tom, if you call me Yankee again I'll kick you." "Well," said he, "You're a Yankee". As good as my word I kicked him and make the kicks just as severe & just as disagreeable as I could. He was older than I & I expected a fight. But instead of attacking me he went [after] the Bishop and complained. I was at once summoned into [the] presence. "Salmon," said the Bishop very gravely & severely "Tom James says you have been kicking him. Is it true." "Yes, Sir." "What did you kick him for?" "Because he called me a Yankee." "Well", said the Bishop, are you not a Yankee. Your father was & I am and we were never ashamed of the name." "Yes, Sir," said I, "I don't mind just being called a Yankee but I wont be called a Yankee *so*"—with a pretty decided emphasis on the last word." The Bishop could not help smiling and dismissed with a reprimand which did not hurt much. I was not called a Yankee, *so,* after that—and had no occasion to kick Tom James again. It was a boy's quarrel. Tom James grew up into incipient manhood and then went to the undiscovered country. Peace & love to his memory.

I went to school as I have said. The school house was a oblong square brick building of two stories on the west side of the town square. I remember little of what happened there. I must have been required to compose; for I remember, on one occasion, that my cousin commended a composition in terms which I thought quite unmerited and which took me entirely by surprise, but which after all made me feel quite proud. I must have been taught some Greek also; for my exercise on an Exhibition occasion probably at the Convention of 1821[10]—was an *original* Greek oration. How I puzzled over it: what trouble I had to turn my English thoughts into Greek form. The Grammar and the Lexicon and the Greek Testament were in great requisition. The subject was Paul & John compared—at any rate Paul was a principal figure; though my memory may be at fault as to John. The subject helped for it allowed me to take sentences from the Testament & so abridge my labor / At length the piece was finished—the platform in the north end of the school room erected—the boys summoned one by one from a little room [over] the east side of it, which served the purpose of Vestry Room, when on Sundays the School room was used for the Church Services—my turn came to front the terrors of an audience—I walked out on the stage—my knees shook—my eyes were dim—but memory served me faithfully & I went through. The Bishop was proud of his Greek orator and I dare say, though I have small remembrance of my own feelings, I thought myself quite a lion.

I was not always industrious. I liked to read stories & would some times have some [interesting] book of narratives[, real] or fictitious, before me when I should have had my lesson book. And once I remember being mean enough to hide my story book & substitute my lesson book as my cousin-preceptor came by & looked inquisitively on my desk. Whether he detected me or not I cannot tell— He made no remark.

So went the days in school. Out of school I did chores—took grain [to mill] & brought back meal or flour—[milked] the cows—[drove] them to & from pasture—took wool to the carding factory over on the Scioto—an important journey to me—built fires and brought in wood in the winter time—helped gather sugar water & make sugar when winter first turned to spring—help plant and sow in the later spring. In short of whatever a boy could do on a farm I did a little.

Temperance Societies had not yet been established and all farmers gave their laborers whiskey especially in the harvest season & even the boys took a little. There was a distillery down the road & it was of my occasional business to fetch whiskey from it and take it to the field for the men. Of course I tasted it, but never contracted any love for it.

Sometimes I was sent to Columbus nine miles south on horseback to make some purchases. I remember yet the firm of Goodale & Buttles—which the boys travestied into good ale in bottles of which the senior partner still survives in honored age[11]—where, one morning, I bought some sickles or scythes & other matters, having risin long before day; mounted old [Sorrel]; & ridden to Columbus determined to be back before breakfast which I [accomplished].

One ludicrous incident of the chore kind impressed itself strongly on my memory. The Bishop [& most] of the older Members of the family went away one morning—he having ordered me to kill & dress a pig which [they were] going to serve for dinner that [day or] next. I had no great trouble in catching & slaughtering a fat young porker. And I had the tub of hot water all ready for plunging him in preparatory to taking off his bristles. Unfortunately however the water was too hot or otherwise in wrong condition; or perhaps, When I [soused] the pig into it I kept him in too long. At any rate when I undertook to take off the bristles [expecting] they would almost come off [of themselves], to my dismay I could not start one of them. The bristles were *set* in pigkilling [prhase]. I pulled & pulled in vain. What should I do[? The] pig must be dressed. In that there must be no failure. I bethought me of my cousins razors—a nice new pair, just suited to a spruce young clergyman as he was. No sooner imagined than done. I got the razors & shaved the pig from toe to snout.

Yours truly
S P Chase

1. In 1866 Chase asked a secretary to copy his letters to Trowbridge, and a fair copy of this letter in Chase's papers at the Historical Society of Pennsylvania may date from that time. The editors referred to the clerk's copy for aid in reading some words in the letterpress version. In the transcription given here, any text that could not be clearly read from the letterpress pages is enclosed in square brackets even if the clerk's copy provides a plausible reading. *Chase Papers,* 1:611.

2. This letter was one of the series of autobiographical accounts Chase wrote to Trowbridge, who used them to prepare *The Ferry-Boy and the Financier* (Boston, 1864), an embellished biography of Chase written for juvenile readers. *Chase Papers,* 1:xii, xxxviii, 611.

3. In recent letters to Trowbridge, Chase had recounted his early schooling in New England and his journey in 1820 as a youth, following his father's death, to Worthington, Ohio, where he joined the household of his uncle Philander Chase, the Protestant Episcopal bishop of Ohio. Chase to Trowbridge, Jan. 21, 23, 1864 (Chase Papers, Hist. Soc. of Pa.).

4. Gen. 22:14.

5. Philander Chase, Jr. (c. 1797–1824), Harvard class of 1818, served under Capt. Thomas Macdonough (1783–1825), who commanded the frigate USS *Guerriere* between 1818 and 1820. Philander Chase, *Bishop Chase's Reminiscences: An Autobiography,* 2d ed., 2 vols. (Boston, 1848), 1:161–70, 332; *DAB,* 12:19–21; George Foster Emmons, *The Navy of the United States* . . . (Washington, D.C., 1853), 12–13; *Quinquennial Catalogue of the Officers and Graduates of Harvard University, 1636–1915* (Cambridge, Mass., 1915), 175.

6. Daniel Drake was early Cincinnati's most famous physician. His son Charles Daniel Drake became a prominent Missouri attorney and politician. *DAB,* 5:425–27.

7. During the War of 1812, Ohio politician and land magnate Duncan McArthur (1772–1839) held the posts of major general of Ohio militia and, later, brigadier general in the U.S. Army. From 1822 to 1824 he represented Ohio in Congress and was elected governor of the state in 1830. *DAB,* 11:549–50.

8. Thomas James (1776–1856), evidently the father of Tom and Nat, had gained notoriety as a local manufacturer of iron. *History of Ross and Highland Counties, Ohio, with Illustrations and Biographical Sketches* (Cleveland, 1880), 210.

9. Alexander and Bazaleel were sons of Sarah Griffith Wells (c. 1789–1839) and Bazaleel Wells (1769–1846), the founder of Steubenville and a producer of woolen goods. Rebecca R. Wells, a sister of Alexander and Bazaleel, Jr., married Philander Chase, Jr. John Alexander Caldwell, *History of Belmont and Jefferson Counties, Ohio* . . . (Wheeling, W.Va., 1880), 477–78.

10. The fourth annual convention of the Protestant Episcopal Church in Ohio, June 6–7, 1821. *Journals of the Annual Conventions of The Protestant Episcopal Church, in the Diocese of Ohio* . . . (Columbus, 1853), 46–64.

11. L. Goodale and A. Buttles were commercial merchants. *Col. Dir. (1845–46),* 20, 36.

FROM RICHARD FULLER

Autograph letter. Chase Papers, Library of Congress (*micro* 31:0223).

Private & Confidential

Baltimore Jany 25. /64[1]

Hon Salmon P Chase—
My dear Sir,

You said to me, the other day, 'I wish to read on that subject but have no time to hear". Will you honor these lines with your prayerful, kind atention? I know you are a devoted lover of your whole country & have no malice against the South; & I can appeal to My Maker that I am ready to lay down my life for the good of that country— I enclose an editorial from one of our papers, requesting you to let me have it again

I know, too, that, without fanaticism, you religiously desire to promote the true interest of the Africans—unhappily, in an evil hour, introduced into this country, & whose presence & bondage is the fatal source of these sad calamities. And my record is on high as to this most difficult of problems. I abandoned, when young a lucrative practice at the Bar, & for 14 years—with no compensation, devoted myself laboriously to a ministry chiefly among & for the slaves. I know & love them; & such are their feelings to me, that my council to them at Port Royal would, at any moment, supersede all the authority of the the military rulers there.

Knowing all this, well aware of your high character for equity & humanity, believing you to be a true Christian, & having experienced your friendship—for which I can only pray that God will reward you—I venture to submit to you &[2] the subjoined suggestions—offered reluctantly—extorted from my diffidence, but which you will assuredly find to be founded in truth.

1st. Pardon me for reminding you that a large portion of the real estates about to be sold at Port Royal belongs to women & children—widows & orphans. The[ir] lands are advertised in an obscure newspaper, & these persons can, of course, know nothing of the proceedgs. Or, if apprised by some accident, how can they possibly pay the tax? They are excluded from the lines; & cannot act for themselves. I am aware that this is done by Act of Congress;[3] but no one can be acquainted with you at all without feeling that you are endowed by God with those rare powers which govern men; & I know that the leaders of Congress would at once defer to your views upon this subject.

2d— Whatever may be the economy projected by the Government the determined policy of those in military power at Port Royal is, to discountenance, & as far as possible prevent Citizens from gaining possession of the lands, and to let the negroes have them. Macchiavelli has truly said that, "next to making freemen slaves, the most difficult thing is to make slaves free";[4] & rest assured that this idea of investing these ignorant, improvident, indolent people with landed estates, & expecting them to improve or cultivate them, is a most Utopian & fanatical delusion. I speak from perfect knowledge. Those who are urging forward this system are men who have grown up with an abstract & absorbing horror of slavery, but who know nothing practically of the matter. With some of them, I fear there is in reality far more hatred of the masters, whom they have been educated to abhor as oppressors, than love for the slave. I have long sought to educate the Africans who came to me by inheritance & marriage; & have believed that, by kindness, & Christian influence, & with a plan of enlistment & discipline similar somewhat to those of the army, the Negroes might be gradually converted into useful, industrious tillers of the soil for wages. Without some such control & regulation, left to regard himself as master of land & to work or not, be assured, my dear Sir, the soil will not be cultivated, the negro will degenerate into a vagrant idler, & the Govermt will have to support him & his family as paupers.

3d. I preached among these people & left them—lamenting that I could do so little; but I left them as virtuous & decent a population as one might hope to find poor fallen human beings to be under such sad disadvantages. More than one officer of the army have called & given me heart rending accounts of the licentiousness now universal among them. I have wept & weep constantly over this. Hired by upright, benevolent citizens who would be their guardians, a paternal supervision would watch over their welfare & interests; but war, especially civil war, is an infernal fire which brings the very dregs of society to the surface. Every day, among those enjoying the confidence & emoluments of the government, we are shocked at the discovery of frauds which, in the most profligate manner, violate all honor, honesty & decency. What must be going on in the remote districts, far from the scrutiny of the Administration, and among a people ignorant, simple, confiding & of easy virtue & readily duped by the selfish and rapacious? To be debauched & defrauded will be their inevitable destiny.

For years have I foreseen this state of things, & in my poor way, I have pleaded with the North & with the South; but have been misunderstood & misrepresented by both. Some of my friends here sold, & advised me to sell; & I could easily have sold these people for $130,000; but welcome any penury rather than sell a human being. Twice, within 20 years, have I made overtures to a number of rich men [at the North] professing to hate slavery, that I would relinquish ½ their value, if they wd subscribe the other half, & join me in some experiment to educate & elevate these people as freedmen; but not a single response could I procure.

Now, their doom is a matter of unceasing prayer & most unutterable solicitude. Let this & my great esteem for you, & your words above quoted be my apology for writing you at such length. I would rather walk miles to converse, than write; but steps are about to be taken which cannot be retraced, & I can only, by this unsatisfactory vehicle, convey a few thoughts of the many which oppress & depress my very soul.

May God in mercy guide & direct & overrule all these things for his glory & the advancement of the Redeemers Kingdom, & the peace & prosperity of the country!

Very sincerely & gratefully
RD FULLER

I beg you will not trouble yourself with any answer to this letter.[5] I have more than once been mortified that I Cd not obtain any the most trivial or manifest [justice], without giving much annoyance to one so absorbed with the public cares—

R. F.

1. Fuller, a Baptist clergyman and native of Beaufort, S.C., presided over Baltimore's Seventh Baptist Church, 1847–71. *DAB*, 7:62.

2. Fuller originally wrote, *to you & to the President,* then neglected to strike through the & when he canceled the phrase *to the President.*

3. In accordance with the second confiscation act, July 17, 1862. *Statutes at Large,* 12:589–92.

4. *Discourses,* Book III, 8:7. Fuller quoted from the same passage during a personal visit with Chase on March 13, 1862. *Chase Papers,* 1:331.

5. "The atrocious rebellion against the National Government has brought great calamities upon the country, and those to which you refer are a part of them," responded Chase on February 4. "It is the part of Christians and patriots to alleviate them as far as practicable. But what can human power do when earthquakes shake the world?" Chase to Fuller, Feb. 4, 1864 (Chase Papers, Hist. Soc. of Pa.).

FROM GEORGE S. DENISON

Autograph letter on letterhead stationery. Chase Papers, Library of Congress (*micro* 31:0326).

Private

United States Custom House,
COLLECTOR'S OFFICE.
New Orleans, January 29th, 1863.[1]

Dear Sir—

I arrived here last Monday morning, having been absent only twenty one days. Gen. Banks had already commenced the execution of the plan I submitted to you, for the reorganization of the State Gov't. His action was in conformity with the letters of the President received here shortly after my departure, & the General's proclamation, issued on the 11th. inst, is enclosed herewith.[2]

The proclamation at first gave considerable dissatisfaction to the Union men, because they had learned to regard the other project as something originated by themselves & it had become their pet plan. This dissatisfaction has nearly or quite disappeared, and nearly all the Union men are working in hearty coöperation. Some few, however, are, even now, thoroughly dissatisfied, among whom, I regret to say, is Mr. Flanders, who, very unwisely, I think, does not hesitate to express his disapprobation. You know his opinion of General Banks, which recently has become much more unfriendly and embittered, but he does not seem to realize how much more important is the success of great principles than the gratification of personal feeling. About this matter I have talked with him earnestly but without effect. The necessary result is, that without assisting or materially affecting Gen. Banks or his policy, he weakens himself. Probably many persons would prefer another Commander than Gen. Banks, but is seems to me wise not to express unavailing regrets but make the best of circumstances as they exist. Gen. Banks friends have to share in the resentment of Mr. Flanders, who has become rather hostile to Mr. Plumly, for no other reason, as I really think, than the fact that he is the earnest & intimate friend of Gen. Banks. With me he is friendly, of course, & I shall do all I can to promote harmony.

The names of Judge Whitaker, Judge Howell,[3] Mr. Hahn, and Mr. Waples (U.S. Dist. Attorney) have been prominently mentioned for Governor, but Hahn & Waples are decidedly the favorites, & Hahn is clear ahead of Waples. Hahn is supported by Gen. Banks, and will probably receive the nomination in the nominating Convention made up from the Union Associations. I regard his election, as almost certain, whether he receives such nomination or not. One of the Senators to be appointed by the Governor will be Mr. Durant, & the other will probably be Mr. Rozier, both men of ability & of radical politics.[4] Tomorrow or on Sunday morning, will appear an appendix to the General's proclamations, giving full information as to the qualifications necessary to voters & all other necessary information. On or about the 1st of April, an election will be held for representatives to Congress, & at the same time the election for Delegates to the Constitutional State Convention.[5] The General thinks proper preparation cannot be made sooner. The whole business goes on prosperously & with certainty of success.

There have been no military movements of consequence. The army in Texas & here, is stationary—except that a respectable force has established itself across the Lake[6] in the direction of Mobile. I should judge, however, that great movements are in preparation, & that Mobile will be heavily attacked before long. Probably, also, an expedition will soon come down from above & go up Red River.[7]

From one of the newspaper slips enclosed herewith, you will see that Mr. Whitaker, Collector of Internal Revenue, & Mr. Collins one of the D'y Collectors of Customs,[8] are doing what they can in relation to the election. From another slip you will see that the planters are to be compelled to work their plantations, or the Gov't will do it for them.

The 1st National Bank opened ten days ago, & is already a success. It is of consequence we should have our bills for circulation with as little delay as possible.

Mr. May has also commenced the business of his office.[9] Gov. Hamilton is still here, but returns to Texas in two days.

There has been a great change for the better in this community in regard to Social relations, which are of more consequence here than in the North. Secessionists begin to find that the Society of Yankees is not so disagreeable as they pretended to believe. Parties, Receptions, & promenade Concerts, have quite thawed their reserve & warmed them into social life again. This has a political bearing, at this time, & Gen. Banks has assisted much in producing this result.

Very Respectfully

Your Ob't Serv't
George S. Denison

To
Hon. Salmon P. Chase
Secretary of the Treasury

1. Denison's error; the year was 1864.

2. Denison, assuming a new role as Banks's ally, had traveled to Washington, D.C., evidently giving both Chase and Lincoln copies of a plan for rapid reorganization of Louisiana's government that responded to the president's instructions of December 24, 1863, and accorded with Banks's proclamation of January 11, 1864. Banks to Lincoln, Dec. 30, 1863, in Basler, *Collected Works,* 7:124–25; Benjamin F. Flanders to Chase, [Jan. 9], 1864 (above); Thomas J. Durant to Chase, Jan. 16, 1864 (above); McCrary, *Lincoln and Reconstruction,* 203–4.

3. Later in the year, J. S. Whitaker, a New Orleans attorney and former municipal judge, received an appointment as chief justice of the Louisiana supreme court, but the state senate rejected the nomination. Rufus K. Howell had presided over the sixth district court since before the war. Edwin L. Jewell, *Jewell's Crescent City Illustrated* (New Orleans, 1873); John Smith Kendall, *History of New Orleans,* 3 vols. (Chicago, 1922), 1:293.

4. New Orleans attorney J. Ad. Rozier was a prominent Unionist and Democrat. Neither Thomas J. Durant nor Rozier ever served in the U.S. Senate. *Nat. Cyc.,* 10:380–1.

5. Banks issued specifics on voter qualifications in General Orders No. 24, February 13, 1864. The election took place on March 28. *Appletons' Annual Cyclopædia,* 4:478–79; *OR,* ser. 3, v. 4:96–98.

6. Apparently Lake Pontchartrain.

7. The Red River campaign represented a major effort by Union forces to strike into the Confederate Southwest. On March 12, Banks and his troops ventured into Louisiana from New Orleans, while another Federal contingent destined for Arkansas headed down the Mississippi River from Vicksburg. The expedition ended in retreat on May 19 after a series of military disasters. Ludwell H. Johnson, *Red River Campaign: Politics and Cotton in the Civil War* (Baltimore, 1958; reprint, Kent, Ohio, 1993); Long, *Civil War Day by Day,* 474, 505.

8. Possibly John C. Collins, identified in other sources as a Treasury agent. McCrary, *Lincoln and Reconstruction,* 228.

9. Chase had appointed Thomas P. May, editor of the *New Orleans Times,* assistant treasurer of the U.S. at New Orleans. May to Chase, July 26, 1864 (Chase Papers, L.C.); Henry Rightor, ed., *Standard History of New Orleans . . .* (Chicago, 1900), 276.

TO JOSEPH MEDILL

Letterpress copy of letter in clerk's hand, signed by Chase. Chase Papers, Historical Society of Pennsylvania (*micro* 31:0354).

January 30,   4.

My dear Sir,[1]

Your note is just received.[2] *I* did not "shut down" on the Five-Twenties loan, but the *law* which limited it to five hundred millions did; and I thought it unwise to ask for authority to extend it, because great numbers had subscribed, expecting that it would command a premium when all taken. All these would be disappointed by the extension of the loan and the injury resulting from their disappointment would not have been countervailed, in my judgment, by the benefits of additional subscriptions.

I have recommended the tax you favor. The question is before Congress and I presume that in due time it will be acted on. I hope the day will come when it will be considered as criminal to issue paper currency without the authority and stamp of the National Government as it is now to issue coin currency. I expressed the opinion in the Report, and still hold it, that to what you justly call the "heterogeneous" currency is due, more than to any other cause, fluctuations in prices.[3]

Very truly Yours,
S P Chase

Joseph Medill, Esq., Tribune,
Chicago, Ill.

1. Medill, part owner of the *Chicago Tribune* since the mid-1850s, played an influential role in Republican politics. *DAB,* 12:491.

2. Medill's letter of January 25 criticized Chase for not issuing more 5–20 bonds and suggested a Federal tax on state bank notes ("heterogeneous currency") to inhibit their circulation and diminish inflation. Medill to Chase, Jan. 25, 1864 (Chase Papers, Hist. Soc. of Pa.).

3. Chase had expressed similar concerns in his most recent annual report to Congress. He was dissatisfied with provisions of the ways and means act of March 3, 1863, that levied a semiannual duty of one percent on state bank notes and exempted portions of the circulation of large banks. Notes issued by state-chartered banks finally passed out of circulation after legislation of March 3, 1865, raised the tax to ten percent and the internal revenue act of June 30, 1864, authorized incentives for their retirement. Chase to John Sherman, May 26, 1864 (below); Hammond, *Sovereignty,* 346–47; *Report of the Secretary of the Treasury . . . 1863,* 19; *Statutes at Large,* 12:709–13, 13:278, 484; *Chase Papers,* 3:371–72, 374.

FROM QUINCY ADAMS GILLMORE

Letter in clerk's hand, signed by Gillmore. Chase Papers, Historical Society of Pennsylvania (*micro* 31:0383).

Head Quarters, Dept. of the South
Port Royal, S.C. Jan 31. 1864.

My dear Sir,

I wrote you on the 23d inst., suggesting Dudley Baldwin Esqr., as a suitable person to be appointed on the board of direct tax commissioners for this State, in case it was decided to make any change in the personel of the board.

I made the remark in that communication that there exists a want of harmony in the Commission. I have examined into the matter very carefully within the last few days and am convinced that I was in error in making that statement, and I take the first opportunity to recall it.

I am also convinced that a majority of the Commission, comprising all its reliable working strength, are in perfect accord in the discharge of their duties.

I have considered it my duty to examine into the scope and character of the new instructions recently issued by the President to the tax commissioners for this state. I am free to express my conviction that the colored man will be the sufferer, if those instructions are enforced, by being thrown into direct competition with white men and speculators, where before he was protected by a carefully prepared law and the liberal and humane instructions issued under it.

I am greatly surprised to learn that I have been represented in Washington as being in favor of the radical changes in the manner of carrying out the law which the new instructions to the commissioners contemplate.[1]

Such is not the case. The only recommendation I have ever made upon the subject is contained in a letter addressed to the General-in-Chief, dated Dec. 14. 1863, and is wholly comprised in the following sentence, viz:—

"The families of *colored soldiers* should be provided for, by allowing them to locate upon and cultivate lands, in advance of the regular survey and sale thereof."[2]

I think the new instructions will defeat the evident intention of the law. Already, difficulties and personal encounters have taken place on some of the plantations among the colored people and between these and the whites, in an attempt to inaugurate operations under the new instructions, through the auspices and advice of other than the tax-commissioners, the legally constituted agents of the Government in this matter.

I recommend that the new instructions be revoked entirely and the old order of things restored: or, if deemed preferable, that the tax-commissioners be called upon for their opinions upon the subject before further action is taken to carry the new instructions into effect.

I see nothing but delay, confusion, discontent and injury to the colored man in any other course.

Very Resp'fully

Your obt. ser't.
Q. A. Gillmore

To,
Hon, S. P. Chase,
Sec. of Treasury
Washington, D.C.

1. Chase had included the instructions with the letter he sent to the direct tax commissioners for South Carolina on December 30, 1863 (above).

2. Gillmore's letter to Henry W. Halleck urged "upon the attention of the Government certain simple measures for bettering the condition of the colored people of this department, colored soldiers in particular." *OR*, ser. 1, v. 28, pt. 2:127.

TO FLAMEN BALL

Letterpress copy of letter in clerk's hand, signed by Chase. Historical Society of Pennsylvania (*micro* 31:0417).

Private

February 2nd, 4.

My dear Mr. Ball,[1]

Yours of the 25th is just received.[2]

I hope you will find somebody to make search for the copies soon. Your suggestion that the search should be extended into the files of the "Philanthropist" is excellent— You have so much to do that I am afraid Trowbridge will get through with his biography before he will hear from you.

You ask for the signs of the times. At present they *seem* to indicate the renomination of Mr. Lincoln. His personal popularity is great and deserved. If to his kindliness of spirit and good sense he joined strong will and energetic action, there would be little left to wish for in him. As it is, I think that he will be likely to close his first term with more honor than he will the second, should he be reelected.

I cannot help being gratified by the preference expressed for me in some quarters: for those who express it are generally men of great weight and high character and independent judgment. I have some reason to think, too, that it is felt to a considerable extent by the masses of the people.— Sometime since, a number of Senators, Representatives and citizens, organized a Committee here with the purpose of bringing forward my name.[3] They think there will be a change in the current which so far as it is not spontaneous is chiefly managed by the Blairs.[4]

Whether they are right in this judgment or not time will tell. Of course, if my name is to be brought forward at all, I shall be glad to have Ohio decidedly on my side. Indeed, if Ohio should express a preference for any other person, I would not allow my name to be used.

I shall be entirely content to retire, as soon as the condition of the finances will permit, to a private station, and hope their condition will permit it before the lapse of many months.

I do not know what prompts the articles in the Gazette. As soon as I saw the first one I directed an examination to be made into the law, and found that it sanctioned the Courts' allowances to Mr. Carson. I think the law, however, is wrong, and shall endeavor to get it amended as soon as practicable.[5]

I am very desirous of getting the incumbrances on the Clifton property released, so as to relieve my bonds. Mrs. Simmons' dower is the principal thing in the way, and your letter encourages me to expect its early removal.[6]

As to the alley onto the privy-vault, you will find on examining the deeds that the right to the vault is in common with the Main street-lot, which extends back to the alley along the rear of my Third Street property. No one else has any right to turn anything into it.— Nor have the owners of the adjoining lot any right to use it for any other purpose, except those for which the vault was made. If nothing better can be done, let the barber-shop on the alley be removed, and the alley opened. It would be much better and cheaper than to allow my Third Street property to be seriously injured by the accumulation of filth beside the shop. Indeed, those who place the filth there must certainly be liable for the injuries to the property, and if the proper representation is made to Mr. Shoenberger, I have no doubt it will be removed.[7]

I should like to sell this property, and all other real estate I have in Cincinnati. Please see what prices can be obtained, and let me know.[8] My time is not likely to be so free that I can devote any portion of it to the care of such property.

Mr. and Mrs. Sprague are in Providence, and Miss Whipple will leave us this week.

Give my very best regards to Mrs. Ball, and the young ladies,[9] and believe me,

Very Cordially Yours,
S P CHASE

Flamen Ball, Esquire,
Cincinnati, Ohio.

1. Ball had served as U.S. attorney for the southern district of Ohio since 1861, three years after he and Chase dissolved their Cincinnati law partnership. *Biographical Cyclopædia,* 3:759.

2. On January 17, Chase had asked Ball to have copies made of an article and letter from the *Cincinnati Gazette* regarding Chase's opposition to Cincinnati's anti-abolitionist riots of 1836. Ball's response, on January 25, agreed to have the task done and suggested a search as well through early issues of the *Philanthropist,* an antislavery periodical from Cincinnati. In addition, Ball solicited Chase's views on the presidential race, reported an impending arrangement to secure a deed from "Mr. and Mrs. Simmons," and told about earthwork related to recent repairs on Cincinnati's Henrie House that caused a privy vault owned by Chase to overflow. Ball to Chase, Jan. 25, 1864 (Chase Papers, L.C.); Chase to Ball, Jan. 17, 1864 (Chase Papers, Hist. Soc. of Pa.).

3. Chase referred to efforts of a group headed by Samuel C. Pomeroy, discussed in Chase to Lincoln, February 22, 1864 (below).

4. Chase suspected all three Blairs: journalist and politician Francis Preston Blair, Sr., and his sons, Francis Preston Blair, Jr., and Montgomery Blair. Chase to Alfred P. Stone, May 23, 1864 (below).

5. At the end of December, the *Cincinnati Daily Gazette* published a series of articles that criticized commercial legislation of July 13, 1861, and May 20, 1862, for allowing Treasury agents such as Enoch T. Carson, surveyor of customs at Cincinnati, to seize cotton owned by suspected Confederates and then collect rewards based on its value. "There should, in a word, be absolute free trade, or absolute prohibition," urged the *Gazette.* "There is no middle ground that will not foster corruption." *Cincinnati Daily*

Gazette, Dec. 25, 31, 1863, Jan. 8, 1864; *Cinc. Dir. (1864),* 79; Greve, *Centennial History,* 2:614; *Statutes at Large,* 12:255–58, 404–5.

6. The "Clifton Farm," a parcel previously owned by Cincinnati founder Israel Ludlow, was located several miles north of the city. Chase's younger daughter, Janet, had inherited an interest in the property through her mother, Sarah Bella Dunlop Ludlow Chase. Chase and Ball had previously corresponded about Simmons and one "Mrs. Thorpe," who also possessed dower rights. It is unclear whether the two women were related, or possibly even the same person with different married names. C. S. Clarkson to Chase, Oct. 23, 1842, July 7, 1848, Ball to Chase, Jan. 25, 1864, Josephine Ludlow quit claim deed, May 13, 1867 (Chase Papers, L.C.); Chase to Ball, Oct. 20, 1863 (Chase Papers, Hist. Soc. of Pa.); *Titus' Atlas of Hamilton County, Ohio. . . .* (Philadelphia, 1869), 7.

7. Ball accused "Schoenberger," possibly Martin Schoenburger, a laborer, of blocking an alley with dirt, thus redirecting water under a barber shop, through Chase's privy vault, and into his cellar. In the 1830s, Chase had acquired commercial and residential property on the north side of Third Street between Main and Sycamore, and a brick store and lot that fronted onto Main and extended back behind the Third Street property. Conveyances from Francis Carr estate, Apr. 26, 1836, May 15, 1838, Ball to Chase, Jan. 25, 1864 (Chase Papers, L.C.); *Cinc. Dir. (1864),* 325.

8. On March 15, Ball reported selling, for $8,000, Chase's store on Main Street. Ball to Chase, Mar. 15, 1864 (Chase Papers, L.C.).

9. Ball and his wife Evelina Chandler Ball had at least four daughters: Eva, Helen, Laura, and Susan. *Chase Papers,* 1:581

FROM ALFRED P. STONE

Autograph letter on letterhead stationery. Chase Papers, Library of Congress (*micro* 31:0485).

Office of the Collector of Internal Revenue,[1]
SEVENTH DISTRICT OF OHIO,
Columbus, O, Feb 4 1864.

Hon S P Chase
Dr Sir.

Ther was a movement made by a number of the members of the Legislature last week to pass, a resolution nominating Mr Lincoln for reelection. I at once busied myself to prevent it, and think, I succeeded. The members meet in caucus to night, but I I am confident no action will be taken in the matter.[2] I think a majority of the members, think that Lincolns renomination is inevitable, and are inclined to go with the current rather than try to stem it. They nearly all say, "if we could only elect Chase, he would make the best President that ever filled the chair, but Old Abe is popular with the Masses and we shall probably have to take him" The current is undoubtedly runing in that direction at present. Your friends are active and will leave no "stone unturned" that will advance your interest.

Parsons and Centre are here and busy with members.[3] I had a long talk with Brough a few days since. He is non-commital, but will oppose action by the Legislature.[4]

Will write you again tomorrow[5]

Truly Yours
A P Stone

1. A former congressman, Alfred Parish Stone served as treasurer of Ohio from 1857 to 1862, when Chase appointed him collector of internal revenue at Columbus. *Bio. Dir. U.S. Cong.*, 1881.

2. The meeting that Stone expected did not take place, but Union party members in Ohio's General Assembly unanimously nominated Lincoln for reelection on February 26. *Cincinnati Daily Commercial*, Feb. 29, 1864; Stone to Chase, Feb. 5, 1864 (Chase Papers, L.C.).

3. Richard C. Parsons and George B. Senter.

4. Ohio voters had elected Union Republican candidate John Brough governor of their state in October. *Biographical Cyclopædia*, 1:298.

5. Stone's letter of February 5 announced the cancellation of the caucus he had expected and assured Chase that he had convinced the speaker of the Ohio House not to raise the issue again. "This will be the last of the matter," wrote Stone. "Your prospects are looking better than they did two weeks since." Stone to Chase, Feb. 5, 1864 (Chase Papers, L.C.).

FROM JOHN T. TROWBRIDGE

Autograph letter. Chase Papers, Historical Society of Pennsylvania (*micro* 31:0454).

Somerville
Feb. 5, 1864

My Dear Sir

An article *extremely personal on yourself* will appear in the next "Atlantic." The idea did not occur to me until a couple of days ago; then I learned that the March No. was already made up & nearly stereotyped; but when I told Mr. Fields my plan, he decided at once to add an extra half-form to the number, for the sake of printing the article.[1] This involves an extra expense to him of some $300: so you see in what estimation you are held in this vicinity. It is a chapter from the book,[2] dressed up so as to stand alone. The position of the Atlantic, & its immense circulation—over 40,000 copies—will bring the subject before the public in a manner which I trust will prove gratifying to your friends. We have decided that the article will create more of a sensation, if its authorship is kept secret for a while. You will please take notice. The book will probably be announced "by the author of" the said article, which will recommend it to a large class which it might not otherwise reach. I have also private reasons for keeping my name in the background; for it has been trumpeted before the public so much lately—in connection with the "Drum[mer]-Boy," articles in the "Atlantic," poems, "Cudjo," &c.,—that I fear the public may sicken of it.[3]

I have continued to receive communications from you, from time to time; for which please accept my sincere thanks. Allow me also to suggest that the publishers of the book are in great haste to get it out, & that a portion of it is already in type.

One of the publishers—Mr. Walker—is going to Washington soon; & as he has requested me to give him a note of introduction to you, I have done so.[4] He wishes to consult you about the title, &, as I guess, some other matters. The title is a great thing with the booksellers, &

they want something *taking*, if it is not so appropriate. Whatever suits them, & is not objectionable to you, I shall readily consent to. They are anticipating a great sale.

Not having heard from Whitman, I do not know whether anything has been done for him or not. If not, permit me to remind you of his case. He gives his time to the hospitals without compensation, & all he desires is something to occupy his forenoons & pay his private expenses. He would be glad of something to do, if it is only copying.[5]

With sentiments of the highest regard, I remain, dear sir,

Sincerely yours,
J. T. TROWBRIDGE

Hon S. P. Chase.

1. "The First Visit to Washington" recounted the story of Chase's arrival in the nation's capital in the 1820s. James Thomas Fields, a partner in the publishing firm of Ticknor and Fields, edited the *Atlantic Monthly. Atlantic Monthly* 13 (Apr. 1864): 448–57; *DAB,* 6:378.

2. That is, *The Ferry-Boy and the Financier.*

3. Recent books written by Trowbridge included *The Drummer Boy. A Story of Burnside's Expedition* (Boston, 1863) and *Cudjo's Cave* (Boston, 1863). Among his poems published recently in the *Atlantic Monthly* were "By the River," 12 (July 1863): 70–72; "The Pewee," 12 (Oct. 1863): 451–53; and "My Brother and I," 13 (Feb. 1864): 156–57.

4. James Perkins Walker (1829–68), senior partner in the Boston publishing firm of Walker, Wise, and Company, had agreed to issue *The Ferry-Boy and the Financier.* "If you regard me as your assassin," Trowbridge wrote to Chase introducing Walker, "then you must look upon him as your undertaker." Trowbridge to Chase, Feb. 3, 1864 (Chase Papers, Hist. Soc. of Pa.); *Appletons',* 6:327; Daniel W. Wise to Chase, Apr. 27, 1864 (Chase Papers, L.C.).

5. For the past year, Walt Whitman (1819–92), the noted American poet, had nursed wounded soldiers around Washington, D.C. In January 1863, he had asked Ralph Waldo Emerson to pen a letter of recommendation to Chase. Trowbridge, who had befriended the poet, took up Whitman's cause with Chase in December and presented Emerson's letter. Years later Trowbridge recounted that Chase expressed concern over Whitman's reputation as author of *Leaves of Grass* and was reluctant to offer him a clerkship. According to Whitman's record of what Trowbridge told him, Chase "considered Leaves of Grass a very bad book." Whitman later obtained a clerkship in the Department of the Interior. *DAB,* 10:143–52; Walt Whitman, *The Correspondence, Volume 1: 1842–1867,* ed. Edwin Haviland Miller (New York, 1961), 61, 64–66, 74, 83, 190–91; John Townshend Trowbridge, *My Own Story: With Recollections of Noted Persons* (Boston, 1903), 386–90; Thomas Donaldson, *Walt Whitman: the Man* (New York, 1896), 156; Emerson to Chase, Jan. 10, 1863 (Personnel Folders of Notable Treasury Employees, Records of Division of Appointments, Gen. Recs. Treasury Dept., Nat. Arch.).

TO JAMES PULLAN

Letter in clerk's hand on letterhead stationery, signed by Chase.
Chase Papers, Library of Congress (*micro* 31:0526).

Treasury Department.
February 6th, 1864.

Dear Sir,[1]

Your note of the first February is received.

I am gratified by the approval of my action in relation to trade by the merchants of Cincinnati. I trust they know me well enough to believe that no restriction upon trade would ever be imposed by me, except upon the strongest reasons of public policy. The less interference there is with perfect freedom of commerce, the better I am suited. It is a mistake to suppose that any *restrictions* ever have been *imposed* by me. The *Act* of Congress of July 17, 1861, *prohibited all* intercourse between loyal and rebel States.[2] The President alone could modify or suspend this prohibition. It was modified and suspended by allowing such trade as could be conducted under Regulations made by me and approved by him. It has been equally his desire and mine to extend the privilege until all restriction might ultimately be safely removed without prejudice to the great object of suppresing the rebellion.

There is great force in what you say in relation to vexations and mischiefs which must necessarily arise from the employment of Local Special Agents. The best intentions and endeavors do not always secure the best men for the duties they have to perform; and imperfections of execution must necessarily attend the carrying out of any great system, especially under new and trying circumstances. Among these imperfections, those arising from the employment of men who turn out to be unfit for their places, is one of the most serious. The sooner we can get rid of Local Special Agents, and indeed of all Agents of every kind, except those which are necessary in times of peace, the better.[3]

Yours very truly,
S P Chase

J. K. Pullen, Esquire,
Cincinnati, Ohio.

1. Cincinnati businessman and banker James Pullan (1805–81) was assessor of internal revenue for the second district of Ohio. *History of Cincinnati and Hamilton County, Ohio: Their Past and Present* . . . (Cincinnati, 1894), 478–79; *Register of Officers (1863)*, 39.

2. The prohibition applied when the president declared a state to be in insurrection. *Statutes at Large*, 12:257.

3. A filing endorsement, apparently added to the letter at the Treasury Department, includes the notation: "Returned. Uncalled for."

TO HENRY W. TRACY

Letterpress copy of letter in clerk's hand, signed by Chase.
Chase Papers, Historical Society of Pennsylvania (*micro* 31:0593).

February 9th, 4.

Dear Sir,[1]

The tone of your note makes me fear that you have taken some offence at the order given to the messenger at my door to admit no one to-day. If such be the case, I regret it.— Members of Congress are always admitted, promptly when possible, but my general [rule] is to devote to their calls each day from ten to twelve, except sometimes on Tuesdays and Fridays, when my time may be required by special duties in reference to the meetings, on those days, with the President. Other gentlemen are admitted during the same hours when consistent with the prior claims of Senators and Representatives, and also from twelve to one after the meeting of the two Houses.—

Without some such rule as this, the transaction of public business would be, as you will readily perceive, absolutely impracticable. Indeed, I find so much of my time now taken up in hearing what is wanted to be done, that, trying very hard to find time to do it, I often fail in the endeavor.

I shall be happy to see yourself and Mr. Grier to-morrow morning between ten and twelve. Or, if Mr. Grier will send me a note of his business to-day, I will put it in the way of being attended to immediately.[2]

Very truly yours,
S P Chase

Hon. H. W. Tracey,
H.R.

1. Henry Wells Tracy (1807–86) represented Pennsylvania in Congress as an Independent Republican, 1863–65. *Bio. Dir. U.S. Cong.*, 1951.

2. On February 8, Robert Cooper Grier of Pennsylvania, associate justice of the U.S. Supreme Court, wrote Chase a letter of introduction for Grier's nephew, Alexander M. Grier. "You may rely with confidence on any statement he may make concerning any matter of business he may have to transact with you," the elder Grier assured Chase. Grier did not specify the nature of his nephew's enterprise. Robert C. Grier to Chase, Feb. 8, 1864 (Chase Papers, L.C.).

TO JOHN T. TROWBRIDGE

Autograph draft (incomplete), Chase Papers, Historical Society of Pennsylvania; letterpress copy of autograph draft (incomplete), Chase Papers, Mss. qC487, ser. 2, letter 74, Cincinnati Historical Society Library, Cincinnati Museum Center for Natural and Cultural History and Science.

Washington, Feb 10, 1864[1]

My dear Sir,

I found Dr. Tyler very kind & very willing to promote my wishes; but alas! there was found no opening for my school in Frederick: so I went on to Washington by the direct stage road.[2] How well I remember the earnest prayer which went up from my heart, that God would here give me work to do, and success in doing it / There was my next hope, & there I had letters to the Rev. Dr. Hawley & the Rev. Mr. Allen.[3] Both were interested in me but neither could help me much. I resolved however to open a school for boys and so, one morning in January, 1827, a *new* advertisement appeared in the National Intelligencer, announcing that a Select Classical School would be opened in the city on the   day of   by Salmon P. Chase.[4] At this time I boarded with Mrs Markland, one the Avenue, whose husband I think, was a clerk under the Government. My roommate was a young doctor—if I remember right a Dane.[5] It troubled me to determine whether I should continue my private prayer, openly or in secret. Duty seemed to require the open manifestation of my religious faith & after some hesitation, I kneeled by a chair the first night we passed together & offered my private worship to our Father who art in Heaven. My roommate did not exactly sympathize with my sentiments; but I think he respected me the more for making them thus quietly but decidedly known.

At this time Mr. Adams' administration had just entered on its second year; and my uncle Dudley was Senator from Vermont, and a supporter of Mr. Adams. He had been an ardent democrat in the days of Madison; and liked Mr. Adams better than many of the Federalists did. These last never quite forgave his support of some prominent measures of Jefferson.[6]

I was not of a very inquisitive disposition and though glad to know and to be noticed by distinguished men never went out of my way to know or be known. Would it have been better had I been of a more inquisitive, more pushing temperament. Certainly I should have more to tell: but should I myself have done more work? I am not sure. Certainly, now, looking back to those days; seeing what opportunities I had to know so much of the foremost men of the land and what little use I made of them, I experience a very lively regret.

But I am before my story.

I remained at Mrs Markland's, hoping for the advent of pupils for the Select Classical School: but for many days none came. My slender means were well nigh exhausted and I began to be very much concerned about my prospects / At length a Frenchman, Mr. Sauveur F. Bonfils—I think his middle initial was F—called on me and made enquiries in reference to placing his young son Columbus Bonfils under my charge.[7] He was so far satisfied that he engaged to send him to me. Here was one pupil—a gleam of hope. How gratified I was! Now, other pupils would pour in! My school would be full and ——; but alas! day after day went by and Columbus Bonfils remained the only name on my list. This would never do. I heard of Clerkships and thought how nice it would be to have one; and while perfoming its duties, to pursue the study of a profession. And why should I not have one. My Uncle was a Senator & a supporter of the Administration. Could he not obtain one for me? Certainly he could. I resolved to ask him. I went to his lodgings—told him my story—how desperate the expectation of scholars seemed—my project of a clerkship—and would he help me. His reply is not likely to be forgotten. "Salmon" said he I once obtained an office for a nephew of mine & he was ruined by it. I then determined never to ask one for another. I will give you fifty cents to buy a spade with[8] but I will not help to put you in a clerkship." Such was the substance if not the language of his reply. I left him greatly dissatisfied. Did it follow because an office did no good to my cousin, I could derive no good from one? But now I am satisfied with his answer. Had I become a clerk, it is almost certain I should have remained a clerk or should have been at least disqualified by Clerk habits for the work I have actually done

Not long after this I received a call from a stranger who announced himself as Mr. Plumley.[9] He told me that he had a boys school, and also a girls school, which he had established later and which demanded most of his time. He could not give the attention to the boys they required & consequently the attendance was falling off— He had heard of me & thought I could take the scholars he had left & make a good school; and if I desired to do so I could. I accepted his proposition with delight & gratitude: and a few days after entered on my duties as teacher. There were ten or twelve boys left in Mr. Plumly's school who with my one engaged pupil Columbus Bonfils formed my first charge.

It was a great pleasure to me when thirty four years afterwards I became Secretary of the Treasury it was in my power to offer unsolicited to this worthy man, who with his excellent wife, were then living in New York in straitened circumstances a respectable position in that city which he now fills creditably.

I continued in charge of this school nearly three years, commencing in February 1827 and closing in the fall or winter of 1829 nearly three years. Among my boys were a number of the sons of leading men, of Mr. Clay Mr. Wirt, Mr. Southard, Gen. Bernard.[10] There was one lad whom I regarded as the most promising of the school, but unfortunately he became, after he left school, a clerk and I found him a clerk in the Treasury Department when I took charge of it.

I became slightly acquainted with quite a number of prominent characters. Too diffident to push myself into notice—possibly perhaps too proud to ask for recognition & preferring to wait for it—too indifferent also—a more serious fault—to what transpired around me to take pains to acquaint myself with the histories & men of the hour—too much inclined to spend what little time I could command in the society of one or another of a small circle of young lady friends—I made much too little use of the advantages which a residence in Washington at that period offered. I was poor and sensitive—a young teacher—needing to be taught & guided myself.

I became a member of the St John's Church under the care of Dr. Hawley, and for a long while was a teacher in the Sunday School. The Superintendency was offered me, but I shrank from accepting it. Another Church was form[ed under] the care of the Rev. H. V. D Johns, with whom [I formed an acquaintance] which became a friendship ending only with his death.[11]

To this church I frequently went with the daughters of Mr. Wirt, of whom two, Elizabeth & Catharine were then just coming into womanhood, rich in the accomplishment of a thorough education, completed by the influence and example of an admirable father and admirable mother.[12] I wish my memory was perfect enough to enable me to describe this most delightful family[,] but were I to attempt it I should fail. Mr. Wirt was one of the handsomest men and one of the completest gentlemen of his time, and among women Mrs Wirt had few equals. How gracefully & with what sweet [manners] she presided over that happy household, I can never forget. I recall her presence now—but how indistinctly as she stood with me one evening under the clusters of the multiflora which clambered all over the garden portico of the house and pointed out to me the stars. There is the faint memory of a sweet voice; a sweet but noble countenance, a little pale; dark hair; clear, gentle, thoughtful, earnest eyes, not without some sparkle of playfulness. That is all.

How many happy hours I spent in that house[.] It is now devoted to some of the uses of this [war] and the family is all scattered. Two of the three boys [are rebels]—the other dead—and all the [girls except one noble and patriotic woman] gone[;] with their father & [mother to make I hope a family in Heaven].[13]

Yours truly
S P Chase

1. Chase's draft of this letter has not survived intact. The first four pages of the eight-page original are in his papers at the Historical Society of Pennsylvania. That manuscript breaks off in mid-sentence. A letterpress copy, which lacks the first page but contains the remainder of the manuscript, may be found in Chase's papers at the Cincinnati Historical Society. The text given here is a composite, the first half of the letter rendered from the surviving portion of the draft in Philadelphia, the second half from the letterpress copy in Cincinnati. The editors used a version of the letter reproduced at *micro* 31:0609 (a copy in a clerk's hand, also located at the Historical Society of Pennsylvania) to supply text that is missing from a torn corner of the letterpress copy and to suggest readings of words that are not clearly legible in the letterpress version.

2. Chase had closed his most recent letter to Trowbridge by recounting circumstances that took him to Washington, D.C., in 1826, including a letter of reference to a resident of Frederick, Md.: "Dr Tyler—Tyler, I am sure; Doctor I think at Frederick City." Chase to Trowbridge, Feb. 8, 1864 (Chase Papers, Hist. Soc. of Pa.).

3. William Hawley and Ethan Allen presided over, respectively, St. John's Church and Christ Church, Episcopal congregations in Washington, D.C. Alexander B. Hagner, "History and Reminiscences of St. John's Church," *Records of the Columbia Historical Society* 12 (1909): 98–103; *Wash. Dir. (1830)*, 8.

4. According to the advertisement, which actually commenced on December 23, 1826, Chase's school would open "on the second Monday in January"—the eighth. *Daily National Intelligencer*, Jan. 6, 1827.

5. Chase might have meant a boarding house run by H. B. Moreland, on the north side of Pennsylvania Avenue. According to Trowbridge's *Atlantic Monthly* article, "The First Visit to Washington," Chase's roommate was David Williams, a clerk in the Treasury Department. *Wash. Dir. (1827)*, 56.

6. Chase referred to John Quincy Adams, Dudley Chase, James Madison, and Thomas Jefferson.

7. Chase had forgotten that his pupil Columbus was not the son of educator St. Sauveur François Bonfils, but of Simon Bernard, a French expatriate who served on the board of planning for U.S. coastal defenses. Chase to Bernard, July 16, 1829, Bernard to Chase, July 17, 1829 (Chase Papers, Hist. Soc. of Pa.); *DAB,* 2:223.

8. The draft in the Historical Society of Pennsylvania breaks off at this point. The remainder of the letter, beginning with *but I will not,* comes from the letterpress copy at the Cincinnati Historical Society.

9. During the Civil War, Chase made Alexander R. Plumley, a Vermont native, weigher in the New York Custom House. *Register of Officers (1863),* 75.

10. Henry Clay, William Wirt, Secretary of the Navy Samuel Lewis Southard, and Simon Bernard.

11. Henry Van Dyke Johns founded the Trinity Episcopal Church in Washington, D.C. The bracketed text in this sentence is missing because of damage to the letterpress copy. The words have been supplied from the clerk's copy in Chase's papers at the Historical Society of Pennsylvania. *Nat. Cyc.,* 5:253.

12. Wirt's second wife, Elizabeth Washington Gamble Wirt.

13. The Wirt sons Chase knew in the 1820s were named William C., Henry (who died in 1850), and Dabney. The Wirts' daughters living in the household during the period described by Chase were, by birth order, Elizabeth, Catharine, Rosa, Ellen, and Agnes. The "noble and patriotic woman" was Elizabeth, who had married U.S. naval officer Louis M. Goldsborough in 1831. John B. Boles, ed., *A Guide to the Microfilm Edition of the William Wirt Papers* (Baltimore, 1971), 18; *Chase Papers,* 1:4, 337.

FROM HORACE GREELEY

Autograph letter. Chase Papers, Historical Society of Pennsylvania (*micro* 31:0615).

New-York,
Feb. 10, 1864.

Dear Sir:

In your last letter; you asked me whether Daniel S. Dickinson would be more acceptable for Collector of our Port than a city merchant.[1] I did not reply, because I understood from Mr. Bailey that no change of Collector was to be made, and I would not needlessly add to the burden of your correspondence.

I now hear that Mr. Barney is likely to be removed, and therefore write to say that, in my judgment, no other living man would be so acceptable for Collector as Daniel S. Dickinson. He has done more for the Union cause than any other man in the State, or any other Breckinridge democrat any where;[2] he belongs to no faction, no clique; he is out of office and poor; he is growing old; and the Unionists every where trust and love him. Appoint any merchant and forty others will ask, 'If a merchant was to be taken, why not I?' and will be disaffected; while all will be heartily satisfied with Mr. Dickinson.

It is said here that either Preston King or Abraham Wakeman is to be appointed.[3] Each is my personal friend; but each is mere clay in the hands of the potter, Weed, who, if either is appointed will control the whole establishment, and by its aid will elect the delegation from our State to the next National Convention.[4] I do not believe it within the power of man to prevent him.

I have had no communication with Mr. Dickinson. I do not know that he would accept the office. I *do* know that he would honor it, and that his appointment would in every way be fortunate.

Apologizing for this long letter, I remain

Yours,
HORACE GREELEY.

Hon. S. P. Chase,
Sec. Treasury,
Washin D.C.

1. On January 14, Chase had suggested Dickinson as a potential nominee for the collectorship if the position opened, "unless you and other friends in New York should come to the conclusion that some eminent merchant should be preferred." Chase to Greeley, Jan. 14, 1864 (Greeley Papers, L.C.).

2. John Cabell Breckinridge, former U.S. vice president, senator from Kentucky, and Democratic candidate for the presidency, sympathized with the southern position on slavery but urged compromise prior to the commencement of the Civil War. *DAB,* 3:8–9.

3. Preston King of New York, chair of the National Republican Committee, served as a Democrat and Free Soiler in Congress, 1843–47 and 1849–53, and as a Republican in the U.S. Senate, 1857–63. Ibid., 10:397; *Bio. Dir. U.S. Cong.,* 1313.

4. The National Union Convention, a gathering of Republicans and War Democrats, met in Baltimore, June 6–7, 1864, and nominated Abraham Lincoln for reelection. *Daily National Intelligencer,* June 8, 9, 1864; Long, *Civil War Day by Day,* 516–17.

FROM WILLIAM P. MELLEN

Draft in various hands, signed by Mellen. Letters Sent: Deputy General Agent, Records of the General Agent, Records of Civil War Special Agencies of the Treasury Department (Record Group 366), National Archives (*micro* 31:0642).

Washington Feby: 11th. 1864.

Sir:

In compliance with the instructions of your letter of Dec. 27th. 1863 to assume the performance of the duties contemplated by the orders of the Secretary of War, in leasing abandoned lands, houses and tenements, I proceeded down the Mississippi River as far as Natchez, and now report my action and the results of my observation.[1]

At Memphis I prepared rules and regulations concerning the renting of abandoned plantations and the employment of Freedmen, which were forwarded to you for approval.[2] These rules provided for radical changes in the system adopted in my Agency last year. Instead of uniform rates per acre, for all lands leased, I fixed a minimum price, and provided that such additional rent should be charged as could be obtained, having regard to the location for comparative safety from raids, condition of buildings and improvements, &c.

The minimum rate is two cents per pound on all cotton raised, and a proportionate sum on other products. In cases where more than one person made application for the same plantation, the leasing was at public Auction at Vicksburg. The *bonus* bid was from (1/10) one tenth of a cent to eight and one quarter (8¼) cents per pound on cotton raised and in proportion for other crops. Average *bonus* two and one third (2⅓) cents per pound on cotton raised. Average rent four and one third (4⅓) cents per pound, equal to seventeen 33/100 dollars per bale.

As the lessees of last year had been assured by General Thomas, and the Commissioners under him, that they should continue this year at Government rates,[3] it was thought unjust to subject them to competition with new applicants. They therefore, have been permitted to continue at the minimum rent.

Of the rent charged, one cent per pound on cotton raised is regarded as a *contribution* towards the support of the young, aged, infirm or helpless Freed people, and is not considered as due to the Government.

The uniform rate of wages to Freedmen last year was seven (7.) dollars to men; five (5.) dollars to women, and half price to children. The employer feeding them, and they clothing themselves. Lost time was deducted from wages.

Believing a uniform rate of wages injudicious, and that to secure cheerful labor increased compensation should be paid, I have divided them into three classes according to age and condition, giving males $15, $20 and $25, and females $10, $14 & 18 per month. In addition to this, the employers to furnish fuel, one acre of ground for garden purposes and separate quarters for each family, without charge, all other expenses of living to be paid by the laborers and all time to be paid for except that voluntarily lost by them.—

Thus the rents are increased from $4 to $8, for each bale of cotton raised as the minimum rate, and wages per month from $7, and $5 to an average of $20, and $14, and instead of the old system of support under slavery I have adopted that usual in the employment of free labor, endeavoring to fix such rates as would yield a sufficient profit to planters to induce immigration and planting by owners of lands; and yet such as would render the system self-supporting and relieve the Government from expense in providing for large numbers now out of employment, and also to stimulate them to willing industry.—

All owners of lands who have remained upon them, or who return to them, taking the oath contemplated by the President's proclamation may occupy and cultivate them without rent:[4] but subject to the contribution of one cent per pound on all cotton raised by them for the support of the helpless Freedmen: and also subject to the same rules in the employment of labor as lessees of abandoned plantations.—

Provision is made to induce each of the Freedmen as are competent and have means or can obtain them from Aid Societies or others, to cultivate small tracts of land on their own account.—

Provision is also made under which planters may contract with Freedmen to give them an interest in the crops produced: these contracts as well as all others for labor to be subject to the approval of the Superintendents of the Freedmen's Home Farms.[5]

Wages of the laborers to be a first lien upon all crops produced, and no shipment to be made until they are paid, or satisfactory arrangement is made for paying them.

Notwithstanding the above named increase in rentals and wages, over six hundred applications have been filed for working plantations specifically named by the applicants, and hundreds of letters have been sent to us, from every section of the Loyal States, expressing desire to enter into the cultivation of southern staples and requesting information—

I find that there are in my Agency, about 30 000 men women and children, now mostly unemployed, and drawing rations from the United States for support and the number is daily increasing.

These must be supported in idleness during this year, Or, they may earn more than their support.

1st. By placing them all in such localities as will render them secure from personal harm and employing them in labor for the Government or,

2nd. By sufficiently protecting the Lessees and other planters who will employ them—

I much prefer the latter course, as likely to be productive of better effects in all their bearings—

But in either case *immediate* action is imperatively necessary. Adequate military protection to this planting interest, must be afforded *at once,* or the hundreds of persons now there, and of others going there, will abandon their contemplated work. The Military forces were mostly unexpectedly withdrawn from the Mississippi by General Sherman to join in his expedition.[6] This created a panic amongst Whites and Blacks in which the former withdrew from the operations they had commenced, or suspended action in commencing. The latter, filled with terror, came crowding to the River banks, imploring protection and many of them were temporarily removed to places of safety—

More than a month has elapsed since work should have been commenced. Another month lost, will end all chance of employment by Lessees and other planters, this year and throw upon the Government, the burden of supporting these thousands.

I believe adequate military protection will cost less than the alternative expense. And that it can be given without interfering with the general military operations. And that if the "Marine Brigade" is increased to 2000 cavalry and mounted Infantry to patrol the River and do scouting duty, with proper transportation; and the number of colored troops now detailed for the purpose of guarding the plantations be increased to Five Regiments to do post duty, and this whole force ordered to the special service of protecting the planting and Freedmen's labor interest in my agency, it will be a very important and most effective branch of the Military service, in incidentally protecting the commerce of the Rivers, and the transportation of supplies to the army throughout my agency. This corps of colored Troops should be required to labor when not engaged in defense against threatened raids, and in this way, could be made self supporting.

If this be done, and an order be issued by the Secretary of War exempting from military seizure all supplies and stock used and employed by Lessees and other Planters, and also exempting from military service, all freed persons employed under the rules except such as shall volunteer, or be regularly drafted into the service, in pursuance of law, and also exempting steamboats employed under authority, in transportation connected with this interest, I feel assured that this years results will be generally satisfactory and profitable[7]

Hundreds of planters who have sent their former slaves beyond our present reach, will then bring them within our protection and employ them under the rules. Thousands of the Freed people, will come thronging within our lines, as soon as they learn that they will be received, employed, and protected who, for months past have been sent back to their former masters to prevent the expense, demoralization and mortality, resulting from the lack of means to provide for them.

I regard this years operations, connected with the Freedmen, as almost as important in their national effects, as the success of our arms. The violent transition from one condition to another of such a mass of labor, must largely effect the industrial and economical interest of the whole country.—

With the protection recommended, if *immediately* given, I feel certain that from four to six hundred thousand acres of land may be cultivated in cotton in my agency this year.— Take the lowest estimate as a basis of calculation and the following results may be expected;

400.000 acres will yield say 400.000 bales of cotton; the one cent per pound contribution paid by all employers for the support of the helpless in my Agency, will give $1.600.000 for that purpose.

The present regulation fee of four cents and internal revenue tax of half a cent per pound on all cotton brought from a State, in insurrection to a loyal State will give $7.200.000.—

One half of this quantity of land rented by the Agents as abandoned by the owners, for one cent per pound upon the cotton raised, will give the Government from this source $800.000.—

Thus the military protection recommended will give an aggregate of $9.600.000.— Add to this the effect upon our manufacturing interests: the reduction of prices of fabrics for families of soldiers and others, and the saving to the Government the expense of supporting the freed people in idleness. Add also the fact that by so doing we shall this year plant the germ of a system for directing and employing this labor, while the numbers of those now within its influence are comparatively small and that a commencement may be made in their improvement and education to prepare them for free labor, the experiences from which may be made available for better informed action in the future when the numbers will be largely increased, and it seems to me sufficient to justify the military protection recommended.

I have already created four districts within my agency on the Mississippi River as follows;

From the mouth of St. Francis River to the Mouth of Arkansas River, T. C. Callicot Assistant agent with office at Helena.[8]

From the Mouth of Arkansas River to the South line of Carroll Parish La, A. McFarland assistant Agent with office at Skipwiths Landing.

From the South line of Carroll Parrish to Grand Gulf, C. A. Montross Assistant agent with office at Vicksburgh.

From Grand Gulf to the Mouth of Red River, William Burnett Assistant Agent with office at Natchez.

These assistant agents lease abandoned plantations, houses and tenements in their respective Districts, and generally supervise the employment and care of the Freedmen.

I have established three "Freedmens Home Farms"; one on the "York Plantation" near Natchez; one on the "Jeff Davis Plantation" on Palmyra Bend, and one on General Pillows Plantation near Helena.[9]

These Home Farms are designed as places of temporary labor for those who are not otherwise employed and for the labor of such as cannot be serviceable to ordinary planters; also for children and the aged and infirm without other homes.—

Of course considerable expenditure will become necessary in connection with these Home Farms, for the construction of proper buildings, purchasing stock, agricultural implements, seeds, supplies &c; the payment of labor, supporting the helpless and education of the young; transportation of freedmen to them or thence to places of employment; medicines and medical attendance and other things incidental to the present condition of this people and of the Country.—

All freed persons brought or coming within our lines, are to be at once transported to these Home Farms where they can be employed until other labor is provided and where the helpless can be more properly and economically cared for than in such "contraband camps" and military posts as are now filled with them and in which they are fed in idleness and demoralized in many ways disgraceful to us and ruinous to them.

To meet the current expenditures incident to this whole business in my agency I would respectfully suggest that authority be given to use temporarily the money on hand or hereafter arising from the sale of captured and abandoned property and from the rents of abandoned houses and tenements.

I think this appropriation will be sufficient, and that this can be repaid out of the products of labor on the Home Farms, and the rents arising from the leases of abandoned plantations, and the contributions paid by employers upon their products, besides leaving a large balance of income to the Government, much more than sufficient to pay all expense of the military protection recommended, in addition to the benefits Government will derive from the protection incidentally given to the Commerce on the River, and the transportation of supplies to the army.

I cannot close this report without acknowledging my obligation for the counsel and assistance of Mr. James E. Yeatman, President of the Western Sanitary Commission. His heart and energies are devoted to the cause of human freedom, and the welfare of those set free. He has accompanied me throughout my tour of inspection, and I am indebted to him for suggesting many of the measures adopted and recommended.

Enclosed herewith, please find the rules and regulations for leasing abandoned plantations and the employment of freedmen above referred to.

Let me again press upon you the importance of prompt action. Every day of delay, we are feeding 30,000 unemployed people and jeoparding the success of this year's operations.

I am
Very Respectfully

Your Obt. Servt.
WM. P. MELLEN
Sup. Sp. Agt. Treasury Department.
1st. Agency.

Hon: S. P. Chase,
Secretary of the Treasury
Washington.

1. Chase and Mellen had discussed the War Department order of October 9, 1863, in correspondence from Chase to Mellen, December 17 and 27, 1863 (both above).

2. Mellen issued the regulations on January 7 and forwarded Chase a copy the following day. Berlin, *Freedom,* ser. 1, v. 3:774–78.

3. The commissioners that Lorenzo Thomas appointed were Louis Dent, George B. Field, and Robert V. Montague. Chase to Mellen, Dec. 27, 1863 (above).

4. That is, the oath contained in Lincoln's Proclamation of Amnesty and Reconstruction, December 8, 1863. Basler, *Collected Works,* 7:53–56.

5. "Home farms" were small plots of land on which former slaves worked under the direction of government officials or Northern philanthropists. Berlin, *Freedom,* ser. 1, v. 3:70–71.

6. On February 3, William Tecumseh Sherman had embarked from Vicksburg on a major military expedition to Meridian, Miss., intent on destroying Confederate railroads and goods. Long, *Civil War Day by Day,* 460.

7. On February 28, Lincoln declared Mellen's system "well intended" but likely "to fall dead within its own entangling details." With Lincoln's blessing, Thomas issued new regulations on March 11 that superseded Mellen's and included provisions for military protection in accordance with orders that Edwin Stanton issued on February 18. *OR,*

ser. 3, v. 4:143, 166–70; Stanton to Chase, Feb. 18, 1864 (Letters Received, Division of Captured Property, Claims, and Land, Gen. Recs. Treasury Dept., Nat. Arch.).

8. Theophilus C. Callicot (b. ca. 1826), Treasury agent at Helena, Ark., previously held the post of speaker in the New York State Assembly. Murphy, *Biographical Sketches*, 265–67; *Brooklyn Eagle*, Dec. 22, 1863.

9. Tennessee attorney Gideon Johnson Pillow (1806–78) was a brigadier general in the Confederate service. Jefferson Davis had owned "Brierfield," about ten miles south of Vicksburg, since the 1830s. *DAB*, 5:124, 14:603–4; *Official Atlas*, pl. 155.

FROM LEWIS B. GUNCKEL

Autograph letter. Chase Papers, Library of Congress (*micro* 31:0690).

(Confidential.)

Senate Chamber.
Columbus. Feb. 12th.

Hon. S. P. Chase.
Dr Sir:

I was a delegate to the Philadelphia Convention in 1856 and opposed your nomination. I regretted, in a little while after, that you were not nominated. *I have been for you ever since.*[1]

There has been a strong disposition, in the General Assembly, to follow the example of other State Legislatures and nominate Mr Lincoln. In common with a few others, I have labored, (and so far successfully) to prevent *any* expression of opinion, on the part of the General Assembly. It is true that popular feeling in this State is now, strongly for Mr. Lincoln. But it was not so, one month ago—it may not be so one month hence. You were never more popular in Ohio, than you are now. Many think Mr Lincoln should be renominated, but they are none the less your friends in that account. If he were out of the way, Ohio would be as nearly unanimous for you, as any State ever is for any Candidate.

Just now, the question of a Legislative nomination is renewed, and urged, because it is said *Mr Chase* and *his friends* are sending out from Washington, secret circulars, charging incompetency, unsoundness &c in Mr Lincoln. I denied, at once, that *anything of the sort*, was done *by you*, or with *your knowledge* or *consent*. Am I not right? Will you not say so, to me, in a letter, which I will hold as strictly confidential, if you so desire? If improper for you to write me at all on the subject, have some friend write me for you. For I would like to be able to deny the charge, authoritively.[2]

Pardon the liberty, I have taken in writing you thus freely, and beleive me,

Truly Your Friend,
LEWIS B. GUNCKEL.

1. Gunckel had attended the 1856 Republican national convention in Philadelphia. He served in the state senate from 1862 to 1865. *Bio. Dir. U.S. Cong.*, 1104.

2. Chase addressed the subject of his potential presidential candidacy in correspondence to Lincoln on February 22 (below).

TO HIRAM BARNEY

Autograph letter on letterhead stationery. Chase Papers, Historical Society of Pennsylvania (*micro* 31:0712).

Treasury Department.
Feb. 13, 1864

My dear Mr. Barney,

Your telegram is just received.[1] I had just written one to you giving leave of absence to enable you to come to Washington forthwith; but on receiving yours determined to write by mail.

I received this morning a letter from the President which surprised and pained me. It contains statements relating to Mr. Bailey, which are evidently founded on Misrepresentations made to him; and, upon the hypothesis that he exercises undue influence in the Custom House, proposes to make you Minister to Portugal & ——— Collector. I put the ——— just as he puts it. He means, I suppose, that the question of successor is left open.[2]

I replied saying that I hoped no definitive action would be taken in a matter which so deeply concerns my Department without conference with me, for which I was ready at any hour convenient to him.

There the matter stands. I think it will be well for you to come at once. It is very probable that when the President comes to understand every thing just as it is he will think it best to take no action at all:—I am confident he will take none in an unfriendly spirit to you, or in disregard of my judgment as to the public interests involved.

Very cordially your friend
S: P: Chase

H. Barney Esq

1. "Business will detain me here till tuesday or Wednesday next," read the telegram. Barney to Chase, Feb. 13, 1863 (Chase Papers, L.C.).

2. Lincoln's letter of February 12 included expressions of concern that John F. Bailey had assumed too much power without proper authorization and that Barney had "ceased to be master of his position." In the original, Lincoln inserted the name of Preston King as Barney's successor, but then deleted it. Barney retained his place as collector of customs in New York until September 1864, when he resigned. Basler, *Collected Works,* 7:181; Barney to Chase, Sept. 5, 1864 (Chase Papers, Hist. Soc. of Pa.).

FROM WILLIAM H. BRISBANE

Autograph letter. Chase Papers, Library of Congress (*micro* 31:0743).

Office of the U.S. Tax Commission
Beaufort So Ca. Feb. 15th 1864

Honored Sir, and Esteemed Friend,

Your Order of the 6th instant came to hand by the last mail. I cannot but feel profoundly thankful to our Heavenly Father that we are thereby saved from that utter confusion into which General Saxton, Mr French & Judge Smith were precipitating us.[1] We have had against a terrible pressure to maintain our position until we could hear from you. And already are Mr French & Judge Smith and others earnestly at work to get your Order of the 6th Instant reversed. From General Saxton I have heard nothing, except by rumor that he is to aid in accomplishing the reversal of it if possible.

I have at all times paid the greatest respect to General Saxton, and you yourself know in what friendly terms I have written & spoken of him. I could not however support his squatter system. The condition of things here under it would be such that no salary or prospect of wealth could tempt me to remain here one year longer. And I told General Saxton that the worst harm I could do him would be to go away & allow his measures full scope. It would ruin his reputation forever. He has followers among those who have appointments they hold at his pleasure; but no man of intelligence here who gets informed of the plans of the Commission but expresses to us his regret that these plans have been interfered with, unless it be those whose interest in these intended preemptions or in their official agencies warp their judgment.

I am sorry for it that General Saxton committed himself to this wild scheme, that out radicals all the radicalism I ever heard of in agrarian history. I had cherished the hope that he would do much good for this people, but he has sadly disappointed me. It appears to me that his sympathies have the entire control over him, & that he leaves no place for the consideration of logical sequences.

I have now but time to subscribe myself

Yours Sincerely
WM HENRY BRISBANE

Hon. S. P. Chase—

1. On December 7, 1862, Saxton had suggested that the Federal government seize Confederate land forfeited for nonpayment of taxes and divide it into small farms to be rented directly to former slaves. According to Brisbane, recent orders issued by Chase exceeded this proposal and violated the law as it existed early in 1864 by permitting such "pre-emptions" beyond the scope of lands designated for charitable purposes. On February 11, Chase suspended the instructions. Berlin, *Freedom,* ser. 1, v. 3:220–22; Brisbane to Chase, Mar. 25, 1864 (Chase Papers, L.C.); Chase to Brisbane, Feb. 11, 1864 (Letters Sent to Collectors and Assessors of Internal Revenue . . . , Gen. Recs. Treasury Dept., Nat. Arch.); Chase to Brisbane, Mar. 1, 1864 (below).

TO CYRUS W. FIELD

Letterpress copy of letter in clerk's hand, signed by Chase. Chase Papers, Historical Society of Pennsylvania (*micro* 31:0757).

February 17th, 4.

My dear Mr. Field,

I am glad to learn from your note of the favorable change in Europe. I regret that I cannot find any copies of the Freedmen's Report.[1] I sent to the War Department for some, but could obtain none.

I have just received the report of the Supervising Special Agent for the Mississippi Valley above Natchez.[2] He has charge of the abandoned plantations in that region. He has leased about two hundred of them, and in several instances to negroes, and applications to lease are exceedingly numerous.— Yesterday a gentleman showed me a statement of the cotton made by some score of Negroes with such opportunities as they could find; scanty enough, you may be sure. They had, however, made on an average, about a thousand dollars a piece during the Season. I received to-day also a letter from Judge Stickney of Florida, who assures me that Florida will be reorganized as a free State within the next sixty or ninety days.—

General Gantt of Arkansas, who was at one time, you know, in the rebel army as Colonel or Brigadier, has just left me.[3] He goes back to Arkansas determined to aid to the utmost of his ability in making the State free as soon as possible. I think it will be one of the first reconstituted upon a free labor basis.

You see what is being done in Louisiana. There can be no doubt, I think, that she will be a free state before the close of the Spring. Already free labor lines both banks of the Mississippi throughout its whole course. And there can be no doubt that slavery is to perish if no Administration of the Federal Government hostile to emancipation shall replace the present. Of this there hardly seems to be a possibility. The opposition, which calls itself sometimes the Conservative, sometimes the Democratic, party, seems to be abandoning the support of slavery as hopeless.

It is now quite certain that an amendment to the Constitution prohibiting slavery throughout the United States will be proposed to the State Legislatures by Congress. Recent votes indicate that the Resolution proposing such an amendment will command the requisite majority of two-thirds in both Houses.[4]

Thus you see that the question of Slavery is in a fair way to be finally disposed of.

Every exertion is being made to fill the ranks of the Armies, so that in the campaign of next Spring the complete crushing of the rebellion may be secured. I am not so sanguine of the immediate and complete success of military operations, as many are.— But of their ultimate success I entertain no doubt, and think there is good reason to believe that it may be achieved within the course of the present year.

The closing of the Five Hundred Millions subscription to the Five-Twenty Bonds is the most important financial success which has been achieved since you left us.[5] The bonds of that loan already command a premium of six per cent. There is an increased demand for the markets of Europe.— It is my purpose to offer another loan within a short time redeemable after ten and payable in forty years. These bonds will be known as the "Ten-Forty Loan," and will bear five per cent. coin interest.[6]

Congress seems resolved to take up the subject of taxation in good earnest. I am anxious to have them provide for at least one-half of our whole expenses in that way. And I hope they will do so. They will certainly impose taxes enough to raise a much larger proportion for current disbursements than heretofore.

There is but one thing that creates the slightest fear in my mind, and that is our vast expenditure, of which I think 25 to 33 per cent. might be avoided. I hope, however, that we have seen the worst of this side, and that after mid-summer we shall be enabled to diminish our expenses rapidly.

There are wild statements about the debt. It amounts now in round numbers, to fifteen hundred millions of dollars, to which may be added for claims of all sorts hereafter to come in, a hundred millions more. This is a good ways from the current assertions that we owe already two thousand millions, twenty-five hundred millions, and as some put it, even three thousand millions.

I have thus given you a birds'-eye view of the situation, and hope you will find it not uninteresting.

Yours very cordially,
S P CHASE

Cyrus W. Field, Esquire,
London, England.

1. That is, the report of the American Freedmen's Inquiry Commission, compiled by Samuel Gridley Howe, James M. McKaye, and Robert Dale Owen and issued on June 30, 1863. Chase discussed the report in correspondence with McKaye, July 25, 1863 (above). *OR,* ser. 3, v. 3:73–4, 430–54.

2. See William P. Mellen to Chase, February 11, 1864 (above).

3. Col. Edward W. Gantt, elected to Congress from Arkansas in 1860, had organized the state's 12th Regiment for the Confederacy and later received a commission as brigadier general. Gantt switched sides after the surrender of troops under his command at Island No. 10, April 7, 1862. In January 1864, Lincoln authorized Gantt to help reconcile free-state factions in Arkansas. Basler, *Collected Works,* 7:154–55; Long, *Civil War Day by Day,* 196; Charles A. Evans, ed., *Confederate Military History . . . ,* 12 vols. (Atlanta, 1899), 10:310–11.

4. The U.S. Senate had passed what became the Thirteenth Amendment on January 11, 1864, but the House did not approve the proposal until January 31 of the following year. The amendment became law after ratification by two thirds of the states on December 18, 1865. Long, *Civil War Day by Day,* 454, 630, 696.

5. Subscriptions for the bonds, authorized by the legal tender acts of 1862, closed on January 21. Field had arrived in England in January to promote his transatlantic telegraph cable. Judson, *Cyrus Field,* 171; *New York Times,* Jan. 23, 1864; Larson, *Jay Cooke,* 147.

6. On March 3, 1864, Congress authorized Chase to offer the loan, supplementary to legislation of March 3, 1863. The Treasury opened subscriptions on March 24, 1864. *New York Times,* Mar. 28, 1864; *Statutes at Large,* 12:709–10, 13:13.

TO GIDEON WELLES

Letter in clerk's hand on letterhead stationery, signed by Chase. Letters Received by the Secretary of the Navy from the President and Executive Agencies, 1837–1886, Naval Records Collection (Record Group 45), National Archives (*micro* 31:0760).

Treasury Department.
February 17. 1864.

Sir:

I have to acknowledge the receipt of your letter of the 12th inst., in reply to mine of the 8th, in which I enclosed a communication from Supervising Special Agent Heaton.[1]

In the letter which I had the honor to address you, after calling your attention to the fact that Mr. Heaton had declined issuing more permits for cutting and bringing out North Carolina ship timber, and to his reasons therefor, I requested your opinion as to whether the interests of the naval service required any such prohibition or restriction as that suggested. I understand your reply to be in the negative, and shall therefore so instruct Mr Heaton.[2]

I deem it proper, however, to express the surprise with which I have read the following passage contained in your letter—a passage which most certainly would not have received your sanction had you not wholly misunderstood the character and objects of the permits issued by the officers of this Department:

"Parties clothed with permits to collect property not their own, and appropriate the avails to their private use, would be likely to pay little regard to the rights of others; and the acts of persons invested with authority to gather where they have not strewn, would lead to distrust, alienation and enmity. The loyal citizens and even the enemy in rebellion will submit to the conquerors who take their property by force under military necessity or by due process of law; but they will not quietly acquiesce in what appears to be a species of robbing for the private benefit of speculating favorites who have contrived to get a permit to commit waste."

I had supposed you to be fully aware that the permits issued by the Treasury Agents simply confer, in the language of the Regulations, "authority to purchase for money other than gold or silver, or to bring out, if raised or already purchased by applicant, any of the products of the country within the lines of national military occupation, except when prohibited by order of the General commanding Department or other special military order, and to transport the same to market."[3] These permits constitute the only means whereby citizens of an insurrectionary district can now legally find a market in the loyal States for their products.

Nor had I hitherto deemed it necessary to assure you, as I now do, that the outrages of which in the above cited passage, and in other portions of your letter you express your disapproval, have received no sanction or color of authority from the action of this Department.

I must add that your letter reads much like a lecture, and is as unacceptable as it is needless. I am sure that *you* neither read nor dictated it.[4]

With great respect,
S P Chase
Secretary of the Treasury.

Hon. Gideon Welles,
Secretary of the Navy.

1. David Heaton's letter of January 28, written from New Bern, N.C., cited evidence of Benjamin F. Butler's hostility toward Treasury agents. In passing, Heaton noted his own unwillingness to issue permits to fell ship timber and his desire to keep the trees "subject to any demand from the War or Navy Departments." Heaton to Chase, Jan. 28, 1864 (Chase Papers, L.C.); Chase to Welles, Feb. 8, 1864 (Letters from Fed. Executive Agents, Naval Records Collec., Nat. Arch.); Welles to Chase, Feb. 12, 1864 (Letters to Fed. Executive Agents, Naval Records Collec., Nat. Arch.).

2. "Over the *cutting* of timber this Department has no jurisdiction," Chase instructed Heaton on February 20, "but permits may be granted to all proper applicants for the purchase and transportation of timber within and from your Agency of the same character and on the same terms as those for other products of the soil." Chase to Heaton, Feb. 20, 1864 (Letters Sent Relating to Restricted Commercial Intercourse and Captured and Abandoned Property, Gen. Recs. Treasury Dept., Nat. Arch.).

3. Section 20, revised Treasury regulations, Sept. 11, 1863. Welles opposed any permits (such as two previously issued by Heaton) that might complicate the straightforward enforcement by the navy of a comprehensive coastal blockade. *Commercial Intercourse,* 19; Welles to Chase, Feb. 12, 18, 1864 (Letters to Fed. Executive Agents, Naval Records Collec., Nat. Arch.).

4. Privately, Welles described this letter from Chase as "miffy." Avowing his authorship of the letter of February 12, Welles conceded in his diary that some of his language may have been "unreserved, and perhaps unfortunate." Still, he "disclaimed any intention to lecture or give . . . offense" to Chase: "The party and political movements just at this time make Chase sensitive, and I award him due allowance." Beale, *Diary of Welles,* 1:527–28; Welles to Chase, Feb. 18, 1864 (Letters to Fed. Executive Agents, Naval Records Collec., Nat. Arch.).

TO THADDEUS STEVENS

Letter in clerk's hand on letterhead stationery, signed by Chase. Committee on Ways and Means, Papers on the Treasury Department, 38th Congress, Records of the U.S. House of Representatives (Record Group 233), National Archives (*micro* 31:0806).

Treasury Department.
February 19, 1864

Sir,

Hon. Mr. Hooper, in behalf of the Committee of Finance,[1] desires me to express my opinion in respect to the expediency of giving the Secretary of the Treasury power to sell the surplus of gold not required for payment of interest, and for other demands for coin.

I have little doubt that such an Act of Congress would tend to restrain speculation and prevent sudden fluctuations in the gold market. A judicious use of such a power may contribute something to the same desirable end.——I feel myself bound to add, however, that in my judgment nothing can largely or permanently reduce the premium on gold or even prevent its increase except reduction in expenditure, provision for a very large proportion of necessary expenditure by taxation, and diminution in the volume of circulation: first, by discouraging all other than National Currency, and secondly, by gradual withdrawal of a portion of the latter, until specie payments can be safely and generally resumed.[2]

Very Respectfully,
S: P: CHASE
Secretary of the Treasury

Hon. Thaddeus Stevens,
Chairman Com. of Finance,
H.R.

1. Here and in the inside address at the foot of this letter, Chase and his clerk confused the names of two congressional financial committees. Stevens chaired, and Republican congressman Samuel Hooper of Massachusetts served on, the House Committee on Ways and Means—not the Committee on Finance, which was in the Senate. *Congressional Globe,* 38th Cong., 1st sess, 1863–64, pt. 1, 18.

2. Chase, in his correspondence to Joseph Medill, January 30, 1864 (above), had expressed concern about continuing circulation of state bank notes. On the issue of resumption of specie payments by the Treasury, see Chase's letter to William Cullen Bryant, December 1 [5], 1863 (above).

TO FRANK E. HOWE

Letterpress copy of letter in clerk's hand, signed by Chase. Chase Papers, Historical Society of Pennsylvania (*micro* 31:0828).

February 20, 4.

My dear Colonel,

I will try to get an extension of leave from Stanton or get your resignation accepted, and will notify you at once of the result.[1]—

What you say about political matters is very interesting, but you must not let these things prevent you from examining closely into the subjects you were sent to inquire into.[2]— I want to get a good report on the operations of the Trade Regulations,[3] the action of officers under them and the custody of the public moneys. Another thing I desire to be particularly informed about, and that is what taxes or fines or other pecuniary contributions are exacted by the military authorities in addition to those collected by the Treasury Agents. I wish to have all possible care taken to avoid the doubling of burdens under civil regulations and military orders.

Assure General Banks for me that I most earnestly desire his complete success in the great work he has to do in the South West. I shall envy him no honors he may win, but shall be most glad to join in bestowing them. I want to be reckoned among his friends and I want to reckon him among mine.

Of course I do not expect him to agree with me as to the expediency or even propriety of every measure I may adopt, to insure financial success, nor do I expect to agree with him in every measure he may adopt to secure success in his military enterprises, including measures for political reconstruction. He sees his work clearer than I can, and so, as I suppose, I see mine clearer than he can.

When Mr. Denison explained to me the general features of the plan of General Banks for reorganizing Louisiana as a Free State,[4] I thought it adequate to its objects and likely to give earlier results than could be obtained in any other way. I inferred also from the fact that the General had conferred with Major Plumley and Mr. Denison that the plan was acceptable to the Free State men generally.

It is with great regret therefore that I have seen indications of dissatisfaction, which seem to have culminated in a division among men who ought to be thoroughly united, and I cannot help thinking that the General, when he found that the Free State Committee were not prepared to accept his plan fully and cordially, did not make such modifications in it, as were necessary to secure harmony. My own sympathies must necessarily be with those who are most earnest and thorough as well as practical. I have been accustomed to look upon Mr. Durant and Mr. Flanders as the best representatives of this class. Mr. Flanders early won my confidence by the straight-forward manliness of his speech and conduct, both when he first visited Washington as a refugee and subsequently during his brief service in Congress; while everything that I have seen coming from Mr. Durant has inspired me with the greatest respect for his abilities and character. I wish, therefore, that General Banks could have seen his way clear to a course of action which would have secured the cordial sympathy and active cooperation of these gentlemen, and the earnest men whom they represent.

The election will be over before you receive this, and what I have said will be of little value except as a frank expression of my personal sentiments.

There is one clause, however, in General Banks' recent order in relation to labor, from which I apprehend bad consequences. I refer to that which requires all persons to take the oath prescribed by the Amnesty Proclamation under penalty of being required to leave the State and go within rebel lines, or into some foreign country.[5] Rather than suffer this penalty many, I fear, will take the oath who are far from loyal in heart or conduct. I have seen recently a number of articles and speeches coming from disloyal men representing the oath as only contingently binding. In other words, as only binding in case the emancipation clauses of the Proclamation shall not be annulled by the Supreme Court or modified or abrogated by Congress. They say they can safely take this oath, because it simply binds to acquiesence in measures to which they are opposed, but which they cannot resist until they become strong enough to reverse them. It is obvious that men who take such an oath upon compulsion, cannot be expected to be useful citizens or to give any valuable aid in the reorganization of the State upon the basis of free labor. I hope this will be considered.

I shall be glad to hear from you soon.

Yours very truly
S P Chase

Col. Frank E. Howe,
New Orleans.

1. Howe, in New Orleans on temporary assignment with the Treasury Department, had resigned his position in the War Department as assistant quartermaster general of volunteers. Edwin M. Stanton accepted the resignation in March and Chase considered appointing Howe supervising special agent soon after, but the assignment apparently never materialized. Chase to Howe, Mar. 19, 1864 (Chase Papers, Hist. Soc. of Pa.); Howe to Chase, Apr. 8, Dec. 15, 1864 (Chase Papers, L.C.).

2. Howe conveyed his first, tentative impressions of Nathaniel Banks and Treasury Department officials on February 6, four days after arriving in New Orleans. "I am surprised, at the strength, and importance of this place, politically," added Howe; "it is to be the great Theatre of action, and can be made available." At least one observer, Thomas P. May, heralded Howe's arrival for its potential to heal a rift between rival political forces under Banks and partisans of Chase in the Treasury Department who supposedly controlled the *New Orleans Times*. Howe to Chase, Feb. 6, May to Chase, Feb. 19, 1864 (Chase Papers, L.C.).

3. The revised Treasury regulations of September 11, 1863. *Commercial Intercourse*, 13–30.

4. See Denison to Chase, January 29, [1864] (above).

5. Section 24 of General Orders No. 23, issued on February 3, 1864. *OR*, ser. 1, v. 34, pt. 2:231.

FROM THOMAS J. DURANT

Autograph letter. Chase Papers, Library of Congress (*micro* 31:0856).

Neworleans. 21. February. 1864

Hon. S. P. Chase,
Secretary of the Treasury
Washington City.
Dear Sir,

I received yesterday your letter of the 6th inst.[1] The condition of affairs in Louisiana is not properly understood. The proclamation of General Banks of the 11th inst, ordering an election of State officers of an executive character under a constition[2] which was odious to the friends of Freedom, and overthrown by the rebellion, necessarily threw things into confusion. How Mr Denison could have approved the action I am entirely at a loss to understand; he could not have perceived its real bearings, and indeed it appears to me that he has not had such an opportunity of rendering himself familiar with the subject as was requisite to the formation of a correct judgment. Mr D. is not conversant with the population of N.O. nor with the history of men who are now conspicuous before the people, his habits do not lead him into association with the citizens, and I do not recollect ever to have seen him at any of the meetings of the Union association.

Enclosed with this I take the liberty of sending you a short pamphlet called "The issue explained" written by one of my friends,[3] and also a hand bill actively circulated through the city by the friends of General Banks' candidate Mr. Hahn, which will display the spirit with which they conduct the canvass. The convention at Lyceum Hall, alluded to in the hand bill is the convention of the Friends of Freedom assembled to choose delegates to the Louisville Convention of 22nd February,[4] which we have been prevented from attending by General Banks' order fixing our election here on the same day; the negro who stood side by side with me on the platform "and participated in the "proceedings", was S. W. Rogers a pastor of one of our colored churches,[5] and his *participation* consisted in offering, at the request of the convention, a prayer to heaven invoking its blessings on the labors of the Convention; and it was generally admitted that a more appropriate or better delivered prayer had seldom been heard from any one. It seemed proper, in a convention of the friends of freedom, to commit no such absurdity before the civilized world, as to refuse permission to the only man on whom freedom was to be conferred, to say that they were in favor of the measure. I send a copy enclosed of the proceedings of the convention.

I was deeply mortified that the plan of state reorganization which had been matured by the "Free State General Committee" should be overthrown. This purpose was announced to me by General Banks in an interview I had with him on the 8th January, when he read me a letter from the President dated 24th Dec. giving him, Genl. B. full power over the subject of reorganization.[6] Up to that time we had been proceeding under a system which had been embodied in an order, from the War Department to Genl. Shepley Military Governor, looking to the call of a convention and to nothing else, and all the union men of the state of every shade of opinion had acquiesced in that system, and were zealously cooperating to bring it about.[7]

What does General Banks do?

He sets aside the order of the war Department both in object and mode of proceeding. He proclaims the Constitution of Louisiana of 1852, to be in force, and orders an election to be held under it.

He declares that the fundamental law of the state is (nevertheless) martial law—which means nothing more than his will and pleasure—and that by virtue of it he changes the Constitution of 1852 to suit his own view; among other thing to enable his soldiers to vote, who by the express terms of that constitution are excluded.

He declares that he will order an election of five members of Congress, although the State is not divided into Districts, and cannot be, as there is no Legislature, and Congress has not acted.

He declares that his Governor, when elected shall appoint two U. S. Senators.

He announces that he will fix the basis of representation in the convention to frame a new constitution at his own will.

Mr Hahn, who is a trickster and a trimming politician, is Genl Banks candidate for the office of Governor. The subordinate agenc[ies] of military Authority employ all their official influence to promote his success, even to threatening to dismiss, and actually dismissing from office, small police men and others who are considered to be unfavorable to him.

Genl Banks organ the Era abuses in the most shameful and indecent manner all those who support Mr Flanders.[8]

All this has the unhappy effect of causing the people to look upon the Major General commanding the Department of the Gulf as a political partisan.

That a military commander should assume and be allowed to exercise such powers as these, is entirely in consistent with the principles of our Goverment; it remains to be seen whether the friends of liberty in Congress will tolerate it. I do not see that any such election can bring a state into the Union, or have any other result than the appointment of a Military Governor of Louisiana by the Major General Commanding instead of by the President.

The Administration has fallen into the error of trying to hurry on civil reorganization at too rapid a rate. Congress should assume control of the whole matter and fix on an immutable basis the civil and political status of the population of African descent, before any state shall be readmitted into the Union.

I feel very grateful for the kind language you use to me. I could not consistently with my self respect run for office under this military order, which contemptuously overthrew the plan I had been so long laboring to promote. I had held the office of Attorney General of Louisiana and Commissioner of Registration, but resigned as soon as Genl Banks proclamation appeared.

The Generals newspaper organ violently and coarsely denounces us as radicals and fanatics, which epithets we, or I at least, may possibly deserve; but the supporters of the Generals Candidate are certainly reactionary, hostile to liberty, and men, who hate and fear the consequences of this rebellion in the improvement and elevation of the colored man. Should such a party be placed in power, through Genl Banks success in electing Mr Hahn, they may thence acquire strength enough to control the election of members of a convention to frame a new constitution, and thus fasten upon us a form of State Goverment founded on no higher sentiment than the "epidermic prejudice". This is the danger before us, unless Congress will interfere.

I have the honor to remain,

With sentiments of the highest respect and esteem

Your most obdt. Servt

THOMAS J. DURANT.

1. Chase had written on February 6 in response to Durant's letter of January 16 (above). Chase encouraged Durant and other radical "Friends of Freedom" to work with Banks, even though Reconstruction in Louisiana had "taken a different turn from what [was] contemplated." Chase commented in reference to Banks's call, on January 11, for state elections: "Mr. Denison, who was here, approved the General's action, and I took it for granted that his opinions were shared by our other friends." Chase to Durant, Feb. 6, 1864 (Chase Papers, Hist. Soc. of Pa.); *OR*, ser. 3, v. 4:22–23.

2. Durant evidently intended to write *constitution* but omitted a syllable after hyphenating at the end of a line.

3. *The Issue Explained* (n.p., 1863).

4. Durant had presided over the Convention of the Friends of Freedom, which met in Lyceum Hall on December 15, 1863. On February 23, 1864, the Louisville "Freedom Convention" passed a platform of seven resolutions that supported a radical program of Reconstruction. *New York Times*, Feb. 23, 1864; *Proceedings of the Convention of the Friends of Freedom . . .* (n.p., [1863]).

5. Stephen Walter Rogers (b. 1821). David C. Rankin, "The Origins of Black Leadership in New Orleans During Reconstruction," *Journal of Southern History* 40 (Aug. 1974): 424.

6. Benjamin F. Flanders and Durant had discussed Lincoln's letter of December 24, 1863, in correspondence to Chase written on January [9] and 16 (above).

7. Orders that the War Department issued to George F. Shepley on August 24, 1863, focused on preparations for a state constitutional convention. *OR*, ser. 3, v. 3:711–12.

8. "Mr. Flanders, it seems, is deaf alike to the voice of patriotism and of reason," claimed the *Era* on February 19 regarding his challenge to Hahn. "If Mr. Flanders persists in committing political suicide, do not let the ends of the cord with which he hangs himself, get twisted about the necks of others."

TO ABRAHAM LINCOLN

Autograph letter. Abraham Lincoln Papers, Library of Congress (*micro* 31:0864).

Washington Feb 22, 1864

My dear Sir

It is probable that you have already seen a letter printed in the *Constitutional Union,* Saturday afternoon, & reprinted in the *Intelligencer* this morning, written by Senator Pomeroy, as Chairman of a Committee of my political friends.[1]

I had no knowledge of the existence of this letter before I saw it in the *Union.*

A few weeks ago several gentleman called on me & expressed their desire, which, they said, was shared by many earnest friends of our common cause, that I would allow my name to be submitted to the consideration of the people in connexion with the approaching election of Chief Magistrate. I replied that I feared that any such use of my name might impair my usefulness as Head of the Treasury Department & that I much preferred to continue my labors where I am & free from disturbing influences, until I could honorably retire from them. We had several interviews. After consultation, and conference with others, they expressed their united judgment that the use of my name as proposed would not affect my usefulness in my present position; and that I ought to consent to it. I accepted their judgment as decisive; but at the same time told them distinctly that I could render them no help, except what might come incidentally from the faithful discharge of public duties;—for these must have my whole time. I said also that I desired them to regard themselves as not only entirely at liberty, but as requested, to withdraw my name from consideration whenever, in their judgment the public interest would be promoted by so doing.

The organization of the Committee, I presume, followed these conversations; but I was not consulted about it; nor have I been consulted as to its action; nor do I even know who compose it. I have never wished that my name should have a moment's thought in comparison with the common cause of enfranchisement & restoration or be continued before public a moment after the indication of a preference by the friends of that cause for another.

I have thought this explanation due to you as well as to myself. If there is anything in my action or position which, in your judgment, will prejudice the public interests under my charge I beg you to say so. I do not wish to administer the Treasury Department one day without your entire confidence.

For yourself I cherish sincere respect and esteem, and, permit me to add, affection. Differences of opinion as to administrative action have not changed these sentiments; nor have they been changed by assaults upon me by persons who profess themselves the special representatives of your views and policy.[2] You are not responsible for acts not your own; nor will you hold me responsible except for what I do or say myself.

Great numbers now desire your reelection. Should their wishes be fulfilled by the suffrages of the people I hope to carry with me into private life the sentiments I now cherish, whole and unimpaired.[3]

With great respect,

Yours truly
S P Chase

The President.

1. The "Pomeroy Circular," a "strictly private" communication issued by Samuel C. Pomeroy, criticized the presidency of Lincoln on three major counts and invited "efficient aid" to organize the election of Chase instead. "We find united in Hon. Salmon P. Chase more of the qualities needed in a President during the next four years than are combined

in any other available candidate," claimed the letter. The *Constitutional Union,* a Washington newspaper, appeared in weekly and daily editions. February 22 was a Monday. *Daily National Intelligencer,* Feb. 22, 1864; Winifred Gregory, ed., *American Newspapers, 1821–1936: A Union List of Files Available in the United States and Canada* (New York, 1937), 86, 92.

2. Spearheaded by the Blair family, attacks on radicals in the Republican party had continued since Montgomery Blair's Rockville, Md., speech in October. On February 27, Frank Blair, Jr., assailed Chase and the Treasury Department on the House floor. "A more profligate administration of the Treasury Department never existed under any Government," charged Blair. "The whole Mississippi valley is rank and fetid with the fraud and corruptions practiced there by his [Chase's] agents." *Congressional Globe,* 38th Cong., 1st sess., 1864, pt. 1, appen., 50; William Ernest Smith, *The Francis Preston Blair Family in Politics* (New York, 1933), 167, 227–28, 236–38, 256–58.

3. Lincoln responded at length on February 29, confessing prior knowledge of the letter, Pomeroy's committee, and "secret issues which I supposed came from it." "I assure you, as you have assured me, that no assault has been made upon you by my instigation, or with my countenance," Lincoln continued. "Whether you shall remain at the head of the Treasury Department is a question which I will not allow myself to consider from any stand-point, other than my judgment of the public service; and, in that view, I do not perceive occasion for a change." Lincoln to Chase, Feb. 29, 1864 (Lincoln Collec., John Hay Lib., Brown Univ.).

FROM LYMAN D. STICKNEY

Autograph letter. Chase Papers, Library of Congress (*micro* 31:0914).

Jacksonville Fla. February 24, 1864

My dear Sir:—

Since my last a serious disaster to our troops in Florida happened about thirty miles west of this place, Gen'l Seymour in command. It was the result of incaution, if not rashness, akin to his assault on Fort Wagner.[1] I accord to him many high qualities of the soldier, but he is without the just balance of a military commander. The Florida campaign opened so well, I hoped, as it might have been avoided by proper discretion, reverse would not befall us.

Gen. Seymour too, is not in accord with us politically, but if he will do the fighting in good style, his copperhead ebulitions might be pardoned.

Maj. Hay now agrees heartily with me about the readiest way of restoring Florida to the Union[2]—to call a convention which shall change the Constitution in what relates to suffrage & Slavery—by making all residents of the State at the time of election, of lawful age, voters—and all the inhabitants thereof *free.* That accomplished, by opening the ports of Fernandina, St Augustine and Jacksonville, removing hindrances to northern emigrants, and giving me the use of a revenue cutter or any seagoing vessel for three or four weeks, I pledge to you that Florida shall be as bright a star as shines in freedom's constellation. In this I speak advisedly, the means given, the end will be gained. This is the only way to make the State what the friends of freedom desire. Maj Hay is sanguine the President will adopt the plan here given.[3]

One has but to see the practical working of the Tax Commission to be convinced of its great value in weeding out the rebellion.[4] Those who are loyal, or who in season return to their loyalty, save their estates, the incorrigibly rebellious only, are cut off from property. Nothing but poverty will humble the pride of these rebel aristocrats. When their spirit is broken they are conquered. Do not, I pray, delay in sending a third man to fill our board. A man of Maj. Sallade's energy and good intention, would do much, very much for our cause, and particularly now.

The Cutter you sent here did me no service / I learn that her machinery broke down several days ago. The Flora, now at New York, is the Vessel best adopted for service on the Florida Coast. Can you not send her with instructions to aid the Tax Commissioners on the Florida Coast? S. S. Warner of Toledo Ohio, chief officer on the C[ua]yhoga is a good republican a good sailor and worthy to command any vessel in your service.[5]

I am under deep obligation for your kindness in procuring a pasport for Mrs Stickney who arrived by the Fulton.[6] She is almost as good a politician as I am, and will do good service in Fla.

Your treasury agent, A. G. Browne, is a good man, his impulses are good, if he gave his thoughts less tongue, no one could find serious objection to him.[7] Of course, you will not think for one moment I write this to impair your good opinion of him.

Ever devotedly Your friend
L. D. Stickney

Hon S. P. Chase

1. Stickney's letter of February 16 foresaw failure in Florida for Lincoln's "ten percent" plan and advocated instead a state constitutional convention at the outset of Reconstruction. On February 20, Federal troops under Truman Seymour (1824–91), brigadier general of volunteers, suffered a major defeat at the battle of Olustee (or Ocean Pond), Fla. To Stickney, the incident echoed a disastrous frontal assault on Fort (or Battery) Wagner, S.C., July 18, 1863, masterminded by Seymour. *DAB*, 17:12; Long, *Civil War Day by Day*, 387, 466; Stickney to Chase, Feb. 16, 1864 (Chase Papers, L.C.).

2. Apparently Lincoln's secretary, John Milton Hay, a major and assistant adjutant general in the U.S. Army, was assessing the political situation in Florida at the president's request. *DAB*, 8:431; Tyler Dennett, ed., *Lincoln and the Civil War in the Diaries and Letters of John Hay* (New York, 1939), 165–66.

3. Seymour's defeat at Olustee prevented Reconstruction in Florida under any plan until after the Civil War. Shofner, *Nor Is It Over Yet*, 10–11.

4. At the time, Stickney and a "Col. Alsop" were the only incumbents of the three-member direct tax commission for Florida. Chase to Stickney, Feb. 25, 1864 (below).

5. Samuel S. Warner was a first lieutenant in the revenue cutter service. The Treasury Department renamed the *Flora* as the *Nemaha* later in the year. Lytle, *Merchant Vessels*, 65, 135; *Register of Officers (1863)*, 47; U.S. Department of Transportation, *Record of Movements*, 418.

6. A sidewheel steamer operating out of New York. Lytle, *Merchant Vessels*, 69.

7. Albert Gallatin Browne, Sr., supervising special agent at Beaufort, S.C. *Register of Officers (1865)*, 66.

TO LYMAN D. STICKNEY

Letterpress copy of letter in clerk's hand, signed by Chase. Chase Papers, Historical Society of Pennsylvania (*micro* 31:0934).

February 25th, 4.

My dear Sir,

I have just received yours of the 16th instant.[1]— I am very glad that Col. Hay is going to return to represent to the President the expediency of modifying his Proclamation.[2] Before it was issued I urged upon him the importance of leaving the number of voters undetermined and of allowing the organization to be made by the unconstrained action of all loyal citizens; leaving the loyal people themselves to determine who should be included under that designation. But my urgency was unavailing[3] / An oath is necessary to determine who are loyal, and I like the form of that given to you better than any I have seen. Even an oath, however, is not sufficient. In my judgment, the true plan is to select three Commissioners of undoubted loyalty, and authorize them to register the loyal citizens; such loyal citizens as may be willing to be registered before a certain day named. These Commissioners should have power to appoint sub-Commissioners, by whom, as well as by themselves, the proper oath of loyalty should be taken, and such other evidences of loyalty given as are entirely satisfactory to the Commissioners. The voters thus registered should either on the day of the completion of the registry or some day shortly thereafter, meet at prescribed places of voting, and vote for for members of a Convention, equal in number to the members of the Legislature before the rebellion. But the Commissioners, in case this number should be found inconvenient, should have power to reduce it. The votes thus cast should be returned to the Commissioners, counted, and certificates of election issued, and the day appointed for the meeting of the Convention, when the delegates should assemble and proceed to form a State Constitution. All other matters might safely be left to the Convention.

Circumstances have prevented me from recommending Major Sallade for appointment, though it was my desire to do so.[4] We will have the Board filled as soon as practicable.— Meantime, you and Col. Alsop can act, unless there is something in the law, which I have not time at this moment to examine, to prevent it.

I hope to be able to send you down a lighter draft Cutter. In the meantime I am glad to know that the "Cuyahoga" is of service, and especially that Lieutenant Warner makes himself so useful.[5]

Wishing you all success, I remain,

Most Cordially Yours,
S: P: Chase

Hon. L. D. Stickney,
Fernandina, Florida.

1. Stickney had mentioned the letter (as "my last") in his correspondence to Chase on February 24 (above).

2. That is, Lincoln's Proclamation of Amnesty and Reconstruction, discussed in correspondence from Chase to Lincoln on November 25, 1863 (above).

3. This sentence is Chase's interlineation. Chase also made other, less substantial, emendations to the letter.

4. In recent letters Stickney had pressed for the appointment of "our friend Sallade" to the tax commission. Stickney to Chase, Feb. 5, 16, 1864 (Chase Papers, L.C.).

5. Chase responded here to praise of Warner in a letter from Stickney on February 5. Stickney to Chase, Feb. 5, 1864 (Chase Papers, L.C.).

TO JANET CHASE

Letterpress copy of autograph letter. Chase Papers, Historical Society of Pennsylvania (*micro* 31:0946).

Washington Feb 2[6], 1864

My darling Nettie,

Your letters have wonderfully improved. The handwriting is good, the spelling almost perfect, and the style extremely agreeable. We are all delighted with them and each that comes has quite a run, as the book people say.

Katie will no doubt give you soon if she has not done so already a full account of the grand review and ball; the latter given by the officers of the 2d. Corps and the former of I know not what divisions of the Army of the Potomac. Miss Sprague & Josie Ludlow had never seen anything of the sort before; and they came back delighted.[1] For my part, when I thought of the suffering which exists throughout the land; of the dangerous condition of our finances; of the urgent necessity for the prosecution of the war, & the speediest possible suppression of the rebellion, I did not feel inclined to participate in such scenes. And yet why should I blame those who did? It is not worth while, under almost any circumstances, to refrain from all amusements; perhaps listlessness & discouragement would creep in and paralyze all action. There are a few earnest souls who seem willing to work without much other pleasure than that of their work and its results. But almost all men and almost all women must have a good deal of relaxation and recreation to keep them in condition to accomplish any thing. In this matter as in many things else the middle is best— Not too much work & not too much amusement and in all innocence & love to God and man.

Claire says she has written you two long letters in French and that you have not replied.[2] Can't you make your exercises [*two words? illeg.*] [*illeg.*]ation writing your french in the form of a letter. I hope you will and that you will keep up the practice. She will be delighted to receive such letters and Katie & I will be glad to read them. And you will find the exercise very improving. Indeed I suppose it is impossible to acquire any real mastery of french without writing it a good deal— Most talking by Americans in French is simply translating quite literally thoughts first conceived in English. The idioms cant be acquired in this way and without a pretty good knowledge and pretty familiar use of them one cant talk well in French. As soon as I can honorably leave the Treasury Department I want to do so; & then I may visit Europe & I shall want you for my interpreter & Secretary. So qualify yourself thoroughly.

Have you ever read the French Translation from the Italian of Silvio Pellicos Treatise on Duties—*des devoirs.*[3] If not I wish you would. The style is beautiful & the sentiments full of piety and devotion; and these things I desire to see in you above all things else.

But here comes Schureman to barberize me and then breakfast—So I must close. Goodbye, darling, and never forget

Your affectionate father
S P Chase

Miss Nettie Chase.

1. The ball apparently occurred in Virginia on February 22. Among those who attended were William Sprague's sister Almira and Josephine Ludlow, the sister of Janet Chase's deceased mother. *Daily National Intelligencer,* Feb. 23, 1864.

2. Claire Albrecht.

3. *Mes Prisons, Suivies des Devoirs des Hommes,* the French translation of Pellico's treatise, was available at the time in many editions. The work originally appeared in Italian in 1834.

TO HORACE GREELEY

Autograph letter. Horace Greeley Papers, Rare Books and Manuscripts Division, The New York Public Library, Astor, Lenox, and Tilden Foundations (*micro* 31:1029).

Washington, Feb. 29, 1864

My dear Mr. Greeley,

The simple fact that I am named in connexion with the next choice of President brings upon me the most unscrupulous attacks of the Postmaster General & his brother & of all whom the former, through his patronage, can enlist in this work.[1]

These attacks, although they cannot hurt me finally, must necessarily find more or less credit with honest friends of Mr. Lincoln, and must impair my usefulness. Except for usefulness, I do not want the Presidency or any other office. And certainly I do not want to be named for any office & remain in a position the duties of which, I am disabled from usefully performing by animosities excited by the fact that I was named for it.

I am doing my utmost to provide means for paying the army and navy & meeting the other great expences of the war; and this with the great disadvantage of never being consulted as to these expences or as to the possibility of lessening them without danger of lessening also the probability of early and complete success. If to these disadvantages are to be added those which must arise from the active & vindictive hostility of the

Blairs, made all the more embarrassing by their uncontradicted claim to be the special representatives of the policy and views of Mr. Lincoln, it is obvious enough that it will be impossible to raise the money that is wanted with any tolerable degree of promptitude and without serious injury to the vast interests dependent on the avoidance of further inflation of the currency.

What, under these circumstances, is my duty?

Perhaps, if my name were withdrawn altogether from consideration, then attacks would be discontinued & I should be left to do my work unembarrassed by them. This would be entirely agreeable to me. Perhaps if I were to retire from the administration the work that I now do might be done more successfully by some other man—Mr. Hooper for example[2]—who entertains the same general views but would not have to encounter the same unfriendly influences. This also would be entirely agreeable to me; and it would set me at liberty to act with the unconditional Union Men as might seem best for the common cause without embarrassment or hindrance.

Give me your counsel.[3]

Your friend
S P Chase

Hon. Horace Greeley

1. For references to Chase's suspicions of Postmaster General Montgomery Blair and his brother Francis Preston Blair, Jr., see the letters to Flamen Ball, February 2, and to Abraham Lincoln, February 22, 1864 (above).

2. Samuel Hooper.

3. In the original, Chase appended and then crossed out the following paraphrase from lines 2 and 29 of Robert Burns's poem, "Tam Glen":

> "Some counsel, dear Tittie, don't Tarry
> Some Counsel unto me come len!"
> *The Poems and Songs of Robert Burns,* 3 vols., ed. James Kinsley (Oxford, 1968), 1:435–36.

TO WILLIAM H. BRISBANE

Letterpress copy of letter in clerk's hand, signed by Chase. Chase Papers, Historical Society of Pennsylvania (*micro* 32:0005).

Unofficial.

March 1st. 4.

My dear Sir,

I have been, and am greatly perplexed by the differences between yourself and Judge Wordding on one side, and Judge Smith, General Saxton, and Mr. French on the other side. Both parties seem equally anxious for the welfare of the colored laborers, which in my judgment should be the paramount object.[1]

Nothing can be more discreditable to the Government, than the distress, in which multitudes of the Freedmen are permitted to remain. I know the task of dealing with their situation is difficult; but I can not help thinking that by mutual concessions among those who have the same objects in view, some plan might be agreed upon which would be practicably useful.

It seems to me that the plan of preemptions by which the colored man will be enabled to obtain a home in the shortest possible time is the best plan.

The President has thought fit to appoint Mr. Cooley in the place of Judge Smith.[2] The preponderance of statements, by those who seem best acquainted with the condition of things in the District, seemed to render this action necessary.

I regret the necessity exceedingly, for I can never forget the early services of Judge Smith to the cause of freedom,—when, to render them, required great courage and genuine manhood.

Please write me a full account of the present condition of things. How many colored families occupy homes which they own? Is it your policy to make them independent cultivators of their own lands, or to make them the dependents of the land-holders?

What will be the effect of having small tracts of twenty acres each, with larger tracts of three hundred and twenty acres in close vicinity? Will not the small tract-holders be obliged to sell out to the larger?

I might go on to ask many such questions, but please consider them as asked,—they will naturally suggest themselves to you. I want a clear idea of the methods and expected practical results of the action you prefer.[3]

Yours very truly
S P Chase

Rev. Wm. H. Brisbane
Beaufort, S.C.

1. Chase had received correspondence from both sides of the dispute. Brisbane wrote on February 15 (above). In January, Rufus Saxton had written of the situation, and Chase later assured him: "My confidence in you and my esteem for you as man & officer remains undiminished." Abram Smith also wrote in February to dissent from his fellow commissioners' reports and to complain of "inexcusable" delays in surveying lands. Saxton to Chase, Jan. 22, 1864 (above); Chase to Saxton, Mar. 15, 1864 (Chase Papers, Hist. Soc. of Pa.); Smith to Chase, Feb. 7, 1864 (Letters Recd. from Exec. Officers, Internal Revenue, Gen. Recs. Treasury Dept., Nat. Arch.).

2. Dennis N. Cooley succeeded Abram Smith on the direct tax commission for South Carolina. Berlin, *Freedom,* ser. 1, v. 3:307.

3. Brisbane is not known to have responded until March 25, when he wrote in defense of limited preemption and complained of Rufus Saxton for generating "all sorts of unnecessary trouble." Brisbane to Chase, Mar. 25, 1864 (Chase Papers, L.C.).

FROM NAPOLEON BONAPARTE BUFORD

Letter in clerk's hand on letterhead stationery, signed by Buford. Letters Received from Executive Officers (AB Series), General Records, Department of the Treasury (Record Group 56), National Archives (*micro* 32:0021).

Head Quarters, District Eastern Arkansas,
Helena, Ark., March 1st. 1864.

Hon. S. P. Chase
Secy. of the Treasury,
Dear Sir:

By your invitation I communicate my ideas derived from experience and observation in the South.

1st. If you knew how hostile the people in the vicinity of the Mississippi River continue to feel toward the Federal Government, you would see how little prospect there is for the enduring restoration of the Union, until a new state of things is brought about either by agreement or conquest—

2nd. The lessees of abandoned plantations are looked upon by the inhabitants with singular hostility— They will be subject to raids, as long as a Guerrilla force remains in the country— The country abounding in swamps and cane-brakes, renders defence of the plantations against predatory incursions impossible, except in localities to which the approaches may be guarded—

3rd. To re-organize the State Government in Arkansas with one-tenth the number of voters at the last presidential election is possible, but what will be the condition of the other nine-tenths? They are hostile now! When will they change their minds?

4th. It is supposed we hold the Mississippi River and its borders. It is true, no hostile vessel navigates its waters, but it is also true that the banks are lined with hostile people. Scarcely a week passes that a boat is not fired into, even though crowded with women and children. The only boats that escape are those licensed at Memphis to trade in cotton and deliver supplies. This class are comparatively safe. The enemy watch Columbus,[1] Memphis, Helena, Lake Providence, Milliken's Bend, Vicksburg, Natchez and Port Hudson with small parties, making it unsafe to get fuel except with strong escorts—

5th. The demoralization is such among the rebels that the oath of allegiance is taken to dupe us: the people being taught that it is not binding on their consciences.

6th. The system of Trade Stores and permits is used by the worshippers of Mammon to supply the enemy with all they can pay for. I have captured 400 prisoners near this post, and all of them have been clothed and equipped with articles received from Memphis— I have conversed with people from this state and from Mississippi every day, and learn that some one member of every family has taken the oath of allegiance for the sole purpose of obtaining supplies. I have sent back to Memphis twelve (12) boats which were violating the laws, and all of them have escaped confiscation. I have remonstrated with the Treasury Agents at Memphis, and they have cast the blame on the Military Authorities at that place. The Head Quarters of the Army of the Tennessee is now in the field, far below here— Genl. Sherman's last order was to leave trade to the care of the Treasury Agents,[2] and they do not seem to me to be looking to the main thing—Conquering a Peace— It is very important to get cotton, and the revenue derived from the trade on the Mississippi is great: but what is the value of both, compared with the cost of the war for even so short a period as three months?

7th. In my opinion, an enduring peace can be brought about only by war measures— From Cairo to New Orleans we are not likely again to encounter a large army. The prohibition of any goods, to pass below Memphis or above New Orleans would shorten the war. This measure, together with success crowning the expeditions that are now in the field would produce great results. The great fleet of boats [crrying] supplies to the army down the river could bring back all the cotton, but it should be paid for in Treasury notes, not in supplies—

8th. In September 1862 I wrote you a plan, from Jacinto, Miss., where I then commanded, proposing that a Judicial Tribunal should accompany the Generals, and confiscate the property of those, only, actually in arms against the Government, and that the loyal purchasers from the north, and the few loyal citizens in the country should reorganize the government, county by county, as it was conquered[3]—I thus have all the men and all their property interests engaged in re-establishing the Union.

9th The slaveholders will never yield, except to force, is my confirmed belief—

I address you because of my sentiments of esteem, and old friendship, and your exalted influence in the councils of the nation—

I am

Your Friend
N. B. Buford

1. Columbus, Ky.

2. Evidently the third section of General Orders No. 2, which Sherman issued on October 25, 1863, from Iuka, Miss.: "Officers need not meddle with matters of trade and commerce, which by law devolve on the officers of the Treasury Department. . . ." *OR,* ser. 1, v. 31, pt. 1:730–32.

3. Buford is known to have written to Chase from Jacinto on October 1, 1862. That letter, however, suggested only that military commanders be given authority to organize civilian governments in conquered territory. Buford to Chase, Oct. 1, 1862 (Chase Papers, Hist. Soc. of Pa.).

FROM HORACE GREELEY

Autograph letter on letterhead stationery. Chase Papers, Historical Society of Pennsylvania (*micro* 32:0068).

Office of The Tribune,
New York, March 2, 1864.

Dear Sir:

Yours of the 29th ult. only reached me today.[1]

I answer at the earliest moment.

As a rule, while I consider the Presidency a thankless and undesirable office—and especially under existing circumstances—I think no man has a right to decline it when it comes to him unsolicited. So I wrote to Mr. Reid[2] last night that I would *not* decline, if I were in your place, but would simply tell the people that I had no care for the place and begged them to do as they thought fit about it irrespective of my wishes. But your letter puts a different aspect on the matter; and I now think you have a perfect right to say that, believing the public interest to be suffering from the Presidential agitation, and that danger exists that it will divide and distract those whose service and coöperation is essential to the National welfare—perhaps to the National existence—you most respectfully request those who may have deemed you worthy of support for next President to regard you as not a candidate, and to unite with you in with-drawing your name altogether from the canvass. That such language on your part would contribute greatly to your own peace and comfort, I cannot doubt; and I do not see that you are called to maintain a position so irksome and embarrassing as yours must be.

But, as to the other matter: I think that, if you decline to be a candidate for President, there is no other man in American who can manage the Finances so successfully as you can. Others may have equal original capacity; but you cannot impart to another that intimate and perfect knowledge of the great machine which nothing but experience can give. But I would say directly to Mr. Lincoln, "I have declined to be a candidate for President, because I deem unity and harmony in our works of vital consequence; and now, if you think I can be spared from my present position, I will surrender that also, in the hope that still greater harmony may be secured. Tell me finally whether I can or cannot leave without embarrassing you or weakening the public service."

That whatever you shall decide to do will be dictated by the loftiest and noblest considerations, is the undoubting faith of very many; but of none more truly than of

Yours,
HORACE GREELEY.

Hon. S. P. Chase,
Washington, D.C.

1. See Chase to Greeley, February 29, 1864 (above).
2. Whitelaw Reid, noted Civil War correspondent for the *Cincinnati Gazette,* librarian of the U.S. House, 1863–66, and eventually Greeley's successor at the *New York Tribune. DAB,* 15:482–83.

FROM RICHARD C. PARSONS

Autograph letter. Chase Papers, Library of Congress (*micro* 32:0077).

Clevd. March 2d /64.

My Dear Gov,

I wrote yesterday, or rather the day before, to Gov Sprague giving him an account of matters in Ohio: As you will have seen, the "Pomeroy Circular" brought matters to a crisis, & the Legislature concluded to move in Caucus at once. When the Legislature was here on the Monday previous, matters stood substantially as when I left Columbus: A *majority* were in favor of letting the whole matter sleep. But you have no idea of the effects produced by that "Circular." It arrayed at once men agt each other who had been party friends always; & finally produced a perfect convulsion in the party: From the best view I could get of the state of things, the feeling was, that *you* were strong enough to defeat Mr. *Lincoln,* but that *his* friends were strong enough to defeat *you* in time. That the division of the party would only produce defeat and disaster, & bring no possible good either to you or Lincoln, & the results would be fatal to both: Hence some decided *Chase* men staid in the Caucus, & finally acted with it, altho' the bulk of them staid away entirely. I did not know of the action until it was over, tho' my friends in Columbus promised to telegraph me at once, if the subject came up again. But it would have been idle to have fought against it at last, as the fear that you & Lincoln were about to be arrayed against each other, & the disastrous consequences that seemed likely to ensue from it, over topped all other considerations, & the resolution in favor of Lincoln was adopted as the best course to pursue:[1]

I have seen the Lincoln feeling growing & spreading of late, & knew well the means that were taken to fan the flame. Lincoln has a vast personal popularity with the people, but this by no means accounts for the concerted action of the Country. Secret societies, organized every where, with their Divisions, Brig Generals, & Major Generals—Leagues &c &c, have all done their work, & the *Indiana* convention was controlled by party leaders of this character perfectly:[2] I begin to think that *Seward & Blair,* anticipated the result that would take place, if you & Lincoln were opposing candidates[3]—that *both* might be sacrificed, & Seward win at last. But of course I cannot judge fully:

As matters now stand here, with so many states already declared for Lincoln,[4] inclusive of Ohio, the question of what is the best course to pursue, so as to prevent any sacrifice of your high reputation, by prolonging a contest that will in the end array our "house against itself," & bring no good to our party at last, seems to me one of the gravest character: I say "no good to our party at last," because I am about convinced that a struggle between you & Lincoln would in the end be prosperous only to some *third* party, whom we do not want, & will not *have,* if possible to prevent it. But our friends at Washington must advise, & judge what is for the best:

Ninety days may change all this state of things, but at present I am discouraged at the condition of affairs, both for our party and our cause:

If you have time, write me,[5] and in the mean time believe me
Faithfully & Sincerely

Your friend.
R. C. PARSONS.

Hon S. P Chase.
&c &c &c

1. Union party members in Ohio's General Assembly had renominated Abraham Lincoln for the presidency on February 26. *Cincinnati Daily Commercial,* Feb. 29, 1864.

2. Lincoln also won the unanimous endorsement of the Indiana Union state convention, meeting in Indianapolis on February 23. *New York Tribune,* Feb. 24, 1864.

3. Parsons wrote again within a few days to report indications that Montgomery Blair was attempting to influence opinion in Ohio against Chase. Parsons to Chase, Mar. 7, 1864 (Chase Papers, L.C.).

4. By March, Lincoln had received endorsements from Union party conventions in at least eleven other states: California, Connecticut, Indiana, Kansas, Maryland, Minnesota, New Hampshire, New Jersey, New York, Pennsylvania, and Wisconsin. *New York Tribune,* Feb. 19, 23, 24, 1864.

5. The editors have not found a reply by Chase. "The action in Ohio, though not what it is represented," wrote Chase to William Orton the next day, "affords me a suitable occasion for gratifying my wish to remove my name from the discussions which are becoming more partizan than patriotic or safe. It shall not be used as a watchword of division." Chase to Orton, Mar. 4, 1864 (Chase Papers, Hist. Soc. of Pa.).

TO HORACE GREELEY

Autograph letter. Horace Greeley Papers, Rare Books and Manuscripts Division, The New York Public Library, Astor, Lenox, and Tilden Foundations (*micro* 32:0099).

Washington, March 4, 1864

My dear Mr. Greeley

Receive my heartfelt thanks for your kind letter.[1] In a day or two I will set myself right and very much as you advise. I have already written to the President— I wrote indeed immediately after seeing the Circular of the Pomroy or Unconditional Union Committee saying that I knew nothing of the Circular till I saw it in print & that the Committee acted in all things without consulting me. I said that I did not desire to administer the Dept. a day without his entire confidence / To this he replied, closing with the statement that there was nothing in the condition of the public interests which called for a change in the headship of my Department: but there was no response in his letter to the sentiments of respect & esteem which mine contained. But this is not remarkable. Whatever appreciation he may feel for public services he never expresses any.[2] So I have worked on.

My immediate object in writing is to call your attention to the aspects in Louisiana. Messrs Durant, Flanders & our truest men are set aside because they are willing that intelligent creoles should vote without regard to complexion. And the paper owned & edited by the Governor elect calls them "Negroheads."[3] Your sagacity will at once see the drift. Negroes may fight but must not vote—may use bullets but not ballots—This seems to me the intensity of meanness. It may be statesmanship.

Most truly your friend
S P CHASE

Hon. Horace Greeley.

1. Greeley's letter of March 2 (above).
2. Chase to Lincoln, Feb. 22, 1864 (above); Lincoln to Chase, Feb. 29, 1864 (Lincoln Collec., John Hay Lib., Brown Univ.).
3. Michael Hahn ran the New Orleans newspaper, *True Delta*. In other letters, also, Chase commented on the use of such epithets. George S. Denison to Chase, Mar. 5, Chase to Benjamin F. Flanders, Mar. 7, Chase to Denison, Mar. 16, 1864 (all below).

FROM GEORGE S. DENISON

Autograph letter on letterhead stationery. Chase Papers, Library of Congress (*micro* 32:0137).

Private

United States Custom House,
COLLECTOR'S OFFICE.
New Orleans, March 5th 1864

Dear Sir—

My letters have not been frequent of late, for the reason that nothing has transpired, except the election, & concerning this, I had explained to you the situation, my own position & the results of which were sure to follow.[1] These results were as I predicted, except that Mr. Hahn's majority was larger & the vote for Mr. Flanders smaller, than was anticipated.[2]

I had & still have, some misgivings as to what you may think of my action in this election, because, being at a distance, you form your opinion of the contest from statements of interested parties. You will know at some future time, if you do not know it now, that I have acted wisely, & pursued the only course honorable for me. After my visit to Washington, I could only follow Gen. Banks' lead. If that visit had never been made, I should probably have done the same thing. This whole contest has been a personal one, & I have failed to detect any difference in the principles of the two parties, of which one is as radical as the other. Probably Mr. Durant and some others do not take this view of the case, & it has been otherwise represented in some of the newspapers, yet I know what I say, is correct.

I enclose Gov. Hahn's inaugural, marking that portion which refers to Slavery. The inauguration was a very brilliant and successful affair.[3]

I hoped that all dissensions in the Union party, would be ended with the election, but I now fear that they will continue. I am reluctant to say anything against Mr. Flanders whom I respect for many good qualities, & I do not say anything against him here. But to you I say that I think he confuses his principles with his interests & desire for personal advancement—that he has great zeal but no wisdom—and that while devoted to your interests, he has injured them and will injure them still more. He wastes his force in the indulgence & gratification of private resentments—he greatly overestimates his own personal influence—he makes no friends & alienates many once his friends. I think you overestimate both his ability & influence. It is not true that the extreme radicals all supported Mr. Flanders. I think an equal or greater number went for Hahn. I have continually endeavored to induce Mr. Flanders & his friends to coalesce with the other Union men, & work in harmony with the majority instead of trying to dictate to them. If he would do this we could control every political movement in the State, & send to the National Convention delegates of our own choice.[4] I hope to succeed but fear not. Such success would be possible if Mr. Flanders could understand what is true, that he is personally unpopular, & therefore every movement inaugurated by him, & in which he is to be the leader, will fail.

Mr. Flanders & Mr. Fellows and the political friends of each, met at a dinner yesterday. I am informed on good authority that a coalition was formed between these two defeated factions, with the object of controlling the State Convention &, through the Convention, of ousting Gov. Hahn, their successful rival.[5] After this is done, each man is to pitch in for himself. Perhaps these indignant Union men, smarting under the sting of recent defeat, expect to vindicate some noble principle by a combination with copperheads, but I don't see it. To a spectator this looks more toward self-aggrandizement at all hazards—and the gratification of personal resentment. The whole project will fail utterly, as I hope will every compact with these pro-slavery semi-secessionists.

We are forming a Chase Club here and meet for organization next Monday. It will comprize some of the best men of the City, of different interests & political affinities. I believe we can control the election of delegates to the National Convention, which we certainly could never do, if Plumly & myself had joined ourselves to the Flanders faction.

Flanders seems to hate Plumly, & I don't know the reason. Plumly has worked hard for you ever since he has been here, & works hard for you now. His commission has not come, & I sometimes fear you have changed your mind about sending it at all. I can only assure you that it will be very bad policy & unjust to with-hold it. It would have been much better to send it at the time first designated. Plumly will undoubtedly be a delegate to the National Convention. He has been very fortunate in his finances lately. Some old stock held by him & regarded as nearly worthless, has risen in value enormously, & brought him nearly Thirty Thousand Dollars. His family have been here this winter and he has lived with some show but not expensively. He has been economical except on one occasion when he gave a party which cost nearly a Thousand Dollars. He has done much good here & no man in the Dep't. has more friends. I make these statements because I do not know what representations may be prompted by Mr. Flanders' hostility to him.

Gen. Banks is doing nothing to futher Mr. Lincoln's renomination. He tells me he is not & I believe him. This is all that we can ask of him, for if he should do anything against Mr. L's renomination, his head would be taken off without delay.

Mr. Whitlaw Reed, who is to be Editor of the N.O. Times, has not yet arrived.[6] I am sorry, for we need him very much. Hahn's paper, the "True Delta" is out for Lincoln, as I supposed it would be.

I see that many Northern papers misconstrue the order which Gen. Banks issued, about people taking the oath & voting at the recent election. This general order was intended to advise & not to compel. No one here supposed or imagined that registration & voting was compulsory, and people voted or did not vote, according to their inclinations.[7]

If not asking too much, I wish you would write me a short letter.[8] I always like to know if my course is approved by you—if not approved, I wish to know it, so that I may do better.

A great military movement up Red River has commenced.[9] The enemy are in large force at Shreveport, where there probably will be a battle. Gen. Banks leaves in three or four days.

Very Respectfully

Your O'bt Serv't
George S. Denison

To
Hon Salmon P. Chase
Secretary of the Treasury

1. Denison's most recent known letter, on February 19, assessed Louisiana politics and predicted Michael Hahn's election as governor on February 22. "Previous to the nomination by the Convention I worked zealously for Mr. Hahn," Denison added, "knowing that his unanimous nomination would heal all dissension. Since then I have *quietly*

done what I could for him." *New Orleans Daily True Delta,* Feb. 23, 1864; Denison to Chase, Feb. 19, 1864 (Chase Papers, L.C.).

2. Hahn and Benjamin F. Flanders, the Union Free Trade and Independent Republican party candidates, received 6,171 and 2,225 votes, respectively. A third candidate, Independent Conservative John Q. A. Fellows, a New Orleans attorney, got 2,959 votes. *New Orleans Dir. (1855),* 85; Rightor, *History of New Orleans,* 609; Sobel and Raimo, *Biographical Directory,* 2:568.

3. Hahn was inaugurated on March 4. "The institution of slavery is opposed alike to the rights of one race and the interests of the other," he proclaimed. "I tell you that I regard its universal and immediate extinction as a public and private blessing." *New Orleans Daily True Delta,* Mar. 5, 1864.

4. The National Union Convention that convened in Baltimore during June 1864.

5. On March 28, Louisiana voters selected delegates to the state's constitutional convention, which met throughout the summer. *Appletons' Annual Cyclopædia,* 4:478; *New Orleans Daily Picayune,* July 23, 1864.

6. The editors have not found evidence that Reid actually assumed the position.

7. General Orders No. 24, issued by Banks on February 13, specified eligibility requirements for voters, who had to take the oath prescribed by Lincoln's Proclamation of Amnesty and Reconstruction. *OR,* ser. 3, v. 4:96–98.

8. Chase replied on March 16 (below).

9. See Denison to Chase, January 29, [1864] (above), for earlier speculation regarding the ill-fated Red River campaign.

TO BENJAMIN F. FLANDERS

Letter in clerk's hand on letterhead stationery, signed by Chase. Special Collections, Dartmouth College Library (*micro* 32:0171).

Treasury Department.
March 7th, 1864.

My dear Sir,

Yours of the 26th is just received. I am not much surprised at the result of the election.[1] All accounts, as well as your letters, had prepared me for it. I regret exceedingly the divisions of the Free State Party, but do not see how they could have been well avoided, otherwise than by allowing the work of reorganization to proceed under the charge of the Free State Committee. When another plan was adopted by General Banks with the sanction of the President, it was right that the friends of the Free State Committee should acquiesce, and acquiesce cheerfully, in what was an inevitable necessity.[2] The first error, as it seems to me, was in not allowing perfect freedom of discussion in regard to the nomination of a candidate for Governor, and perfect freedom of action by loyal citizens. All the troubles appear to me to have flowed from this error.—

I notice that the same slang terms,—such as "Negro-heads," "Negro-Equality men," and the like, with which Anti-Slavery men have been always assailed,—were applied very freely to you and your friends. I am only sorry that the epithets were not better deserved.— Nothing, in my judgment, is clearer than that in States where the colored people constitute so large a proportion of the population as in the States upon the Gulf, they should be allowed to vote if qualified by having borne arms in defence of the Country, or by sufficient education. A rule upon this subject could be easily adopted, which would secure all interests and rights without prejudice to established order.

But it is not worth while to comment on this subject further. The petition of the colored Creoles to the President and to Congress will bring the subject before the Country.[3]— I earnestly hope that all friends of State Organization on the basis of the prohibition of Slavery will now act together and secure that main object.

I understood sometime ago, and I think from a letter of yours, that you proposed to resign the Supervising Special Agency after the election.[4] Please let me know what your purpose now is. Will you retain the Presidency of the Bank or the Supervising Special Agency? The duties of the two places are incompatible, as I suppose.

I see that your opponents were very free in imputations of the use of your Agency to secure your own election. These imputations I have no doubt are groundless, but I shall be glad to have your assurances that no permits have been granted or withheld, and no appointments made or denied, otherwise than if your name had not been before the electors.

Very Sincerely Your Friend,
S P Chase

Hon. Benj. F. Flanders,
New Orleans.

1. Flanders' letter analyzed Louisiana's gubernatorial election of February 22. According to Flanders, Nathaniel P. Banks insured an outcome favorable to his candidate by ordering all city, state, and military personnel to vote for Hahn. "The effect of the election has been very bad," continued Flanders. "The question of negro suffrage & equality which was invoked to defeat me . . . has roused all the base prejudice and passions common to the ignorant and vulgar." Flanders to Chase, Feb. 26, 1864 (Chase Papers, Hist. Soc. of Pa.).

2. For Banks's plan, see Thomas J. Durant to Chase, January 16, 1864 (above), and Banks to Lincoln, December 30, 1863, in Basler, *Collected Works,* 7:124–25.

3. On January 5, more than a thousand "colored citizens" of Louisiana petitioned Congress and the president for the right to vote. *New Orleans Daily True Delta,* Apr. 6, 1864.

4. See Flanders to Chase, December 12, 1863 (above).

FROM HENRY VILLARD

Autograph letter. Chase Papers, Library of Congress (*micro* 32:0213).

244 Pennsylvania Avenue[1]
March 7th 9 AM

Dear Sir,

It being possible, that, in the pressure of public business, you may have overlooked the letter of Mr Sherman to the Editor of the "Gazette", I beg to enclose it.[2] I honor the author for it. The moral courage, independence of popular delusions and manly disregard of possible personal consequences, it discloses, present a most striking and refreshing contrast with the halting, hesitating, calculating advocacy of your cause by others, that profess to be your friends. A few such frank words from those, that guide the public mind, do a thousand times more good than nerveless, editorials after the Greeley fashion. To me the discouraging feature of my profession is, that, while I have access to the columns of newspapers, I cannot control their contents, & I cannot understand, why those, that have it, dare not exercise it independently.

I enclose also two other clippings: one with the version of the nature of your correspondence with Mr Lincoln telegraphed to the Commercial & the other containing a dispatch on the same subject to the New-York Tribune. You will see that they differ essentially.[3] The Tribune dispatch was sent at my instance; but I regret to say that the Correspondent of that paper, to whom I spoke in regard to the matter, framed it so as to come altogether short of the form and substance I wanted conveyed in justice to you.

I hope that the good motive I have in writing the following, will prevent my being considered presumptuous and obtrusive with unsolicited opinions by you. You know I have good opportunities for observation among both your friends and your enemies & my sincere interest in your public career impels me to state frankly what I believe to be true in regard to questions of such great importance to you.

Your enemies are bent upon forcing you not only out of the way of Mr Lincoln, as to the Presidential succession, but also out of the Cabinet. You can gratify them no more than by doing of your own accord, what they are trying to accomplish by every means within their reach. To allow the latter to be successful, would be—I express not only my own, but also the opinion of some of your truest and most prominent friends—a grave mistake; to frustrate them a true triumph over those that wish you ill. I cannot help considering your case as that of the Generals, who permitted themselves to be driven, by personal vexations, into asking to be relieved from active commands and now rue the step in continued retirement. Of course, matters may take such a turn as to make a continuance of your official relations intolerable and impossible; but would it not be better not to yield, until the persecution of your enemies becomes so vindictive, as to make sure, that the indignation of the people will be aroused and turned against them?

I always thought, that you sacrificed yourself for the country upon exchanging a seat in the Senate with one in the Cabinet. That sacrifice may not be appreciated *now,* as it should be; but I am confident it will be, sooner or later. And, I think sincerely, that the further self-sacrifices, you are making, by continuing in a position, that is perhaps becoming more and more unpleasant to you, will enhance the ultimate, popular appreciation of your services to the country.

Begging you again to forbear with the liberty I have taken in the above and to apprise me of your decision in regard to the publication of the correspondence,

I am very respectfully
H VILLARD

Hon S P Chase

1. German-born Henry Villard (1835–1900), best known later in the century as a railroad promoter in the Pacific Northwest, reported for the *New York Herald,* the *New York Tribune,* and his own news agency during the Civil War. *DAB,* 19:273–75.

2. John Sherman's undated letter, which appeared in the *Cincinnati Daily Gazette* on March 3, 1864, addressed issues raised by the Pomeroy Circular. "I prefer the nomination of Governor Chase to that of Mr. Lincoln, as I believe Governor Chase has more executive ability than Mr. Lincoln," wrote Sherman, "but I am entirely willing to abide the action of the Union Convention at Baltimore."

3. The articles referred to Chase's letter to Lincoln, February 22 (above), and the president's response on February 29. According to the *New York Tribune,* Lincoln offered assurances that he "did not perceive any occasion" for a new Treasury secretary. In the *Cincinnati Commercial,* however, he supposedly left the matter to Chase's discretion. *Cincinnati Commercial,* in the *New York Times,* Mar. 5, 1864; *New York Tribune,* Mar. 7, 1864.

TO JOHN T. TROWBRIDGE

Letterpress copy of letter in clerk's hand. Chase Papers, Mss. qC487, ser. 2, letter 92, Cincinnati Historical Society Library, Cincinnati Museum Center for Natural and Cultural History and Science (*micro* 32:0342).

Washington March 13, 1864

My dear Sir[1]

The Garner Case comes next in order and is invested with a peculiar interest by its tragic circumstances.[2]

It is impossible to state the facts except in the merest outline; but even an outline will convey a pretty accurate idea of the whole transaction.

In the night of the 2[*illeg.*]th[3] of January 1856, a party of slaves escaped from Boone County in Kentucky into Storrs township adjoining Cincinnati on the Ohio river. Among the persons composing the party were an old man named Simon Garner and his wife—so far as a slave woman could be a wife—Mary; a son of the old man, also named Simon, and Margaret his wife, and their four children.[4]

They took refuge in a colored man's house,[5] near the river bank below Millcreek, a stream which divides Storrs from Cincinnati. They were tracked immediately, and a warrant for their apprehension was obtained the next morning, Monday [*torn*] 28th from one Pendery, a Commissioner appointed by Judge McL[*illeg.*][6] under the Fugitive Slave Act of 1850.— Provided with this warrant, the United States Marshal—named Robinson—with a gang of officers and the slave-claimants, hastened to the house where the fugitives had taken refuge. Their entrance was resisted. Young Simon, who was armed with a six-shooter, fired four shots on the party of official and unofficial slave-hunters before he and his companions were seized. While this was going on, his wife Margaret, who was naturally of a violent disposition and now frenzied by excitement, seized a butcher-knife and, declaring that she would kill all the children before they should be taken across the river, actually succeeded in killing one, a little girl of three years of age, named Mary.

The survivors were taken in custody and conveyed to the Police Station House.

The friends of the slaves procured the same day a writ of habeas corpus returnable before the Probate Judge of the county, which was executed by the sheriff so far as to take the slaves in custody and convey them to the county jail.[7]

The Probate Judge immediately proceeded to Columbus to confer with me as to the proper course of procedure.

The hostility to abolition under which some men included all earnest antislavery action, was at this time intense in Southern Ohio, and nowhere more intense than in Cincinnati. At the election which had been held for Governor only three months before, I had received, in Hamilton County which includes Cincinnati, only forty-five hundred and sixteen votes out of twenty-three thousand two hundred and eighty. The rest, divided between the democratic and Know-Nothing candidates, represented hostility to my political and especially to my antislavery opinions and principles.[8]

I had been Governor just fourteen days when the Probate Judge called to confer with me.[9] It was not necessary for me to inform him that in my judgment the Fugitive Slave Act was unconstitutional and void: it had been proclaimed on too many occasions to leave in ignorance a man so well informed. Nor did I think it right to make any suggestions to a Magistrate concerning a decision to be made by him. What he naturally desired to know and had a right to know was, whether the Executive of the State would sustain the process of the State in the midst of a community in which, by most persons, any decision against the claims of Masters would be regarded as little better than treason to the Constitution & the Union.

I did not hesitate to assure him that the process of the State Courts should be enforced in every part of the state, whether in Hamilton or any other county; and authorized him to say to the sheriff that in the performance of his duty he would be sustained by the whole power at the command of the Executive.

The case, for some reason satisfactory to the friends of the Slaves, was not brought to a hearing before the Probate Judge on the writ then issued. Proceedings under it were abandoned, and the sheriff had already on Tuesday, and upon the return of the Judge, notified the

Federal Marshal,[10] that he did not regard the fugitives as in his custody, (though they might remain in jail,) but as in that of the officers of the United States.

The Slave Act Commissioner, under whose warrant the seizure had been made, then declared his purpose to proceed to hear the case on the claim for surrender; but delays of various kinds were interposed until on Friday, February 8, the Grand Jury reported an indictment against the two Garners and their wives for the murder of the child Mary, and, all four being still in jail, they were again taken into custody by the sheriff. The three children remained in jail also, and were regarded as in the custody of the Marshal.

Matters remained in this condition for some days, until the Marshal applied to United States District Judge Leavitt for a habeas corpus against the sheriff for the four fugitives, for the purpose of bringing them before him to determine, not whether they were unlawfully deprived of liberty, but whether the sheriff was entitled to their custody under the criminal process of the State rather than the Marshal under the Slave Act Commissioners' Warrant. It was a manifest abuse of the writ of habeas corpus, thus to convert it into a summary replevin; but the counsel for the sheriff, one of whom in conversation with the Judge had heard him express the opinion that the prisoners could not be removed from custody under arrest for crime by any proceeding under the Fugitive Slave Act, made no opposition to the allowance of the writ.[11] It was accordingly granted, and a hearing was had on Tuesday the 26th February upon the return of the sheriff that he held the four persons indicted under the process of the State to abide their trial on the charge of murder.

After the argument before Judge Leavitt was closed, the Judge allowed the Fugitive Slave Law Commissioner to take his seat and announce his decision, in the proceeding commenced by his warrant. As was expected he denied to the fugitives the claims to freedom asserted in their behalf, and ordered that all should be delivered to their respective claimants.

The Slave Act Commissioner in this case was a weak, mercenary fellow; but his decision is written in judicial style, and bears the marks of a very different order of intellect from his. Who wrote it?

Meanwhile another writ of Habeas Corpus had been issued by Judge Burgoyne, the Probate Judge, for the three children, on which a hearing was had before him on the same day, Tuesday February 26th, on which Pendery the Slave Act Commissioner delivered his decision as just stated. After arguments on the Constitutionality of the Slave Act, and particularly that part of it which makes the United States Commissioners Judges in cases arising under it, he deferred his judgment until Saturday following, having made a special order that the children should not be removed from the jurisdiction of the Court until final decision.

On Thursday [morn]ing, however, Judge Leavitt announced his decision in the case which had been argued before him. He declared, to the surprise of every one, unless some had foreknowledge of his conclusions, that the custody of the sheriff as against the claims of the Marshal under the Fugitive Slave Act was unlawful, and ordered the former to deliver the indicted prisoners to the latter.

With this order the Marshal at once proceeded to the jail, where the sheriff delivered to him not only the four indicted prisoners, but also the three children, notwithstanding the order of the Probate Judge as to the latter. All the fugitives were immediately hurried into an omnibus, which was surrounded by a number of special deputy Marshals—there were five hundred of these specials appointed, the purchase of whose claims for fees, it is said, afforded good chances for speculation to the Marshal and his regular deputies and the Slave Act Commissioner—and immediately driven to the river, and taken across on the Ferry Boat to Kentucky. Hardly an hour elapsed after Judge Leavitt had made his order before the fugitives were lodged in a Kentucky jail.

I had observed the proceedings in these cases with great interest, and with deep solicitude for the fate of the slaves. All that I could do in their behalf, under the circumstances then existing, was done. They were represented by able counsel, and the power of the State was pledged to maintain the process of the State. No one imagined that any Judge could be found who would undertake to transfer by a proceeding in Habeas Corpus, prisoners indicted under State law to Federal custody under the Fugitive Slave Act. Nor did any one imagine that persons held under an order of a State Court during the pendency of a Writ of Habeas Corpus, would be carried off beyond the jurisdiction and in violation of that order. But such a Judge was found, and such an abduction was perpetrated.

I could not prevent this any more than I could prevent the commission of other outrages. I could not foresee such transactions, and if I could have foreseen, I had no more power to prevent them than any private citizen possessed;—except in the single contingency that the sheriff might need the power of the State to enforce the execution of process in his hands. Except in that contingency I had no power other than [moral], the whole weight of which was given to the side of the fugitives, in every form of encouragement, counsel and support, to those engaged in their defence. I was not in Cincinnati during the proceedings. The Legislature was in Session. I had only a fortnight before the seizure of the fugitives entered an office wholly without experience in its duties, and my constant presence was required at Columbus. Had I been at Cincinnati, I do not now see that I should have been likely to add anything to the ability or the zeal with which the cause of the fugitives was defended, or to suggest anything which did not occur to them. And certainly if they on the spot could devise no way to prevent the surrender and carrying off of the fugitives under the unanticipated circumstances of that day, it is not wonderful that I could devise none, while a hundred and twenty miles off and wholly uninformed of the outrage which was being enacted.

Some Abolitionists distant from the scene have blamed me since because I did not in some way prevent the carrying back to slavery of Margaret Garner.[12] They saw the tragic circumstances of her case and felt peculiar sympathy for her; but they did not see the extraordinary efforts made to save her. That these efforts were were unsuccessful all humane persons must lament; but how more effort could be made or with what more likelihood of success, no one has yet pointed out. And no one conversant with the circumstances and concerned in the efforts made in her behalf, has found fault with what I did. All those approved my action and were grateful for my support. It must be remembered that Margaret was but one of seven fugitives, each of whom was entitled if not to equal sympathy, certainly to equal rights and equal efforts for their protection. None of them were forgotten or neglected.

After they were surrendered the Prosecuting Attorney sent me copies of the indictment and proceedings, and suggested that though the indicted prisoners could hardly be considered as having fled from justice in Ohio, yet it might be proper to regard them as having constructively done so, and to issue a requisition for their delivery to an Agent of the State to be brought back within its jurisdiction.[13] I felt keenly the humiliation of being reduced to this mode of asserting the right of the State to the custody of persons indicted under her laws. It was obvious that when returned to the custody of the sheriff they would be in precisely the same relations as when they were taken from his custody by Judge Leavitt's order, and there would be no legal obstacles which did not exist to the original order to a repetition of it. A friend,[14] however, volunteered, if I would issue a requisition, to go with the Agent and purchase the freedom of the three children, and it seemed probable, if the others could be brought back, that an arrangement might be made also with their claimants for the relinquishment of [their] claims on them. So I overcame my reluctance to adopt the theory of constructive escape and issued the requisition.

My agent, and the gentleman who had volunteered to accompany him, immediately [departed] on their mission and obtained a warrant of extradition from the Governor of Kentucky, who doubtless gladly embraced the opportunity of making a precedent of constructive escape, which he hoped [wo]uld be useful to claimants of slaves found in Ohio, but not actual fugitives from a Slave State.[15]

With the Warrant thus obtained the Agent proceeded to Louisville, but the slave-masters cont[rived] to evade him, and the slaves were sent South notwithstanding all efforts to recover them.

Subsequently, hearing that Margaret had been brought back to Covington, I wrote the Prosecuting Attorney to go over and demand her. He went and was told that she had been there but had been again sent South. It is doubted whether she was in fact ever brought there.

Nothing has been heard of the Garner family since. Perhaps the Rebellion has restored the Liberty of which the cause of the Rebellion caused the loss; and we may yet hear of these slaves as among those rejoicing in the new found freedom which God's Providence has given to so many.

J. T. Trowbridge Esq
Somerville, Mass

1. Although unsigned, this letterpress copy, which shows interlineations by Chase, appears to record his final intentions for the text of the letter. A draft in Chase's hand is among his papers at the Historical Society of Pennsylvania and may be seen at *micro* 32:0350.

2. Much of Chase's correspondence with Trowbridge during March concentrated on fugitive slave cases in which Chase had been involved. Chase sent all of his accounts of fugitive cases, including this one dated March 13 and another dated March 20 (below), to Trowbridge on March 21. Chase had discussed the Margaret Garner case in letters to Henry Ward Beecher, Horace Greeley, and William Dennison, December 26, 29, 31, 1863 (all above). Chase to Trowbridge, Mar. 21, 1864 (Chase Papers, Cinc. Hist. Soc.).

3. Chase's draft has *28th.*

4. Two boys, aged six and four, three-year-old Mary, and a nine-month-old girl. Coffin, *Reminiscences,* 562–63; Yanuck, "Garner Fugitive Slave Case," 50–52.

5. The home of Elijah Kite. Yanuck, "Garner Fugitive Slave Case," 51.

6. Chase's draft has *McLean.* He referred to John L. Pendery, the commissioner, and John McLean, associate justice of the U.S. Supreme Court.

7. The probate judge was John Burgoyne, who handed the writ to Deputy Sheriff E. Jefferson Buckingham. *Cinc. Dir. (1855),* 34; *Cinc. Dir. (1856),* 41; Yanuck, "Garner Fugitive Slave Case," 54.

8. Incumbent governor William Medill ran for the Democrats. The Know-Nothings (American party) nominated Allen Trimble, a former state legislator. *Appletons',* 4:285; Sobel and Raimo, *Biographical Directory,* 3:1196–97.

9. Chase's first inauguration as governor of Ohio occurred on January 14, 1856. Salmon P. Chase, *Inaugural Address of Salmon P. Chase, Governor of the State of Ohio . . .* (Columbus, 1856).

10. Hiram H. Robinson.

11. Edward Mills and George Hoadly, Jr. provided legal counsel to Sheriff Gazoway Brashears. Chase to William Dennison, Dec. 31, 1863 (above); Hoadly to Chase, Jan. 6, 1864 (Chase Papers, L.C.).

12. For example, Theodore Parker and Wendell Phillips. Chase to Henry Ward Beecher, Dec. 26, 1863 (above); Parker to Chase, July 17, 1856, in *Chase Papers,* 2:444–46.

13. Hamilton County's prosecuting attorney was Joseph Cox (b. 1822), who later became a judge on Ohio's First Judicial Circuit. According to Cox, the slaves "did not *flee*

from justice in this State but were *taken* out of the State by the overwhelming force of the United States Marshall and his posse." Cox to Chase, Feb. 29, 1856 (Chase Papers, L.C.); George Irving Reed, ed., *Bench and Bar of Ohio: A Compendium of History and Biography*, 2 vols. (Chicago, 1897), 1:135–39.

14. Edward Stowe Hamlin, at that time a Cincinnati attorney. *Bio. Dir. U.S. Cong.*, 1122; Hamlin to Chase, Mar. 11, 1856 (Chase Papers, L.C.).

15. The Ohio agent and the governor of Kentucky were Joseph Cooper and Charles S. Morehead, respectively.

TO JANET CHASE

Letterpress copy of autograph letter. Chase Papers, Historical Society of Pennsylvania (*micro* 32:0391).

Washington, March 15, 1864

My darling Nettie,

You must never be ashamed of any thing you do when you do your best.

If you don't begin to write French you will never learn; and you can write to no one with more assurance of being set right kindly than to Claire.[1] So don't fail to write if only a page & send your letter every week.

Your last letter to me is not quite so correct as your other letters have been of late. "Babarous" is not, and yet is—barbarous; & "conscious stricken" is not conscience stricken.

I am not in the habit of writing or expressing my opinions very freely: for on some points I am not certain they are correct and on others they differ so much from those most current, that I fear the expression of them may be ascribed to a wrong motive & to do harm rather than good.

But to you, my dear child, who, though in some respects a little too thoughtless & careless, are, in others, quite a woman in intelligence and judgment, I believe I will hereafter write more freely.

And, perhaps, I cannot interest you more than by telling you what I have just done about the Presidency and why I did it.

I have declined to be considered as a candidate for that office. A good many of the best and most earnest men of the country desired to make me a candidate; but I always felt that being so considered would greatly impair my usefulness as Secretary of the Treasury and subject me to attacks from the mere partizans of the President as a candidate for reelection against which I could not defend myself without neglect of duties more important to the country. There was so much dissent from this view and I was so unwilling to seem even to shrink from responsibilities which many insisted I ought to assume, that I allowed myself to be named. It was not long before my apprehensions were realized. The two Blairs assailed me indirectly & directly;[2] the most ungenerous influences were used to injure me; my relations with the

President were in danger of becoming unfriendly; and it was becoming daily more & more clear that the continuance of my name before the people would produce serious discords in the Union Organization and might endanger the success of the measures & the establishment of the principles I thought most indispensable to the welfare of the country.

While things were in this condition a majority of the Union Members of our Legislature declared Mr. Lincoln to be the first choice of Ohio and her soldiers.[3] I had already said that the wishes of our friends in Ohio would be controlling with me, and I gladly accepted this action of the Union Members as an indication of their wishes, & redeemed my promise by asking that no further consideration might be given to my name.

I expect Mr. Lincoln will be nominated for relection and I expect to support him as I did in 1860 & for the same reason that he is presented by the majority of those with whom I act as the representative of the views and principles which I believe sound & important.

There, darling, is a dish of politics. I have almost hated to write it; but shall be satisfied & pleased if I have gratified you.

Your affectionate father
S P CHASE

Miss Nettie Chase

1. Claire Albrecht.
2. Francis Blair, Jr., and Montgomery Blair.
3. Richard C. Parsons discussed the nomination, which the legislators made on February 26, in correspondence to Chase on March 2 (above).

TO GEORGE S. DENISON

Letter in clerk's hand on letterhead stationery, signed by Chase. George S. Denison Papers, Library of Congress (*micro* 32:0412).

Treasury Department.
March 16th, 1864.

My dear Sir,

I have received your letter and read it with great interest.[1] It was natural and almost inevitable that you should support Mr. Hahn for Governor, though I am not sure that I should have done so had I been in your place. Mr. Hahn never inspired confidence in me, nor as I think in the earnest friends of our cause here. He appeared to me to be a politician, not desiring to do wrong, but not bold in doing right. I advocated zealously his admission to a seat in Congress, but some of his earliest votes disappointed me.

Mr. Flanders, on the contrary, gained my confidence almost from our first interview. I never saw anything like duplicity, falsehood or trimming, about him. I feel as sure of his integrity as I do of yours. In regard to both my assurance is complete. I should therefore have preferred Mr. Flanders to Mr. Hahn.—

Another thing. I see that the supporters of Mr. Hahn pride themselves upon conservatism—upon that meanest of all conservatisms—which reproaches the friends of the oppressed as "Negro-heads" and "Negro-Equality Men." I never feared these epithets, though they have been constantly launched at me almost from the beginning of my political life, and I would not surrunder the principles which the epithets are intended to stigmatise for the Presidency or for a higher office, if there were one. You may easily infer that my sympathies would have been with the supporters of Mr. Flanders rather than with those of Mr. Hahn.

After all, however, I cannot tell what I should have done under the circumstances which actually existed at New Orleans. I approved heartily the design of General Banks to make Louisiana a free State in the shortest possible time,[2] and had I been in the place of the Free State leaders, I think I should have endeavored to co-operate with him in carrying out his purpose. I understand that General Banks did in fact endeavor to bring Mr. Durant and Mr. Flanders into co-operation with him, and only took the line of separate action when he found himself unable to induce them to join with him. Of course, he could not go back, and if they would not go with him, he was obliged to act with those who would.

I regret this failure of co-operation, because I cannot be sure what use will be made of the results which have thus far been obtained, and because I fear great mischiefs from divisions both in Louisiana and elsewhere.

You have doubtless seen my letter asking that no further use should be made of my name in connection with the Presidential canvas.[3] The determining consideration which induced me to write it was the action of the Union men of the Ohio Legislature;[4] but that action was itself the result of causes which had a wider operation.

They operated even in New Orleans, and I have no doubt that the political and military power there has been wielded with a view to the re-election of the President, while there has been hardly a word said in support of the Administration of my Department, the most difficult and certainly not the least successful. Within the last few days a Senator has told me that the President read to him a letter from General Banks, in which the latter assured the former that the election of Governor Hahn would promote the good of the country and "your *interest.*"[5]

It is of no consequence to me personally what delegates are sent from Louisiana to the Baltimore Convention.[6] I shall be glad if they are men who sympathize with the Unconditional Union men of Missouri, Kentucky, Virginia, Maryland and Delaware. The safety of the country requires such men.

I cannot believe that any coalition is formed between the friends of Mr. Flanders and the supporters of Mr. Fellows. If it exists it must soon show itself, and as you say it must "fail utterly." Since writing this sentence I have seen Mr. Hutchins who assured me that there is no ground for the statement.[7]

Nor can I believe that Mr. Flanders in what he has done was governed by mere aspiration for place. I learned from Col. Howe that General Banks would have acceded to the nomination of Mr. Flanders, if he would have co-operated in the General's plan. If this be so, Mr. Flanders might have reached the Gubernatorial chair very easily.— That he did not seek it in this way—that he accepted a nomination with the certainty of defeat from the first, may prove pertinacity and even obstinacy, but it does not prove ambition and self-love.

I say this in justice to Mr. Flanders. You are quite right in seeking to bring the Union men together. If Mr. Hahn redeems his pledges, and goes in earnest for a prompt establishment of a free State, unsullied by compromises in the form of negro apprenticeships or like devices for the continuance of servitude, there can be no ground for permanent divisions.[8]

Yours very Cordially,
S: P: CHASE

Geo: S. Denison, Esq.
New Orleans.

1. See Denison to Chase, March 5, 1864 (above).

2. As described in Thomas J. Durant to Chase, January 16, 1864 (above), and Banks to Lincoln, December 30, 1863, in Basler, *Collected Works,* 7:124–25.

3. Chase had addressed the letter to Ohio state senator James C. Hall on March 5. Chase to Hall, Mar. 5, 1864 (Chase Papers, Hist. Soc. of Pa.), also published in the *New York Times,* Mar. 11, 1864; Gilkey, *Ohio Hundred Year Book,* 175.

4. See Richard C. Parsons to Chase, March 2 (above), for a discussion of the nomination, which occurred on February 26.

5. Banks to Lincoln, Feb. 26, 1864 (Lincoln Papers, L.C.).

6. The national Union convention to be held in Baltimore in June.

7. This sentence is an insertion in Chase's handwriting.

8. For Michael Hahn's inaugural statements regarding slavery, see Denison's letter to Chase, March 5, 1864 (above).

TO JOHN T. TROWBRIDGE

Autograph draft. Chase Papers, Library of Congress (*micro* 32:0543).

Washington Mar 20, 1864

My dear Sir,

It is difficult for any one, now, to form a correct idea of the terror which possessed the minds of almost all men during the period which elapsed between the first outbreaks of violence against the abolitionists and the organization of a powerful party founded on opposition to

Slavery extension. It pervaded all classes & all professions. It colored legislative, administrative & judicial decisions. All who had any political aspirations through the favor of the two great parties,—& who had not save the few who dared to cling to the weaker side in the faith that it was the right side—felt that it was necessary to propitiate the ascendant Slave Power. Good men, fearing civil convulsion as the consequence of resistance submitted and endeavored to persuade themselves, that due respect for law required submission. Good men in Judicial seats made the law by construction what the Slave Power desired to have it, & persuaded themselves that prudent and due regard for the alleged intent of the Constitution and for the slaveholding claims under it warranted their construction. And sometimes confessions extorted by terror or wishes expressed under duress real or imagined, of poor creatures claimed as slaves were accepted as sufficient grounds of judicial action.

It was curious to see how much respect was paid to slavecatchers. During the trial of the Parish Case the coarse & vulgar agent of the slaveholder Driskell sat at the same table with Judge McLean, and was treated with distinguished consideration:[1] and in other cases, wherever the slaveholder or his agents appeared there were exhibitions of flunkeyism which it is impossible to give an idea of.

It was a remarkable illustration of the unwillingness of Judges to meet questions where the logic was on the side of the alleged fugitive but the consequences of decision in his favor would be fatal to slaveholding pretensions when the Supreme Court of Ohio directed the publication of my argument in support of the principle of universal freedom outside of states in which slavery was sustained by law & constitution, and yet avoided the assertion of the principle by their decision.[2] Illustrations equally remarkable may be found in repeated cases where Judges turned sharp corners to avoid decisions adverse to slaveholding interests and sometimes actually reversed their own previously declared opinions.

An instance not of this sort just mentioned, but illustrative of the general tendency was furnished by the action of a Judge in Cincinnati, whose estimable character forbids the idea that he departed [conscionably] from the line of judicial duty.[3]

In March 1855 just after the Rosetta case A man named Harle, calling himself the Rev. Mr. Harle arriving at Cincinnati on his way from Maysville in Kentucky to Missouri with two slaves named Emanuel & Alfred landed with the slaves at Cincinnati & took them, chained, across the landing to the down river boat.[4] They were later taken from his custody by the Writ of Habeas Corpus and brought before Judge Storer of the Superior Court. It was a clear case of an attempted transit through a free state by a slaveholder taking his slaves with him, & the question was could a slaveholder bring his slaves into the state for that purpose & retain his control over them as slaves within its jurisdiction. The case was fully argued by Mr. Walker & myself for the alleged slaves & by Mr. Chambers and another for the claimant.[5] I summed up the whole case thus: "The Constitution of Ohio says that in this state there shall be no slavery. Mr. Harle says there shall be slavery in Ohio. Which is law here the Constitution or the will of Mr. Harle?" The Judge reserved his decision. On the day before that fixed for its delivery the Judge with one the lawyers for the claimant—the counsel for the so called fugitives knowing nothing of the matter—went to the jail where the negroes were questioned by the counsel as to their wishes to go with Harle. They said they wanted to go. The Judge then returned to the Court Room & directed them to be brought in. He then questioned them again and they again professed a wish to go with Harle. He then made an order permitting them to go, and a Sheriff deputy attended them to the river to prevent any attempts to compel them to remain! There was, of course, no decision in the case. Had the decision been made & had the negroes after the discharge to which they were believed to be entitled chosen to go with Mr. Harle there would have been nothing to complain of. I think there would have been a [decision] & an opportunity of free election had not the proslavery sentiment been still very strong, and the idea of duty to masters rather than to men been so widely diffused & deftly planted in the public mind by the judicial decisions already made.

Even after the organization of the Republican Party, which followed the great popular movement excited by the repeal of the Missouri Prohibition and, in Ohio, placed me in the Governor's Chair,[6] the proslavery feeling, which now began to take the softer name of conservatism, exerted even within its ranks, an exceedingly powerful influence. It led to the selection, in [force] the largest number, of extremely moderate men as candidates of the Party. It was this spirit which prompted the qualified language of Mr. Lincoln's inaugural on the subject of slavery and led him to pronounce distinctly in favor of the execution of the Fugitive Slave Act;[7] and gave occasion to the discreditable transactions in its execution which took place at several places, particularly at Cleveland & Chicago.[8] It has not even yet altogether lost its control; though the progress of opinion, through the war, has been such that, unless some fatal compromise shall take place, it can never resume its old sway over the minds of men.

Yours very truly
S P Chase

J. T. Trowbridge Esq

1. In 1847, Kentucky slaveholder Peter Driskell had brought suit in Ohio, under the Federal fugitive slave law of 1793, against Francis Drake Parish of Sandusky, one of

Chase's clients, for allegedly helping a runaway slave. Driskell's agent was "Col. Mitchell." *Chase Papers,* 1:181; *Weekly Ohio State Journal,* July 28, 1847.

2. Chase's comments apparently refer to the argument he delivered on appeal in 1837 in defense of antislavery spokesman James G. Birney, accused of harboring the alleged runaway Matilda in violation of the Federal fugitive slave statute. *Birney v. Ohio,* 8 Ohio 230 (1837); John Niven, *Salmon P. Chase: A Biography* (New York, 1995), 57.

3. Bellamy Storer, a former Whig congressman and judge of Cincinnati's Superior Court, 1854–72. Robson, *Biographical Encyclopædia,* 451.

4. Earlier in 1855, Chase had unsuccessfully defended sixteen-year-old Rosetta Armstead, an escaped slave from Kentucky, from being forced back into servitude under the fugitive slave act of 1850. According to one contemporary newspaper, Baldwin Harle (or "Haurl," by one account) of Missouri had recently purchased Emanuel Points and Alfred Raney from Vincent Tabb, a resident of Dover, Ky. *Chase Papers,* 1:244; *Cincinnati Commercial,* Mar. 17, 1855; *National Era,* Mar. 29, 1855.

5. Joining Chase was his former law partner, Timothy Walker, previously judge of Hamilton County's Court of Common Pleas. Cincinnati attorneys Francis T. Chambers and Algernon Sydney Sullivan represented Harle. *Appletons',* 5:740; *Cincinnati Commercial,* Mar. 17, 19, 1855; *Cinc. Dir. (1855),* 43; *DAB,* 19:363.

6. The Kansas-Nebraska act, approved on May 30, 1854, explicitly repealed the Missouri Compromise, which forbade the establishment of new slave states north of latitude 36° 30'. The following fall, a storm of protest swept Chase and other antislavery politicians into office throughout the North. Stephen E. Maizlish, *The Triumph of Sectionalism: The Transformation of Ohio Politics, 1844–1856* (Kent, Ohio, 1983), 199–203; Roseboom, *Civil War Era,* 281–86; *Statutes at Large,* 10:277–90.

7. Lincoln's first inaugural, delivered on March 4, 1861, repeated a campaign promise not "to interfere with the institution of slavery in the States where it exists" and endorsed the legitimacy of the fugitive slave act of 1850. *Daily National Intelligencer,* Mar. 5, 1861.

8. The Cleveland incident was apparently the Oberlin-Wellington rescue case, in which a U.S. district court in April 1859 convicted two antislavery activists under the fugitive slave act for helping runaway slaves to escape from Federal officials. Roseboom, *Civil War Era,* 346.

TO JOHN T. TROWBRIDGE

Letter on letterhead stationery, in Chase's and clerks' hands, signed by Chase. Chase Papers, Historical Society of Pennsylvania (*micro* 32:0548).

Treasury Department.
March 21st, 1864.

Dear Sir,[1]

The New York Convention, which was in Session at the same time,[2] adopted resolutions in favor of the exclusion of slavery from the territories, and nominated Mr. Van Buren for President and Gen. Dodge of Wisconsin for Vice President. A resolution was also adopted authorizing the delegates of the New York Democracy to the Convention at Baltimore to attend and take part in any Convention of the Free States which might be called for the purpose of collecting and concentrating the popular will in relation to the Presidency.[3]

When the Convention of the 9th of August met, the New York delegates under this resolution took their seats as members.[4] The attendance was very large. Eighteen States were represented by 465 delegates, and there was moreover an immense mass Convention, numbered by tens of thousands. Gen. Dodge had declined, or rather rejected the nomination for the Vice Presidency tendered him by the New York Convention, and Mr. Van Buren had not accepted the nomination for the Presidency. The whole subject of national nominations was therefore considered as open, Mr. Hale having placed his name at the disposal of the Convention.[5] It was the pleasure of the Ohio delegation that I should take a very active part in the proceedings of both of the Mass Convention & the Convention of Delegates. At an informal meeting which preceded the organization of the former there were indications of a division as to platform. Knowing Mr. Preston King's sentiments, I took the liberty of calling upon him for a speech, and at its conclusion moved that he be requested to reduce its leading propositions to writing and that his speech should be considered as the platform recommended by the meeting. This notion seemed to allay all jealousies on the part of the New York Democrats, and was unanimously agreed to. The next day the mass convention assembled, and Mr. King reported resolutions embodying the propositions of his speech. They declared, (1st) That it was the duty of the Federal Government to relieve itself of all responsibility for the extension or continuance of slavery wherever it had constitutional authority to do so, and was responsible for its existence; (2d) that it had neither responsibility nor constitutional authority to interfere with slavery within the States; and (3d) that it had authority and should promptly exercise it to prevent the extension of slavery into free territory, and to prohibit its existence in such territory by an Act of Congress. These resolutions were received with universal approbation. Mr. Adams presided over the mass Convention.[6] A Committee on Resolutions was appointed, consisting of three persons from each State represented. I was one of the members of this Committee from Ohio, and the resolutions reported were almost entirely drafted by me. They were, however, very carefully considered by the Committee, and very fully discussed before they received its sanction. The resolution on the tariff was adopted at the instance of Mr. White of New York.[7]—

The delegate Convention for the nomination of candidates for the Presidency and Vice Presidency met in the Church near the Square on which the mass convention was assembled.[8] I had the honor to preside over this Convention. To ascertain the views of members in respect to the Presidency an informal ballot was taken, the result of which showed a clear majority for Mr. Van Buren over all others.— Mr. Hale received nearly the whole vote not given to Mr. Van Buren. After the preference of the Convention had been thus shown, Mr. Leavitt of Massachusetts moved the unanimous nomination of Mr. Van Buren, and was earnestly seconded by Mr. Lewis of Ohio.[9] As these two gentlemen had been the most active & able as well as the most zealous friends of Mr. Hale, the motion was adopted without hesitation and by acclamation. Mr. Adams was nominated, also by acclamation, for Vice President. The nominations thus made were announced by me as President of the Convention of delegates to the mass convention and were received with the most enthusiastic demonstrations.

Thus ended the work of this great convention, to the assembling and acting of which is attributed, and I think justly, the passage of the bill organizing the territory of Oregon with the prohibition of slavery, which was then pending in the Senate of the United States.[10]—

In the canvas which followed I took a very active part, but confined my labors almost wholly to Ohio. The election showed both the power of party and the power of principles. Except in Ohio & Massachusetts the Whig party almost everywhere supported the nominees of the Philadelphia Convention,[11] and except in New York, the Democratic party almost everywhere supported the nominations of the Baltimore Convention. In New York, the recognized organization of the democratic party was in the hands of the friends of Mr. Van Buren. His vote, therefore, in that State was very large. In Massachusetts and in the northern counties of Ohio, the profound Anti-Slavery convictions of the people made it impossible for them to support national nominees without any declaration against the extension of slavery. Mr. Van Buren received in all 291.678 votes out of 2.882.121, the whole number given.— Of these votes 120.000 were given in New York, 38.133 in Massachusetts, and 35.494 in Ohio. General Taylor was elected.

Immediately after the election, the Northern Democracy which had supported General Cass, claiming that under the doctrines maintained by him, slavery, though not prohibited by law, could find no ingress into the territories, passed by an easy transition into the profession of the doctrines entertained by the Independent Democracy which had supported Mr. Van Buren. Everywhere indications became visible of a disposition to unite upon the platform of slavery prohibition. Resolutions were adopted in many of the States both by the Old Line and Independent Democrats, uniting the two organizations, and in others where actual union did not take place, there was more or less concert of action. In Ohio I was elected to the Senate by the united votes of the Old Line and Independent Democrats, and took my seat in that body in March 1849. I was not, however, satisfied that the union between the two organizations could be perfect or permanent until in a National Convention, the Old Line Democracy of the Free States should either succeed in obtaining the adoption of a national platform, declaring the Party independent of slave-holding dictation, or by breaking the bond of adhesion to the slave interest by open separation

I therefore declined to go into the Democratic Caucus of the Senate, or commit myself to the organization otherwise than by supporting its candidates in Ohio so long as the party in that State should maintain an anti-slavery position. The event justified my apprehensions.— It soon became evident that the leaders of the Democratic party were not prepared to surrender the supposed advantages of their slave-holding alliance. In 1850 the Compromise Measures, including the Fugitive Slave Act, were supported by almost the entire party in Congress, though opposed by a majority of the Ohio representatives. They were almost universally denounced by the Democratic press in Ohio, and for a time it seemed possible that they might be repudiated by the Northern Democracy.

When the Convention met at Baltimore, however, it soon became apparent that no such hope was to be realized. Resolutions were adopted approving the Compromise measures, and denouncing all agitation of the Slavery question, by which was understood all resistance to the pretensions of slave holders. Gen. Pierce was nominated for President, and, Mr. King of Alabama for Vice President. The Whig Convention nominated General Scott for President, and Mr. Graham of North Carolina for Vice President.[12] Its platform was almost identical in spirit and substance with that of the Democratic Convention. After these nominations and declarations I did not hesitate what course to take. I addressed at once a letter to Mr. Butler of New York, declaring my own determination to adhere to the principles announced at Buffalo, and to act with the only party faithful to them, that is to say, with the Independent Democracy which had maintained its organization, and had called a Convention to meet at Pittsburgh.[13] I earnestly urged him and the Democrats who had acted with him at Buffalo, to maintain the ground they had then taken.

I shall ever lament that this appeal was not heeded. The party of freedom had given, while unorganized in 1840, one vote in every 350 of all the votes cast in the United States, for its candidates. (1)[14] In 1844 it had given one vote in 44, and in 1848 it had given one vote in 10, and almost one in 9. This, it must be remembered, was the proportion in the free States of the whole vote of the United States. The proportion in the free States considered by themselves must, of course, have been much larger. It cannot be doubted, I think, that had the New York Democracy adhered to the principles avowed in 1848, and refused to support the Baltimore nominations upon a platform repugnant to the sentiments and convictions of a large majority of the Northern people, a vote would have been given for the nominees of the Independent Democracy which, if not sufficient to elect its candidates, would have ensured the election of General Scott, and consequently the union of nearly the whole Democratic Party, in the course of the following year, upon the principles of the Independent Democracy. The Democracy of the Union, united upon these principles, would have been invincible, and slavery, excluded from the National territories, would have been ameliorated, diminished, and finally abolished in the States by State action. The rebellion, in all probability, would have been avoided and the Union would have been preserved unbroken, and preserved not for Slavery, but for freedom. I took great pains to explain these views to many, and a good deal of apprehension was manifested by certain Slave State Senators lest they should be adopted.

The New York Democrats, however, saw the matter otherwise than I. They went over almost unanimously to the support of Mr. Pierce, who was of course elected. Their defection and that of those influenced by their example in other States, reduced the vote of the Independent Democracy from 291.678 in 1848 to 157.296 in 1852. The whole number given was 157296, and the Independent Democratic vote was one in 20. Near three fourths of the whole defection was in New York.

The agreement of the two old parties upon substantially one platform, and the election of General Pierce, devolved upon the Democratic party the whole responsibility of that platform. The reorganization of parties became inevitable, and as the platform of the Independent Democracy alone represented antagonism to the Compromise Democracy, it was also evident that the principles of that party must form a basis of opposition to the Administration; which must inevitably be driven into new concessions to the slave power.

It was not long before this logic of events exhibited its natural consequence in the introduction of the Nebraska Bill into the Senate, with its clause repealing the Missouri prohibition. At first there was great uncertainty among Whig Senators and Representatives as to the course which ought to be pursued. The entire body of Southern Whigs in Congress went over to the Administration upon this question, and very few Democrats either North or South ventured to oppose the repeal of the prohibition. A few of the Independent Democrats conferred together, and resolved to draw up an appeal to the people, to be signed by all those opposed to the repeal. An appeal was accordingly drawn up by me,—the same which was afterwards printed and widely circulated,—but it was found impossible to procure the signatures desired. Almost all seemed to dread committing themselves against slavery. It was then proposed to issue the appeal with the signatures of the Ohio Senators and Representatives alone.[15] Some were ready to sign it, but others were unwilling. So, finding unanimity even in Ohio unattainable, the paper was signed by the Independent Democratic Senators and Representatives alone, and sent forth as their appeal to the people against the meditated wrong.[16] It was copied everywhere and read everywhere. The people, always in advance of the politicians upon questions of principle, took the alarm, and their potential voice was heard in Congress. The doubting were decided, and the timid took courage. The alliance of the Administration Senators and Representatives with the whole body of the Southern Whigs, secured, it is true, the passage of the bill; but the Senators and Representatives who voted against it, represented a majority of the people of the free States. It was no longer doubtful upon what ground the reorganization of parties would take place. It must necessarily find its only bond of union in opposition to the extension of Slavery.

A vain attempt was made to turn the current of public sentiment into other channels by the organization of the American or "Know Nothing" party; but its first National Convention was broken up by a division upon the slavery question, and the party, after a brief existence, disappeared from political contests.[17]

While the American party was yet powerful, I, though not a member of the organization was nominated for Governor of Ohio by an Anti-Nebraska Convention in which the Americans, so called, had a decided majority.[18] Opposition to slavery, however, was so much stronger in their hearts than zeal for the principles of the organization, that my nomination was carried by a vote of nearly two to one. The canvas which followed was unusually sharp. A considerable number of Whigs, retaining the animosities excited by my election to the Senate, refused their support, and joined in strenuous efforts to defeat me by withdrawing enough votes from the Anti-Nebraska force to secure the election of the Administration candidate. Their efforts were unsuccessful and I was elected. I at once addressed myself to the duties of my new position. I sought to promote all practicable reforms; encouraged by all the means in my power the interests of education; endeavored to reorganize the military system of the State; and omitted no opportunity of making the voice of Ohio heard on the side of freedom and justice.[19] At the same time, I endeavored as far as practicable to conciliate opposition founded in misapprehension, and succeeded finally in organizing a compact and powerful party based on the great principles of freedom and free labor.—

One of my most trying duties arose from the misconduct of the State Treasurer. He succeeded a brother-in-law who had misapplied nearly half a million of dollars belonging to the State.[20] The defalcation was concealed from me and from all the State officers almost a year and a half. The Treasurer had accomplished this by representing the money as having been actually received from his predecessor and as being actually in the Treasury, and by deceiving the Legislative Committees and the officers of the State who examined its condition. At length finding it impossible to procure sufficient funds to pay the July interest of 1857, he disclosed the existence of the defalcation to the State Auditor,[21] who communicated the fact to me. I at once called upon the Treasurer and after some conversation insisted upon his resignation. He denied my authority to require it. I admitted I had no such authority, but said to him that as he had represented the money which had been abstracted as being actually in the Treasury and as he now admitted it was not there, he was by his own showing a defaulter, and I could not assume his explanation of the defalcation to be true until established by proof. I went on to say that the Constitution authorized the Governor to fill any State office made vacant by disability, and that I should take the responsibility if he did not resign, of assuming a defalcation and instituting a prosecution against him as the author of it, the first step in which would be his arrest; and of considering his arrest as creating a disability; and thereupon of appointing his successor. He then asked time to consider and to confer with his legal advisers, to which I readily assented and appointed two o'clock as the hour at which I would call and learn his decision. I left and called again at the hour agreed upon. He at once handed me his resignation and his successor was appointed, gave bond and entered upon his office the same afternoon.[22]

Few things have ever given me greater pain than the necessity of this action. The Treasurer was a generous, open hearted man, of fine talents, and greatly beloved by his friends, among whom there were few who cherished for him a warmer regard than I did myself. Excepting this transaction I do not know that his fidelity to any trust was ever questioned. He has since served the country faithfully at the head of an Ohio regiment in the field.[23] Duty required the action which I took. It was necessary to protect the interests of the State, and to defend the party which had entrusted to me the executive power of the State from virtual responsibility for the defalcation. The credit of the State was saved, and means were promptly provided for the payment of the July interest.

Against my wishes I was soon after renominated for Governor by acclamation.[24] The election of Mr. Buchanan in the preceding year, the lassitude and depression which usually follows ill success in a Presidential canvas and above all the defalcation, which the opponents of the State Administration did not hesitate to charge upon me, made the canvas for reelection peculiarly disagreeable and difficult. I was obliged to go thro' the whole State and explain the facts to the people everywhere.— There was no Congressional election to awaken an interest in national topics and secure the aid of candidates for Congress pleading their own cause before their constituencies. Notwithstanding all disadvantages, however, I was reelected though by a small majority, and remained in office two years longer, pursuing the same general course as hitherto.

In the last year of my second term, John Brown's famous raid upon Harper's Ferry occurred,[25] and reports were spread through Virginia that large bodies of men were being organized in Ohio with a view to rescue him from his Virginia captors. Governor Wise addressed a letter remonstrating against these organizations and threatening to pursue any invaders of Virginia into the State of Ohio. I replied in substance that his apprehensions of military organizations in Ohio were unfounded, and that I trusted he would not undertake to follow into Ohio any alleged offenders against Virginia, for the legislation of Ohio was adequate to the fulfilment of all her duties to her sister states and the Executive of Ohio was bound to repel any aggression upon her soil.[26]

At the close of my term, Governor Dennison succeeded me, and I was soon after elected to the Senate for the second time. The Presidential election followed in the same year. The Republicans of Ohio honored me by a declaration of their preference in the State Convention, which was held to appoint delegates at large to the nominating Convention.[27] The Ohio Convention however did not nominate, as did many other State Conventions, the district delegates, but left the selection of these to district Conventions. This gave an opportunity to the partisans of other candidates to foment divisions, and secure the selection in several districts of delegates unfriendly to me. The result was the division of the Ohio delegates in the nominating Convention[28] and the destruction of their influence.— Without its united support there was not much ground for expecting much support from other delegations in which I had numerous friends ready to unite with the Ohio delegation had that delegation been itself united. Notwithstanding these disadvantages, my support was respectable, though not sufficient to warrant any expectation of success. Mr. Lincoln was nominated, and I gave him my cordial support.

After his election he invited me to Springfield to confer with me as to the selection of his cabinet.[29] He said that he had felt bound to offer the position of Secretary of State to Mr. Seward as the generally recognized leader of the Republican party, intending if he should decline it to offer it to me. He did not wish that Mr. Seward should decline it, and was glad that he had accepted, and now desired to have me take the place of Secretary of the Treasury. He had feared there might be some objections to this in Pennsylvania, but had been assured none would be urged.— I replied that I did not wish and was not prepared to say that I would accept that place if offered. A good deal of conversation followed in reference to other possible members of the Cabinet, but everything was left open when we parted, and I returned to Columbus.

Shortly after this, in December, South Carolina seceded, and everything indicated great irresolution and timidity on the part of the Administration. I wrote a very earnest letter to General Scott, entreating him as head of the Army to take the necessary measures to secure the public safety and rely upon the Country for its sanction and support. The General replied very kindly, but did not evince a disposition to assume the responsibility of the crisis.[30] In February, Virginia invited a conference of the States at Washington, and appointed Commissioners on her part.[31] This conference doubtless was intended as a means of extorting new concessions to the Slave interest from Congress. To prevent injurious results it seemed necessary that there should be a general representation from all the States—from free as well as from the Slave States which had not become involved in secession. I was one of the Commissioners selected by the Governor to represent Ohio.[32] Unfortunately I was the only one who was prepared to resist the purchase of peace by undue concessions. I was quite willing to give to the Slave States the strongest assurances that no aggressions upon their rights or real interests were meditated, but I was not at all willing to disguise from them the fact that the further extension of slavery could not be allowed.— The death of Judge Wright and the appointment of Mr. Wolcott in his place gave me one resolute and like-minded associate in the Commission, but we were a minority.[33] The vote of Ohio in the Conference was steadily on the side of submission. The Commissioners whose general views agreed with mine, finally determined to propose to refer all matters of difference to a National Convention, and in the meantime to arrest the progress of disunion by assurance that no invasion of State rights over the subject of slavery or over any other subject, was meditated or would be attempted. In support of this proposition, I addressed the Conference with great earnestness and with great plainness. I warned them of the consequences which must follow secession, and implored them not to reject the only proposition which in my judgment was likely to save the Country from a Civil War. The proposition was nevertheless rejected; and the vote of Ohio was cast for its rejection.[34] Instead of it, a proposed amendment to the Constitution, making large concessions to the slave interest, was forced through the Convention in disregard of its rules and submitted to Congress. There, as I had predicted, it received little favor.[35] I am not certain that anything which the Conference could have done would have saved the country from the insurrection which has since assumed such fearful proportions of civil war. It is only certain that nothing which was done had the slightest salutary effect upon the disastrous course of events. The Convention was an abortion.

Before its adjournment the President arrived in Washington, having come through Baltimore in the night and in disguise.[36] It was said that this was necessary to defeat a plot for his assassination. I cannot think it was necessary. At any rate, it seemed to me that the President elect should not have entered otherwise than openly and by daylight. Meantime Congress was full of schemes for pacificication; all of them involving more or less an abandonment of the principles which had been deliberately proclaimed by the Republicans in relation to slavery. Threats were openly made that unless such abandonment should be conceded, there should be no inauguration. To these menaces, I, for one, replied, "Inauguration first, adjustment afterwards," and these words were caught up and repeated by loyal newspapers as a popular motto. They were not perhaps without their influence.

Notwithstanding these menaces the inauguration took place without disturbance and in the presence of a vast multitude.— The President, without any conference with me on the subject, sent in my name to the Senate as Secretary of the Treasury. I had already taken my seat as a Senator, but did not happen to be in the chamber when the nomination was sent in, and knew nothing of it until a few minutes afterwards when, returning to my place, I was informed that it had been unanimously confirmed as soon as made.[37] I went at once to the President and expressed my disinclination to accept the position. After some conversation, in the course of which he referred to the embarrassments which my declination would occasion him, I said I would give the matter some further consideration, and advise him the next day of my conclusion. Some rumor of my hesitation got abroad, and I was immediately pressed by most urgent remonstrances against any declination on my part. I finally yielded to this, and surrendered a position every way more desirable, to take charge of the disordered finances of the country under circumstances most unpropitious and forbidding.[38]

Immediately after the organization of the Cabinet, the question of what should be the policy of the Government in respect to the seceded States demanded the most serious attention. Anderson with his little Company of soldiers was holding Fort Sumter,[39] and the first question was, Shall he be relieved? General Scott declared that complete relief was impracticable with a less force than twenty thousand men.[40] He thought, however, that the Fort might be defended for several months if reinforced and provisioned. But that reinforcements and provisioning were impracticable as the fire of the enemy's batteries would be concentrated upon any vessel which might make the attempt, both while entering the harbor, and especially when endeavoring to land men and cargos at the Fort. The President finally determined to make the attempt to send provisions to the garrison.

Information that the attempt would be made was transmitted to the Governor of South Carolina and its receipt was promptly followed by an order from the rebel authorities to reduce the Fort.[41] How this was accomplished is historical, and it is also historical how the country was aroused by the rebel guns which opened on the Fort. The call for seventy-five thousand men immediately followed.[42] It soon became evident that nothing beyond the mere defence of Washington was to be accomplished by this force.

I took the liberty of urging upon General Scott to occupy Manassas and compel the rebels to evacuate Harper's Ferry and the Valley of the

Shenandoah. It has since become evident that this might have been then done, and it is even probable that a vigorous use of the force then at the disposal of the Government might have driven the rebels from Richmond. The action proposed, however, was thought to involve too much risk. The rebels were suffered for weeks to occupy Alexandria with an insignificant force, to excite insurrection in Baltimore, and to destroy the national property at Norfolk, except that which was destroyed under orders by ourselves.[43] At last, after long delays, Baltimore was recovered, Alexandria was occupied by National troops, and the rebels were driven from Harpers Ferry. Meanwhile it had become evident that the Seventy-five thousand men originally called for would not be sufficient. To replace them I took the liberty to propose to call for sixty-five thousand volunteers. This proposition, after having been modified so as to include an increase of the regular army was sanctioned by the President, who, with the consent of the Secretary of War, directed me to prepare the necessary orders. I invited to my assistance Col. Thomas, Major McDowell, and Capt. Franklin; and after a good deal of consideration the Orders since known as Nos. Fifteen and Sixteen were framed, the one for the enlistment of volunteers and the other for regular regiments.[44]

Major McDowell contributed the largest amount of information & suggestion; while the two other officers were by no means wanting in both. It was my part to decide between different opinions & to put the whole in form.

The object I had in view in all this was—as there was no law authorizing the raising of the force required—to prepare a regular system & plan in conformity with which all new enlistments should be made, clear & intelligible in itself, and capable of being laid before Congress when convened in a form which would be likely to receive its sanction. The orders were promulgated in May.

There were wide departures from this plan however. Great irregularities prevailed. Regiments were raised under verbal authorities from the President & the Secretary of War & under written Memoranda of which no record was preserved. So that the Orders failed to secure the principal objects I had in view, beyond the simple provision of force—order & system, & so efficiency & accountability.

During this time great efforts were made in Kentucky & in Missouri to precipitate those states into rebellion; and I was called on to take a very considerable part in the measures adopted to prevent their success. The President & Secretary of War indeed committed to me for a time the principal charge of whatever related to Kentucky & Tennessee & I was very active also in promoting the measures deemed necessary for the safety of Missouri. When Rousseau, then a Union Senator in the Kentucky Legislature from Louisville, came to Washington to seek means of raising men for the defence of the Union, I took his matters in charge; obtained for him a Colonel's Commission and an order which I drew myself authorizing him to raise twenty companies.[45] I was also charged with the care of Nelson's work; drew most of the orders under which he acted; & provided the necessary means to meet expences.[46] So also I was called on to frame the orders under which Andrew Johnson was authorized to raise regiments in Tennessee.[47] These duties brought me into intimate relations with these officers: particularly with the first two. They were worthy of the confidence reposed in them by the President. I doubt if more valuable work has been done with so much activity, economy & practical benefit in raising & using men, by almost any others. Nelson's movement into the interior of Kentucky, & establishment of Camp Dick Robinson was, especially, most opportune.[48] I think that this movement saved Kentucky from secession. I am quite sure that without the organization of Nelson & Rousseau she would not have been saved from that Calamity.

General Cameron, while Secretary of War, conferred much with me. I never undertook to do any thing in his Department except when asked to give my help & then I gave it willingly. In addition to western border-state matters the principal subjects of conference were slavery & the employment of colored troops. We agreed very early that the necessity of arming them was inevitable; but we were alone in that opinion. At least no member of the Administration gave it open support, while the President & Mr. Blair[49] at least were decidedly averse to it. The question of the employment of the colored people who might refuge within our lines soon became one of practical urgency. Gen Butler wrote from Fortress Monroe in May 1861 asking what disposition should be made of such persons.[50] The Secretary conferred with me & I submitted my suggestions to him in the form of a letter which he adopted with slight modifications. Gen Butler again wrote in July, and being again consulted & again submitted suggestions which were adopted. In the first of these letters of Gen. Cameron Gen. Butler was directed to refrain from surrendering alleged fugitives from service to alleged masters. In the second he was directed to employ them under such organizations & in such occupations as circumstances might suggest or require.

I have thus far said nothing of my financial labors, preferring to reserve what little account I can give of them till the last.

The Treasury when I took charge of it was almost literally empty. The receipts were very small, and most of what did come in was in Treasury notes. I therefore addressed myself at once to the negotiation of a loan.

Having conferred with my predecessor General Dix and other gentlemen whose judgments I relied on, I issued proposals for my first loan on the 22d. of March 1861.[51] The Amount offered was $8.000.000, the right of rejecting bids regarded as disadvantageous being reserved to the Government. The bonds to be issued were six per cents redeemable after twenty years; and not doubting that they were worth intrinsically more than par I was not willing to acknowledge that the credit of the Nation was so impaired that the Secretary of the Treasury obliged to make a loan, was obliged, also, to take whatever brokers & capitalists might see fit to offer for bonds.

The bids were opened on the 2d. of April; and amounted to $27,182,000, at rates varying from 85 for 100 to par. There was only one bid so low as 85 & only one so high as 100. The last previous loan had been negotiated by my predecessor on the 23d. of February 1861 at rates varying from 90.15 to 96.10; while previous loans had been negotiated at rates still more disadvantageous.[52] It seemed a fit occasion now to give bidders to understand that bonds of the United States were not to be put into the market for the best price that could be got, & without reserve. I therefore rejected all bids below 94. There was some dissatisfaction among disappointed bidders at lower rates; but the effect of the decision was certainly useful to the country.

I continued to borrow money under existing laws. On the 11th April just before Sumter I borrowed 4.901.000 on two years Treasury Notes at a small premium: and on the 25th of May, I borrowed, on twenty years bonds, $7,310,000 at from 85 to 93, declining all bids below 85; and, on two years Treasury Notes, $1,684,000 at par.

These loans, considering the condition of the country at the time were remarkable successes. The average rate of discount on the bonds sold below par was less than six per cent, while the average rate of all loans, under par, previously made in times of war, was over twelve & a half percent.

I was indebted for my success in great part, to the confidence and support, most generously given me, of a number of distinguished citizens having large influence in financial circles, and I endeavored to merit what they gave by frankness, fairness and firmness.

Congress assembled on the 4th. of July 1861 and soon afterwards passed an act to authorize a National Loan and for other purposes. Under this act, and acts amending it, I took measures to secure the funds necessary to carry on the war.[53]

With this object I invited representatives from the Banking Institutions of New York, Boston and Philadelphia to meet me in New York, and they promptly responded to my invitation.[54]

Our conferences were full and unreserved. I explained to them the situation of the country: the large inevitable expenditure for the suppression of the rebellion: my hopes of vigorous prosecution of all measures necessary to that great end: my wishes for economy; my views of the inexpediency of high rates of interest which might suggest a possibility of future inability to pay it. They, on their side, explained the position of the Banks; their disposition to sustain the Government; and their inability to take more bonds than their disposable capital allowed without a prospect of an early sale and distribution. They thought my ideas as to interest rather too stringent; and on some other points they thought me rather illiberal—not sufficiently considerate perhaps of the interests they represented. I was obliged to be very firm and to say, "Gentlemen, I am sure you wish to do all you can, & I hope you will find that you can take the loans required on terms which can be admitted. If not, I must go back to Washington and issue notes for circulation; for, gentlemen, the war must go on until this rebellion is put down, if we have to put out paper until it takes a thousand dollars to buy a breakfast."

The result of the conference was an agreement by the Banks of the three cities to unite as associates, and advance to the Government fifty millions of dollars, at once or as wanted, on the Secretary's drafts in favor of the Assistant Treasurers;[55] in consideration of which, I on my part agreed to appeal to the People for subscriptions to a National Loan, on Three years notes bearing 7–30 per cent interest, and convertible into Twenty years Bonds bearing six per cent. and to pay over the proceeds of these subscriptions to the Banks in satisfaction of their advances so far as they would go and to deliver to them 7–30 Notes for any deficiency.[56]

This agreement was faithfully fulfilled. I opened books of subscription to the National Loan in all parts of the loyal States and the people responded with alacrity. About forty five millions were thus subscribed and paid to the Banks and the remainder was made good by the delivery of the promised Seven Thirties.

This operation enabled the Banks to make a second advance of fifty millions on nearly the same terms. It had become evident that the popular subscription would not continue as large and prompt as at first, and the inconveniences of its management by the Department had proved to be very great. The accounts of the Subscription Agents were therefore closed, and the notes for the second loan were delivered directly to the Bankers who distributed them as best suited themselves. This simplified the transaction to the Treasury; and the arrangement, though not quite so advantageous to the Banks, as the first, was, every way, more convenient.

By these two loans I obtained one hundred millions of dollars, paying under the immediate exigency a rate of interest only one and three tenths per cent higher than the ordinary rate of six per cent and that only for three years. The sums needed beyond the amounts thus obtained were supplied by the negotiation of notes at two years and sixty days and by issuing United States Notes as circulation.

The Banks declined to make another loan of fifty millions for 7–30 Notes and I was obliged by the absolute necessity of providing means for military and naval disbursement, to offer another description of securities. The Act authorizing a National Loan provided for the disposal of six per cent bonds with such deduction from their face value, as would make them equivalent to seven per cent. bonds redeemable after twenty years, disposed of at par. I was extremely reluctant to avail myself of this power, but the emergency was great, and there was no other resource, and I submitted. Fifty millions in six per cent. bonds were equal to $45.795.478.48 in seven per cent. bonds redeemable after twenty years; and accordingly I gave the Banks fifty millions in six per cent bonds for $45.795.478.48 in coin.

The Banks had constantly urged me to forego the further issue of United States Notes, and draw directly upon them for the sums subscribed, and placed on their books to the credit of the Government. "In what funds will my drafts be paid?" I asked. "We in New York are entirely willing to pay in coin," was the reply. "But how will it be in Boston? how in Philadelphia? How, if you in New York give the draft holder a check on Cincinnati or St. Louis, will the check be paid?" "In whatever funds the holder of the draft or check is willing to receive." "That is to say," I answered, "in coin, if the holder insists on coin, and the bank is able and willing to pay; but in Bank Notes if he will consent to receive Bank Notes. I cannot agree to this, gentlemen. You ask me to borrow the credit of local banks in the form of circulation. I prefer to put the credit of the people into notes and use them as money. If you can lend me all the coin required or show me where I can borrow it elsewhere at fair rates, I will withdraw every note already issued, and pledge myself never to issue another; but if you cannot, you must let me stick to United States Notes, and increase the issue of them just as far as the deficiency of coin may require." This resolution, seen to be unalterable, was followed by important consequences.

The negotiation of the Seven per cent. loan (for such it really was), took place on the 16th of November.[57] The bankers could not pay their subscription in coin unless unless they could find a market for their bonds, and prices declined instead of advancing. It soon became plain that the bank note circulation could not be sustained at the par of coin, unless made receivable by the Government, and that it could not be made so receivable without risk of serious and perhaps irretrievable financial embarrassment and disorder. In other words it became plain that a general bank suspension was inevitable except by sacrifices which the banks would not make. The banks of New York suspended on the 30th December 1861, and their example was followed throughout the country. This suspension made it certain that the Government could no longer obtain coin on loans in any adequate amounts: some of the banks indeed which had subscribed to the seven per cent. loan declined to pay their subscriptions in coin, and even asked to be relieved from payment in notes of the United States. Under these circumstances I had no choice but to suspend payment of these notes in coin, and take measures to provide a currency in which loans could be negotiated and the transactions of the Government carried on. I wished to avoid the necessity of making notes of any kind a legal tender; and proposed several modes of doing it. To none could the unanimous assent of the banks be obtained. Some of them manifested a disposition to discredit the National Circulation wholly, whether issued in notes bearing interest or issued in notes bearing no interest; and if possible force upon the country the circulation of the suspended banks. Several bankers refused to receive the United States Notes on deposit. This way of things was the high road to ruin; and I did not hesitate as to the remedy. I united at once with those who desired to have the United States Notes made a legal tender, and by joining them decided the success of that measure.[58]

Yours truly,
S P CHASE

J. T. Trowbridge, Esq.

1. Portions of this long letter are in the handwriting of two different clerks (with emendations by Chase), and six pages in the middle of the manuscript are in Chase's hand. Trowbridge extracted a substantial portion of this letter for inclusion in an appendix, titled "National Work," to his biography of Chase (Trowbridge, *Ferry-Boy,* 321–29). Trowbridge marked numerous changes on the manuscript letter (such as changing Chase's first-person references to third person) and struck through large portions of text. The appendix in his book reflects those alterations. The editors have attempted to reproduce the letter here as it was when Chase sent it to Trowbridge. This transcription, in other words, does not show Trowbridge's emendations insofar as they can be distinguished from cancellations, insertions, and changes made by Chase and his clerks before they sent the letter. A letterpress copy of the pages in Chase's hand, now among his papers at the Cincinnati Historical Society, helps determine the sequence of changes in that portion of the letter.

2. The opening of this letter does not appear to follow in sequence any of the extant autobiographical letters to Trowbridge.

3. Meeting June 22–23, 1848, the Utica, N.Y., Free-Soil convention nominated former president Martin Van Buren and Henry Dodge, previously the governor of Wisconsin Territory and one of that state's first U.S. senators. The Democratic national convention, which met in Baltimore, May 22–25, 1848, selected Lewis Cass, U.S. senator from Michigan, and William O. Butler, former congressman from Kentucky, as its presidential and vice-presidential candidates. *Bio. Dir. U.S. Cong.,* 754–55; *DAB,* 3:371, 5:348–49, 19:152–57; *Daily National Intelligencer,* May 23–27; *New York Evening Post,* June 24, 26, 1848.

4. The Buffalo, N.Y., Free-Soil convention, August 9–10, 1848. *National Era,* Aug. 17, 1848.

5. John Parker Hale, antislavery U.S. senator from New Hampshire, was presidential candidate for the Liberty party in 1847. *DAB,* 8:105–6.

6. Charles Francis Adams of Massachusetts, vice-presidential nominee of the Buffalo convention and U.S. ambassador to Britain during the Civil War. *National Era,* Aug. 24, 1848; *DAB,* 1:40–48.

7. The resolution called for "such a tariff of duties as will raise revenue adequate to defray the necessary expenses of the Federal Government, and to pay annual instalments of our debt and the interest thereon." Joseph Livingston White, a New York attorney, was a former Whig congressman from Indiana. *Bio. Dir. U.S. Cong.,* 2040; *National Era,* Aug. 17, 1848.

8. The delegate convention met in Buffalo's Universalist Church. Richard H. Sewell, *Ballots for Freedom: Antislavery Politics in the United States, 1837–1860* (New York, 1976), 156.

9. Joshua Leavitt made the motion, seconded by Methodist clergyman and educator Samuel Lewis of Cincinnati. *National Era,* Aug. 17, 1848; *Appletons',* 3:706.

10. The measure was approved on August 14, 1848. *Statutes at Large,* 9:323–31.

11. The national Whig convention, June 7–9, 1848, nominated Zachary Taylor, hero of the U.S. war with Mexico, and former New York congressman Millard Fillmore as presidential and vice-presidential candidates. *Bio. Dir. U.S. Cong.,* 995; *DAB,* 18:352; *Daily National Intelligencer,* June 8–12, 1848; Joseph G. Rayback, *Free Soil: The Election of 1848* (Lexington, Ky., 1970), 194–200.

12. Meeting in Baltimore during the first week of June 1852, Democrats chose Franklin Pierce, U.S. senator from New Hampshire and brigadier general in the war with Mexico, and William Rufus Devane King (1786–1853), U.S. senator from Alabama. Gen. Winfield Scott and William Alexander Graham (1804–75), former U.S. senator, governor of North Carolina, and secretary of the U.S. Navy, won nomination at the Whig national convention, which also gathered in Baltimore, June 16–19, 1852. *DAB,* 7:480–81, 10:406–7, 14:577, 16:510; *Daily National Intelligencer,* June 2–6, 17–19, 21, 1852.

13. Chase's "letter" of July 15, 1852, clearly intended as a manifesto for publication, appeared in the *National Era* in July 1852 and was also issued separately as a pamphlet. The letter's nominal recipient was New York attorney and antislavery politician Benjamin Franklin Butler (not the Massachusetts politician and Civil War general of the same name). The Free Democratic convention, held in Pittsburgh August 11–12, 1852, selected John P. Hale and George W. Julian, a former antislavery congressmen from Ohio, as its presidential and vice-presidential candidates. *National Era,* July 29, Aug. 26, 1852; Chase to Butler, draft, [July 15, 1852] (Chase Papers, Hist. Soc. of Pa.); *The Radical Democracy of New York and the Independent Democracy: Letter from Senator Chase . . .* ([Washington, D.C., 1852]); *DAB,* 3:356, 10:246.

14. Chase inserted this number to refer to a footnote he placed at the bottom of the page: "(1) American Almanac 1860 p. 201." Tables showing popular votes for presidential elections, 1824–56, appear in *The American Almanac and Repository of Useful Knowledge, for the Year 1860* (Boston, 1859), 201–2.

15. In 1854, Chase and Benjamin F. Wade represented Ohio in the U.S. Senate. Ohio's congressmen were Edward Ball (1811–72); George Bliss; Lewis D. Campbell; Moses Bledso Corwin (1790–1872); David T. Disney; Alfred P. Edgerton; Andrew Ellison (1812–c. 1860); Joshua R. Giddings; Frederick W. Green (1816–79); Aaron Harlan (1802–68); John Scott Harrison; Harvey H. Johnson (1808–96); William D. Lindsley; Matthias H. Nichols; Edson B. Olds; Thomas Ritchey (1801–63); William Robinson Sapp (1804–75); Wilson Shannon; Andrew Stuart (1823–72); John L. Taylor; and Edward Wade. *Bio. Dir. U.S. Cong.,* 157, 570, 830, 962, 1089, 1134, 1265, 1720, 1767, 1891.

16. The "Appeal of the Independent Democrats in Congress, to the People of the United States" circulated in newspapers and pamphlets starting in January 1854. The signers were Chase, Congressman Alexander DeWitt (1798–1879) of Massachusetts, Charles Sumner, Joshua Giddings, New York congressman Gerrit Smith, and Edward Wade. Ibid., 903, 1829; *Chase Papers,* 2:382.

17. The convention met in Philadelphia, June 8–15, 1855. Tyler Gregory Anbinder, *Nativism and Slavery: The Northern Know Nothings and the Politics of the 1850s* (New York, 1992), 167–70.

18. Gathering in Columbus on July 13, 1855, the convention selected Chase by a margin of 225 to 144. Roseboom, *Civil War Era,* 303–5.

19. Chase's first inaugural, January 14, 1856, vowed to promote universal education and urged upon state lawmakers "the judicious encouragement of voluntary [military] organization." Chase, *Inaugural Address,* 4.

20. William H. Gibson held the office from 1856 to 1857. His brother-in-law, John G. Breslin, served from 1852 to 1856. For more on the "Breslin defalcation," see also *Chase Papers,* 1:285–93, 2:452–57. *A Biographical Record of Fairfield County, Ohio, . . .* (New York, 1902), 266–71; Reed, *Bench and Bar of Ohio,* 1:202–4; Gilkey, *Ohio Hundred Year Book,* 453.

21. Francis M. Wright.

22. Alfred P. Stone. *Chase Papers,* 1:286.

23. Gibson commanded the 49th Ohio Regiment during the Civil War. Reed, *Bench and Bar of Ohio,* 1:203.

24. At Ohio's Republican state convention, on August 12, 1857. *Columbus Gazette,* Aug. 14, 1857.

25. Abolitionist John Brown and his followers took the Federal arsenal at Harpers Ferry, Va., on October 16–17, 1859. *DAB,* 3:133.

26. Henry A. Wise apparently addressed letters with similar contents to Chase and to President James Buchanan on November 25, 1859. Wise's letter to Buchanan and Chase's reply of December 1 were printed in the *New York Times* on December 9. Chase to Wise, Dec. 1, 1859 (Chase Papers, Ohio Hist. Soc.); *DAB,* 20:423.

27. The Ohio General Assembly elected Chase to his second term in the U.S. Senate on February 2, 1860. The Ohio Republican convention declared its preference on March 1. *Cincinnati Daily Gazette,* Mar. 2, 1860; *Columbus Gazette,* Feb. 3, 1860.

28. The national Republican convention, Chicago, May 16–18, 1860. *Chicago Tribune,* May 17–19, 1860.

29. Lincoln to Chase, Dec. 31, 1860, in Warden, *Chase,* 364.

30. South Carolina seceded from the Union on December 20, 1860. For Chase's letter to Winfield Scott, December 29, 1860, see *Chase Papers,* 3:43–44. Long, *Civil War Day by Day,* 12–13.

31. Virginia's representatives at the conference, which met from February 4 to 27, 1861, were: John White Brockenbrough (1806–77), judge of the U.S. court for the western district of Virginia; former U.S. senator William C. Rives; former congressmen James Alexander Seddon (1815–80) and George William Summers (1804–68); and ex-president John Tyler. Long, *Civil War Day by Day,* 32, 42; *DAB,* 15:635–37, 16:545–46, 18:206–7, 19:92; *Daily National Intelligencer,* Feb. 11, 1861; Wakelyn, *Biographical Dictionary,* 110.

32. As Ohio's commissioners, Governor William Dennison appointed, along with Chase, Ohio legislator Franklin T. Backus (1813–70); former U.S. senator Thomas Ewing, Sr.; Congressman William S. Groesbeck; Judge Reuben Hitchcock; Congressman Valentine B. Horton; and John C. Wright, former congressman, Ohio supreme court justice, and editor of the *Cincinnati Gazette. Daily National Intelligencer,* Feb. 11, 1861; *Appletons',* 1:129, 6:624–25; *Biographical Cyclopædia,* 3:730–31; *DAB,* 6:237–8, 8:13–14, 9:239.

33. Wright died on February 13, 1861, and was succeeded on the commission by Christopher P. Wolcott, whom Chase had appointed attorney general of Ohio in 1856. *Appletons',* 6:624; Samuel A. Lane, *Fifty Years and Over of Akron and Summit County* (Akron, 1892), 553.

34. Amos Tuck of New Hampshire presented the proposal on February 6, and Chase spoke in support the same day. The conference rejected the amendment by a vote of 9 to 11 immediately after Chase's speech. *Daily National Intelligencer,* Feb. 11, 1861; Salmon P. Chase, *How the South Rejected Compromise in the Peace Conference of 1861. Speech of Mr. Chase, of Ohio* (New York, 1863), 2–11.

35. Among other provisions, the amendment would have divided remaining U.S. territory along a line of 36° 30', forbidden acquisition of new territory without the approval of a majority of all senators from free and slave states, prohibited Federal interference with slavery in any state, and prevented states from refusing to cooperate with Federal officials to capture fugitive slaves. In effect, the House killed the amendment on March 1, 1861, by refusing to suspend rules that prevented it from considering new legislation from the Senate during the last three days of the congressional session. Chase, *How the South Rejected Compromise,* 1–2; Lucius Eugene Chittenden, *Report of the Debates and Proceedings of the Peace Convention Held at Washington, D.C., February 1861* (New York, 1865; reprint, New York, 1971), 440–52; *Congressional Globe,* 36th Cong., 2d sess., 1860–61, pt. 2, 1332–33.

36. Lincoln arrived in Washington, D.C., on February 23, 1861. Long, *Civil War Day by Day,* 41.

37. Lincoln (as president) and Chase (as senator) took oaths of office on March 4. On the following day Lincoln nominated Chase secretary of the Treasury. *Congressional Globe,* 36th Cong., 2d sess., 1860–61, pt. 2, 1433; *Daily National Intelligencer,* Mar. 5, 1861; U.S. Senate, *Journal of Executive Proceedings,* 11:289.

38. Chase to Lincoln, Mar. 6, 1861 (Lincoln Papers, L.C.).

39. Major Robert Anderson, U.S.A. *DAB,* 1:274.

40. Scott to Lincoln, Mar. 12, 1861 (Lincoln Papers, L.C.).

41. South Carolina's governor at the time was Francis Wilkinson Pickens. Confederate Secretary of War LeRoy Pope Walker (1817–84) issued the orders on April 10 to Brig.

Gen. Pierre G. T. Beauregard, commander of Confederate troops at Charleston. *DAB,* 2:111, 14:560, 19:351–52; *OR,* ser. 1, v. 1:297.

42. On April 15. Long, *Civil War Day by Day,* 59.

43. The U.S. Navy abandoned its facilities at Norfolk, Va., on April 20. The Baltimore riots lasted from April nineteenth to the twenty-first. Ibid., 62–63.

44. Lincoln's proclamation of May 3, 1861, made in cooperation with Simon Cameron, called for a total of nearly 83,000 new volunteers, regulars, and sailors. The War Department issued Orders 15 and 16 the following day. Working with Chase were Adjutant General Lorenzo Thomas; Irvin McDowell, who served in Washington at that time; and William Buel Franklin, who had recently superintended construction on the U.S. Capitol dome and the Treasury Building. Basler, *Collected Works,* 4:353–54; *DAB,* 3:438, 6:602, 12:29, 18:441; Heitman, *Historical Register,* 1:434; *OR,* ser. 3, v. 1:151–57.

45. Chase's comment might refer to the commission Rousseau received as colonel of the 3d Kentucky Infantry on September 9, 1861. *DAB,* 16:194.

46. For Chase's interaction with William Nelson during the latter's recruitment of Unionist forces in Kentucky during 1861, see *Chase Papers,* 3:80–88, 90–91.

47. In March 1862, Lincoln appointed Andrew Johnson military governor of Tennessee. *DAB,* 10:83.

48. The camp was located near Bryantsville, Garrard County, in eastern Kentucky. William Nelson to Chase, Aug. 24, 1861 (Chase Papers, L.C.).

49. Montgomery Blair.

50. Benjamin F. Butler to Winfield Scott, May 24, 1861, in *OR,* ser. 1, v. 2:648–51.

51. Chase offered the loan under legislation of February 8, 1861. *Report of the Secretary of the Treasury, on the Finances, Containing Estimates of the Public Revenue and Public Expenditures, . . .* 37th Cong., 1st sess., 1861, S. Ex. Doc. 2, 31; *Statutes at Large,* 12:129–30.

52. The loan act of February 8, 1861, passed during the tenure of John A. Dix as secretary of the Treasury, had authorized the sale of up to $25 million in government debt. *New York Times,* Feb. 22, 1861; *Statutes at Large,* 12:129–30; *Bio. Dir. U.S. Cong.,* 18.

53. The national loan act, approved July 17, 1861, was amended on August 5 of that year and on February 12, 1862. *Statutes at Large,* 12:259–61, 313–14, 338.

54. Chase's trip to New York for negotiations with the "Associated Banks" that provided loans to the government lasted from August 9 to 15, 1861. Chase to Lincoln, Aug. 9, 1861 (Lincoln Papers, L.C.); Chase to George Harrington, Aug. 15, 1861 (Letters Received from Asst. Treasurers, Gen. Recs. Treasury Dept., Nat. Arch.); Hammond, *Sovereignty,* 85–86; *Chase Papers,* 3:113–15.

55. In 1861, the assistant treasurers were John J. Cisco (New York), Benjamin Farrar (St. Louis), Ezra Lincoln (Boston), and James H. Walton (Philadelphia). *Register of Officers (1861),* 22.

56. Another analysis later offered by A. S. Bolles, in *Lippincott's Monthly Magazine* 38 (July–December 1886): 200–206, depicted the bankers as "faithful allies and supporters of the government." For details of the agreement, which was signed on August 15, see *The Bankers' Magazine, and Statistical Register,* n.s., 11 (September 1861): 161–63, and the *New York Times,* Aug. 16, 1861.

57. *New York Times,* Nov. 18, 1861.

58. In an epigram penned for an unknown recipient on March 24, 1864, Chase declared: "When public Exigencies require Coin must become paper: when public exigencies allow paper must become coin." (HM8289, Huntington Lib.).

FROM JOHN J. CISCO

Letterpress copy of autograph letter. John J. Cisco Letterbook, Missouri Historical Society, St. Louis (*micro* 32:0587).

United State Treasury,
New York March 21st 1864.

Dear Sir,

I have received your letter of the 18th instant, requesting me to collect the opinions of men of experience and sagacity upon the two questions, "First, whether any use of the power to sell gold vested in the Secretary will be beneficial; Secondly, what use".[1]

While the subject was under discussion in Congress; after the passage of the Gold Bill,[2] and since the receipt of your letter, I have had frequent conversations with our most experienced and sagacious financiers, and find their views generally accord with my own. I will now proceed to state briefly what those views are.

I do not regard the present or even a much greater accumulation of gold in the Treasury as an evil, On the contrary I think the time will come when it will prove a great blessing to the country. That time will be, when we are about to resume specie payments, (An event which should be constantly held in view, and which I trust is not very far distant.) Then this accumulation will naturally flow out of the Treasury into our Banks, and give them the strength they will need, and cannot have without a large reserve of coin.

A large gold reserve in my judgment, should always be held by the Government. It is an unmistakable evidence of strength, which makes a powerful impression on the public mind, not only here, but in Europe, and influences to a great extent investments in our bonds.

If you sell the gold not needed for the payment of interest on the public debt, and thereby reduce its value, as compared with paper, it will be purchased and sent to Europe, to bring out still larger importations of needless articles of luxury, which have already assumed such fearful proportions beyond the exports of our own products, that it is viewed with alarm by those who look to the true interests of the Country. This prodigality of our people can only be checked at this time by increasing the duties, and by withholding the facilities for procuring the coin to pay for purchases abroad.

There is now a large and increasing demand for our bonds to go to Europe, stimulated by the high price of exchange, and the comparative small cost at which they are placed there, Reduce the value of gold materially, and it will be transmitted instead of your bonds.

The authority to sell gold vested in you, may I think be beneficial, even if it is not used. More speculators will not be likely to purchase for a rise, knowing that you have the power to crush them at any moment. Under such circumstances their interests would naturally prompt them to operate for a fall.

For the foregoing reasons, I am of the opinion that the interests of the Government will not be promoted by the sale of its surplus gold. Should you differ with me however, then I trust you will confine your sales exclusively to Importers to enable them to pay duties. The large number of this class of Merchants who are now compelled to purchase gold daily from the Brokers for this purpose is undoubtedly one of the causes of the comparative high price.[3]

In regard to the manner of carrying out the sales of gold, I agree with you that the privileges extended to the importers of New York must be extended to all, and that the average price here for each week should be ascertained, and transmitted by telegraph, at the close of business hours on Saturday, to the Department and from thence to all the different ports, The best plan in carrying out this arrangement would be, I think, to allow the Assistant Treasurers and Depositaries[4] to sell, and issue Specific Certificates to the credit of the Collectors and receivable only for duties from the parties to whom they are issued. The Collectors receiving these Certificates will pursue the same course now practiced, in having the amount daily placed to the credit of the Treasurer[5] of the United States.

If you decide to sell precisely as any other holder would, and not confine your sales to importers, you should do it confidentially. The effect unquestionably, would be greater, in keeping the time, place and amount secret, than it would be to sell in open market through my Office.

I do not think any better mode can be adopted in selling Exchange on London, than that heretofore practiced by the Department. The Bank of Commerce is the only large institution in the Country dealing to any great extent in foreign exchange. All its operations hitherto have been so well and prudently managed, that not the least suspicion was excited that the Government was an interested party; but if I were to undertake to sell exchange, it would be instantly known that I was operating for Government, and the effect could not but be prejudicial.

I fully agree in what you say in relation to the three great measures necessary to bring about sound finances, and I sincerely trust that Congress may adopt the plan suggested by yourself as the means of attaining so desirable a result.

Yours very truly,
John J Cisco

Hon S P Chase,
&c &c &c.

1. Chase had also discussed sales of gold and of exchange in England. "Heretofore when the Department has had exchange to sell, the sales have been made confidentially through the Bank of Commerce," he wrote. "Can you suggest a better mode for future sales?" In addition, Chase expressed his desire for more economical expenditures by Congress, for taxation to cover at least half the amount of expenditures, and for measures to bring all banks under Federal control: "Without these three measures, I am hopeless of sound finances; with them and with the State bank currency out of existence, it is my confident belief that specie payments could be resumed in six weeks." Chase to Cisco, Mar. 18, 1864 (Chase Papers, Hist. Soc. of Pa.).

2. A joint resolution of Congress approved on March 17 authorized the Treasury secretary "to dispose of any gold in the treasury of the United States not necessary for the payment of interest of the public debt." *Statutes at Large,* 13:404.

3. On March 19, the price of gold rose to about 162, from a low of around 151 as the year opened. Its peak for 1864, reached on July 9, was approximately 266. *Appletons' Annual Cyclopædia,* 4:377.

4. Legislation of August 5, 1861, authorized Chase "to select and appoint one or more depositories in each state for the deposit and safe-keeping of the moneys arising from the taxes." *Statutes at Large,* 12:309.

5. Francis E. Spinner.

TO JOHN T. TROWBRIDGE

Letter in clerk's hand, signed by Chase. Chase Papers, Historical Society of Pennsylvania (*micro* 32:0613).

Treasury Department
March 22, 1864.

Dear Sir,[1]

I had already urged on Congress the adoption of a system of National Currency to be furnished to Associations organized under National authority, and secured by the pledge of National Securities. Congress was not yet prepared for so decided a measure as this.— When upon the first issue of United States Notes I had expressed the opinion that the exigencies of the War might furnish the occasion for the establishment of a truly national currency, the idea was received with little favor and less faith.

Very few, when I brought a plan for a National Currency before Congress, were prepared to accept it either as desirable or practicable.[2] A majority of both the House and Senate financial Committees were incredulous or hostile. Only Mr. Hooper of Massachusetts, a gentleman whose sound judgment and large knowledge of financial subjects, gave great and deserved weight to his opinions, encouraged me by open support; and the most he could do was to obtain leave to bring in the bill authorizing a National Banking System and providing for a National Currency, and procure an order for the printing of it.— Out of Congress, Robert J. Walker, distinguished by his brilliant administration of the Treasury when himself Secretary, and by his great ability, gave the plan the sanction of his approval. Encouraged by such judgments, I was not daunted by the general opposition. I knew that so great a revolution in the currency of the Country could not be expected to command general and immediate assent, and I was not dissatisfied with the delay, because it gave me an opportunity of preparing for the transition by the issue of United States Notes, which, made a legal tender, were sure to obtain universal currency. Their currency would prevent in some degree the irregular and and dangerous increase of bank note circulation, which would otherwise take place, and furnish the means by which that circulation could be redeemed. Congress authorized the issue of this circulation and also provided for the issue of Five Hundred Millions in bonds redeemable after five years, and payable twenty years from date, which afterwards became well known under the name of "Five-Twenties."[3] To support the credit of the notes they were made convertible into these bonds, and the interest on the bonds was made payable in coin. This was doubtless wise at the beginning, but it soon became evident that the right of conversion at the pleasure of the holder of the notes would prevent the bonds from being taken in sufficient amounts to supply the demands of the War. I urged the financial committees to repeal the provision for conversion, but in vain.[4] Congress adjourned and I was left with no other means of raising money in large sums, except by the issue of United States Notes and the conversion of the Five-Twenties. I endeavored to stimulate conversions by the appointment of Agents, but without very great success. I was obliged to depend chiefly upon U.S. Notes. When Congress again met met in December 1862, I again represented the inconvenience of the clauses in the Five-Twenty Act, authorizing conversion and requiring sales at market rates, and again urged the necessity of an Act authorizing the organization of a National Banking System and thus providing a permanent national currency. A decided majority in both Houses was at first opposed to these measures. At length however, though with great difficulty, a majority was induced to adopt my views. The National Banking Act was passed and the privilege of conversion was limited to the first of July 1863.

I had made strenuous endeavors to dispose of the 5–20 bonds by way of loan, but the best offer I could obtain for a single loan of fifty millions was 97½ or 98 for a hundred, involving the loss on each 50.000.000# of the 500.000.000#,—beyond all expenses of preparation, transportation, and all risks,—of a million to a million and a quarter of dollars; that is to say, of from Eight to ten millions of dollars on the whole loan. These were the best terms. It was impossible to tell how much worse might have to be submitted, if the usual modes of making loans should be resorted to. I therefore determined on another plan. I had already engaged the services of Mr. Jay Cooke as General Agent, and arranged with him to obtain subscriptions throughout the whole country through sub-Agents for whom he was to be responsible. This arrangement, aided by the legislation of Congress, now worked very well.[5]— Mr. Cooke sent his Agents everywhere, and through newspapers gave the widest possible publicity to the loan, and secured great favor towards it. He was responsible for all his Agents, for all expenses and for all risks, and the whole compensation was three-eighths of one per cent., of which one-eighth only was compensation to him for services and responsibilities, and even from this 8th large amounts were deducted for actual expenditures. The result was that the whole five hundred millions of loan was taken by the end of January, and the subscriptions were in excess of nearly eleven millions of the amount authorized.

The employment of Mr. Cooke did not exclude the employment of the Treasurer, the Assistant Treasurers and Designated Depositaries of the United States throughout the country. They received all the subscriptions they could obtain and allowed one-eighth of one per cent. to those who bought for resale. Mr. Cooke's exertions contributed very largely to the subscriptions made with those officers. The whole expense of the loan was #1.400.000, as against a loss of from eight to ten millions at the least which would have attended the ordinary course of negotiation.—

I had been told by the most experienced financial men that the Five-Twenty negotiation would prove a failure, for bonds redeemable after five years would find no takers except at inadmissible discounts. I resolved to attempt the negotiation, because of my extreme aversion to binding the country to pay high rates of interest for long periods of time. While the subscription for Five-Twenties was going on, National Banks were being organized under the banking law, and is still going on. It has become tolerably certain that the system will be a success and will furnish to the country a safe, sufficient and uniform currency. It is greatly to be regretted that Congress has not been willing to impose heavier taxes on the State Bank circulation, so as to effectually restrict and discourage it. This is now the greatest necessity. There is every reason to expect that bonds may now be negotiated under the recent act at 5 per cent. interest, and there can be no doubt that if the necessary legislation can be obtained and the war pushed to an early and successful termination, that the credit of the country will be preserved unimpaired, & that the great results, including the resumption of specie payments, which I have kept steadily in view from the beginning, will be attained.

Very truly yours,
S P CHASE

J. T. Trowbridge, Esq,
Somerville.

1. As he did with Chase's letter of March 21 (above), Trowbridge made alterations on the manuscript of this letter and incorporated its text directly into the "National Work" appendix of his biography. The editors have reproduced the letter as Trowbridge received it from Chase, ignoring the changes made for publication in Trowbridge's book. Trowbridge, *Ferry-Boy*, 329–32.

2. Chase originally made the proposal in his annual report to Congress, December 9, 1861. *Report of the Secretary of the Treasury, on the State of the Finances, for the Year ending June 30, 1861*, 37th Cong., 2d sess., 1861, S. Ex. Doc. 2, 17–20.

3. The first legal tender act, which included authorization for the 5–20 bonds, was approved on February 25, 1862. *Statutes at Large*, 12:345–48.

4. For Chase's frustration with the convertibility clauses of the greenback acts, see *Chase Papers*, 3:225–26, 291–92, 358–60, 369–71.

5. Legislation of March 3, 1863, sanctioned the arrangement with Cooke. *Statutes at Large*, 12:709–13.

TO HENRY WINTER DAVIS

Letterbook copy in clerk's hand. Letters Sent Relating to Restricted Commercial Intercourse and Captured and Abandoned Property (BE Series), General Records, Department of the Treasury (Record Group 56), National Archives (*micro* 32:0648).

Treasury Department
March 25th. 1864.

Hon. Henry Winter Davis,
Ch'n Com. on Rebellious States,[1]
Ho of Reps.
Sir.

In accordance with the provisions of the Executive Order promulgated in General Orders No. 331 of the War Department, dated 9th. of October last, the Supervising Special Agents of the Treasury Department have assumed charge of the abandoned plantations, etc, within our military lines in the States heretofore declared to be in insurrection;[2] but for want of legal authority in the premises very little has been or can be done toards cultivating them or ameliorating the condition of the freed people in those sections of the country.

Men of energy and means are ready and anxious to fairly test the problem of compensated labor in the rebel States, as soon as the necessary legislation can be had. For the want of this hundreds of thousands of fertile acres produce little or nothing; while thousands of freedmen whose willing labor is needed on the abandoned plantations, remain in worse than idleness, all destitute, many suffering and some actually perishing. This condition of theirs imposes heavy and unnecessary burdens on the charity of humane people, and an onerous tax upon Government. The prospect of a valuable crop for the current year is greatly impaired by delay. Prompt and efficient action by Congress may yet be of great and enduring service. Evry consideration of sound policy, therefore, no less than the dictates of humanity seems to require speedy and decisive action on the subject; and I earnestly hope your Committee will do all in its power to secure it.

The draft of a Bill which will answer for immediate purposes has already been transmitted to the Committee and a copy is herewith enclosed.[3]

With great respect.
S. P. Chase
Sec Treas.

Similar letter, same date addressed to Hon. Charles Sumner, Ch'n Com: on Slavery and Freedmen. U. S. Senate.[4]

1. In December 1863, the House of Representatives appointed Davis to its Select Committee on Rebellious States. *House Journal,* 38th Cong., 1st sess., 1863–64, 63.

2. The supervising special agents at the time were: William P. Mellen of the first special agency (Mississippi Valley); Hanson A. Risley, second special agency (primarily Virginia and West Virginia east of the Alleghenies); David Heaton, third special agency (North Carolina); Albert G. Browne, Sr., fourth special agency (South Carolina, Georgia, and Florida); and Benjamin F. Flanders of the fifth special agency (Texas and the lower Mississippi Valley). For General Orders No. 331, see *OR,* ser. 3, v. 3:872. *Letter of the Secretary . . . Special Agents,* 2.

3. Legislation that authorized Treasury agents to lease confiscated plantations and employ former slaves on them was approved on July 2, 1864. *Statutes at Large,* 13:375–78.

4. In January the Senate had formed a select committee of seven members, including Sumner, "to take into consideration all propositions and papers concerning slavery and the treatment of freedmen." *Senate Journal,* 38th Cong., 1st sess., 1863–64, 74, 78.

TO WILLIAM E. DODGE

Printed copy. Jacob W. Schuckers, *The Life and Public Services of Salmon Portland Chase* (New York, 1874), 400 (*micro* 39:0939).

WASHINGTON, *March* 31, 1864.

. . . .[1] I thank you for transmitting to me a copy of the resolutions of the Chamber of Commerce, adopted on the 17th instant.[2]

The merchants of New York may rest assured that I shall most gladly do whatever for me is possible for the security and prosperity of business.

But it must be borne in mind that nothing short of a return to specie payments can secure stability in the value of currency. Even specie payments, it is well known, do not fully accomplish that object. The value of money, as well as of all other subjects, fluctuates in obedience to great laws, the operations of which cannot always be foreseen or provided for.

Our present difficulties arise mainly from excessive expenditure without adequate taxation. They arise in almost an equal degree from the presence in the channels of circulation of an element—I mean the notes of State banks—which cannot be regulated or even understood by the national authorities.

If these two causes of disturbance be removed by the action of Congress, and we have what I greatly hope, vigor and success in the war, I see no reason why resumption of specie payments need be very long deferred.[3]

I have no control over the volume of expenditure or over the amount of taxation, or over the volume of circulation as affected by the issues of State banks, or over the conduct of the war. I feel myself like one undertaking to navigate a ship without a chart among forces of winds and currents which he cannot measure or manage. I can only do my best, hoping the best, and trusting Him with whom are the issues of all events.

1. The ellipses appear in Schuckers's book, their significance unexplained. New York entrepreneur William Earl Dodge (1805–83) was a partner in metal conglomerate Phelps, Dodge and Company. *DAB,* 5:352–53.

2. Among resolutions passed at the meeting of the New York Chamber of Commerce was one "relative to the simplification of the process of passing goods through the

Custom-house" and another "suggesting that the Government advertise at what premium, from week to week, gold or certificates of deposit therefore, can be had for use at the office of the Assistant Treasurer." *New York Times,* Mar. 18, 1864.

3. See Chase's letters to Joseph Medill, January 30, 1864, and to Thaddeus Stevens, February 19, 1864 (both above), for previous expressions of concern about state bank note circulation and specie payments. The internal revenue act of 1864, signed on June 30, raised duties and internal revenue. Long, *Civil War Day by Day,* 530; *Statutes at Large,* 13:223–306.

FROM FRANK E. HOWE

Autograph letter. Chase Papers, Library of Congress (*micro* 32:0792).

Unofficial

Steamer Washington"[1]
Near Alexandria 1st. April '/64

Hon S. P. Chase
Very dear Sir,

Confirming my respects of the 18th. pr "Evening Star",[2] I would report that after two very useful & pleasant interviews between Mr Flanders & General Banks, particulars of which I take it for granted the former has submitted to you together, with the official correspondence which was the fruit of those interviews, I have to inform you that at the urgent request of Mr Flanders I left very suddenly with Genl Banks for this place[3]—& the object of this letter is to give you a plain statement of incidents & impressions—

On our way up which was somewhat perilous General Banks matured a plan, by which the country, would get the benefit of the produce of this country, under restrictions, the proceeds to be held by the Treasury Dept. On reaching the mouth of Red River, the Capt of Gun Boat informed us, that Admiral Porter had seized all the Cotton he could get hold of, and had burned a great deal—

None of us believed this—but reaching Alexandria—a novel, and to me a sad sight presented itself— There were Gun Boats with large Barges filled with this troublesome commodity— On shore the scene was ludicrous & sad There were marines black & white under commissioned Officers, driving cattle, large forces of 200 each, & less, escorting mule teams of waggons (which they brought with them) filled with Cotton, some times on top, old pictures, with Cows & Calfs hitched on behind—& often some fine hunting dog which they had gobbled up— I saw seven marines at the end of a rope twenty feet long, the other end round the horns & neck of a Bull, who had become infuriated, & who dashed from one side of the road to the other, swinging the whole squad, then he pulled, they holding on with all their force, when he made a charge upon them, *slacking the rope,* tumbling them all in a heap, & rushing over them—when others despatched him with an axe—this, opposite a church green, was a sad phase of war.

A school teacher, a young *loyal* woman who had suffered greatly, but who had quietly invested her confederate pay in *seven* bales of cotton, had it taken by Porter, & it had left for Cairo—but when Porter heard these facts, he promptly & in a kind manner, permitted her to pick out seven better bales from his stock, but the Admiral will never hear of all the cases of this character— Sad indeed was the sight of the village stores, particularly a drug store, and some of the houses I went into—that had been sacked by the marines, the people said, headed by officers—it was worthy of a New York Mob. A Rosa Bonheur painting costing $500—I am told was taken from one house[4]— The Admiral keeps a fine stud of horses, equal almost to anything I have seen in Europe—has 12 on board his Flag Ship[5]—and 11 in his stable which stable with the horses, he has gobbled on this campaign— Its funny to see him *aboard* of a fine Stallion, with two officers as a staff—when taking a fast gait, you are impressed with the thought, that there must be a heavy ground swell, or roll, on— Marines on mules in squads of 20 is also a novel sight, one mule getting annoyed at the sailor grip of the bit & laying down breaking a gobbled looking glass, by which Jack intended to adorn himself through, instead of the reflection of a pail of water, his more becoming element. These scenes present a great contrast, to Banks former occupation of Alexandria,[6] & the Rebel Lees invasion of Penn where private property and, houses were respected—But we must not stop here in viewing this picture, I am satisfied, by information received by Genl Banks before his march, & by his plans, if left to work them out—not a Bale of Cotton would have been burned—

I think by the action of the Navy Fifty thousand bales have been burned & Gov Wells[7] & other martyrs to the Union cause think One hundred thousand bales have been burned, and predict that Three hundred thousand bales will go in another week, if the Navy pursue this course—

I have seen a great deal of Southern society—particularly the women of this country— I am convinced we shall have a severe fight at Shreveport[8]— The wives and daughters of officers who are in the confederate Army tell me—they have told them, that if they do not hold Shreveport against the Yankees—they will never be welcomed again by them, to their old Southern Homes.

The bitterness of the women will be the severest element, we shall have to contend with, in progress of reconstruction— My belief is that Kirby Smiths, Dick Taylor, Genl Green, and perhaps McGruder Armies are in good condition[9]— I am sure they are well enough clothed—& certain they are well fed.

Mrs Shepard wife of a Confederate Officer—shew me in Alexandria, an order on the Commissary, for her to draw every 10 days—100 lbs Flour 50 lbs Beef 25 Lard 25 lbs sugar 25 Salt 25 Corn Meal, for which she paid $50 in confederate money, she then sold it to the parties she boarded with for for $350 Confederate money—& repeated this every 10 days as her right, & the right of every women whose husband was in Conf Army as an Officer— Her husband was only Captain— This Mrs Shepard was a Miss Kenner, was educated at Miss Haines school in New York;[10] they own the Golden Grove plantation here, (40 miles from New Orleans); were offered Five hundred & fifty thousand dollars for it the year before the war and today she hardly knows how to clothe her two little children—she is about 25 years old—bitter & insane upon this subject—wont take the oath—

I have represented this, with other cases, to General Banks, many of whom he has sent through the lines, as he will this one. While we have plenty of such cases as these to contend with in the Red River country, we have cheering assurances of returning loyality, in the large number of people daily entering our lines—availing themselves of every possible means of transportation— Teams with whole families— But the most useful features, are the bands of Jay Hawkers— The first night of our arrival Genl Banks authorised certain parties to go into the woods, and inform the men who had been living over a year there, if they would come in, he would arm them— The next morning I almost wept on visiting their rendezvous to see over 200, of as hard & severely tried a sett of men as I ever saw— They said *"their turn had come now"* and mounted as they were, on worn out & jaded animals, the first exploit of theirs, was to capture a Staff Officer & men of Genl Greens— Our Army was nearly two days marching through Alexandria, and every where they met Banks, recd him with hearty cheers—they had then marched 200 Miles, and were as fresh & buoyant in spirits as you would wish— After they had passed, the refugees from the woods, poured in to enlist— Colored people swarmed the road sides; we sent off 600, first load to New Orleans—mostly women & children.

The river is astonishing the oldest residents by rapidly falling—this may affect seriously the operations of the Gun Boats.

My intention is to accompany Genl Banks until Shreveport falls, of which he feels certain—and be back in New Orleans, about the 20th. of April (perhaps earlier) with a settled Policy in my pocket as regards "Trade Regulations" which I will promptly submit to you— I know this letter is too long, but I only expect you will glance it over— It has been written hurriedly, and I hope will be regarded by you as private

With high regard

Your Obt Svt
FRANK E. HOWE.

1. Howe, at the time acting as a special agent for the Treasury, wrote this letter near Alexandria, La., apparently on board the *George Washington,* a U.S. Mail sidewheel

steamer of 804 tons out of New York, or one of many other vessels named *Washington*. *New Orleans Times Picayune*, Mar. 30, 1864; Lytle, *Merchant Vessels*, 75, 199.

2. Howe's letter of March 18 informed Chase about successful attempts to prevent fees from being assessed for passes and permits, reported on a local commission evidently formed to study local banks, and presented evidence that Nathaniel Banks intended to cooperate with Howe's investigations. The *Evening Star* was a sidewheel steamer based in New York. Howe to Chase, Mar. 18, 1864 (Letters Recd. from Exec. Officers, War Dept., Gen. Recs. Treasury Dept., Nat. Arch.); Lytle, *Merchant Vessels*, 60.

3. Banks had embarked on the ill-fated Red River campaign on March 12. Long, *Civil War Day by Day*, 474.

4. Rosa Bonheur (1822–99), a French painter noted for her studies of animals. Thorne, *Chambers's Biographical Dictionary*, 177.

5. David Dixon Porter's flagship, a former blockade runner, was the USS *Malvern*, a side-wheeled iron steamer of 647 tons. The U.S. Navy had captured the vessel on November 9, 1863. *DAB*, 15:88; *ORN*, ser. 2, v. 1:133.

6. Federal forces took Alexandria, La., on March 16, 1864. Long, *Civil War Day by Day*, 475.

7. James Madison Wells (1808–99), a native Louisianan and antisecessionist, won election as lieutenant governor in February 1864. *DAB*, 19:641–42.

8. Effective defensive measures by the Confederates at the battles of Sabine Crossroads (also known as Mansfield) and Pleasant Hill, La., April 8 and 9, 1864, prevented Federal troops from taking Shreveport during the Red River campaign. Long, *Civil War Day by Day*, 482–83.

9. Lt. Gen. Edmund Kirby Smith presided over the Confederate Trans-Mississippi Department. His subordinates, Richard Taylor, Thomas Green (1816–64), and John Bankhead Magruder, all major generals, commanded the District of West Louisiana, cavalry in the Trans-Mississippi Department, and the District of Texas, respectively. *Appletons'*, 2:746; *DAB*, 10:425, 12:205, 18:340.

10. Josephine Kenner Shepard, a relative of Chase's third wife, was a daughter of Louisiana planter William Butler Kenner. Her husband was Charles M. Shepard. Henrietta B. Haines directed the boarding school in New York City that Chase's older daughter, Kate, had attended. Stanley Clisby Arthur, *Old Families of Louisiana* (New Orleans, 1931), 159; Sarah Bella Dunlop Ludlow Chase to Kate Chase, Dec. 11, 1850 (Chase Papers, Hist. Soc. of Pa.); *Chase Papers*, 1:83; Haines to Chase, July 5, 1851 (Chase Papers, L.C.); *New York Dir. (1851–52)*, 231.

TO CYRUS W. FIELD

Letterpress copy of letter in clerk's hand, signed by Chase. Chase Papers, Historical Society of Pennsylvania (*micro* 32:0881).

April 6, 4.

My dear Mr. Field,

I have just received your note of the 12th March. I send by this mail a few copies of speeches which may perhaps afford some correct ideas of things here.

We are expecting much from General Grant, who seems to be busy in organizing a great and I hope decisive campaign.[1] Our news from Louisiana is good. The rebels are being steadily pushed back by overwhelming forces. It is a pity they won't stop and fight. If they would, the work might be finished sooner, but as it is there is little reason to doubt the complete recovery of the Trans-Mississippi country this year; and I see no reason why Grant may not expel rebellion within the same time from the whole country this side of the Mississippi.

I don't like the way reconstruction is managed.— It is to be much regretted that the President does not stand by the loyal men who in the Slave States have stood most firmly by the Union, and almost worshipped him because of his Proclamation. I mean of course the loyal blacks. Why should not the black man, who has fought the battles of his country or has otherwise proved his loyalty to our cause, and has sufficient intelligence to exercise the right of suffrage properly,—why should not such a man be permitted to vote? I see no reason against it. On the contrary, I see in the present condition of the rebel districts a grand opportunity to organize State Governments upon intelligent suffrage; that is to say by securing in the Constitutions of the reconstructed States the right of suffrage to all who can read and write, and have a fair understanding of the Constitution of the country. Unfortunately, as I think, the President does not see matters in this light. He seems to think that to give negroes, however intelligent, the right of suffrage would jeopard the success of the Union Party at the next election, when he himself will doubtless be the candidate for reëlection.

Our most troublesome question now is that of the finances. I am appealing to Congress to give me a Bank Bill so amended as to ensure the speedy conversion of the State into National Banks; to impose taxes on State Bank Notes which will expel them from circulation within a reasonable time,—say two years,—and to levy general taxes which will give us a revenue equal to at least one half the expenditure. If they will do these things, our finances will be safe from everything but military disaster.

Yours very truly,
S P Chase

P.S. Our friends in the House dissatisfied with some amendments forced into the Bank bill have had it laid on the table today: So that it is killed for the present. It will I trust be immediately revived & carried through[2]

Cyrus W. Field, Esquire,
London, England.

1. Ulysses S. Grant, who in March had been promoted to lieutenant general and given command of all U.S. armies, would soon issue orders for a set of simultaneous campaigns involving movements by the Army of the Potomac in Virginia, William Tecumseh Sherman's army into Georgia, Nathaniel Banks against Mobile, Benjamin F. Butler up the James River toward Richmond, and Franz Sigel in the Shenandoah Valley. The operations were to commence in May. Long, *Civil War Day by Day,* 473, 483, 492, 501.

2. The postscript is in Chase's hand. Samuel Hooper had introduced the bill, H.R. 333, in March as a replacement for the February 1863 "national currency act" that had established the national banking system. Progress on the measure came to a halt over amendments that would have exposed national banks to state and local taxation and restricted the banks' rate of return to seven percent. Chase to Horace Greeley, Apr. 6, 1864

(below); H.R. 333 (Orig. Bills, 38th Cong., Recs. of U.S. House of Representatives, Nat. Arch.); *New York Tribune,* Apr. 8, 1864; *Congressional Globe,* 38th Cong., 1st sess., pt. 2, 1864, 1451–53; *Chase Papers,* 3:368.

TO HORACE GREELEY

Autograph letter on letterhead stationery. Horace Greeley Papers, Rare Books and Manuscripts Division, The New York Public Library, Astor, Lenox, and Tilden Foundations (*micro* 32:0883).

Private

Treasury Department.
Apl. 6, 1864

My dear Mr. Greeley,

The National Bank Bill as the telegraph has probably already informed you was laid on the table on the motion of Mr Stevens; & the motion to reconsider also laid on the table. This puts it beyond resurrection except by a new bill or a bill in the Senate.[1]

This is a severe blow and should not have been given by our friends. Mr. Hooper and Mr. Stevens I fear acted too much from impulse.

It is in vain for me to strive to maintain the public credit and still more in vain to think of keeping down the price of gold unless we can have an exclusive national currency, & it is vain to hope for an exclusive National Currency unless we can have such amendments of the National Banking System as will facilitate the conversion of the State Banks into National Banks.

The points on which the fatal differences occurred were a uniform rate of interest for all banks organized under the bill of 7%. and the taxation of the National Banks by the States. I think both points important. There should be a uniform rate of 7% for interest & the National Banks should not be taxable by State & Municipal authorities:—but the bill should have been saved even had it been necessary to yield these points and sent to the Senate where it could be amended.

Why can't you say in the Tribune that it is as wrong in principle to issue & circulate a piece of paper money without the imprint & sanction of the nation as it is to issue & circulate a piece of metallic money.[2] Fix this thought in the popular mind & it will go a great way toward the establishment of a national currency.

I hope still for the reviving of the Banking bill: not that I have any great love for National rather State Banks per se, but because I believe the first Constitutional and the latter unconstitutional and because I know that A National Banking System under our existing circumstances is *indispensable* to the maintenance of the National Credit.

I write just now on this theme because it is of most pressing importance: but even more important, in real & permanent influence, is a sufficient tax bill. I have urged this subject until I fear I am thought importunate. But what can I do? The Army must be paid—the Navy must be paid—the public creditors must be paid. We *cannot* pay unless we can keep gold down. And we cannot keep gold down if our disbursements are to be kept flowing in so large excess over income.

Plenty of nostrums are suggested to me: but nostrums wont save us. We must have at least half our expenses paid by taxation and we must have an exclusive National Currency in which taxes can be paid. Give me these two things and with God's blessing, I will maintain the National Credit against every thing except great disasters in the field.

Pray let the Tribune speak. Let the issue go to the People National Currency and Adequate Taxation with Specie Payments and National Success, or State Currency and Deficit Taxation with Paper payments & National failure.

Your friend
S: P: CHASE

Hon H Greeley

1. Thaddeus Stevens quickly introduced a substitute for Hooper's bank bill. The new measure, designated H.R. 395, passed with amendments to become "An Act to provide a National Currency," June 3, 1864, a detailed revision of regulations for the system of national banking associations. Chase to Cyrus W. Field, April 6, 1864 (above); *Statutes at Large,* 13:99–118; H.R. 395 (Orig. Bills, 38th Cong., Recs. of U.S. House of Representatives, Nat. Arch.).

2. Greeley described the resulting article in a letter to Chase, April 7 (below).

FROM HORACE GREELEY

Autograph letter on letterhead stationery. Chase Papers, Historical Society of Pennsylvania (*micro* 32:0909).

Office of The Tribune,
New York, April 7, 1864.

My Dear Mr. Chase:

I have your note of last evening respecting the failure of the Bank bill; and I have *tried* to write such an article as is needed, which you will find in to-morrow's Tribune.[1] I fear it will not altogether please you; but I have given to it my best thought.

I fear you cannot borrow all you need on a five per cent. bond, and do not see why you should not pay all that may be required—even *ten* per cent. on temporary loan if you must. I would go back to the popular Five-Twenties, if I thought I could float Two or Three Hundred Millions of them; or I would issue Two Hundred Millions more of 7 per cents like the old 7.30.s. Do not let one or two per cent. in the rate of interest keep the Government in beggary when there is money enough to be had by those who will pay the market price for it.

I know you feel that this would diminish the value of the *present* outstanding Public Securities; but I say No—it would diminish their

Greenback *price*—not their actual, real *value*. I presume you will not question that a Five-Twenty at par with Gold at 130, is actually higher than the same bond at 112 (Greenback) when Gold is 165. And yet all we need is a recognition of this truth to take us right out of our present trouble, which is damaging the business of the country more than you can realize. We have strikes upon strikes for higher wages; and *The Tribune* now pays 17 cents per pound for Paper that it has bought for years at 8, 9 and 10. Of course, we see hard times, and must till Gold goes down. And to send it down you must fund at least Five Hundred Millions by the 4th of July.

Pardon my freedom, and believe me

Yours,
HORACE GREELEY.

Hon. S. P. Chase, Treasury.

1. For the previous day's note, see Chase to Greeley, April 6, 1864 (above). Greeley's article of April 8 promoted greenbacks as the sole national currency, higher excise taxes to diminish imports, and another national loan. *New York Tribune,* Apr. 8, 1864.

TO SIDNEY GEORGE FISHER

Letterpress copy of letter in clerk's hand, signed by Chase. Chase Papers, Historical Society of Pennsylvania (*micro* 33:0003).

April 8th, 4.

Sir,[1]

It will give me great pleasure to comply with your request by sending you the financial Reports since the inauguration of Mr. Lincoln,[2] and I will add to them some of Mr. Walker's Letters, which will shed light, not merely on the Currency System, but on collateral financial subjects.

To me no truth is more clear than that the fiduciary currency of every country must be under the direct control of the National Government, and that without such control unity of operation and uniformity of value cannot be secured. I am no believer in irredeemable paper money. The National Banking System will be a failure unless the National Currency is made the just equivalent of gold and silver. To bring about this equilibrium is my earnest desire, and my labors will fail of one of their great objects if I do not attain it.— To its attainment I feel that legislation imposing taxes at least equal to one-half of the National Expenditure and excluding the circulation of local currency of every description other than National Currency, is indispensable.

Very truly Yours,
S P CHASE

Sidney E. Fisher, Esq.[3]
Philadelphia.

1. In July, Philadelphia lawyer and author Sidney George Fisher (1809–71) published an article in the *North American Review* that supported U.S. government policy on legal tender notes. *DAB,* 6:410–11; Fisher, "A National Currency," *North American Review* 99 (July 1864): 204–45.

2. Chase had issued four reports, the *Report of the Secretary of the Treasury on the Finances* of July 1861 and three annual reports issued in December of each year: *Report of the Secretary of the Treasury, on the State of the Finances, for the Year Ending June 30, 1861,* 37th Cong., 2nd sess., 1861, S. Ex. Doc. 2; *Report of the Secretary of the Treasury, on the State of the Finances, for the Year Ending June 30, 1862,* 37th Cong., 3rd sess., 1862, S. Ex. Doc. 1; and *Report of the Secretary of the Treasury . . . 1863.*

3. Chase's clerk erred in writing Fisher's middle initial.

TO JAY COOKE

Letterpress copy of letter in clerk's hand. Chase Papers, Historical Society of Pennsylvania (*micro* 33:0034).

Treasury Department,
April 10, 1864.

[My] Dear Sir,

Will you do me the favor of calling on Mr. Cisco and conversing with him [freely] on the condition of the gold market. He will, I am sure, confer freely with you. I have written to him about the practicability of using a portion of the surplus gold and exchange in breaking down the speculation price; and I have named to him two persons through whom I thought the work might be done. He approved of one who, however, cannot immediately be brought into action; and did not approve of the other.[1] I think he shares the confidence I repose in you and will be ready to express his views to you, and if anything can be done you two gentlemen can certainly devise the way of doing it. He has my full authority for such action as he may think wise and prudent, and you can, I am sure, execute any plan which requires secrecy and skill.

It was in reference to this matter that I desired to consult with you, and therefore telegraphed you yesterday to come to Washington. I have seen to-day Mr. H. D. Cooke and am satisfied that it is better for you to go to New York and aid so far as you can in arranging the difficulties in the Fourth National.[2] This letter will answer every purpose of a personal interview.

It is of immense importance to bring down the price of gold. I have authorized Mr. Cisco to raise the rate of interest of the temporary loan, if he thinks it expedient.[3] This I hope will withdraw considerable amounts of legal tenders from circulation; for I do not reissue anything I receive on account of temporary loan.

I think, also, of offering a loan of say 50 millions of six per cents of 81; expecting for them a handsome premium. I wish to arrest the upward tendency of gold, and at the same time discontinue the sale of it to merchants.

I know these measures are only expedients and that no measures can be really successful so long as the local banks retain the control of the currency and Congress delays necessary taxation. I am very confident, however, that within the next three weeks sufficient taxation will be imposed and the circulation of the local banks put in a way of rapid withdrawal.[4] In the meantime expedients may be justified.

You will please keep all knowledge of this letter to yourself and Mr. Cisco. I do not retain a copy; but will thank you to keep the original until it is convenient to have one made.

Yours Faithfully[5]

Jay Cooke, [Esq]

1. Chase suggested Ludwig Marx, associated with New York merchants Knauth, Nachod, and Kühne, and John Thompson (1802–91), a financial publisher and banker who established the First National Bank of New York in 1863 and the Chase National Bank in 1877. Cisco disapproved of Thompson. Chase to Cisco, Apr. 7, 1864, in Jessy Emilie Young, "Some Unpublished Letters of Salmon P. Chase" (master's thesis, Columbia Univ., 1922), 62–63; Cisco to Chase, Apr. 8, 1864 (Cisco Letters, Mo. Hist. Soc.); *DAB,* 18:462–3; *New York Dir. (1863),* 481, 587.

2. Cooke had spearheaded organization of New York's Fourth National Bank in December 1863. In April 1864, a dispute over management erupted between the bank's board and its president, George Opdyke, that was not resolved until the end of the year. Ellis Paxson Oberholtzer, *Jay Cooke: Financier of the Civil War,* 2 vols. (Philadelphia, 1907), 1:343–50.

3. As of April 9, Cisco had authorization to raise the rate on temporary loans to six percent. Chase to Cisco, Apr. 9, 1864 (Letters Sent, Loan Division, Recs. of Bureau of Public Debt, Nat. Arch.).

4. Chase had discussed state bank note circulation and the need for higher taxes in letters to Joseph Medill, January 30, 1864, Thaddeus Stevens, February 19, 1864, and William E. Dodge, March 31, 1864 (all above).

5. No signature is visible on the letterpress copy. The complimentary closing is in Chase's handwriting.

TO THADDEUS STEVENS

Letter in clerk's hand on letterhead stationery, signed by Chase. Committee on Ways and Means, Papers on the Treasury Department, 38th Congress, Records of the U.S. House of Representatives (Record Group 233), National Archives (*micro* 33:0057).

Treasury Department.
April 11, 1864

Sir,

The circulation of corporation notes as money under dissimilar laws of different States contributes largely to the depreciation of the National Currency and constitutes at this moment a most serious danger to the National Finances.[1]

The law making United States Notes a legal tender in payment of debts[2] did not except debts evidenced by these notes; and therefore operated as a virtual repeal of the State laws by which the corporations issuing them were required to redeem them in coin.— Availing themselves of this legislation, these corporations have made the United States Notes the basis of their own issues; and inasmuch as these notes themselves cannot at present be exchanged for coin, redemption has become merely nominal.

No reduction in the volume of National issues, under these circumstances, can work material benefit to the circulation; for every such reduction merely makes room for fresh corporation issues, which are not always or even generally restricted to the amount of United States Notes withdrawn. Thus the issues of the State Corporations create a constantly increasing excess in the volume of currency as compared with the requirements of actual transactions: and this excess works progressive depreciation.

To arrest this depreciation is an absolute necessity, and to effect this object I see no better or more certain means than judicious measures for the exclusion from circulation of all Notes intended to circulate as money, and not authorized by national legislation.

There can be no hardship in such measures; for all corporations now authorized to issue notes under State laws can be changed by proper proceedings into National Banking Associations. The only effect will be to bring all circulation under National control and prevent increase without sanction of Congress.

And not only is there no hardship; but the security which will be given by a unifom currency to all transactions of business will be a positive advantage to all institutions of discount.

Even if there be in some cases a degree of hardship[3] it is only that which should be, and by patriotic and loyal institutions will be, cheerfully borne, as a sacrifice necessary to the public safety and welfare.

To the convenience of the people in the payment of internal taxes;— to the negotiation of loans;—and to the faithful discharge of National obligations to the Army, the Navy, and the public creditors, one currency and that a national currency, is indispensable. The time seems to have come when Congress under the Constitution, should provide such a currency and make it the exclusive circulation of the country, by asserting and maintaining the doctrine that the National Currency belongs to the Nation, and that the emission of notes for circulation as money by private, municipal or state authority is as indefensible as the emission of coin by the same authority, and as subject to restriction and prohibition by Congress under the Constitution.

With a view to the proper assertion of this power by Congress, and as a measure well adapted to prevent the further depreciation of the currency, and to secure its progressive improvement until the attainment of uniformity shall make the assumption of specie payments practicable, and thus give all circulation its highest value, I transmit for the consideration of the Committee and of Congress the accompanying bill.[4]

Very Respectfully,
S P Chase
Secretary of the Treasury.

Hon. Thaddeus Stevens,
Chairman Com. Ways and Means,
H.R.

1. By "corporation notes," Chase referred to the circulating notes of banks incorporated under various state laws.

2. That is, the first legal tender act, passed in February 1862. *Statutes at Large,* 12:345–48.

3. The clerk wrote *some hardship*; Chase struck through *some* and wrote, as an interlineation, *in some cases a degree of.*

4. Chase's proposal would have taxed state bank notes at the rate of three percent annually and declared them illegal one year after the bill's passage. The final version, included as part of the internal revenue act of 1864, allowed the notes to continue circulating but taxed them at one percent per year and levied additional charges that varied with the size of the bank. "A Bill to prevent depreciating the currency," [Apr. 11, 1864] (Orig. Bills, 38th Cong., Recs. of U.S. House of Representatives, Nat. Arch.); *Statutes at Large,* 13:277–78.

TO WILLIAM P. FESSENDEN

Copy in clerk's hand on letterhead stationery. Abraham Lincoln Papers, Library of Congress (*micro* 33:0077).

Treasury Department.
April 12th. 1864

Sir.[1]

Notwithstanding the diminished amount of United States Notes in circulation, and the gradual withdrawal from use as currency of interest bearing United States Notes made a legal tender for their face, the price of gold continues to advance.[2] This effect can only be attributed to one of two causes, and is probably due in part to each: First, to the increase of notes of local banks; and Secondly, to the efforts of speculators. I have already submitted through you to the consideration of the Committee of Ways and Means a bill intended as a remedy for the first evil.[3] I now beg leave to submit to its consideration a bill intended as a remedy for the second.

The first bill, if it becomes a law, will have, I doubt not the most salutary consequences. The effects of the second will probably be more immediate, though perhaps not of such permanent importance.[4]

I ask for both a candid consideration, and if approved, the favorable action of Congress.

It must not be thought, however, that I regard either or both of these measures as adequate remedies for financial disorders. Nothing short of taxation to one-half of the amount of our current expenditures and a reduction of those expenditures to the lowest point compatible with efficiency will ensure financial success to the Government. And without military successes, all measures must fail.

Very Respectfully yours.
(SIGNED) S. P. CHASE
Secretary of the Treasury.

Hon. Wm. P. Fessenden,
Chairman Com. on Finance,
U.S.S.

1. Chase wrote an identical letter to Thaddeus Stevens on the same day, which also included a draft for proposed legislation to outlaw speculation in gold. This was the "second" bill mentioned below. After amendment, the act passed both houses of Congress on June 16 and was signed the following day. Chase to Stevens, Apr. 12, 1864 (Letters Sent to Committees of Congress, Gen. Recs. Treasury Dept., Nat. Arch.); *Congressional Globe,* 38th Cong., 1st sess., 1863–64, 1640, 3062; *Statutes at Large,* 13:132–33.

2. Gold rose in price from about 161 to 165 between the beginning of March and April 12. *Appletons' Annual Cyclopædia,* 4:377; John J. Cisco to Chase, Mar. 21, 1864 (above); *New York Times,* Apr. 12, 1864.

3. See Chase to Thaddeus Stevens, April 11, 1864 (above).

4. The price of gold remained high despite U.S. government sales, which ended on April 19 or 20, and the bill's eventual passage. By the end of April, gold sold for approximately 179 and topped 200 as June closed. From July to December its price fluctuated between 194 and 267. *Appletons' Annual Cyclopædia,* 4:377; Chase to John J. Cisco, Apr. 19, 1864 (Letters Sent, Loan Division, Recs. of Bureau of Public Debt, Nat. Arch.); Cisco to Chase, Apr. 20, 1864 (Cisco Letters, Mo. Hist. Soc.).

TO NATHANIEL P. BANKS

Autograph letter on letterhead stationery. Nathaniel P. Banks Papers, Library of Congress (*micro* 33:0086).

Treasury Department.
Apl. 13, 1864

Dear General,

This letter will reach you, I hope, in the midst of decisive successes. The rebellion must be crushed this summer, or we shall be plunged into the greatest financial difficulties. The immense disbursements incident to the preparations for the campaign just begun are well nigh overwhelming in their demands.[1]

Our immediate anxieties are absorbed by this great necessity: but there are other matters almost as urgent. It is my firm belief that this war has grown out of national injustice in Slavery. It must be delayed in prosecution as it has been, by the continuance of this injustice. You have been the honored instrument of making Louisiana a Free State. While I regret some of the incidents in the accomplishment of this work I rejoice in the work itself. It is good & great: but to make it fruitful as it should be, more is needed. You are a Massachusetts man & in Massachusetts all men are equal before the law. Your action must be tried by Massachusetts standards. It pained me greatly that men supposed to represent your ideas & supporting your preferred candidate for Governor[2] thought fit to stigmatize the free state men who did not see questions of expediency & principle with their light, as Negro Equality Men. Depend upon it, dear General, no permanent honor is to come to any body from such a spirit. There is a grand opportunity in Louisiana to establish institutions on the solid basis of justice and wisdom. Let all who are alike qualified have political rights alike. Let the right to vote be determined not by nativity or complexion, but by intelligence, character & patriotism: Let all vote who have proved their devotion to their country by service in the field & all who, being unconvicted of crime or misdemeanor, can read & write & after the first election are found to possess a competent knowledge of the Constitutions of the State & the United States. It is not difficult to regulate suffrage on this or some such basis. Let the Constitutional Convention authorize an enrollment of the voters who possess these qualifications, by providing for commissions in each Parish to Examine those who desire to exercise the elective franchise & giving to all found qualified, certificates of qualification as electors.[3] After the first General Assembly shall be elected the Legislature can be authorized to provide for the [necessary] examinations. These are only hints of modes of which practical details can be arranged. Better will doubtless suggest themselves. The important point is to have suffrage extended equally to all equally qualified.

If this can be accomplished in Louisiana, the example will be followed in all the Gulf states: and probably in all the states now in rebellion. And what an honor to lead in such a work, which more than anything that can be devised will consolidate Union & ensure against future disturbances!

May this honor be yours! It will be if you will.

Your friend
S P Chase

Maj Gen. N. P. Banks

1. The Red River campaign.

2. Michael Hahn. Benjamin F. Flanders to Chase, Jan. 23, 1864 (above).

3. Louisiana's revised constitution of September 5, 1864, granted state legislators the authority to pass such measures, but they refused to proceed. *Appletons' Annual Cyclopædia,* 4:479.

TO ABRAHAM LINCOLN

Autograph letter on letterhead stationery. Abraham Lincoln Papers, Library of Congress (*micro* 33:0114).

Treasury Department.
April 14 1864

My dear Sir,

I send you a copy of my letter to the Committee on Finance to which I referred yesterday and add another the same Committee which was sent yesterday.[1]

The first urges the exclusion from circulation of all credit currency not sanctioned by Congress

The second urges the repression of gold speculation.

Both measures are of great importance—the first of the greatest.

If Congress will make these measures laws and add a National Banking Act which will make the National Banking system safe & at the same time time acceptable, and a Tax Law which will yield, with duties on imports, four hundred millions of revenue, or half at least of the expenditure, there will be no need to fear financial disasters—unless we shall have unexpected military disasters.

I have taken the liberty heretofore and perhaps too pertinaciously to urge all possible economy compatible with efficiency: but I hope that the importance of it will be thought a sufficient justification

I am glad to understand that the military work of suppressing the rebellion is now to prosecuted with system & the utmost vigor. With system & vigor and economy in the conduct of the war and with the financial measures I have indicated we may confidently expect, through the Divine favor, an early & successful termination of the struggle and the restoration of peace with an unbroken Union of Free States.

Yours very truly
S P Chase

The President

1. Chase actually referred to two sets of identical letters sent to chairs of the House and Senate financial committees. Chase to Thaddeus Stevens, Apr. 11, Chase to William P. Fessenden, Apr. 12, 1864 (above); Chase to Fessenden, Apr. 11, 1864 (Lincoln Papers, L.C.); Chase to Stevens, Apr. 12, 1864 (Letters Sent to Committees of Congress, Gen. Recs. Treasury Dept., Nat. Arch.).

TO ABRAHAM LINCOLN

Autograph letter. Abraham Lincoln Papers, Library of Congress (*micro* 33:0249).

New York, April 15, 1864[1]

My dear Sir,

Two topics seem to occupy exclusively the attention of New York—Speculation and the Metropolitan Fair.[2] Today the tidings from Paducah create a momentary diversion—something this way "A horrible affair that at Paducah!" "Yes, really 'twas terrible." Then a little pause—then, "how's gold now?"[3]

The sales which have been made here yesterday & today seem to have reduced the price; but the reduction is only temporary, unless most decisive measures for reducing the amount of circulation & arresting the rapid increase of debt be adopted. These measures can only be put in operation by Congress, and Congress will be slow to act with the promptitude absolutely indispensable unless you manifest a deep sense of their importance and make members feel that you regard their adoption as essential to the success of your administration.

Thus far every financial measure has been crowned with success; but I have always warned gentlemen in Congress and in the Administration that debt could not be increased indefinitely by selling bonds & issuing notes; and the time has come when taxation and retrenchment must play their parts. They ought to have been called into activity a year ago; but is not yet too late. Without them it is my duty to say emphatically *there is no hope* of continued financial success.

Next to taxation and retrenchment a uniform national currency is most important. This can be accomplished only through the passage of the National Banking Law now before Congress; or by some bill embracing its leading amendments of the act of last year. In my judgment the Banks organized under this law should pay their full share of taxation,—but they should be taxed under National & not under State laws. The National Government will need to pay interest on debt, current expences, &, so long as the war lasts, its extraordinary expences, vast sums from taxes. Duties on imports are the only exclusive resource of the Nation as distinguished from the states. Why should not the National Banks & their property and franchises be added? I see no good reason: while uniform taxation by Congress would put all the Banks throughout the country upon an equal footing and secure the unity & completeness of the System. Some of the New York Members have urged their subjection to state taxes, & some concessions have, I think unwisely, been made to their wishes. It would be much better could they be prevailed on to yield their wishes to the public good.

The National Banking bill should be followed by the bill to tax local bank circulation & prohibit after some fixed period its further issue.

These two bills will give us what we must have, if success is wanted, a national currency.

If you concur with me in these judgments, may I not hope that you will send for such members as are disposed, from any cause, to be lukewarm or opposed & urge them to give their needful support to the bills. Mr. Hooper in the House and Mr. Sherman in the Senate will gladly furnish you all necessary information as to the views of Senators & Representatives.

Since I have been writing a gentleman has come in who tells me that Gold after declining to 171 & 170 was carried up again on the news of the disaster at Paducah, exaggerated as much as possible, interested & unfriendly persons, to 174.

I hope to be able to go to Philadelphia tomorrow and to return to Washington, Monday Evening or Tuesday Morning.

With the greatest respect & regard

Yours truly
S P CHASE

The President

1. Although Chase's date could plausibly be 25—and this letter was filed by that date in Lincoln's papers—the New York dateline, the reference to skirmishing at Paducah, and a retained copy in Chase's papers at the Historical Society of Pennsylvania all indicate a date of April 15.

2. Chase arrived in New York late on April 13 and left for Philadelphia on the sixteenth. His purpose apparently was to manage the Federal response to dramatic increases in the price of gold. The Metropolitan Fair, which opened on April 4, was a fund-raising benefit conducted in behalf of the U.S. Sanitary Commission. Chase to John J. Cisco, Apr. 13 (Telegrams Sent, Gen. Recs. Treasury Dept., Nat. Arch.); Chase to Jay Cooke, Apr. 10 (above); Horace Greeley to Chase, April 16 (below); Chase to George Harrington, Apr. 16, 1864 (Harrington Papers, Mo. Hist. Soc.); Chase to Andrew Johnson, Apr. 16, 1864 (Susan Walker Papers, Cinc. Hist. Soc.); *New York Times*, Apr. 4, 1864.

3. According to later reports, troops under Confederate general Nathan Bedford Forrest had attacked Federal forces at Paducah, Ky., on April 14 and looted the town under a flag of truce. Long, *Civil War Day by Day*, 485; *OR*, ser. 1, v. 32, pt. 1:549–50.

FROM HORACE GREELEY

Autograph letter on letterhead stationery. Chase Papers, Historical Society of Pennsylvania (*micro* 33:0143).

Office of The Tribune,
New York, April 16, 1864.
5 P.M.

Dear Sir:

I had to visit Albany yesterday in behalf of my book; and I returned to-day in season to have met you had I not supposed you would remain till 7 P.M. I reached the Sub-Treasury just after you had left.[1]

I write to beg you to issue an appeal to all loyal men and women, over your own signature, asking every one to take $50 or over in the Ten-Forty Loan, explaining what it is, what are the inducements to take it, and how the money is to be employed, and entreating them to *trust themselves*. Show them that this will pay the armies, contract the currency, kill speculation, and finish the monopolists of Food, &c., &c. You can safely assure them that, if they will put up Five Hundred Millions before the 4th of July, you will restrict the currency by at least half that amount. (I think a great deal more, by compelling the State Banks to contract). I beg you to make a bold, [*illeg.*], stirring appeal, such as you so well can, and ask every loyal journal in America to publish it as an act of patriotic duty. The People only want to see what is to be done, and *how* it is to be done, and they will do it. Their hearts were never sounder than they are to-day. And if we should have a victory in May, you can borrow all you want.

If you should want more money than you are authorized to accept on 10–40s, try another 7.30. or other temporary loan, and make a fresh appeal. We are bound to go through, and ought to do it with full pockets.

I mean to visit Washington five or six weeks hence, if you do not return to us meantime. My faith increases.

Yours,
HORACE GREELEY.

Hon S. P. Chase, Sec. Treasury.

1. On April 10, Greeley had completed the first volume of *The American Conflict . . .*, 2 vols. (Hartford, 1864, 1866). The U.S. subtreasury in New York was located at the corner of Wall Street and Nassau. Glyndon Van Deusen, *Horace Greeley: Nineteenth-Century Crusader* (Philadelphia, 1953), 301; *New York Dir. (1864)*, 6.

TO HORACE GREELEY

Autograph letter on letterhead stationery. Horace Greeley Papers, Rare Books and Manuscripts Division, The New York Public Library, Astor, Lenox, and Tilden Foundations (*micro* 33:0152).

Treasury Department.
Apl. 19, 1864

My dear Mr. Greeley,

Your letter was put into my hands in Philadelphia yesterday morning.[1] I will try to prepare an appeal unless too much badgered. It is hardly worth while however, for I cannot do the work half so well as you have already done it in the Tribune. Still I will try my hand.[2]

The Speculators got a very bad black eye last week; but will rally of course. The scare did Congress good: though many members persist in saddling the National Banks with State taxation. This if persisted in is going to be very mischievous. It will make parties every where about much or little taxation, and hurt our side. Let these Banks & the Capital in them be reserved as exclusive subjects of National taxation and let them be taxed by an uniform rule all over the country as much as they can bear. In this way we get a fruitful source of revenue & shall soon be able to let off many vexatious small taxes. Besides National Banks should in principle be sublect only to National Taxation just as foreign commerce is. Let the States have the real estate exclusively & concurrently private personal property & transactions; Let the Nation have exclusively foreign commerce & National Banks & concurrently private personal property & transactions. Such a division will work well.

Yours cordially
S P CHASE

Hon. H. Greeley

1. See Greeley to Chase, April 16, 1864 (above).
2. The editors have not located such an appeal.

TO JAY COOKE

Letterpress copy of autograph letter. Chase Papers, Historical Society of Pennsylvania (*micro* 33:0450).

May 5, 64

My dear Mr. Cooke,

I hope my *wrathiness* was not excessive.[1] Indeed it was vexation in thinking that all my labors to serve our country had found recompense, so far as Mr. Lincolns special friends were concerned and with his apparent—but as I hope & believe merely apparent—endorsement, only in outrageous calumny. I seldom consult personal considerations in my public conduct and so suppressed my inclination to resign my office & denounce the conspiracy of which the Blairs are the most visible embodiment. After returning from Baltimore I conferred with Gov. Brough[2] & other friends who were earnest in advising against resignation, & I yielded to their judgment, which indeed coincided with my own, though exceedingly contrary to my impulses. Immediately afterwards I was obliged to visit Philadelphia & was absent from Wednesday Morning until Saturday night. On Monday I learned that the Ohio Delegation had taken the matter up & that one of them had called on the President who disavowed in the most explicit terms all connexion with & responsibility for Blairs assault, & expressed his decided disapproval of it.[3] As this was merely verbal, however, the delegation determined to call on the President in a body and make & obtain a distinct statement in writing—on their part of their advice, my action, & their convictions on what was due from the President to me, to Ohio & to the country & on his part such reply as he should see fit to give.[4]

Thus the matter now stands. It seems now only simple justice to me that every friend who believes I have done my duty should by voice, pen and press utter the sentiments which this outragous attack must kindle in honest minds of indignation against the unworthy men who have set on foot & propagated these vile calumnies.

Yours faithfully
S P Chase

Jay Cooke Esq

1. On April 23, Frank Blair, Jr., had delivered a scathing attack on the floor of the U.S. House that accused Cooke, Chase, and his Treasury agents—"blood-hounds," in Blair's words—of fraud and corruption wielded to advance Chase's presidential aspirations. In a meeting with Lincoln shortly after, the president reassigned Blair to active duty as a major general of volunteers. Chase learned about both events and surmised Lincoln's complicity in Blair's attack later the same day en route to a fair in Baltimore to benefit the U.S. Sanitary Commission. "I was shown to Mr. Chase's presence in a car set apart for his use," Albert Gallatin Riddle, former Free-Soil congressman from Ohio, later recalled. "He was alone, and in a frightful rage, and controlled himself with difficulty while he explained the cause. The recital in a hoarse, constrained voice, seemed to rekindle his anger and aggravate its intensity. The spacious car fairly trembled under his feet." Basler, *Collected Works,* 7:312; *Congressional Globe,* 38th Cong., 1st sess., 1864, 1828–32; *DAB,* 15:591; Albert Gallatin Riddle, *Recollections of War Times: Reminiscences of Men and Events in Washington, 1860–1865* (New York, 1895), 266, 267.

2. John Brough served as Republican governor of Ohio, 1864–65. *DAB,* 3:94–95.

3. According to Riddle, Lincoln disavowed Blair's speech in a two-hour interview on May 2 with Riddle and Ohio congressman Rufus Paine Spalding. "If you intend to make it the occasion of pursuing a personal warfare," Lincoln supposedly warned Blair prior to the speech, "you had better remain silent." *Bio. Dir. U.S. Cong.,* 1849; Riddle, *Recollections,* 269–76.

4. On May 3, Union members of the Ohio congressional delegation requested an interview with Lincoln for the following day. Whether that meeting transpired is not known. Ohio congressman James M. Ashley did confer with Lincoln on May 5. Ashley to Lincoln, May 3, 1864 (Lincoln Papers, L.C.); Miers, *Lincoln Day by Day,* 3:256.

TO ABRAHAM LINCOLN

Autograph letter on letterhead stationery. Abraham Lincoln Papers, Library of Congress (*micro* 33:0482).

Treasury Department.
May 6, 1864.

Sir,

In obedience to your direction to prepare and give you in writing my opinion as to what course the Government should take in relation to the Massacre, by the rebels, of our colored soldiers with their white officers, after surrender, at Fort Pillow, I respectfully submit the following views.[1]

All soldiers enlisted and mustered into the service of the Nation should, in my judgment, be placed, in all respects, upon the same footing, without regard to complexion, and this equality, so far as protection is concerned was pledged to the colored soldiers by the Presidents Order of July 30, 1863.[2]

To redeem this pledge it becomes necessary to retaliate the slaughter, in violation of the laws of war, of the officers & men who surrendered at

Fort Pillow by the execution of an equal or equivalent number of rebel officers & soldiers.

It does not seem probable that the selection for execution of equal numbers would so surely arrest the perpetration of such atrocities as those of Fort Pillow as would the selection an equivalent number of officers of high rank: for the Slaveholding class, which furnishes such officers, holds very cheap the lives of the nonslaveholding classes which furnish the privates.

I think, therefore, that among the rebel prisoners of highest rank, now held by the United States, there should be taken a number, equivalent, according to the rules of exchange, to the number of officers & men murdered at Fort Pillow & that notice of the selection should be given by the Lieutenant General to the General commanding the rebel armies, accompanied by a demand for information whether the Fort Pillow murders are sanctioned by the rebel authorities.[3]

Should an affirmative answer be returned or should it become otherwise manifest that those atrocities will not be disavowed but repeated, then the pledge given by the order of July 30, 1863 should be promptly and decisively redeemed.

With great respect,
S P CHASE

The President

1. The alleged atrocity occurred on April 23, when Confederate cavalry under the command of Nathan Bedford Forrest took the Federal post of Fort Pillow, Tenn. Lincoln solicited opinions from all members of his cabinet on May 3. Long, *Civil War Day by Day*, 484; Lincoln to cabinet members, May 3, 1864, in Basler, *Collected Works*, 7:328.

2. According to General Orders No. 252, "for every soldier of the United States killed in violation of the laws of war, a rebel soldier shall be executed; and for every one enslaved by the enemy or sold into slavery, a rebel soldier shall be placed at hard labor on the public works." "Order of Retaliation," July 30, 1863, in Basler, *Collected Works*, 6:357.

3. The cabinet never articulated an official response to the incident at Fort Pillow. If accepted, Chase's advice would have required Ulysses S. Grant to initiate the message. Not until February 1865, when Robert E. Lee received an appointment as commanding general, did the Confederacy have a similar position beneath its commander-in-chief, Jefferson Davis. *DAB*, 7:496; John G. Nicolay and John Hay, *Abraham Lincoln: A History*, 10 vols. (New York, 1917), 6:483; Emory Thomas, *The Confederate Nation, 1861–1865* (New York, 1979), 282.

TO JOHN C. HAMILTON

Letterpress copy of letter in clerk's hand, signed by Chase. Chase Papers, Historical Society of Pennsylvania (*micro* 33:0576).

Private

May 13, 1864.

Dear Sir,[1]

I have received your letter of the 9th instant, and thank you for it.—Friendly suggestion or criticism is never unwelcome to me.

I think I see the financial condition very clearly, and there are few things to which my attention is called by friends or opponents which have not already been subjects of anxious reflection.— I think there is no real difficulty in carrying our finances safely and triumphantly through this war, except that which has embarrassed and retarded the war itself.— Congress is unwilling to take the decisive steps which are indispensable to the highest degree of public credit, and the executive does not, I fear, sufficiently realize[2] the importance of an energetic and comprehensive policy in all departments of Administration.— It is the part of Congress, by adequate taxation, to provide for so large a portion of current expenditure as to reduce the amounts to be borrowed within limits which leave no doubt as to the ability of the country to provide both for principal and interest. It is its duty also to set apart such funds for the payment of interest and for the reduction of principal as will be seen and confessed by all impartial minds to be sufficient for the object; and it is its farther duty to limit expenditures to objects of the most urgent importance, and restrict them by the most rigid economy compatible with efficiency.

Congress shrinks from adequate taxation; it shrinks from the necessary appropriation of specific funds; it takes but little oversight either of the character or of the amount of expenditure.— Here are our greatest difficulties. They may prove insuperable. We cannot borrow at moderate rates of interest under legislation which does not inspire confidence, and we cannot borrow at extravagant rates without incurring annual charges beyond the possibility of payment.

Let Congress give me the measures I require, and let the President give me the support of economical and efficient administration, Civil and Military, and I will undertake to resume specie payments at a week's notice and to maintain them; and yet borrow at five per cent. all the money which will be required to carry on the war for two years longer.

What I can do under other circumstances is not so clear. I can only, so long as I remain at the head of the Treasury Department, do all in my power.

Yours very truly and respectfully,
S P Chase

Jno: C. Hamilton, Esquire,
No. 17 W. 20 St.
N.Y.

1. New York attorney John Church Hamilton (1792–1882) was one of Alexander Hamilton's sons. *Appletons'*, 3:60.

2. The phrase, *I fear, sufficiently realize* is Chase's interlineation after cancellation of a word as written by the clerk.

TO JESSE BALDWIN

Letterpress copy of autograph letter. Chase Papers, Historical Society of Pennsylvania (*micro* 33:0665).

Private

Washington, May 18, 1864

Dear Sir,[1]

I have too sincere a friendship for you to be indifferent to any thing you say or write. It may not always be in my power to agree with friends or to manifest my sentiments towards them as they or I would wish, but they are never forgotten, nor do their services to our common cause ever cease to be gratefully remembered.

Your letter and the petition enclosed with it have both been carefully read.

I do not agree with you in thinking that the Constitution prohibits the issue of legal tender notes under [the aut]hority of Congress: but I do concur in the opinion [that] an inflated paper currency is a great evil & should be reformed as soon as possible.

The difficulty is in the practicability of the reform; so long as expenditure so largely overgoes income.

In my judgment if Congress will "[perfect] a good & judicious excise law," and give the Country a National Banking System instead of State Banking Systems and State Banking without System it will not be difficult to return to specie payments. We must pay as we go or very nearly that; if we want to maintain credit at its highest point. As long as Government spends four or five times as much as it collects, there can be no permanent financial safety. It was well enough to borrow at first, when the military authorities told us that the rebellion would be suppressed "in a year" or after a "short sharp decisive struggle;" but as soon as it became manifest that borrowing [was going] to any amount over a [thousand] or at most fifteen hund millions Congress ought to have provided taxes sufficient to make it certain that the debt should not be carried beyond say two thousand or at most twenty five hundred Millions. It is not too late even now for Congress by retrenchment and taxation to ensure this: but retrenchment and taxation are not popular & Congressmen want to be popular. To be sure a crash will come & then there will be a reckoning; but every one says, "after *me* the deluge."[2]

Your redemption plan would be good if there were not a better; but where would you get coin unless redemption of specie payments comes first to pay the first instalment of redemption bonds. In my judgment the first step is to economize & systematize expenditure; [next] the most energetic energy in the prosecution of the War; next exclusion of State Bank Notes from circulation; next [adequate] taxation; next resumption sustained by the [whole] power of the Government. Many details I cannot notice; but the general outline indicates where in my judgment lies the path of safety.

You say nothing about your family. I shall be glad to know how you all are; and what you are doing.

Sincerely your friend
S P Chase

Jesse Baldwin Esq.
Youngstown, O

1. Baldwin represented Mahoning County in the Ohio House, 1860–61. Gilkey, *Ohio Hundred Year Book,* 240.

2. The expression, *après moi le déluge,* gained currency during the reign of Louis XV of France. *La Grande Encyclopédie: Inventaire Raisonné des Sciences, des Lettres et des Arts,* 31 vols. (Paris, 1886–1902), 22:649; Paul Augé, ed., *Larousse du XXe Siècle,* 6 vols. (Paris, 1928–33), 1:293.

TO JOHN BROUGH

Letterpress copy of autograph letter. Chase Papers, Historical Society of Pennsylvania (*micro* 33:0705).

May 19, 4

My dear Governor,

Few things, in my public experience, have given me so much satisfaction, as your manifestations of sympathy and friendship, when I conferred with you as to the course I ought to take on the occasion of Blair's malignant assault apparently endorsed by the President.[1] I have followed your counsel then given, though at a great cost of personal feeling, because I was sure it was the counsel of a patriot & a friend. I shall never forget your expressions of personal interest, so manifestly prompted by the heart. I felt them through and through. If I ever have an opportunity to show the gratitude I feel you shall see how real it is.

The terrible rains have arrested the progress of Grant & have given the rebels an opportunity to mass a large force against Butler & force him back to his entrenchments.[2] In one point of view this seems well enough, for the more Butler has against him the fewer there will be to dispute the advance of Grant. Today the skies look as if we should have some days of clear weather: My anxiety is very great; but departmental administration allows me no voice in military matters—not even in those which most nearly concern the Treasury—and I can therefore only wait, & pray, & hope.

It has become quite apparent now that the importunity of Mr. Lincoln's special friends for an Early Convention in order to make his nomination sure was a mistake both for him & for the country. The Convention will not be regarded as an Union Convention; but simply as a Blair-Lincoln Convention, by a great body of citizens whose support is essential to success. Few except those already committed to Mr. Lincoln will consider themselves bound by a predetermined nomination. Very many, who may ultimately vote for Mr Lincoln, will wait the course of events, hoping that some popular movement for Grant or some other successful general will offer a better hope of saving the country. Others, and the number seems to be increasing, will not support his nomination in any event; believing that our ill success, thus far, in the suppression of the rebellion is due mainly to his course of action & inaction; & that no change can be for the worse.

But these are speculations merely from my standpoint. You see the field more clearly, because through less mist, and can cast the horoscope better than I. May God direct all sight. "My heart's desire & prayer to Him for (America) is that (S[he]) may be saved".

I went out yesterday to see our troops; the hundred days men—but not having taken sufficient care to inform myself of localities failed to find any of them. I shall go again tomorrow.[3]

The Treasury Investigation will, I think, show that the Department has kept up with the demands of the times, and fully vindicate my plan of executing a large part of the work of preparing bonds & notes in the Treasury Building. The improvements in Machinery made by the much abused Mr. Clark have alone made the mechanical execution of the immense work possible.[4]

Faithfully yours
S P Chase

His Excellency
John Brough,
&c &c &c

1. Chase also discussed his response to Blair's speech of April 23 in a letter to Jay Cooke, May 5 (above).

2. May 19 marked the eleventh day of the battle of Spotsylvania, Va., in which Federal forces under Ulysses S. Grant faced Robert E. Lee's Army of Northern Virginia. On May 18, Confederate Pierre G. T. Beauregard had pressed Benjamin F. Butler's Army of the James into a corner formed by the James River on the north and the Appomattox River to the south. According to one newspaper report on May 18, "offensive operations had been necessarily suspended until the roads became passable." *Daily National Intelligencer,* May 18, 1864; Long, *Civil War Day by Day,* 496–506.

3. On April 21, Brough and the governors of Indiana, Illinois, Iowa, and Wisconsin offered to recruit a total of 85,000 infantry troops in U.S. service for the limited term of 100 days. Lincoln accepted the offer two days later. Basler, *Collected Works,* 7:312–13.

4. In 1862, the Treasury Department assumed a responsibility previously borne by outside contractors to print and cut its own paper currency under the direction of Spencer Morton Clark, head of the National Currency Bureau. On May 3, a select committee of the U.S. House commenced an investigation into the wisdom of this arrangement and into allegations that Clark and Gustavus A. Henderson, a clerk in the Treasury Department, had corrupted female employees. In its final report on June 30, from which a minority dissented, the committee endorsed the department's control of printing and dismissed the charges of immorality as "shameful and unfounded." It also recommended that other allegations of fraud in the Treasury Department be referred to the Joint Committee on the Conduct of the War. Baker, *History,* 287–328; *Treasury Department,* 38th Cong., 1st sess., 1864, H. Rep. 140; Chase to George Harrington, Nov. 19, 1863 (above); *Register of Officers (1863),* 42; *Wash. Dir. (1864),* 127.

FROM GIDEON WELLES

Letter in clerk's hand on letterhead stationery, signed by Welles.
Letters Received from the Navy Department, General Records, Department of the Treasury (Record Group 56), National Archives (*micro* 33:0753).

Navy Department,
Washington, May 20th 1864,

Sir:

I have the honor to call your attention to delay in the payment of requisitions from this Department, and to state that many of the Contractors who are running their establishments almost exclusively for the Government, in some instances night and day, are seriously embarrassed for the want of funds, and unless speedily releived will be compelled to postpone the completion of their work.

The embarrassment occasioned by a delay in the payment of such bills is not confined to the Contractors but reaches thousands of Mechanics who are dependent upon their daily labor for their support.

Persons who have been in the habit of furnishing supplies inform the Department that they cannot sell to Government upon the same terms that they would to individuals—so great is the un certainty and so long the delay in receiving payment.

Of late payments to Contractors have almost entirely ceased and the evil is so serious that I have thought it best to call your special attention to the matter hoping that a remedy may be devised.[1]

I have the honor to be,

Very Respectfully,
Gideon Welles
Secretary of the Navy—

Hon, S. P. Chase
Secretary of the Treasury.

1. "In the absence of legislative provision for adequate revenues from the taxation there is no available resource except loans," responded Chase, "and it is extremely difficult to obtain, in this way, the means required to meet the very large expenditures under the direction of the War and Navy Departments." Chase to Welles, May 24, 1864 (Letters Sent to Cabinet, Gen. Recs. Treasury Dept., Nat. Arch.).

TO ALFRED P. STONE

Letterpress copy of autograph letter. Chase Papers, Historical Society of Pennsylvania (*micro* 33:0780).

Washington May 23, 1864

My dear Colonel,

All right as to the note. The people are crazy or I am. I dont *see* the recent military successes.[1] Most earnestly do I pray that we may see them hereafter. All under God depends on Grant. So far he has achieved very little and that little has cost beyond computation. Still my hope is in him. He seems the ablest & most persistent man we have. Sherman has done well & apparently more than Grant. I think he has good opportunities if Mr. Lincoln will only let the black loyalists have a fair chance—that is let them come into the army on a perfectly equal footing as to pay, chances of promotion, & right to vote on the soil which they help recover from rebellion, with white loyalists. Such a policy, honestly adopted & manfully carried out, will save us. Nothing short of it, in my opinion, will. Without such a policy Sherman must grow weaker & weaker as he advances; and Savannah, if he ever reaches it, may be his Moscow.[2]

I have not written a word to Ohio I believe on the subject of the villainous malignant, & lying assault on me by the Blairs—for the Congressional General was only the Mouthpiece of the trio—and its apparent endorsement by Mr. Lincoln.[3] I did not want to say any thing by way of appeal, in my personal behalf,—against an endorsement of Mr. Lincoln while the great outrage, not on me only but on the Constitution, implied in sending back Blair to the Army in the way & under the circumstances he was sent back remains on the record unredressed. I would not write this were it possible for the letter to reach you in time to affect the action of the Convention. If the facts don't speak to the people I have no desire to speak to them, at present.

Yours sincerely
S: P: CHASE

Col. A. P. Stone

1. Stone had apparently notified Chase about proposed resolutions to renominate Lincoln for the presidency and to "congratulate the country on the success of our army," which the Ohio Union state convention subsequently adopted on May 25. *Cincinnati Daily Commercial,* May 26, 1864.

2. Grant was pushing the Army of the Potomac southward through Virginia toward Richmond, slowed by battles with Lee's troops at the Wilderness and Spotsylvania. As part of a multi-pronged strategy initiated early in May, William Tecumseh Sherman, commanding the Federal armies of the Tennessee, the Cumberland, and the Ohio, had moved from Chattanooga and was advancing slowly toward Atlanta. Chase anticipated Sherman's movement to the coast at Savannah, Ga., deep into enemy country beyond sources of aid and supplies, and feared the possibility of a result similar to what had befallen Napoleon I in his disastrous campaign into Russia in 1812. Sherman reached Savannah in December 1864 and early the next year began to advance northward through the Carolinas. Long, *Civil War Day by Day,* 483, 492–96, 498–99, 504–7, 597, 613; *DAB,* 17:95–96; Thorne, *Chambers's Biographical Dictionary,* 931.

3. For Chase's reaction to Frank Blair, Jr.'s speech of April 23, see Chase to Jay Cooke, May 5, 1864 (above).

TO JOHN J. CISCO

Autograph letter on letterhead stationery. John J. Cisco Papers, Miscellaneous Manuscripts Collection, Library of Congress (*micro* 33:0793).

Treasury Department.
May 24 1864

My dear Sir,

Your letter of yesterday gave me the first real pain I have experienced from any act of yours since we have been connected by official relations.[1]

In your practical wisdom, steadfast integrity & indefatigable labors I have found invaluable support; while your personal kindness has ever made it a pleasure to me to confer with you & to profit by your counsels.

The fact that now propose to withdraw from your responsible post under the constraint of imperative considerations arising from the condition of your health impaired in the public service greatly enhances the regret which your intended resignation by itself excites.

I wish it were possible for you leave your post in charge of some other officer long enough to regain your health without severing your connexion with the Department; and if you have not already weighed this thought I hope you will do so.

If you have weighed it and have, nevertheless, decided on tendering your resignation there will be no choice but to accept it; hoping and praying that you may find, in relief from official duties and anxieties and amid new scenes and circumstances that renovation of health for which you seek and for which you lay down the office you have filled so long, so worthily and so usefully.

Most truly & faithfully

Your friend,
S: P: Chase

John J. Cisco, Esq

1. Cisco evidently corresponded with Chase at least twice on May 23. He requested details on the terms of a $50 million loan that Chase proposed to offer, but that letter says nothing about any intention to resign. Cisco to Chase, May 23, 1864 (Cisco Letters, Mo. Hist. Soc.).

FROM GIDEON WELLES

Letter in clerk's hand on letterhead stationery, signed by Welles. Letters Received from Executive Officers (AB Series), General Records, Department of the Treasury (Record Group 56), National Archives (*micro* 33:0839).

Navy Department,
Washington, 25 May, 1864.

Sir:

I have the honor to acknowledge the receipt of your letter of the 11th. inst., suggesting the expediency "of the purchase by each Department of the coin it may need for its special disbursements and the keeping of its accounts exclusively in lawful currency."[1]

Careful consideration has been given to your suggestion, which it seems to me is open to many and very serious objections. Practically, so far as this Department is concerned, it cannot be carried into execution without an entire revolution in the present method of paying drafts upon the Department—a method which has been in practice since its organization.

No inconsiderable portion of the foreign expenses of the naval service is now paid by drafts upon Baring, Bros. & Co, London, who are reimbursed at heavy expense, it requiring in our lawful but depreciated paper, with the present rate of exchange, discount on drafts &c., more than two dollars in our lawful currency to secure one dollar in specie when payments are made. I am not prepared to admit that the cost of reducing our domestic currency into gold, which is the basis for exchange, and the true measure of value everywhere, is a proper charge upon this Department. Although we have for the last two years met this expense, no estimates or appropriations for this difference have been made, nor can it be designed by Congress that the funds, or any portion of them appropriated for the use of the Navy should be paid in a currency not available to meet its expenses.

It is only where drafts payable in gold if drawn directly upon the Department, can be more readily and advantageously disposed of, than if drawn upon the Barings, that such has been the custom, as at Panama, and at some of the West India Islands, &c.

Requisitions to meet the payment of such drafts, accompanied by the drafts themselves, are made upon the Treasury Department, and I am not aware that the Navy Department is authorized to make such requisitions greater than the face of the draft. To do so would be to introduce a practice liable to abuse by abandoning one of the checks hitherto considered necessary for the protection of the Government.

At the points I have named, and at others, drafts not payable in gold cannot be negotiated, owing to the fluctuation in the value of our paper currency, and I apprehend that it would seriously embarrass the service to disturb existing arrangements or customs in these respects.

I need not assure you that the expenses of this Department payable in gold have always been confined to the smallest possible limit, the officers and others on foreign service being allowed to draw gold only for their actual expenses abroad, and though blankets and very many other articles similar to those furnished the Indians, form a part of the naval supplies, I have not required gold for their purchase; and for the expenses of the Department in California and at other points within the United States "where coin is the chief or only currency", payments greatly to the disadvantage of the Department as well as those in its service, have been made in our depreciated currency.

The express authority of Congress was deemed necessary to authorize the Treasury Department to purchase and dispose of gold [Acts March 17, 1862 and March 17, 1864][2] and without such authorization, and an appropriation expressly to meet the expense, I do not feel myself authorized to enter the market as a purchaser of gold.

The wisdom of unsettling the policy of the government, previously and always safely pursued, and requiring the Navy Department to discharge certain fiscal duties properly pertaining to, and heretofore performed by, the Treasury, I do not acquiesce in, and must respectfully remonstrate against the change. Our foreign liabilities are contracted and must be discharged on the true money basis.

The proposition that foreign bills shall not be paid by the Treasury as has been done in all time because based on true values, but that the Navy Department shall now take upon itself these fiscal duties, is such a revolution and will be so liable to error and abuse, as to render it in every point of view objectionable.

The domestic bills and liabilities of the Navy Department I shall endeavor to meet by requisitions on the Treasury to be paid in the lawful paper money of the government, facilitating as far as possible the arrangements and operations of the Treasury, but the requisitions for foreign bills payable in gold had better be met by the Treasury as in all past time. The requisitions of the Navy on the Treasury will specify the necessity for specie when it exists, but the requisitions and the bills should correspond and be for the amount actually drawn for, without alteration while in their transit to the Treasury by intermediate Agents empowered to purchase gold from day to day at the expense of the government, when the government has gold in its vaults which the Treasury has recently been authorized to sell.

I have to honor to be,

Very respectfully,
GIDEON WELLES
Secretary of the Navy.

Hon.
S. P. Chase,
Secretary of the Treasury.

1. Chase had written to the heads of the departments of War, Navy, and the Interior to state that those departments' requisitions for payments in coin "in the aggregate make a heavy draft for coin and create misapprehensions as to the amount of the actual expenditure of the several Departments reckoned in lawful money.— The Acts of Congress do not seem to contemplate payments in coin, except for interest and principal of the public debt.—" Chase to William H. Seward, with notation of similar letters sent to other departments, May 11, 1864 (Letters Sent to Cabinet, Gen. Recs. Treasury Dept., Nat. Arch.).

2. Legislation of March 17, 1862, authorized the Treasury secretary to "purchase coin with any of the bonds or notes of the United States." A joint resolution of Congress two years later permitted him to sell gold in the Treasury "not necessary for the payment of interest of the public debt." *Statutes at Large,* 12:370, 13:404.

TO JOHN SHERMAN

Autograph letter on letterhead stationery. John Sherman Papers, Library of Congress (*micro* 33:0854).

Treasury Department.
May 26, 1864

My dear Sir,

I enclose two drafts of a National Bank taxation clause—one marked A. providing for the appropriation of the whole tax to the payment of interest or principal of the public debt & repealing the real estate direct tax law, and another marked B. dividing the proceeds of the tax between the National & the loyal States. In either form the clause will be vastly more beneficial to the country than in the form of the bill whether original or amended.[1]

I also enclose a draft of a section providing for tax on Banks not National [in] the Internal Revenue Act.[2] It substantially restores the House proposition limiting it to Banks of the States.

Some discrimination in favor of the National System which affords substantial support to the Government as compared with the Local System which [is] circulating notes in competition with those issued by [the] Government seems to me indispensably necessary.

It is impossible to prevent the depreciation of the currency unless Congress will assume its constitutional function & control it: and it is idle to try to make loans unless Congress will give the necessary support to public credit.

I am now compelled to advertise for a loan of fifty millions & to avoid as far as practicable the evils of sales below par must offer the last bonds of '81.[3] Should the provisions I ask for be sanctioned I shall anticipate a satisfactory premium. Should they be denied I may still be able to negotiate one loan on pretty fair terms: but I dread the effects on future loans.

Hitherto I have been able to maintain the public credit at the best points possible with a surcharged circulation. My ability to do so is due mainly to the legislation of the session of 1862–3.[4] I must have further legislation in the same direction if it is desired to maintain that ability.

Yours truly
S P Chase

Hon John Sherman

1. Sherman served on a conference committee responsible for reconciling House and Senate amendments to the bank bill, H.R. 395. The final version, signed on June 3, 1864, did not incorporate the clauses suggested by Chase. *Congressional Globe,* 38th Cong., 1st sess., 1864, pt. 1, 2476, 2621; *Statutes at Large,* 13:99–118.

2. For earlier suggestions regarding the bill, see Chase to Thaddeus Stevens, April 11, 1864 (above). Chase also discussed the need for additional taxes in correspondence to William E. Dodge, March 31, 1864 (above). As passed, the internal revenue act of 1864 provided "That any bank ceasing to issue notes for circulation, and which shall deposit in the treasury of the United States, in lawful money, the amount of its outstanding circulation, to be redeemed at par, under such regulations as the Secretary of the Treasury may prescribe, shall be exempt from any tax upon such circulation." *Statutes at Large,* 13:278.

3. On July 17, 1861, Congress had authorized a national loan of $250 million, payable in twenty years. Ibid., 12:259–61.

4. Notable financial legislation of the Thirty-seventh Congress included the first and second legal tender acts, February 25 and July 11, 1862, the internal revenue act of July 1, 1862, and the national banking act (national currency act) of February 25, 1863. Ibid., 12:345–48, 432–89, 532–33, 665–82.

TO RICHARD SMITH

Letterpress copy of letter in clerk's hand, signed by Chase. Chase Papers, Historical Society of Pennsylvania (*micro* 33:0876).

Private

May. 27th, 4

My dear Sir,

I notice in your money article of the 24th some comments upon an article copied from the New York Tribune which I think put the saddle on the wrong horse entirely.[1] The expenses of the Government average $2.500.000 a day: often they considerably exceed that amount. $2.500.000 a day is in round number $65.000.000 a month. Now there are only two ways to provide this sum; one is by borrowing; the other is by issuing legal tender notes in some form. Suppose I advertise for a loan of sixty-five millions to pay the expenses of one month at six per cent., at what rate would the bonds be taken? The six per cent. bonds of 1881 sold yesterday at 114.[2] The real value, accrued interest deducted, is between 112 and 112½. Now suppose sixty-five millions put on the market, what price could be obtained? Possibly 110. Suppose another sixty-five millions put on the market next month: what price then? Doubtful if par. It is easy to see that to obtain money by loans in this way, however it might suit the ideas of some people, who suppose that the capacity of absorbing loans is infinite, would hardly work in practice.

All that can be done by loans in any form is to absorb what naturally seeks investment in this description of securities, and if this capacity of absorption be *crowded,* the effect of the glut will be found in the rapid diminution of the price of bonds until they become entirely unavailable.—

How idle it is then to clamor about raising money by loans exclusively; about selling the bonds for what they will bring, and all that. Under existing circumstances the best that can possibly be done is to get all that can be got by loans without greatly damaging those already in the market, and to meet the remainder of expenses by legal tenders so made as to inflate the circulation as little as possible. It was no choice of mine to issue the 5 per cent. legal tenders;[3] it was a necessity created by the inadequacy of revenue as compared with expenditures, and by the impossibility of making loans at any rate of interest.

It is a great mistake, however, to think that the currency is inflated by the amount of the issues. About two hundred millions of notes were issued. The issue no doubt inflated the currency, but an issue of forty or fifty millions of non-interest paying legal tenders would have inflated it equally. The truth is that the currency was surcharged when the issue began, and the true remedy was taxation enough to pay so large a proportion of expenses that the residue could have been provided for by loans. And the only real remedy for the evils of our present situation is, greater taxation, diminished expenditure, and preparation for a return to specie payments.

Some people seem to think that I ascribe the inflation of the currency to the State Banks. What I do say is, that the National Government *has been obliged* to issue its legal tender notes, and that I do not see *any such necessity* for the issue of paper money by the State Banks. The two circulations together make the inflation. Which can be withdrawn with the greatest advantage to the Government?— That is the question; not what caused the inflation. I know of no just claim which the State Banks have to make money for the country. I *know* that it is a *necessity* for the nation to have it. I think then that the State Bank currency should be withdrawn, and that no currency should be allowed except the National. So far as this consists of legal tenders, their issue and circulation are a direct gain to the country by a saving of interest, and if not issued in excess the benefit would be unmixed. So far as it consists of notes of National Banks, it is recommended by the indispensable necessity of such institutions to make a uniform National currency permanent; by the benefits derived from the support afforded by them to the credit of Government bonds, and by the convenience and utility of these institutions to the Government.

I have said more than I intended, and quite crudely, but your intelligence will enable you to see my meaning, and you will be satisfied I hope that if I cannot altogether prevent inflation I do all that is possible under existing circumstances. I hope that the legislation of Congress at this session, though long delayed, and the victories of our armies, though eager expectation still remains unsatisfied, will before long enable as to pay more as we go, and make it possible to do so by reducing and systematizing expenditure.—

Very truly Yours,
S P Chase

Richard Smith, Esq., "Gazette,"
Cincinnati, O.

1. Smith, a Republican, wrote for the *Cincinnati Gazette.* The article from the *Gazette* responded to rumors, reported in the *New York Tribune* on May 21, that the U.S. Treasury intended to offer a new series of Treasury notes. "The fact is, the legal tender business has been run too far," asserted the article, "and the interests of the public and of the national finances require that Congress shall put a stop to it. Better far to pay eight percent for money than to make any further issue of legal tender notes, in any shape or form, for the simple reason that these cannot be put out in any form or under any restriction, that they will not inflate the currency." *Cincinnati Daily Gazette,* May 24, 1864; Charles Frederic Goss, *Cincinnati the Queen City,* 4 vols. (Chicago, 1912), 4:277–78.

2. That is, bonds issued under legislation of July 17, 1861, mentioned by Chase on May 26 in his letter to John Sherman (above).

3. Regarding the issue of interest-bearing legal tender notes authorized by legislation of March 1863, see Chase to John J. Cisco, August 31, 1863, and January 4, 186[4] (above).

TO WILLIAM CULLEN BRYANT

Letterpress copy of letter in clerk's hand, signed by Chase. Chase Papers, Historical Society of Pennsylvania (*micro* 33:0923).

May 30, 4

My dear Sir,

I was surprised to see in the Evening *Post* a statement calculated to create the impression that the Secretary of the Treasury is still issuing legal tender notes.[1] The truth is that during this month the legal tender issues have been reduced nearly half a million of dollars, and the five per cent. Treasury Notes nearly fourteen millions. I have been doing my utmost to prevent inflation. The Banks without any plea of necessity are increasing their issues, to the infinite danger of the country. The Secretary of the Treasury does not increase the circulating issues of the Government by a single dollar, except under the pressure of the most imperious necessity. The Banks of the city of New York by certified checks turn their accumulated deposits into currency, and thus give a greater impulse to inflation than any single cause. Why not look at the matter just as it is, and claim for the country the exclusive use of the circulation, and urge that the Banks be compelled to withdraw their circulation, the presence of which is now so mischievous.

Very truly Your Friend,
S P Chase

Wm. C. Bryant, Esq.
New York.

1. Chase may have referred to an allusion in a letter to the *Post* by L. Bonnefoux that encouraged a new national loan. *New York Evening Post,* Apr. 11, May 17, 1864.

TO FREDERICK KÜHNE

Letterpress copy of letter in clerk's hand, signed by Chase. Chase Papers, Historical Society of Pennsylvania (*micro* 34:0003).

June 1, 4.

Dear Sir,[1]

I am much gratified by the result of your action. I cannot agree with you that the sale of Government bonds will permanently reduce the price of gold. The surcharge of the circulation is the difficulty. This consists wholly of bank notes and bank credits, in the forms of certificates of deposit and certified checks. If the bank note circulation were out of the way gold would be nearly at par.

It is said by unreflecting persons, Why does not the Government reduce its circulation, for the banks won't reduce theirs? The answer is simple: In the first place, the Government circulation is a necessity both to the Government and to the people; while the bank note circulation is simply a contrivance for the benefit of the banks which issue it; and in the second place, if the Government should reduce its circulation the banks, under existing circumstances, would increase theirs, and so the evil instead of being diminished would be increased.

It may be expedient and even necessary to sell Government long bonds,[2] but it will not remedy the evils we suffer permanently. The most that can be expected from such a sale is temporary relief. Taxation and a sound currency are the only cure.—

Very truly Yours,
S P Chase

F. Kühne, Esqr.
N.Y.

1. Chase had authorized Kühne, the German consul in New York and a member of the New York business partnership of Knauth, Nachod, and Kühne, to sell government specie on the open market in an attempt to drive down the price of gold. Chase to Jay Cooke, Apr. 10, 1864 (above); John J. Cisco to Chase, June 6, 1864 (below); *New York Dir. (1863)*, 481, 490.

2. That is, bonds issued on a long-term basis.

FROM JOHN J. CISCO

Letterpress copy of letter in clerk's hand, signed by Cisco. John J. Cisco Letterbook, Missouri Historical Society, St. Louis (*micro* 34:0098).

Unofficial.

New York June 6, 1864.

Dear Sir:—

I have, from the morning of the 31st. Ultimo. up to the close of business hours today, sold about $4.365.000. in gold, through Messrs Stuart and Kühne without either knowing the operations of the other.[1]

Their sales have been very judiciously managed and with a view to produce the best possible effect. A combination was formed here to put gold up to 200. and I have not a doubt but that it would have risen to over that figure on any of the days of our operations if we had not stopped its progress by continually feeding the market in small doses.

I have gone as far in my sales as I deem it prudent without further instructions. Please advise me by telegraph if I shall stop at this point or continue further.

I enclose you a slip cut from the Washington correspondence of the N.Y. Herald of today, which caused quite a sensation and alarmed everybody here.[2] Gold ran up to 194½. Notwithstanding our efforts to keep it down.

Faithfully Yours,
John J Cisco

Hon. S. P. Chase.
&c, &c, &c, &c,

1. James Stuart (1802–79) and Joseph Stuart (1803–74) were partners in the New York banking firm of J. and J. Stuart and Co. James Stuart was also a director of the

Hanover Bank, in the same city. *New York Dir. (1863),* 844; *New York Times,* Nov. 19, 1874, Mar. 27, 1879.

2. "Owing to the largely increased expenses of the government," reported the newspaper, " . . . it is estimated that four millions a day will hardly be sufficient to meet the accumulating requisitions upon the Treasury." According to the *Herald,* Chase intended to continue issuing five-percent legal tender notes, but to substitute six-percent legal tenders in the near future.

TO HORACE GREELEY

Autograph letter on letterhead stationery. The Pierpont Morgan Library (*micro* 34:0151).

Treasury Department.
June 10, 1864

My dear Sir,

Thanks for books—*ditto* for promise as to notice of R.J.W.[1] Mean to find time to read former,

Was in New York during most of the daylight of Tuesday Wednesd[ay] & Thursday; but so absolutely the prey of the money folk that I had only time for one glance at my daughter.[2] So did not see you: though I wished to badly.

I mean to go in for a foreign loan now though it galls me. If Congress would have given a good tax law last December and we could have managed to get along without the great bounties it would not have been necessary.[3] But the price of gold must & shall come down or I'll quit and let somebody else try. Oh! if Congress would only see and act!

Your friend
S P Chase

Hon H Greeley.

1. On June 7, Greeley had sent Chase a copy of the first volume of his new book, *The American Conflict* . . . , 2 vols. (Hartford, 1864, 1866), and agreed to print a notice that extolled the efforts of Robert J. Walker in behalf of the Union. Included in the piece, which appeared in the *New York Tribune* on June 13, was a brief review of Walker's recent publication, *American Slavery and Finances.* Greeley to Chase, June 7, 1864 (Chase Papers, Hist. Soc. of Pa.).

2. Chase had left Washington, D.C., for New York on the evening of Monday, June 6, at the request of the chairman of the loan committee of the Associated Banks. Chase to Abraham Lincoln, June 6, 1864 (Conn. Hist. Soc.).

3. On June 20, Chase asked John J. Cisco to prepare a foreign loan under authorization of the ways and means act of March 3, 1863. Federal outlays for enlistment bounties totaled more than $300 million during the war. Chase to Cisco, June 20, 1864 (below); *Statutes at Large,* 12:709–10, 13:219; Eugene Converse Murdock, *Patriotism Limited, 1862–1865: The Civil War Draft and the Bounty System* (Kent, Ohio, 1967), 19.

TO SIMEON NASH

Letterpress copy of letter in clerk's hand, signed by Chase. Chase Papers, Historical Society of Pennsylvania (*micro* 34:0235).

June 15th, 4.

Dear Sir,[1]

I am always glad to receive your letters, even though I do not always have time to answer them as I wish.[2]

I quite agree with you as to the renomination of the President. It was required by the general sentiment of the Union men, and to oppose it could be hardly anything else than factious. So I thought, and therefore took my name out of the canvas. I do not see how any sincere man, who holds the views expressed in the Baltimore Platform can excuse himself from a zealous support of the nominees of the Convention,[3] unless indeed some great popular movement should take place—contrary to all present likelihood—in favor of General Grant or some such leader.— I am [*torn*]rry to see some very good men taking part in the Fremont movement.[4] I cannot think it will be persisted in.

I agree with you partly on the negro question. It is quite probable that in Ohio the people are not yet ready for universal suffrage but I do not think any very earnest Union men in Ohio would object to letting negroes vote *here* or in the States in insurrection. They are certainly the most loyal part of the people of the South, and I, for one, would not hesitate to trust them with ballots as well as with bullets. Perhaps you have seen my letter to the New York meeting, saying as much.[5]

[*torn*] financial troubles do not spring from the 5 per cent. loan. That was taken more rapidly than the 5/20 loan, but like that loan was not taken in sufficient amounts to meet expenditures, increased lately beyond any former precedent.— I am now opening the bids of a Six per cent. loan redeemable after 1881,[6] and I find very few of those which are from the West above par. Of course such bids will not be accepted, but the fact that they are offered shows that whatever rate of interest the Government may be willing to give upon a standing loan, the subscriptions will be governed not so much by the rate as by the disposition of the people to invest. This must be taken, however, within limits. A very high rate or a very low rate, would repel investers.

I have no influence with the Cincinnati *Gazette* men. They attack me sometimes,—indeed pretty often,—but I keep on never minding it, and am equally philosophical when other people are attacked.

I should have been very glad to see you in Washington, had you made your appearance here. That one reason of your being confined to Ohio is a large practice is not unpleasant; but I am sorry to learn that another is the condition of Mrs. Nash's health. I hope that your Summer's trip will prove the means of its restoration.

It will be impossible to make financial people agree with you about making duties payable in currency. We must have gold for the payment of interest on the public debt; but it is not likely that any way of getting it will prove so cheap, or on the whole so satisfactory as that of getting it in payment of import duties.

Very truly Yours,
S P Chase

Hon. Simon Nash,
Gallipolis, Ohio.

1. Nash (1804–79), a legal author, former Ohio state senator from Athens County, 1839–43, and judge on the state's court of common pleas, wrote to Chase with political advice throughout the war. *DAB,* 13:388–89; Gilkey, *Ohio Hundred Year Book,* 291; Nash to Chase, Dec. 21, 1861, May 2, Sept. 5, 1862, Jan. 18, 1864 (Chase Papers, L.C.).

2. Nash had written on June 10, endorsing Lincoln's renomination at the Union party national convention in Baltimore, June 6–7. The letter also encouraged less talk about "social equality" for African Americans, criticized the 10–40 five-percent loan of March 3, 1864, and urged Chase to pressure the *Cincinnati Gazette* not to attack Lincoln and to discuss African Americans less often. In closing, Nash lamented his inability to visit Washington, D.C., in the spring due to his wife's poor health, but looked forward to a vacation of unknown destination later in the summer. Nash to Chase, June 10, 1864 (Chase Papers, L.C.); *Daily National Intelligencer,* June 8, 9, 1864; Long, *Civil War Day by Day,* 516–17; *Statutes at Large,* 13:13.

3. Included in the Union party platform were expressions of support for the integrity of the nation, the unconditional surrender of rebels, and slavery's "complete extirpation." For Lincoln's running mate the convention selected Andrew Johnson. *New York Tribune,* June, 9, 1864.

4. John C. Frémont received the nomination of radical Republicans who gathered in Cleveland on May 31. Long, *Civil War Day by Day,* 511–12.

5. Chase sent the letter to James S. Wadsworth and others as part of a "mass celebration" in New York on June 4 in honor of Ulysses S. Grant. Chase to Wadsworth et al., June 3, 1864 (Chase Papers, Hist. Soc. of Pa.), printed in the *New York Times,* June 5, 1864.

6. See Chase to John Sherman, May 26, and to Richard Smith, May 27, 1864 (both above).

TO JOHN J. CISCO

Letterpress copy of autograph letter. Chase Papers, Historical Society of Pennsylvania (*micro* 34:0303).

June 20 64

My dear Sir,

You will receive today the statement of the Public Debt as it existed on the 14th instant, made up from the books of the Department and returns to the date.[1] It is as nearly accurate as such a statement can be. Returns from all Officers & Depositories received to that date do not give the condition as it existed on the same day; and there must be, of course, some variation between the true condition on that day & the condition exhibited by the returns. But this variation is incidental to all statements relating to an increasing & diminishing debt. The Amount of Bonds issued, of United State Notes in Circulation, of all facts indeed already settled & recorded is, it is believed, strictly accurate.

I have been greatly disappointed by the action of some parties from whom I hoped the most strenuous aid in upholding the National credit—and among these parties I especially regret to find the Fourth National Bank. What could have induced that Institution to put in its disparaging bid?—very little better than Mr. Gallatins $5000 at 101.[2]

The Loan Bill was reported last evening & postponed till Wednesday when it will come up, & I hope, be passed.[3] As I shall have no authority to negotiate a foreign loan or indeed any other except to complete the 75 millions loan & to sell the 10/40s until that act passes, I shall not be able to accomplish any good, that I can see, by coming earlier.[4] Meantime I shall be glad to have you prepare a form of bond to be disposed of abroad for my examination: and ascertain at what rate the Government can undertake to pay guilders in Amsterdam without loss or disadvantage.[5]

I have written to Mr. Duer asking him if he will accept the position of your successor. If not I shall fall back in Mr. Stewart, who must accept, I do not see why he should not; for after a few years service should he desire to retire the best financial positions in New York will court his acceptance.[6]

Yours faithfully
S P CHASE

John J Cisco Esq.

1. On June 14, the national debt stood at $1,719,395,168.88, plus interest charges of $71,699,730.15. *Letter of the Secretary of the Treasury, Communicating . . . a Statement Showing the Full Amount of the Public Debt . . . ,* 38th Cong., 1st sess., 1864, S. Ex. Doc. 52.

2. Among the founders of New York's Fourth National Bank was Jay Cooke. James Gallatin presided over what became the city's Gallatin National Bank. Chase had received bids for a loan authorized in 1861. Chase to Simeon Nash, June 15, 1864 (above); *New York Times,* May 30, 1876; Oberholtzer, *Jay Cooke,* 1:343–49.

3. The ways and means bill was finally approved on June 30. *Statutes at Large,* 13:219–22.

4. Chase apparently referred to $75 million that remained to be sold of the 10–40 bonds authorized by the ways and means act of March 3, 1863. *Statutes at Large,* 12:709–10, 13:219.

5. Cisco recommended that the current form of U.S. bond be modified slightly to allow payment of interest coupons in Amsterdam, and also advised Chase of exchange rates between Dutch guilders and U.S. gold dollars. Cisco to Chase, June 22, 25, 1864 (Cisco Letters, Mo. Hist. Soc.); Chase to Cisco, June 23, 1864 (Chase Papers, Hist. Soc. of Pa.).

6. Poor health had recently forced Cisco to resign as assistant treasurer in New York, effective June 30. New York bankers Denning Duer and John Aikman Stewart had both rejected Chase's offer. Stewart later reconsidered and held the post briefly in 1864–65. Chase to Cisco, June 28, 1864 (Cisco Papers, Misc. Mss. Collec., L.C.); Chase to Abraham Lincoln, June 28, and Chase to Cisco, July 1, 1864 (below); Duer to Chase, June 22, 1864 (Chase Papers, L.C.); Chase to William Curtis Noyes, June 17, 1864 (Chase Papers, Hist. Soc. of Pa.); *DAB,* 18:11; *New York Dir. (1863),* 247.

TO WILLIAM P. FESSENDEN

Letter in clerk's hand, signed by Chase. Committee on Finance, Committee Papers, 38th Congress, Records of the U.S. Senate (Record Group 46), National Archives (*micro* 34:0308).

Treasury Department,
June 20th, 1864.

Sir,

I have already frequently expressed to you my conviction that expenses and taxes should be brought into such relations that at least one half the former may be defrayed by income derived from the latter.[1]—

The internal revenue bill now before the Committee of Conference on disagreements between the two Houses, according to the best estimates made in this Department, will not produce during the next fiscal year more than #250.000.000.[2]

It is impossible to state with any precision the amount that may be expected from customs. It is not safe, however, to set it down at more than #60.000.000.

What the expenses will be cannot be foreseen. If those of the past year be taken as the criterion they will reach in round numbers #900.000.000. It may be hoped that military success will enable the Government to reduce this amount, but it would be unsafe to state it at less than #750.000.000.

You will see therefore that the revenue will fall short of one half by at least #65.000.000.

In my judgment it is indispensable that at least this amount of additional revenue be provided. Indeed a much larger amount may and should be raised in order to ensure certain provision at reasonable rates of the amount required by the expenditures of the war. I name #65.000.000 as the lowest additional sum which can be made to suffice.

How this additional sum can best be raised belongs properly to the consideration of Congress and of the Financial Committees of the two Houses. I beg leave to suggest, however, that it can be most certainly obtained through the imposition of an additional tax on spirits and by a special war tax on incomes.[3]— Better, it seems to me, a tax of ten or even twenty per cent. on all incomes than the rapid accumulation of National debt attended, as it must be, by the rapid deterioration of National credit.

Very truly Yours,
S P Chase
Secretary of the Treasury.

Hon. Wm. P. Fessenden, Ch. Com. on Finance,
U.S.S.

1. For example, see Chase's letter to Fessenden of April 12, 1864 (above).

2. Lincoln signed the internal revenue act on June 30. *Statutes at Large,* 13: 223–306.

3. As enacted, the internal revenue act of 1864 levied a new tax of $1.50 per gallon of distilled spirits after July 1, 1864, and two dollars after February 1, 1865. In addition, the measure contained provisions for a graduated tax that ranged from five percent on incomes of $600 to $5,000 up to ten percent on incomes higher than $10,000. *Statutes at Large,* 13:243, 281.

TO BENJAMIN F. WADE

Letterbook copy in clerk's hand. Letters Sent to Committees of Congress (D Series), General Records, Department of the Treasury (Record Group 56), National Archives.

Treasury Department[1]
21. June 1864.

Hon. B. F. Wade,
Chm. etc U.S.S.
Sir:

Reports of irregularities and abuses in the action of the officers of the Treasury Department, charged with duties relating to trade with and in insurrectionary districts, induced me sometime since to send an Agent to examine into their truth or falsity.— The result led me to believe that the reports though much exaggerated, had some foundation; and one Assistant Special Agent against whom the most serious and best supported allegations were made has been suspended from service and pay.[2]—

With the means of examination at the control of this Department, however, it is impossible satisfactorily to ascertain to whom just responsibility attaches for supplies furnished to rebels through our Military lines, and for fraudulent transactions in cotton and other staples of the country.—

Therefore, and especially in view of the fact that the whole subject has been referred by the House of Representatives to the Committee on the conduct and expenditures of the war of which you are Chairman, I take the liberty of suggesting that it be examined by your Committee at as early a date as practicable.[3]—

I shall gladly afford every aid in my power for the prosecution of the investigation.—

Very Ry &c
S. P. Chase,
Secy of the Try

1. Another letterbook copy of this letter is in Chase's papers at the Historical Society of Pennsylvania and appears at *micro* 34:0329.

2. The "reports" were evidently accusations presented by Francis Preston Blair, Jr., in his April 23 speech on the House floor. On May 24, Chase formally suspended Ralph S. Hart, assistant special agent at Natchez, Miss., for allegedly extorting fees. The investigator was Thomas Heaton, another assistant special agent. Chase to Hart, May 24, 1864 (Letters Sent to Special Agents, Recs. of Bureau of Customs, Nat. Arch.); Robert Frank Futrell, "Federal Trade with the Confederate States, 1861–1865: A Study of Government Policy" (Ph.D. diss., Vanderbilt Univ., 1950), 318–23; *Letter of the Secretary . . . Special Agents,* 2.

3. Wade chaired the Joint Committee on the Conduct of the War. According to Chase, subsequent study by the committee freed Hart "of all censure" and exonerated the Treasury Department. Chase to William Curtis Noyes, July 11, 1864 (below); *DAB,* 29:304.

TO PARKE GODWIN

Letterpress copy of autograph letter. Chase Papers, Historical Society of Pennsylvania (*micro* 34:0363).

June 23, 64

My dear Sir,[1]

The Evening Post has of late contained several articles on my financial measures which, in my judgment, were injurious instead of useful. I do not object to criticism; but when a man who is certainly trying to do his best and is allowed to possess an average share of sense & information, is put in a very difficult position, under heavy burdens, it seems to me that he is entitled to support, until it can be clearly demonstrated that there is a better way, & this demonstration should primarily at least be addressed to him instead of being offered to the public. I am very willing that any body should take my place; but while I remain it the good of the country requires that I should have help—not opposition.

The Evening Post in an article printed a day or two since and in yesterdays paper also lays it down as a principle that all bids for a loan should be accepted: and this though in the notice the right to decline all offers deemed disadvantageous was expressly reserved.[2] Under this principle the bids under par should have been accepted; and had Mr. Ketchum[3] or any other of the low bidders, foreseeing that the whole loan would not be offered for at par & over offered to take the residue, say five millions, even at ten cents on the dollar or one cent on one mill the offer should have been accepted. To adopt such a principle & faithfully carry it out would be to surrender the Government to combinations of speculators.

So also the Evening Post recommends the issue of six per cent. notes convertible into legal tenders principal & interest on demand.[4] This plan was urged on me by Mr. Ketchum. It was clear to me that it was a simple proposition that the Government should issue six per cent notes payable on demand; and that if adopted one of two effects must follow; either the Government must withdraw & keep in reserve a large proportion of ordinary notes to meet demands for conversion or must issue additional notes to meet such demands: the first, would make the issue unavailable as a resource and at the same time always expose the Treasury to runs by combinations willing to create a panic; while the second would put it into the power of combinations & even of powerful individuals or institutions to inflate the currency at will.

These considerations decided my action. I have heard all sides—patiently reflected on all propositions—and without a particle of interest or feeling to sway me one way or the other, have decided as I thought the public interest required. I am still satisfied that I have decided rightly.

The Evening Post also censures pretty harshly the Gold act.[5] I am not an admirer of that sort of legislation generally; but what is there in this particular act of which honest friends of the Government can complain? It prohibits no fair & real transactions; but merely fictitious and gambling transaction. Certainly the Eveng Post would not extend the principles of free trade so far as to protect combinations of swindlers. If the act, fairly interpreted, imposes embarrassment on legitimate transactions it should be amended; but its object is good & its principle in my judgment should not be abandoned.

Knowing your candor & fairness, and your real desire to support the Government in the present crisis—I send you these hastily written notes. Before closing I must thank you for insisting on adequate taxation & reduction of expenditures. These are the true remedies. We must prepare to resume specie payments and this by making it possible to raise what money is needed beyond the supply of taxes at moderate rates; and possible also to reduce national circulation by bond loans and by substituting for State Bank Notes the currency of the National Banks.[6] If this last substitution was accomplished & a sound uniform currency thereby ensured, a good system of taxation with organization & economy in expenditure would enable me to secure a resumption just as soon as it would be safe—immediately or within a year.

Your friend
S P Chase

Parke Godwin Esq

1. Godwin edited the *New York Evening Post* with William Cullen Bryant. *DAB*, 7:351–52.

2. The argument appeared in articles printed in the *Evening Post* on June 17 and 22.

3. New York banker Morris Ketchum.

4. "In the shape we recommend," asserted the paper, "we believe that they would all be retained by the community as investment, and by a part of the community—men of small means—who could not be reached in any other way." *New York Evening Post*, June 17, 1864.

5. Legislation signed on June 17 prohibited speculation in gold. In "Gold Up to the Skies," the *Evening Post* described it as "absurd legislative tinkering" by "ignoramuses" enacted in violation of "the laws of trade" and thus responsible for recent increases in the price of gold. Congress soon repealed the measure by means of a one-sentence act approved July 2, 1864. *New York Evening Post*, June 22, 1864; Chase to William P. Fessenden, Apr. 12, 1864 (above); *Statutes at Large*, 13:132–33, 344.

6. Chase had pressed this argument since at least the beginning of the year. Chase to Joseph Medill, Jan. 30, to Thaddeus Stevens, Feb. 19, Apr. 11, 1864, to William E. Dodge, Mar. 31, to Jay Cooke, Apr. 10, and to John Sherman, May 26 (all above).

TO JOHN MURRAY FORBES

Letterpress copy of autograph letter. Chase Papers, Historical Society of Pennsylvania (*micro* 34:0427).

June 25,

My dear Sir,

You are quite right. The People who really want the War to be prosecuted are willing to pay the cost in taxes; why won't Congress see it & act upon it.[1] Why too does any man who knows we must have soldiers object to their being recruited where they can be had; only providing against interference with States which have quotas to raise?

As to taxes the case is clear enough. There is no possibility that expences can be reduced next fiscal year below $750.000.000. They are more likely to reach 900.000.000 as they do this year. Now then take 750 mills. There is little chance of raising more than $1000000 a day from sale of bonds; but say 1.100.000 and you get about 400.000.000 a year: that leaves 350.000.000 to be obtained from taxes. Now no prudent man under such circumstances would think of less than $400.000.000 of taxes, & upon this amount I have constantly insisted. I have exhausted all power of appeal; except a simple statement that I cannot undertake to attempt to carry on the Department with a less provision.

How strange it is that when State Banks hold a loan from the people in circulation of $150.000.000 legislators will insist that the people shall call in & cancel their own notes instead of requiring the State Banks to call in & cancel theirs!

But don't you gentlemen deceive yourselves. We can't get down from the present inflation caused as much by the Banks as by the Government—by the former without necessity—by the latter under necessity the most stringent at a jump. We must go down gradually. I am getting in all the Five per cent legal tenders as fast as I can. I shall do it with the proceeds of loans as far as possible; but I have no hope that loans will produce all that is wanted. For what I cannot provide in this way I must issue Six per cent compound interest legal tenders.[2] This at least puts inflation into what Mr. Lincoln calls a course of gradual extinction.[3]

Your friend
S P Chase

J. M. Forbes Esq

1. In a letter written to Chase on June 23, Forbes and others had suggested a national sales tax of one percent. Forbes et al. to Chase, June 23, 1864 (Chase Papers, L.C.).

2. Chase issued such notes, which were legal tender for their face value, under authority of the ways and means act of March 3, 1863. Ten dollars was the smallest denomination offered, and on the reverse of each note a schedule showed the increase in value as interest was compounded semiannually to maturity in three years. *Statutes at Large,* 12:710; Robert Friedberg, *Paper Money of the United States: A Complete Illustrated Guide with Valuations,* 6th ed., rev. by Jack Friedberg (New York, 1968), 18, 56; *Report of the Secre-*

tary of the Treasury on the State of Finances, for the Year 1864, 38th Cong., 2d sess., 1864, H. Ex. Doc. 3, 3, 7, 18, 38–39.

3. Chase alluded to language in the famous "House Divided" speech that Lincoln delivered in Springfield, Ill., on June 16, 1858: "Either the *opponents* of slavery, will . . . place it where the public mind shall rest in the belief that it is in the course of ultimate extinction; or its *advocates* will push it forward, till it shall become alike lawful in *all* the States. . . ." Basler, *Collected Works,* 2:461–62.

TO JAY COOKE

Autograph letter. Jay Cooke Papers, Historical Society of Pennsylvania (*micro* 34:0454).

Treasury Department
June 26, 1864

My dear Sir,

I have carefully considered the plan of negotiation proposed by Mr. Marx & Mr. Kuhne and am disposed to adopt its principle. It will be necessary to modify details somewhat. Having provided otherwise some three millions of exchange (say 1.500.000 in gold) it does not seem to me so important to conclude the details at once as it is to attend to the legislation here in the last days of the Session: As soon as Congress shall adjourn I mean to go to New York and devote myself wholly to these matters until finally concluded.[1]

Accept my warmest thanks for your disinterested & patriotic zeal and services. You notice I dare say the malignant falsehoods which are constantly printed against you and me because of my employment of your energy & skill in the negotiation of the 5–20 Loan: Like falsehoods are circulated about the 75 Mill Loan.[2] The falsifiers omit to notice that a large share of your firm's bids were declined. I do not believe that if you had represented your firm the bids would have been so low. They say that my rate for acceptance was fixed with reference to favored parties who had some means of knowing what it would be: How mean this falsehood is! I did not know myself what the rate would be until the bids had been opened, and the amounts at the several rates from par & under to 3; from 3 to 4; & from 4 upwards had been ascertained. Had the statement of these amounts impressed me with the conviction that the majority of intelligent bids regarded 3 as a *fair* rate I should have accepted all at 3 & upwards. As it was I accepted all at four or over not because *I* thought *four* the sufficient rate but because it was the rate indicated as fair by the bids / Not a soul had an intimation what rate would be adopted & could not for I did not know myself.

But why speak of these things. Calumny has a thousand tongues and is as immortal as Sin—dying & reviving continually

Your friend
S P Chase

Jay Cooke Esq

1. The first session of the Thirty-eighth Congress adjourned on July 4. By that time, although he could not have anticipated it on June 26, Chase's resignation from the cabinet had been offered and accepted. On July 15, he visited New York as a private citizen. Chase to Lincoln, June 29, Lincoln to Chase, June 30, 1864 (below); *Chase Papers,* 1:481; *Bio. Dir. U.S. Cong.,* 175.

2. Cooke was under attack for the wealth he acquired as the government's loan agent. On January 5, 1864, the House asked Chase to give a detailed account of Cooke's dealings with the Treasury Department. Chase's report, submitted on April 2, concluded that "the services rendered by the general agent and the sub-agents could not have been as successfully performed, nor, indeed, performed at all by the Treasury Department itself." *Jay Cooke & Co. . . . ,* 38th Cong., 1st sess., 1863–64, H. Ex. Doc. 66, 4; *House Journal,* 38th Cong., 1st sess., 1863–64, 103; Larson, *Jay Cooke,* 160.

TO ABRAHAM LINCOLN

Autograph letter on letterhead stationery. Abraham Lincoln Papers, Library of Congress (*micro* 34:0499).

Treasury Department.
June 28 1864

My dear Sir,

I have telegraphed Mr. Cisco begging him to withdraw his resignation and serve at least another quarter. If he declines to do so I must repeat that, in my judgment, the public interests require the appointment of Mr. Field.[1] One of the gentlemen named by Senator Morgan is over seventy & the other, I think, over sixty years old, and neither has any practical knowledge of the duties of the office.[2] They are both estimable gentlemen and were the times peaceful & the business of the office comparatively small & regular, I should gladly acquiesce in the appointment of either. But my duty to you & to the country does not permit it now. I have already after conference with Senator Morgan offered, with his concurrence, my recommendation to your consideration to three gentlemen, each admirably qualified, but each has declined.[3] I now recommend Mr. Field because among those who will take the place I think him best qualified and only for that reason. But this, especially in these times, should be a controlling reason.

That you may see that I am warranted not only by my personal observation, but by the opinions of the best men in my judgment I enclose, with this, several papers which have been sent to me.

Yours most truly
S P Chase

The President.

P.S. As soon as Mr. Cisco's answer comes I will send it to you.[4] If he declines I trust you will act without delay. The office will be without a head on the 1st of July & the bond to be given is ($400.000) four hundred thousand dollars.

1. On June 27, Chase had sent Lincoln a letter of recommendation and also a formal nomination form for Assistant Secretary Maunsell B. Field, John J. Cisco's former deputy,

to succeed Cisco as assistant treasurer at New York. The next day, meeting reluctance on Lincoln's part to nominate Field, Chase telegraphed Cisco to "respectfully but earnestly" ask him to remain in his position "at least one quarter longer." Chase urged Cisco: "Let nothing except the absolute requirements of your health prevent your consent." Chase to Lincoln, June 27, 1864 (Lincoln Papers, L.C.); Chase to Cisco, telegram, June 28, 1864 (Cisco Papers, Misc. Mss. Collec., L.C.); *Chase Papers,* 1:466–67.

2. In an interview with Chase on June 27, U.S. Senator Edwin D. Morgan, previously governor of New York, had suggested either sixty-six-year-old Richard Milford Blatchford, a New York attorney, or Dudley Sanford Gregory, a sixty-four-year-old banker from New Jersey. *Chase Papers,* 1:463–64.

3. Chase had already offered the position to Denning Duer, John Aikman Stewart, and William Curtis Noyes. Chase to Cisco, June 20, 1864 (above); Chase to Noyes, June 17, 1864 (Chase Papers, Hist. Soc. of Pa.); Chase to Noyes, July 11, 1864 (below).

4. Cisco both wrote and telegraphed on June 28 withdrawing his resignation (but mistakenly dated his letter June 27). The telegram read: "I cannot resist your appeal & therefore consent to the temporary withdrawal of my resignation." On June 29, Chase sent Cisco's reply to Lincoln. Cisco to Chase, June 2[8], 1864 (Cisco Letters, Mo. Hist. Soc.); same to same, telegram, June 28, 1864 (Lincoln Papers, L.C.); Chase to Abraham Lincoln, June 29, 1864 (below).

TO ABRAHAM LINCOLN

Autograph document on letterhead stationery. Abraham Lincoln Papers, Library of Congress (*micro* 34:0496).

Treasury Department.
June 28, 1864

Memorandum for President

Mr Field is recommended by many of the most reliable business men of New York, such as Jonathan Sturgis, Peter Cooper, Phelps, Dodge & Co, as well as by prominent Republicans such as John A. King Horace Greeley & others[1]

His capacity and integrity are not called in question by any body.

The office cannot be made useful to the Government & especially to the Treasury Department unless administered with the same disinterested integrity & impartiality with which Mr. Cisco has conducted it. Mr. Field would not claim to be the equal of Mr. Cisco, in administrative capacity, but will, I think, endeavor to equal him in fairness & honesty of administration

The office should not be controlled in administration by mere party considerations. Appointments should doubtless be given to faithful friends of the Government; but should be made otherwise exclusively on grounds of integrity & capacity. Mr. Field is a Republican & would give proper political considerations due weight; but he would not allow them improper influence.

1. Jonathan Sturges (1802–74) and Peter Cooper (1791–1883) were New York merchants. Chase had corresponded with William E. Dodge of Phelps, Dodge and Company earlier in the year. John Alsop King (1788–1867) was a former Whig congressman and Republican governor of New York. *DAB,* 4:409–10, 10:394–95; *Appletons',* 5:734; Chase to Dodge, Mar. 31, 1864 (above).

FROM ABRAHAM LINCOLN

Autograph letter. Lincoln Collection, John Hay Library of Rare Books and Special Collections, Brown University (*micro* 34:0519).

Private

Executive Mansion
Washington D.C. June 28, 1864

Hon. Secretary of the Treasury
My dear Sir:

When I received your note this forenoon suggesting a verbal conversation in relation to the appointment of a successor to Mr. Cisco, I hesitated because the difficulty does not, in the main part, lie within the range of a conversation between you and me.[1] As the proverb goes, no man knows so well where the shoe pinches as he who wears it. I do not think Mr. Field a very proper man for the place; but I would trust your judgment, and forego this, were the greater difficulty out of the way. Much as I personally like Mr. Barney, it has been a great burden to me to retain him in his place, when nearly all our friends in New-York were directly, or indirectly urging his removal. Then the appointment of Judge Hogeboom to be General Appraiser, brought me to, and has ever since kept me at the verge of open revolt.[2] Now, the appointment of Mr. Field would precipitate me in it, unless Senator Morgan, and those feeling as he does could be brought to concur in it. Strained as I already am at this point I do not think I can make this appointment in the direction of still greater strain.

The testimonials of Mr. Field, with your accompanying notes were duly received, and I am now waiting to see your answer from Mr. Cisco.[3]

Yours truly
A. LINCOLN

1. In addition to his letter of June 28 (above) explaining his recommendation of Field, Chase also wrote a brief note to the president: "I shall be glad to have a conversation with you on the subject of the appointment of Mr. Cisco's successor at any time & place convenient to you." Chase to Lincoln, June 28, 1864 (Lincoln Papers, L.C.).

2. The Senate had confirmed John T. Hogeboom as general appraiser of the New York Custom House on April 7, 1864. U.S. Senate, *Journal of Executive Proceedings,* 13:479–80.

3. See Chase's letter and memorandum to Lincoln, June 28 (above).

TO JOHN J. CISCO

Autograph letter on letterhead stationery. John J. Cisco Papers, Miscellaneous Manuscripts Collection, Library of Congress (*micro* 34:0527).

Treasury Department.
June 29, 1864

My dear Sir,

I am very grateful for your telegram and letter.[1] It relieves me from a very painful embarrassment and from serious apprehensions. I could not remain here and see your office made parcel of the machinery of party, or even feel serious apprehensions that it might be. The only drawback upon my satisfaction comes from my concern for your health and from my anxiety about the condition of public affairs. I pray God that no harm may come to you from your self sacrifice, and that our dear country may soon see brighter days.

The Internal Revenue Bill is not sufficient and I must take the responsibility of recommending tax enough to bring up our whole income to four hundred millions a year, and wait till Congress acts or adjourns[2] / Meantime I am getting bonds ready with coupons payable in Amsterdam: Say so to Mr. Kuhne & Mr. Marx & say also that the best way to reduce the price of gold & to sustain public credit is to make revenue & expences come as near together as possible. The less we want the more easily we can get it.[3]

I asked Mr. Kuhne if I remember rightly for the form of a coupon; perhaps I asked you. At any rate I have received one—I now send one & ask that it may be returned with any observations thought important.

Yours most truly
S P Chase

John J Cisco Esq

I have just received Mr. Kuhne's form of coupon. It is unnecessary therefore to enclose one

1. See Chase's letter to Abraham Lincoln of June 28 (above) with regard to Cisco's withdrawal of his resignation.
2. For more on this recommendation, see Chase to Lincoln, June 30, 1864 (below).
3. Chase had written Cisco earlier (June 20, 1864, above) concerning arrangements to sell coupon bonds in the Netherlands.

TO ABRAHAM LINCOLN

Autograph letter on letterhead stationery. Abraham Lincoln Papers, Library of Congress (*micro* 34:0559).

Treasury Department.
June 29, 1864

My dear Sir,

I have just received your note and have read it with great attention.[1] I was not aware of the extent of the embarrassment to which you refer. In recommendations for office I have sincerely sought to get the best man for the places to be filled without reference to any other classification than supporters and opponents of your administration. Of the latter I have recommended none; among the former I have desired to know no distinction except degrees of fitness.

The withdrawal of Mr. Cisco's resignation, which I enclose,[2] relieves the present difficulty; but I cannot help feeling that my position here is not altogether agreeable to you; and it is certainly too full of embarrassment and difficulty and painful responsibility to allow in me the least desire to retain it.

I think it my duty therefore to enclose to you my resignation.[3] I shall regard it as a real relief if you think proper to accept it; and will most cheerfully render to my successor any aid he may find useful in entering upon his duties.[4]

With the greatest respect,

Yours truly
S P Chase

The President

1. Lincoln to Chase, June 28, 1864. (above).

2. Cisco to Chase, June 2[8], 1864 (Cisco Letters, Mo. Hist. Soc.).

3. "I respectfully resign the office of Secretary of the Treasury which I have the honor to hold under your appointment," read the letter. Chase to Lincoln, June 29, 1864 (Lincoln Papers, L.C.).

4. Lincoln officially accepted Chase's resignation on June 30 and offered the job to former Ohio governor David Tod, who declined. Lincoln's second choice, Senator William P. Fessenden, accepted the appointment on July 1. *Chase Papers,* 1:470; Long, *Civil War Day by Day,* 530–31.

TO ABRAHAM LINCOLN

Letter in clerk's hand on letterhead stationery, signed by Chase.
Abraham Lincoln Papers, Library of Congress (*micro* 34:0601).

Treasury Department.
June 30, 1864.

Sir,

I enclose a letter which I have thought my duty to address to the Committee of Ways and Means, and also copies of two accompanying documents marked "A" and "B."[1] The importance of providing by the Tariff and Internal Tax bill for at least one-half of the National Expenditure during the fiscal year commencing to-morrow can hardly be overstated. The bills which have actually passed Congress will not, in my judgment, produce this amount within a hundred millions of dollars. The Insurrectionary Trade bill, if passed, may add 25 millions to the income, leaving a deficit still of about eighty millions.[2] These figures may not be entirely correct, nor do I claim absolute correctness for those in the letter to the Committee. They are, however, sufficiently correct for practical purposes.

If you concur with me in the opinion that the additional taxes proposed are exceeding important, if not indispensably necessary, I beg leave to suggest the expediency of a recommendation of the increase by yourself to Congress.

With greatest respect

Yours,
S P Chase

The President.

1. On June 29, Chase had sent identical letters to Thaddeus Stevens, chairman of the House Committee on Ways and Means, and to William Fessenden, chairman of the Senate Committee on Finance. These long letters addressed measures by which revenue might be increased to carry a larger portion of expenditures, thereby reducing dependence on borrowing. Enclosure "A" contained projections of revenue in the coming fiscal year under pending internal revenue legislation, while the document labeled "B" comprised suggestions by William Orton for means of increasing internal revenues. Chase to Stevens, June 29, 1864 (Papers on Treasury Dept., 38th Cong., Committee on Ways and Means, Recs. of U.S. House of Representatives, Nat. Arch.); copy of letter to Stevens (Lincoln Papers, L.C.); Chase to Fessenden, June 29, 1864 (Committee Papers, 38th Cong., Committee on Finance, Recs. of U.S. Senate, Nat. Arch.).

2. Lincoln signed internal revenue and tariff acts on June 30 and the trade bill on July 2. *Statutes at Large,* 13:202–18, 223–306, 375–78.

FROM ABRAHAM LINCOLN

Autograph letter on letterhead stationery. Lincoln Collection, John Hay Library of Rare Books and Special Collections, Brown University (*micro* 34:0606).

Executive Mansion.
Washington. June 30, 1864.

Hon. Salmon P. Chase
My dear Sir

Your resignation of the office of Secretary of the Treasury, sent me yesterday, is accepted.[1] Of all I have said in commendation of your ability and fidelity, I have nothing to unsay; and yet you and I have reached a point of mutual embarrassment in our official relation which it seems can not be overcome, or longer sustained, consistently with the public service.

Your Obt. Servt.
A. LINCOLN

1. See Chase's letter to Lincoln of June 29 (above).

TO WILLIAM CULLEN BRYANT

Letterpress copy of autograph letter. Chase Papers, Historical Society of Pennsylvania (*micro* 34:0597).

Washington June 30, 1864

My dear Sir,

Your good opinion has always been valued as among my chief treasures—because it is the honest opinion of a candid & just observer: I have never expected it to extend to all the measures the exigencies of the country have compelled me to adopt: and yet looking back I see now no measure which my judgment condemns except that required by the New York Banks—the issue of legal tender coupons.[1] My grand objects have been first to provide for the demands of the War; and second, to secure the substitution of a national bank note currency for state bank note currency, and through the last resumption of specie payments, and so permanence & strength in financial order. I think if we could compare notes, very little difference would be found between us in opinions.

But it of little importance to the country now what my financial views may be. A sense of duty to myself and to the country—imperative you will think I hope it must have been—constrained me to tender yesterday my resignation to the President; & it has been accepted today. So I am no longer Secretary. If I feel some regret that I cannot carry out my ideas to consummation, it is compensated by the sense of relief from crushing responsibilities.

With this act terminates, I trust, my whole connexion with official life. Place has never been anything to me but opportunity for work; and I gladly surrender all claims upon it in favor of those who may prize it more.

Please say to Mr. Godwin that I no longer care to know who Public Service is.[2]

Yours most truly
S P CHASE

Wm. Cullen Bryant, Esq

1. Of the five-percent interest-bearing legal tender notes issued under authority of the ways and means act of March 1863, some had narrow "coupons" printed at one end, to be clipped off in redemption for interest every six months. As William Fessenden, Chase's successor as secretary of the Treasury, described the situation, the coupon notes "have been found particularly objectionable, as, though withdrawn to a certain extent while the interest is maturing, they are liable to be periodically rushed upon the market." Chase, and subsequently Fessenden, tried to substitute legal tender notes with compounded interest, "as being more likely to be withdrawn and held until maturity, as an investment." *Report of the Secretary of the Treasury . . . 1864,* 18; Chase to John D. Van Buren, Apr. 17, 1865 (Chase Papers, Hist. Soc. of Pa.); Chase to John Murray Forbes, June 25, 1864 (above); *Statutes at Large,* 12:710; for illustration of a similar form of coupon note, see Friedberg, *Paper Money,* 18–19, 66–68.

2. On June 24, "Public Service," a "loyal private banker," had published a column in the *New York Evening Post* critical of Chase and the Treasury. Two days later Chase asked Bryant for the author's name. Bryant's reply, on June 28, told of Parke Godwin's intention to answer the letter. Bryant also directed Chase to a *Post* article of the same day, written in Chase's defense "with no little ability" by "Veritas and Justitia." Chase to Bryant, June 26, Bryant to Chase, June 28, 1864 (Chase Papers, Hist. Soc. of Pa.); William Cullen Bryant II and Thomas G. Voss, eds., *The Letters of William Cullen Bryant,* 6 vols. (New York, 1975–92), 4:368.

TO JOHN J. CISCO

Letterpress copy of autograph letter. Chase Papers, Historical Society of Pennsylvania.

Washington, July 1 1864.[1]

My dear Mr. Cisco,

I ought to have written you yesterday but could not get the time. It is due to you that the circumstances of my resignation be fully explained.

The persistent attacks of Montgomery Blair & his brother[2] had created for me great embarrassments here. The President manifested no unkindness; but it was very unpleasant to be associated in the same administration, even in offices so separated as the Treasury & Post Office Department with a man who omitted no opportunity to vent his spite & utter his slanders behind my back. And it was not very agreeable to me that the President in his regards seemed to put us very much [on a level]—with some—perhaps considerable—balance on the Blair side.

Then Congress had failed to respond to the necessities of the Treasury in such a manner as I thought [the needs] of the time required. The National Banking had been deprived of much of its value as an instrument for good and the taxes on the Banks under it had been cut down to half what they should have been in order to allow taxation under state authority.[3] I asked that the full tax might be imposed & its product placed in the Treasury as a basis for loans. The Internal Revenue law too had been passed in such a shape that I was satisfied it would not yield half enough to provide for the disbursements of the fiscal year which begins today, & I thought that nothing less than half would secure revenue enough to make loans of the balance at any reasonable rate practicable. There seemed little hope that Congress would levy additional taxes to meet the emergency.

So with fearful burdens upon me[,] I was likely to left to struggle against the hostility of one or more members of the Cabinet, with only a negative support from the President, and without resources sufficient to make a successful administration of the finances probable if possible.

Of course I could not wish to remain; but I do not know that these considerations would have induced me to resign. Had there been no other I think I should have held on to the helm, &, if the ship went [down,] let it be seen that pilot was faithful.

But the Captain of the Ship refused to let the pilot have the command: and of course his function ended. You ask How? And you shall be answered.

You know what endeavors I made to secure a suitable successor for you. The post was offered to three gentlemen in succession of all shades of political opinions prevailing among the supporters of the general policy of the administration & by each declined. I cared but little about their political status—[so] they were truly loyal & fully qualified, & certain make an honest & faithful administration of the office their main end if they should accept. After receiving the final decision of Mr. Stewart I determined to offer the place to Mr. Field & called on Senator Morgan to confer with him about it.[4] He made no objection to Mr Field; but said that the chairman of some political committee had called on him quite indignant about the political complexion of your office & insisting it should be reformed. He produced a list of all the officers & clerks under you, with letters indicating the political party set opposite the name of each. I told Senator Morgan that I did not believe that any considerable number of clerks in your office were opponents of the administration: though I had no doubt that many were democrats as indicated by the letter D—and the Ds were plenty on the list I assure you—[but democrats] I thought[,] like Andrew Johnson, Daniel S. Dickinson or John A. Dix. I said also that I could not admit the propriety of making an appointment of an Assistant Treasurer in New York on mere party or rather factional grounds / I was alarmed at the spirit manifested by procuring the list, and felt certain that if the Office should be made any thing like a political machine the public interests must suffer & my administration be greatly embarrassed if not irretrievably damaged. I said a [good] deal in this [sense] to the Governor, assuring him at the same time of my respect for all of the gentlemen he named;[5] but objecting to them as not immediately prepared by practical acquaintance to enter upon the duties of the Office and moreover as not being either young enough or if young enough not sufficiently versed in the business, to warrant confidence that the business of the office would be carried on as it should be. I expressed the belief also that if either should go into the Office & undertake to carry out political reforms by removals for mere political causes, the results would [be very apt] to be disastrous. He did not seem satisfied with my views nor yet much dissatisfied. I told him I must act that day (the 27th) as your resignation would take effect on the 30th. I then left him saying I would consider what he had said.

I did reflect and with every disposition to gratify him; but one of the gentlemen [he named was from the interior of the State and an entire] stranger to me, & the other two, though very worthy personally, were not practically acquainted with the office and were likely moreover I fear to carry too much politics into the administration of the office. After a full consideration I recommended to the President the appointment of Mr. Field[6] & supposed the [matter ended]; not supposing that he would allow interference with me in the selection of an officer in such important & confidential relations with me on any other ground than that of fitness.

The next day, however, I received a note from him expressing his reluctance to nominate Mr. Field because of Senator Morgans persistent opposition.[7] I replied [first] by a note asking a personal interview & afterwards, not receiving an answer, by a letter & [memorandum] stating particularly my reasons for [preferring] Mr. Field at this junct[ure].[8] In this note I informed him that I had telegraphed you begging you to withdraw your resignation.[9] This I had done when from the delay of his answer to my note suggesting personal conversation I had become pretty sure that there would be some difficulty.

To this letter I received an answer from the President stating the embarrassments to which he had been subject[ed], through certain appointments in the [Custom] House at New York; and that the appointment of Mr. Field would create additional embarrassment of the same sort, unless Senator Morgan & those feeling as he does could be brought to concur in it.[10]

This was a distinct [declaration] that in the appointment of your successor it was necessary for me to satisfy Senator Morgan & those who think as he does[,] and it determined me to tender my resignation. I could not hold the office of Secretary of the Treasury, under condition that I should be controlled in the Selection of an Assistant Treasurer of New York by any body other than the President or without his permission to select from among loyal & faithful men for that place the fittest man who would accept it & with whom my relations could be as cordial & confidential as they have ever been with yourself.

I replied therefore to the Presidents letter stating generally the rule which, in my opinion, should govern selections for official trusts; and adding that though your resignation relieved the present difficulty I could not but feel that my position here was not altogether agreeable to him and was certainly too full of embarrassment and difficulty & painful responsibility to allow in me the least desire to retain it, and that I therefore enclosed my resignation [&] should regard it as a real relief if he should think proper to accept it.[11]

To this he answered the next day accepting my resignation[, &] stating that of all he had said in commendation of my ability & fidelity he had nothing to unsay; but that he & I had reached a point of mutual embarrassment in our official relations which, it seemed, could not be overcome or longer sustained, consistently with the public Service.[12]

And so closed with the financial year my connexion with the Treasury Department.

Yours most truly
S P Chase

John J Cisco Esq

1. A clerk's copy of this letter is in Chase's papers at the Library of Congress (reproduced at *micro* 34:0615). The editors consulted that version to assist with readings of words that are difficult to read in the letterpress copy.

2. Francis Preston Blair, Jr.

3. Chase had repeatedly expressed similar concerns since the beginning of the year. Chase to Jay Cooke, Apr. 10, to William E. Dodge, Mar. 31, to Parke Godwin, June 23, to Joseph Medill, Jan. 30, to John Sherman, May 26, and to Thaddeus Stevens, Feb. 19, Apr. 11, 1864 (all above).

4. Chase offered the position to Denning Duer, William Curtis Noyes, and John Aikman Stewart before suggesting Maunsell B. Field. Chase and Morgan met on June 27. Chase to Lincoln, June 28, 1864 (above); *Chase Papers,* 1:463–64.

5. In the meeting Chase understood Morgan to suggest Richard Milford Blatchford and Dudley Sanford Gregory as candidates. At some point, Morgan also recommended Thomas Hillhouse (1816–97), a financier from Geneva, N.Y., and a former assistant adjutant general of U.S. volunteers. *Chase Papers,* 1:463–64; Morgan to Lincoln, June 28, 1864, in Basler, *Collected Works,* 7:413; *Nat. Cyc.,* 8:247.

6. Chase to Lincoln, June 27, 1864 (Lincoln Papers, L.C.).
7. Lincoln to Chase, June 28, 1864 (above).
8. For the "note" requesting a conference, see Chase to Lincoln, June 28, 1864 (Lincoln Papers, L.C.). The letter and memorandum, both also written on June 28, are reprinted above.
9. Chase to Cisco, telegram, June 28, 1864 (Cisco Papers, Misc. Mss. Collec., L.C.).
10. Lincoln to Chase, June 28, 1864 (above).
11. Chase to Lincoln, June 29, 1864 (above).
12. Lincoln to Chase, June 30, 1864 (above).

TO HORACE GREELEY

Letterpress copy of autograph letter. Chase Papers, Historical Society of Pennsylvania (*micro* 34:0682).

Washington July 4, 1864

My dear Mr Greeley,

What can I say that will express my heartfelt gratitude for your most generous article on my withdrawal from Mr. Lincoln's cabinet?[1] Nothing except that it is heartfelt and lasting as life.

I enclose to you copies of the correspondence which immediately preceded my resignation.[2]

There is one matter which does not appear on the face of it which no doubt entered into the final result pretty largely. Somebody had made a list of all the officers & clerks & if I remember rightly even messengers in Mr. Cisco's office distinguishing by the letter *D* all those denominated democrats & by the letter U perhaps or R all those admitted to be Unionists or Republicans. The Democrats were made to constitute a very great majority, perhaps nine tenths of the whole. This list was brought to Senator Morgan and by him handed to me as an argument for making now an appointment which would have political significance. Now I never accepted the maxim that "the spoils belong to the victors."[3] I agree that when, in the result of a party struggle, [one] political organization having marked and distinctive principles is brought in to power in place of another representing opposite ideas, the Head of the prevailing party is bound to make his appointments, unless in some rare cases, from the members of it. But to make indiscriminate removals is in my judgment pernicious to the public services. Removals should be made for cause & sometimes political difference is cause enough—always when carried to the extent of [factious] speeches and acts against the Administration or its head. Where men quietly and faithfully perform their duties, however, and perform them well, I should be slow to remove because of honest differences as to political principles or policy.

In Mr. Cisco's case I was entirely confident that most of the officers marked *D* were just such democrats as Dickinson or Tremain[4] or Cisco himself and I was wholly averse to an appointment of "such political significance" as would result in removals for differences in wing or division, or, in that office unless the circumstances of particular cases, should justify and require it, even for party differences.

I was alarmed by the prospect of consequences almost sure to follow the inauguration of such a course of action, and unwilling to be responsible for the Treasury with its chief office administered for the purpose of giving it effect. It was this feeling which added strength to my conviction that I *must* not admit the principle that "the appointment must have the concurrence of Senator Morgan & those who thought as he did—" I was obliged to insist that the appointment should be made mainly on the ground of special fitness for the place, and I felt profoundly the duty of claiming that, as the office was next in importance financially to my own and as I must be in constant & confidential correspondence & consultation with its chief, the successor of Mr. Cisco should be a gentleman known to me & acceptable to me as well as fit for the place.

The President would not agree to this. He even declined to have a personal conference concerning the matter.[5] This action with many antecedent circumstances convinced me that he did not feel satisfied with my position in his administration.

The rest is shown by the letters: except what you know otherwise of the hostility inside which embarrassed me at every step[6] and the neglect of Congress to make what I conceived to be necessary provision for financial success.

Your friend,
S P Chase

Please let Mr. Tilton see this letter & the correspondence & confer with him as to what should be said in the Independent.[7]

1. The article, printed in the *Tribune* on July 1, praised Chase as "one of the very few great men left in public life since the almost simultaneous decease of Messrs. Clay, Webster and Calhoun. . . . No man lives," it asserted, "who can bring larger powers to the work or devote them more unreservedly, unselfishly, to the welfare of his country."

2. Chase also reviewed the correspondence in a letter to John J. Cisco on July 1, 1864 (above).

3. The author of the list was Charles Jones, who chaired New York's Union State Committee. William L. Marcy of New York made the statement about "spoils" on the floor of the U.S. Senate on January 25, 1832. *Chase Papers,* 1:464; *Register of Debates in Congress,* 22d Cong., 1st sess., 1832, 1325.

4. Lyman Tremain, a former Democrat, had been elected attorney general of New York State in 1858. *Bio. Dir. U.S. Cong.,* 1953.

5. Lincoln to Chase, June 28, 1864 (above).

6. Most notably, the speech of Francis Preston Blair, Jr., on April 23. Chase to Jay Cooke, May 5, 1864 (above).

7. On July 7, Greeley published an article in Theodore Tilton's *Independent* that praised Chase, reviewed his career, and attributed his resignation to relations with the president that were "less cordial and trustful than were absolutely required by the arduous nature of his duties and the difficulties of his position."

TO WILLIAM CURTIS NOYES

Letterpress copy of autograph letter. Chase Papers, Historical Society of Pennsylvania (*micro* 34:0782).

Washington July 11, 1864.

My dear Sir,

Your very welcome letter reached me last Friday.[1] It is a real consolation to me that you approve my action.

It was indeed unavoidable, without acquiescence in terms incompatible as I thought with any honorable or any useful performance of my duties.

A long experience had convinced me that I was out of place in Mr. Lincoln's administration. Nothing but the urgency of friends and the hope of being serviceable to the country has kept me in connexion with it for more than a year.

My hopes of usefulness, however, were never stronger than as the recent Session of Congress approached its close.

The Investigation of the Treasury Department was closed: and if its result did not entirely silence accusation against one of my subordinates they did free him of all censure in the judgment of the Union Members of the Committee and as I cannot helping thinking in the honest opinion of the opposition members also. They not only vindicated the Department completely, but demonstrated the economy, vigilance & success of that branch of its work which had been chiefly assailed.[2]

The legislation of Congress, though not what I wished was better than at any former Session, and might be improved at the next. The taxation was not adequate to the support of the highest degree of credit, but it afforded ground on which an appeal might be made with probable success for the loans necessary for the service until next winter.[3] I felt that I would get on with tolerable military success and I hoped with a good degree of confidence great success. Congress had also conferred on the Department larger powers than heretofore in relation to abandoned plantations, to the care of freedmen, to trade, and to the purchase and sale of products of rebel states & had thus opened new paths, through fields of usefulness hitherto only partially explored.[4]

All these circumstances, and others connected with the completion of works begun, naturally made me somewhat reluctant to give up my trust to another. I never that nobody could understand or feel it as I did.

But my recommendation of Mr. Field as the Successor of Mr. Cisco revealed a feeling toward me on the part of Mr. Lincoln of which I had not suspected the existence. Had you accepted the appointment when tendered to you it would probably have never been manifested.[5] He objected to Mr. Field because of Senator Morgans persistent opposition to him and desired me to name one of three gentlemen named by him.

Under ordinary circumstances I should not have objected to either of the three, but just now I felt that I needed either more practical acquaintance with the duties of the office or greater capacity of labor and more adaptability than I supposed either of them to possess. Besides all the gentlemen had already been named to me by Senator Morgan and I had considered all he had said with every wish to satisfy him if I could, and I felt that it was wrong and ungenerous in him to press the matter before the President by way of appeal from me. No officer of the Department was more important to me and there was none in whose appointment it was more indispensable to the success and even safety of my administration that I should have a controlling voice subject only to the President should he think think the man named by me unfit. For many reasons I could not submit to have it controlled by any Senator. I asked therefore for a personal conference with the President, & telegraphed Mr. Cisco begging him to withdraw his resignation. No answer to my request coming from the President I sent him a paper stating the general principles which governed my selection and submitting the testimonials which warranted, in my judgment, the selection of Mr. Field. I also stated that I had telegraphed Mr. Cisco. To this he replied that he had not consented to a personal interview because the matter was out of the range of personal conversation between us; that he had been greatly troubled by retaining Mr. Barney & by the appointment of Judge Hogeboom; that Mr. Field's appointment would be in the same direction; and that he could not make it unless I could get Senator Morgan to concur.

Mr. Cisco had, in the mean time withdrawn his resignation; but only temporarily & might at any time renew it; and the letter satisfied me that the control of my Department, at a most vital point was to be taken from me and placed in outside hands. Mr. Lincoln I was sure would never have written it had my position here been agreeable to him, and I could not help feeling that I could not expect anything like cordial support against the bitter though causeless hostility which he knew to exist against me in as well as out of his councils.

It was my plain duty under these circumstances, as I thought to tender my resignation. He could accept or invite a conference if I was mistaken for mutual explanations. He showed I was right by his acceptance of it.

What the future has in store you as I can not guess. There is great and almost universal dissatisfaction with Mr. Lincoln among all earnest men. They doubt whether he can be reelected: they fear the consequences of his reelection. As yet however they have allowed themselves to be drawn along by the organized political forces which suppressed discussion before his renomination by cries of disloyalty against those who doubted its expediency.

I expect to be in New York before the close of the week and have some thought of going abroad for the Summer. Should it be possible I shall be very glad to accept your invitation & pass a day or two with you at Litchfield.[6]

We are in a sort of siege here.[7] An assault on the fortifications north of my house, some six or seven miles was expected this morning; but I have heard no guns & presume the rebels thought better of it.

Yours faithfully
S P CHASE

1. "With all sensible, honest and really loyal people your resignation was regarded as a public misfortune," wrote Noyes on July 7. "There is any amount of dissatisfaction with the present combination of officials," he continued, "and proper and *wise* combinations could throw it to the winds." The letter closed with an invitation for Chase to visit Noyes in New England, "to talk over these matters." Noyes to Chase, July 7, 1864 (Chase Papers, L.C.).

2. Chase discussed the investigation, conducted by the Committee on the Conduct of the War, in correspondence to Benjamin F. Wade, June 21, 1864 (above).

3. For similar expressions of a recurring theme see Chase's letter to John J. Cisco, July 1, 1864 (above).

4. In accordance with legislation of July 2, 1864. *Statutes at Large,* 13:375–78.

5. Chase had offered Noyes the position of assistant treasurer at New York on June 17. For additional accounts of events leading to Chase's resignation, see Chase to Cisco, July 1, and Chase to Horace Greeley, July 4, 1864 (both above). Chase to Noyes, June 17, 1864 (Chase Papers, Hist. Soc. of Pa.).

6. Chase left Washington, D.C., on July 13 and arrived in New York on the fifteenth. From August 13 to 17 he visited Noyes in Litchfield, Conn. *Chase Papers,* 1:479–81, 488–89.

7. On July 11, Confederate raiders under Jubal A. Early reached the outskirts of Washington, D.C., probed the city's defenses, and burned the Blair family home at Silver Spring, Md. The following night they withdrew and headed southward. Long, *Civil War Day by Day,* 537–38.

FROM WILLIAM P. MELLEN

Autograph letter. Chase Papers, Historical Society of Pennsylvania (*micro* 34:0857).

Cincinnati Augt. 10, 1864

My dear Mr. Chase

I have received your letters of 3d & 5th inst.[1]— I reached here too late to insist upon the withdrawal of your name from the convention. I should certainly have taken the responsibility of doing it if I had been here and seen "the situation"— Your telegram to me at Washington did not reach there until after I left on Thursday night.[2] Your letter of the 3d I found here. I was disappointed by the delay, but supposed you had advised others fully & did not regard it important to answer me.— I have been very much chagrined by the whole affair. The mismanagement has been shocking. Your name was not withdrawn, nor was a fight made for you. If either had been done the result would not have be so mortifying. You were suffered to appear to compete for the nomination and yet no effort was made to nominate you. The great statesman of the age, *seems* to have been *beaten* by—Ben Eggleston! and that too, in your own home by two to one![3] I am informed that it was arranged that Hoadley was to withdraw your name on Sat. morn. but that he was prevented by Dixon and Potter,[4] and your letter agreeing to accept was read instead. Well may you pray to be saved "from your friends" / I have felt inclined to write an article with extracts from your letters to set you right, but am advised that this would probably provoke angry discussion, and that it will probably be correctly understood any way.— I hope so.

About Presidential matters. I learned reliably in Washington that a secret movement is being made by leading war democrats in favor of Brough / They think McClellan is neither fish nor flesh. If the war democrats get the control of the Convention at Chicago, it will be a struggle probably between McC. & Brough. If this grows vindictive, who is so likely to be agreed to by both as you? If democrats there are as smart as democrats have heretofore been, I can hardly doubt the result.— There is also talk of a compromise ticket with McClellan and Pendleton, as the nominees. I dont believe any body can prognosticate upon any reliable basis.[5]

I am very glad to hear from *you* such opinions of Brough. I have also heard Genl. Rosecrans name mentioned.

The dissatisfaction with Mr. Lincoln grows to abhorrence. I dont believe he can be elected. Every day satisfies the public more and more, that instead of the "Honest old Abe" they believed him to be, he has been a cunning trickster unscrupulously devising for *himself*—that instead of administering his office with fidelity to the country, individuality rather than nationality has influenced his action. His treatment of you and retaining Blair, has contributed largely to this eye-opening process. Have you seen the paper of Ben. Wade and Winter Davis? Every one who has read it whom I have heard express an opinion of it, says "Amen."[6]

I understand the meaning of the call for a convention on the 22nd Sept. to be, that if a peace man is nominated at Chicago and the dissatisfaction with Mr. Lincoln continues, a new candidate combining the war democrats, the Freemont men, and the dissatisfied republicans may be put into the field.[7] So far as I can learn no *individual* has been named. What a day it would be for the Country, if at last the real patriots and true men of all parties, should select you as the man of the nation. It seems to me that if God directs human affairs and has decreed success to our cause, this may be the means through which it is to be accomplished.

I am very busy preparing to go to General Sherman. If you are at the helm, I too should expect great results from labor under the new regulations[8] / I like Mr. Fessenden, but the difference between "now and then" is very apparent. Of course I shall do all I can.

I am glad you are having a good time. From the tenor of your letter I infer that you have abandoned going to Europe.[9] Relaxation and rest were needed and will do you good. What are you going to write this winter?

It will give me a great deal of pleasure to hear from you often.[10] You know that there is no man on earth whom I admire so much, respect so highly, and love so devotedly as you, and if I were more righteous I would pray harder for you.

Please remember me kindly to Mrs Sprague and believe me

Faithfully &c
WM P. MELLEN

1. Chase's letter of August 3 has not been found. Writing from Massachusetts on August 5, he discouraged "friends" from considering him as a candidate for Ohio's first congressional district at a Union party convention scheduled for Cincinnati on August 6. He also discussed his plans to visit Cincinnati in the fall, settle "east of the mountains," and commence writing on some unidentified project. Chase then endorsed John Brough as a presidential candidate. "Fortunate would it be for the country if Lincoln, Fremont, & all would give way & let the Union vote be concentrated upon him," he wrote. Chase to Mellen, Aug. 5, 1864 (Clara H. Mellen Papers, Bowdoin Coll.); *Cincinnati Daily Commercial,* Aug. 8, 1864.

2. Responding to word from Mellen that opposition to Chase's nomination for Congress "could be overcome by active exertion," Chase wrote the following telegram on August 3 but was unable to send it until the fourth: "Unanimous nomination would command acceptance but cannot compete & must not be regarded as competitor." *Chase Papers,* 1:485.

3. Benjamin Eggleston, "an illiterate, brawling caucus-monger," according to one account, was a Cincinnati merchant and former state legislator. Eggleston received eighty-four votes to Chase's thirty-nine. "The proposing of Mr. Chase's name was received with cheers and hisses—the latter in the ascendency," reported the *Cincinnati Daily Commercial* of August 8. *Bio. Dir. U.S. Cong.,* 955.

4. Evidently M. D. Potter, editor of the *Cincinnati Commercial. Cincinnati Commercial,* Aug. 6, 1864; *Cinc. Dir. (1864),* 299.

5. At their national convention in Chicago, August 29–31, Democrats nominated George B. McClellan and George Hunt Pendleton, a Peace Democrat, as presidential and vice-presidential candidates. *Chicago Tribune,* Aug. 30–Sept. 1, 1864.

6. Accusing Lincoln of seizing dictatorial powers, the Wade-Davis Manifesto of August 5 protested the president's recent pocket veto of legislation that would have enabled radicals in Congress to control Reconstruction. Montgomery Blair remained in the cabinet until September 23, when Lincoln took advantage of his standing offer to resign. William Dennison succeeded Blair as postmaster general. Long, *Civil War Day by Day,* 552; *New York Tribune,* Aug. 5, 1864; Basler, *Collected Works,* 8:18, 20.

7. Plans for the convention of radicals at Buffalo on September 22 never materialized. Donnal V. Smith, *Chase and Civil War Politics* (Columbus, Ohio, 1931; reprint, Freeport, N.Y., 1972), 148–49.

8. The new regulations for trade "with and in States and parts of States declared in insurrection" were issued on June 30. *Report of the Secretary of the Treasury . . . 1864,* 294–350.

9. Earlier, Chase had considered visiting Europe with his daughters. Chase to Charlotte Eastman, July 11, 1864 (Chase Papers, Hist. Soc. of Pa.); Chase to John Trowbridge, July 17, 1864 (Houghton Lib., Harvard Univ.).

10. Chase responded to Mellen on August 17, denying that he had ever authorized use of his name for the congressional race. "It was unkind to me to use my name under the circumstances . . . ," wrote Chase. "Henceforth I trust that I may be let alone so far as political positions are concerned. I want none of them." Chase to Mellen, Aug. 17, 1864 (Clara H. Mellen Papers, Bowdoin Coll.).

TO GEORGE OPDYKE

Autograph letter. John Austin Stevens Papers, New-York Historical Society (*micro* 34:0888).

Bost[on] Aug. 19, 1864

My dear Mr. Opdyke

It was impossible for me to go to New York without breaking engagements made before receiving your telegram.[1] I sincerely hope that the deliberations of the gentlemen who will confer under your roof may be fruitful of benefit to our country, never more in need of wise counsel & fearless action by and among patriotic men. Mr. Noyes knows my views perhaps as well as any body, & expects to be present at your meeting. But my views are, by no means, as clear as I could wish, and I should be very glad to have the advantage of the clearer & better knowledge of other & better informed gentlemen.

Your friend
S P CHASE

Hon George Opdyke

1. Opdyke and others displeased over the prospect of Lincoln's reelection had called a meeting in New York for the evening of August 19 to discuss drafting some other candidate more to their liking. *Chase Papers,* 1:491; Smith, *Chase and Civil War Politics,* 149–50.

FROM WHITELAW REID

Autograph letter. Chase Papers, Historical Society of Pennsylvania (*micro* 34:0894).

Washington,
22d Aug. 1864.

Dear Mr Chase:—

Returning here today from a month's rest by the sea-side, I hear, in several quarters, of a desire, not to say an effort, to get you to come out in a letter counselling harmony in the support of Mr Lincoln. Some of the gossips have it that, if you will do so, you will be made to oust ready Mr Raymond, & take the French mission.[1]

I was shown today by a friend, very zealous for you, (if it were not unkind, I would say more zealous than wise,) a private letter from you, somewhat similar to the one they want to get for publication; & was asked if I didn't think such a letter would be of great service to *you*?

Will you pardon my intrusive forwardness, if I drag up an old quotation? "Timeo Danaos, et dona ferentes," which, being translated, means, "Confound their foreign missions!"[2]

Seriously:— Isn't it wise to wait for the Chicago Convention; & for the speedy crystallization of elements that is likely to follow? I know that Mr Greeley, (& for that matter, politicians of all grades, in New York,) hold Mr. Lincoln's election, under present circumstances, to be an impossibility. And I am sure that, carefully studying popular feeling, as I have done within the past five or six weeks, from Cincinnati & Washington, to Kennebunk & Rye Beach, I can't reach any other conclusion.

Mr. Lincoln himself is very much frightened. He has been telegraphing Greeley, begging him to come on here; which the latter in no wise inclines to do.[3]

I'm very sorry, as it turned out, that you were mixed up in the 1st District contest.[4] I would have written you, as soon as I reached Cincinnati, advising you that Eggleston's nomination was a foregone conclusion; but I didn't know where to address you.

Pardon the freedom of the suggestion I have hinted at above. I feared some of your friends here were urging on you a doubtful course; & while I didn't doubt that your decision would be sound, in any event; I thought it would do no harm if you knew that all your friends didn't think alike.

Sincerely Yours,
WHITELAW REID.

To/
Hon. S. P. Chase,
Ex. Secretary. &c &c &c,
Care. Hon. S. Hooper,
Boston.

1. Rumors at the time inaccurately suggested that Henry Jarvis Raymond, editor of the *New York Times* and chair of the National Union Committee, coveted the position, which William L. Dayton already occupied. Francis Brown, *Raymond of the Times* (New York, 1951), 255, 270.

2. Reid's translation was more playful than precise. The Latin quotation, which is from Virgil's *Aeneid* (bk. 2, l. 48), actually translates into a well-known comment expressing distrust of the Trojan horse: "I fear the Greeks, even when they bring gifts." Angela Partington, ed., *The Oxford Dictionary of Quotations,* 4th ed. (New York, 1992), 712; Norbert Guterman, comp., *A Book of Latin Quotations with English Translations* (Garden City, N.Y., 1966), 130–31.

3. Reid apparently referred to telegrams sent on August 6 and 8, in which Lincoln urged Greeley to visit Washington for discussions about ill-fated attempts by Greeley to encourage peace negotiations with Confederate representatives in Canada. Basler, *Collected Works,* 7:482–83, 485; Long, *Civil War Day by Day,* 534, 536, 540, 554.

4. William P. Mellen discussed the episode in his letter of August 10 (above).

TO WILLIAM P. FESSENDEN

Autograph letter on letterhead stationery. Chase Manhattan Archives (*micro* 34:0918).

REVERE HOUSE.[1]
BOSTON.
Boston, August 27, 1864

My dear Sir,

I have not had time to consider any thing deliberately since I saw you, and what I may say may not have much value.[2] I write only to fulfil my promise to you, by giving you hastily my view of the Financial situation.

I assume that the daily disbursements, or engagements, amount, on the average to $2.700.000, counting week days only. This will make a total of $845.000.000 in round numbers for the year 1864–5. Take from this sum the amount required for coin interest & other coin payments & supplied from customs say $70.000.000; and there remains for other objects $775.000.000 to be supplied from loans & revenue other than customs. The rate of receipts of Internal Revenue since July 1, indicates an income from this source of about $18.000.000 per month or $216.000.000 a year; which sum will be increased by the receipts from the Special Income tax to 236 or 240.000.000.[3] To this may be added $25.000.000 from purchase & sale of products of rebel states, if our armies are successful & the Treasury derives from this source all it legitimately may. This sum may be large[r]; but taking it as correctly estimated the whole amount of revenue, except customs, may be set down at $265.000.000 for the year. Take this sum from the estimated expenditures; and you have the amount $510.000.000 to be provided by loans in some form—say in round numbers $1.600.000 each week day. If there is to be a reduction of the circulation, which I hoped & expected to effect of say $10.000.000 per month, the sum of $120.000.000 must be added. But this will not increase the total of the debt but merely change its form. The real increase will be represented by the loans made to meet disbursements beyond revenue.

How to obtain these loans is the question of most pressing importance! How to obtain them in such a way as to improve rather than injure the public credit and the general interests depending on the condition of the currency is a question of equal importance, if not of such pressing exigency.

When I left the Department a large amount of Five per cent Legal Tenders had been withdrawn, say $70.000.000. I expected to replace them in part with Compound Interest Notes;[4] leaving say ten millions absolutely withdrawn; and I wished to add to the amount withdrawn ten millions a month; of which part would be replaced by the National Currency issued by the National Banks. In this way I expected to accomplish a safe & gradual reduction in the volume of currency; with a view to the resumption of specie payments as soon as practicable, without too great prejudice to the large interests involved. In this anticipation I assumed that the legislation of Congress, though not likely to cause any considerable reduction of the State Bank Circulation, would prevent its increase.

The amount of liabilities beyond all provision for them was about $13.000.000; or if the intended reduction of ten millions should be added $23.000.000. To meet this I advertised the balance of the

$75.000.000 loan, declined, say $33.000.000, fixing the minimum at four per cent premium; below which previous offers had not been accepted. Some offers under this advertisement had already been made when I resigned &, I did not doubt that I should obtain offers for the whole, if not under the advertisement then in the papers, yet by subscriptions or under another advertisement. This would have enabled to clear the table of requisitions and left me ten millions & the revenue to meet future demands for a few days till I could arrange for the disposition of the 7.30s & 10/40s at home & of other bonds abroad.

The advertisement was, properly enough, withdrawn after my resignation; and it was my hope & expectation that you would find a better resource than the 1881s in a loan of $50.000.000. from the Associated Banks; some of the leading managers of which, hostile to me because of my support of the National Banking System, would, I thought, be likely to give you the benefit of their influence.[5] My expectation was not realized. You got nothing from those Banks but compliments.

Since then you have done what I proposed to do in appealing to the People for subscriptions to the 7.30s.[6] But as yet you have not disposed of any other bonds than the 10/40s. It seems to me that you should.

The subscriptions for the 7.30s & the 10/40s equal my expectations under the present plan of disposing of them. But my experience had satisfied me, as I have already said to you, that the plan of a General Agency, adopted in obtaining subscriptions for the 5/20s was better than the plan of numerous Agents, (National Banks & others under them), with Supervision in the Treasury Department, which I adopted in obtaining subscriptions for the 10/40s, and which is now continued both in regards to the 10/40s & the 7/30s. I have not forgotten the calumnies, for which my employment of Mr. Cooke as General Agent was made the occasion;[7] and, I confess, it was with a view to avoiding these calumnies that I adopted a different plan for the 10/40s. But having become satisfied that the first plan was best for the country, I had determined to return to it & disregard the calumnies. If you think it best to adhere to the present plan, I cannot suggest any improvement in it; unless it be that the Advertising Agent should be directed to pay more attention to the 10/40s, and that the efforts of the National Banks & others should be stimulated by larger rewards. *I* think the present compensation is or ought to be sufficient; but it is so important to raise money enough to meet all demands promptly that it seems advisable to consider whether effort may not be stimulated by increase.

When I last saw you we had some talk about receiving certificates of indebtedness in payment for bonds in whole or in part. I have no doubt they should be so received rather than allow the present depreciation: but may not the same end be accomplished without the discredit which will attach to their receipt for bonds? Why not suspend all payments in certificates till the outstanding amount is reduced to proper limits—say almost $150.000.000. The reduction might be hastened by the purchase, through a confidential agent, of a few millions. This operation by improving their value would greatly benefit the holders & would enhance the public credit.

If you resolve on a reduction through a loan, I think the best plan to be adopted is to make them receivable for a limited time[,] for 10/40s.

Your main reliance for funds must be on the bonds of 1881, the 5/20s, the 10/40s & the 7.30s.

It will be wise I think to dispose of the $33.000.000 undisposed of, of the 75.000.000 loan:[8] nor should I hesitate to add to this amount enough to make the total amount of 1881s issued, (after all exchanges of the old 7.30s are completed) some even number of hundreds of millions. These bonds can be disposed of now, I think, at a premium of not less than 4%. Possibly more may be obtained.

Then the sale of the new 7.30s & the 10/40s should be pushed in every possible way. I have already suggested a General Agent and with or without such an agent the most liberal & active advertising & the most liberal encouragements to purchasers for resale & to the National Banks acting as agents.

The 5/20s should, it seems to me be reserved to meet the demand in Europe. I have never seen the way clear to a foreign loan properly so called; but I thought that the market for bonds already opened might be greatly extended & improved. I was about making the attempt when the action of the President in relation to appointments in the Department caused my resignation. I proposed to furnish bonds with coupons payable in Amsterdam, and to establish abroad the same kind of Agencies for distribution which had been established at home. Of course I could not have National Banks abroad; but it seemed to me not impossible to find solid & active banking houses, which could & would perform substantially the same functions in relation to the sale of bonds.

From these sources & by these means, if confidence in the administration can be maintained, with fair measures of military success, I do not doubt that the Treasury can be supplied till the meeting of Congress. Then the State Banks must be induced to come into the national System or required to cease from issuing notes for circulation; & such taxes must be issued as will bring the amount to be raised by loans within the limits of the natural demand for bonds.[9] Such legislation by the last Congress would have saved many millions. By the next Congress it will be indispensable. National Currency & adequate taxation are indispensable to the success of the Treasury Department. With these & with public confidence in the Administration nothing need be apprehended.[10]

I have written in haste & therefore too much—but I have fulfilled, as well as I could, my promise.

Yours very truly
S P Chase

Hon Wm Pitt Fessenden.

I have not been able to make a copy of this. Will you direct young Davis to make one, & send it under Cover to me to the care of Gov. Sprague. I expect to go to Concord this afternoon.[11]

1. A hotel on Bowdoin Square. *Chase Papers,* 1:483.
2. Chase and Fessenden met in Boston on August 18. Ibid., 490.
3. For details about the tax, which was approved on June 30, see Chase to Fessenden, June 20, 1864 (above).
4. See Chase's correspondence to John M. Forbes, June 25, and to William Cullen Bryant, June 30, 1864 (both above), concerning efforts to substitute six-percent compound interest legal tender notes for five-percent coupon notes.
5. See, for Chase's resort to sales of bonds authorized in 1861, his letter to John Sherman, May 26, 1864 (above); and, for the consortium of "Associated Banks," Chase to John T. Trowbridge, Mar. 21, 1864 (above).
6. Fessenden issued the appeal on July 26. *New York Times,* July 26, 1864.
7. Chase expressed similar sensitivity in a letter to Jay Cooke on June 26 (above).
8. The ways and means act of June 30, 1864, repealed legislation supplementary to the act of March 3, 1863, except for provisions to issue $75 million, which the Treasury Department had already advertised for sale. *Statutes at Large,* 13:13, 219.
9. Legislation of March 3, 1865, that addressed these issues helped seal the fate of state-chartered banks. Hammond, *Sovereignty,* 347; *Statutes at Large,* 13:484.
10. Chase continued the sentence with *except,* then blotted the word.
11. Chase intended to visit Concord, N.H. James M. Davis, one of the clerks who had assisted with Chase's Treasury correspondence, evidently continued in a similar role under Fessenden. *Chase Papers,* 1:495, 3:xxv–xxvi; *Register of Officers (1865),* 18.

TO SAMUEL HOOPER

Letterpress copy of autograph letter. Chase Papers, Historical Society of Pennsylvania (*micro* 35:0041).

Washington, Septr. 16, 1864

My dear Sir,

Yours of the 13th has just reached me and I beg you to accept my warmest thanks for this new proof of your real friendship.[1] When I look back to the support you originally gave me both by counsel & by action and think of its continuance during the years I devoted to our Finances, and the indispensable necessity of it to the success which crowned my efforts, I feel sentiments of gratitude & respectful affection, which I should find it difficult to express without seeming guilty of exaggeration.

I fear your opinion that I should be able to [res]ume the charge of the Department and avert the disasters which menace our financial condition is hardly well founded. I really do not see what I could do which may not as well be done by Mr. Fessenden. He seems to have the general confidence as fully as ever I did, & he certainly merits it. It is apparent also that the more he becomes accustomed to the work, he masters it more easily. Since I have been here I have been a good deal with & once or twice when he has received people on business of importance. He seems, already, to have gained quite a systematic control over the practical [workings][2] of the Department. To be sure the greatest difficulties lie in the direction you indicate: but in that who could accomplish more than he can? Money can be only attained through taxes & loans. The scale of taxation is fixed until the next Congress—and I see nothing that can be done in the way of loans which he is not doing; unless it be to return to the Agency System at home & establish it abroad. To return to it at home he is so manifestly disinclined, and after the experience I had of base imputation for resorting to it I cannot blame him. He feels inclined to it abroad however & will, I think, take early measures of a practical character.

There is one difficulty which applies alike to all modes of raising money—I mean the inordinate demand. Our expences are largely increased by high prices & the putting of the three hundred thousand new troops—for such I understand will be the result of [volunteering] & the draft under the new call—into the field will precipitate a vast amount of requisitions on the Treasury.[3] True increased economy in administration through the efforts of Mr. Stanton will make the demand somewhat less than it would otherwise be, but it will still be enormous & I fear beyond the ability of any Secretary [to] provide.

You are right in thinking I could have secured better results had the President not thought fit to create the occasion—& even the necessity if I would preserve my self-respect—for my resignation: than I could hope for now were I to resume the charge of the Department. So could Mr. Fessenden had he been in the Department from the beginning of the Administration: and I see no reason to doubt now that he can secure, by going over all that I could by resuming.

I would not shrink from the attempt, to accomplish even the work you think possible, however, could I be assured of real cooperation on the part of the President as well as of Congress. I should have no doubt of being able to secure the latter; but I see no reason to hope for the former. I do not distrust at all that I should have the President's good will; but I do not believe it possible to rouse him to the active interest & earnest & resolute action in his whole administration which have become essential to financial success.

Since I have been here I have followed the advice of friends who assured me of his wish for cordial relations between us as well as my own sense of duty by calling on him. He received me kindly & this evening I have, on his invitation visited him at Soldiers Home.[4] At each interview others were present & nothing transpired beyond ordinary talk on ordinary topics. If he has any inclination for any other, he will doubtless make some opportunity for it; but nothing in his manner or tone leads me to think that he appreciates the financial situation or supposes that I could be of service. I rather think that he supposes he has gained more by the appointment of Mr. Draper as Collector[5] & Mr. Wakeman as Surveyor of New York than he could have gained by my continuance in the Department or by the most earnest devotion of his own time and labor to the difficulties which surround it. Things may change in this respect; but experience does not, in my judgment, warrant the expectation. We can only hope.

In relation to the canvass now in progress I propose to do as you wish. I have already authorized the sending of word to Cincinnati that I will speak there whenever suitable arrangements shall be made; and am entirely ready to do all in my power to secure the result which Mr. Lincoln desires.[6] I am confirmed rather than shaken in the opinion I expressed in my last letter of the importance of sustaining him for reelection & after reelection. All the good we can secure, as it seems to me, for our country must be secured through him. The Democratic Party seems to have taken pains to say to all loyal men "I *will* drown; no body *shall* help me:" The loyal people will hardly interfere as the compassionate bystanders did in the case of the poor Frenchman.

I really wish you could be here. It now looks as if I might remain through next week: but your presence may be & probably will be more useful if I am not here. It is not likely, I fear, that any practical results can be accomplished which would warrant the exposure of your health to any detriment. Should you come, however, either now or some weeks hence you will not find that any thing said or done or left intentionally unsaid or undone, by me, has created the slightest "impediment" to the completest good understanding you can desire:

I regret to say that my impression of the military situation has not been improved by what I have learned here—Sherman is fortifying at Atlanta evidently under the impression that the war is to be protracted; Grant does not seem to take the earnest personal control on the Army of the Potomac which is essential to the earliest possible success; there appears to be an idea here that it is not wise even if were certainly practicable to capture & hold Mobile.[7] Little or nothing can be confidently expected until the armies are recruited up to their full strength. I hoped for more than the indications promise at present; but I am as confident as ever of final success and am *pretty sanguine* that it can be practically accomplished within the next six months. I have been too often disappointed to feel certain.

If I shall have left the city before your answer can come hither, it will be forwarded.[8]

I congratulate you on the unanimity of the Republican State Convention of Massachusetts. Gov. Andrew & the other State officers must feel the compliments they have received.[9]

Most sincerely & faithfully yours
S P CHASE

Hon. S. Hooper.

1. Chase returned home from his trip to New England on September 14. Writing in response to a letter of September 9, Hooper encouraged Chase to support Lincoln's reelection campaign and explored the possibility of Chase regaining the helm at the Treasury Department. "Any man succeeding you at such a time as the present must be weaker and have less opportunity for the exercise of ingenuity in directing the affairs of the Treasury," wrote Hooper. *Chase Papers,* 1:503; Hooper to Chase, Sept. 13, 1864 (Chase Papers, Hist. Soc. of Pa.).

2. Chase wrote *business* and *workings,* one over the other, and his final intention is difficult to discern from the letterpress copy.

3. Lincoln's proclamation of July 18, based on legislation of July 4, called for five hundred thousand new troops. A draft was to be used after fifty days to meet any portion of the quota that remained unfilled. Basler, *Collected Works,* 7:448–49; *Statutes at Large,* 13:379–80.

4. The day Chase returned to Washington, September 14, he visited the Treasury Department, where both William Pitt Fessenden and Hugh McCulloch advised him to play a role in the coming election campaign. Fessenden saw Lincoln, who invited Chase to call. The next day Chase had an interview with the president and noted that Lincoln "recd. me quite cordially." On the sixteenth, Chase and Edwin M. Stanton included the Soldiers' Home, the Lincolns' summer residence, on the route of a carriage ride, but evidently did not see the president at that time. In the evening of that day Chase paid a call on Lincoln, this time recording the event as "talk with President indifferent but cordial." *Chase Papers,* 1:503–4.

5. Simeon Draper (1804–66), a politician, New York merchant, and chair of his state's Union party, served a brief stint in 1864–65 as the successor to Hiram Barney's position as collector of customs at New York. *Appletons',* 2:229.

6. From September 24 until the election on November 8, Chase campaigned in Ohio, Kentucky, Pennsylvania, Michigan, Chicago, and St. Louis, speaking in behalf of Lincoln and the Union-Republican ticket. Chase to Kate Chase Sprague, Sept. 17, 1864 (below); *Chase Papers,* 1:507–10.

7. Union victory in the naval battle of Mobile Bay on August 5 opened the prospect of a siege of Mobile, Ala., but Federal forces did not occupy the city until the Confederates withdrew in April 1865. Long, *Civil War Day by Day,* 551–52, 673–74.

8. Responding on September 20, Hooper continued to maintain hope that Chase might be reinstalled at the head of the Treasury. Hooper's letter also detailed a plan to issue special legal tender notes in small denominations to pay sailors and soldiers. Hooper to Chase, Sept. 20, 1864 (Chase Papers, Hist. Soc. of Pa.).

9. The Massachusetts state Republican convention, meeting in Worcester on September 16, passed a platform that endorsed the national Union ticket, expressed support for continuing the war, and nominated incumbent governor John A. Andrew for reelection. *Appletons' Annual Cyclopædia,* 4:510; *DAB,* 1:280–81.

TO KATE CHASE SPRAGUE

Autograph letter. Chase Papers, Library of Congress (*micro* 35:0049).

Washington, Sep. 17, 1864

My dear Katie,

I have just returned from hearing an excellent sermon on the proper observance of Sunday: but I trust it is no violation of it to write you.[1]

Every telegram has been opened in the hope that it might announce your arrival well & safe, at Providence, if not at the Beach.[2] As yet I have been disappointed and now that there has been time enough for a letter to come and none has come I cannot help feeling a great deal of anxiety. I am confident, however, that I shall not have to wait for some intelligence from you much longer.

I have seen the President twice since I have been here.[3] Both times third persons were present & there was nothing like private conversation. His manner was evidently intended to be cordial & so were his words: and I hear of nothing but good will from him. But you know he is not at all demonstrative either in Speech or Manner—not at all in these respects what I like. I feel that I do not know him, & I found no action on what he says or does.

It is my conviction that the cause I love & the general public interests will be best promoted by his election, and I have resolved to join my efforts to those of almost the whole body of my friends in securing it. Whether it can be secured I do not know; but I think it can be. My apprehensions arise from the manifestations I see of a purpose to compromise, if possible, by sacrificing all that has been done for freedom in the rebel states—to purchase peace for themselves—the whites—by the reenslavement of the blacks. I cannot think that God will bless any who entertain such thoughts.

I am invited to address a great Mass Meeting in Cincinnati on the Evening of Saturday next, and also by the National Union Association to speak at Mozart Hall, in Cincinnati, on any Tuesday or Saturday evening after next Saturday. I think of accepting the first invitation & letting my answer to the other be determined by circumstances.[4]

I propose therefore to go to Cincinnati next Thursday: leaving either Baltimore or New York in the morning or evening of that day as may be most convenient. Col. Howe has some thought of going with me, & I shall write him tonight to let you know. If you & Nettie will go—or either of you—please make arrangements to leave Baltimore or New York as you may prefer, and telegraph me so that I shall know by Wednesday Morning—or afternoon will do.[5] I must learn so that I can meet you at one place or the other: I was going to say unless you will take Col H's escort the whole way—but this wont do as he goes—if he goes at all to accompany me.

With warmest love to Nettie & Ida[6] & kindest remembrances to all

Your affectionate father
S P Chase

Mrs Kate C. Sprague

1. The sermon was delivered by Bernard Harrison Nadal, pastor of the Wesley Chapel in Washington, D.C. *Chase Papers,* 1:504.

2. William Sprague owned a farm at Narragansett Beach, near Wakefield, R.I. Chase to Kate Chase, Aug. 19, 1863 (above); Chase to Charles Sumner, June 25, 1865 (Chase Papers, L.C.).

3. See Chase's letter of September 16 to Samuel Hooper (above).

4. At Cincinnati's market space on September 24, Chase delivered an address in support of the national Union ticket. His speech at Mozart Hall, on Saturday, November 12, celebrated Lincoln's reelection, secured through balloting on November 8. *Chase Papers,* 1:507, 510; *Cincinnati Daily Gazette,* Nov. 14, 1864.

5. Chase left Washington on Wednesday, September 21, en route to Cincinnati via Baltimore. His daughters intended to join him in Baltimore, but then declined to make the journey. *Chase Papers,* 1:506; Chase to Kate Sprague, Sept. 23, 1864 (Chase Papers, Hist. Soc. of Pa.).

6. Ida Nichols, William Sprague's niece.

TO GEORGE S. DENISON

Autograph letter. HM 23246, The Huntington Library, San Marino, California (*micro* 35:0068).

Washington, Septr. 20. 1864.

My dear Mr. Denison,

Your letter of the 6th is just received, and like all your letters has interested me much.[1]

I have not seen the new Constitution of Louisiana; but if it provides for complete emancipation would vote for it, though I should prefer to see a provision also for the extension of suffrage to all persons unconvicted of crime.

It is with great regret that I read & hear of so much dissatisfaction with Mr. Flanders. I wish he had more of the spirit of accommodation than he seems to have; but his very integrity perhaps makes him unbending. I have said to Mr. Fessenden that I should if in his place sustain him, unless he should be proved less honest than I think him, or unless it should be clearly established that his continuance in office would prejudice instead of promoting the public interests.

It is sad to contrast the work in Louisiana with the work in Georgia & Tennessee under Sherman or the work in Virginia under Grant. I always wished Gen Banks success, & shall be glad now to see the tide turn in his favor. If I felt otherwise I should be ashamed of myself and endeavor to crush out the feeling.

What is Plumley doing? I learn that he boasted of being very active in procuring the removal of Graham & Waples, which seems to me to have been wrong. He wrote me in a very bad spirit in reply to a letter which I meant to be entirely kind though frank.[2] Of course he must choose his path; but I fear his will not conduct him to good ends.

We have news today of a brilliant victory by Sheridan. I hope it will expedite the capture of Richmond.[3] But I fear the end of the rebellion, is yet remote, unless peace be purchased by disunion & disgraceful compromise. There is in my judgment but one way to reconstitute revolted states in loyal relations; and that is by making all loyal [citizens] equal before the law & furnishing all with the safeguard of the ballot. The next best mode to this is that which most nearly approaches it.

There has been & is a great deal of dissatisfaction with Mr. Lincoln; but it is very clear to me that the best interests of the country require his reelection, and I shall give him my active support. It is not probable that my action will be appreciated as I would wish; but no matter. I must be satisfied with doing what I believe to be right & patriotic.

Write to me whenever you can and give me all the particulars of what goes on which you think interesting or useful.[4]

Very sincerely your friend & cousin
S P Chase

George S. Denison Esq

1. Denison's letter of September 6 reported on ratification of Louisiana's new constitution and a congressional election, both of which occurred on September 5. "The fact is, this whole civil reorganization in Louisiana is a cheat & a swindle and everybody knows it," he asserted. Denison to Chase, Sept. 6, 1864 (Chase Papers, L.C.); Long, *Civil War Day by Day,* 567.

2. Early in 1865, Lincoln nominated Cuthbert Bullitt and Charles A. Peabody to replace James Graham and Rufus Waples as U.S. marshal and U.S. attorney, respectively, for the eastern district of Louisiana. The letter from Benjamin R. Plumly, apparently written on April 30, replied to correspondence of February 23 and March 8 in which Chase accused Plumly of disloyalty to the antislavery movement and of using his position for monetary gain. "I am forced to regard your letter as worse than disingenuous," wrote Plumly, "for you were fully informed that for many months I had held no office, to prostitute, even if I were so disposed, having been rudely displaced by your Supervising Spl. Agent without a word of notice or complaint." Chase to Plumly, Mar. 8, 1864 (Chase Papers, Hist. Soc. of Pa.); U.S. Senate, *Journal of Executive Proceedings,* 13:369, 384, 14:91; Plumly to Chase, Apr. 30, 1864 (Chase Papers, L.C.).

3. On September 19, Philip H. Sheridan's Army of the Shenandoah decisively defeated troops under Confederate Jubal A. Early at Winchester, Va. Union forces did not take Richmond until April 3, 1865. *DAB,* 17:80; Long, *Civil War Day by Day,* 571, 665.

4. Denison responded with two letters on October 8. In one, he informed Chase that Louisiana's new constitution empowered, but did not require, the legislature to extend the franchise to African Americans. "To do more than this would have been an exercise of more justice generosity & magnanimity than was possessed by the Convention," he explained. The other letter repeated stories of anticipated military action against Mobile, Ala., offered a negative assessment of Benjamin F. Flanders, and informed Chase that Benjamin Rush Plumly had assumed the chair of Louisiana's Board of Education for Freedmen. Denison to Chase, Oct. 8, 1864, two letters (Chase Papers, L.C.)

TO EDWIN M. STANTON

Autograph letter. Edwin M. Stanton Papers, Library of Congress (*micro* 35:0132).

Cincinnati, Oct. 13, 1864

My dear Sir,

Your telegram, announcing the death of the Chief Justice was received this morning.[1] As a lawyer he leaves a name behind him which any lawyer might be proud of; as a man I have rarely known one more kind & genial. I differed widely from him on political questions—let the veil drop upon the differences.

Within the last three or four months I have been assured that it was the Presidents intention, to offer the place to me in case of a vacancy. I think I should accept it if offered: for I am weary of political life & work. What do you think.

This will be handed you by Hassaurek who is dreadfully distressed about his brother & feels that he must go & see personally what can be done.[2] Let me beg you to do all you can for him. He is worthy & so is his brother who is a prisoner.

Your friend
S P CHASE

Hon. E. M. Stanton.

1. Early on the morning of October 13, Stanton telegraphed Chase with the news that Roger Brooke Taney had died the night before. Stanton to Chase, Oct. 13, 1864 (Chase Papers, Hist. Soc. of Pa.); *DAB,* 18:294.

2. Friedrich Hassaurek, currently U.S. minister to Ecuador, sought the exchange of his half brother, Leopold Markbreit, whom the Confederates held as a military prisoner. *Chase Papers,* 1:515.

FROM HORACE GREELEY

Autograph letter on letterhead stationery. Chase Papers, Historical Society of Pennsylvania (*micro* 35:0160).

Office of The Tribune,
New York, Oct. 19, 1864.

Dear Sir:

I have yours of the 15th this morning, and shall print your speech in bold, and as soon as possible—perhaps to-morrow.[1] We are overwhelmed with Election matter, but there will always be room for such speeches.

As to the Chief Justiceship, I hear but one voice; yet there are whispers that [Mrs.] L. is committed to Ira Harris, while I have heard (but do not believe) that Gov. Dennison favors Noah H. Swayne. Gov. Morgan went on to Washington on Monday night to urge your appointment. And I can hear of no counter movement in this quarter.

I think you ought not only to accept the appointment if tendered, but to change your residence to Maryland, on some pleasant farm near Baltimore, so as to exert the influence of your character and position over the destinies of that new born State. I cannot feel that our Anti-Slavery work is half done so long as the Blacks remain politically under the feet of the Whites. I look for a great anti-negro reaction the moment the War is over—an uprising of all that is [ruffianly] under the direction of all that is rascally in the land to revenge on the poor negroes the humiliation and [discomfiture] of the slaveholders. This brutality will have to be resisted every where, but we especially need genius as well as character on the Bench to administer the proper legal discipline to its contrivers as well as their tools. I pray you to consider this. Maryland is destined to bear a leading, unenviable part in this predestined rebound of the Rebellion; and the Baltimore roughs will need the promptest and sternest judicial discipline to convince them that the good old days, when negroes might be knocked down, maimed or ravished with impunity exist no longer. You should not only be Chief Justice, but be living where you can [inspire] and direct the judicial [*illeg.*] needed to bring these miscreants to order.

As to our State, we shall carry it by about the majority of 1860. Military disaster might reduce this, but nothing less than the surrender of Grant's army could overcome it.

Yours,
HORACE GREELEY.

Hon. S. P. Chase,
Cincinnati, Ohio

1. On October 20, the *New York Tribune* printed a campaign speech that Chase had delivered in Covington, Ky., on the evening of October 13. *Chase Papers,* 1:508.

TO GEORGE S. DENISON

Autograph letter. George S. Denison Papers, Library of Congress (*micro* 35:0249).

Cincinnati, Nov. 11, 1864.

My dear Mr. Denison,

Your two letters of the 8th ult. are received & welcome as your letters always are.[1] I wish that in addition to the information you give of civil & military movements you would add impartial sketches of your prominent men, as seen by friends and as seen by enemies. I desire to be informed & it may become important that I should be informed fully as to persons as well as things.

I enclose the rough draft of a letter I sent Gen. Banks after reading his letter to Senator Lane.[2] Please return it & tell me what you think of it. It seems to me to put myself right—I count nothing on any effect on him.

That Mr. Plumley is making himself so useful gives me real pleasure. I never doubted that his heart was right with our general cause & especially with the oppressed of all races, not excepting the colored. I did not like his method of political action & found it difficult to reconcile some things he did & omitted with his personal professions to me; but I never entertained an unkind sentiment towards him. In one respect I thought he failed to understand me & it was a respect in which no one perhaps likes to be misunderstood. He seemed to think that in my administrative action as head of the Treasury Department I could be influenced by my own political hopes or apprehensions, and I did not like to be thought capable of this. He seemed to me to adopt General Banks maxim that "success is duty"; to which that other saying "Ends sanctify means" is too apt to be a corollary.[3] If I judged him wrongly I shall be glad—and more than glad—highly gratified to be convinced of it.

I am very sorry to read what you say of Mr. Flanders. I resisted the effort to remove him, because I thought the removal would be unjust to him; and because it seemed to me to be mainly urged by persons whose characters would certainly receive no new illumination from a comparison with his. I hate to consent to the removal of an honest man, even though there be sufficient ground in unacceptable temper & manners or in want of ability—of which last nobody accuses Mr. F——. When I see the Secretary, however, as I may before long, I shall think it my duty to let him see what you say.

The Constitution is better than I expected—but I wish that its suffrage articles were more liberal to loyal men without distinction of color and less liberal to disloyal men. I am still clearly of opinion that when the colored race furnishes a large proportion of the population there should be no discrimination between it & the White men in respect to suffrage. Doubtless there are evils & inconveniences in equality—but there are greater in inequality. Had the question been *settled* by the constitution speedy acquiescence would have followed; & then strenuous endeavors to raise the intellectual standard of all the uninformed Negro ballots in my judgment are as necessary in rebel states reorganized as negro bullets.

We have been on the brink of civil war in the north. Nothing, but divided counsels of opposition leaders saved us from it. The strength & ramifications of the conspiracy, now being exposed at Indianapolis, of which the recent attempts at St Albans, Sandusky, Chicago & plans of attack on other places were parts are frightful.[4] It is now effectually suppressed by the activity of the Government and by the voice of the people in the election.

We do not yet know certainly the result in New York: but think we have the State. If so and if we have also, as we expect, the Pacific States McClellan has but twenty one votes.[5] He ought not to have one. Considered as men Mr. Lincoln is immensely his superior: considered as Representatives of Ideas & Principles & Measures this superiority becomes immeasureable. Of course I did everything in my power to contribute to the great victory just achieved. Not to have done so would have been infidelity to the great cause to which my life has been devoted & I claim no merits for what I could not omit to do without forfeiting my own self respect.

Perhaps you know that it is supposed by many that Mr. Lincoln will offer me the seat vacated by the death of Judge Taney. I should have gone to Washington this week had I not been unwilling even to seem to seek the appointment. I expect now to go as soon as the question is decided. Katie & Nettie will spend the winter there. I am not at all sanguine that the vacant seat will be offered me. I should like the offer better than the seat. I think I should take it, but am afraid I should not much relish the transfer from the active responsibilities of life to the quiet work of the bench.

I need not repeat that your letters are always welcome and you must not wait for answers always. If possible write at least twice a month and give me all the insight you can.[6] I will write, as often as I can.

Your friend always
S P CHASE

Geo. S. Denison Esq

1. For summaries, see Chase's letter to Denison, September 20, 1864 (above).

2. Nathaniel P. Banks's letter of September 24, written to Senator James H. Lane of Kansas, defended Reconstruction policies followed in Louisiana since January. Chase's draft response to the letter inquired about the identity of a Treasury official in New Orleans who, according to Banks, previously held a Confederate military commission. Chase also expressed qualified support for Louisiana's new constitution but faulted it for restricting suffrage. He criticized Banks for supposedly favoring specific candidates for office. Banks's reply to Chase is printed at November 16 (below). Chase to Banks, Nov. 8, 1864 (Chase Papers, Hist. Soc. of Pa.); excerpts from Banks to Lane, Sept. 24, 1864, in the *New York Times,* Oct. 1, 1864.

3. "The ends sanctify the means" is a proverb that, in various forms, dates back at least as far as Sophocles in the fifth century B.C. Sophocles, *Electra,* William Sale, trans. (Englewood Cliffs, N.J., 1973), 33; Burton E. Stevenson, ed., *The MacMillan Book of Proverbs, Maxims, and Famous Phrases* (New York, 1948; reprint, 1966), 681.

4. In September, charges were filed in military court against alleged Confederate sympathizers suspected of fomenting armed insurrection in the upper Middle West. The trials, conducted in Indianapolis, continued into November. At St. Albans, Vt., Confederate raiders from Canada had robbed three banks on October 19. The incident near Sandusky, Ohio, involved Confederate agents who seized two Lake Erie steamers on September 19, intending to free prisoners of war held nearby. In Chicago, officials exposed a plot on November 6 to gain control of the city and free Confederate soldiers confined at Camp Douglas. Klement, *Dark Lanterns,* 172–83; Long, *Civil War Day by Day,* 571–72, 585–86, 593.

5. New York, California, Nevada, and Oregon were among the states won by the Union ticket. *Appletons' Annual Cyclopædia,* 4:173, 574, 588, 643.

6. Denison responded on November 25, identifying Thomas P. May as the Federal official whom Banks had accused of being a former Confederate military officer. Denying the charge, Denison went on to defend provisions for suffrage in Louisiana's new constitutions. He also rejoiced over Lincoln's reelection, introduced new U.S. legislators from the state, and explained his rejection of an earlier offer to become assistant treasurer in New Orleans. Denison to Chase, Nov. 25, 1864 (Chase Papers, L.C.).

TO CHARLES SUMNER

Autograph letter. Chase Papers, Library of Congress (*micro* 35:0255).

Cincinnati Nov. 12, 1864

My dear Sumner,

The triumphant close of the canvass leaves me a few moments in which to acknowledge your kind letter of the 24th.[1]

I know the principles which govern your relations with the Administration & shd. honor you less if they were other than they are.

As yet nothing has reached touching the *decision* of the President as to the vacant seat; though what I have heard indicates that his purpose of offering it to me is unchanged.

Quite recently it has been told me that, last spring, when it was so probable that the vacancy would immediately occur, a paper was drawn up & signed by the other Judges—whether the new or all was not said—recommending the appointment of Judge Swayne.[2] I do not know how this may be but I do know that just before the adjt. of the Court, Judge Field expressed a very strong wish for my appointment & that Judge Miller has recently expressed the same.[3] However this may be the paper, if prepared, must have been in the Presidents hands at the time of his conversations with you before & other Senators since my resignation and it will certainly no more affect his intention now than then.

I have heard from others before I read it in your note that the President told the Senate Committee that he & I could not get along together in the cabinet. Doubtless there was a difference of temperament and, on some points, of judgment. I may have been too earnest & Eager while I thought him not earnest enough & too slow. On some occasions indeed I found it was so. But I never desired anything else than his complete success & never indulged a personal wish incompatible with absolute fidelity to his Admn. To assure that success I labored incessantly in the Treasy. Dept. with what results the world knows. When I found that the use of my name in connexion with the Presidency would interfere with my usefulness in the Dept. I seized the opportunity offered by the expression, by a majority of the Union members of the Ohio Legislature of a preference for him, to ask that no further consideration might be given to my name.[4] After that I advised all friends who consulted me, in reference to the action of the Baltimore Convention, to give him their support. After that nomination I joined no movement to bring forward another candidate, but, at the proper time, gave all the aid in my power to his reelection.

It would be uncandid not to say that I felt hurt & wronged by the circumstances which preceded & attended my resignation and that I was far from satisfied with the indications that Mr. Lincoln sympathized more with those who assailed & disparaged than with those who asserted & maintained the views held by me in common with the great majority of the supporters of his Admn.

But I felt greatly reassured on the last point by his timely & pointed notice "to whom it may concern"[5] & it did not cost me much of a struggle to put duty & conviction in the government of my personal sentiments—the less because I always thought him honest in purpose & not unfriendly in heart.

I think now there would never have been any difficulty about our getting along together could he have understood my sentiments just as they were & allowed me to understand his freely & unreservedly.

But,

Let the dead Past bury its dead,
and let the future know us by our labors
to take
Occasion by the hand & make
The bounds of freedom wider yet.[6]

Faithfully yours
S P Chase

Hon Chs. Sumner

1. On October 14, Sumner wrote about urging Lincoln to appoint Chase as chief justice, in accordance with assurances supposedly given by the president "last spring." Chase thanked Sumner five days later, and Sumner responded on October 24 with an elaboration of Lincoln's original statement. At that time, Sumner told Chase, Lincoln "confessed that you & he could not get along together in the cabinet, but that he should be glad to make you C.J." Chase to Sumner, Oct. 19, 1864 (Chase Papers, L.C.); Sumner to Chase, Oct. 14, 24, 1864 (Chase Papers, L.C.).

2. David Davis apparently first suggested Associate Justice Noah Swayne as a replacement for Taney as chief justice sometime during the winter of 1863–64. Other candidates besides Chase and Swayne included Edward Bates, Francis Blair, Jr., New York attorney William M. Evarts, Ira Harris, and Edwin M. Stanton. Davis to Lincoln, Oct. 22, 1864 (Lincoln Papers, L.C.); Fairman, *Reconstruction and Reunion,* 8–12; Horace Greeley to Chase, Oct. 19, 1864 (above).

3. The Supreme Court had adjourned on April 18, to reconvene in December. Associate justices Stephen Johnson Field and Samuel Freeman Miller were Lincoln appointees. Chase later recalled of Field's endorsement: "It took me by surprise; but was very grateful to my feelings." Chase to Field, Apr. 30, 1866 (Chase Papers, Hist. Soc. of Pa.); Minutes, Apr. 18, Dec. 5, 1864 (Recs. of Supreme Court, Nat. Arch.).

4. The members had stated their "preference" on February 26, 1864. Chase withdrew his name from consideration on March 5, 1864. Chase to Hall, Mar. 5, 1864 (Chase Papers, Hist. Soc. of Pa.), also published in the *New York Times,* Mar. 11, 1864; *Cincinnati Daily Commercial,* Feb. 29, 1864.

5. On July 18, 1864, Lincoln had written a statement, addressed "To Whom it may concern," to be used by Horace Greeley in discussions with Confederate peace envoys. Concerned that he not appear unwilling to consider an armistice, yet reluctant to offer the Confederacy easy terms that would allow a cease-fire preserving the status quo, Lincoln used the statement to frame conditions for negotiation. "Any proposition which embraces the restoration of peace," he wrote, "the integrity of the whole Union, and the abandonment of slavery, and which comes by and with an authority that can control the armies now at war against the United States will be received and considered by the Executive government of the United States." Basler, *Collected Works,* 7:451; David Herbert Donald, *Lincoln* (New York, 1995), 522–23.

6. Chase copied the first line of this poem from Henry Wadsworth Longfellow, "A Psalm of Life." Longfellow, *The Complete Writings of Henry Wadsworth Longfellow . . . ,* 11 vols. (Boston and New York, 1904), 1:20.

FROM NATHANIEL P. BANKS

Autograph letter. Chase Papers, Historical Society of Pennsylvania (*micro* 35:0271).

Washington D.C.
16"— November. 1864.

Dear Sir,

Yours of the instant I received yesterday[1]— The paragraph in my letter to which you refer, relates to Mr. May assistant Treasurer of the

United States. He is understood to have served as captain in the Rebel army, and to have been commissioned as captain, previous to the occupation of New Orleans, by the Federal government.[2]—

It was not mentioned in disparagement to him as a public officer, or as a private citizen. He is in all respects an honorable and loyal man—

The fact was mentioned as an illustration of the difficulty which attended the exclusion of such persons, from the rights of citizenship by the Constitution of the State, when they were recognized by the government, of the United States, in appointment to responsible officers, by both civil and military Departments— It seemed a sufficeint justification of the action of the Convention, and reference was made thereto, for that reason only—

I understood your approval of the re-organization of the State, to have reference, only, to the form of government proposed, and not to the candidates for office. My impression is now and was then just as you state your intention to have been— I had myself nothing to do with the selection of Candidates or the election of officers— The success of Mr. Hahn was not at all owing to the influence of the government or its officers, civil or military, but solely to the number of offices held and controlled by Mr Flanders, and the impossibility of his combining any considerable number of men, or different interests, in his support— This was the result purely of personal and mental infirmities— In addition to this disqualification, he held the chief Treasury office, to which he thoght all other treasury offices were subordinate, was President of the 1st. National Banks—was generally understood to be interested in contracts for completion of the Custom House, and had demanded, in person, of the President, the removal of the military officers of the Department— Governor Hahn was a very different man. He held no office—had made war upon no officer of the govt.: was interested in no emoluments from the general govt.: and was able, without effort from the amenity of character and disposition to unite in his support, all nationalities classes, and interests— He did not receive the united vote of the citizens of Louisiana who had enlisted in the army—on the contrary, Mr Flanders recd. the votes of such soldiers as preferred him, and in some places—as at Port Hudson he—Mr. F—— received *every vote,* Governor Hahn not one—

Neither was Mr Flanders defeated on account of his opinions in relation to the negroes.— He repudiated, publicly, as a candidate the idea that he was in favor of giving them, the Elective franchise, or equal rights with the whites— His failure was in consequence of his assuming the right to all appointive & elective offices in the state, and his unwillingness, and perhaps inability to act with other people, or to allow them to act with him. This unhappy temper he has shown I am informed, in his department towards officers connected with him in the Treasury Department— No one has suffered from it more than himself and his friends— I never have complained of his course, but it wld. be unreasonable to require *me* to support or approve it—

It is to be regretted that the Convention did not meet more decisively some of the questions connected with the elevation of the negro race, but it was a great deal to demand as much as they performed—and I doubt if other states would have done, under the same circumstances—as much.

I asked in Faneuil Hall, how many votes Massachusetts would give for the same, constitution,—if it were applicable to her condition, as to that of Louisiana and the answer was *not one!*[3]

I have been here three days. I came hoping to gather courage—for the future, but I regret to say that I do not see evidence of the spirit that is required to surmount all our troubles— It may be otherwise— I have strong convictions as to the course the government shd. pursue—but I prefer to follow others always so I say little— This much I believe however, that our delverance will come from greatness of admistration rather than from success in war.

With the highest respect

I am, as always Your Obt: Servant
N. P. BANKS

1. For a discussion of Chase's letter to Banks, initially drafted on November 8, see Chase to George S. Denison, November 11, 1864 (above).

2. Federal forces landed at New Orleans on April 25, 1862. Long, *Civil War Day by Day*, 203–4.

3. Banks delivered a campaign speech at the Boston landmark on October 30. According to one report—which did not record any query and response about support for the Louisiana constitution—he "alluded to the new Constitution of Louisiana, and described the proceedings of the convention which framed it, and said there was no better on the face of the earth." He also urged the U.S. government and Northerners to give Louisianans and their constitution "that support which the people of New England, which the people of the central States and the great West receive from the hands of the general government." *Boston Daily Advertiser*, Oct. 31, 1864.

FROM SAMUEL HOOPER

Autograph letter. Chase Papers, Historical Society of Pennsylvania (*micro* 35:0305).

Boston Novr: 20th 1864

My dear Sir,

Accept my thanks for the congratulations on my election and the kind expressions in yours of the 14th Inst. My opponent was Judge Abbott, who would be indignant at the idea that he was not the best man on that side to run against me.[1] As the direct and only argument used against my re-election was the support I had given to the financial measures of the administration, I think my large majority may be fairly considered an endorsement of your financial policy. I have not yet received the report of the speech in which you gave a sketch of that policy—but hope it will come as I wish much to read it.[2]

The past week I attended the meeting of the Stockholders of the Suffolk Bank here when they voted to organize under the National law; and this morning I have a letter from our friend Mr Russell of New York informing me that the Directors of the Bank of Commerce of N.Y. had decided unanimously to do the same, all of them being present at the meeting, except one who was in Europe.[3]

Ten days since I expressed in a note to Mr Fessenden my anxiety in consequence of certain reports—lest Mr Lincoln may not keep the promise he made to him as well as to myself & others. In reply Mr Fessenden assures me *"there is no danger about Mr. Chase"*. While I was in Washington & within a week after the death of Judge Taney—Mr Fessenden repeated to me what the President had said to him,—that he should fulfill the promise he made in regard to filling the vacancy if the Chief Justice died—and Mr Fessenden, affecting not to understand him, asked what he referred to—when the President repeated the promise, and added, that he should make the appointment after the elections were over. As the rumors refer now to Mr. Stanton,—and Mr Fessenden has said we may not be disturbed by any rumors concerning himself or Mr Stanton,—my faith in the promise of the President is not shaken. At the same time I shall be better satisfied when the appointment is announced. Colfax is here—and says the West, so far as he knows it, is unanimous in your favor, and that he had so written to the President.[4] Here your appointment will give great satisfaction.

If Genl. McLellan wishes to be the Senator from New Jersey—I see no objection to it—and like the idea because I think he would give the public an opportunity to judge of his true character.[5]

I propose to be at Washington on Friday or Saturday, the 2d & 3d Decr:, leaving here early enough to pass a day or two in New York on the way there.

Yours with great regard,
S Hooper

The Hon: S. P. Chase

1. Hooper had won reelection to his third term in Congress earlier in the month. His opponent was Boston attorney and Democratic politician Josiah Gardner Abbott (1814–91). *Bio. Dir. U.S. Cong.,* 507–8; *Boston Daily Advertiser,* Nov. 8, 1864; *DAB,* 9:203.

2. Perhaps a reference to Chase's speech at Mozart Hall, Cincinnati, on November 12, which included a review of Treasury Department policies under his administration. Chase to Kate Chase Sprague, Sept. 17, 1864 (above); *Cincinnati Daily Gazette,* Nov. 14, 1864.

3. New York merchant Charles Handy Russell served as one of the directors of the Bank of Commerce. *Chase Papers,* 1:323.

4. Schuyler Colfax sent Lincoln at least two such letters, one on October 23 and another on November 3. Colfax to Lincoln, Oct. 23, Nov. 3, 1864 (Lincoln Papers, L.C.).

5. New Jersey was one of only three states that George B. McClellan carried in the election of 1864. In January 1865, McClellan and his wife left for Europe, where they remained for the next three years. *DAB,* 11:584; Stephen W. Sears, ed., *The Civil War Papers of George B. McClellan: Selected Correspondence, 1860–1865* (New York, 1989), 627.

FROM SCHUYLER COLFAX

Autograph letter on letterhead stationery. Chase Papers, Historical Society of Pennsylvania (*micro* 35:0398).

Thirty Eighth Congress
HOUSE OF REPRESENTATIVES.
UNITED STATES OF AMERICA
Washington City Dec 5 1864

Private

Dear Governor,

Arriving here Friday, after a delightful lecturing & visiting tour in New England, & a splendid Banquet given me at Phil,[1] I found your letter of the 13th remailed. While in N. England, I urged every M.C. I saw to write Mr. Lincoln about C.J.,[2] Alley & Hooper assured me it was all right & certain:[3] I told them it was not; I knew what adverse Washn. influences there were & how influential.

Friday night I had a long talk with the President. He told me of various objections he had heard, which he added, did not influence him, *but he repeated them.* Some were sinister ones, whose paternity I think I can recognize, & which, I told Mr. Lincoln, were unworthy of their author. Another was that your ambition was the Presidency, & that a Presl. candidate should not be C.J. to use it as a stepping stone, impairing the strength & impartiality of the Judiciary. I asked Mr. Lincoln if you had not yourself once told him your preference to be C.J. rather than President. He replied yes; & I added that, if appointed, I felt certain you would dedicate the remainder of your life to the Bench. I did not say it to the President, but I may say it here frankly, that I never did fancy C.J. McLean being a candidate for President.[4]

I have been urging M.C.s to day to go up & see the President. Mr Sumner saw him Sat night, I hear, & found him, as I did undecided. Gen Wilson told me last night he would go specially. And Grinnell,[5] Wilson, & others told me they would go to day or to night.

I neglected to add one thing to the President, which struck me after I left the White House might have influenced him, if his mind was evenly balanced—to ask him if, with all this overwhelming public sentiment in your favor, he appd. some one else, History might not say that he did so because you had dared to be a candidate for the Presl. nomination against him. It would have touched him on a point of honor & magnanimity. I asked Garfield yesterday to hint it to him to day.

I write in great haste, for I am overwhelmed with business, & found over 200 letters here, awaiting attention & replies.

Yours truly
SCHUYLER COLFAX

Dennison[6] Sat night told me he was not taking part. And I told him I was, & that in the West & New England there was only one feeling. Senator Lane of Inda., (who was not for you for President, you remember,) told the President to day emphatically, "Every Union man in Indiana *desires* Gov Chase's appt. & every Democrat *expects* it." The fact is, I have never seen public opinion so overwhelmingly & unitedly settled on any one, as on yourself for this position. Whatever the result, it is indeed a proud testimonial of confidence.

1. The banquet took place in Philadelphia's Assembly Building on Thursday, December 1. *New York Times,* Dec. 3, 1864.
2. That is, Colfax spoke to members of Congress about the pending appointment of a chief justice.
3. Massachusetts congressmen John Basset Alley and Samuel Hooper.
4. During his tenure as an associate justice of the Supreme Court, John McLean had often been considered a candidate for the presidency. *DAB,* 12:128.
5. Clergyman, community promoter, and Republican leader Josiah Bushnell Grinnell (1821–91) of Iowa sat in Congress from 1863 to 1867. *DAB,* 8:4–5.
6. William Dennison.

TO ABRAHAM LINCOLN

Autograph letter. Abraham Lincoln Papers, Library of Congress (*micro* 35:0404).

Washington, Decr. 6, 1864

My dear Sir,[1]

On reaching home tonight I was saluted with the intelligence that you this day nominated me to the Senate for the office of Chief Justice.[2] I cannot sleep before I thank for this mark of your confidence, & especially for the manner in which the nomination was made.[3] I shall never forget either and trust that you will never regret either. Be assured that I prize your confidence & good will more than nomination or office.

Faithfully yours
S: P: CHASE

The President

1. A copy of this letter, in Chase's hand, is at the New-York Historical Society. Presumably a retained copy, it bears a filing endorsement in Jacob Schuckers's handwriting.
2. The version at the New-York Historical Society reads *you have this day,* with *have* as an interlineation. The second session of the Thirty-eighth Congress opened on December 5. The next day Lincoln sent Chase's nomination to the Senate, which immediately approved the appointment. On December 15, Associate Justice James M. Wayne swore

Chase in as chief justice and Chase assumed his place with the court. U.S. Senate, *Journal of Executive Proceedings,* v. 14, pt. 1:1; Minutes, Dec. 15, 1864 (Recs. of Supreme Court, Nat. Arch.).

3. On the same day Lincoln presented his annual message to Congress, which included an expression of confidence in the conduct of government finances over the past year and an endorsement of Chase's banking policies. The version of this letter at the New-York Historical Society has *thank you for this mark,* and also begins a new paragraph at the start of this sentence. Basler, *Collected Works,* 8:136–53.

Bibliography

SOURCES CITED BY ABBREVIATED TITLES

Appletons'	James Grant Wilson and John Fiske, eds. *Appletons' Cyclopædia of American Biography.* 6 vols. New York, 1887–89.
Bio. Dir. U.S. Cong.	*Biographical Directory of the United States Congress 1774–1989 . . . Bicentennial Edition.* Washington, D.C., 1989.
Chase Papers	John Niven et al., eds. *The Salmon P. Chase Papers.* Kent, Ohio, 1993–.
DAB	American Council of Learned Societies. *Dictionary of American Biography.* 20 vols. New York, 1928–36.
DNB	Leslie Stephen and Sidney Lee, eds. *The Dictionary of National Biography.* Reprint ed., 21 vols. London, 1973.
Nat. Cyc.	*The National Cyclopaedia of American Biography.* 63 vols. New York, 1891–1984.
OR	*The War of the Rebellion: A Compilation of the Official Records of the Union and Confederate Armies.* 128 vols. Washington, D.C., 1880–1901.
ORN	*Official Records of the Union and Confederate Navies in the War of the Rebellion.* 30 vols. Washington, D.C., 1894–1922.
Register of Officers (1861)	*Register of Officers and Agents, Civil, Military, and Naval, in the Service of the United States, on the Thirtieth September, 1861.* Washington, D.C., 1862.

Register of Officers (1863) — *Register of Officers and Agents, Civil, Military, and Naval, in the Service of the United States, on the Thirtieth September, 1863.* Washington, D.C., 1864.

Register of Officers (1865) — *Register of Officers and Agents, Civil, Military, and Naval, in the Service of the United States, on the Thirtieth September, 1865.* Washington, D.C., 1866.

Who Was Who — *Who Was Who in America.* Chicago, 1943–.

CITY DIRECTORIES

Cinc. Dir. (1855) — *Williams' Cincinnati Directory, City Guide and Business Mirror.* Cincinnati, [1855].

Cinc. Dir. (1856) — *Williams' Cincinnati Directory, City Guide and Business Mirror.* Cincinnati, [1856].

Cinc. Dir. (1863) — *Williams' Cincinnati Directory, City Guide and Business Mirror, for the Year Commencing June, 1863.* Cincinnati, [1863].

Cinc. Dir. (1864) — *Williams' Cincinnati Directory . . . June 1864.* Cincinnati, [1864].

Col. Dir. (1845–46) — *Kinney's Directory of Columbus, for 1845–6.* Columbus, 1845.

New Orleans Dir. (1855) — *Cohen's New Orleans Directory to 1855.* New Orleans, 1855.

New York Dir. (1851–52) — *The New York City Directory, for 1851–1852.* New York, [1851].

New York Dir. (1863) — H. Wilson, comp. *Trow's New York City Directory.* New York, 1863.

New York Dir. (1864) — H. Wilson, comp. *Trow's New York City Directory.* New York, 1864.

Providence Dir. (1865) — *The Providence Directory, for the Year 1865.* Providence, R.I., 1865.

St. Louis Dir. (1854–55) — *The St. Louis Directory, for 1854–55.* St. Louis, 1854.

Wash. Dir. (1827) — *The Washington Directory.* Washington, D.C., 1827.

Wash. Dir. (1830) — *The Washington Directory.* Washington, D.C., 1830.

Wash. Dir. (1862) — Thomas Hutchinson, comp. *Boyd's Washington Directory.* Washington, D.C., 1862.

Wash. Dir. (1863) — *Hutchinson's Washington and Georgetown Directory.* Washington, D.C., 1863.

Wash. Dir. (1864) — Andrew Boyd, comp. *Boyd's Washington Directory. Containing Also a Business Directory of Washington, Georgetown and Alexandria.* Washington, D.C., 1864.

OTHER SOURCES CITED

Appletons' Annual Cyclopædia and Register of Important Events. . . . 42 vols. New York, 1862–1903.

Baker, L. C. *History of the United States Secret Service.* Philadelphia, 1868.

Basler, Roy P., ed. *The Collected Works of Abraham Lincoln.* 9 vols. New Brunswick, N.J., 1953–55.

Beale, Howard K., ed. *The Diary of Gideon Welles.* 3 vols. New York, [1960].

Berlin, Ira, et al., eds. *Freedom: A Documentary History of Emancipation, 1861–1867.* 4 vols. to date. Cambridge, Eng., 1982–.

The Biographical Cyclopædia and Portrait Gallery with an Historical Sketch of the State of Ohio. 6 vols. Cincinnati, 1883–95.

Chase, Salmon P. *"Going Home to Vote." Authentic Speeches of S. P. Chase, Secretary of the Treasury, during his Visit to Ohio. . . .* Washington, D.C., 1863.

———. *How the South Rejected Compromise in the Peace Conference of 1861. Speech of Mr. Chase, of Ohio.* New York, 1863.

———. *Inaugural Address of Salmon P. Chase, Governor of the State of Ohio. . . .* Columbus, 1856.

Coffin, Levi. *Reminiscences of Levi Coffin: The Reputed President of the Underground Railroad. . . .* Cincinnati, [1876].

Commercial Intercourse with and in States Declared in Insurrection, and the Collection of Abandoned and Captured Property. Washington, D.C., 1863.

Fairman, Charles. *Reconstruction and Reunion, 1864–88, Part One.* Vol. 6 of Paul A. Freund, gen. ed., *The Oliver Wendell Holmes Devise History of the Supreme Court of the United States.* New York, 1971.

Friedberg, Robert. *Paper Money of the United States: A Complete Illustrated Guide with Valuations.* 6th ed., rev. by Jack Friedberg. New York, 1968.

Gerteis, Louis S. *From Contraband to Freedman: Federal Policy Toward Southern Blacks, 1861–1865.* Westport, Conn., 1973.

Gilkey, Elliot Howard. *The Ohio Hundred Year Book: A Hand-Book of the Public Men and Public Institutions of Ohio. . . .* Columbus, 1901.

Greve, Charles Theodore. *Centennial History of Cincinnati and Representative Citizens.* Chicago, 1904.

Hammond, Bray. *Sovereignty and an Empty Purse: Banks and Politics in the Civil War.* Princeton, 1970.

Harrington, Fred Harvey. *Fighting Politician: Major General N. P. Banks.* Philadelphia, 1948.

Heitman, Francis Bernard. *Historical Register and Dictionary of the United States Army. . . .* 2 vols. Washington, D.C., 1903.

Holli, Melvin G., and Peter D'A. Jones, eds. *Biographical Dictionary of American Mayors, 1820–1980: Big City Mayors.* Westport, Conn., 1981.

Johns, John E. *Florida During the Civil War.* Gainesville, Fla., 1963.

Johnson, Rossiter, ed. *The Twentieth Century Biographical Dictionary of Notable Americans. . . .* 10 vols. Boston, 1904; reprint, Detroit, 1968.

Judson, Isabella Field, ed. *Cyrus W. Field: His Life and Work [1819–1892].* New York, 1896.

Klement, Frank L. *Dark Lanterns: Secret Political Societies and Treason Trials in the Civil War.* Baton Rouge, 1984.

Lanman, Charles. *Biographical Annals of the Civil Government of the United States. . . .* Washington, D.C., 1876.

Larson, Henrietta M. *Jay Cooke: Private Banker.* Cambridge, Mass., 1936.

Letter of the Secretary of the Treasury, Transmitting . . . A List of the Special Agents of the Treasury Department and their Assistants. 38th Cong., 1st sess., 1864, S. Ex. Doc. 31

Long, E. B. *The Civil War Day by Day: An Almanac, 1861–1865.* Garden City, N.Y., 1971.

Loyal Publication Society. *The Conditions of Reconstruction. . . .* New York, 1863.

Lytle, William M., comp. *Merchant Steam Vessels of the United States, 1807–1868.* Mystic, Conn., 1952.

McCrary, Peyton. *Abraham Lincoln and Reconstruction: The Louisiana Experiment.* Princeton, 1978.

McLaughlin, Charles Capen, et al., eds. *The Papers of Frederick Law Olmsted.* 6 vols. to date. Baltimore, 1977–.

Merli, Frank. *Great Britain and the Confederate Navy, 1861–1865.* Bloomington, 1965.

Miers, Earl Schenck, ed. *Lincoln Day by Day: A Chronology, 1809–1865.* 3 vols. Washington, D.C., 1960.

Murphy, William D. *Biographical Sketches of the State Officers and Members of the Legislature of the State of New York. In 1862 and '63.* Albany, 1863.

Nevins, Allan. *The War for the Union.* 4 vols. New York, 1959–71.

New York Custom-House. 38th Cong., 1st sess., 1864, H. Rep. 111.

Oberholtzer, Ellis Paxson. *Jay Cooke: Financier of the Civil War.* 2 vols. Philadelphia, 1907.

Official Atlas of the Civil War. New York, 1958.

Reed, George Irving, ed. *Bench and Bar of Ohio: A Compendium of History and Biography.* 2 vols. Chicago, 1897.

Report of the Secretary of the Treasury, on the Finances, Containing Estimates of the Public Revenue and Public Expenditures. . . . 37th Cong., 1st sess., 1861, S. Ex. Doc. 2.

Report of the Secretary of the Treasury on the State of Finances, for the Year 1864. 38th Cong., 2d sess., 1864, H. Ex. Doc. 3.

Report of the Secretary of the Treasury, on the State of the Finances, for the Year Ending June 30, 1863. 38th Cong., 1st sess., 1863, H. Ex. Doc. 3.

Riddle, Albert Gallatin. *Recollections of War Times: Reminiscences of Men and Events in Washington, 1860–1865.* New York, 1895.

Rightor, Henry, ed. *Standard History of New Orleans. . . .* Chicago, 1900.

Robson, Charles, ed. *The Biographical Encyclopædia of Ohio of the Nineteenth Century.* Cincinnati, 1876.

Rose, Willie Lee. *Rehearsal for Reconstruction: The Port Royal Experiment.* Indianapolis, 1964.

Roseboom, Eugene H. *The Civil War Era, 1850–1873.* Vol. 4 of Carl Wittke, ed., *The History of the State of Ohio.* Columbus, 1944.

Schuckers, Jacob W. *The Life and Public Services of Salmon Portland Chase.* New York, 1874.

Shofner, Jerrell H. *Nor Is It Over Yet: Florida in the Era of Reconstruction, 1863–1877.* Gainesville, Fla., 1974.

Simon, John Y., et al., eds. *The Papers of Ulysses S. Grant.* 20 vols. to date. Carbondale, Ill., 1967–.

Smith, Donnal V. *Chase and Civil War Politics.* Columbus, Ohio, 1931; reprint, Freeport, N.Y., 1972.

Sobel, Robert, and John Raimo, eds. *Biographical Directory of the Governors of the United States, 1789–1978.* 4 vols. Westport, Conn., 1978.

Thorne, J. O., ed. *Chambers's Biographical Dictionary.* Rev. ed. New York, 1969.

[Trowbridge, John Townsend]. *The Ferry-Boy and the Financier.* Boston, 1864.

———. "The First Visit to Washington." *Atlantic Monthly* 13 (Apr. 1864): 448–57.

U.S. Department of Transportation. *Record of Movements: Vessels of the United States Coast Guard, 1790–Dec. 31, 1933.* Washington, D.C., 1989.

U.S. Senate. *Journal of the Executive Proceedings of the Senate of the United States. . . .* Washington, D.C., 1828–; reprint ed., New York, 1969.

Wakelyn, Jon L., ed. *Biographical Dictionary of the Confederacy.* Westport, Conn., 1977.

Walker, Robert J. *American Slavery and Finances.* London, 1864.

Warden, Robert B. *An Account of the Private Life and Public Services of Salmon Portland Chase.* Cincinnati, 1874.

Yanuck, Julius. "The Garner Fugitive Slave Case." *Mississippi Valley Historical Review* 40 (1953): 47–66.

Index

Page references for notes that identify individuals are in bold type (with **1**:, **2**:, and **3**: indicating biographical references in Volumes 1–3 of the *Chase Papers*).

The Salmon P. Chase Papers, Volume 4
was designed by Will Underwood;
composed in 10/12 ITC New Baskerville
with Bulmer display type
on a Macintosh Power PC system with postscript output
by The Book Page, Inc.;
printed by sheet-fed offset lithography
on 60-pound Glatfelter Smooth Natural acid-free stock
with halftones printed on 70-pound enamel gloss stock,
Smyth sewn and bound over 98' binder's boards
in ICG Arrestox B grade cloth
by Braun-Brumfield, Inc.;
and published by

The Kent State University Press
KENT, OHIO 44242